Lecture Notes in Computer Science 13618

More information about this series at https://link.springer.com/bookseries/558

Frank Hopfgartner · Kokil Jaidka · Philipp Mayr ·
Joemon Jose · Jan Breitsohl (Eds.)

Social Informatics

13th International Conference, SocInfo 2022
Glasgow, UK, October 19–21, 2022
Proceedings

 Springer

Editors
Frank Hopfgartner (iD)
Universität Koblenz-Landau
Koblenz, Germany

Philipp Mayr (iD)
GESIS – Leibniz-Institut für
Sozialwissenschaften
Cologne, Germany

Jan Breitsohl (iD)
University of Glasgow
Glasgow, UK

Kokil Jaidka (iD)
National University of Singapore
Singapore, Singapore

Joemon Jose (iD)
University of Glasgow
Glasgow, UK

ISSN 0302-9743   ISSN 1611-3349 (electronic)
Lecture Notes in Computer Science
ISBN 978-3-031-19096-4   ISBN 978-3-031-19097-1 (eBook)
https://doi.org/10.1007/978-3-031-19097-1

This Springer imprint is published by the registered company Springer Nature Switzerland AG
The registered company address is: Gewerbestrasse 11, 6330 Cham, Switzerland

Preface

This volume contains the proceedings of the 13th Conference on Social Informatics (SocInfo 2022), held in Glasgow, UK, during October 19–21, 2022. This conference series has always aimed to create a venue of discussion for computational and social sciences researchers, acting as a bridge between these two different and often separated academic communities. SocInfo 2020 had to face challenges brought on by the COVID-19 pandemic and was conducted virtually to better adapt to the travel difficulties and restrictions. SocInfo 2021 never materialized, and in this context, SocInfo 2022 made the brave attempt to revive the conference series. However, we faced numerous challenges, including finding a proper venue and sponsorships. SocInfo 2022 was organized as a hybrid conference to accommodate those affected by COVID-related difficulties. Nevertheless, the conference's goal remained unchanged: to provide a forum for academics to explore methodological novelties in the computational and social science fields and identify shared research trajectories. Despite the difficulties brought by the pandemic, the organizers received a vast number of diverse and interdisciplinary contributions, ranging from works that ground information system design on social concepts to papers that analyze complex social systems using computational methods or explore socio-technical techniques using social sciences methods.

We have received 102 paper submissions this year which were reviewed by 26 Senior Program Committee members and 129 Program Committee members with a strong interdisciplinary background from all over the world. The Program Committee members reviewed all submissions and provided the authors with in-depth feedback on how to improve their work. Similar to previous years, SocInfo 2022 employed a double-blind peer-reviewing process involving a two-tiered Program Committee. Based on reviewers' input, the Program Committee co-chairs selected 22 full and eight short papers for oral presentation. In addition, seven abstract submissions were accepted for poster presentation, as well as four papers presenting late-breaking results.

At the conference in Glasgow, SocInfo 2022 hosted three keynote speakers, namely Michael Haenlein (Professor of Marketing at the University of Liverpool), Piyushimita (Vonu) Thakuriah (Professor at Rutgers University), and Edgar Meij (Head of the Search and Discovery group at Bloomberg).

We would like to thank all authors and attendees who contributed to making SocInfo 2022 a prime forum to present and discuss research on social informatics. Moreover, we express our sincere gratitude to everyone who helped in organizing the conference. Finally, we would like to emphasize our appreciation for the efforts of the Program Committee members who dedicated their time and efforts to guarantee that submissions adhered to the highest standard expected from SocInfo.

Finally, we hope that these proceedings will constitute a valid input for your research interests and that you will continue the scientific exchange with the SocInfo community.

October 2022

Frank Hopfgartner
Kokil Jaidka
Philipp Mayr
Joemon M. Jose
Jan Breitsohl

Organization

General Chairs

Joemon M. Jose   University of Glasgow, UK
Jan Breitsohl   University of Glasgow, UK

Program Committee Chairs

Frank Hopfgartner   Universität Koblenz-Landau, Germany
Kokil Jaidka   National University of Singapore, Singapore
Philipp Mayr   GESIS, Germany

Senior Program Committee

Marcelo Armentano	UNICEN, Argentina
Leif Azzopardi	University of Strathclyde, UK
Matthew Barr	University of Glasgow, UK
Fausto Giunchiglia	University of Trento, Italy
Cathal Gurrin	Dublin City University, Ireland
Martin Halvey	University of Strathclyde, UK
Benjamin Kille	Norwegian University of Science and Technology, Norway
Yunhyong Kim	University of Glasgow, UK
Styliani Kleanthous	Open University of Cyprus, Cyprus
Tsvi Kuflik	University of Haifa, Israel
Monica Lestari Paramita	University of Sheffield, UK
Elisabeth Lex	Graz University of Technology, Austria
Andreas Lommatzsch	TU Berlin, Germany
Suvodeep Mazumdar	University of Sheffield, UK
Raksha Pavagada Subbanarasimha	IIIT Bangalore, India
Lena Podoletz	University of Edinburgh, UK
Srinath Srinivasa	IIIT Bangalore, India
Padmini Srinivasan	University of Iowa, USA
Aixin Sun	Nanyang Technological University, Singapore
John Ternovski	Georgetown University, USA
Thanassis Tiropanis	University of Southampton, UK
Michele Tizzoni	ISI Foundation, Italy
Antonela Tommasel	ISISTAN, CONICET-UNICEN, Argentina

Klaus Troitzsch	University of Koblenz-Landau, Germany
Milena Tsvetkova	London School of Economics and Political Science, UK
Davide Vega	Uppsala University, Sweden

Program Committee

Palakorn Achananuparp	Singapore Management University, Singapore
Mikhail Alexandrov	Russian Presidential Academy of National Economy and Public Administration, Russia, and Autonomous University of Barcelona, Spain
Hamed Alhoori	Northern Illinois University, USA
Iuliia Alieva	Carnegie Mellon University, USA
Stuart Anderson	University of Edinburgh, UK
Panagiotis Andriotis	University of the West of England, UK
Makan Arastuie	Seagate, USA
Muhammad Atif Qureshi	TU Dublin, Ireland
Ebrahim Bagheri	Ryerson University, Canada
Divya Bansal	PEC University of Technology, India
Dominik Batorski	University of Warsaw, Poland
Felix Biessmann	Berlin University of Applied Sciences, Germany
Livio Bioglio	University of Turin, Italy
Matteo Böhm	Sapienza University of Rome, Italy
Kalina Bontcheva	University of Sheffield, UK
Marco Brambilla	Politecnico di Milano, Italy
Ulrik Brandes	ETH Zürich, Switzerland
Kevin Matthe Caramancion	Mercyhurst University, USA
Kathleen M. Carley	Carnegie Mellon University, USA
Colin Campbell	University of Mount Union, USA
Fabio Celli	Maggioli R&D, Italy
Nina Cesare	University of Washington, USA
Charalampos Chelmis	University at Albany, USA
Min Chen	CISPA, Germany
Ninghan Chen	University of Luxembourg, Luxembourg
Yi-Shin Chen	National Tsing Hua University, Taiwan
Dimitris Christopoulos	MU Vienna, Austria, and Edinburgh Business School, UK
David Corney	Full Fact, UK
Andrew Crooks	University at Buffalo, USA
Mithun Das	Indian Institute of Technology Kharagpur, India
Marco De Nadai	Fondazione Bruno Kessler, Italy
Amruta Deshpande	Graphika Inc., USA

Djellel Difallah	New York University, USA
Ly Dinh	University of Illinois Urbana-Champaign, USA
Sofia Dokuka	National Research University Higher School of Economics, Russia
Victor M. Eguiluz	Institute for Cross-Disciplinary Physics and Complex Systems, CSIC-UIB, Spain
Reza Farahbakhsh	Télécom SudParis, France
Dennis Feehan	University of California, Berkeley, USA
Gerhard Fuchs	University of Stuttgart, Germany
Sabrina Gaito	University of Milan, Italy
Floriana Gargiulo	GEMASS, CNRS and Sorbonne University, France
Francesca Greco	Sapienza University of Rome, Italy
Barbara Guidi	Università di Pisa, Italy
Riccardo Guidotti	University of Pisa, Italy
Claudia Hauff	Delft University of Technology, The Netherlands
Denis Helic	Graz University of Technology, Austria
Julia Hsin-Ping Hsu	George Mason University, USA
Pan Hui	HKUST, China, and University of Helsinki, Finland
Ali Hürriyetoğlu	Koc University, Turkey
Adriana Iamnitchi	Maastricht University, The Netherlands
Tunazzina Islam	Purdue University, USA
Gholamreza Jafari	Shahid Behesti University, Iran
Alejandro Jaimes	AiCure, USA
Pablo Jensen	IXXI, ENS Lyon, France
Seungwon Eugene Jeong	University of Bristol, UK
Kenneth Joseph	University at Buffalo, USA
Shubhra Kanti Karmaker	Auburn University, USA
Kazuhiro Kazama	Wakayama University, Japan
Andreas Koch	University of Salzburg, Austria
Sergei Koltcov	National Research University Higher School of Economics, Russia
Olessia Koltsova	National Research University Higher School of Economics, Russia
Cem Kozcuer	Berliner Hochschule für Technik, Germany
Ponnurangam Kumaraguru	IIIT Delhi, India
Hemank Lamba	Carnegie Mellon University, USA
Renaud Lambiotte	University of Oxford, UK
Walter LaMendola	University of Denver, USA
Georgios Lappas	University of Western Macedonia, Greece
Deok-Sun Lee	Korea Institute for Advanced Study, South Korea

Contents

Short Papers

Late-Breaking Papers

Full Papers

Communities, Gateways, and Bridges: Measuring Attention Flow in the Reddit Political Sphere

Cesare Rollo[1], Gianmarco De Francisci Morales[2], Corrado Monti[2(✉)],
and André Panisson[2]

[1] University of Turin, Turin, Italy
cesare.rollo@unito.it
[2] CENTAI, Turin, Italy
gdfm@acm.org, {monti,panisson}@centai.eu

Abstract. Online social media have attracted large and vibrant communities, which shape how people interact online. Platforms such as Reddit provide a safe harbor for groups to discuss a variety of topics, including politics and even conspiracy theories. We propose a framework, dubbed *attention-flow graph*, to investigate the flow of users across Reddit communities from a network perspective. This graph concisely summarizes how users shift their attention from one subreddit to another over time, and allows to capture its community structure. In addition, it enables the operationalization of the concepts of gateways and bridges: particular subreddits that support the transition of users towards specific communities. We apply this framework to identify political and conspiracy communities, thus discovering their bridges and gateways. We find that conspiracy theories help attracting users to the alt-right community from occultist subreddits, but also by diverting users from the radical left.

Keywords: Social media · Network science · Conspiracy · Echo chambers

1 Introduction

The effect of social media on how the general public forms its opinion is a pressing issue of the last decades, due also to their role in several contemporary political events, such as Donald Trump's election (Enli 2017). Some researchers argue that their usage has been accompanied by a growth in mass ideological polarization (Kubin and von Sikorski 2021). At the same time, surveys have reported a large growth in affective polarization (Iyengar et al. 2012)—individuals unwilling to socialize across ideological boundaries. These phenomena have been linked to selective exposure: users prefer information sources that agree with their views (Stroud 2010), and sort themselves into communities of like-minded individuals, i.e., "echo chambers" (Cinelli et al. 2021). Whether this tendency has been exacerbated by social media is an open debate (Boxell et al. 2017).

F. Hopfgartner et al. (Eds.): SocInfo 2022, LNCS 13618, pp. 3–19, 2022.
https://doi.org/10.1007/978-3-031-19097-1_1

Some particularly concerning examples of echo chambers are provided by conspiracy theories such as QAnon, that have led to outbursts of violence;[1] or the growth of far-right extremism in the U.S., which has been nurturing recent terrorist events, such as the 2022 Buffalo Attack (Abbas et al. 2022). Models of online radicalization highlight the effect of social interactions in the process, and in particular the "influence of like-minded individuals and the online community on the individual's new worldview" (Neo 2019). Thus, it is important to study the places where this connection happens, and how *gatekeepers* of information shape the worldview within the echo chamber (Garimella et al. 2018a).

The original work on gatekeeping (Lewin 1947) referred to the power of gate-keepers to decide which messages may pass through their channels. More modern views of gatekeeping re-imagine it within the context of user-generated content and social media. In this context, users do not act as filters, rather they decide, in an ecosystem of complex processes which may involve algorithms (Thorson and Wells 2016), which items the collective attention focuses on (Bruns 2003). Indeed, the paradigm shifts from editors keeping the gates of publishing, to users pointing out which sources (gates of information) to watch, thereby fostering the dissemination of specific worldviews (Welbers and Opgenhaffen 2018). We adopt a similar view in this work, and ask ourselves which forums can have a role in supporting a shift in the attention of Reddit users towards specific topics and ideas. Given the decentralized, peer-to-peer nature of the modern information gathering process, it is natural to approach it from a network perspective.

It is well-known that new ideas tend to flow into a community via boundary spanners and brokers (Burt 2004). At the same time, bridges, which span structural holes (Burt 1992), connect separate communities, while gatekeepers facilitate or hinder information flows (West 2017). In particular, we are interested in which communities serve as entry points and precursors to other communities—noticeably, conspiracy and hoaxes-spreading ones. In this sense, our work is similar in spirit to the ones by Klein et al. (2019) and Phadke et al. (2022). However, we develop a general framework to analyze the flow of attention within Reddit, which can identify precursors to engagement with specific communities.

Much of the attention has been focused on Facebook (Quattrociocchi et al. 2016), Twitter (Garimella et al. 2018a), and YouTube (Ribeiro et al. 2020b; Fabbri et al. 2022). Our goal is to empirically explore this phenomenon by using Reddit as the object of study. Reddit, which self-defines as "the front page of the Internet", is a social news and discussion website which has consistently ranked among the top ten most visited websites worldwide over the past years.[2] It is organized in topical forums called subreddits, each dedicated to a specific topic of discussion; users typically subscribe to and participate in multiple subreddits of interest. Its role in the development of far-right and conspiratorial attitudes has been extensively scrutinized (Massachs et al. 2020; Phadke et al. 2022). Indeed, these studies have shown that the fora frequented by users are powerful

---

[1] https://www.theguardian.com/us-news/2020/oct/15/qanon-violence-crimes-timeline.

[2] https://en.wikipedia.org/wiki/Reddit.

indicators for their future trajectories. For instance, dyadic interactions with members of conspiracy communities are the most important social precursors to joining conspiracy communities (Phadke et al. 2021). Furthermore, engagement with specific communities (e.g., men's rights activists) has been identified as a gateway towards alt-right extremism (Mamié et al. 2021). Therefore, places that act as melting pots for users within and without the conspiracy community are fundamental to understand the pathways taken by users.

We propose a graph-based approach to analyze the flow of attention across communities on Reddit. Fabbri et al. (2022) proposed a similar approach to study how YouTube videos can represent a gateway that introduce users to a radicalization path. This concept is modeled as a path on a what-to-watch-next graph that leads user to harmful content. In our case, we look for specific subreddits that have a comparable role in shifting the attention flow of users towards a community. To do so, we draw inspiration from the work by Davies et al. (2021) which analyses user migration within Reddit. They find an interesting interplay between user migration and controversies, increasing politicization, and the rise of conspiracy theories. We wish to leverage this interplay to uncover the underlying common structure between user attention and (political) topics.

Our approach based on the *attention-flow graph* provides a way to identify the main communities within Reddit based on the flow of users within them (Cai et al. 2019), rather than on the static view used by co-participation networks (Phadke et al. 2022; Waller and Anderson 2021). Similar approaches have been already used to analyze behavior on Reddit (Massachs et al. 2020; Ribeiro et al. 2020a), however they have been mostly ad-hoc. The attention-flow graph is a way to formalize and systematize this type of analysis. As such, the attention-flow graph allows to identify important landmarks in the pathways across the website such as *gateways* from and *bridges* to other communities. In particular, while subscription information is not public, the production of content on a subreddit can be seen as a proxy for membership (Datta and Adar 2019). Finally, although our specific insights regard political and conspiratorial communities, our methodology is more general, and can be applied to the study of any topic on Reddit. For instance, while out of the scope of the current study, the attention-flow graph can be used to study the effect of moderation within the platform (e.g., banning of subreddits) (Chandrasekharan et al. 2017; Horta Ribeiro et al. 2021).

2 Data

Reddit is a social news aggregation and discussion platform. It has been recognized as an influential one, especially for the alt-right and conspiratorial communities: Zannettou et al. (2017) have shown that fringe communities on Reddit are comparatively successful in spreading their content to more mainstream media.

Discussions on Reddit are organized in topical communities called *subreddits*. Users (known as *redditors*) can publish *posts* in subreddits, and *comment* on other posts and comments, thus creating a tree structure for the overall discussion. In addition, users can also *upvote* a message to show approval, appreciation, or agreement (and their opposites with a *downvote*). The *score* of a message is the number of upvotes minus the number of downvotes. In this study, we restrict our attention to posts (rather than comments), since they are a better proxy for the active involvement of a user in a specific subreddit. Each subreddit focuses on a specific topic, thus subscribers to the same subreddit can be seen as sharing similar interests. For instance, some subreddits gather politically-aligned groups of users by limiting their participants to supporters of a political group or figure (e.g., in r/The_Donald, moderators explicitly state that the community is for 'Trump Supporters Only' and that dissenting users will be removed).

We extract all Reddit posts from 2017 to 2020 from the PushShift dataset (Baumgartner et al. 2020). To account only for users positively engaged with a community, we keep only posts with score greater than one. We exclude smaller subreddits by selecting only those that have at least one month with at least 50 distinct users publishing a post on it. Finally, we take care of automated accounts by removing users who posted on more than 50 distinct subreddits for at least one month and users with bot in their username (except common dictionary words). In the end, we obtain a data set with 242 220 979 posts submitted by 3677 137 users in 25 877 subreddits.

3 Methods

In the following, we first state our definition of *attention flow* (Sect. 3.1) and how it can be transformed into a graph (Sect. 3.2). Then, we operationalize of the concepts of communities, gateways, and bridges by using this graph (Sect. 3.3).

3.1 Attention Flow

Our first goal is to formalize the concept of attention flow across subreddits, meant to capture how much each subreddit at time step t' contributes to the user base of another subreddit at a time step $t > t'$. In practice, we always consider $t = t' + 1$, where the time step represents one month.

Let $\mathcal{U}$ be the set of users and $\mathcal{S}$ be the set of subreddits. Define $c_{u,s}^{(t)}$ as the number of interactions of user $u \in \mathcal{U}$ with subreddit $s \in \mathcal{S}$ at time step t, and $\mathbf{C}^{(t)} \in \mathbb{N}^{|\mathcal{U}| \times |\mathcal{S}|}$ as the corresponding matrix for all users and all subreddits at time step t. We define the attention matrix $\mathbf{B}^{(t)}$ as the row-normalized form of $\mathbf{C}^{(t)}$, and each row $\mathbf{b}_u^t$ as the attention vector of user u at time step t. Therefore, for each user u and subreddit s, we quantify how much the user's attention changes between t and t' as follows:

$$\mathbf{\Delta b}_{u,s}^t = \begin{cases} \mathbf{b}_{u,s}^t - \mathbf{b}_{u,s}^{t'} & \text{if } \mathbf{b}_{u,s}^t \cdot \mathbf{b}_{u,s}^{t'} = 0 \\ 0 & \text{otherwise} \end{cases}$$

This representation highlights the subreddits s that are adopted or abandoned by user u between t' and t, represented in a vector $\mathbf{\Delta b}_u^t$ where the adopted subreddits are represented as positive flow $\mathbf{\Delta^+ b}_u^t$, and the abandoned ones as negative flow $\mathbf{\Delta^- b}_u^t$. By evenly matching the negative flows with the positive ones, we define the attention flow of user u as the outer product $\mathbf{F}^{(t,u)} = \widehat{\mathbf{\Delta}^-\mathbf{b}_u^t} \otimes \mathbf{\Delta}^+\mathbf{b}_u^t$. Where $\widehat{\mathbf{\Delta}^-\mathbf{b}_u^t}$ is the l_1-normalized form of the absolute values in $\mathbf{\Delta}^-\mathbf{b}_u^t$.

Each user u active in both t' and t determines a per-user attention flow matrix $\mathbf{F}^{(t,u)} \in \mathbb{R}^{|\mathcal{S}| \times |\mathcal{S}|}$ where $f_{i,j}^{(t,u)}$ represents how much of the attention of user u was transferred from subreddit i to subreddit j between the time steps t' and t. By aggregating over users, $\mathbf{F}^{(t)} = \sum_{u \in \mathcal{U}} \mathbf{F}^{(t,u)}$ represents how much of all users' attention migrated from subreddit i to subreddit j.

3.2   Network Construction

Next, we devise a suitable network representation from the attention flow previously defined, by aggregating multiple time steps. $\mathbf{F}^{(t)}$ can be seen as the adjacency matrix of a weighted directed network, which represents the overall attention flow of users among subreddits. Thus, the set of matrices $\{\mathbf{F}^{(t)}\}_{t=1,\dots T}$ represent a temporal flow graph that encodes the user flow among subreddits.

Since network weights represent user flow, they depend on the popularity of both source and target nodes, i.e., the number of users that post on those subreddits in the considered time interval. Node strength s is thus strongly correlated with subreddit popularity. As a consequence, for each node, the main in- and out-neighbors are subreddits with higher popularity, that at all time steps absorb and consume attention from all the others. To avoid this effect, we *rescale* edge weights to dampen their dependency on node popularity: $\widetilde{F_{ij}} := \frac{F_{ij}}{\sqrt{\sum_k F_{ik} \cdot \sum_k F_{kj}}} = \frac{F_{ij}}{\sqrt{s_i^{out} \cdot s_j^{in}}}$. We empirically find that re-scaling by the geometric mean of the in/out-strenghts works best (see Appendix A).

Finally, we define the aggregated network over multiple time steps as $\mathcal{F} = \frac{1}{T} \sum_{t=1}^T \mathbf{F}^{(t)}$. Henceforth, we refer to this network as the *attention-flow graph* (AFG). This graph is dense, but most weights have very small values (median 10^{-3}, see Appendix B). Section 4.1 shows that pruning low-weight edges is beneficial to community detection, and the threshold can be determined experimentally.

3.3   Communities, Gateways, and Bridges

The definition of *attention-flow graph* allows to operationalize the concepts of communities, gateways, and bridges. We use the Stochastic Block Model (SBM) to uncover the underlying community structure of the AFG.[3] A major advantage of using SBM for community detection derives from being a sound statistical model, which lowers the chance to overfit (mistake stochastic fluctuations for actual structure) compared to maximizing modularity (Guimera et al. 2004).

Each community represents a collection of subreddits where users regularly migrate from one to another, while moving to a subreddit external to the community is rare. Indeed, they represent a community that is interested in similar

---

[3] Specifically, we use a degree-corrected version of the stochastic block model (Karrer and Newman 2011), with the addition of the degree sequence $k = \{k_i\}$ of the graph as an additional set of parameters (Peixoto 2017).

themes. However, they can loosely be seen as *echo chambers*: assuming a user on Reddit reads the same subreddits they participate to, it is unlikely for an individual, during their trajectory on Reddit, to be exposed to content produced outside this bubble. Moreover, if two users belong to distinct communities, their interaction is less likely.

The extraction of such communities enables us to investigate the role of specific nodes in connecting them. In particular, when considering a user that is active inside a community X, we seek to understand which are the likely pathways that drive them towards a different community Y. By modeling the users' movement across subreddits as random walks (where the weighted adjacency matrix $\mathcal{F}$ is the transition matrix of a Markov process), the stationary distribution of walkers that (re-)start their walk from X is given by the Personalized PageRank (PPR) in community X (Garimella et al. 2018b). Thus, we can quantitatively determine which are the specific subreddits $s \in Y$ that are more likely to be crossed by a random walker that belongs to X, and which as bridges from X to Y.

Definition 1 (Bridge node). *A subreddit s belonging to a community Y is a* bridge *from the community X (for $X \neq Y$) if it has a high probability of being reached by a random walk with uniform probability of restart in all $s' \in X$.*

This definition captures the subreddit's property of being a transition point for users that walk away from a community X, heading towards community Y.

Similarly, to find subreddits acting as attractors for X, we can apply a complementary definition, by using the PPR from outside of X.

Definition 2 (Gateway node). *A subreddit $s \in X$ is a* gateway *for community X if it has a high probability of being reached by a random walk with uniform probability of restart in all $s' \notin X$.*

Note that the definition of a *bridge* requires to consider a pair of communities (X, Y), starting and arrival, while we define *gateways* only by referring to a unique entry point for community X. By applying these definitions, we obtain for each community a ranking of its top gateway and bridge nodes. Informally, a bridge between X and Y redirects the flow from X to Y, i.e., is an attractor point to Y from X. The subreddits thus identified as bridges can act as transition nodes, through which users typically transit while shifting their attention from one community to another; alternatively, they can represent meeting points for users that have different interests. Conversely, a gateway for X is an ingress point for the whole community X, irrespective of its source. Users ending up in a gateway node have a higher chance of being absorbed into that community. The next section reports some concrete examples within the Reddit political sphere.

4   Results

This section illustrates the results obtained by applying the process described so far to the Reddit data set, with a focus on political and conspiratorial communities. First, we show how we validate our graph construction and community

Table 1. Adjusted mutual information (AMI) scores between ground-truth subreddit categorizations at 3 levels of depth and SBM communities resulting from edge-pruning thresholds at different percentiles.

Hierarchy	Pruning 0th	25th	50th	75th
Level 1	0.230	0.249	0.280	**0.300**
Level 2	0.283	0.307	0.340	**0.369**
Level 3	0.278	0.293	0.345	**0.409**

detection by using a human-curated data set (Sect. 4.1). Then, we restrict our attention to the political communities (Sect. 4.2), and show how they are connected to each other. Finally, we focus on their gateways and bridges, particular subreddits that support the transition of users from one ideological side to another (Sect. 4.3).

4.1 Preprocessing and Validation

As mentioned in Sect. 3.2, the attention-flow graph is very dense; thus, as a preprocessing step, we prune its edges by removing those with smaller weight. To choose the threshold of this pruning process, and to validate the quality of the communities we find, we compare our results to a human-curated data set[4] created by redditors to categorize subreddits into topics. It organizes topics within three levels, e.g., the subreddit r/chicagobulls belongs to the *NBA* subtopic, which in turns is part of *Sport*. The data set contains 2017 labeled subreddits, of which 1255 appear in the time frame we consider. Of those, 1211 are also labelled with a second subtopic level, and 712 with a third more specific one.

Table 1 reports the adjusted mutual information (AMI) between the benchmark categorizations and the SBM communities, with edge-pruning thresholds set at different percentiles. First, we observe that with any choice of threshold, the community detection obtains a good fit with respect to the ground truth. In fact, it obtains AMI scores between 0.278 and 0.409 for the finer categorization level—values in line with state-of-the-art results of applications of community detection on real data (George et al. 2020). Secondly, we note that in all levels of depth, we obtain the highest correspondence with the ground truth at the 75th percentile. As such, we consider this threshold in the rest of our analysis.

The giant component of the final pruned network has 24 529 nodes with 581 990 directional edges. A total of 140 communities, with a median size of 122 nodes each, are found by SBM. By inspecting the results, we observe that such communities are based on their topic or partisan affiliation, as expected.

4.2 Political Communities

Among all the identified communities, we focus on those related to politics and conspiracies. In particular, we identify four communities of particular interest.

---

[4] https://www.reddit.com/r/ListOfSubreddits/wiki/listofsubreddits.

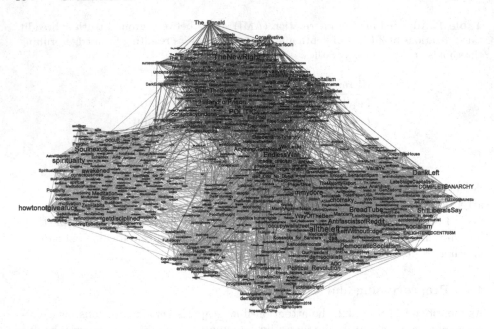

Fig. 1. Subgraph of the attention-flow graph with political and conspiratorial communities. Each one is represented by a color: *Alt-right* (green), *Radical Left* (blue), *Liberal* (orange), and *Esoterism* (purple). (Color figure online)

Liberal. This community covers a wide range of politics and current news topics, mainly from a liberal/centrist point of view. In fact, it includes democratic-wing subreddits such as `r/JoeBiden` or `r/YangForPresidentHQ`, communities opposed to more left-wing politicians (`r/Enough_Sanders_Spam`), and to right-wing ones (`r/EnoughTrumpSpam`). It also contains many generalist, political communities such as `r/politics`. This fact is not surprising, since Reddit appears to have a liberal bias in its user base (Shatz 2017).

Radical Left. This community is a meeting point for leftist users. Among its most popular subreddits we find in fact left-wing politicians such as Bernie Sanders (`r/SandersForPresident`), and more radical communities such as `r/ChapoTrapHouse` (a popular radical left podcast) and `r/LateStageCapitalism` (dedicated to anti-capitalistic satire), or intellectuals (`r/chomsky`).

Alt-Right. This community attracts users aligning with the so-called "alt-right" movement. It is mainly composed of right-wing groups (`r/TheNewRight`) and Donald Trump's supporters (`r/The_Donald`), but it also hosts subreddits related to right-wing conspiracy theories (Marwick and Partin 2022) such as `r/greatawakening` and `r/conspiracy` (both involved with the QAnon theory). Also some traditional conservative subreddits (such as `r/Conservative` and `r/Republican`) are embedded inside this community, albeit their size is smaller.

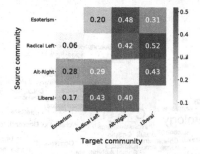

Community	$|V|$	$|E|$
Alt-Right	128	2079
Radical Left	112	2011
Liberal	113	1517
Esoterism	139	1595

(a) **Number of nodes** $|V|$ **and internal edges** $|E|$ **of each community.**

(b) **Probability that a random walk on the attention-flow graph starting in source community** s **reaches a target community** t **(with** $t \neq s$**).**

Fig. 2. Statistics on the four political communities considered.

Esoterism. This community is not strictly related to politics but its main topic can be viewed as an extension of the classical conspiracy theories to the spiritual sphere. In fact, among its main subreddits we can find groups related to esoterism and occultism such as r/Paranormal, r/Glitch_in_the_Matrix, and r/occult.

The subgraph induced by these four communities in the attention-flow graph includes a total of 492 subreddits and 7202 edges. By using a standard force-directed layout, we depict such a subgraph in Fig. 1. Figure 2a shows the size of these communities, which appears to be well-balanced, ranging from 112 to 139 subreddits in each community. Instead, we observe different distances between each pair of clusters. Figure 2b reports the probability of a random walker starting in source community s to reach a target community t (for $s \neq t$). This proximity measure shows that the *Radical Left* and *Liberal* groups are close to each other, while *Esoterism* is more connected to *Alt-Right*.

4.3 Political Bridges and Gateways

By applying our definitions of *bridge* and *gateway* nodes to the AFG, as given in Sect. 3.3, we investigate the pathways driving user to different political groups.

Bridges. First, we focus on *bridge nodes* (Definition 1) identified in the four communities of interest. Table 2 shows a ranking of the top subreddits in terms of PPR, for each starting community, considering the attention-flow subgraph induced by these communities. Generally—as shown in Fig. 2b—the *Radical Left* and the *Liberal* community are close, as the top bridge for each arrives from the other. The same holds for the *Alt-Right* and the *Esoterism* communities. Nevertheless, while all the top-3 bridges starting in the *Liberal* community arrive in the *Radical Left* one, the opposite is not true, as *Radical Left* has bridges to the *Alt-Right* community, e.g., through r/WikiLeaks and r/ConspiracyII.

Now, let us focus on the top bridge subreddit for each community, represented in Fig. 3. We start with the one with the largest PPR—the subreddit that is more

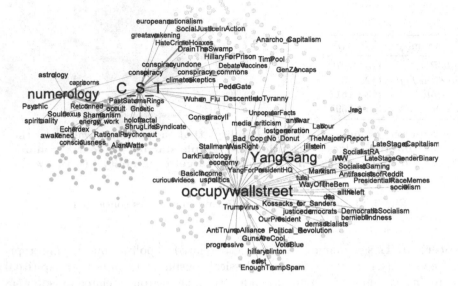

Fig. 3. Same subgraph represented in Fig. 1 with emphasis on the top bridge of each community (see Table 2) and their neighbors.

Table 2. Top-3 bridge nodes for each starting community.

Bridge Subreddit	Start	Arrival	PPR ($\times 10^{-4}$)	Bridge Subreddit	Start	Arrival	PPR ($\times 10^{-4}$)
r/numerology	Alt-Right	Esoterism	4.49	r/occupywallstreet	Liberal	Radical Left	7.61
r/jimmydore	Alt-Right	Radical Left	3.44	r/MarchAgainstNazis	Liberal	Radical Left	4.70
r/Lyme	Alt-Right	Esoterism	3.11	r/tulsi	Liberal	Radical Left	4.02
r/YangGang	Radical Left	Liberal	5.54	r/C_S_T	Esoterism	Alt-Right	4.33
r/WikiLeaks	Radical Left	Alt-Right	4.39	r/ConspiracyII	Esoterism	Alt-Right	3.10
r/ConspiracyII	Radical Left	Alt-Right	4.25	r/CriticalTheory	Esoterism	Radical Left	3.00

powerful as a bridge between communities—r/occupywallstreet, a subreddit dedicated to the Occupy Wall Street movement. This movement, born after the financial crisis of 2008, focuses on the problem of growing inequalities in U.S., and argues that politicians—including the liberal administrations—are too influenced by the interests of finance. Our framework reveals that this subreddit acts as a powerful bridge from the *Liberal* community to the *Radical Left* one.

Conversely, the main bridge from the *Radical Left* community is towards the *Liberal* one, and it is r/YangGang. This subreddit is dedicated to supporters of Andrew Yang, a candidate for the U.S. Democratic presidential primaries in 2020. The demographic of Yang's supporters overlaps significantly with Reddit's (Skelley 2019), which may explain the popularity of the subreddit. While some of Yang's proposals (Universal Basic Income, support for Medicare For All)

Table 3. Top-3 gateway nodes for each community.

Gateway Subreddit	Community	PPR ($\times 10^{-4}$)	Gateway Subreddit	Community	PPR ($\times 10^{-4}$)
r/TheNewRight	Alt-Right	17.99	r/Jewish	Liberal	8.80
r/The_Donald	Alt-Right	16.22	r/AntiTrumpAlliance	Liberal	8.44
r/multiculturalcancer	Alt-Right	14.37	r/Liberal	Liberal	8.31
r/Anti_Communism	Radical Left	13.88	r/numerology	Esoterism	1.83
r/sendinthetanks	Radical Left	13.65	r/occult	Esoterism	1.56
r/GenZedong	Radical Left	13.08	r/cults	Esoterism	1.51

can be considered left-leaning, Yang does not ascribe himself to the left (e.g., one of his slogans was "not left, not right, forward") and attracts liberal voters (ibid), which explains the role of his supporters' subreddit in the network.

Moving to the right end of the political spectrum, the subreddits r/C_S_T (abbreviation for *Critical Shower Thoughts*) and r/ConspiracyII act as bridges from the *Esoterism* community to the *Alt-Right* one. r/C_S_T collects "politically incorrect" casual thoughts, a type of content known to be connected to the roots of alt-right movements (Massachs et al. 2020). r/ConspiracyII is highly focused on political conspiracy theories, that eventually culminate in supernatural or pseudo-scientific beliefs. Thus, the "bridge" property highlighted by our framework suggests that such subreddits attract users interested in esoterism/occultism towards the alt-right political faction, via involvement in the universe of conspiracy theories. Interestingly, r/ConspiracyII is also one of the top-3 bridges tapping into the *Radical Left* and leading users' attention to the *Alt-Right*. This observation supports the idea that conspiracy theories are "diversionary narratives" (Wu Ming 1 2021), appealing to a critical view of today's society, but serving the purpose to focus such views within a conservative framework (Jolley et al. 2018). Finally, the last of the four top bridges is r/numerology, an accessible occultist subreddit—interested in mystical and esoteric aspects of numbers—which drives alt-right users towards the *Esoterism* community.

Gateways. To find *gateway nodes* (Definition 2), we compute for all the subreddits in a given community c their PPR outside c (restricted to the 4 communities of interest). However, the random walkers can span the entire network and eventually pass through other communities before reaching the target c. Table 3 reports a summary of the top gateways, which, as expected, differ from bridge nodes. These subreddits are in fact important entry points, in general, for users in a given community. For instance, a user gravitating towards the *Alt-Right* community is more likely to enter it from r/TheNewRight (a subreddit discussing the alt-right movement in general), r/The_Donald (dedicated to Trump's supporters), or r/multiculturalcancer (which attacks the idea of a multicultural society). In particular, r/TheNewRight and r/The_Donald display a much larger PPR than all the other gateways we find: this fact suggests the importance of particular subreddits—and of the Trump presidency—in attracting individuals to the *Alt-Right* community.

These rankings of gateway nodes tell us which are the main entry points of each community for a random walker, but they do not provide us with any information regarding their origin. We investigate this aspect by computing the inflow received by each gateway node from the other (possibly non-politicized) communities in the whole AFG. We compute the inflow of a node s from a community c as the sum of the weights of the in-links to s from any node in c. We label all neighboring communities by observing its largest subreddits, as done for the four communities of interest; the list of largest subreddits for all the mentioned communities are available in Table 4.

We report some examples of particular interest in Table 5. The subreddit r/Ani_Communism, a powerful gateway node for the *Radical Left* group, self-describes as *"The subreddit of Anime Revolutionaries"*. Interestingly, the closest community to r/Ani_Communism is not related to politics, but instead seems to be mainly focused on videogames, including subreddits such as r/LilliaMains (a character of the League of Legends videogame), r/ColdWarZombies (a fantasy war game), and r/PS5restock. As such, its role as an entry point towards *Radical Left* for many Reddit users interested in gaming seems relevant. Similarly, r/The_Donald, gateway for the *Alt-Right* community, displays some of the same communities among its top inflows, such as *Videogames/Fantasy*, but also relevant differences—e.g., a community related to Twitch streamers. Finally, r/numerology, gateway for *Esoterism*, is the most different, as it draws user attention from parts of the network far from politicized communities, such as those related to gaming hardware and crypto-currencies.

5 Conclusion and Future Work

In this work, we analyzed the flow of user attention on Reddit, focusing on the political and conspiratorial communities. We first materialized this flow as a network of subreddits, where links represent user flowing from a subreddit to another. This compact representation allowed us to study four years of user participation to Reddit in a concise format. We did so by relying on the concepts of communities, gateways, and bridges—typically employed in network science—on this attention-flow graph. Thanks to this framework, we identified four main political and conspiratorial communities on Reddit. We then investigated which subreddits have a pivotal role in supporting the flow of users from one community to the other. This way, we discovered, for instance, that the Occupy Wall Street movement supports users flowing from a liberal perspective to a leftist one; and that conspiracy theories helps attracting users to the alt-right community from occultist subreddits, but also from the radical left community.

Our contribution is therefore twofold: on the one hand, we provide a concrete, principled method to study user attention flow on Reddit from a network perspective; on the other hand, our results help to shed light on the topic of opinion formation. Still, our work has limitations: first, our approach is tailored on the community-based Reddit ecosystem, and not immediately applicable to other social media; second, we rely on posts as a proxy for participation, since there is no data for subscriptions. Nevertheless, we are able to identify how Reddit supports the growth of conspiratorial communities, and what is the role of such communities in the wider political ecosystem. Such empirical findings can form the basis for further studies on the political movements of our times, as well as helping community managers of social media to identify the most harmful communities, that could foster the spread of hoaxes and conspiracy theories.

Appendix

A   Weight Rescaling

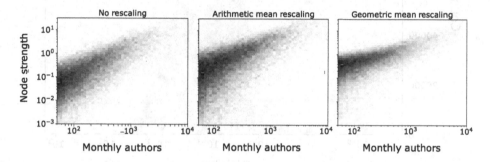

Fig. 4. Distribution of the subreddits in the space defined by their number of monthly users and their (rescaled) node strength in the attention-flow graph, i.e., the sum of the weight of all of their links.

In order to define the weights of the links in the attention-flow graphs, we wish to focus on links that are deviating from the most popular subreddits. E.g., the constant flow of users towards a generalist subreddit such as r/pictures is not as interesting for our purposes as the flow between two topical communities. For this reason, we rescale the weight w of a link between two subreddits (s, s') in order to reduce the correlation of w with the number of users of s and s'. Thanks to our framework, we are able to perform such normalization using only information coming from the node weights themselves. In fact, we rescale each weight by the mean of the total weights of the links incident on the head and the tail of each link. We compare two types of means: arithmetic and geometric. Figure 4 reports this comparison, clearly showing that the geometric mean succeeds in this goal, as it dampens the dependency between the resulting subreddit node strength (i.e., the sum of the weights w of all of their links in the attention flow graph) and the number of monthly users in each subreddit.

B   Pruning Thresholds

As shown in table Table 1, community detection algorithm benefits from edge pruning. In fact, the weights distribution of the attention-flow graph, plotted in Fig. 5, spans over several orders of magnitudes and the considerable amount of lightly weighted links adds a background noise in the network, which is detrimental for the community detection.

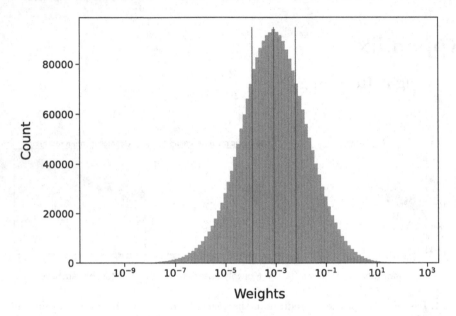

Fig. 5. Weights distribution of the attention-flow graph, with the investigated pruning thresholds at 25th, 50th and 75th percentiles indicated by red vertical lines. (Color figure online)

C   Mentioned Communities

In Table 4, we report the top-10 largest subreddits by userbase for all the mentioned communities: the four politicized communities of interest, and their neighboring communities mentioned in Table 5.

Table 4. Top-10 subreddits by userbase for mentioned communities.

Label	Top 1 subreddit	Top 2 subreddit	Top 3 subreddit	Top 4 subreddit	Top 5 subreddit	Size
Alt-Right	The_Donald	worldpolitics	conspiracy	greatawakening	CBTS_Stream	128
Esoterism	Dreams	Incels	Paranormal	witchcraft	Glitch_in_the_Matrix	139
Liberal	Coronavirus	PoliticalHumor	politics	CoronavirusMemes	China_Flu	113
Radical Left	ChapoTrapHouse	SandersForPresident	SelfAwarewolves	PresidentialRaceMemes	LateStageCapitalism	112
LGBTQ+	TeenAmIUgly	pointlesslygendered	TransTryouts	latebloomerlesbians	okbuddyhetero	155
Entertainment	KeanuBeingAwesome	frenworld	whatsthatbook	ConsumeProduct	okboomer	293
Videogames/Fantasy	keoXer	MarioJudah	EajParkOfficial	PS5restock	ainbowroad	1291
Gaming Hardware	PS5	XboxSeriesX	buildapc	Amd	nvidia	110
Twitch	LaStalla	EIDL	BPTmeta	Homyatol	Panetty	674
Satire	mildly_interesting	TheCircleTV	covfefe	PolHumor	net_neutrality	198
Crypto-currencies	CryptoCurrency	Bitcoin	btc	ethtrader	ethereum	13
Anime	Genshin_Memepact	codevein	Helltaker	DevilArtemisUniverse	JuJutsuKaisen	285
Self-help	AmItheAsshole	relationship_advice	depression	NoFap	Tinder	104

Label	Top 6 subreddit	Top 7 subreddit	Top 8 subreddit	Top 9 subreddit	Top 10 subreddit
Alt-Right	Conservative	WatchRedditDie	JordanPeterson	NoNewNormal	Libertarian
Esoterism	DecidingToBeBetter	IWantToLearn	step1	spirituality	tarot
Liberal	YangForPresidentHQ	CoronavirusUS	HongKong	EnoughTrumpSpam	JoeBiden
Radical Left	ABoringDystopia	OurPresident	TheRightCantMeme	WayOfTheBern	VaushV
LGBTQ+	femboyhooters	questions	comingout	TheClickOwO	aromantic
Entertainment	Boomerhumour	shower_thoughts	screenshots	opienanthony	disenchantment
Videogames/Fantasy	CanadaPS5	Pxlsspace	PlayGodfall	theblackvoid	usps_complaints
Gaming Hardware	OculusQuest	battlestations	hardwareswap	oculus	GlobalOffensiveTrade
Twitch	USCIS	DarioMocciaTwitch	interestingnewsworld	pga2k21	barexam
Satire	podemos	zuckmemes	AskABrit	EpsteinMemes	NickerNation
Crypto-currencies	CryptoMarkets	Bitcoincash	BlockChain	CryptoCurrencies	dashpay
Anime	TowerofGod	SDSGrandCross	PampamilyangPaoLUL	KanojoOkarishimasu	obeyme
Self-help	ApplyingToCollege	offmychest	CasualConversation	stopdrinking	ADHD

Table 5. Top-5 communities by normalized inflow for three gateway nodes.

(a) r/Ani_Communism

Community	Inflow
Videogames/Fantasy	0.699
Radical Left	0.201
LGBTQ+	0.045
Satire	0.039
Anime	0.004

(b) r/The_Donald

Community	Inflow
Alt-Right	0.411
Videogames/Fantasy	0.133
Satire	0.081
Entertainment	0.059
Twitch	0.049

(c) r/numerology

Community	Inflow
Satire	0.604
Crypto-currencies	0.256
Esoterism	0.075
Self-help	0.039
Gaming Hardware	0.016

References

Abbas, T., Somoano, I.B., Cook, J., Frens, I., Klein, G.R., McNeil-Willson, R.: The buffalo attack-an analysis of the manifesto (2022). https://icct.nl/publication/the-buffalo-attack-an-analysis-of-the-manifesto/

Baumgartner, J., Zannettou, S., Keegan, B., Squire, M., Blackburn, J.: The pushshift reddit dataset. In: Proceedings of the International AAAI Conference on Web and Social Media, vol. 14, pp. 830–839 (2020)

Boxell, L., Gentzkow, M., Shapiro, J.M.: Is the internet causing political polarization? evidence from demographics. Technical report, National Bureau of Economic Research (2017)

Bruns, A.: Gatewatching, not gatekeeping: collaborative online news. Media Int. Aust. **107**(1), 31–44 (2003)

Burt, R.S.: Structural Holes: The Social Structure of Competition. Harvard University Press, Cambridge (1992)

Burt, R.S.: Structural holes and good ideas. Am. J. Sociol. **110**(2), 349–399 (2004)

Cai, B., Decker, S., Zheng, C.: The migrants of reddit: an analysis of user migration effects of subreddit bans. Preprint (2019)

Chandrasekharan, E., Pavalanathan, U., Srinivasan, A., Glynn, A., Eisenstein, J., Gilbert, E.: You can't stay here: the efficacy of reddit's 2015 ban examined through hate speech. Proc. ACM Hum.-Comput. Interact. **1**(CSCW), 1–22 (2017)

Cinelli, M., De Francisci Morales, G., Galeazzi, A., Quattrociocchi, W., Starnini, M.: The echo chamber effect on social media. PNAS: Proc. Natl. Acad. Sci. **118**(9), e2023301118 (2021). https://doi.org/10.1073/pnas.2023301118. http://www.pnas.org/lookup/doi/10.1073/pnas.2023301118

Datta, S., Adar, E.: Extracting inter-community conflicts in reddit. In: Proceedings of the International AAAI Conference on Web and Social Media, vol. 13, pp. 146–157 (2019)

Davies, C., et al.: Multi-scale user migration on reddit. AAAI (2021)

Enli, G.: Twitter as arena for the authentic outsider: exploring the social media campaigns of Trump and Clinton in the 2016 US presidential election. Eur. J. Commun. **32**(1), 50–61 (2017)

Fabbri, F., Wang, Y., Bonchi, F., Castillo, C., Mathioudakis, M.: Rewiring what-to-watch-next recommendations to reduce radicalization pathways. In: Proceedings of the ACM Web Conference 2022, pp. 2719–2728 (2022)

Garimella, K., De Francisci Morales, G., Gionis, A., Mathioudakis, M.: Political discourse on social media: echo chambers, gatekeepers, and the price of bipartisanship. In: WWW 2018: The Web Conference, pp. 913–922 (2018a)

Garimella, K., De Francisci Morales, G., Gionis, A., Mathioudakis, M.: Quantifying controversy on social media. ACM Trans. Soc. Comput. **1**(1), 3 (2018b)

George, R., Shujaee, K., Kerwat, M., Felfli, Z., Gelenbe, D., Ukuwu, K.: A comparative evaluation of community detection algorithms in social networks. Procedia Comput. Sci. **171**, 1157–1165 (2020)

Guimera, R., Sales-Pardo, M., Amaral, L.A.N.: Modularity from fluctuations in random graphs and complex networks. Phys. Rev. E **70**(2), 025101 (2004)

Horta Ribeiro, M., et al.: Do platform migrations compromise content moderation? evidence from r/the_donald and r/incels. Proc. ACM Hum.-Comput. Interact. **5**(CSCW2), 1–24 (2021)

Iyengar, S., Sood, G., Lelkes, Y.: Affect, not ideologya social identity perspective on polarization. Public Opin. Q. **76**(3), 405–431 (2012)

Jolley, D., Douglas, K.M., Sutton, R.M.: Blaming a few bad apples to save a threatened barrel: the system-justifying function of conspiracy theories. Polit. Psychol. **39**(2), 465–478 (2018)

Karrer, B., Newman, M.E.: Stochastic blockmodels and community structure in networks. Phys. Rev. E **83**(1), 016107 (2011)

Klein, C., Clutton, P., Dunn, A.G.: Pathways to conspiracy: the social and linguistic precursors of involvement in reddit's conspiracy theory forum. PLoS ONE **14**(11), e0225098 (2019)

Kubin, E., von Sikorski, C.: The role of (social) media in political polarization: a systematic review. Ann. Int. Commun. Assoc. **45**(3), 188–206 (2021)

Lewin, K.: Frontiers in group dynamics: II. Channels of group life; social planning and action research. Hum. Relat. **1**(2), 143–153 (1947)

Mamié, R., Horta Ribeiro, M., West, R.: Are anti-feminist communities gateways to the far right? Evidence from reddit and Youtube. In: 13th ACM Web Science Conference 2021, pp. 139–147 (2021)

Marwick, A.E., Partin, W.C.: Constructing alternative facts: populist expertise and the QAnon conspiracy. New Media Soc. 14614448221090201 (2022)

Massachs, J., Monti, C., De Francisci Morales, G., Bonchi, F.: Roots of trumpism: homophily and social feedback in donald trump support on reddit. In: WebSci 2020: 12th International ACM Web Science Conference, pp. 49–58. WebSci (2020)

Neo, L.S.: An internet-mediated pathway for online radicalisation: RECRO. In: Violent Extremism: Breakthroughs in Research and Practice, pp. 62–89. IGI Global (2019)

Peixoto, T.P.: Nonparametric Bayesian inference of the microcanonical stochastic block model. Phys. Rev. E **95**(1), 012317 (2017)

Phadke, S., Samory, M., Mitra, T.: What makes people join conspiracy communities? Role of social factors in conspiracy engagement. Proc. ACM Hum.-Comput. Interact. **4**(CSCW3), 1–30 (2021)

Phadke, S., Samory, M., Mitra, T.: Pathways through conspiracy: the evolution of conspiracy radicalization through engagement in online conspiracy discussions. In: Proceedings of the International AAAI Conference on Web and Social Media, vol. 16, pp. 770–781 (2022)

Quattrociocchi, W., Scala, A., Sunstein, C.R.: Echo chambers on Facebook. Available at SSRN 2795110 (2016)

Ribeiro, M.H., et al.: The evolution of the manosphere across the web. arXiv preprint arXiv:2001.07600 (2020a)

Ribeiro, M.H., Ottoni, R., West, R., Almeida, V.A., Meira Jr, W.: Auditing radicalization pathways on Youtube. In: Proceedings of the 2020 Conference on Fairness, Accountability, and Transparency, pp. 131–141 (2020b)

Shatz, I.: Fast, free, and targeted: Reddit as a source for recruiting participants online. Soc. Sci. Comput. Rev. **35**(4), 537–549 (2017)

Skelley, G.: What We Know About Andrew Yang's Base. Five Thirty Eight (2019). https://fivethirtyeight.com/features/what-we-know-about-andrew-yangs-base/. Accessed 18 Aug 2022

Stroud, N.J.: Polarization and partisan selective exposure. J. Commun. **60**(3), 556–576 (2010)

Thorson, K., Wells, C.: Curated flows: a framework for mapping media exposure in the digital age. Commun. Theory **26**(3), 309–328 (2016)

Waller, I., Anderson, A.: Quantifying social organization and political polarization in online platforms. Nature **600**(7888), 264–268 (2021)

Welbers, K., Opgenhaffen, M.: Social media gatekeeping: an analysis of the gatekeeping influence of newspapers' public Facebook pages. New Media Soc. **20**(12), 4728–4747 (2018)

West, S.M.: Raging against the machine: network gatekeeping and collective action on social media platforms. Media Commun. **5**(3), 28–36 (2017)

Wu, M.: La Q di Qomplotto: QAnon e dintorni: come le fantasie di complotto difendono il sistema. Edizioni Alegre (2021). https://edizionialegre.it/notizie/the-q-in-conspiracy/

Zannettou, S., et al.: The web centipede: understanding how web communities influence each other through the lens of mainstream and alternative news sources. In: Proceedings of the 2017 Internet Measurement Conference, pp. 405–417 (2017)

Don't Take It Personally: Analyzing Gender and Age Differences in Ratings of Online Humor

J. A. Meaney[1]([⊠])(ID), Steven R. Wilson[1,2](ID), Luis Chiruzzo[3](ID), and Walid Magdy[1](ID)

[1] School of Informatics, University of Edinburgh, Edinburgh, UK
jameaney@ed.ac.uk, wmagdy@inf.ed.ac.uk
[2] Oakland University, Rochester, MI, USA
stevenwilson@oakland.edu
[3] Universidad de la República, Montevideo, Uruguay
luischir@fing.edu.uy

Abstract. Computational humor detection systems rarely model the subjectivity of humor responses, or consider alternative reactions to humor - namely offense. We analyzed a large dataset of humor and offense ratings by male and female annotators of different age groups. We find that women link these two concepts more strongly than men, and they tend to give lower humor ratings and higher offense scores. We also find that the correlation between humor and offense increases with age. Although there were no gender or age differences in humor detection, women and older annotators signalled that they did not understand joke texts more often than men. We discuss implications for computational humor detection and downstream tasks.

Keywords: Computational humor · Offense detection · Online texts · Demographics

1 Introduction

Computational Humor Detection is a fast-growing area of research and has produced at least one humor detection challenge per year since 2017 with Hashtag Wars in SemEval 2017, [18], the Spanish-language HAHA task in Iberlef 2018 [4] and 2019 [5], Assessing Humor in Edited Headlines in 2020 [11] and HaHackathon in 2021 [17]. With participation in these challenges increasing year on year, organisers are beginning to refine their conception of humor, and to incorporate some of the vast, inter-disciplinary findings of the broader humor research community.

One vital branch of this research is that humor is known to vary along the lines of demographic characteristics. Factors such as age [14], gender [10], personality [21] and other demographic variables all modulate responses to humor. Humor tasks have struggled to incorporate such demographic awareness into

© The Author(s), under exclusive license to Springer Nature Switzerland AG 2022
F. Hopfgartner et al. (Eds.): SocInfo 2022, LNCS 13618, pp. 20–33, 2022.
https://doi.org/10.1007/978-3-031-19097-1_2

their tasks, and instead tend to average over all humor ratings - which removes nuance and subjectivity from the data [16], as well as possibly decreasing the generalizability of humor detection systems.

A second salient finding from the broader humor literature is that humor is closely linked to offense [15] and indeed, can be used as a mechanism to mask hateful or offensive content. Several competitions have modelled hate speech [1] [27], which is related to offense, but HaHackathon was the first humor detection competition to co-model humor and offense. As the concept of offense is less tangible than humor, it was split in two:

1. *General offense* meaning that a text targets a group of people simply because they belonged to that group and/or is likely upsetting to a lot of people.
2. *Personal offense*, targeting a group that the reader belongs to or cares about.

Although the annotators of this dataset provided demographic data about their age and gender, this was not released as part of the humor detection task, and this is the first analysis of the impact of these age and gender on the humor and offense ratings in this large dataset. The analysis aims to uncover if humor and offense are as meaningfully linked in big datasets as they are in small-N studies, while validating evidence that there are gendered differences in the distribution of humor ratings [24], as well as tolerance of aggressive humor.

As in [10], we are mindful of the use of *gender* to specify a cultural phenomenon, indicating men and women as socially-defined groups, rather than a biological distinction.

1.1   Related Work

Gender and age differences have been the subject of many studies in the fields of psychology, sociology, education, and management studies. Svebak et al. [24] found that "overall humor scores" were higher for men than they were for women. However, it should be noted that "overall humor" was narrowly assessed, using only three items, with each representing one of the dimensions of the Situational Humor Questionnaire. The same work reported that humor appreciation declines with age: the mean scores for total sense of humor on average declined across the age cohorts from highest score in the 20s to lowest score among those aged 70. More recently, an Italian study of covid-related humor [3] reported that increasing age, as well as being female was related to finding pandemic humor more aversive and less funny.

In terms of gender differences, perhaps the most replicated result is that men tolerate aggressive humor more than female respondents do [10]. Proyer and Ruch [20] report that men tended to score higher on kagelaticism - the joy of laughing at others, which suggests that as long as a joke does not target men explicitly, it may be offensive towards other groups, without impacting men's humor ratings. Interestingly, Knegtmans et al. [12] found that participants whose social power had been manipulated to place them in a high-power state rated jokes which targeted others as less offensive, and gave higher humor ratings.

No differences in the appreciation of nonsense humor [13], or neutral jokes [7] were found.

1.2   Research Questions (RQ)

1. Is there a correlation between annotators' perceptions of humor and offense? Does this vary by age and gender?
2. Are there differences in humor *detection* and *comprehension* between groups?
3. Are there differences in the distributions of humor and offense ratings between groups?

Using a dataset of >120k ratings of humor and offense [17], we find a slight negative correlation between humor and offense, which varies as a function of gender and age. The negative link between humor and offense increases as annotators age. We also find a stronger correlation between general offense and humor for women, but male annotators only linked these concepts when they signalled that they were personally offended. There were no significant differences between groups when it came to correctly identifying texts as jokes (i.e. humor detection), but there were differences when it came to humor comprehension. More women than men indicated that they did not get a joke, and women of all age groups had higher rates of using the label "I don't get it" than men of all age groups. In terms of the distribution of ratings, women were more likely to use lower humor ratings and higher offense ratings, while men showed the opposite trend. In terms of age groups, the oldest group tended to report that they didn't get a joke more than any other group, while annotators ages 26–40 were least likely to use this label, and also gave the highest humor ratings overall. Older groups were more likely to use higher ratings of general and personal offense, while younger annotators were less likely to use these.

2   Dataset Description

The dataset features the texts and ratings used in the humor and offense shared task HaHackathon at SemEval 2021 [17]. Including non-humorous texts, this comprises 202,369 ratings of 10,000 texts. Each text has an average of 20.2 ratings, with no text having fewer than 17 votes. There were 1,821 unique annotators (mean age 40.45 years, SD = 15.64 years), and each annotator rated an average of 111.13 texts. The highest number of texts rated by one person was 307.

Of the 10,000 texts in the dataset, 2,000 were sourced from the Kaggle Short Jokes Dataset[1]. Half of the Kaggle texts were selected because they referred to one of the common targets of online hate speech outlined by Silva et al. [22], e.g. women, members of the LGBT community, religious/racial minorities, and this target was the butt of the joke. These texts were deemed likely to elicit ratings

---

[1] https://github.com/amoudgl/short-jokes-dataset.

of offense from some annotators. The other half of the Kaggle texts referred to a common hate speech target, but did not make it the butt of the joke.

The other 8,000 texts were sourced from Twitter, from a mix of humorous and non-humorous accounts. Amongst the non-humorous accounts, there were several which advocate for, or provide information to common targets of hate speech. This ensured that mentions of these targets were not limited to humorous texts only.

Annotators were asked up to three sets of questions about each text: one related to humor and two related to offense.

1. **Humor detection/rating:** annotators were asked if the intention of the text was to be humorous. This binary response question was aimed at gauging the genre of the text, and annotators were asked not to judge based on whether they found it funny, but whether it contained indicators of the humor genre, e.g. a setup and punchline, puns, absurd content, etc. If the annotator selected 'yes', they were asked to rate how funny they found it from 1–5. There was also the option to select 'I don't get it' if the text was identified as humorous, but the humor was not understood. If the annotator selected 'no', they were not asked any further questions about this text.
2. **General offense detection/rating:** If a text had been labelled as humorous, annotators were asked if they thought the text targeted a group simply because they belonged to a group, or if they thought the text would be offensive to a large number of people. In the case of a 'yes' response, they were asked how generally offensive they thought the text was from 1–5.
3. **Personal offense:** If a text had been labelled as humorous, we asked annotators if they were personally hurt by the text, or were hurt on someone else's behalf, and if so, to rate how much from 1–5.

The pool of annotators comprised 4 age groups: 18–25, 26–40, 41–55, 56–70. In order to avoid a lack of shared cultural knowledge, all annotators were native English speakers and citizens of the United States. Although we aimed to be inclusive of diverse genders, the dataset included only four annotators who preferred not to disclose their gender. As they rated a total of 384 texts, they were excluded from the gender analysis, for reasons of statistical power.

Annotators provided informed consent before beginning the annotation, and the procedure was approved by the Ethics Committee of the corresponding author's institution. Other demographic data about the annotators, such as gender and personality traits, was also provided as part of the dataset.

3   Methodology

Given that the humor and offense annotations were reported using an ordinal scale, for RQ1, we used the Spearman rank correlation [23] to report the correlations between these variables. The Spearman rank correlation is a generalisation of the Pearson correlation which is used for discrete and ordinal data which captures the strength and direction of the relationship between two variables by ranking the values of each variable, summing the square differences and calculating the covariance of the ranks. This returns a correlation coefficient, ρ, ranging from -1 to $+1$, the magnitude of which indicates the strength of the relationship and the sign signifies the direction. It also returns a p-value - the probability that the value of the coefficient could occur under the null hypothesis.

To answer RQ2, we calculated the proportion of annotators from each group (i.e., gender or age group) that mislabeled (failed to *detect*) or misunderstood (failed to *comprehend*) each text. The resulting distributions were non-normal, so we chose non-parametric tests, which do not assume an underlying distribution. As we have only two values for gender in the dataset, we used a Wilcoxon Signed Rank test [26] to examine the null hypothesis that the samples from male and female annotators came from the same distribution. This is similar to a paired t-test, and it ranks the absolute value of the pairs of differences to calculate the test statistic, w. With this test, we report the Common Language Effect Size (CLES): the proportion of pairs where the values for one group are higher than the other.

For more than two groups, i.e., our age variable, which had four bins, we use the Friedman test [8], which is similar to a repeated measures ANOVA. Again values are ranked and the test compares the mean rank of each group for statistical significance. In the case of a significant result, we ran post hoc pairwise Wilcoxon tests. We used the Bonferroni correction to adjust the p-values for multiple comparisons, reducing the risk of false positive results.

For RQ3, we first used the Wilcoxon and Friedman tests to determine if one group tended to give higher or lower ratings than another. We then used a chi-square test of homogeneity to examine how the distributions differed from each other. This test determines if the frequencies of each possible value of the dependent variable are distributed in the same way across the different groups. The test calculates the expected frequencies of each rating by each group by multiplying the number of annotators in each group by the true probability that any annotator would pick each answer. This expected frequency is then compared to the observed frequency.

4   Results

4.1   RQ1: Is There a Correlation Between Humor and Offense?

For the following analysis, we excluded texts which had been labelled as 'not humorous' by our annotators, and removed outliers (e.g. texts that had fewer than 3 humor ratings). This left 121,622 ratings of 6,918 texts.

Overall, there was a small negative correlation between humor and general offense ($\rho = -0.13$, $p < 0.05$), and this grew stronger for humor and personal offense ($\rho = -0.19$, $p < 0.05$), which suggests that offensive content is negatively related to humor appreciation. There was a strong correlation between general and personal offense ($\rho = 0.60$, $p < 0.05$), indicating that these concepts are linked, but are not identical.

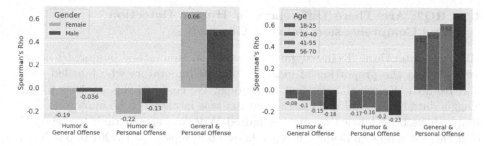

Fig. 1. Correlations between humor and offense by gender and age

Correlations Between Ratings by Gender. When examining the correlations between ratings split by gender, an interesting trend emerged (Fig. 1). There was almost no relationship between humor and *general* offense for men, however *personal* offense ratings were negatively correlated with humor ratings. Conversely, for female annotators, both types of offense were more strongly correlated with a reduced humor rating for female annotators.

Correlations by Age. A second interesting trend emerged in terms of age: the older the annotators were, the stronger the negative link between general *and* personal offense on humor ratings was (Fig. 1). The oldest group had the most prominent negative correlation between humor and both types of offense, as well as the strongest correlation between the two offense metrics.

Correlations by Age and Gender. Although splitting 20 ratings per text into 8 groups (for four age groups by two gender groups) would cause issues of data sparsity and statistical power, we noted that the trend of an increasingly negative correlation between humor and offense continues when this is broken down by age and gender (Fig. 2). Female annotators relate lower humor scores to higher offense scores increasingly with age, and this trend is much less pronounced in male annotators.

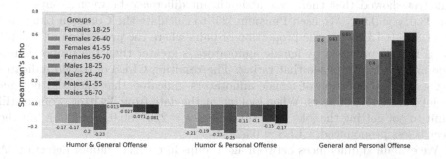

Fig. 2. Correlations between humor and offense by age and gender

4.2   RQ2: Are There Differences in Humor Detection and Comprehension Between Groups?

Humor Detection. To investigate differences in annotators' humor *detection*, we looked at the proportion of male and female annotators who labelled each text from the Kaggle data as 'not humorous'. We confined this analysis to the Kaggle data because all texts in this dataset was intended to be humorous, and should have been labeled as such. A paired Wilcoxon signed rank test showed that there was no significant difference between groups ($z = 134201.0$, $p = 0.29$) (Table 1).

Table 1. Mislabeling and misunderstanding in the Kaggle Jokes

	Male	Female
Proportion of annotations from each group	42.92%	57.08%
'Not Humor' ratings from each group	3.79%	3.70%
Unique texts with 1+ label of not-humorous	22.91%	25.42%
'I don't get it' ratings from each group	5.77%	7.35%
Unique texts with 1+ rating of 'I don't get it"	33.04%	45.81%

We used a similar procedure to test if there were significant differences between age groups in terms of humor detection. A Friedman test showed that there were no significant differences between groups ($\chi^2 = 6.976$, $p = 0.07$).

Humor Comprehension. After labeling a text as humorous, one of the options for humor rating was 'I don't get it'. This indicated that the annotator had recognized that the text was intended to be humorous, but that they lacked the knowledge to fully understand the joke. We first looked at the Kaggle dataset, and calculated the number of 'I don't get it' votes from men and women, as a proportion of the total votes per text from each group. A paired Wilcoxon signed rank test showed that there was a significant difference between groups ($z = 214403.0$, $p < 0.05$). We used Pingouin [25] to calculate the Common Language Effect Size (CLES), i.e. the proportion of pairs where the proportion of 'I don't get it' ratings provided by female annotators is greater than the proportion of male annotators who gave that rating. The resulting CLES of 0.5540 indicates that a larger proportion of female annotators indicated that they did not get the joke in 55.45% of pairs. When looking at the data from Twitter, women still admit to not getting the joke more than men ($z = 2298680.0$, $p < 0.05$), but the effect is less pronounced, CLES = 0.5223.

We examined differences between age groups in terms of humor detection. A Friedman test showed that there were no significant differences between groups ($\chi^2 = 0.0012$, $p = 0.06$).

4.3   RQ3: Are There Differences Between Groups in Distributions Humor and Offense Ratings?

When looking at the distribution of ratings across the 6 possible values (1–5 and '*1 don't get it*') for the entire dataset (both Kaggle and Twitter), a χ^2 test of homogeneity demonstrated that there were significant differences between the distributions of humor ratings between men and women ($\chi^2 = 202.25$, $p < 0.05$) and showed that women were more likely to select 'I don't get it', while men were more likely to use higher ratings. We also explored if this difference translated into different average humor ratings per text and a Wilcoxon signed rank showed that men gave significantly higher ratings than women on humor ($z = 9684516.5$, $p < 0.05$) and the CLES score of 0.5333 indicated that men gave higher humor ratings in 53.33% of pairs.

For general offense, a χ^2 test of homogeneity showed significant differences between groups ($\chi^2 = 430.85$, $p < 0.05$), and examining the expected versus observed counts showed that the trend seen in the humor ratings was reversed: men were more likely to choose low offense ratings and women were more likely to select higher values. In terms of averaged general offense ratings, group differences were significant ($z = 4260050.5$, $p < 0.05$, CLES $= 0.4704$), with men giving higher offense ratings in 47.04% of pairs.

Similarly, for personal offense, a χ^2 test of was significant ($\chi^2 = 1195.94$, $p < 0.05$) with a more pronounced trend showing that women were more likely to select a high personal offense rating, and men systematically under-selected high ratings. This led to significant differences in the average personal offense ratings per text, where men gave higher personal offense scores in only 41.5% of pairs ($z = 1234096.5$, $p < 0.05$, CLES $= 0.4146$).

When looking at age groups, a χ^2 test showed significant differences in humor ratings between age groups ($\chi^2 = 239.98$, $p < 0.05$). The oldest group, 56–70, were most likely to report 'I don't get it', while annotators aged 26–40 were least likely to use this, and most likely to give high ratings. In terms of general offense, there were significant group differences ($\chi^2 = 540.936$ $p < 0.05$), and annotators 18–40 were more likely to give lower general offense ratings, while those aged 41–70 used fewer low ratings than expected, and the group ages 56–70 was most likely to give the highest possible offense rating of 5. Group differences were more pronounced in personal offense ratings ($\chi^2 = 1387.43$, $p < 0.05$) where the two youngest groups gave consistently lower than expected ratings of personal offense, while the older group gave consistently higher ratings. This resulted in significant differences in the average personal offense scores between groups ($\chi^2 = 38.223$, $p < 0.05$).

5   Qualitative Analysis

The negative correlation for female annotators between humor and general offense, which was uncovered in the above analysis, is succinctly illustrated in Fig. 3. Texts which are offensive for women tend to earn a lower humor rating, while general offense is more tolerated by men.

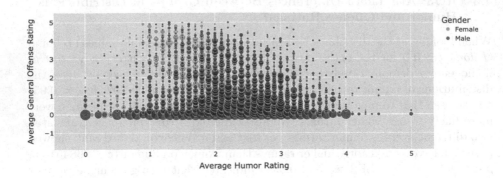

Fig. 3. Relationship between humor and offense by gender

To examine what type of texts male and female annotators differed on with regard to general offense ratings, we selected the top 40 texts where there was at least a 1.5 point difference between the mean general offense score given by male and female annotators. We labeled the topic or target of the texts and five annotators rated whether the content was aggressive or not. Annotators were instructed that a text should be deemed aggressive if it contained violent content or used racial slurs, and inter-annotator agreement was relatively high (Fleiss's $\kappa = 0.3815$) (Fig. 2).

Table 2. Sample texts where annotators differed on general offense

Text	Humor		G. Offense	
	Female	Male	Female	Male
Why are the labia on Japanese women oriented sideways instead of vertically? Goes better with their eyes	1.0	2.2	4.2	1.3
In my spare time, I help blind kids I mean the verb, not the adjective	1.3	2.0	2.2	0.17
Two condoms walk by a gay bar... One says to the other, "Wanna go inside and get shitfaced?"	2.6	1.6	0.85	2.4
What did the Jewish pirate say when he heard his wife died? Argh, shiva me timbers	1.6	1.6	1.0	2.1

There was a sizeable overlap of topics, with women finding texts about the LGBT community more offensive than men, while male annotators found texts about religion more generally offensive. The texts that were offensive to women tended to be aggressive, while men were more tolerant of this. Interestingly, men selected several texts which were not intended to be jokes (e.g. were drawn

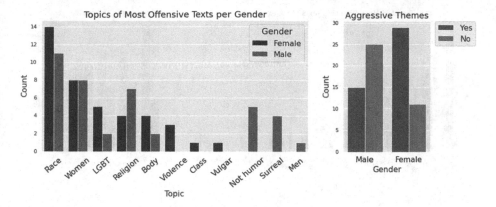

Fig. 4. Topics and aggression where gender groups disagreed on general offense ratings

from accounts supporting targets of hate speech) as both humorous and offensive (Fig. 4).

We followed a similar procedure to examine the texts where offense ratings from different age groups differed from each other. We compared the mean general offense rating from each group to the average general offense rating from the other 3 groups combined, and looked at the top 40 texts where there was at least a 1.5 point difference. Several topics predominate, namely race, women, body (e.g. disability, body weight). The texts rated as more generally offensive by younger groups focused on these topics, but as age increased, so did the variety of topics featured. The texts selected by group 1 (the youngest group) featured more which were aggressive in nature, but as age increased, aggression was less linked to offense (Fig. 5).

6 Discussion

We used a large dataset of texts rated for humor and offense, along with some demographic information about the annotators to explore differences between age and gender groups. We looked at how the groups link humor and offense, differences in humor detection and comprehension, as well as differences in the distributions of ratings.

RQ1: We found that female annotators negatively link humor and offense more strongly than men. Male annotators do not link general offense with diminished humor ratings. In fact, they link humor and offense to a lesser extent, and only when personally offended.

As regards age groups, the correlation between humor and offense was weakest in the youngest group, and grew steadily with age - as did the link between general and personal offense.

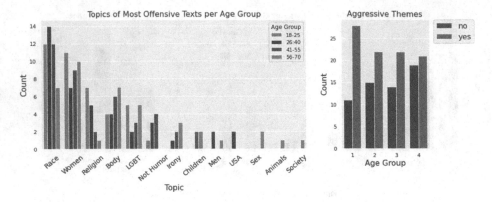

Fig. 5. Analysis of topics and aggression where age groups disagreed on general offense ratings

RQ2: There were no differences in gender or age groups in terms of humor detection. However, when it came to humor comprehension, women selected 'I don't get it' more often than men.

RQ3: In terms of the distributions of ratings, women gave lower humor ratings and higher offense ratings, while men showed the opposite trend. Amongst the age groups, annotators 26–40 gave the highest ratings and the fewest reports of 'I don't get it'. In line with findings from RQ1, younger groups gave lower offense ratings and older groups reported higher offense.

Some of the findings above are well attested in the humor literature, albeit in smaller-N studies. Hofmann et al. [10] report that men's tolerance of aggressive humor is one of the most consistent findings in the humor field, with seven out of eight studies mentioned replicating this result. Our qualitative work shows that in the texts on which men and women differed most on general offense, aggression featured more prominently for women. Perhaps relatedly, Proyer and Ruch [20] report that men score higher on katagelasticism - the joy of laughing at others. This may be reflected in the fact that general offense does not diminish male annotators' humor ratings, only personal offense does.

A more surprising result is the increasingly strong negative correlation between humor and offense as age progressed. This contradicts the oft-touted idea of *Generation Snowflake*, which contends that those born after 1995 tend to be the most overly reactive to offensive material [9]. The older age groups - 40–55 and 56–70 - gave higher ratings of offense than their younger counterparts, and our qualitative analysis indicated that the older groups gave higher offense ratings to a wider variety of topics.

The finding that women used the 'I don't get it' label more than men is a result that may benefit from some contextualisation from the humor literature. Bell [2] found that when shown incomprehensible jokes, women tended to explicitly state that they did not get it, while men implicitly signaled it by asking concept-checking questions. It is not possible to know whether this was the case here, but it is true that the qualitative results uncovered that men were mentioning not humorous texts as both humorous and offensive.

6.1 Implications

Given the gender and age group differences in ratings of humor and offense, it is evident that humor detection systems which average over all annotators' ratings fail to model the subjectivity that is inherent to this task. These systems may not generalise well on downstream tasks, such as content moderation, and may not be effective at moderating aggressive content if they are tuned to men's preferences, or alternatively may be more restrictive if tuned to women's preferences. Furthermore, as sociologists have pointed out [15], the line between humor and offense is continually under revision in most societies, therefore not only are these responses subjective, but they are a moving target. We should focus on incorporating frameworks to include demographic knowledge in our systems, which can constantly be updated to reflect society's changing definitions of humor and offense.

6.2 Limitations

It is a limitation that the dataset did not afford the opportunity to explore the interaction between age and gender. As each text has approximately 20 annotations per text, splitting these into 8 groups to model age and gender would not have provided sufficient statistical power. Similarly, it is a limitation that there were insufficient annotations from gender non-conforming annotators, as there is a dearth of literature on their reactions to humor and offense. The lack of annotators that self-identify with genders other than female and male has been noticed in the past in different tasks as well [6,19].

A final constraint is that we are modelling only one half of the humorous interaction - the recipient of the joke. Excluding the teller of the joke can deny the recipient some important context needed to enjoy the joke, and different tellers can mitigate the responses. Future work should include this dimension.

7 Conclusion

We present the first analysis of the demographic data provided with the HaHackathon data - a large dataset used to train systems for computational humor detection. Our findings indicate that women negatively link humor to offense, while men only do so if they are personally offended. Links between humor and offense grew with age. There were no differences in humor detection by gender or age groups, but women and older annotators indicated that they did not understand jokes more than men. Distributions of humor and offense ratings replicated findings from humor research, namely that men gave higher humor ratings and lower offense ratings. We hope that these findings will inform future frameworks for computational humor detection and dataset creation.

Acknowledgements. This work was supported in part by the EPSRC Centre for Doctoral Training in Data Science, funded by the UK Engineering and Physical Sciences Research Council (grant EP/L016427/1) and the University of Edinburgh.

References

1. Basile, V., et al.: SemEval-2019 task 5: multilingual detection of hate speech against immigrants and women in twitter. In: Proceedings of the 13th International Workshop on Semantic Evaluation, pp. 54–63 (2019)
2. Bell, N.D.: Responses to incomprehensible humor. J. Pragmat. **57**, 176–189 (2013)
3. Bischetti, L., Canal, P., Bambini, V.: Funny but aversive: a large-scale survey of the emotional response to Covid-19 humor in the Italian population during the lockdown. Lingua **249**, 102963 (2021)
4. Castro, S., Chiruzzo, L., Rosá, A.: Overview of the HAHA task: humor analysis based on human annotation at IberEval 2018. In: IberEval@ SEPLN, pp. 187–194 (2018)
5. Chiruzzo, L., Castro, S., Etcheverry, M., Garat, D., Prada, J.J., Rosá, A.: Overview of haha at IberEval 2019: humor analysis based on human annotation. In: IberLEF@ SEPLN (2019)
6. Excell, E., Moubayed, N.A.: Towards equal gender representation in the annotations of toxic language detection. In: Proceedings of the 3rd Workshop on Gender Bias in Natural Language Processing, pp. 55–65 (2021)
7. Ferstl, E.C., Israel, L., Putzar, L.: Humor facilitates text comprehension: evidence from eye movements. Discourse Process. **54**(4), 259–284 (2017)
8. Friedman, M.: The use of ranks to avoid the assumption of normality implicit in the analysis of variance. J. Am. Stat. Assoc. **32**(200), 675–701 (1937)
9. Haidt, J., Lukianoff, G.: The coddling of the American mind: how good intentions and bad ideas are setting up a generation for failure. Penguin UK (2018)
10. Hofmann, J., Platt, T., Lau, C., Torres-Marín, J.: Gender differences in humor-related traits, humor appreciation, production, comprehension, (neural) responses, use, and correlates: a systematic review. Curr. Psychol. 1–14 (2020)
11. Hossain, N., Krumm, J., Gamon, M., Kautz, H.: SemEval-2020 task 7: assessing humor in edited news headlines. arXiv preprint arXiv:2008.00304 (2020)
12. Knegtmans, H., Van Dijk, W.W., Mooijman, M., Van Lier, N., Rintjema, S., Wassink, A.: The impact of social power on the evaluation of offensive jokes. Humor **31**(1), 85–104 (2018)
13. Köhler, G., Ruch, W.: Sources of variance in current sense of humor inventories: how much substance, how much method variance? (1996)
14. Kuipers, G.: The humor divide: class, age and humor styles. In: Good Humor, Bad Taste, pp. 71–101. De Gruyter Mouton (2015)
15. Lockyer, S., Pickering, M.: Beyond a Joke: The Limits of Humour. Springer, London (2005). https://doi.org/10.1057/9780230236776
16. Meaney, J.: Crossing the line: where do demographic variables fit into humor detection? In: Proceedings of the 58th Annual Meeting of the Association for Computational Linguistics: Student Research Workshop, pp. 176–181 (2020)
17. Meaney, J., Wilson, S., Chiruzzo, L., Lopez, A., Magdy, W.: SemEval 2021 task 7: hahackathon, detecting and rating humor and offense. In: Proceedings of the 15th International Workshop on Semantic Evaluation (SemEval-2021), pp. 105–119 (2021)

18. Potash, P., Romanov, A., Rumshisky, A.: SemEval-2017 task 6:# hashtagwars: learning a sense of humor. In: Proceedings of the 11th International Workshop on Semantic Evaluation (SemEval-2017), pp. 49–57 (2017)
19. Prabhakaran, V., Davani, A.M., Diaz, M.: On releasing annotator-level labels and information in datasets. In: Proceedings of the Joint 15th Linguistic Annotation Workshop (LAW) and 3rd Designing Meaning Representations (DMR) Workshop, pp. 133–138 (2021)
20. Proyer, R.T., Ruch, W.: Enjoying and fearing laughter: personality characteristics of gelotophobes, gelotophiles, and katagelasticists. Psychol. Test Assess. Model. **52**(2), 148–160 (2010)
21. Ruch, W.: The Sense of Humor: Explorations of a Personality Characteristic, vol. 3. Walter de Gruyter, Berlin (2010)
22. Silva, L., Mondal, M., Correa, D., Benevenuto, F., Weber, I.: Analyzing the targets of hate in online social media. In: Proceedings of the International AAAI Conference on Web and Social Media, vol. 10 (2016)
23. Spearman, C.: The proof and measurement of association between two things. Am. J. Psychol. **15**(1), 72–101 (1904)
24. Svebak, S., Martin, R.A., Holmen, J.: The prevalence of sense of humor in a large, unselected county population in Norway: relations with age, sex, and some health indicators (2004)
25. Vallat, R.: Pingouin: statistics in python. J. Open Source Softw. **3**(31), 1026 (2018)
26. Wilcoxon, F.: Individual comparisons by ranking methods. In: Biometrics Bulletin, no. 6, vol. 1, pp. 80–83 (1945). http://www.jstor.org/stable/3001968
27. Zampieri, M., et al.: SemEval-2020 task 12: multilingual offensive language identification in social media (OffensEval 2020). arXiv preprint arXiv:2006.07235 (2020)

#IStandWithPutin Versus #IStandWithUkraine: The Interaction of Bots and Humans in Discussion of the Russia/Ukraine War

Bridget Smart$^{(\boxtimes)}$ (iD), Joshua Watt (iD), Sara Benedetti (iD), Lewis Mitchell (iD), and Matthew Roughan (iD)

The University of Adelaide, Adelaide, Australia
{bridget.smart,joshua.watt,sara.benedetti,lewis.mitchell,
matthew.roughan}@adelaide.edu.au
http://set.adelaide.edu.au/mathematical-sciences

Abstract. The 2022 Russian invasion of Ukraine emphasises the role social media plays in modern-day warfare, with conflict occurring in both the physical and information environments. There is a large body of work on identifying malicious cyber-activity, but less focusing on the effect this activity has on the overall conversation, especially with regards to the Russia/Ukraine Conflict. Here, we employ a variety of techniques including information theoretic measures, sentiment and linguistic analysis, and time series techniques to understand how bot activity influences wider online discourse. By aggregating account groups we find significant information flows from bot-like accounts to non-bot accounts with behaviour differing between sides. Pro-Russian non-bot accounts are most influential overall, with information flows to a variety of other account groups. No significant outward flows exist from pro-Ukrainian non-bot accounts, with significant flows from pro-Ukrainian bot accounts into pro-Ukrainian non-bot accounts. We find that bot activity drives an increase in conversations surrounding angst (with $p = 2.450 \times 10^{-4}$) as well as those surrounding work/governance (with $p = 3.803 \times 10^{-18}$). Bot activity also shows a significant relationship with non-bot sentiment (with $p = 3.760 \times 10^{-4}$), where we find the relationship holds in both directions. This work extends and combines existing techniques to quantify how bots are influencing people in the online conversation around the Russia/Ukraine invasion. It opens up avenues for researchers to understand quantitatively how these malicious campaigns operate, and what makes them impactful.

Keywords: Bot nets · Information flow · Sentiment analysis · Linguistic analysis · Disinformation campaigns · Influence campaigns · Twitter

F. Hopfgartner et al. (Eds.): SocInfo 2022, LNCS 13618, pp. 34–53, 2022.
https://doi.org/10.1007/978-3-031-19097-1_3

1   Introduction

Social media is a critical tool in information warfare, playing a large role in the 2022 Russian invasion of Ukraine [6,30]. Disinformation and more generally *reflexive control* [38] have been used by Russia and other countries against their enemies and internally for many years [10]. A relative newcomer in this space – Twitter – has already been extensively used for such purposes during military conflicts, for instance in Donbass [10], but its role in conflicts is evolving and not fully understood. Both sides in the Ukrainian conflict use the online information environment to influence geopolitical dynamics and sway public opinion. Russian social media pushes narratives around their motivation, and Ukrainian social media aims to foster and maintain external support from Western countries, as well as promote their military efforts while undermining the perception of the Russian military. Examples of these narratives include allegations: that Ukraine was developing biological weapons [40], that President Volodymyr Zelenskyy had surrendered [5,16], and that there is a sustained campaign showing the apparent success of 'The Ghost of Kiev' [18]. Some of the information being pushed is genuine, and some is malicious. It is not easy to discriminate which is which.

Understanding and measuring information flows and various language features has previously allowed researchers to understand community dynamics and identify inauthentic accounts and content [1,31,36]. Here we apply and extend these techniques to understand and quantify the influence of bot-like accounts on online discussions, using Twitter data focussed on the Russian invasion of Ukraine. In essence we seek to determine whether the malicious influence campaigns work as intended.

Our dataset consists of 5,203,764 tweets, retweets, quote tweets and replies posted to Twitter between February 23rd and March 8th 2022, containing the hashtags #(I)StandWithPutin, #(I)StandWithRussia, #(I)SupportRussia, #(I)StandWithUkraine, #(I)StandWithZelenskyy and #(I)SupportUkraine [39]. See Sect. 3 for further details. A summary plot of the data is shown in Fig. 1. The figure also shows a measure of the proportion of bot traffic over the same time period, as estimated by the bot-detection tool Botometer [33].

In all time series figures, we present five significant events that provide context for our findings: when the conflict begins (24th February 2022), when the fighting in Mariupol begins (26th February 2022), when Russia captures Kherson (2nd March, 2022), when Russia captures the Zaporizhzhia nuclear power plant (4th March 2022) and when Ukrainian authorities first attempt to evacuate Mariupol (8th March 2022). These events are linked to noticeable changes in the volumes of related tweets, and in our analysis we delve deeper to understand how information is flowing. As a result, we learn how bots are influencing the online conversation by measuring what communities are talking about online, and how this discussion evolves. We use lexicon and rule based techniques to create an approach that is robust, transferable and able to be quickly applied to large volumes of data.

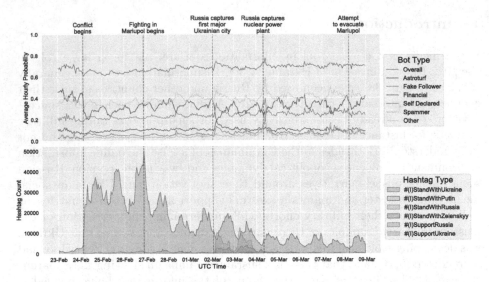

Fig. 1. Average hourly probabilities of bots tweeting query hashtags (top). Hourly frequency of the query hashtags (bottom). The time period we consider is the first fortnight after Russia's invasion of Ukraine. Both plots also include five significant events over this time period. Note that the query hashtags can be found in Sect. 3. We can observe a significant spike in the bot activity of several bot types on the 2nd and 4th of March. The spike in bot activity on the 2nd of March aligns with Russia's capture of Kherson, and also aligns with a significant increase in pro-Russia hashtags. This spike in activity was due to an increase in activity of pro-Russian bots – likely used by Russian authorities. The spike in bot activity on the 4th of March aligns with when the use of pro-Russia hashtags diminished, but also when Russia captured the Zaporizhzhia nuclear power plant. This spike was due to an increase in activity of pro-Russian bots (before being removed) and an increase in activity of pro-Ukrainian bots – likely by pro-Ukrainian authorities in response to Russian bots.

We employ time-series analysis techniques to understand how bot-like activity impacts the wider group of participants, by measuring linguistic content, sentiment and their lagged effect on future discussions. We use the Linguistic Inquiry and Word Count (LIWC; pronounced "Luke") [29] and Valence Aware Dictionary for Sentiment Reasoning (VADER) [13], dictionary based models to measure the linguistic features and sentiment of our dataset. To measure bot activity, we classify a random sample of 26.5% of accounts which posted at least one English language Tweet in the dataset using Botometer [33].

This work extends existing techniques to understand how bot-like accounts spread disinformation on Twitter and measure the effect of these malicious campaigns. The main contributions are:

– An extension of existing information flow techniques to examine aggregated group activity. We establish statistical significance of information flows between accounts grouped by national lean and account type. The highest information flows are out of pro-Russian non-bot accounts. Information flows into non-bot account groups are only significant for balanced and pro-Ukraine accounts, with pro-Russian non-bot accounts only exhibiting a net outward information flow of information.

– We establish a significant relationship between bot activity and overall non-bot sentiment (with $p = 0.000376$), but find this relationship is significant for both positive and negative lags, indicating there may be confounding factors.
– An analysis of the effect which bot activity has on emotions in online discussions around the Russia/Ukraine conflict. We find that bots significantly increase discussions of the LIWC categories: Angst, Friend, Motion, Time, Work and Filler. The strongest relationship is between Self Declared bot activity and words in the 'Work' category (with $p = 3.803 \times 10^{-18}$), which includes words relating to governance structures like 'president' and 'government'.
– A dataset[1] of Twitter users who participated in discussions around the Russian Invasion of Ukraine [39].

2   Related Work

Many works have analysed bot-like accounts on social media [9,15,25]. Authors have shown bots are present in social networks, especially with regard to political campaigns/movements [25]. Keller and Klinger [15] showed social bot activity increased from 7.1% to 9.9% during German election campaigns, using bot probabilities before and during the election campaign. Furthermore, Stella et al. [37] showed bots increase exposure to negative and inflammatory content in online social systems. These authors used various information networks to find that 19% of overall interactions are directed from bots to humans, mainly through retweets (74%) and mentions (25%) [37]. A more socially-focused approach by Cresci et al. [9] measured Twitter's current capabilities of detecting social spambots. They assess human performance in discriminating between genuine accounts, social spambots, and traditional spambots through a crowd-sourcing campaign. Notably, these works focus on analysing structural aspects of communication networks between bot and non-bot accounts, whereas we will examine information flows directly, using the full content of tweets.

Information flows in online social networks have been used to reveal underlying network dynamics, and employed to understand how individual users exert influence over one another online. Typically these flows are measured using statistical and information-theoretic measures of information flows [1,31,36], to understand if significant information flows exist between groups, particularly between bot and non-bot accounts. In social media, existing approaches only consider account-level information flows, while our work considered aggregated information flows.

---

[1] Dataset available at https://figshare.com/articles/dataset/Tweet_IDs_Botometer_results/20486910.

The use of bots by Russian authorities has been widely observed: *e.g.*, Collins [7] found 5,000 bots were pushing protests against *Russiagate haux,* a political event concerning relations between politicians from US and Russia; and Shane [35] suggested Russia created 'Fake Americans' to influence the 2016 US election. Moreover, Purtill [32] found that Russia had a massive bot army in spreading disinformation about the Russia/Ukraine conflict. Muscat and Siebert [22] have suggested that both Ukraine and Russia are utilising bot armies in their cyber warfare. However, the extent to which these bots drive particular discussions and influence the behaviour of humans on social media during the Russia/Ukraine conflict is relatively unexplored. We aim to address this question through our analysis of information flows, sentiment, and linguistic features.

3   Data Collection and Preprocessing

We used the Twitter API (V2) to collect all tweets, retweets, quotes and replies containing case-insensitive versions of the hashtags #(I)StandWithPutin, #(I)StandWithRussia, #(I)SupportRussia,   #(I)StandWithUkraine, #(I)StandWithZelenskyy and #(I)SupportUkraine [39]. These Tweets were posted from February 23rd 2022 00:00:00 UTC until March 8th 2022 23:59:59 UTC, the fortnight after Russia invaded Ukraine. We queried the hashtags with and without the 'I' for a total of 12 query hashtags, collecting 5,203,746 tweets. The data collected predates the beginning of the 2022 Russian invasion by one day. These hashtags were chosen as they were found to be the most trending hashtags related to the Russia/Ukraine war which could be easily identified with a particular side in the conflict.

We first extracted all of the Twitter-labelled English tweets from the dataset. Of these, we calculated the proportion of words which appear in each LIWC category for a given tweet. These proportions are what we refer to as the 'LIWC Data'. The unique accounts in this filtered data set were randomly sampled to calculate account-level Botometer labels, since Botometer uses language dependent features.

Twitter's takedown of Russian accounts on the March 3rd may lead to bias issues within our data, as the activity of these accounts will not be present in our dataset. However, analysis showed that the content spread by these accounts persisted depsite the takedown[2].

3.1   Categorising Accounts via National Lean

The query hashtags from each tweet were extracted and the total number of pro-Ukrainian (ending in Ukraine or Zelenskyy) and pro-Russian (ending in Russia or Putin) hashtags were counted and used to establish the national *lean* of a tweet. If the number of pro-Ukranian query hashtags exceeded that of the pro-Russian hashtags, the tweet was labelled as 'ProUkraine', and labeled as 'ProRussia'

---

[2] https://twitter.com/timothyjgraham/status/1500101414072520704.

conversely. If the counts were balanced, the tweet was labelled 'Balanced'. Where applicable, the lean of an account was taken to be the most commonly occurring national lean across all tweets from that account.

We found that 90.16% of accounts fell into the 'ProUkraine' category, while only 6.80% fell into the 'ProRussia' category. The balanced category contained 3.04% of accounts, showing that accounts exhibiting mixed behaviour are present in the dataset.

We explored other methods for categorising accounts, e.g., labelling accounts as 'ProUkraine' or 'ProRussia' if they use only those types of hashtag. However, as we were primarily concerned with aggregated activity, we elected to prioritise labelling each account by their 'usual' behaviour.

3.2 Bot Classifications

We use Botometer [41] to quantify the extent of bot activity in the dataset by assigning scores to a random sample of accounts. Note that we used Botometer's 'English' scores throughout this paper – these scores utilise both language dependent and language independent features during classification [41]. Botometer provides an 'overall' bot score, referred to as the complete automation probability (CAP) and scores corresponding to six distinct sub-types: AstroTurf, Fake Follower, Financial, Self Declared, Spammer and Other.

The rate limits allowed us to randomly sample 26.5% of unique accounts in our dataset which posted at least one English Tweet. This random sample leads to an approximately uniform frequency of Tweets from accounts with Botometer labels across the time frame we considered.

Due to rate limit constraints, the Botometer scores were calculated post-collection, so a small number of accounts may have been removed or scores may be calculated using activity after our collection period.

While it is more appropriate to use Botometer's CAP score as a measure of how bot-like an account is, rather than as a classification tool, it was necessary to label accounts to establish and understand information flows between account groups. Using the recommended cutoff of 0.43, we categorised each labelled account into one of the six Botometer categories or as 'NotBot' [33]. Where an account was not queried, it was labelled as 'FailedToClassify'.

The process for each account is as follows:

1. If the maximum Botometer score is greater than 0.43 then the corresponding category label is assigned to that account.
2. Else if the maximum score is smaller than 0.43, the account is categorised as 'NotBot'.
3. Otherwise the account is labelled as 'FailedToClassify'.

The results of classification were 1,347,082 'FailedToClassify', 218,382 'Not-Bot', 192,633 'Other', 29,627 'Fake Follower', 29,622 'AstroTurf', 1,976 'Spammer', 1,723 'Self Declared' and 662 'Financial' accounts.

4   The Role of Bots in the Overall Discussion

Figure 1 shows the average hourly bot probability for different bot types (top), and the hourly frequency of query hashtags (bottom). There is an initial spike in the #(I)StandWithUkraine tweets, which is also most dominant overall. Interestingly, the #(I)StandWithPutin and #(I)SupportPutin hashtags spike on 2nd-3rd March, just after Russia captured its first Ukranian city (Kherson). We believe these spikes in support of Putin are predominately due to the presence of bots, as indicated by the increase in overall bot activity around this time. This observation was independently made by researcher Timothy Graham around this time [32]. On March 4th, Twitter removed over 100 users who pushed the #(I)StandWithPutin campaign for violating its platform manipulation and spam policy [8]. This may lead us to underestimate the impact of pro-Russian media after this date, as information may be spreading from alternative sources or shifting to different hashtags.

In Fig. 1 we can see the daily cycles in activity. Figure 2 enhances that view by showing the daily cycle based on the hour of day (centred around the mean). Note that the 'AstroTurf' cycle is opposite to that of all other types. Astroturfing accounts are active at opposite times to the other bot types. There are two potential explanations: either the Astroturfing accounts are from a different timezone to a majority of the accounts, or, Botometer uses timezone to determine whether an account is Astroturfing.

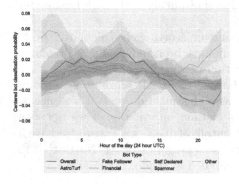
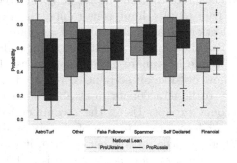

Fig. 2. Average hourly Botometer results showing the daily cycle. The time series observed in Fig. 1 (top) is averaged based on the hour of the day (UTC time).

Fig. 3. Probabilities of bot types based on national lean and bot classification. National lean and bot classification are described in Sects. 3.1 and 3.2.

Figure 1 (top), also shows a spike in bots on March 2nd and 4th. The first spike aligns with Russia capturing Kherson, but also when the #(I)StandWithPutin and #(I)StandWithRussia hashtags were trending. We observed the mean overall Botometer score of active pro-Russia accounts increased from 0.535 (1st March) to 0.593 (2nd March), whereas the mean over-all Botometer score of active pro-Ukrainian accounts decreased from 0.585 (1st March) to 0.562 (2nd March). Hence, this further suggests that bots were responsible for making the pro-Russia hashtags trend on these dates. The second spike in bot activity on March 4th is more difficult to explain. On this date Russia captured the Zaporizhzhia nuclear power plant, but also a handful of pro-Russian accounts were removed by Twitter. The mean overall Botometer score of active pro-Russia accounts significantly increased from 0.535 (3rd March) to 0.613 (4th March) and the mean overall Botometer score of active pro-Ukrainian accounts slightly increased from 0.573 (3rd March) to 0.603 (4th March). As a result, this spike in bot activity is due to the presence of pro-Russian bots (before they were removed) and the presence of pro-Ukrainian bots advocating against the pro-Russian accounts. Nonetheless, there is an obvious presence of bots over the duration of the first fortnight after Russia's invasion of Ukraine.

The time of day effects are most pronounced for the AstroTurf and Other bots, whereas the activity of Fake Follower, Financial, Self Declared and Spammer bots are less impacted by the time of day. This may be because AstroTurf and Other bots are pushing campaigns specific to certain countries, and hence sharing content aligned with those timezones. The spike in Other bots occurs at 10:00 UTC which corresponds to 1:00 pm Ukrainian time. Matthews [21] suggested that noon to 1:00 pm is the most popular time to tweet in any timezone. Hence, the Other bots are likely to be increasing their engagement in Ukraine by being most active around this time.

Figure 3 shows pairwise box plots of the Botometer type probabilities based on whether the accounts are pro-Ukraine or pro-Russia. The most commonly-used bot type for both campaigns is the Self-Declared bots, suggesting that authorities have identified these bots to be most useful in a information warfare campaign. Furthermore, we observe a fairly consistent spread of bot types for both campaigns. Pro-Russian accounts have a mean CAP score of 0.42, while pro-Ukrainian accounts have a mean score of 0.43, with medians 0.36 and 0.34 respectively. However, the median probability of an account being an AstroTurf bot is slightly higher for pro-Ukrainian accounts than pro-Russian accounts. Additionally, the median probability of a Self-Declared bot is slightly higher for pro-Russian accounts compared to pro-Ukrainian accounts. This highlights that pro-Ukrainian accounts may be utilising more Astroturfing in their information warfare, whereas pro-Russian accounts may be utilising more Self-Declared bots.

5   Information Flows Between Bots and Human Accounts

5.1   Information-Flow Estimation Methods

We measure the influence of accounts on overall online discussion using the following symmetric net information flow measure from the time-stamped writings of a source S to target T [36]:

$$\Delta(T||S) = \frac{\hat{h}(T||S)}{\sum_X \hat{h}(T||X)} - \frac{\hat{h}(S||T)}{\sum_X \hat{h}(S||X)}. \tag{1}$$

Here $\hat{h}(\mathcal{T}\|\mathcal{S})$ is the non-parametric cross entropy rate estimator [1,17]:

$$\hat{h}(\mathcal{T}\|\mathcal{S}) = \frac{N_{\mathcal{T}} \log_2 N_{\mathcal{S}}}{\sum_{i=1}^{N_{\mathcal{T}}} \Lambda_i(\mathcal{T}|\mathcal{S}_{\leq t(T_i)})}, \tag{2}$$

where $N_{\mathcal{S}}$ and $N_{\mathcal{T}}$ are the number of symbols written by the source and target, respectively, and Λ_i^l denotes the length of the shortest substring, l starting at index i which does not appear in the first $i + l - 1$ symbols. See [2] for an example of Λ_i^l estimation. We aggregate content by account type rather than on an account level to measure the information flows between account types and establish their significance.

We use the language analysis tools Valence Aware Dictionary and Sentiment Reasoner (VADER) [13] for sentiment analysis, as well as the Linguistic Inquiry and Word Count (LIWC) [29] to establish relationships between conversation features and bot-activity. We then use the Granger causality test to determine whether one time series X is useful in forecasting another time series Y with some time lag p.

We do this by fitting two linear models. The first model we include only the lagged values of Y:

$$Y_t = \alpha_{1,0} + \alpha_{1,1} Y_{t-1} + \cdots + \alpha_{1,p} Y_{t-p} + \epsilon_{1,t}, \tag{3}$$

where we define $\epsilon_{i,t}$ as the error term of model i at time t and $\alpha_{i,j}$ as the parameter of model i at lag j. Next, we augment the model to also include the lagged values of X:

$$Y_t = \alpha_{2,0} + \alpha_{2,1} Y_{t-1} + \cdots + \alpha_{2,p} Y_{t-p} + \beta_1 X_{t-1} + \cdots + \beta_p X_{t-p} + \epsilon_{2,t}. \tag{4}$$

The null hypothesis, that X does not Granger-cause Y, is accepted via an F-test if and only if no lagged values of X are retained in the regression model observed in Eq. 4.

5.2   Aggregated Information Flows

We apply information-flow measures to content aggregated by account type, to understand inter-community information flows. Rather than using an aggregate statistic on individual information flows, the proposed aggregated flow approach allows the symmetric and normalisation properties of the net information flow measure [36] to be preserved. This process improves the quality of the entropy estimate for the group behaviour, by increasing the available sequence length and mitigating the effect of slow convergence of the estimator. In this section we also develop a significance test for net information flow.

Each account is labeled by both bot classification and national lean, and the content within these account groups is aggregated. The cross entropy between each of these groups is calculated pairwise, and these values are normalised according to Eq. 1.

These pairwise cross entropy estimations produce a fully connected network. We then perform a statistical test for whether aggregated net information flows are significant between groups, allowing a network of significant information flows to be constructed (Fig. 4).

To approximate the null distribution for the difference between median outgoing flow rates between each group, we randomly shuffle group labels for each tweet, reconstruct aggregated sequences, then calculate net information flows. These aggregated net flows are used to calculate the differences in group median out-flows and construct the empirical null distribution, which is used to calculate an empirical p-value for the observed values. These aggregated net information flows reveal that generally information flows out of the pro-Russian accounts, with the exception of the pro-Russia FailedToClassify and pro-Russian Fake Follower account groups (Fig. 4). This indicates that these account groups may be predominately interacting with other accounts within the same group, rather than accounts with other leans or types. The 'ProRussia NotBot' account group has the largest outward information flows and significant flows to a range of other groups, having a positive information flow into both 'ProUkraine' and 'Balanced' account groups.

This indicates that these Russian non-bot accounts influence a variety of user groups with the greatest between group information flows. This may indicate that human-controlled accounts, or accounts which appear less bot-like, have more influence in our social network, potentially due to their behaviour or perception. While the 'NotBot' label is derived from the Botometer score, this label does not mean these accounts are not malicious or automated.

Most of the significant information flows between 'ProUkraine' account groups is between groups with the same lean. This may indicating that more information flows between the accounts within each of these groups rather than to accounts in other groups. 'ProUkraine' groups have the highest self entropy rates, meaning that these groups do not just aggregate information from other account groups, but influence other accounts within the same group (Fig. 4(d)).

The Balanced account groups show information flows to all other national-lean types, and connect otherwise disjoint parts of the information flow network. These accounts may act as a bridge for information to move between 'ProRussia' and 'ProUkraine' accounts. Most of these groups have small but significant information flows to other groups, with information tending to flow out of these groups.

Notably, the few significant information flows into non-bot account groups indicate some influence from 'bot-like' accounts on non-bot accounts. However, these account groups have stronger outward net information flows then inward flows, suggesting that while they tend to have influence on the content of other 'bot-like' accounts, they do not influence non-'bot-like' users generally.

When account-level flows are considered rather than the aggregated flows presented here, several similar significant flows exist between 'bot-like' and non-'bot-like' accounts.

6 How Bot Accounts Influence Linguistic Features of the Conversation

Having characterised bot activity and identified significant information flows, we now aim to explore the content of these relationships. We first consider relationships between bot activity and sentiment, with a focus on understanding if bot-like accounts have a significant impact on the compound sentiment of non-bot accounts, measured using the CAP Botometer score and weighted average compound sentiment. The linguistic impact is then quantified by using LIWC to develop a statistical framework for understanding the relationship between bots activity and emotional/linguistic content.

6.1 Bot Activity and Overall Sentiment

To understand how bots drive non-bot sentiment, we begin by cleaning and preparing two time series. The first is the mean CAP Botometer score, which acts as a proxy for the total proportion of bot-like activity on the network. The second is the CAP-weighted mean compound sentiment. Weighting the VADER compound sentiment by the complement of the Botometer CAP score provides a measure of non-bot sentiment without making account labelling assumptions. It is robust to threshold choices, and provides a meaningful measure of the overall sentiment of the dataset.

Each time series is aggregated hourly. The first 50 h are removed from both time series since there is a comparatively small tweet volume over that period. The mean CAP Botometer score has a linear trend, which is removed via a linear regression. Both time series are standardised to have mean zero to ensure they comply with the assumptions to perform Granger causality analysis. We also removed the daily periodic cycle (Fig. 2) from each time series.

The cross correlations are then calculated for various lags to understand the effect of mean CAP Botometer score on the CAP-weighted mean compound sentiment. A maximum lag of 12 h is considered. A positive relationship exists between the cleaned time series, indicating there is a correlation between the activity of 'bot-like' accounts and the compound sentiment of the non-'bot-like' accounts. There is a significant relationship between the two series, with $p = 3.76 \times 10^{-4}$.

Since effects cannot occur simultaneously, we consider the lagged effect of bot activity on non-bot compound sentiment, finding a positive cross correlation for both positive and negative lags (Fig. 5). This shows that bot activity increases when sentiment increases, but also that sentiment increases with increases in bot activity. Figure 5 indicates that the relationship between sentiment and bot activity is complicated, with marked events driving spikes in the compound sentiment of not-'bot-like' accounts. There are also spikes in the mean compound sentiment of other account lean types, which may be due to events which we did not consider in our analysis. This indicates that there may not be an overall effect on the non-bot compound sentiment due to bot activity, although this relationship may exist on an individual account level.

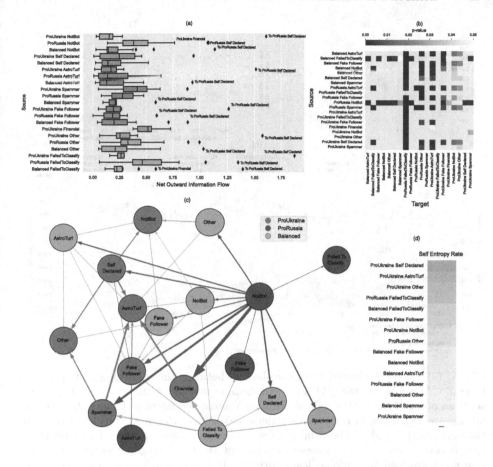

Fig. 4. (a) Aggregated net outward information flows by account type and national lean. The outward flows for each aggregated group predominantly fall in the $(0, 0.5)$ range, however 'ProRussia NonBot', 'ProUkraine Financial', 'ProUkraine Spammer' and 'ProRussia FailedToClassify' net flows tend to be greater. Values above the 80th percentile are labelled – the majority of these represent flows into the 'ProRussia Self Declared' group. (b) Heatmap of empirical p-values for each intergroup net information flow, showing significance of the difference in median outbound flows between groups. This test is used to form the network shown in (c). (c) Significant net information flows between groups. Not pictured are aggregated groups with inadequate sample size. Each aggregated group is coloured by national lean; edges are weighted by magnitude of net information flow. Significant flows out of 'ProRussia NotBot' accounts indicate that information flows from these accounts to other groups, most commonly groups with a balanced or 'ProUkraine' lean. Most intergroup flows for groups with a 'ProUkraine' lean are to other groups with 'ProUkraine' lean, with no significant flows from 'ProUkraine' account groups to 'ProRussia' account groups. (d) Lists the 15 highest self entropy rate values for the aggregated groups, with the top three groups all having a 'ProUkraine' lean.

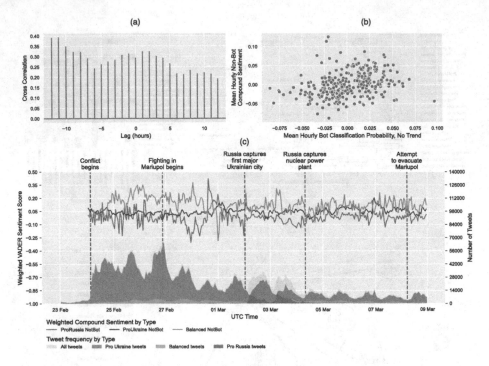

Fig. 5. (a) Shows the lagged cross correlations between the mean hourly Botometer Overall CAP score and the CAP weighted mean compound sentiment. Each lag represents an offset of the CAP weighted mean compound sentiment in hours. These correlations are significant in both lag directions. (b) Considering a scatterplot of the two timeseries with trend and burn-in samples removed, reveals a positive linear relationship between them. (c) The timeseries represent the CAP weighted mean compound sentiment grouped by national lean, with 'ProRussia', 'ProUkraine' and 'Balanced' accounts considered separately. To aid interpretation of these timeseries, the tweet frequency of each type (from all accounts) and some significant event markers are given. Before the 2nd of March there was minimal activity from 'ProRussia' accounts, so the CAP weighted mean compound sentiment estimate has high variance and is of low quality. After March 3rd, there is a spike in Balanced CAP weighted mean compound sentiment, from Balanced accounts, suggesting that these accounts were producing more positive tweets overall, potentially in response to humanitarian corridors opening.

6.2   Bot Activity and Linguistic Discussion Features

Using LIWC, we explore how different types of bots drive emotions and discussions around the Russia/Ukraine conflict. We produce hourly averages for overall LIWC proportions and the Botometer probabilities. This results in a set of time series, all over 336 h. We utilise the Granger Causality Test (Sect. 5.1) on these time series to determine whether the activity of certain bots Granger-cause more or less discussion around particular LIWC categories.

We apply pairwise Granger Causality Tests between each Botometer time-series, X, and each LIWC timeseries, Y, for $p = 12$ lags/hours (see Eq. 3 and 4 in Sect. 5.1). This time window is chosen as it is reasonable to assume a majority of the effects from bots will occur over this time frame. The validity of this assumption is explored below.

We use the F-score from the Granger Causality Test as a measure of how 'influential' a type of bot is on each LIWC category. To get a sense of direction for these relationships, we use the sign of the largest β coefficient from Eq. 4 in Sect. 5.1. We multiply the sign of this coefficient by the F-score from the Granger Causality Test to obtain a measure of strength and direction, referring to this as the Bot Effect Strength and Direction. Moreover, we use the lag of the largest β coefficient from Eq. 4 in Sect. 5.1 to represent the most prolific lag in the relationship. We use the p-value from the Granger Causality Test to determine whether the effects are significant, and perform a Bonferroni Adjustment to adjust for multiple hypothesis tests. The results are displayed in Fig. 6, where we have only included the significant relationships. The number in the centre of each square represents the most prolific lag – we interpret this as the number of hours until

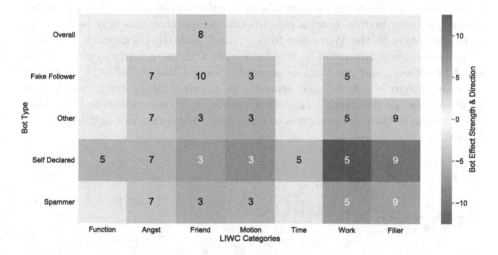

Fig. 6. A series of pairwise Granger Causality Tests are performed to examine whether the activity of bot types is Granger-causing changes in discussions of the LIWC categories. The heat maps colour describes the bot effect strength and direction from the Granger Causality Test (over 12 h/lags) between the time series of hourly bot proportions and the time series of hourly LIWC category proportions. The number in the centre describes the most prolific lag in the Granger Causality Test. We calculate the bot effect strength using the F-score from an F-test on the Granger Causality linear models. Moreover, we calculate the bot effect direction and most prolific lag using the sign and lag (respectively) of the largest β coefficient from Eq. 4 in Sect. 5.1. We perform a Bonferroni Adjustment on the p-values from the Granger Causality Tests and only show the Bot Types and LIWC Categories with a significant adjusted p-value (< 0.05).

the effects of the bot activity are most pronounced. Figure 6 shows that bots do have a significant impact on discussions of certain LIWC categories. To better understand what each of these LIWC categories represent, we generated word clouds of the words from each LIWC category that appeared in the dataset. The size of the words represent their relative frequency in the data – the larger the word the more frequently it occurs. The word clouds for Angst, Motion and Work are shown in Figs. 7a, 7b and 7c, respectively. For a full discussion of the words associated with various LIWC categories, see Pennebaker and Francis [28]. In Fig. 6, the self-declared bots have greatest amount of influence on a number of discussions. In particular, the self-declared bots increase discussions around angst, friends, motion, time, work and the usage of filler words, but decrease the usage of function words. Moreover, it is apparent that these bots most strongly influence discussion of the work category (with a most prolific lag of five hours). Figure 7c shows that most of the discussion around work is involved with governing bodies, with 'president' and 'governments' being the most commonly used words. While it is difficult to assert exactly why these bots are driving more discussions of work, we gain further understanding by also observing that self declared bots Granger-cause more angst (with a most prolific lag after 7 h). Combining these two observations suggests that self-declared bots drive more angst about governing bodies. From a pro-Russian perspective, this may be to cause more disruption in the West, and from a pro-Ukrainian perspective, this may be to cause more disruption in Russia. Figure 3 shows a fairly even probability of pro-Russia and pro-Ukraine accounts being self-declared bots. Although the exact origin of self-declared accounts is unknown, it is worth noting that we considered predominately English accounts. It is therefore more likely that the intention of these accounts was to drive more disruption in English-speaking countries.

(a) Angst Category   (b) Motion Category   (c) Work Category

Fig. 7. Word Clouds which demonstrate the frequency of words in particular LIWC categories.

Observe that Fake Follower, Spammer and Other bots also increase angst (all with the most prolific lag after 7 h). Figure 7a shows that a majority of angst-related words are surrounding fear and worry. Hence, we argue that self-declared, fake follower, spammer and other forms of automated account types combine to increase fear in the overall discussion of the Russia/Ukraine war. This observation has been hypothesised by many authors [24,26], but a detailed analysis has been lacking and may be of concern for many governments and defence organisations.

Figure 6 further shows that fake follower, self-declared, spammer and other bot types also increase online discussion around motion. In Fig. 7b, we see a number of motion related words that are potentially associated with staying or fleeing the country. Combining this with increases in Angst suggests that bots could be influencing people's decisions surrounding whether to flee their homes or not. Druziuk [11] noted that bots have allowed "Ukrainians to report to the government when they spot Russian troops", but the usage of bots to influence people on staying/leaving the country is something not observed before. However, it is difficult to denote whether this is being done in support of Ukraine, Russia or both.

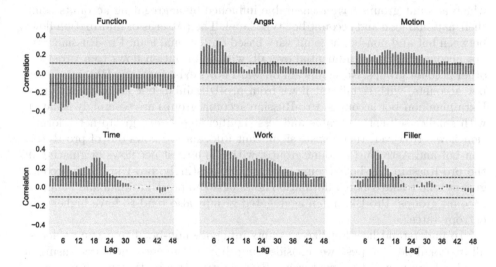

Fig. 8. Lagged cross correlations between the hourly Self Declared bot proportions and the significant hourly LIWC Category proportions (significance is determined from the results in Fig. 6). We consider 48 h/lags for each of these plots and represent the significance threshold using a horizontal dotted line. This shows the extent to which the bots drive changes in online discussion and how long these effects can persist for.

In Fig. 6 the most prolific lag is mostly consistent for a given LIWC category, but varies greatly for bot type. Hence, the time which bots effect a given discussion on the war depends mainly on the topic of discussion and not on the type of bot. For instance, we observe that Fake Follower, Self-Declared, Spammer and Other bots all most prolifically effect discussions of work after five hours. To further examine the effects of the lag on discussion of different LIWC categories, we plot cross correlations in Fig. 8. These plots represent the cross correlation between Self-Declared bot proportions and a number of significant LIWC categories (in Fig. 6) over 48 h.

The direction of the effect for each LIWC variable in Fig. 8 is consistent with Fig. 6, further validating our results. This direction is consistent for all significant lags, justifying our decision to choose the largest parameter in the regression model as an indication of direction in Fig. 6. For some LIWC categories the effects of Self-Declared bots linger over many lags but for others the effects diminish relatively quickly. For instance, the effects on the work category and the function category are significant for lags almost up to 48 h, whereas the effects on the angst and filler categories diminish within 24 h.

7   Conclusion

This work investigates if and how bot-like accounts influence the online conversation around the Russian invasion of Ukraine during February 2022. We showed which account groups have measurable influence by aggregating accounts using their national lean and account bot-type label. The patterns of information flows between bot and non-bot account vary based on national lean: Pro-Russian non-bot accounts are most influential overall, with information flows to a variety of other account groups. No significant outward flows exist from pro-Ukrainian non-bot accounts, with significant flows from pro-Ukrainian bot accounts into pro-Ukrainian non-bot accounts. Pro-Russian account groups are seemingly isolated, with smaller self-entropy rates and less significant between group net information flows. However, there exists significant information flows out of pro-Russia non-bot and AstroTurf account groups, with the largest net flows originating in the pro-Russian non-bot account groups. Contrastingly, pro-Ukrainian account groups tend to have more information flows between pro-Ukrainian and balanced account groups. Pro-Ukrainian aggregated groups also tend to have higher self-entropy rates.

To understand how bot-like accounts influence non-bot like accounts across all national lean types, we consider non-bot sentiment, measured using a weighted compound sentiment score. By weighting this by the overall bot probability, this compound sentiment reflects the overall sentiment of non-bot-like accounts across the network. The relationship between this sentiment and the bot activity is significant but occurs in both directions, with sentiment and bot activity both impacting each other.

Finally, we identify the effect of bot-like accounts on LIWC linguistic discussion features. Self-declared bots have the largest impact, showing significant relationships with word in the Function, Angst, Friend, Motion, Time, Work and Filler categories. To find the direction and significance of these relationships we use pairwise Granger causality tests. We find bots generally increase word usage in these categories with a 3–10 h lag. Self-declared bots show the strongest relationship with Work discussions, i.e., words pertaining to governing bodies ("president", "government" and "leadership"). We also see bot accounts increase the use of words in the angst category which contains words related to fear and worry ("shame", "terrorist", "threat", "panic").

In future work, we will explore information contained on the network of interactions between users recorded in the tweets using a network science approach [3,4,23]. We will also further explore diverse ways to classify the national lean of authors based on their published Twitter content. Preliminary results indicate heavy-tailed distributions in timing lags that differ between account types, suggesting differences in coordinated activity signatures [20]. We will examine coordination campaigns and coordination networks [12,14,19,27,34] to quantify the impact of coordinated activity in the social network structure and to further investigate its influence on social media users.

Using a number of approaches we describe a framework to understand the impact of bots on the network, explore how malicious campaigns operate and measure their effect on online discussion. Our approach is applicable to any social media content presenting polarisation between distinct groups and can be applied to other data to understand how malicious campaigns operate.

Acknowledgements. B.S. would like to acknowledge the support of a Westpac Future Leaders Scholarship. L.M. and M.R. are supported by the Australian Government through the Australian Research Council's Discovery Projects funding scheme (project DP210103700). L.M. also acknowledges support from the Australian Defence Science and Technology Group ORNet scheme.

References

1. Bagrow, J.P., Liu, X., Mitchell, L.: Information flow reveals prediction limits in online social activity. Nat. Hum. Behav. **3**(2), 122–128 (2019). https://doi.org/10. 1038/s41562-018-0510-5
2. Bagrow, J.P., Mitchell, L.: The quoter model: a paradigmatic model of the social flow of written information. Chaos Interdisc. J. Nonlinear Sci. **28**(7), 075304 (2018)
3. Barabási, A.L.: Network Science. Cambridge University Press, Cambridge (2016)
4. Caldarelli, G.: Scale-Free Networks: Complex Webs in Nature and Technology. Oxford University Press, Oxford (2007)
5. Champion, M., Krasnolutska, D.: Ukraine's TV comedian President Volodymyr Zelenskyy finds his role as wartime leader, February 2022. https://www. japantimes.co.jp/news/2022/02/26/world/volodymyr-zelenskyy-wartime-president/
6. Chen, E., Ferrara, E.: Tweets in time of conflict: a public dataset tracking the twitter discourse on the war between Ukraine and Russia. arXiv preprint arXiv:2203.07488 (2022)
7. Collins, B.: After Mueller report, Twitter bots pushed 'Russiagate hoax' narrative (2019). https://www.nbcnews.com/tech/tech-news/after-mueller-report-twitter-bots-pushed-russiagate-hoax-narrative-n997441. Accessed 19 June 2022
8. Collins, B., Korecki, N.: Twitter bans over 100 accounts that pushed #IStand-WithPutin, March 2022. https://www.nbcnews.com/tech/internet/twitter-bans-100-accounts-pushed-istandwithputin-rcna18655

9. Cresci, S., Di Pietro, R., Petrocchi, M., Spognardi, A., Tesconi, M.: The paradigm-shift of social spambots: evidence, theories, and tools for the arms race. In: Proceedings of the 26th International Conference on World Wide Web Companion, WWW 2017, pp. 963–972, Companion, International World Wide Web Conferences Steering Committee, Republic and Canton of Geneva, CHE, April 2017. https://doi.org/10.1145/3041021.3055135

10. Doroshenko, L., Lukito, J.: Trollfare: Russia's disinformation campaign during military conflict in Ukraine. Int. J. Commun. 15, 4662–4689 (2021)

11. Druziuk, Y.: A citizen-like chatbot allows Ukrainians to report to the government when they spot Russian troops - here's how it works. Business Insider, April 2022. https://www.businessinsider.com/ukraine-military-e-enemy-telegram-app-2022-4. Accessed 19 June 2022

12. Giglietto, F., Righetti, N., Rossi, L., Marino, G.: It takes a village to manipulate the media: coordinated link sharing behavior during 2018 and 2019 Italian elections. Inf. Commun. Soc. 23(6), 867–891 (2020). https://doi.org/10.1080/1369118X.2020.1739732

13. Hutto, C., Gilbert, E.: Vader: a parsimonious rule-based model for sentiment analysis of social media text. In: Proceedings of the International AAAI Conference on Web and Social Media, vol. 8, pp. 216–225 (2014)

14. Keller, F.B., Schoch, D., Stier, S., Yang, J.: Political astroturfing on twitter: how to coordinate a disinformation campaign. Polit. Commun. 37(2), 256–280 (2020)

15. Keller, T.R., Klinger, U.: Social bots in election campaigns: theoretical, empirical, and methodological implications. Polit. Commun. 36(1), 171–189 (2019). https://doi.org/10.1080/10584609.2018.1526238

16. Klepper, D.: Russian propaganda 'outgunned' by social media rebuttals. AP NEWS, March 2022. https://tinyurl.com/3x9anuta. Section: Russia-Ukraine war

17. Kontoyiannis, I., Algoet, P.H., Suhov, Y.M., Wyner, A.J.: Nonparametric entropy estimation for stationary processes and random fields, with applications to English text. IEEE Trans. Inf. Theory 44(3), 1319–1327 (1998)

18. Laurence, P.: How Ukraine's 'Ghost of Kyiv' legendary pilot was born. BBC News, May 2022. https://www.bbc.com/news/world-europe-61285833. Accessed 19 June 2022

19. Lukito, J.: Coordinating a multi-platform disinformation campaign: internet research agency activity on three us social media platforms, 2015 to 2017. Polit. Commun. 37(2), 238–255 (2020). https://doi.org/10.1080/10584609.2019.1661889

20. Mathews, P., Mitchell, L., Nguyen, G., Bean, N.: The nature and origin of heavy tails in retweet activity. In: Proceedings of the 26th International Conference on World Wide Web Companion, pp. 1493–1498 (2017)

21. Matthews, B.: Best time to tweet for clicks, retweets and engagement. Empower Agency, June 2015. https://empower.agency/best-time-to-tweet-clicks-retweets-engagement/. Accessed 19 June 2022

22. Muscat, S., Siebert, Z.: Laptop generals and bot armies: the digital front of Russia's Ukraine war, March 2022. https://eu.boell.org/en/2022/03/01/laptop-generals-and-bot-armies-digital-front-russias-ukraine-war. Accessed 19 June 2022

23. Newman, M.: Networks. Oxford University Press, Oxford (2018)

24. Nguyen, K.: How Putin's propaganda is sowing seeds of doubt to deny sympathy for Ukraine. ABC News, April 2022

25. Orabi, M., Mouheb, D., Al Aghbari, Z., Kamel, I.: Detection of bots in social media: a systematic review. Inf. Process. Manag. 57(4), 102250 (2020). https://doi.org/10.1016/j.ipm.2020.102250

26. Osborne, C.: Ukraine destroys five bot farms that were spreading 'panic' among citizens, March 2022. https://www.zdnet.com/article/ukraine-takes-out-five-bot-farms-spreading-panic-among-citizens/
27. Pacheco, D., Hui, P.M., Torres-Lugo, C., Truong, B.T., Flammini, A., Menczer, F.: Uncovering coordinated networks on social media: methods and case studies. In: Proceedings of the AAAI International Conference on Web and Social Media (ICWSM), pp. 455–466 (2021)
28. Pennebaker, J.W., Francis, M.E.: Cognitive, emotional, and language processes in disclosure. Cogn. Emot. **10**(6), 601–626 (1996). https://doi.org/10.1080/026999396380079
29. Pennebaker, J.W., Francis, M.E., Booth, R.J.: Linguistic inquiry and word count: LIWC 2001, vol. 71. Lawrence Erlbaum Associates, Mahway (2001)
30. Polyzos, E.S.: Escalating tension and the war in Ukraine: evidence using impulse response functions on economic indicators and twitter sentiment. Available at SSRN 4058364 (2022)
31. Pond, T., Magsarjav, S., South, T., Mitchell, L., Bagrow, J.P.: Complex contagion features without social reinforcement in a model of social information flow. Entropy **22**(3), 265 (2020). https://doi.org/10.3390/e22030265
32. Purtill, J.: When it comes to spreading disinformation online, Russia has a massive bot army on its side. ABC News, March 2022
33. Sayyadiharikandeh, M., Varol, O., Yang, K.C., Flammini, A., Menczer, F.: Detection of novel social bots by ensembles of specialized classifiers. In: Proceedings of the 29th ACM International Conference on Information and Knowledge Management, pp. 2725–2732, October 2020. https://doi.org/10.1145/3340531.3412698
34. Schoch, D., Keller, F.B., Stier, S., Yang, J.: Coordination patterns reveal online political astroturfing across the world. Sci. Rep. **12**(1), 4572 (2022). https://doi.org/10.1038/s41598-022-08404-9
35. Shane, S.: The fake Americans Russia created to influence the election. The New York Times, September 2017. https://www.nytimes.com/2017/09/07/us/politics/russia-facebook-twitter-election.html. Accessed 19 June 2022
36. South, T., Smart, B., Roughan, M., Mitchell, L.: Information flow estimation: a study of news on Twitter. Online Soc. Netw. Media **31**, 100231 (2022). https://doi.org/10.1016/j.osnem.2022.100231. https://www.sciencedirect.com/science/article/pii/S2468696422000337. ISSN: 2468–6964
37. Stella, M., Ferrara, E., Domenico, M.D.: Bots increase exposure to negative and inflammatory content in online social systems. Proc. Natl. Acad. Sci. **115**(49), 12435–12440 (2018). https://doi.org/10.1073/pnas.1803470115. https://www.pnas.org/doi/abs/10.1073/pnas.1803470115
38. Thomas, T.: Russia's reflexive control theory and the military. J. Slav. Mil. Stud. **17**(2), 237–256 (2004). https://doi.org/10.1080/13518040490450529
39. Watt, J., Smart, B.: Tweets discussing the Russia/Ukraine War, August 2022. https://doi.org/10.6084/m9.figshare.20486910.v4. https://figshare.com/articles/dataset/Tweet_IDs_Botometer_results/20486910
40. Wong, E.: U.S. fights bioweapons disinformation pushed by Russia and China. The New York Times, March 2022. https://www.nytimes.com/2022/03/10/us/politics/russia-ukraine-china-bioweapons.html. Accessed 19 June 2022
41. Yang, K.C., Ferrara, E., Menczer, F.: Botometer 101: social bot practicum for computational social scientists, January 2022. https://doi.org/10.48550/arXiv.2201.01608

Evaluating the Impact of AI-Based Priced Parking with Social Simulation

Jakob Kappenberger$^{(\boxtimes)}$, Kilian Theil , and Heiner Stuckenschmidt

Mannheim Center for Data Science, Mannheim, Germany
jakob.kappenberger@uni-mannheim.de,
{kilian,heiner}@informatik.uni-mannheim.de

Abstract. Across the world, increasing numbers of cars in urban centers lead to congestion and adverse effects on public health as well as municipal climate goals. Reflecting cities' ambitions to mitigate these issues, a growing body of research evaluates the use of innovative pricing strategies for parking, such as Dynamic Pricing (DP), to efficiently manage parking supply and demand. We contribute to this research by exploring the effects of Reinforcement Learning (RL)-based DP on urban parking. In particular, we introduce a theoretical framework for AI-based priced parking under traffic and social constraints. Furthermore, we present a portable and generalizable Agent-Based Model (ABM) for priced parking to evaluate our approach and run extensive experiments comparing the effect of several learners on different urban policy goals. We find that (1) outcomes are highly sensitive to the employed reward function; (2) trade-offs between different goals are challenging to balance; (3) single-reward functions may have unintended consequences on other policy areas (e.g., optimizing occupancy punishes low-income individuals disproportionately). In summary, our observations stress that fair DP schemes need to account for social policy measures beyond traffic parameters such as occupancy or traffic flow.

Keywords: Urban informatics · Fair machine learning · Social simulation

1 Introduction

Urban parking represents a significant source of inefficiency for municipalities. The number of cars in city centers is growing and, on average, cars are parked 23 out of 24 h a day [31]. As the supply of parking space is fixed in the short-term, a large share of individual motorized traffic is cruising for parking [11], which has further adverse effects on congestion. Beyond that, environmental challenges and the vocal demand for safe and livable inner cities pressure policymakers to reduce curbside parking and develop efficient solutions for parking management [17,30]. Consequently, major US and European cities such as San Francisco and Madrid [8] experiment with innovative tools such as DP to regulate demand.

F. Hopfgartner et al. (Eds.): SocInfo 2022, LNCS 13618, pp. 54–75, 2022.
https://doi.org/10.1007/978-3-031-19097-1_4

While related work examines the efficacy of such schemes concerning optimal occupancy [27], their impact on other facets of urban life (such as social equity) appears far less thoroughly researched. For example, reducing overall traffic with more aggressive pricing strategies might disproportionately affect low-income drivers. Moreover, both in municipal practice and academic research, dynamically priced parking is usually based on simple conditional rules. Thus, the potential of Machine Learning (ML) for pricing, which may offer improved performance, seems not yet fully explored. This holds in particular for RL, a variant of ML, that, enabling dynamic reactions to the state of its subject while optimizing varying target functions, appears well suited for this task.

We address these research gaps by systematically exploring the effects of RL-based DP for parking in inner cities. Our key contributions are:

- **Theory**: Conceptualizing the findings of related work, we introduce a theoretical framework for AI-based DP of urban parking space.
- **Models**: Combining an ABM with RL, we implement a portable and generalizable environment to evaluate the impact of dynamically priced parking in inner cities. To this end, we extended the NetLogo traffic grid model [34] to simulate priced parking within a prototypical city block layout. Furthermore, we implemented a comprehensive set of RL reward functions to optimize occupancy, congestion, and social composition.
- **Analysis**: We systematically analyze the impact of this system on stationary and moving traffic (e.g., occupancy, traffic flow) as well as the social composition of traffic participants in the city center. We present a preliminary catalog of unintended consequences as useful guidelines for practitioners and urban policymakers.

In the following, this paper is structured as follows: the remainder of Sect. 1 provides an overview of parking policy as a theoretical foundation and summarizes other studies on priced urban parking; Sect. 2 introduces our ABM and the RL-based learners to optimize traffic and social outcomes; Sect. 3 discusses our simulation findings; Sect. 4 concludes and summarizes avenues for future research.

1.1 Background: Parking Policy

Efforts by local authorities to impact traveling patterns and traffic in city centers can be viewed through the lens of Transport Demand Management (TDM). This concept defines "any action or set of actions aimed at influencing peoples' travel behavior in such a way that alternative mobility options are presented and/or congestion is reduced" [21]. Policies altering the provision of public parking spaces form a crucial part of the family of TDM measures. Such a policy can be defined as "a decision about how much land to give over to parking and the terms and conditions of use of that space" [20].

We loosely adapt the framework developed by Mingardo et al. [22], who identify four main objectives of parking policy:

1. Contributing to better accessibility and mobility in the municipal area;
2. Improving the quality of life in the city;
3. Supporting the local economy;
4. Raising municipal revenue.

City authorities have several policy instruments to manage the supply of parking spaces directly and their demand indirectly. Pricing parking represents the final and most powerful regulatory level [22]. Traditionally, parking has been priced via two static strategies: (1) *marginal cost pricing*, where the price of a parking spot corresponds to the municipal costs of providing it [10]; and (2) *market pricing*, where the parking price is obtained from comparable municipalities, e.g., via benchmarking [19]. A significant disadvantage of marginal cost pricing is the complexity of factoring in all relevant material and social costs, e.g., increased risk of accidents or decreased quality of life. As municipalities rarely account for all of those, this strategy usually yields underpriced parking spaces [28]. Charging a static market price, on the other hand, is difficult to impossible due to the strong seasonality (by day, week, or year) parking demand is subject to [19, p. 148]. Thus, starting in the 1950s, this gave rise to *DP* strategies [33], which allow municipalities to react to demand fluctuations by charging higher prices in times of high demand and vice versa. In practice, such systems have already been deployed in cities like Madrid or San Francisco. Nevertheless, these schemes usually only feature slow and limited price adjustments and have been criticized for their possible negative social impact [4]. This motivated us to experiment with RL algorithms that are able to set prices dynamically and continuously while considering a more comprehensive range of effects (e.g., on congestion or social composition).

1.2 Related Work

Multiple studies have attempted to model priced parking in inner cities [12]. Arnott et al. [2] examine how parking fees affect congestion caused by rush-hour traffic in the morning. Using a bottleneck model (i.e., a car queue congesting a road in the city center), they find that location-dependent pricing succeeds in eliminating congestion. As part of his work on the cost of free parking, Shoup [30] presents a model considering a variety of variables: the prices of on- and off-street parking, parking duration, time spent searching for parking, and costs for passengers due to cruising for parking. Thus, the author illustrates that even unpriced parking incurs societal costs, e.g., due to cruising for parking. Regarding pricing, Shoup [30] compares market pricing of curbside parking to providing it for free. The findings include that when curbside parking is cheaper than adjacent off-street parking, cruising for parking is often a rational strategy.

Moving beyond mathematical modeling, scholars have also used computational methods such as ABMs to model parking in city centers. An early example is *PARKAGENT*, an ABM proposed by Benenson et al. [3]. The authors center their attention on residential parking and find that additional parking supply linearly affects search time and walking distance of drivers in their model. Similarly, Dieussaert et al. [6] created *SUSTAPARK* to provide a Java framework for the simulation of cruising for parking and its effects on traffic. The model represents a road network with parking lots, private garages, and curbside parking. Based on different activity goals, drivers devise a parking strategy incorporating the distance to the destination, expected search time, and parking fees.

As of recently, ML methods have increasingly entered the domain of parking models. However, studies using ML tend to focus on occupancy prediction and do not consider additional factors such as congestion or social costs. For instance, Amato et al. [1] use convolutional neural networks for visual parking lot occupancy detection. Based on historical data collected in the pilot phase of SFpark, the DP system deployed in San Francisco, Simhon et al. [32] use ordinary least squares and elastic net regression for predicting occupancy and determining prices. They find that model performance is particularly sensitive to the fees of adjacent zones. Saharan et al. [29] run a MATLAB simulation determining prices via conditional programming. The authors conclude that this scheme reduces parking fees in low occupancy settings and leads to rising prices in areas with strong demand. Generally, existing research in this field appears to focus on supervised ML methods for price prediction in discrete intervals.

In summary, several studies have attempted to simulate parking behavior realistically by considering a variety of factors and actors. The focus of these efforts usually lies on the development of the models instead of analyzing their outcomes. This informs the motivation for our work to explore traffic-centered outcomes such as occupancy and congestion in combination with social consequences. Furthermore, we were interested in exploring RL, which enables real-time adjustments of parking prices and, thus, is particularly suited for optimizing multiple outcomes at once, allowing us to study trade-offs between different policy goals.

2   Methodology

2.1   Agent-Based Model Used in This Study

A prototype of our ABM was developed by graduate students participating in a research seminar taught by the second and third author of this paper. In this seminar, students extended NetLogo's traffic grid model [34] with a parking use case under dynamic pricing constraints. As outlined in the following, this model was extensively refined and extended for the purpose of this study; Fig. 1a provides an overview of the visual interface. Statistics for available parking space, demand for parking, and traversing traffic were empirically calibrated based on open government and municipal data of Mannheim, the municipality our simulation is modeled after. We discuss the elements of our ABM (environment, agents and attributes, rules) following the framework established by Gilbert [9].[1]

---

[1] All code required for reproducing this study is available at https://github.com/JakobKappenberger/ai-priced-parking.

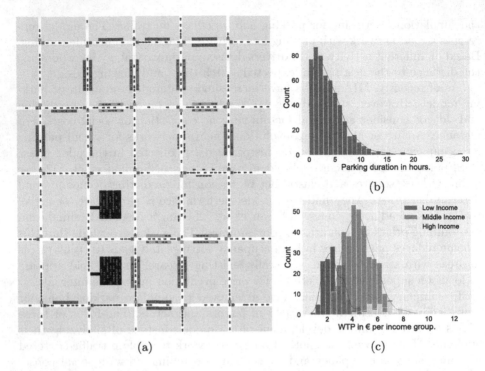

(b)

(c)

Fig. 1. (a) shows the visual interface of the ABM for parking. (b) and (c) depict the distributions of parking duration and Willingness to Pay (WTP), respectively.

Environment. The model's environment is defined by a grid layout of roads and blocks (cf. Fig. 1a). Located at the curbside, the yellow, green, teal, and blue patches designate parking spaces that are randomly scattered across the grid. Stripes of parking places situated opposite to one another are grouped. The coloring, indicating the different Controlled Parking Zones (CPZs) in the model, is then assigned depending on the distance of the groups to the center of the map, with the brightness of the colors decreasing the larger this distance grows. Due to their centrality, the green and, mainly, the yellow CPZ can be interpreted as most closely resembling the Central Business District (CBD) of the simulated city center. Beyond that, this model also introduces parking garages to account for off-street parking represented by the large blocks of black patches scattered across Fig. 1a.

Agents and Attributes. The central agents of our model are cars moving across the grid. For each car cruising for parking, a random parking duration is drawn from the distribution shown in Fig. 1b, which was adopted from Jakob and Menendez [13].

For every car, an income is randomly drawn from a log-normal distribution. Related work shows that the income of up to 99% of the population can be approximated with a two-parameter log-normal distribution [5]. This distribution is given by:

$$f(x) = \frac{1}{x\sigma\sqrt{2\pi}} \exp\left[-\frac{1}{2}\left(\frac{(\ln(x) - \mu)}{\sigma}\right)^2\right] \qquad \sigma = \sqrt{2\ln\frac{\bar{x}}{\tilde{x}}}, \ \mu = \ln(\tilde{x}) \quad (1)$$

We calibrated the parameters $\bar{x}$ (the population mean) and $\tilde{x}$ (the population median) based on the income distribution of Germany. Following the OECD [26], cars are divided into three income classes: Incomes between 75% and 200% of $\tilde{x}$ are assigned the "middle-income" class. Deviations above or below this mark are called "high-" or "low-incomes", respectively.

The variable Willingness to Pay (WTP) captures the amount of money a driver is willing to pay for parking per hour. Although income is a significant determinant of WTP, studies stress the importance of behavioral factors such as perceived comfort and security [15]. To account for this individual variance, we randomly draw the WTP for each driver from a gamma distribution dependent on their income class.[2] This procedure resulted in the WTP distributions shown in Fig. 1c. Finally, specifying whether they are willing to park on a parking place without paying, the agents own the attribute *parking-offender?*.[3]

Behavioral Rules. All cars navigate the grid with previously assigned goals. For traversing cars, this goal is one of the exit points of the street network. For cars seeking to park, destinations are assigned with probabilities inversely proportional to their distance to the center of the grid, accounting for the higher popularity of the CBD. After target assignment, cars curate a list of the closest parking opportunities and elect the shortest route to the first one. Upon arrival, cars attempt to park in the road of their assigned target. If no spot is available (or if spots are too expensive), cars move to the next list item. Similar to Shoup [30], garages are only considered if there is no curbside parking at a cheaper cost since curbside parking is generally considered the more attractive option.

Once a car has entered the street with its parking location of choice, it requests the fee of the closest available CPZ. If the fee is within the WTP, the car parks and the fee is added to the municipality revenues; if the fee exceeds the WTP, the driver will resume searching. We assume that WTP increases proportionally to the time spent cruising for parking. If a car belongs to the group of potential parking offenders, it will calculate the probability of getting

---

[2] Due to a lack of empirical evidence, the parameters of the distribution were manually calibrated to preserve the correlation between income and WTP and to ensure the functioning of the underlying parking routines in the model, i.e. to avoid excluding low-income drivers completely from parking.

[3] To achieve a distribution in line with empirical evidence (approximately 0.28 vehicles per 100m road [23]), we calibrated the parameter to render a quarter of the drivers potential parking offenders.

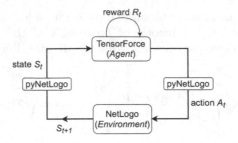

Fig. 2. Interaction between TensorForce *(Agent)* and NetLogo *(Environment)*.

caught. For this calculation, we assume rational actors with complete knowledge of the environment (i.e., the number of controls per hour and the fine as a multiple of the parking price are known *a priori* to offenders). Upon completion of their parking time, cars leave the CPZ and navigate towards the edge of the grid, where they are replaced with newly set up cars. In contrast, cars unable to find parking are not replaced once they leave the map. This preserves the change to the social distribution in the model that this behavior introduces.

2.2 AI-Based Dynamic Pricing

To introduce an RL-based AI agent to our NetLogo ABM, we used the *pyNetLogo* library [14]. This extension allows for communicating with NetLogo's API to control the model from within a Python session. As RL framework, we used *TensorForce* [16].[4]

Our workflow is depicted in Fig. 2: We designed a custom TensorForce environment acting as a wrapper for the ABM and a communication interface for the TensorForce agent. The custom environment receives the current state of the NetLogo simulation, computes the appropriate reward, and sends the actions determined by the agent back via pyNetLogo. A time step t occurs in intervals of 900 ticks in the model to allow the RL agent to adjust prices every 30 min simulated. At every time step t, the TensorForce agent queries the current state S_t from the environment, simulated by NetLogo. Table 1 in Appendix A shows the information contained in S_t.

Based on these numerical state representations, TensorForce calculates a reward R_t according to the reward function supplied to the agent (an overview of reward functions used in this paper is provided in Sect. 2.2). Completing time step t, TensorForce transmits the next actions A_t via pyNetLogo to the ABM. Individual actions can originate from an integer range from 0 to including 20. The action values are then divided by 2 to freely set fees for a CPZ between €0 and €10 in €0.50 intervals. This strategy has the advantage of enabling immediate reactions to occupancy changes and, conceptually, an easier process of credit

---

[4] We chose this library based on a detailed review of RL frameworks by Nguyen et al. [24].

assignment for the agent.[5] After the fee changes have been realized in NetLogo and the simulation has continued to run for another half hour of simulated time, the environment sends S_{t+1}. This process repeats until the episode is complete, prices have been adjusted 24 times, and the terminal state has been reached. Thereafter, the environment in NetLogo is reset, and the next episode begins.

Reward Functions. Designing an appropriate and well-performing reward function for a given RL problem is a crucial and difficult challenge [7]. We define reward functions (shown in Fig. 4 in Appendix A) that are linked to the main objectives of parking policies mentioned above except for the goal of maximizing profit, which is not a major concern in public policy.

For $r_{occupancy}$, the desired range of occupancy of the individual CPZs between 75 and 90% was chosen in accordance with the goal of having "one or two spaces per block remain on average unoccupied" stated in the literature [30]. Figure 4a shows the shape of this function with rewards for values larger than the upper end of the target corridor normalized to $[0, 1]$. A full degree of utilization for a given CPZ represents a rather undesirable state that the agent should seek to avoid in favor of values in the target range or marginally below. During the subsequent experiments, R_t is computed by applying $r_{occupancy}$ to the *CPZ_occupancy* of every CPZ contained in S_t, summing up the outputs and dividing them by the number of CPZs to render the final range of $r_{occupancy}$ in the interval between $[0, 1]$.[6]

r_{cars}, r_{social}, and r_{speed} all share a quadratic shape to encourage faster convergence by the agent. While r_{cars} minimizes the number of cars traversing the model grid to promote the second goal of parking policy, namely improving the quality of life in the city area, r_{social} and r_{speed} maximize the share of low-income drivers and the average speed of the non-parking cars driving in the grid, respectively. These functions are mainly coupled to the policy goals of accessibility and mobility.

$r_{composite}$ takes multiple individual reward signals into account. Due to TensorForce's lack of Multi-Objective Reinforcement Learning (MORL), we modeled r_t as a weighted sum of its elements, which is a common fallback for such cases [18]. The function is given as:

$$r_{composite}(x, y, z) = \frac{1}{2}r_{occupancy}(x) + \frac{1}{4}r_{cars}(y) + \frac{1}{4}r_{social}(z)$$

$$x = \text{overall\_occupancy}_t, \ y = \text{n\_cars}_t, \ z = \text{normalized\_share\_low}_t$$

(2)

---

[5] A limiting factor is a relatively high volatility of prices and a lack of *a priori* knowledge of them by the agents. Therefore, in a real-world use case, policy measures would have to guarantee drivers a reserved parking space with a price fixed prior to them entering the city.

[6] The choice to use the occupancy levels of the individual CPZs instead of the global one was made as it otherwise would have been conceivable that the agent balances under- and full utilization of different CPZs to achieve a favorable score nonetheless.

We omitted r_{speed} to obtain a parsimonious model and as it should strongly correlate with r_{cars}. $r_{occupancy}$ contributes half of the final value R_t due to its distinguished position among all optimization functions and as it is the variable that municipalities can influence most. Notably, in contrast to $r_{occupancy}$, $r_{composite}$ relies on the global occupancy to avoid an added layer of abstraction. The remainder of the output of $r_{composite}$ is contributed in equal shares by r_{cars} and r_{social}. Therefore, the function optimizes the occupancy of different CPZs under environmental and social constraints.

2.3   Experiments

Model Configuration. Two different versions of the ABM for parking in the city grid were created for training and evaluation. For the former, shorter computation times were critical to achieving the number of episodes required for model-free RL. Using a larger scale evaluation model, we expect it to be more representative of our empirical calibration and thus yield more conservative and robust results.

To obtain a representative model configuration, we conducted hyperparameter tuning to calibrate the model based on government data supplied by our partnering municipality: The number of 47K cars entering and leaving the city squares was translated to the 12 h period modeled and number of simulated blocks in the ABM. Afterwards, the model was run in its static baseline configuration with different values for its initial hyperparameters to achieve both a representative overall traffic volume and a share of cruising cars consistent with studies related to our use case [11]. For the training configuration, we then searched for the number of cars necessary to create a simulation as similar as possible to our evaluation model. The resulting parameter configurations as well as visualizations of the tuning process can be inspected in Appendix A and B. While the RL training was conducted for 50.000 episodes per reward function, we ran the evaluation model for 500 iterations to achieve robust results for analysis.[7]

Baselines. As a benchmark, we deployed two baselines: To mirror the predominant pricing strategies in many municipalities, we implemented a *static* baseline pricing, which charges €3.6 per hour for the two central CPZs and €1.8 for parking in the two more peripheral areas of the map.[8] To account for more modern pricing schemes, we used a simple DP scheme as a *dynamic* baseline: A CPZ's fee is increased by €0.25 if more than 90% is occupied. Conversely, prices are lowered by €0.25 when the individual utilized capacity falls under 75% and by €0.50 if it amounts to less than 30%. Each of the 500 runs was then scored using a simpler version of $r_{occupancy}$ that, every half hour, awards every CPZ a score of 0.25 if its occupancy lies in the desired range between 75 and 90%. Finally, we selected the run with the median accumulated score over the sample. For the RL

---

[7] Running 35 simulations in parallel on a Intel Xeon Gold 6230 processor, training took approximately 39 h for $r_{occupancy}$.

[8] This tariff was chosen following the pricing policy in Mannheim.

experiments, this procedure was mirrored using the respective reward functions to score a given experiment.

Hyperparameter Tuning. For every reward function, we fine-tuned the hyperparameters of the Proximal Policy Optimization (PPO) algorithm using *HpBandster*'s implementation of Bayesian Optimization and Hyperband (BOHB). Every parameter vector was evaluated after 5,400 episodes of training over four iterations of successive halving. For reproducibility, our final hyperparameter configurations per reward function are listed in Appendix B, Table 3.

3   Results and Discussion

Figure 3 compares the median performance of all reward functions and the baselines across four different dimensions.[9] Appendix C contains in-depth results with CPZ fees, occupancy, number of cars, social composition, and car speed per reward function against the time of day. Our evaluated dimensions correspond to three out of four goals of parking policy. "Maximize speed" and "preserve social composition" measure the mobility and the accessibility component of the first goal. "Minimize cars" is a proxy for improving the quality of life in the urban area.

Overall, we find that the effects of an RL system determining parking fees depend heavily on its reward function. $r_{occupancy}$ and r_{social} work best to optimize their respective dimension. However, as $r_{occupancy}$ also outperformed r_{cars} and r_{speed} regarding the number of vehicles and average speed, respectively, dedicated learners did not always achieve the best results for the dimension they were trained to optimize. This shows that the four evaluated dimensions are not orthogonal; optimizing the utilized capacity of parking space, e.g., is correlated with maximizing speed per vehicle. The baselines were outperformed by at least one RL learner in any given dimension. In the following, we will discuss the results in more detail along all employed reward functions and the four dimensions depicted in Fig. 3.

The simple static baseline pricing exhibits one particularly strong dimension as it posts the second-best performance retaining accessibility of low-income agents. Nevertheless, this feat appears counterbalanced by the strategy's poor results in the remaining dimensions. In particular, since the strategy delivers the second-worst performance minimizing cars and worst occupancy score, its overall output once more demonstrates the shortcomings of following static pricing mentioned above.

In contrast, the DP baseline appears to be a strong benchmark in multiple examined dimensions. While its effect on accessibility appears rather undesirable since the analyzed run yielded one of the lowest shares of low-income agents in

---

[9] Analyzing a reward function's median run should yield robust results concerning its reward score. However, individual features (e.g., the vanishing speed of cars from certain income classes) are likely still influenced by randomness.

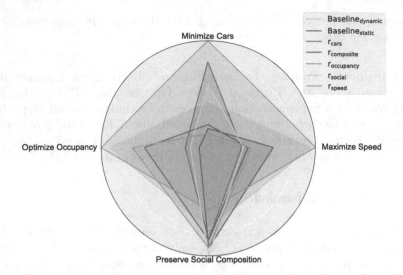

Fig. 3. Performance of the reward functions (and the baselines) relative to the best run regarding the respective dimension. Dimension "optimize occupancy" shows the timeshare that CPZs are held in the desired occupancy range. "Maximize speed" is the mean value of the average normalized speed during the runs. The scores on the remaining dimensions were determined by the value of the respective indicator at the end of the day, i.e., the number of vehicles and the Jensen–Shannon Divergence between the initial and the final social distribution, respectively.

the simulation, the dynamic baseline achieved the second-best performance for CPZ occupancy as well as the mobility dimension.

Turning to $r_{occupancy}$, its impact appears to surpass expectations. The policy learned results in the best performance regarding occupancy, thus succeeding in managing the available parking supply efficiently. Moreover, compared to the dynamic baseline, the function appears even more versatile. The pricing learned by maximizing $r_{occupancy}$ also delivers the best performances concerning quality of life as well as mobility. However, its favorable score compared to the other learners notwithstanding, the aggressively priced fees of $r_{occupancy}$ result in the highest share of low-income drivers having to leave the city after not finding parking spaces. Therefore, the accessibility of lower-income groups is significantly lowered.

r_{social} excelled in the dimension it is directly optimizing, with the most stable social distribution in the model of any pricing strategy, thus retaining accessibility to the simulated inner city. Conversely, it performed poorly in most remaining facets analyzed. For instance, by recording one of worst average car speeds, r_{social} demonstrates the negative influence of free or cheap curbside parking on traffic flow often criticized in the literature [30,31]. Furthermore, since half of the CPZs are constantly at full capacity, the agent also failed to manage the occupancy of curbside parking opportunities effectively. Nonetheless, remarkably, the agent training with r_{social} displaced the third-most cars from parking in the city center as its pricing strategy involves offering parking in the most popular CPZs for free as well as pricing the remaining parking space so aggressively that all strata of society appear to be equally impacted.

Unfortunately, the hypothesized similarity of the outcomes produced by r_{cars} and r_{speed} manifests itself in a unexpected manner. The agent struggled to learn optimal strategies for both reward functions as it converged on very static policies that do not succeed in reliably clearing the road network without causing congestion from the cars attempting to leave it. Therefore, future research should experiment with different reward functions for the policy goals of promoting quality of life as well as mobility.

The overall performance of $r_{composite}$ can be described with the phrase "jack of all trades, master of none" since the policy achieved average performances across almost all dimensions. In particular, however, the aim of restraining $r_{occupancy}$ (which contributes half of the reward in $r_{composite}$) by adding components of r_{social} and r_{cars} does not appear to bear fruit; this can be seen as it only improves over the vanilla occupancy function regarding social composition, while scoring lower for occupancy, average speed, and minimizing cars. Hence, the combined function exhibits inferior properties regarding the goals of securing accessibility and mobility. However, it remains to stress that the use of dedicated MORL approaches may have a positive impact in this matter, as it would allow the leaner to identify its influence on its individual components more reliably.

4   Conclusion

This paper studied the effects of AI-based DP for curbside parking in inner cities. Our key contributions are:

- **Theory**: Amalgamating the related literature on DP for urban parking, we developed a theoretical framework for AI-based DP of urban parking space.
- **Models**: Combining an ABM with RL, we introduce the first portable and generalizable environment to systematically evaluate the effects of dynamically priced parking concerning traffic flow, occupancy, and social composition.
- **Analysis**: Overall, our experiments demonstrate that the outcomes are highly sensitive to the chosen reward function. Furthermore, almost all learners had adverse effects of varying degrees on low-income drivers' ability to park in the city center. This finding stresses the importance of designing DP schemes in a socially equitable manner. We translate these findings into a preliminary catalog of potentially adverse policy effects (see below).

On a high level, our core findings are:

You Can't Have Your Cake and Eat It. Designing an optimal parking policy under numerous side constraints requires extensive trade-offs. Although performing well concerning social composition, our composite learner underperformed concerning occupancy, traffic flow, and number of vehicles.

Optimizing for Single Dimensions May Have Unintended Consequences. For example, optimizing the utilized capacity of parking space also has the worst effect on social composition and the best effect on congestion; optimizing solely for social composition, however, led to more congestion and inefficiencies regarding occupancy. Given a fixed good, managing demand with dynamic prices equal across all income cohorts will always disproportionately impact those of low income. Thus, we argue that DP schemes should be evaluated holistically and incorporate social policy measures beyond traffic parameters.

Finally, there are several starting points for future research: A general issue of modeling priced parking is the scarcity of empirical evidence [25]. Consequently, future iterations of the ABM should be underpinned by additional empirical data, e.g., to calibrate utility functions, WTP, model the parking decision process, and further increase the validity of the findings. Since the presented study combines two expensive methods (an ABM and RL), it would be interesting to analyze the performance trade-offs inherent to using computationally cheaper approaches, e.g., supervised ML, in the same context. Lastly, future research could revolve around developing additional composite reward functions balancing unintended societal consequences of purely traffic-oriented learners.

Acknowledgements. This research was conducted as part of the grant "Consequences of Artificial Intelligence for Urban Societies (CAIUS)," funded by Volkswagen Foundation. We would like to thank the students of our spring 2020 research seminar "Social Simulation," who developed an early prototype of our ABM in NetLogo: Madeleine Aziz, Jens Daube, Paul Exner, Jakob Kappenberger (née Gutmann), Jonas Klenk, and Aamod Vyas. We furthermore would like to thank Frederic Gerdon and the other members of project CAIUS for their helpful feedback to an earlier version of this article.

A   Methodology

Table 1 lists the information contained in S_t, and Fig. 4 shows four out of the five deployed reward functions. Figures 5 and 6 visualize the hyperparameter tuning processes that resulted in the utilized model configurations for the ABM.

Table 1. Variables contained in state S_t.

Variable	Description
ticks	Ticks passed so far in the simulation
n_cars	Share of originally spawned vehicles currently in simulation
overall_occupancy	Overall occupancy of all curbside parking places
mean_speed	Normalized average speed of all non-parking cars
normalized_share_low	Normalized share of low-income cars
CPZ_occupancy	Current utilized capacities of all four CPZs
garages_occupancy	Occupancy of garage(s) (average if multiple)

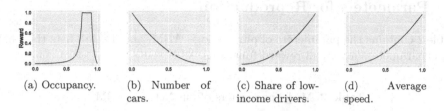

(a) Occupancy.   (b) Number of cars.   (c) Share of low-income drivers.   (d) Average speed.

Fig. 4. Reward functions for learning optimal parking prices.

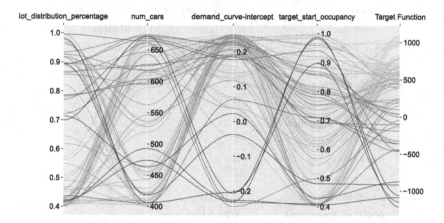

Fig. 5. Result of Bayesian hyperparameter tuning for 100 episodes for the evaluation model. The target function optimizes for the desired volume of traffic and average share of cruising cars of 30% (consistent with Shoup [11]) (higher is better).

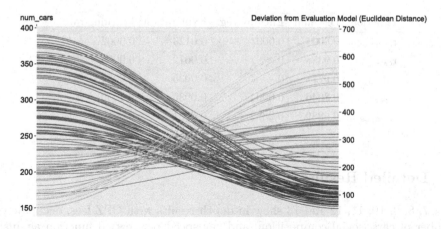

Fig. 6. Result of random hyperparameter tuning for 100 episodes for the training model. The target function minimizes the euclidean distance to the evaluation configuration in terms of the dimensions described in Sect. 3 (lower is better).

B   Parameters for Reproduction

Table 2 contains the parameters of our Netlogo ABM, and Table 3 lists the final hyperparameters across all reward functions.[10]

Table 2. Model parameters of our NetLogo ABM.

Variable	Value
ticks	21,600
num-cars	286 (training), 601 (evaluation)
max-x-cor	28 (training), 40 (evaluation)
max-y-cor	30 (training), 50 (evaluation)
num-garages	1 (training), 2 (evaluation)
lot-distribution-percentage	0.5
target-start-occupancy	0.51
demand-curve-intercept	0.25
initial fee of all CPZs	€2.0
fines-multiplier	5
controls-per-hour	1
pop-mean-income	€26,105
pop-median-income	€23,515
temporal-resolution	1,800

Table 3. Final hyperparameters across all reward functions.

Function	Discount	Entropy reg.	Exploration	Learning rate
$r_{occupancy}$	0.8004	0.0001	0.0126	0.0002
r_{cars}	0.9358	0	0.0012	0.0006
r_{social}	0.9778	0	0.0035	0.0052
r_{speed}	0.8046	0.0004	0.0035	0.0459
$r_{composite}$	0.9889	0.2882	0.0031	0.0010

C   Detailed Results

Figs. 7, 8, 9, 10, 11, 12 and 13 show in-depth results with CPZ fees, occupancy, number of cars, social composition, and car speed per reward function against the time of day.

---

[10] All experiments were conducted with a batch size of 36. Following Kuhnle et al. [16], entropy regularizations < 0.00001 were set to 0.

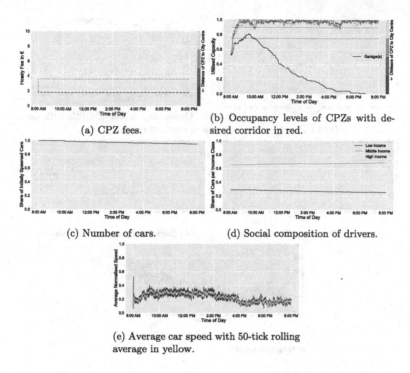

(a) CPZ fees.

(b) Occupancy levels of CPZs with desired corridor in red.

(c) Number of cars.

(d) Social composition of drivers.

(e) Average car speed with 50-tick rolling average in yellow.

Fig. 7. Results of the median static baseline run. (Color figure online)

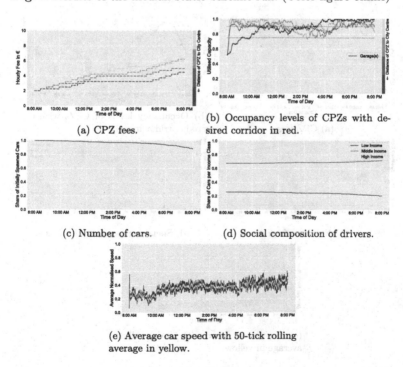

(a) CPZ fees.

(b) Occupancy levels of CPZs with desired corridor in red.

(c) Number of cars.

(d) Social composition of drivers.

(e) Average car speed with 50-tick rolling average in yellow.

Fig. 8. Results of the median dynamic baseline run. (Color figure online)

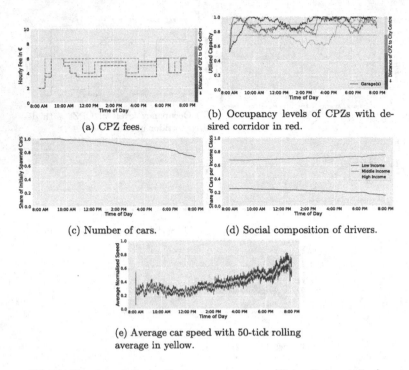

(a) CPZ fees.

(b) Occupancy levels of CPZs with desired corridor in red.

(c) Number of cars.

(d) Social composition of drivers.

(e) Average car speed with 50-tick rolling average in yellow.

Fig. 9. Results of the median $r_{occupancy}$ run. (Color figure online)

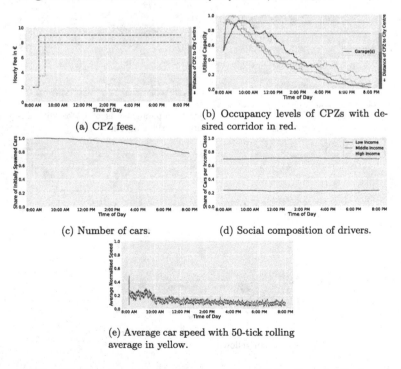

(a) CPZ fees.

(b) Occupancy levels of CPZs with desired corridor in red.

(c) Number of cars.

(d) Social composition of drivers.

(e) Average car speed with 50-tick rolling average in yellow.

Fig. 10. Results of the median r_{cars} run. (Color figure online)

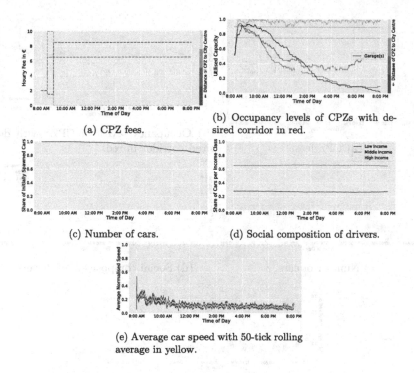

(a) CPZ fees.

(b) Occupancy levels of CPZs with desired corridor in red.

(c) Number of cars.

(d) Social composition of drivers.

(e) Average car speed with 50-tick rolling average in yellow.

Fig. 11. Results of the median r_{social} run. (Color figure online)

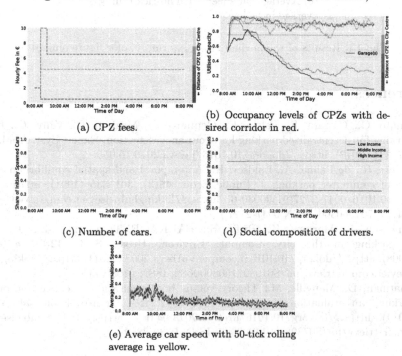

(a) CPZ fees.

(b) Occupancy levels of CPZs with desired corridor in red.

(c) Number of cars.

(d) Social composition of drivers.

(e) Average car speed with 50-tick rolling average in yellow.

Fig. 12. Results of the median r_{speed} run. (Color figure online)

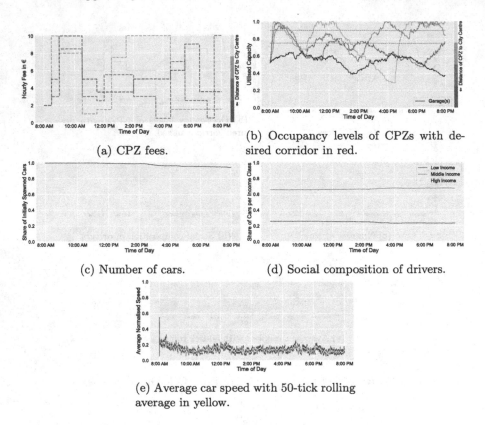

(a) CPZ fees.

(b) Occupancy levels of CPZs with desired corridor in red.

(c) Number of cars.

(d) Social composition of drivers.

(e) Average car speed with 50-tick rolling average in yellow.

Fig. 13. Results of the median r$_{\text{composite}}$ run. (Color figure online)

References

1. Amato, G., Carrara, F., Falchi, F., Gennaro, C., Meghini, C., Vairo, C.: Deep learning for decentralized parking lot occupancy detection. Expert Syst. Appl. **72**, 327–334 (2017). https://doi.org/10.1016/j.eswa.2016.10.055
2. Arnott, R., de Palma, A., Lindsey, R.: A temporal and spatial equilibrium analysis of commuter parking. J. Public Econ. **45**(3), 301–335 (1991). https://doi.org/10.1016/0047-2727(91)90030-6. https://linkinghub.elsevier.com/retrieve/pii/0047272791900306. ISSN 0047-2727
3. Benenson, I., Martens, K., Birfir, S.: PARKAGENT: an agent-based model of parking in the city. Comput. Environ. Urban Syst. **32**(6), 431–439 (2008). https://doi.org/10.1016/j.compenvurbsys.2008.09.011. https://linkinghub.elsevier.com/retrieve/pii/S0198971508000689. ISSN 0198-9715
4. Chatman, D., Manville, M.: Theory versus implementation in congestion-priced parking: an evaluation of SFpark, 2011–2012. Res. Transp. Econ. **44**, 52–60 (2014). https://doi.org/10.1016/j.retrec.2014.04.005. https://linkinghub.elsevier.com/retrieve/pii/S0739885914000067. ISSN 0739-8859

5. Clementi, F., Gallegati, M.: Pareto's law of income distribution: evidence for germany, the United Kingdom, and the United States. In: Salzano, M., et al. (eds.) Econophysics of Wealth Distributions, pp. 3–14. Springer, Milano (2005). https://doi.org/10.1007/88-470-0389-X_1. ISBN 978-88-470-0329-3 978-88-470-0389-7

6. Dieussaert, K., Aerts, K., Steenberghen, T., Maerivoet, S., Spitaels, K.: SUSTAPARK: an agent-based model for simulating parking search. In: 12th AGILE International Conference on Geographic Information Science Hannover, pp. 1–11. Association for Geographic Information Laboratories in Europe, Hannover (2009). https://agile-online.org/conference_paper/cds/agile_2009/agile_cd/pdfs/133.pdf

7. Eschmann, J.: Reward function design in reinforcement learning. In: Belousov, B., Abdulsamad, H., Klink, P., Parisi, S., Peters, J. (eds.) Reinforcement Learning Algorithms: Analysis and Applications. SCI, vol. 883, pp. 25–33. Springer, Cham (2021). https://doi.org/10.1007/978-3-030-41188-6_3

8. Friesen, M., Mingardo, G.: Is parking in Europe ready for dynamic pricing? A reality check for the private sector. Sustainability 12(7), 2732 (2020). https://doi.org/10.3390/su12072732. https://www.mdpi.com/2071-1050/12/7/2732. ISSN 2071-1050

9. Gilbert, N.: Agent-Based Models. SAGE Publications Inc, Thousand Oaks (2020). https://doi.org/10.4135/9781506355580. https://methods.sagepub.com/book/agent-based-models-2e. ISBN 978-1-5063-5560-3 978-1-5063-5558-0

10. Glazer, A., Niskanen, E.: Parking fees and congestion. Reg. Sci. Urban Econ. 22(1), 123–132 (1992). https://doi.org/10.1016/0166-0462(92)90028-Y. https://linkinghub.elsevier.com/retrieve/pii/016604629290028Y. ISSN 0166-0462

11. Hampshire, R., Shoup, D.: How much traffic is cruising for parking? Transfers Magazine, vol. 4 (2019). https://transfersmagazine.org/magazine-article/issue-4/how-much-traffic-is-cruising-for-parking/

12. Inci, E.: A review of the economics of parking. Econ. Transp. 4(1–2), 50–63 (2015). https://doi.org/10.1016/j.ecotra.2014.11.001. https://linkinghub.elsevier.com/retrieve/pii/S2212012214000562. ISSN 2212-0122

13. Jakob, M., Menendez, M.: Parking pricing vs. congestion pricing: a macroscopic analysis of their impact on traffic. Transportmetrica A: Transp. Sci. 17(4), 462–491 (2021). https://doi.org/10.1080/23249935.2020.1797924

14. Jaxa-Rozen, M., Kwakkel, J.H.: PyNetLogo: linking NetLogo with python. J. Artif. Soc. Soc. Simul. 21(2), 4 (2018). https://doi.org/10.18564/jasss.3668. http://jasss.soc.surrey.ac.uk/21/2/4.html. ISSN 1460-7425

15. Jeihani, M., Ardeshiri, A., Du, J., Rakha, H.: Drivers willingness to pay progressive rate for street parking. Technical report, U.S. Department of Transportation, January 2015. https://www.mautc.psu.edu/docs/MAUTC-2013-04.pdf

16. Kuhnle, A., Schaarschmidt, M., Fricke, K.: Tensorforce: A Tensorflow Library for Applied Reinforcement Learning (2017). https://github.com/tensorforce/tensorforce

17. Litman, T.: Parking Management Best Practices. Routledge, New York (2019). ISBN 978-0-367-33012-5, oCLC: 1110487321

18. Mannion, P., Devlin, S., Mason, K., Duggan, J., Howley, E.: Policy invariance under reward transformations for multi-objective reinforcement learning. Neurocomputing 263, 60–73 (2017). https://doi.org/10.1016/j.neucom.2017.05.090. https://linkinghub.elsevier.com/retrieve/pii/S0925231217311037. ISSN 0925-2312

19. Manville, M.: Parking pricing. In: Ison, S., Mulley, C. (eds.) Transport and Sustainability, vol. 5, pp. 137–155. Emerald Group Publishing Limited, Bingley, UK (2014). https://doi.org/10.1108/S2044-994120140000005019. https://www.emerald.com/insight/content/doi/10.1108/S2044-994120140000005019/full/html. ISBN 978-1-78350-919-5 978-1-78350-920-1

20. Marsden, G.: Parking policy. In: Ison, S., Mulley, C. (eds.) Transport and Sustainability, vol. 5, pp. 11–32. Emerald Group Publishing Limited, Bingley, UK (2014). https://doi.org/10.1108/S2044-994120140000005016. https://www.emerald.com/insight/content/doi/10.1108/S2044-994120140000005016/full/html. ISBN 978-1-78350-919-5 978-1-78350-920-1

21. Meyer, M.D.: Demand management as an element of transportation policy: using carrots and sticks to influence travel behavior. Transp. Res. Part A: Policy Pract. **33**(7–8), 575–599 (1999). https://doi.org/10.1016/S0965-8564(99)00008-7. https://linkinghub.elsevier.com/retrieve/pii/S0965856499000087. ISSN 0965-8564

22. Mingardo, G., van Wee, B., Rye, T.: Urban parking policy in Europe: a conceptualization of past and possible future trends. Transp. Res. Part A: Policy Pract. **74**, 268–281 (2015). https://doi.org/10.1016/j.tra.2015.02.005. https://linkinghub.elsevier.com/retrieve/pii/S0965856415000221. ISSN 0965-8564

23. Morillo, C., Campos, J.M.: On-street illegal parking costs in urban areas. Procedia - Soc. Behav. Sci. **160**, 342–351 (2014). https://doi.org/10.1016/j.sbspro.2014.12.146. https://www.sciencedirect.com/science/article/pii/S1877042814062478. xI Congreso de Ingenieria del Transporte (CIT 2014). ISSN 1877-0428

24. Nguyen, N.D., Nguyen, T.T., Nguyen, H., Creighton, D., Nahavandi, S.: Review, Analysis and Design of a Comprehensive Deep Reinforcement Learning Framework. arXiv e-print 2002.11883 (2021). https://arxiv.org/abs/2002.11883

25. Nourinejad, M., Roorda, M.J.: Impact of hourly parking pricing on travel demand. Transp. Res. Part A: Policy Pract. **98**, 28–45 (2017). https://doi.org/10.1016/j.tra.2017.01.023. https://linkinghub.elsevier.com/retrieve/pii/S0965856415303396. ISSN 0965-8564

26. OECD: Under Pressure: The Squeezed Middle Class. OECD, May 2019. https://doi.org/10.1787/689afed1-en. https://www.oecd-ilibrary.org/social-issues-migration-health/under-pressure-the-squeezed-middle-class_689afed1-en. ISBN 978-92-64-54283-9 978-92-64-15034-8 978-92-64-98251-2 978-92-64-69927-4

27. Pierce, G., Shoup, D.: Getting the prices right: an evaluation of pricing parking by demand in San Francisco. J. Am. Plann. Assoc. **79**(1), 67–81 (2013). https://doi.org/10.1080/01944363.2013.787307. http://www.tandfonline.com/doi/abs/10.1080/01944363.2013.787307. ISSN 0194-4363, 1939-0130

28. Proost, S., Van Dender, K.: Optimal urban transport pricing in the presence of congestion, economies of density and costly public funds. Transp. Res. Part A: Policy Pract. **42**(9), 1220–1230 (2008). https://doi.org/10.1016/j.tra.2008.03.009. https://linkinghub.elsevier.com/retrieve/pii/S0965856408000864. ISSN 0965-8564

29. Saharan, S., Kumar, N., Bawa, S.: An efficient smart parking pricing system for smart city environment: a machine-learning based approach. Future Gener. Comput. Syst. **106**, 622–640 (2020). https://doi.org/10.1016/j.future.2020.01.031. https://linkinghub.elsevier.com/retrieve/pii/S0167739X19322496. ISSN 0167-739X

30. Shoup, D.: The High Cost of Free Parking. Planners Press, American Planning Association, Chicago, updated edn. (2011). ISBN 978-1-932364-96-5, oCLC: ocn742069668

31. Shoup, D.: Free parking or free markets. In: Shoup, D. (ed.) Parking and the City, 1st edn, pp. 270–275. Routledge, New York (2018). https://doi.org/10.4324/9781351019668. https://www.taylorfrancis.com/books/9781351019651. ISBN 978-1-351-01966-8

32. Simhon, E., Liao, C., Starobinski, D.: Smart parking pricing: a machine learning approach. In: 2017 IEEE Conference on Computer Communications Workshops (INFOCOM WKSHPS), Atlanta, GA, pp. 641–646. IEEE, May 2017. https://doi.org/10.1109/INFOCOMW.2017.8116452. http://ieeexplore.ieee.org/document/8116452/. ISBN 978-1-5386-2784-6

33. Vickrey, W.: Statement to the joint committee on Washington, DC, metropolitan problems (with a foreword by Richard Arnott and Marvin Kraus). J. Urban Econ. **36**(1), 42–65 (1994). https://doi.org/10.1006/juec.1994.1025. https://linkinghub.elsevier.com/retrieve/pii/S0094119084710254. ISSN 0094-1190

34. Wilensky, U.: Netlogo Traffic Grid Model (2003). http://ccl.northwestern.edu/netlogo/models/TrafficGrid

Linguistic and News-Sharing Polarization During the 2019 South American Protests

Ramon Villa-Cox[1](✉)(iD), Helen Shuxuan Zeng[1](iD),
Ashiqur R. KhudaBukhsh[2](iD), and Kathleen M. Carley[1](iD)

[1] Carnegie Mellon University, Pittsburgh, PA 15213, USA
{rvillaco,shuxuanz,carley}@andrew.cmu.edu
[2] Rochester Institute of Technology, Rochester, NY 14623, USA
axkvse@rit.edu

Abstract. In computational social science, two parallel research directions exploring – news consumption patterns and linguistic regularities – have made significant inroads into better understanding complex political polarization in the era of ubiquitous internet. However, little or no literature exists that presented a unified treatment combining both these research directions. When working on social events from countries that do not speak English as a first language, computational linguistic resource availability is often a barrier to sophisticated linguistic analyses. In this work, we analyze an important sociopolitical event, the 2019 South American protests, and demonstrate that (1) a combined treatment offers a more comprehensive understanding of the event; and (2) these cross-cutting methods can be applied in a synergistic way. The insights gained by the combination of these methods include that polarization in users' news sharing patterns was consistent with their stances towards the government and that polarization in their language mainly manifested along ideological, political, or protest-related lines. In addition, we release a massive dataset of 15 million tweets relevant to this crisis.

Keywords: Linguistic polarization · News-sharing polarization · South American protests

1 Introduction

Political polarization is a widely-studied topic across multiple research disciplines [18,27]. In computing and information systems literature involving social media data, two parallel lines of research – network-focused and language-focused – have made significant inroads into better understanding of complex political polarization in the era of ubiquitous internet. However, little or no literature exists melding these two research directions in a synergistic way. Also, there exists a stark contrast between research attention on political polarization involving countries speaking English as first language (specifically the US) and countries speaking languages other than English. A major contributing factor

F. Hopfgartner et al. (Eds.): SocInfo 2022, LNCS 13618, pp. 76–95, 2022.
https://doi.org/10.1007/978-3-031-19097-1_5

to this attention difference is the sheer mismatch in natural language processing (NLP) resources between English and most other languages [24].

In this paper, we focus on a major political event *outside US* in a language *different from English* and show that the synergy between network-focused methods applied on news sharing patterns and language-focused methods can offer us a better understanding of the manifestation of polarization. We consider the 2019 South American protests, a major event that affected multiple countries yet received little or no attention from the computational social science community.

A central theme in all these protests was a massive online presence and the reported involvement of international and regional actors that sought to influence their evolution. While social media response during protests has received research attention, little or no publicly available data exists to further our understanding. We release a dataset of over 15 million tweets with weakly labeled stance of approximately 500k users. Via this substantial corpus, we analyze the online polarization during the South American protests along two dimensions: Polarization in language and in news sharing patterns.

Our contributions in this paper are the following.

• *Methods*: We present a novel method to mine stance in Twitter data that requires minimal supervision. The mined stances are used to segregate the user pool into two groups: one in favor of the government, and the other, against it. The user stances, and their subsequent grouping, set up the basis for our study of the polarization observed in these networks. Our work relies on a domain expert who has comprehensive knowledge about the sociopolitical issues the countries studied. Having access to annotation expertise can be a double-edged sword. On one hand, the performance of machine learning systems benefits from superior annotation quality [1]. On the other hand, expert annotators are costly. Our method relies on a weakly labelled approach to minimize labelling efforts. However, the risk of relying on automated methods for tasks with social impact is well-documented [17,25]. We show that a recently proposed unsupervised method to quantify linguistic polarization [18] can be used in a synergistic way to validate our weakly labelled approach. We also demonstrate this method's suitability in characterizing and quantifying linguistic polarization in countries not speaking English as the first language and experiencing a completely different sociopolitical crisis. We further validate these partitions by presenting strong evidence of polarization in news sharing and information diffusion by users, consistent with their stances towards the government.

• *Social*: We look at a globally important event: the series of South American protests that took place in multiple countries in 2019. We observe that linguistic polarization mainly manifested along ideological, political or protest-related lines. Moreover, we find strong evidence of the polarization in users' news sharing patterns, consistent with their stances towards the government. These can have pervasive effects on public discourse and political literacy.

• *Resource*: To the best of our knowledge, no large scale social media dataset relevant to protests spanning multiple countries exist. We hope that the rich network and semantic structure present in the data will be helpful not only for assessing polarization during these events but to advance stance classification efforts in the Spanish language.

2   Background

In 2019, a series of protests shocked the region of South America that started in Ecuador with Chile, Bolivia and Colombia soon following. Except in Bolivia, the protests resulted from left-wing movements seeking to resist austerity measures being imposed in each country. In Bolivia, the protests were a right-wing response to an alleged electoral fraud undertaken by the government in favor of the president seeking reelection. These protests had a massive online presence with reported involvement of international actors that sought to influence their evolution. These include international news agencies like RT en Español, funded by the Russian government, or TeleSUR and NTN24, funded in part by the Venezuelan government, that were more critical of local governments (except for Bolivia) and provided more favorable coverage of the protesters. In contrast, local news agencies tended to be more critical of them and favorable towards the government[1]. For this work, we collected a dataset of 100 million tweets from 15+ million users around each protest (Appendix A contains description of the data collection methodology, ethical considerations, and the timeline of the protests).

3   Related Work

Protests in the Age of Social Media. There is a long standing debate in political science concerning the role that media (social media in particular) plays in collective action during political unrest. This line of research can be further categorized into network-focused and language-focused studies. The former utilizes network-based methods centered around Twitter collections of protests to show that (1) protest communication networks are often fragmented and underutilized [14]; (2) peripheral participants play a critical role in the diffusion of protest messages [5]; and (3) the directionality of these networks can be leveraged to characterize the different roles played by individuals [6]. To our knowledge, little or no work has combined network-based and language-based methods to understand the nature of polarization. In what follows, we provide a brief overview of the research that has explored these separate, but related, dimensions of polarization.

Polarization in Language. Political polarization has been widely studied across several disciplines with extensive focus on partisan US politics. Notable examples include studies on climate change [4,11], gun control/rights [9], Supreme Court confirmations [7], economic decisions [23], congressional votes [26], polarization

---

[1] https://www.nytimes.com/2020/01/19/us/politics/south-america-russian-twitter.html.

in media [28], etc. Recently, [18] presented a quantifiable framework for polarization that leverages machine translation. Our use of this framework establishes its generalizability as we consider: (1) a different social media platform (the framework has been solely applied to YouTube data [18,19]); (2) a language different from English; (3) and a completely different socio-political context.

Polarization in News Consumption. Much of the recent research on polarization in news consumption has centered around the cognitive dimension, while the social aspects have hardly been investigated [22]. Most echo chambers encountered empirically are a result of social media practices that exhibit polarized content engagement, rather than exposure [12]. On a similar note, a review of numerous studies on Facebook showed that observed polarization is driven more by selective exposure resulting from confirmation bias than by filter bubbles or echo chambers [31]. Polarization has also been identified as an important driver for diffusion of misinformation. This has been observed in the context of disinformation campaigns around the release of popular Marvel movies [2,3] and in the diffusion of scientific, conspiracy theory and satiric Facebook articles [8].

Weak-Labeling of Social Media Data. Utilizing weak signals in social media to train models has been explored in the past, achieving mixed results. In the field of ideology detection, several lines of work have focused on Twitter interactions to exploit a user's endorsement (given by retweeting, following, or liking behavior) of political figures to predict their general partisanship [13,15,34,35], or to forecast the results of an election [32,33]. In this work, we build upon these approaches by leveraging hashtag usage of labeled political figures to reduce the risks of using non-informative hashtags. Moreover, as described in the following section, this offers our proposed methodology different levels of validation to assess the robustness of the labels obtained.

4   Weak Labeling Methodology

We propose a weak labeling methodology that requires minimal labeling effort and leverages a user's endorsement of politicians' tweets and hashtag campaigns with defined stances towards the protest. The reliance in these two signals provide different levels of validation to assess the robustness of the labels obtained. We believe that this methodology holds promise for the development of large-scale databases for the analysis of similar contentious events (with active involvement of local political figures). A description of the annotation process follows next.

Political Figures. A set of 25 of the most prominent verified partisan actors for and against the protests were identified in each of the countries. These seed users included the most prominent members of each government involved with the protests (president, interior/defence minister, etc.). We also identified other leaders of the government's coalition party that were vocally supportive of the government (in Twitter). Similarly, we identified the movements/parties that were in opposition of the government (by promoting the protests) and included their most vocal/prominent members. We then compiled the list of their Twitter

Table 1. Distribution of labeled political figures and stance hashtags.

	Political figures		Stance-tags	
	Against	Pro	Against	Pro
Bolivia	83	31	180	91
Chile	164	183	452	254
Colombia	148	182	204	180
Ecuador	124	113	318	141

friends (people who they follow), ordered them by follower count, and labeled the stance of partisan actors. These actors were classified as: politicians or political organizations, media figures or militants (self-described partisan influencers). The labeling procedure was as follows. A domain expert fluent in Spanish and with knowledge of the events that took place around each of the protests was presented the user card (including their description and location) of a labeling candidate and their timeline (tweets and retweets done by the user) in the period corresponding to the protest of the relevant country. Based on this information, the domain expert determines the type of user being considered and whether she was "in favor" (1), "against" (0), or if their stance was undetermined (–1) towards the government of the relevant country. 1,028 users are labeled by the domain expert. Table 1 summarizes the stance distribution.

Stance-Tags. We construct a set of trailing hashtags (dubbed "stance-tags") that were consistently used in "in favor" or "against" the government of each country. We label a first set of 778 hashtags as follows. Annotators fluent in Spanish and aware of the relevant events were presented tweets using these hashtags during the period corresponding each protest. The annotators determine if the candidate hashtag was used primarily in tweets taking a position "in favor" (1), "against" (0), or neutral/undetermined (–1) towards the protests or government.

Next, we expand this set of hashtags by others that co-occurred exclusively with tweets for one side of the labeled set, yielding 838 extra hashtags. This second set was not as thoroughly validated and were only pruned by removing hashtags unrelated to the protest or deemed too general. We finally augment these with any missing hashtags used exclusively by labeled political figures from one side of the argument. As before, this set was only validated by a cursory analysis to remove any hashtag unrelated to the protests. This augmentation step added 227 new hashtags, and the final distribution is presented in Table 1.

4.1   Determining User Stances

Our weak labeling methodology relies on the hypothesis that users are more likely to tweet (or retweet) hashtags or political figures that are aligned with their stances during these events. Hence, weak-stance labels are assigned to a user if their percentage of tweets with a consistent stance-tag is above a given probability threshold. This threshold was set to 90% as determined via validation experiments performed on the hand-labeled political figures. Further details

Table 2. Number of weakly-labeled users and their original tweets (not including retweets). We also include the corresponding counts for users in the two-hop neighborhood of labeled users.

		Bolivia	Chile	Colombia	Ecuador
Against	Users	58 727	221 641	79 908	51 545
	Tweets	2 079 286	7 648 773	2 258 276	1 248 620
Pro	Users	54 776	33 327	28 310	25 566
	Tweets	1 447 120	2 167 763	1 164 129	493 509
Neighbors	Users	668 815	860 824	556 821	457 241
	Tweets	7 803 498	8 518 147	4 978 669	4 307 034

of this exercise and of the stance distribution obtained by each weak signal are presented in Appendix B. The final user stance was determined by combining the labels obtained by both signals, allowing us to validate the stances assigned to the users. There was a 41.9% overlap of users labeled by both methodologies, while 46.8% of the users were labeled based on their hashtags and 11.3% only based on their endorsement of political figures. Whenever a there was an inconsistency between the label assigned by both methodologies (or if one method assigned an inconsistent label for a user), we deemed that label inconsistent. Importantly, in the worst case (Bolivia) a 10.6% of the users had an inconsistent stance, which provides evidence for the robustness of the labels constructed. The final distribution of the consistent weakly-labeled users and the number of original tweets (not including retweets) posted by them is presented in Table 2. We include counts for users in the two-hop neighborhood of labeled users (these IDs are part of the data released), as we expect that the rich network structure present in the data will be helpful not only for assessing polarization but to advance stance classification efforts in languages other than English. The dataset is shared through Zenodo[2] and further details are discussed in Appendix A.1.

5 Linguistic Polarization

We employ a recently-proposed framework [18] to quantify linguistic polarization in large-scale text discussion datasets. In the original paper [18], the authors applied this framework to English YouTube comments in the context of polarization in US cable news networks viewerships. Our results indicate that the methodology is generalizable to discussions on a different political crisis, in a different language (Spanish), and manifested in a different social media platform (Twitter). This framework assumes that two sub-communities (e.g., the sub-community favoring the protest and the sub-community opposing the protest) are speaking in two different *languages* (say, $\mathcal{L}_{pro}$ and $\mathcal{L}_{against}$) and obtains single-word translations using a well-known machine translation algorithm [30]. Since $\mathcal{L}_{pro}$ and

---

[2] Publicly available at: https://doi.org/10.5281/zenodo.6213032.

Table 3. Pairwise similarity between languages for: Pro and Against government communities (Stance-Split) and a baseline from two random samples from the combined corpus (Randomized-Split). Similarity metrics are constructed with corpora of the same size. The sub-sampling process was repeated six times and we report the mean and standard deviation (in parenthesis). The evaluation set is computed by taking the top 5K most frequent words of the combined corpora.

	Stance-Split (%)	Randomized-Split (%)
Bolivia	57.11 (1.31)	93.37 (0.61)
Chile	68.21 (1.46)	91.37 (0.62)
Colombia	64.22 (1.13)	91.94 (0.67)
Ecuador	56.50 (1.12)	93.52 (0.53)

$\mathcal{L}_{against}$ are both in fact Spanish, ideally, any word w in $\mathcal{L}_{pro}$ should translate to itself in $\mathcal{L}_{against}$. However, when a word w_1 in one language translates to a different word w_2 in another, it indicates w_1 and w_2 are used in dissimilar contexts across these two *languages* signalling (possible) disagreement. These disagreed pairs present a quantifiable measure to compute differences between large scale corpora as greater the number of disagreed pairs the farther two sub-communities are. Let our goal be to compute the similarity between two languages, $\mathcal{L}_{source}$ and $\mathcal{L}_{target}$, with vocabularies $\mathcal{V}_{source}$ and $\mathcal{V}_{target}$, respectively. The similarity measure between two languages along a given translation direction computes the fraction of words in $\mathcal{V}_{source}$ that translates to itself. The larger the value of this similarity measure, the greater is the similarity between a language pair. We constructed $\mathcal{L}_{pro}$ and $\mathcal{L}_{against}$ by combining all the main tweets by a user of a given stance (this includes tweets not related to the protests) ensuring that a retweeted tweet in included only once. We follow the same experimental design and preprocessing steps as described in [18]. Using a well-known machine translation algorithm, we translate the top 10k words in one language to the other and examine disparities. Following [18], we use stop-words as anchors for the translation as these are the most likely to maintain their meaning across the different groups.

How Can We Linguistically Validate Our Weakly Labelled User Stances? We first highlight how linguistic polarization can provide corroborating evidence and validate weakly labelled user stances. We contrast this linguistic polarization measure against a baseline similarity metric calculated by repeating the process with randomized splits (of the same size) for each of the countries. Our intuition is a randomized split will exhibit lesser linguistic polarization than a split guided by stance. Table 3 indeed shows that is the case. This results lends further credence to our method to determine stance and indicates how these methods can be applied in a synergistic way. We further note that the largest polarization was observed in Bolivia and Ecuador, while the lowest was observed in Chile (this difference being significant at a 95% threshold).

We next contextualize the observed linguistic polarization by highlighting notable examples of the mistranslated word pairs. Due to space constraints, in Table 4 we present examples only for Bolivia and Ecuador (the results are consistent across all the countries studied). We find linguistic polarization mainly

Table 4. Notable instances of linguistic polarization by topic for Ecuador and Bolivia.

Country	Theme	L_{pro} (translation)	$L_{against}$ (translation)
Ecuador	Idiological	Fascistas (fascists)	Comunistas (communists)
		Neoliberal (neoliberal)	Progresista (progressive)
	Protest	Chapas (police -informal-)	Infelices (Bastard)
		Decreto883 (Policy)	Derogatoria (derogate)
	Political	Jarrin (Government official)	CONAIE (Protest leaders)
		Lasso (supportive politician)	Correa (opposition politician)
Bolivia	Idiological	Comunismo (communism)	Neoliberalismo (neoliberalism)
		Socialismo (socialism)	liberalismo (liberalism)
	Protest	Derrocar (overthrow)	Derrotar (defeat)
		Masistas (president supporter)	Maleantes (malefactors)
	Political	Almagro (OEA's Secretary)	Delincuente (Delinquent)
		Evo (president's name)	Asesino (assassin)

Table 5. Pairwise similarity between languages of different countries computed for: Top) pro-protest communities, and Bottom) against-protest communities.

L_{pro}		Bolivia	Chile	Colombia	Ecuador
	Bolivia	-	51.98 (1.47)	46.00 (0.70)	42.98 (0.91)
L_{pro}	Chile	51.98 (1.47)	-	69.22 (0.82)	54.42 (0.74)
	Colombia	46.00 (0.70)	69.22 (0.82)	-	51.64 (0.57)
	Ecuador	42.98 (0.91)	54.42 (0.74)	51.64 (0.57)	-

$L_{against}$		Bolivia	Chile	Colombia	Ecuador
	Bolivia	-	51.70 (0.47)	50.10 (1.2)	50.74 (1.13)
$L_{against}$	Chile	51.70 (0.47)	-	62.96 (0.64)	65.48 (1.72)
	Colombia	50.10 (1.2)	62.96 (0.64)	-	57.58 (0.93)
	Ecuador	50.74 (1.13)	65.48 (1.72)	57.58 (0.93)	-

manifested along ideological, political and protest-related lines. Terms related to left-leaning ideologies in one community tend to be discussed in similar contexts as right-leaning terms (e.g., Socialism mistranslates to Fascism); terms related to law and order in one group are discussed in a similar context as the other discusses oppression (an informal term for police mistranslates to bastard or vandals to protesters). Importantly, we find that the motivations for the protests mistranslate to each other. For example, in the case of Ecuador, Decreto883[3] mistranslates to derogate which was one of the calls of the protests movements (a similar pattern is shown for Bolivia with the "overthrow" term). Finally, opposition leaders are discussed in similar contexts as government representatives.

To test the robustness of the methodology to differences in dialects, we apply it to compare stances between the countries. The middle and bottom sections of Table 5 include the pairwise similarity of languages for pro- and

---

[3] This refers to the decree 883 which proposed austerity measures and started the protests in the country.

against-government communities between countries. Note that, for both stance types, the language similarity is significantly lower for pairs that contrast Bolivia with any other country. This is consistent with the fact that Bolivia is the only country which has a left-leaning government and hence right-leaning protesters. Moreover, even with the added noise of local colloquialisms, we are still able to recover the ideological polarization between protest movements, when compared to Bolivia ("neoliberalism" still mistranslates to "communism" or "socialist" to "nazi"). These differences do not exist when comparing protests movements with similar ideological motivations (e.g. "socialist" in Ecuador translates to "socialist" in Chile). Importantly, we can use this methodology to mine knowledge from the corpora, as we find that local political leaders from the protest in one country mistranslate to their counterparts in the other country (e.g. "Correa" in Ecuador mistranslates to "Petro" in Colombia – an opposition leader).

6   Polarization in News Sharing Behavior

To assess the polarization observed in user's news sharing behavior, we identified the 853 main regional and local news outlets operating in each country (or major reporters) collecting their names, Twitter handles and the URLs for their main domain. International media includes agencies like CNN and others from Venezuela and Russia to explore regional influence campaigns on the protests. However, tweets sharing news articles from these outlets can have rich topical diversity ranging from sports to politics. We thus need a filter to detect articles relevant to the protests. We built a neural text classifier [20] using FastText embeddings pre-trained on the combined stance dataset to classify the tweets into two categories: relevant and irrelevant to the protests. This classifier achieves an accuracy of 92% on a held-out test set (details are presented in Appendix C).

Community Detection Among News Agencies. We keep the 383 subset of news outlets that, after the filtering process, are either directly retweeted by a user or that have a user tweet/retweet a URL corresponding to their domain (see Table 10 in Appendix C). We then explore the community structure of these news outlets based on the homogeneity of their user bases. We define the bipartite network $\mathcal{G} = (\mathcal{N}, \mathcal{U}, \mathcal{E})$ where $\mathcal{N}$ is the set of news outlets; $\mathcal{U}$ is the set of users who have retweeted the posts of news outlets in $\mathcal{N}$, or tweeted (retweeted) a URL corresponding to one of the news agencies. The bipartite graph, $\mathcal{G}$, can be described as a matrix $\mathcal{M}$ for which $\mathcal{M}_{i,j} = 1$ when user j shared (retweeted) news agency i, and 0 otherwise. We then define the co-occurrence matrix $\mathcal{C}^N = \mathcal{M}\mathcal{M}^T$, which counts the number of users shared by two news agencies in $\mathcal{N}$.

Via the application of the Louvain clustering algorithm on the resulting network, we find that media outlets are divided into three clusters: a) major local media; b) regional Russian and Venezuelan media, including local left-leaning media; and c) local Venezuelan media. This implies that outlets are not only clustered geographically but also ideologically, as the local media cluster includes the major media organizations in each country, which were reportedly more likely to support the local governments (with the exception of Bolivia where the situation is reversed). Our clustering results support the hypothesis that media with similar stances are more likely to share homogeneous user bases providing additional validation for our proposed partitions.

6.1   Quantifying the Polarization

We next explore the diversity in the user bases of the news outlets in a given cluster to estimate the polarization in news sharing by users with different stances. To this end, we compute the ratio of retweets from pro-government users for the regional Russian and Venezuelan news media clusters. We find that in Chile, Colombia and Ecuador, 90% of these outlets have 10% or less of the diffusion of their articles coming from pro-government users. Of the remaining 10% of these outlets, the relevance of this user base was less than 20%. Whereas in Bolivia, the reverse is observed, as almost all news outlets in this cluster had at least 80% of their retweets coming form pro-government users (there was only one outlet that had 70% of this user base). This is consistent with the political orientation of the media organizations in this cluster and their documented support of the Bolivian government [16, 29], while Ecuador, Chile and Colombia had more right-leaning governments at the time of the protests. The results provide further evidence of polarization in news sharing behavior, as users are more likely to retweet news aligning with their stances.

We further explore if the observed level of polarization can be accounted by the asymmetry in the user stance distribution found in each country. For each news outlet in the two clusters analyzed, we compute the relative entropy of their user bases. For each news agency n, its relative entropy is defined as follows:

$$H(n) = -p_{pro} * log\frac{p_{pro}}{g_{pro}} - (1 - p_{pro}) * log\frac{1 - p_{pro}}{1 - g_{pro}} \tag{1}$$

where p_{pro} is the ratio of retweets for news media n from pro-government users and g_{pro} is the overall ratio of pro-government users in that country. The relative entropy $H(n)$ evaluates how p_{pro} differs from g_{pro} - the lower the value of $H(n)$, the more disproportional the level of polarization is with respect to the asymmetries observed in the stance distribution. The maximum possible value 0 of $H(n)$ is obtained when a news organization's user base matches the stance distribution for the country. Figure 1 shows, for each of the countries studied, the distribution of relative entropy for news media in the clusters of local media and regional Russian and Venezuelan media. We observe that for all countries, regional media from Russia and Venezuela are disproportionately polarized. Moreover, in the case of Bolivia, we observe the highest level of relative polarization, an observation that is consistent with the language polarization levels described in the previous section.

6.2   Polarization Through News Media Transitions

We finally analyze user transitions among the different clusters of news media. We adapt a methodology previously used to examine the transition behavior of users browsing websites related to the topic of gun rights/control [21].

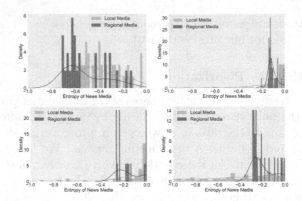

Fig. 1. Distribution of relative entropy for local (blue cluster) and regional Russian and Venezuelan media (red cluster) in Bolivia (top left), Chile (top right), Colombia (bottom left) and Ecuador (bottom right). (Color figure online)

Table 6. Transition matrix and summary mobility indices for Bolivia, Chile, Colombia and Ecuador

(a) Transition Matrix.

Country		Local media	Regional media
Bolivia	Local media	95.26%	4.74%
	Regional media	3.67%	96.33%
Chile	Local media	64.35%	35.65%
	Regional media	21.13%	78.87%
Colombia	Local media	91.4%	8.6%
	Regional media	18.01%	81.99%
Ecuador	Local media	80.43%	19.57%
	Regional media	7.59 %	92.41%

(b) Summary Mobility Indices.

Country	IR	ML	MR
Bolivia	95.87%	2.05%	2.08%
Chile	73.5%	13.19%	13.31%
Colombia	88.38%	5.84%	5.78%
Ecuador	89.21%	5.24%	5.55%

Specifically, we seek insights about how the political orientation of news media influences the type of news outlets that a user will retweet next[4] after having retweeted news supporting or objecting the protest. For each user, we represent her retweeting history as a Markov chain of the cluster of outlets the retweeted news come from. Then, we describe the distribution of the transition probabilities by an n-state transition matrix P_n, with elements $p_{ij} = \text{Prob}(X_{t+1} = j | X_t = i)$. We note that the row-wise sums are equal to 1. State 0 represents when the user shares news articles from the local news cluster, and state 1 from the cluster of regional Russian and Venezuelan media. Table 6a summarizes the transition matrix for Bolivia, Chile, Colombia and Ecuador.

---

[4] An outlet can be retweeted either directly or indirectly via a tweet originating from their account, or a third party tweet containing a url with their domain.

To analyze the underlying trends of these matrices, we employ Summary Mobility Indices, which have been widely used in economics and sociology. They describe the direction of the mobility in the following way:

- Immobility Ratio: IR $= \sum_{i=1}^{n} p_{ii}/n$
- Moving Up (Left): MU (ML) $= \sum_{i<j} p_{ij}/n$
- Moving Down (Right): MD (MR) $= \sum_{i>j} p_{ij}/n$

where n is the number of states. As mentioned previously, the cluster of Russian and Venezuelan media is comprised of left-leaning outlets, including smaller media operations local to each country. We therefore rename the moving up index (from local media to Russian, Venezuelan media) as moving left (ideologically), and the moving down index as moving right (ideologically). The Summary Mobility Indices for different countries are included in Table 6b. We note that the majority transitions are to the same state, which indicates users tend to share articles from the same community where the stances of the information align with their own. The likelihood of transitioning out of a user's community is generally low. In this regard, the transition matrices suggests (1) presence of eco-chambers in the midst of the protests and (2) confirmation bias in the way users choose to share content. Moreover, the observed polarization levels in news transitions are consistent with what was described for the language polarization in the previous section, with Chile showing the lowest level of polarization and Bolivia the highest.

7 Discussions

In this work, we explore polarization in user behavior based on their stance towards the government during the 2019 South American protests. We employ a novel method that requires minimal supervision to label the stance of users. We make our resulting dataset publicly available. We focus on polarization in language and in news media sharing and show that together, the analyses shed vital insights. Our linguistic polarization results indicate that polarization largely manifests along ideological, political, and protest-related lines. We also find strong evidence of polarization in news sharing and information diffusion by users, consistent with their stances towards the government. The news media in our dataset clusters with the political stances of their content. We find consistent evidence of polarization in the way users choose to share news on Twitter, as users tend to stay in the community of news media that shares information they are more likely to agree with. Moreover, we show the important role that regional Russian and Venezuelan news outlets like RT en Español and TeleSUR, played in the social media discussion of the protests throughout the region. This shows how effective these outlets have been in gathering an audience of left-leaning users in the region, an initiative that has been identified by other studies of these news outlets [16, 29]. Finally, we observe that along both dimensions of polarization explored, we obtain consistent results, with Chile showing the lowest level of polarization and Bolivia the highest.

Limitations: Our proposed weak-labeling methodology is not able to determine users with neutral stances towards the government (or the protests). This limits the scope of the analysis presented in this work to users with two defined stances towards the event: for or against. Characterizing the neutral users and estimating their prevalence in these events merit deeper exploration as they can potentially serve as the bridge between polarized communities. Moreover, even though our findings suggest that polarization in news sharing is consistent with users' stances, we are not able to ascertain if this is due to confirmation bias in part of the users, or a result of their exposure to said content because of filter bubbles.

A   Data Collection

Table 7. Collection period and number of tweets collected for each country.

	Collection Period (in 2019)	Number of Tweets (Millions)
Bolivia	October 15 to November 24	23.5
Chile	October 10 to November 24	59.6
Colombia	November 10 to December 24	20.4
Ecuador	September 25 to October 24	19.1

The dataset consists of 100 million tweets from 15+ million users collected using Twitter's API v1 around the protests that transpired in countries studied. For each event, we built the queries by first identifying the most prominent hashtags/terms (using Twitter's trending terms in the country). After some days of streaming, we determined the most frequent relevant hashtags not yet included and taking special effort to include hashtags used by different groups (for and against the each government). We included these to our query which were collected via weekly REST grabs (to ensure their collection from the start). By repeating this process each week, we built up the set of more than 500 hashtags. To improve the quality of the conversational structure present in the data, we also re-hydrated any missing targets or ancestors (up to 5 levels above in the conversation tree) of replies or quotes. Table 7 presents the relevant descriptive statistics for the collection. To better contextualize our work, we first present a brief overview of the main events that transpired in each of the countries.

Ecuador • Protests started in October 3, 2019 as a response to an austerity package (the 883 Decree) which involved the removal of fuel subsidies. Protests leaders included indigenous movements (CONAIE) and followers of former president Rafael Correa. After two weeks of violent clashes, the temporary reallocation of the seat of government, and the paralyzation of large part of the economy; President Moreno agreed with indigenous leaders to withdraw the 883 Decree. We used 191 terms and hashtags for the collection, that included for example: #EcuadorEnCrisis, #ParoNacionalYa, #EcuadorEnResistencia, #ToquedeCacerolazo, etc.

Chile • Chile is one of the wealthiest countries of South America but also one with highest inequality. On October 7, 2019 protests started because of a rise in the cost of subway tickets in Santiago (the capital), which lead to clashes between the police and protesters. Overtime this translated to a demand for structural change, and for constitutional reform. On November 15, the National Congress signed an agreement to hold a national referendum to rewrite the constitution. The protests continued well into 2020, and due to COVID the referendum was rescheduled to October 2020, when it was overwhelmingly approved with 78% of the vote. We used 244 terms and hashtags for the collection, that included for example: #ChileEnHuelga, #ChileProtests, #YoNoMarcho, #ToqueDeQuedaYA, #FueraPiñeraDictador, #ChileDesperto, etc.

Bolivia • Former President Evo Morales, who was the longest-serving leader in South America with 13 years in office, was accused of wrongdoing in his fourth term election. On October 21, protests started around his reelection and demanding the nullification of the elections. On November 10 an audit team from the Organization of American States (OAS) questioned the integrity of the election. The same day following pressure from the armed forces, Evo Morales announced his resignation. Protests continued until the end of November, primarily by those that sought Morales' return. We used 244 terms and hashtags for the collection, that included for example: #EleccionesBolivia2019, #BoliviaDiceNo, #GolpeDeEstadoEn-Bolivia, #FraudeElectoralEnBolivia, #EvoEsDemocracia, etc.

Colombia • The protests in Colombia were a response to economic and political reforms proposed by President Ivan Duque. On November 21, massive protests started throughout the country demanding the end of austerity measures. Protesters displayed flags of Chile and Ecuador, banners reading "South America woke up", and chanted anti-violence slogans. The protests continued throughout the year, with multiple clashes between the public and the armed forces. We used 201 terms and hashtags for the collection, that included for example: #CarcelParaPetro, #ApoyoALaFuerzaPublica, #ColombiaDesperto, #ESMAD, #ParoNacional25N, etc.

A.1   Ethical Considerations

We make our data publicly available and, to adhere to Twitter's terms and conditions for sharing data, we do not share the full JSON of the collected tweets[5]. Instead, we provide their respective tweet or user IDs, the type of tweet (Original, Reply or Quote), and in the case of weakly labeled users or tweets,

---

[5] Note to reviewers: to uphold the anonymization policies for submission, we will make the link publicly available before publication.

their assigned label. Since the Tweets will have to be re-hydrated, if a user deletes a tweet (or their account), it will not be available for analysis ensuring that the user's *right to be forgotten* is preserved. However, for the hand-labeled political figures (described later), given their public role during these events, we not only provide their user ID but also their user name and user type. We also release the full set of labeled stance tags.

B   Weak-Labeled Dataset

We determine the user stance based on how prominently they tweet (or retweet) a hashtag from a given stance or retweet a labeled political figure. In this appendix we provide further details of the validation methodology used to prune the set of stance-tags and further details of the weak-labels obtained by each signal.

B.1   Stance-Tags Validation

Our weak labeling methodology relies on the hypothesis that users are more likely to tweet (or retweet) hashtags or political figures that are aligned with their stances during these events. Hence, weak-stance labels are assigned to a user if their percentage of tweets with a consistent stance-tag is above a given threshold. To test this hypothesis, we apply our methodology (just based on stance-tags) to predict the stance of the political figures labeled. We can also use this exercise to determine a suitable threshold for the stance assignment. We limit our analysis to the 88.1% of labeled users that tweeted (or retweeted) at least 5 tweets containing a stance stag. We also present results excluding the set of extra 229 stance-tags obtained using this set of users in order to have a better assessment of the performance in the wild. Figure 2 presents the accuracy of the methodology at different probability thresholds. As expected, higher thresholds are more conservative in the assignment of a label (the percentage of

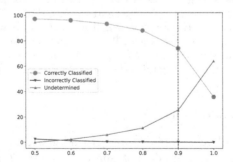

Fig. 2. Performance of the weak labeling methodology on the labeled political figures at different probability thresholds. The chosen threshold for the construction of the dataset is indicated by the dashed vertical line.

undetermined users increases) but also decrease the likelihood of missclassification. However, in the most aggressive classification threshold, only 2.6% of the users are missclassified, which supports our starting hypothesis.

For the construction of the dataset released in this work, we opt for a conservative 90% threshold, which results in 74.2% correctly classified users but only a 0.3% (2 users) classification error. The reason for this conservative approach is that our validation set is comprised of highly political users, which could result in a higher likelihood of missclassification among more casual users [10].

Nonetheless, we are able to considerably increase the performance of this methodology (with the 90% threshold) by first including the aforementioned 229 hashtags, used exclusively by user of each side, which improves the accuracy to 80.0%. Lastly, we prune our hashtag set by removing tags that were used too frequently by users of a different stance. This results in the removal of 46 hashtags and brings the final classification accuracy of our proposed weak-labeling methodology to 88.6%.

B.2   Assignment of User Stances

We assign the User stance based on how prominently they tweet (or retweet) a stance tag or retweet a labeled political figure. The threshold used to determine the stance was obtained during the hashtag validation procedure described above and set at 90%.

Table 8. Government Stance of users based on hashtag usage.

	Pro	Against	Inconsistent	Total
Bolivia	46 040	57 654	2 717	106 411
Chile	20 478	220 648	381	241 507
Colombia	16 460	55 883	154	72 497
Ecuador	18 909	48 478	230	67 617

Hashtag Usage. Users were assigned a stance if they used stance tags either in their tweets (or retweets) or in their user description. In both cases, a stance was assigned to a tweet (or description) if it contains hashtags with the same stance, otherwise it was deemed inconsistent. As before, we only proceeded with users that had at least 5 tweets with a consistent stance or if at least one description was consistent. As less than 1% of labeled users were labeled based on their descriptions, we do not desegregate results based on the origin of the label. A stance was assigned to a user if at least 90% of their tweets had the same stance. The number of users classified and their distribution is presented in Table 8.

Endorsement of Political Figures. The procedure followed to assign a stance to a user based on their endorsement of political figures, follows the same logic as before. As such, users were assigned a stance if at least 90% of their retweets of labeled political figures are from users with the same stance. As before, we only proceed with users that had at least 5 retweets of these users. The number of users classified and their distribution is presented in Table 9.

Table 9. Government stance of users based on endorsement of political figures.

	Pro	Against	Total
Bolivia	29 573	17 444	47 017
Chile	29 548	78 735	108 283
Colombia	22 165	60 082	82 247
Ecuador	20 957	32 243	53 200

C   Filtering Irrelevant Media Tweets

We started with a dataset of news agencies and journalist for the countries explored (this was obtained from the NetMapper software[6]). It had several limitations and was expanded by searching for the most important news agencies operating in each country, manually checking who they follow and adding agencies that were not included. This resulted in a list of 853 news agencies (or major reporters) detailing their Twitter handles and main URL (if available). Notably, the list included agencies from Venezuela and Russia that predominately operate in the region, this is important as we explore influence campaigns on the protests. We then proceeded to identify the agencies that were either directly retweeted by a user or that had a user tweet/retweet a URL corresponding to

Table 10. Number of news agencies in each country. *The regional category includes regional Venezuelan and Russian media among others.

	Bolivia	Chile	Colombia	Ecuador	*Regional
# Agencies	52	95	69	99	69

Table 11. Distribution of the labeled tweets and resulting predictions after classification.

	Labeled Tweets (#)		Predicted (#)	
	Total	Deduplicated	Tweets	Users
Relevant	78 318	7 177	1 024 166	276 754
Not relevant	53 671	8 156	675 496	247 324

---

[6] https://netanomics.com/netmapper-government-commercial-version/.

their domain. The number of news agencies from each country resulting from this process is shown in Table 10.

However, news articles identified in our data set cover topics ranging from the protests to sports. When studying the polarization of news consumption during the political event, it is important to first remove tweets which are irrelevant to the protests. It is not obvious if a tweet from a news agency is relevant or not, but many tweets in our data set contain the URL of an article that they reference. For this reason, we determined the relevance to the protest of a small set of the 900 most tweeted URLs in our dataset distruted among the different countries. We complemented this dataset with an additional set of URLs labeled by extracting subsection metadata from them. If the subsection referenced sports, culture or technology, the URL was labeled as irrelevant to the protests. Then, we assigned the URL label to any tweet that used it. The final sample distribution are presented in Table 11. We note that even though we are able to assign a label to more than 100k tweets, most of them contained duplicated text (as news media tend to tweet the same thing multiple times). The classification was done with the unduplicated dataset.

To classify the relevance of the tweets, we built a CNN text classifier [20] using 300 dimensional FastText embeddings trained on the combined datasets (both by stance and country) used to analyze the language polarization. We used 100 filters on 3 layers with filter sizes 3, 4 and 5 and a dropout rate of 50%. We achieved an accuracy and F1-score of 92% in a held-out test set. After predicting the labels of tweets (relevant or irrelavant to the protests), we obtain a dataset of 1,024,166 relevant and 675,496 irrelevant tweets. The distribution of the data set is shown in Table 11. The analysis of polarization in news consumption patterns presented in this works was done only on the tweets that are relevant to the protests.

References

1. Alhazmi, K., Alsumari, W., Seppo, I., Podkuiko, L., Simon, M.: Effects of annotation quality on model performance. In: 2021 International Conference on Artificial Intelligence in Information and Communication (ICAIIC), pp. 063–067 (2021)
2. Babcock, M., Cox, R.V.C., Kumar, S.: Diffusion of pro-and anti-false information tweets: the black panther movie case. Comput. Math. Organ. Theory **25**(1), 72–84 (2019)
3. Babcock, M., Villa-Cox, R., Carley, K.M.: Pretending positive, pushing false: comparing captain marvel misinformation campaigns. In: Shu, K., Wang, S., Lee, D., Liu, H. (eds.) Disinformation, Misinformation, and Fake News in Social Media. LNSN, pp. 83–94. Springer, Cham (2020). https://doi.org/10.1007/978-3-030-42699-6_5
4. Baldwin, M., Lammers, J.: Past-focused environmental comparisons promote proenvironmental outcomes for conservatives. Proc. Natl. Acad. Sci. **113**(52), 14953–14957 (2010)
5. Barberá, P., et al.: The critical periphery in the growth of social protests. PLoS ONE **10**(11), e0143611 (2015)

6. Beguerisse-Díaz, M., Garduno-Hernández, G., Vangelov, B., Yaliraki, S.N., Barahona, M.: Interest communities and flow roles in directed networks: the twitter network of the UK riots. J. R. Soc. Interface **11**(101), 20140940 (2014)
7. Darwish, K.: Quantifying polarization on twitter: the Kavanaugh nomination. arXiv abs/2001.02125 (2020)
8. Del, M., et al.: The spreading of misinformation online. Proc. Natl. Acad. Sci. **113**(3), 554–559 (2016)
9. Demszky, D., et al.: Analyzing polarization in social media: method and application to tweets on 21 mass shootings. In: NAACL-HLT 2019, pp. 2970–3005. Association for Computational Linguistics (2019)
10. Evans, A.: Stance and identity in twitter hashtags. Lang. Internet **13**(1) (2016)
11. Fisher, D.R., Waggle, J., Leifeld, P.: Where does political polarization come from? Locating polarization within the us climate change debate. Am. Behav. Sci. **57**(1), 70–92 (2013)
12. Garrett, R.K.: The "echo chamber" distraction: disinformation campaigns are the problem, not audience fragmentation. J. Appl. Res. Mem. Cogn. **6**(4), 370–376 (2017). https://www.sciencedirect.com/science/article/pii/S2211368117301936
13. Golbeck, J., Hansen, D.: Computing political preference among twitter followers. In: Proceedings of the SIGCHI Conference on Human Factors in Computing Systems, pp. 1105–1108 (2011)
14. González-Bailón, S., Wang, N.: Networked discontent: the anatomy of protest campaigns in social media. Soc.l Netw. **44**, 95–104 (2016)
15. Gu, Y., Chen, T., Sun, Y., Wang, B.: Ideology Detection for twitter users via link analysis. In: Lee, D., Lin, Y.-R., Osgood, N., Thomson, R. (eds.) SBP-BRiMS 2017. LNCS, vol. 10354, pp. 262–268. Springer, Cham (2017). https://doi.org/10.1007/978-3-319-60240-0_32
16. Gurganus, J.: Russia: Playing a Geopolitical Game in Latin America. Carnegie Endownent for Peace (2018)
17. Hovy, D., Spruit, S.L.: The social impact of natural language processing. In: Proceedings of the 54th Annual Meeting of the Association for Computational Linguistics (Volume 2: Short Papers), pp. 591–598 (2016)
18. KhudaBukhsh, A.R., Sarkar, R., Kamlet, M.S., Mitchell, T.M.: We don't speak the same language: interpreting polarization through machine translation. In: AAAI 2021, pp. 14893–14901 (2021)
19. KhudaBukhsh, A.R., Sarkar, R., Kamlet, M.S., Mitchell, T.M.: Fringe news networks: dynamics of US news viewership following the 2020 presidential election. In: WebSci 2022: 14th ACM Web Science Conference 2022, pp. 269–278. ACM (2022)
20. Kim, Y.: Convolutional neural networks for sentence classification. In: EMNLP 2014, pp. 1746–1751, October 2014
21. Koutra, D., Bennett, P.N., Horvitz, E.: Events and controversies: Influences of a shocking news event on information seeking. CoRR abs/1405.1486 (2014). https://arxiv.org/abs/1405.1486
22. Ling, R.: Confirmation bias in the era of mobile news consumption: the social and psychological dimensions. Digit Journal. **8**, 1–9 (2020)
23. McConnell, C., Margalit, Y., Malhotra, N., Levendusky, M.: Research: Political Polarization Is Changing How Americans Work and Shop. Harvard Business Review (2017)
24. Mohammad, S., Kiritchenko, S., Sobhani, P., Zhu, X., Cherry, C.: Semeval-2016 task 6: detecting stance in tweets. In: Proceedings of the 10th International Workshop on Semantic Evaluation (SemEval-2016), pp. 31–41 (2016)

25. Olteanu, A., Castillo, C., Diaz, F., Kıcıman, E.: Social data: biases, methodological pitfalls, and ethical boundaries. Front. Big Data **2**, 13 (2019)
26. Poole, K.T.: Howard: the polarization of American politics. J. Polit. **46**(4), 1061–1079 (1984)
27. Poole, K.T., Rosenthal, H.: The polarization of American politics. J. Polit. **46**(4), 1061–1079 (1984)
28. Prior, M.: Media and political polarization. Annu. Rev. Polit. Sci. **16**, 101–127 (2013)
29. Rouvinski, V.: Understanding Russian priorities in Latin America. Kennan Cable 20 (2017)
30. Smith, S.L., Turban, D.H.P., Hamblin, S., Hammerla, N.Y.: Offline bilingual word vectors, orthogonal transformations and the inverted softmax. In: 5th International Conference on Learning Representations, ICLR 2017 (2017)
31. Spohr, D.: Fake news and ideological polarization: filter bubbles and selective exposure on social media. Bus. Inf. Rev. **34**(3), 150–160 (2017)
32. Swamy, S., Ritter, A., de Marneffe, M.C.: "i have a feeling trump will win.................": forecasting winners and losers from user predictions on twitter. In: Proceedings of the 2017 Conference on Empirical Methods in Natural Language Processing, pp. 1583–1592 (2017)
33. Tsakalidis, A., Aletras, N., Cristea, A.I., Liakata, M.: Nowcasting the stance of social media users in a sudden vote: the case of the greek referendum. In: Proceedings of the 27th ACM International Conference on Information and Knowledge Management, pp. 367–376 (2018)
34. Wong, F.M.F., Tan, C.W., Sen, S., Chiang, M.: Quantifying political leaning from tweets, retweets, and retweeters. IEEE Trans. Knowl. Data Eng. **28**(8), 2158–2172 (2016)
35. Xiao, Z., Song, W., Xu, H., Ren, Z., Sun, Y.: TIMME: Twitter ideology-detection via multi-task multi-relational embedding. In: Proceedings of the 26th ACM SIGKDD International Conference on Knowledge Discovery & Data Mining, pp. 2258–2268 (2020)

"The Times They Are-a-Changin": The Effect of the Covid-19 Pandemic on Online Music Sharing in India

Tanvi Kamble[1], Pooja Desur[1](✉), Amanda Krause[2], Ponnurangam Kumaraguru[1], and Vinoo Alluri[1]

[1] International Institute of Information Technology, Hyderabad, India
tanvi.kamble@researchiiit.ac.in, pooja.desur@studentsiiit.ac.in,
{pk.guru,vinoo.alluri}@iiit.ac.in
[2] James Cook University, Townsville, QLD, Australia
amanda.krause1@jcu.edu.au

Abstract. Music sharing trends have been shown to change during times of socio-economic crises. Studies have also shown that music can act as a social surrogate, helping to significantly reduce loneliness by acting as an empathetic friend. We explored these phenomena through a novel study of online music sharing during the Covid-19 pandemic in India. We collected tweets from the popular social media platform Twitter during India's first and second wave of the pandemic (n = 1,364). We examined the different ways in which music was able to accomplish the role of a social surrogate via analyzing tweet text using Natural Language Processing techniques. Additionally, we analyzed the emotional connotations of the music shared through the acoustic features and lyrical content and compared the results between pandemic and pre-pandemic times. It was observed that the role of music shifted to a more community focused function rather than tending to a more self-serving utility. Results demonstrated that people shared music during the Covid-19 pandemic which had lower valence and shared songs with topics that reflected turbulent times such as *Hardship* and *Exclusion* when compared to songs shared during pre-Covid times. The results are further discussed in the context of individualistic versus collectivistic cultures.

Keywords: Musical emotions · Online music sharing · Covid pandemic · Social surrogacy · Lyrics

1 Introduction

The Covid-19 pandemic has significantly impacted everyday life with multiple state and nation-wide lockdowns around the world. Long isolation periods, increasing rates of unemployment, and with hundreds of thousands catching the virus daily, the pandemic caused an unprecedented socio-economic crisis [30]. India in particular had one of the highest Covid-19 infection rates and is the

F. Hopfgartner et al. (Eds.): SocInfo 2022, LNCS 13618, pp. 96–113, 2022.
https://doi.org/10.1007/978-3-031-19097-1_6

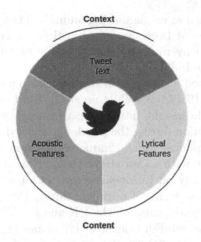

Fig. 1. Our study focuses on analyzing the context of music sharing from tweet text and the content of music sharing using acoustic features and lyrical themes.

second worst affected country[1] in terms of reported Covid-19 cases and deaths [11,31]. These distressing times paired with months of isolation periods had people searching for coping mechanisms and proxies for physical social interactions.

Social media provides a constant means of communication with the outside world having a network reach much larger than any physical one. It enables users to keep in touch with their friends and family through posts and messages [5]. As the pandemic limited in-person interactions, social media use, enabling people to meet their social needs, was at an all time high [34]. Twitter affords a space to share thoughts and mood states, especially through music. Music that is shared on Twitter servers various functions, be it to either promote favorite artists or as a way to express feelings about the music shared, amongst others. From an evolutionary point of view sharing music has shown to help in social bonding, building a sense of community, and convey emotional states [23].

Music can play the role of an empathetic friend by acting as a social surrogate [29] and be used as a coping mechanism. It can elicit several emotions including feelings of being connected to others and being understood and can help boost mood when one is feeling down [18]. When users share music online along with how it made them feel and how it has helped them, comparisons can be made as to how music played the role of a social surrogate before and during the pandemic. It is possible that the kind of music one listens to or wants others to listen to during times of crisis can convey the coping mechanisms used by people to some extent. It has been seen that COVID-19 restrictions have led to lifestyle changes including change in trends in music consumption. People streamed songs from their balconies more during the initial lockdowns [15], exploring new styles and groups of music [3], and there was an increase observed in the listening time

---

[1] https://www.worldometers.info/coronavirus/countries-where-coronavirus-has-spread.

[4,8]. Past work has looked at music sharing online [37] but as per our knowledge, work in this sphere has not been done during times of crisis. Furthermore, no studies have examined why music is shared online or what need it fulfills by sharing, especially in the Indian context.

Recent times witnessed a slow rise in studies investigating music trends during Covid-19 [10,12,13,16,17,33]. While no study has looked into online music sharing, they do provide insight into music consumption trends. A study on German media consumption during the pandemic showed that media (including music, books, movies amongst others) induced nostalgia during Covid-19 functioned as a way to cope with social stress (fear of isolation) during lockdown periods [35]. Another study on European countries found that music consumption on Spotify changed in terms of nostalgia during the pandemic [36].

Another study on popular music in the UK and the US during the pandemic demonstrated a negative trend in valence of lyrics and higher reference of interpersonal dependence in lyrics [25]. However, there are differences in how countries consume and associate with music [19,27]. Individualistic cultures such as UK and US use music as a tool for self expression. On the other hand, collectivistic cultures, which include Asian countries like Japan, India, and China, use music typically to add positivity to their lives [27]. Emotional connections to music and coping mechanisms are different for individualistic cultures where people are self-sufficient and achievement-oriented as compared to collectivistic cultures where people are interdependent and family-oriented [19].

In this study we focus on India, a culturally rich country and that has a deep relation to music. A study of 3,000 Internet users showed that 80 per cent of Internet users called themselves as 'music-lovers' [14] in India. Despite being one of the largest countries in terms of population, music sharing trends have not been studied. Work has been done on the evolving Indian music industry [1,7,20] but a focus on the trends of the overall population is lacking. Moreover, on average, an Indian spends 19.1 h a week listening to music which is higher than the global average of 18 h [14]. Thus, it is important to consider how and why users share music online in India. A large Twitter user base of 23 million Indians provides opportunities for a large scale study. A study on India could further enhance the comparison of the function of music between collectivistic and individualistic cultures.

This paper aims to analyse online music sharing of Indians during the pandemic. To this end, we take a two-pronged approach to analyzing tweets posted during this time (see Fig. 1). We first analyze tweet text to understand the role music plays as a social surrogate via NLP techniques. Subsequently we analyze the musical content being shared by examining emotional connotations derived via acoustic features and lyrics. Additionally, we examine lyrical themes shared during the pandemic. We compare all of the above with pre-pandemic times to identify changes/trends.

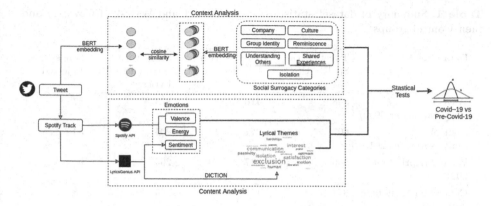

Fig. 2. Pipeline of extracting emotion, lyrical themes, and the function of music from tweets. Red circles represent BERT word embeddings and the purple, yellow, and blue circles symbolize the different embeddings obtained from social surrogacy statements belonging to different categories. (Color figure online)

2 Methodology

2.1 Dataset

Using the Twitter API[2], we collected tweets that were geo-tagged as India that contained a Spotify URL for tracks during the first and second wave of the pandemic (see Fig. 2). As per the WHO[3] dashboard of Covid-19 cases, the peak of Wave-1 and Wave-2 in India was recorded on September 14, 2020 and May 3, 2021 respectively. Judging by the steepness of both the peaks, we considered a period of two months around the Wave-1 peak and one month around the Wave-2 peak as our Wave-1 and Wave-2 time periods respectively. To compare this with a control group, we collected similar tweets during the same period of months as Wave-1 (referred to as Control-1) and Wave-2 (referred to as Control-2) in 2019. The same period of months was taken in order to avoid temporal music sharing differences that can occur as a result of seasonal trends. We collected a total of 1,364 tweets that were posted during both waves of the pandemic. One tweet can have multiple track URLs shared in them, but each song of the tweet is added separately to the dataset. We limited our analysis to tweets in English. A total of 54.3% of the tweets collected during Wave-1 and 48.2% of tweets collected during Wave-2 had English tweet text. Detailed statistics about the dataset are given in Table 1. From the Spotify URL, the name and artist of the song was retrieved using the Spotify ID. With this information, we collected lyrics for each track, using the LyricsGenius and azlyrics API.[4]

---

[2] https://developer.twitter.com/en/docs/twitter-api.
[3] https://covid19.who.int/region/searo/country/in.
[4] https://lyricsgenius.readthedocs.io/en/master/.

Table 1. Summary of dataset statistics across Wave-1 and Wave-2 of Covid-19 and their Control groups -

Data Group	Tweets with Spotify URL	Tweets with English Songs	Songs with correct English Lyrics	Songs Rejected
Wave-1 (July-November 2020)	808	416	323	87
Control-1 (July-November 2019)	607	271	204	54
Wave 2 (April-June 2021)	556	317	263	94
Control-2 (April-June 2019)	351	177	155	48

2.2   Tweet Analysis

From each tweet, we examined the *context* and the *content* of the music associated with it. Context of the music shared refers to the tweet text accompanying it. It gives a glimpse into why a user shared that particular track. We used this text to consider if the music may have played a role of a social surrogate. On the other hand content refers to both the musical and lyrical features of the song. We looked at the emotional connotations of the content by extracting the acoustic features from the music and sentiment and themes from the lyrics.

Context Analysis. In order to capture the functions played by music, we used a set of 30 statements formulated in past work [29] as demonstrations of music functioning as a social surrogate.[5] These include statements such as "It reminds of certain periods of my life or past experiences" or "I can identify with the musicians or bands". These 30 statements were originally collected as a result of a survey where participants described how media plays a role of a social surrogate in their lives and was then adapted to music [29]. These statements belong to 7 overarching categories – *Company, Reminiscence, Shared Experiences, Isolation, Understanding Others, Culture, and Group Identity.* The category *Company* describes the role of music in helping to feel less lonely and providing comfort. *Reminiscence* is when music elicits feeling of nostalgia through a person or experience. *Shared Experiences* covers how music helps people to feel understood and identify with the music/artists. The category *Isolation* involves feelings of wanting to isolate socially and not talk to others but finding solace in music. *Understanding Others* includes how music brings about feelings of belonging and understanding others and the world. When music helps to connect to one's culture and allows people to express cultural uniqueness the surrogacy role falls under the category *Culture.* Music that helps people to identify to a

---

[5] Refer to Appendix 1.

subculture and belong to a particular social group the role falls under the category *Group Identity*. Examples of tweets which came under the above categories include "Reminder to listen to this song when feeling underconfident" (*Shared Experiences*) or "Something that reminds me of my childhood" (*Reminiscence*).

To get the context of the music shared, we first preprocessed the text of each tweet to remove links, hashtags, and emojis. In order to filter out tweets that did not represent the function of music as a social surrogate, we manually removed tweets that fell under the *Non social surrogacy* category. These tweets consisted of keywords/strings such as "mood", "stream this song" or "listen to this". A total of 502 tweets were identified as showing roles of social surrogacy of which 150 and 165 belonged to time periods Wave-1 and Wave-2 respectively and 111 and 76 belonged to Control-1 and Control-2 respectively. Only this set was used for further tests. An automated approach was used to categorize each of these filtered tweets into one of the seven social surrogacy categories. The sentence embedding of the resulting text of the tweets was calculated by using a BERT transformer.[6] Similarly, the sentence embedding for each of the 30 statements was calculated. Cosine similarity which was used as a distance metric to represent semantic similarity was calculated between each tweet and each of the 30 statements in the embedding space. A tweet was allocated into the corresponding category of the most similar statement embedding (provided the similarity was greater than 0.5). Thus, a tweet was only mapped to either one or zero of the seven social surrogacy categories. Some examples of tweets along with the allocated groups are shown in Table 2. This automated approach provided a way to observe the ways music served as a surrogate during the pandemic without the intrusion of human bias. It also allowed us to investigate which categories of surrogacy such as *Reminiscence* or *Isolation* were more prevalent than others when users shared music online during the considered time periods.

Table 2. Examples of tweet text categorized into Social Surrogacy Categories using BERT embeddings

Tweet text	Most Similar Surrogacy Statement	Category
song i remember from childhood	It reminds me of certain periods of my life or past experiences	Reminiscence
the joy of discovering music thats totally you	I can identify with the musicians or bands	Shared Experiences
Dedicated to the Nocturnal	I want to isolate myself from my surroundings	Isolation

Content Analysis. In some cases, the song name returned from the Spotify API[7] did not match the song in LyricsGenius API owing to gibberish lyrics. We

---

[6] https://huggingface.co/docs/transformers/model_doc/bert.
[7] https://spotipy.readthedocs.io/en/2.19.0/#.

weeded out such songs (n = 236) from the pool of English songs (n = 1,181). This happened for songs which were remixed-versions or were sung live and hence such songs were removed.

Emotions. We examined the emotional connotations of the music shared in two ways - by using the acoustic features of the songs and by performing a sentiment analysis on the lyrics. To obtain the acoustic features, we used the Spotify API in order to extract valence and energy of the song which provides insight to its emotional connotation. Valence is indicative of the pleasantness/positiveness of the track while energy is self-explanatory. We then performed sentiment analysis on the lyrics using a lexicon and rule-based sentiment analysis tool called VADER.[8] It is used in grammar-free texts like social media.

Lyrical Analysis. We performed topic modelling on the lyrics using DICTION software[9] to extract the topics of the songs that were shared during the different data groups. DICTION is a language analysis software that uses dictionaries to determine the topic(s) of a given text. There are 40 topics[10] each of which has a dictionary of words associated with it where no two dictionaries have the same words. It calculates the frequency of the words from the text to determine the topics. We decided to use DICTION as it is a good choice for topic modelling for free-grammar text like songs and poem since it has a word to word mapping [2,6,22,25]. Further details about DICTION and the custom lists have been discussed in the appendix. We ran DICTION on the lyrics of the songs belonging to Covid-19 and control periods for all the 40 topics, and divided the frequency of words by the total number of words to normalize the scores.

2.3   Statistical Tests

The contextual information and musical content was compared between the following time periods: Wave-1 (n = 323) versus Control-1 (n = 204), Wave-2 (n = 263) versus Control-2 (n = 155), and Covid-19 as a whole referred to as Wave-1 + Wave2 (n = 586) versus pre-Covid period of 2019 referred to as Control-1 + Control-2 (n = 359). Context-wise, a frequency table was created for comparing observed frequencies which were the Covid-19 periods and the expected proportions which were the corresponding control groups. A chi-square goodness of fit test [24] was performed to observe if the proportions were significantly different. Content-wise, we used the non-parametric Mann Whitney U test (MWU) to examine the difference between valence and energy (the acoustic features) across the conditions. For the lyrical analysis, MWU tests were also performed on results of DICTION analysis between each of the above mentioned time periods. The Benjamini-Hochberg procedure was used to account for

---

[8] https://github.com/cjhutto/vaderSentiment.

[9] https://dictionsoftware.com/.

[10] 40 topics include 31 dictionary based variables, five master variables which are a combination of the dictionary based variables and four calculation based variables. The last four variables rely on calculations such as word count, word size rather than dictionary matches. Details about the variables are given in Appendix 2.

running multiple statistical tests for all the comparisons listed above. The results of these tests are reported in the next section.

3 Results

3.1 Context Analysis

The percentage of total tweets lying in each social surrogacy category during Wave-1 and Control-1 are shown in Fig. 3. The chi-square goodness of fit test was significant (p = 0.028), suggesting that the proportions of tweets amongst the social surrogacy categories were significantly different between Wave-1 and Control-1. Post hoc multiple z-test comparisons were done to observe which categories showed significant differences in proportions. Two of the social surrogacy groups – *Reminiscence* and *Group Identity* had a significant decrease in the proportion of tweets falling into these categories during Wave-1. On the other hand, the chi-square test was non-significant across the distribution of proportions when comparing Wave-2 and Control-2, or Covid-19 as a whole (Wave-1 + Wave2) and pre-Covid-19 period (i.e. Control-1 + Control-2).

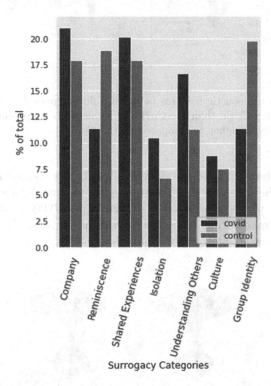

Fig. 3. Distribution of tweets into social surrogacy categories during Wave-1 and Control-1 (covid and control in legend respectively).

3.2   Content Analysis

Emotions. Figure 4 displays distributions of valence and energy derived from acoustic features for different conditions. Results of the Mann Whitney U tests revealed that valence of music shared during Covid (Wave-1 and Wave-2 combined) was significantly lower (U = 613715, p = 0.006) than pre-Covid time period. Similar results were observed when comparing Wave-1 with Control-1 where valence was significantly lower during Wave-1 (U = 231695, p = 0.037) while energy was found to be higher (U = 229345, p = 0.018). No significant differences were observed in either valence or energy of music shared when comparing Wave-2 with Control-2.

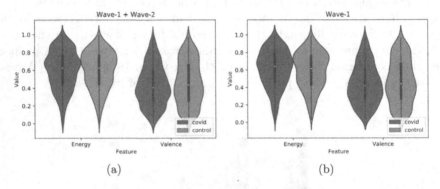

Fig. 4. Comparison of acoustic features between different periods. (a) Valence is significantly lower during Covid than pre-Covid. (b) Valence is significantly lower during Wave 1, while Energy is higher as compared to the Control-1.

Sentiment analysis on lyrics as shown in Fig. 5 was also performed. During comparison only the time periods of Wave-2 against Control-2 showed differences that were statistically significant (U = 33920.5, p = 0.0005) according to the Man Whitney U test. During Wave-2 the lyrics of the songs had a lower mean sentiment (0.24) as compared to the Control-2 (0.39).

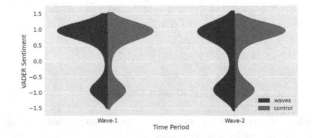

Fig. 5. Sentiment Analysis of Lyrics of the songs according to the different time periods. Mean Sentiment of Wave-1 was higher than Control-1 but it was vice-versa for Wave-2 and Control-2.

Lyrical Themes. We observed that different lyrical themes were shared in different time periods. Table 3 summarises the results of the Mann-Whitney U tests conducted on the various DICTION categories.

Wave-1 demonstrated an increased sharing of music with lyrical themes signifying *Exclusion* (U = 33874.0, p = 0.005) and *Hardship* (U = 34698.5, p = 0.041), when compared to Control 1. Similar pattern was observed when comparing the Covid-19 time period to pre-Covid-19 time periods where topics of *Exclusion*(U = 103193.0, p = 0.049) and *Hardship* (U = 102221.0, p = 0.05) were shared more as well. The topic of *Motion* was shared more in Wave-1 than Control-1 (U = 38425.5, p = 0.04) but was shared less in Covid-19 group as a whole than pre-Covid times as a whole (U = 100560.0, p = 0.018). Wave-2 witnessed an increase in music with lyrical themes representing *Communication* (U = 12557.0, p = 0.012) when compared to Control-2. Another observation to be made was that the values of *Satisfaction* increased in the songs shared during Wave-1 when compared with Control-1 (U = 38066.5, p = 0.026) but the opposite happened when we observed Wave-2 and Control-2.

Table 3. DICTION variables for different time periods that show significant differences with $p < 0.05$ in Man Whitney U Test ($*p < 0.01$). An arrow indicates an increase or decrease in the songs shared in the time period.

Wave-1 (vs. Control-1)	Exclusion* ↑, Satisfaction ↑, Hardship ↑, Motion ↑
Wave=2 (vs. Control-2)	Communication ↑, Satisfaction* ↓
Wave-1 + Wave-2 (vs. Control-1 + Control-2)	Hardship ↑, Exclusion ↑, Motion ↓

4   Discussion

Our study examined the effect of the Covid-19 pandemic on the type of music that was shared online via Twitter in India. Overall music sharing seems to be different during Covid-19 and pre-Covid-19 times. The number of music related tweets posted by users to share a certain song on Spotify increased during Wave-1. This increase in music sharing online could be attributed to higher rates of social media usage during periods of isolation in the pandemic [32], or to how music sharing builds a sense of community [28] which was needed during the pandemic. A portion of the increase should be credited to the fact that Spotify was released in India during 2019, and as its popularity began to grow, the number of users sharing Spotify links increased subsequently. Apart from the increase in number of tweets there were several differences observed in the context and content as discussed below.

We examined how music might function as a social surrogate during the pandemic. Tweets which fell under the categories *Company* (in which people use music to feel less lonely and find comfort) and *Shared Experiences* (which covers music experiences that help people to feel understood) made up 41% of the total tweets containing music collected during the pandemic. During Wave-1, music acted as a social surrogate through the role of *Group Identity* to a lesser amount then pre-pandemic times. *Group Identity* involves feeling a sense of belonging to a particular social group on a smaller scale, such as identifiying with a particular artist or associating oneself with a fan group. India, a collectivistic community, has shown to put a great importance on community, and as the pandemic brought about distressing times, the sense of community tended to expand, which is reflected by more music shared that was not targeted towards a specific subgroup. This result suggests that perhaps people may have felt a less pressing desire to separate into smaller subgroups and preferred to experience and share music with a larger, more diverse demographic to fulfil their need for community.

Similarly the proportion of tweets falling into the category *Reminiscence* which is more self directed (reminds one of their past experiences or a person), also decreased during Wave-1. While past work [35] has demonstrated that media associated with a sense of nostalgia was consumed more during the Covid-19, this study was done on a individualistic culture (Germany). India has shown a different trend where the role of self-involved social surrogacy categories reduced during the pandemic. Our interpretation is that music was shared to foster a sense of greater community rather than for personal preferences.

Music shared online in India during Wave-1 was more negatively valenced but had higher overall energy values in terms of acoustic features. The valence and energy values mirror the feelings caused by the turbulent times the country experienced. This is in line with results from a study on UK and US where songs with negatively valenced lyrics were found to be more popular during the pandemic as compared to before [25]. Typically since negative valence of music is congruent to negative valence derived from lyrics [9], these results are comparable and the cultures seem to show a similar change in trends over the period of the pandemic. Lyrical themes of *Exclusion* (describes the sources and effects of social isolation [25]) and *Hardship* (terms of natural disaster, problems faced, and human fears) were observed more in India during the pandemic and these themes also reflect the distressing times. There was also more *Satisfaction* (terms associated with positive affective states [25]) related lyrical themes which has to do with positive affective states, although valence was negative. This could be an attempt to try to balance the negative mood of the music with positive words while still reflecting the current hard times of the pandemic. This result opposes results done on a study of individualistic culture where lyrical themes of Satisfaction were less predominant during the first six months of the pandemic [25], albeit limited to top charts on Spotify. Nevertheless, these results concerning the lyrical themes of shared music highlight the similarities and differences between the consumption and sharing of music in individualistic and collectivistic cultures.

Wave-2 was much more disastrous for India [26] than Wave-1. Music sharing online evidenced a decrease in the sentiment of lyrics as well as a decrease in the themes of *Satisfaction*. One potential explanation in Wave-1 themes of *Satisfaction* arose by trying to build up hope but by Wave-2 the decrease showed the opposite trend. Additionally, music shared with themes of *Communication* (terms of social interaction either with one person or a group) increased during Wave-2. From an evolutionary point of view, music has been used as a social bonding tool and reveals a person's emotional states to others [23]. In this way themes of *Communication* in music expose a desire to reach out and bond with others which could explain this increase. Overall the combined duration of Wave-1 and Wave-2 brought about music sharing with more negative valence than pre-Covid-19 times, with lyrical themes of *Hardship* and *Exclusion* thereby mirroring the dire situation of the pandemic.

In sum, our study is the first that looks at music sharing trends online during the pandemic. Music shared online provides a glimpse into the emotional state of a person. Studying the text accompanying the sharing of a song online helps reveal the role music can play in our lives and its benefits during distressing times. While this study has shown that collectivistic and individualistic cultures both reported negative trends in valence of music during the pandemic, Wave-1 in India reflected a glimmer of hope with the increase in lyrical themes of *Satisfaction*. Furthermore, India as a collectivistic culture has a tendency to put the well being of a community at large above ones own. This is well demonstrated by the role that *Group Identity* and *Reminescence* played as a social surrogate which decreased during the pandemic.

The social surrogacy approach which summarizes the various functions music plays as a social surrogate can be extended to study music shared in other countries. It can also be extended to data collected from other social media platforms. Future research on this topic could also benefit from a mixed methods approach, where manual annotation of the tweets could complement the automated approach, although it may not be feasible and scalable for a large number of datapoints. While our study was limited to music with lyrics in English, future work can accommodate music and tweets in other languages using advanced NLP techniques. While the sharing of songs with English lyrics in India is a consequence of a western influence, the consumption of global products does not necessitate a change in a culture's core values. For instance, despite the popularity of Bollywood and the influence of Indian music in Western countries, like UK and USA, [21] these countries are still categorized as individualistic [12]. Lastly, we note that we have collected the music shared only on the Twitter platform, and as such the music analysed in the present study is not a complete representation of the music listened to by the Indian population as a whole. Future work could also explore the use of other platforms and collaborative playlists.

Acknowledgement. This research was partially funded by IHUB at IIIT Hyderabad.

5   Appendix

5.1   Appendix 1

The 30 statements that were used to model the role of music as a social surrogate and their assigned categories as per [29] are given in Table 4.

Table 4. Social Surrogacy statements corresponding to each group

Social surrogacy category	Statement
Company	It keeps me company.
	It can make me feel less lonely.
	It comforts me when I'm sad.
Culture	It mirrors the history and culture of my country.
	It makes me feel connected to my culture.
	It is a good way to express the uniqueness of our culture.
Group Identity	I would like to identify with a particular subculture.
	It helps me to show that I belong to a particular social group.
	It makes me feel connected to all the people who like the same kind of music.
	I would like to take the artists as role models
	It makes me feel connected to others.
Isolation	I don't want to talk to anybody.
	I like to have some sound in the background.
	I want to isolate myself from my surroundings.
	I don't want to hear the surrounding sounds.
Reminiscence	It reminds me of the people that I used to listen to the music with.
	It reminds me of a particular person.
	It reminds me of certain periods of my life or past experiences.
	It helps me reminisce.
Shared Experience	I can recognize myself in the lyrics.
	The songwriter has made similar experiences as I have.
	I like to immerse myself into the lyrics.
	I can identify with the musicians or bands.
	I can sing along with it.
	It makes me feel like somebody else feels the same as I do.
Understanding Others	It helps me understand the world better.
	It makes me feel connected to the world.
	It tells me how other people think.
	It makes me feel like I belong.
	It helps me to understand what is going on in others people's heads.

5.2   Appendix 2

DICTION 7.0, as mentioned earlier, is a content analysis software which uses dictionaries of topics to perform word to word mapping and gives a score related to each topic. The value of each variable for a song is a float value. Even though

Table 5. 31 dictionary based variables

Variable name	Variable definition
AMBIVALENCE	Words expressing hesitation or uncertainty like confusion, mystery, etc.
ACCOMPLISHMENT	Words expressing task-completion, modes of expansion like grow, buy, employ, produce, etc.
AGGRESSION	Words of human competition and forceful action, social domination, energy, personal triumph
BLAME	Terms of social inappropriateness, unfortunate circumstances like cruel, miserly, painful, etc.
CENTRALITY	Terms denoting institutional regularities and/or substantive agreement on core values. Words like indigenous terms, typicality, etc.
COGNITION	Words referring to cerebral processes, both functional and imaginative
COLLECTIVES	Singular nouns connoting plurality that function to decrease specificity like army, crowd, country, world, etc.
COMMUNICATION	Terms referring to social interaction, both face-to-face, mediated, social actors, social purposes, etc.
CONCRETENESS	No thematic unity other than tangibility and materiality. Words of sociological units, occupational groups, political alignments
COOPERATION	Terms designating behavioral interactions among people that often result in a group product like words of designations of formal work relations and informal associations
DENIAL	Words of negative contractions, negative function words like not, nothing, etc.
DIVERSITY	Words describing individuals or groups of individuals differing from the norm
EXCLUSION	Terms describing the sources and effects of social isolation
FAMILIARITY	Words including common prepositions (across, over, through), demonstrative pronouns (this, that) and interrogative pronouns (who, what), and a variety of particles, conjunctions and connectives (a, for, so)
HARDSHIP	Containing words related to natural disasters, hostile actions, injustice, human fears and griefs
HUMAN INTEREST	standard personal pronouns, family members and relations and generic terms friend, baby, human.
INSPIRATION	Words of Abstract virtues deserving of universal respect
LEVELING TERMS	Words used to ignore individual differences and to build a sense of completeness assurance like everyone, absolute, each, fully, etc.
LIBERATION	Terms describing the maximizing of individual choice and the rejection of social conventions
MOTION	Terms connoting human movement, physical processes, journey, speed etc.
NUMERICAL TERMS	Words indicating numbers or numerical operations like sum, percentage or quantitative topics like mathematics
PASSIVITY	Words ranging from neutrality to inactivity like inertness, compliance, docility, etc.
PAST CONCERN	The past-tense forms of the verbs contained in the Present Concern dictionary
PRAISE	Social, Intellectual, entrepreneurial, moral and Physical Qualities
PRESENT CONCERN	A selective list of present-tense verbs like general physical activity, social operations, task-performance, etc.
RAPPORT	This dictionary describes attitudinal similarities among groups of people like terms of affinity, deference, etc.
SATISFACTION	Terms associated with positive affective states, undiminished joy, moments of triumph
SELF-REFERENCE	Terms of first-person references
SPATIAL TERMS	Terms referring to geographical entities, physical distances, and modes of measurement
TEMPORAL TERMS	Terms that fix a person, idea, or event within a specific time-interval, thereby signaling a concern for concrete and practical matters
TENACITY	Forms of the verb 'to be'. These verbs connote confidence and totality

it is a frequency, homographs are incremented as decimals instead of '1' in the DICTION software. The 40 categories of DICTION can be divided into the following sub-categories:

1. **Dictionary based variables**: Each variable has a dictionary of words associated with it. There are 10,000 words classified into a total of 35 discrete variables. The number of words in each dictionary range from 10 to 745. Table 5 contains a brief description of each of the 35 variables.
2. **Calculation Based Variables:** Four DICTION variables result from calculations rather than dictionary matches. They are calculated using a formula which envolves data like the number of words in the text, length of each word, occurrences of each word, etc. Table 6 explains the different Calculation based variables.

Table 6. Four calculation based variables

Variable name	Variable definition
COMPLEXITY	Average number of characters-per-word
INSISTENCE	All words occurring three or more times that function as nouns or noun-derived adjectives are identified
EMBELLISHMENT	A selective ratio of adjectives to verbs
VARIETY	Type-Token Ratio, ratio of number of different words in a passage to the passage's total words

3. **Master Variables:** The five master variables provide the most general understanding of a given text. They are a combination of the Dictionary-based and Calculation-based variables. The are formed by converting all subaltern variables to z-scores, combining them via addition and subtraction, and then by adding a constant of 50 to eliminate negative numbers. For example, Optimism, which is [Praise + Satisfaction + Inspiration] - [Blame + Hardship + Denial] to which 50 is added standardizes the six variables. Table 7 gives an idea about what the master variables signify.

Table 7. Five Master Variables which are a combination of the Dictionary based variables

Variable name	Variable definition
ACTIVITY	Language featuring movement, change, the implementation of ideas and the avoidance of inertia
CERTAINTY	Language indicating resoluteness, inflexibility, and completeness and a tendency to speak ex cathedra
COMMONALITY	Language highlighting the agreed - upon values of a group and rejecting idiosyncratic modes of engagement
OPTIMISM	Language endorsing some person, group, concept or event or highlighting their positive entailments
REALISM	Language describing tangible, immediate, recognizable matters that affect people's everyday lives

References

1. Agarwal, P., Karnick, H., Raj, B.: A comparative study of Indian and western music forms. In: ISMIR (2013)
2. Anglada-Tort, M., Krause, A.E., North, A.C.: Popular music lyrics and musicians' gender over time: a computational approach. Psychol. Music **49**(3), 426–444 (2021). https://doi.org/10.1177/0305735619871602
3. Cabedo-Mas, A., Arriaga-Sanz, C., Moliner-Miravet, L.: Uses and perceptions of music in times of covid-19: a spanish population survey. Front. Psychol. **11** (2021). https://doi.org/10.3389/fpsyg.2020.606180. https://www.frontiersin.org/article/10.3389/fpsyg.2020.606180
4. Carlson, E., Wilson, J., Baltazar, M., Duman, D., Peltola, H.R., Toiviainen, P., Saarikallio, S.: The role of music in everyday life during the first wave of the coronavirus pandemic: a mixed-methods exploratory study. Front. Psychol. **12** (2021). https://doi.org/10.3389/fpsyg.2021.647756. https://www.frontiersin.org/article/10.3389/fpsyg.2021.647756
5. Clark, J.L., Algoe, S.B., Green, M.C.: Social network sites and well-being: the role of social connection. Current Directions Psychol. Sci. **27**(1), 32–37 (2018)
6. Cook, S.L., Krupar, K.: Defining the twentieth century and impacting the twenty-first: Semantic habits created through radio and song. ETC: Rev. General Semant. **67**(4), 412–434 (2010). https://www.jstor.org/stable/42579071
7. Evans, A.E.: Music in India: an overview. In: The 2016 Symposium (2016)
8. Fink, L.K., Warrenburg, L.A., Howlin, C., Randall, W.M., Hansen, N.C., Wald-Fuhrmann, M.: Viral tunes: changes in musical behaviours and interest in coronamusic predict socio-emotional coping during covid-19 lockdown. Humanities Soc. Sci. Commun. **8** (2021). https://doi.org/10.1057/s41599-021-00858-y
9. Fiveash, A., Luck, G.: Effects of musical valence on the cognitive processing of lyrics. Psychol. Music **44**, February 2016. https://doi.org/10.1177/0305735615628057
10. Gibbs, H., Egermann, H.: Music-evoked nostalgia and wellbeing during the united kingdom covid-19 pandemic: Content, subjective effects, and function. Front. Psychol. **12** (2021). https://doi.org/10.3389/fpsyg.2021.647891. https://www.frontiersin.org/article/10.3389/fpsyg.2021.647891

11. Goel, I., Sharma, P., Kashiramka, P.: Effects of the covid-19 pandemic in India: an analysis of policy and technological interventions. Health Policy Technol. **10**, December 2020. https://doi.org/10.1016/j.hlpt.2020.12.001

12. Granot, R., et al.: "help! i need somebody": music as a global resource for obtaining wellbeing goals in times of crisis. Front. Psychol. **12** (2021). https://doi.org/10.3389/fpsyg.2021.648013. https://www.frontiersin.org/article/10.3389/fpsyg.2021.648013

13. Howlin, C., Hansen, N.C.: Music in times of covid-19, March 2022. https://doi.org/10.31234/osf.io/z94fq. https://psyarxiv.com/z94fq

14. Industry, T.I.M.: Digital music study (2019)

15. Lehman, E.T.: "washing hands, reaching out" - popular music, digital leisure and touch during the covid-19 pandemic. Leisure Sci. **43**, 273–279 (2020)

16. Levstek, M., Barnby, R.M., Pocock, K.L., Banerjee, R.: "it all makes us feel together": Young people's experiences of virtual group music-making during the covid-19 pandemic. Front. Psychol. **12** (2021). https://doi.org/10.3389/fpsyg.2021.703892. https://www.frontiersin.org/article/10.3389/fpsyg.2021.703892

17. Martínez-Castilla, P., Gutiérrez-Blasco, I.M., Spitz, D.H., Granot, R.: The efficacy of music for emotional wellbeing during the covid-19 lockdown in Spain: an analysis of personal and context-related variables. Front. Psychol. **12** (2021). https://doi.org/10.3389/fpsyg.2021.647837. https://www.frontiersin.org/article/10.3389/fpsyg.2021.647837

18. Mas-Herrero, E., Marco-Pallares, J., Lorenzo-Seva, U., Zatorre, R.J., Rodriguez-Fornells, A.: Individual differences in music reward experiences. Music Perception **31**(2), 118–138 (2013). https://doi.org/10.1525/mp.2013.31.2.118

19. Miyamoto, Y., Ma, X., Petermann, A.G.: Cultural differences in hedonic emotion regulation after a negative event. Emotion **14**(4), 804 (2014)

20. Muthusamy, S.: Music industry in economic development of india. ANJAC J. Humanities Soc. Sci. **3**, 1–9 (2012). ISSN: 0976–4216

21. NAWAZ, P.K.M.: An introduction to the globalization of Indian music (2019)

22. North, A.C., Krause, A.E., Kane, R., Sheridan, L.: United kingdom "top 5" pop music lyrics. Psychol. Music **46**(5), 638–661 (2018). https://doi.org/10.1177/0305735617720161

23. Patel, A.D.: Music, biological evolution, and the brain (2010)

24. Pearson, K.: X. on the criterion that a given system of deviations from the probable in the case of a correlated system of variables is such that it can be reasonably supposed to have arisen from random sampling. The London, Edinburgh, and Dublin Philosophical Magazine and Journal of Science 50(302), 157–175, July 1900. https://doi.org/10.1080/14786440009463897

25. Putter, K.C., Krause, A.E., North, A.C.: Popular music lyrics and the covid-19 pandemic. Psychol. Music, 03057356211045114 (0). https://doi.org/10.1177/03057356211045114

26. Ranjan, R., Sharma, A., Verma, M.: Characterization of the second wave of covid-19 in India, April 2021. https://doi.org/10.1101/2021.04.17.21255665

27. Saarikallio, S., Alluri, V., Kulmunki, I., Toiviainen, P.: Emotions of music listening in Finland and in India: comparison of an individualistic and a collectivistic culture. Psychol. Music **49**, 030573562091773 (2020). https://doi.org/10.1177/0305735620917730

28. van der Schyff, D., Silverman, M.: Music in the Community, November 2019

29. Schäfer, K., Eerola, T.: How listening to music and engagement with other media provide a sense of belonging: an exploratory study of social surrogacy. Psychol. Music **48**(2), 232–251 (2020)

30. Shang, Y., Li, H., Zhang, R.: Effects of pandemic outbreak on economies: evidence from business history context. Front. Public Health **9** (2021). https://doi.org/10.3389/fpubh.2021.632043. https://www.frontiersin.org/article/10.3389/fpubh.2021.632043

31. Shukla, M., Pandey, R., Singh, T., Riddleston, L., Hutchinson, T., Kumari, V., Lau, J.Y.F.: The effect of covid-19 and related lockdown phases on young peoples' worries and emotions: Novel data from India. Front. Public Health **9** (2021). https://doi.org/10.3389/fpubh.2021.645183. https://www.frontiersin.org/article/10.3389/fpubh.2021.645183

32. Tsao, S.F., Chen, H., Tisseverasinghe, T., Yang, R., Li, L., Butt, Z.: What social media told us in the time of covid-19: a scoping review. Lancet Digital Health **3**, January 2021. https://doi.org/10.1016/S2589-7500(20)30315-0

33. Vidas, D., Larwood, J.L., Nelson, N.L., Dingle, G.A.: Music listening as a strategy for managing covid-19 stress in first-year university students. Front. Psychol. **12** (2021). https://doi.org/10.3389/fpsyg.2021.647065. https://www.frontiersin.org/article/10.3389/fpsyg.2021.647065

34. Wong, A., Ho, S., Olusanya, O., Antonini, M.V., Lyness, D.: The use of social media and online communications in times of pandemic covid-19. J. Intensive Care Soc. **22**(3), 255–260 (2021)

35. Wulf, T., Breuer, J., Schmitt, J.: Escaping the pandemic present: The relationship between nostalgic media use, escapism, and well-being during the covid-19 pandemic. Psychology of Popular Media, September 2021. https://doi.org/10.1037/ppm0000357

36. Yeung, T.Y.C.: Did the covid-19 pandemic trigger nostalgia? evidence of music consumption on spotify, August 2020

37. Zangerle, E., Pichl, M., Gassler, W., Specht, G.: #nowplaying music dataset: Extracting listening behavior from twitter. In: Proceedings of the First International Workshop on Internet-Scale Multimedia Management. p. 21–26. WISMM 2014. Association for Computing Machinery, New York (2014). https://doi.org/10.1145/2661714.2661719

The Side Effect of ERC-20 Standard in Social Media Platforms

Barbara Guidi(ID) and Andrea Michienzi(✉)(ID)

Department of Computer Science, University of Pisa, Pisa, Italy
guidi@di.unipi.it, andrea.michienzi@unipi.it

Abstract. With the advent of blockchain technology, Online Social Media are moving towards integrating blockchain-based reward systems into their platforms. A reward system could help fight the spread of fake news by giving economic rewards to the users who contribute the most to the growth of the platform. Reddit recently proposed the Reddit Community Points, a rewarding system implemented on top of the Ethereum and Gnosis blockchains. Content creators can gain ERC-20 tokens, based on the votes they receive. These community tokens, called DONUTS, should be spent inside the Reddit platform, however, ERC-20 tokens can be easily traded or exchanged outside the platform. In this paper, we propose a study concerning the side effect of implementing community tokens as ERC-20 tokens. The analysis takes DONUTS as a case study and shows that the vast majority of tokens are transferred to and from decentralised exchange services, showing that users are not in favour of keeping the earned tokens to be used on the Reddit ecosystem. We also highlight that users are interested in entering the speculative market of blockchain tokens.

Keywords: Blockchain · SocialFi · Rewarding system · Ethereum · Reddit · Community tokens

1 Introduction

Online Social Media (OSMs) are among the most popular Internet services available nowadays, with more than 4.6 billion active users[1]. The rapid and widespread of OSMs highlighted several issues of these platforms, including the ones connected to data and the privacy of the users [3,15], the presence of bots, spammers, and misinformation channels which spread fake news [7,8,17], and censorship [9].

Developers and researchers identified that the typical centralised architecture of OSMs was a potential weak point, and new decentralised solutions were proposed [5]. Thanks to the introduction of blockchain technology in this scenario, a new generation of platforms, called Blockchain Online Social Media (BOSM) [10], emerged. An important aspect of BOSMs is the introduction of the reward

---

[1] https://datareportal.com/reports/digital-2022-global-overview-report.

© The Author(s), under exclusive license to Springer Nature Switzerland AG 2022
F. Hopfgartner et al. (Eds.): SocInfo 2022, LNCS 13618, pp. 114–127, 2022.
https://doi.org/10.1007/978-3-031-19097-1_7

system, geared toward economically incentivising users to a constructive use of the social platform. The introduction of rewards on OSMs is the starting point of the definition of a new Decentralised Finance (DeFi), called Social Finance (SocialFi)[2], which is the combination of DeFi with the Social activity. Through a rewarding system users that contribute constructively to the well-being of the platform are rewarded, such as when users create a socially impactful piece of content for the community.

One of the strongest motivations behind introducing a reward system in BOSMs is to fight the spread of fake news, as people should create truthful and insightful to have access to rewards. Censorship is easily eliminated thanks to the underlying blockchain technology. However, rewarding systems can be cheated on by bot accounts, that are capable of automatically performing sets of actions, to maximise their economic gain on the platform. On top of that, introducing an economic aspect in OSMs can have a serious impact on the content created by users, leading to information bubbles, single though, and echo chambers, because users are attracted only to those topics that generate high economic rewards. This can be amplified considering that the rewards on these platforms are tokens based on the common ERC-20 standard.

Current OSMs are trying to introduce social services by exploiting the concepts used in BOSMs. A platform that decided to embrace blockchain is Reddit. Reddit [1], with more than 430 million monthly active users[3] is a one-of-a-kind OSM, where its users, called *redditors* are able to create pieces of content with the most disparate type of media content in thematic communities, called subreddits, within which users are encouraged to deal with the specific topics addressed by the subreddit only. Recently, Reddit introduced the Reddit Community Points (RCP), which are a form of a community token, named DONUT, implemented on top of the Ethereum blockchain, and used to reward the contribution of redditors. The aim of the community tokens in Reddit is to incentivise redditors to create excellent content by rewarding RCP. RCPs are meant to be spent within the subreddit to gain additional perks, such as purchasing a special membership.

Reddit started the experiment of RCP to reduce the dependence of subreddits on centralised actors and make them autonomous and governed by the users participating in the subreddit itself. RCP represents one of the first examples of SocialFi in OSMs. The governance of the token is managed through a Decentralised Autonomous Organisation (DAO) [6,14] and users can participate in it based on the tokens owned. The DAO is able to manage multiple aspects of the RCP, including the number of tokens emitted and how they are distributed to contributors. While the introduction of a rewarding system can be a strong incentive for users to contribute to the platform constructively, the way redditors decide to use the earned tokens is still unclear. In this paper, we aim to show that community tokens implemented as ERC-20 can be used out of their initial context. As a case study, we analyse the DONUT tokens, proposed for

---

[2] https://hackernoon.com/socialfi-and-how-it-empowers-the-social-media-user-in-the-web-30-landscape.

[3] https://thrivemyway.com/reddit-statistics/.

the /r/EthTrader subreddit, both on Ethereum and Gnosis chains. We decided to focus on this token because it is the most mature of all the RCP tokens and, being deployed on a mainnet, it is a token that can be immediately exchanged on the market via Decentralised Exchanges (DEXs). More in detail, we extract the token transfers and study how tokens are transferred among the addresses. The study shows the impressive amount of activity related to DEXs, and for this reason, we also investigate how users tend to swap tokens for one another. The analyses show the evident side effect of the introduction of ERC-20 tokens as Community tokens. Indeed, the community tokens are principally used outside the community where they are proposed, and instead of collecting DONUTs through social activity, users can easily acquire them through DEXs. Additionally, users are inclined toward swapping DONUT tokens for other tokens that give easy access to investment opportunities. Lastly, this paper highlights that wealthy people can effortlessly acquire a large number of DONUT tokens, giving them access to the decision process of the DAO that governs the token. To the best of our knowledge, this is the first study concerning the impact of SocialFi, and in particular the impact of ERC-20 tokens, on Social Media. Furthermore, this is the first study about the Reddit Community Points.

The rest of the paper is organised as follows. Section 2 provides the relevant background concerning the Ethereum blockchain and blockchain-powered rewarding systems. Section 3 provides a description of the main features of Reddit, while Sect. 4 provides a detailed description of the Reddit Community Points. Section 5 provides a set of analyses that cover how users make use of the tokens earned, with a focus on how users swap them for other liquid tokens. Section 6 concludes the paper, pointing out possible future works.

2   Background

In this Section, we provide a set of concepts that are relevant to this paper. Given its key role in the decentralisation process of many social services, we start by providing the basic notions concerning blockchain technology, while we discuss the benefits of adopting it in a social scenario later in the Section.

2.1   Blockchain and Smart Contracts

A blockchain is one of the possible implementations of distributed digital ledger technology (DLT). It consists of a list of transactions among a set of users in a P2P network that is grouped in blocks, and each block is chained (contains a link) to the previous block. The blockchain is managed by a network of computers that build trust among the involved parties with the usage of cryptographic techniques. Blockchain technology has several important properties, including decentralisation, persistency, anonymity, tamper freeness and auditability [20].

Recent blockchains, such as Ethereum, allow users to have more complex interactions with each other, thanks to smart contracts [4]. Smart contracts are programs stored on a blockchain that can be invoked by users. Being stored on a blockchain, their code is public, auditable, and cannot be changed [19]. Thanks to these properties, it is possible to build complex applications that go beyond trading digital assets between users. To invoke a function of a smart contract, a transaction must be issued with the address of the contract as the destination of the transaction and the function, along with the parameters of the call, in a dedicated field of the transaction. During the execution of one of their functions, a contract may call another contract's function, however in this case there is no need to create a new transaction, but all the subsequent calls generated by the transaction are stored in the transaction logs.

2.2 The ERC-20 Standard

The blockchain offers natural support for economic applications. Ethereum was the first blockchain to bring this support to the next level, by integrating smart contracts in the scenario of Decentralised Finance. In particular, Ethereum provides smart contract interfaces for interacting with digital tokens, so that the interaction with these digital assets is standardised [18]. One of the most well-known standards is the ERC-20 standard, which consists of a smart contract interface that can be used to implement a smart contract that manages a fungible crypto asset. The execution of a contract implementing the ERC-20 interface cannot be modified because, following the standard, an ERC-20 token contract must be created by another contract that self-destructs upon the creation of the ERC-20 token contract.

The major difference between transferring ERC-20 compliant tokens as opposed to transferring Ether, lies in the nature of the transaction. Indeed, when transferring Ether, a canonical transaction is required. Instead, in the case of an ERC-20 token transfer, the payer must send a transaction to the contract managing the token and call a specific function that transfers the funds from the payer address to the payee address. The smart contract code will, in turn, update the balance of the users involved in the token transfer, according to its code.

2.3 Blockchain-Based Rewarding Systems

With the introduction of blockchain technology, OSM platforms are going under a profound revolution that includes the introduction of a rewarding system to fight phenomena like fake news spreading. Thanks to this approach, a new kind of decentralised finance has been proposed, the so-called Social Finance (SocialFi). Steem is a blockchain that supports the development of social applications thanks to its rich set of transactions and an embedded rewarding system that rewards users based on their social contribution [12,16]. Steemit is the main application built on top of the Steem blockchain [13]. The Hive blockchain originated as the effect of a hard fork from the Steem blockchain [2], but is progressively changing its approach to avoid being controlled by a single entity.

Yup [11] is a one-of-a-kind approach because it implements a multi-chain (EOS and Ethereum) rewarding system that integrates with existing platforms.

Users can vote on pieces of content created on other OSM, and they receive rewards if other users give the same rating. Likestarter is a platform that enables DAO for crowdfunding projects on top of the Ethereum blockchain. It adopts a multi-token approach: a token for the governance of the DAO, and a liquid token used to support the project [21]. Minds has an approach similar to Reddit's, meaning that the platform is centralised, but the rewarding system is implemented through a smart contract deployed on the Ethereum blockchain.

3   Reddit

Reddit is a social media platform in-between a forum and an OSM that serves multimedia content, mostly text and images, delivered through countless subreddits, which are thematic communities. Reddit is heavily focused on the contribution provided by its community: redditors are at the same time content creators, curators, and consumers. In particular, consumers feed on the content created by content creators, but can also evaluate the pieces of content published, through the so-called upvotes and downvotes, helping some content to reach a widespread social virality.

3.1   The Reddit Community Points

Reddit Community Points (RCP) were introduced in 2019, as a community token to incentivise Reddit's users to create pieces of content with remarkable quality. The incentive system of the RCP is based on the idea of awarding cryptocurrency tokens based on the social impact generated by each piece of content, measured according to the feedback provided by the other users of Reddit.

As of the beginning of 2022, RCPs are available only for the "r/EthTrader" subreddit, whose tokens are called *DONUTS*, implemented on the Ethereum and Gnosis chains. Experimental versions of RCPs are available for other subreddits, implemented on Redditspace chain[4], a testing network layer-2 blockchain for Gnosis, dedicated to the deployment of RCP.

RCPs are awarded to users who contributed in the respective subreddit (i.e. contributors of /r/EthTrader will receive DONUTs), as explained in the official documentation[5]. The amount of tokens distributed at each round is not fixed. It starts at 5 million for the first distribution and is reduced by 2.5% for each subsequent distribution. Tokens are assigned 50% to the contributors (users who created pieces of content for the subreddit), 10% to moderators (special users that moderate the subreddit), and the remaining 40% are set aside for community projects. As concerns the rewarding model and all the other details related to token distribution, the DAO of the specific subreddit can adjust values and decide their own rules.

---

[4] https://testnet.redditspace.com/.

[5] https://www.reddit.com/community-points/documentation/distribution-process.

3.2   What Are DONUTs

DONUTs are ERC-20 tokens that represent community contribution and engagement within the subreddit /r/EthTrader. They can be seen as a Social Token, and in particular as a Community Token. A community token is centred around communities rather than individuals and is usually used to regulate access and participation within the respective community[6]. Redditors earn DONUTs simply by participating and contributing content to the subreddit. DONUTs can be used within the subreddit for multiple community activities:

- **Voting.** Users can spend DONUTs to increase vote weight in community governance polls.
- **Special Membership.** DONUTs can be used to purchase special memberships, which brings a number of aesthetic perks.
- **Banner Advertising.** DONUTs can be used to purchase control of the top banner of the subreddit, which is often used for advertising purposes. Ownership of the banner follows a Harberger Tax system, in which the owner must pay a daily tax in order to retain it.
- **Tipping.** Users can also show special appreciation to content creators by sending tips in the form of DONUTs.

Being part of the Ethereum and Gnosis economic system, DONUTs can also be spent outside the platforms.

DONUTs were initially launched as an additional function of the /r/ EthTrader subreddit, fully implemented on Reddit's private servers. In December 2019, for transparency reasons, they were moved to the Ethereum blockchain, implemented as an ERC-20 token contract. Due to the high transaction fees on the Ethereum blockchain, DONUTS are currently distributed also on the Gnosis chain. Since its introduction on the blockchain, the token has attracted a lot of interest, and it is now listed on decentralised exchanges like Uniswap, thus gaining an actual economic value.

3.3   DONUT Tokenomics

DONUT tokens are minted and distributed every 4 weeks to registered users, based on their contribution to the /r/EthTrader subreddit. While there is a correlation between the number of upvotes and downvotes received by the pieces of content created by each user in the 4 weeks time period and how many DONUTs a user receives, the ratio is not 1:1. DONUTS are also awarded for other purposes, such as liquidity incentives, further development of the token, and subreddit moderation. At each distribution, 4 million new DONUTs are created and are distributed to the users of the /r/EthTrader subreddit, according to Table 1. To receive the tokens earned, users have to provide the gas fee needed to execute the relative transaction.

The tokens spent in the /r/EthTrader subreddit are burned, thus leaving the circulation to help regulate inflation. However, since the tokens are available on

---

[6] https://outlierventures.io/research/understanding-social-tokens/.

Table 1. DONUT token distribution

Type of contribution	Tokens allocated
Posts	1.02 M DONUTs per distribution
Comments	680 K DONUTs per distribution
Bonus to posts	680 K DONUTs per distribution
Community treasury funds	510 K DONUTs per distribution
Tipping & Content curation	340 K DONUTs per distribution
Uniswap liquidity incentives	400 K DONUTs per distribution
Honeyswap liquidity incentives	200 K DONUTs per distribution
Moderation	170 K DONUTs per distribution

both the Ethereum public blockchain and the Gnosis layer-2, token exchanges also come into play. In particular, Uniswap and Honeyswap are the two endorsed DEXs, the former being on Ethereum and the latter on Gnosis, that manage a liquidity pool for the DONUT token. The aim of the liquidity pool is to provide a market for people to acquire or sell DONUT tokens. Both liquidity pools work according to a formula of the constant product so that people are encouraged to trade evenly with the pool. Users can also provide liquidity to the pools and are incentivised to do so by a set of rewards, shown in Table 1.

4   Analysis of the DONUT Tokens

In this Section, we provide an analysis of the usage of the DONUT tokens as part of the RCP programme on the /r/EthTrader subreddit. We gather the token transfers stored on Ethereum and Gnosis chains in a dataset reported in Table 2. The dataset consists of more than 85,000 token transfers performed between the 4th of December 2019 (date of launch on the blockchain) and the 8th of January 2022, most of which were performed on the Gnosis chain.

Table 2. Dataset of the DONUTs transfers on Ethereum

Ethereum		Gnosis	
Holders	Transfers	Holders	Transfers
9,885	34,709	3,592	51,671

4.1   DONUTs Token Transfers

Figures 1a and b show the bivariate distribution of the number of DONUT transfers per user, on the Ethereum chain and on the Gnosis chain respectively. The Figures show a skewed distribution, where most users sent and received tokens

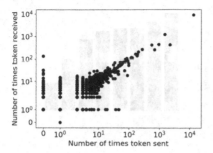

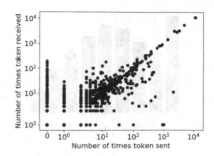

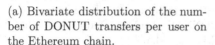

(a) Bivariate distribution of the number of DONUT transfers per user on the Ethereum chain.

(b) Bivariate distribution of the number of DONUT transfers per user on the Gnosis chain.

Fig. 1. Distribution of the number of times DONUTS tokens were transferred.

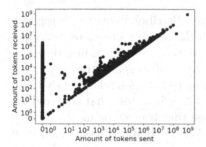

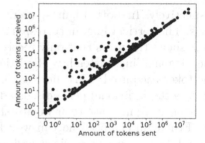

(a) Bivariate distribution of the number of DONUTS transferred per user on the Ethereum chain.

(b) Bivariate distribution of the number of DONUTS transferred per user on the Gnosis chain.

Fig. 2. Distribution of DONUTS token transferred.

less than 10 times, while a few transferred DOUNTS thousands of times. In the case of the Ethereum chain, the address of the Uniswap DONUT-WETH liquidity pool, transferred tokens more than 10,000 times. This shows how users are interested in exchanging DONUTs for Wrapped Ether and have access to the investment opportunities available on Ethereum, instead of spending DONUTs inside the subreddit, in respect to the original goal. Among the other most active users, we identify other DEXs, and the ERC-20 genesis address, which is used to mint and burn tokens. On the Gnosis chain we see a similar situation, where the most active addresses belong to contracts that implement DEX services, like Uniswap and Baoswap. Considering that DONUTs have been proposed as community tokens, the fact that the most recurrent addresses belong to DEXs hints that users may be more interested in using them as a tool to enter the cryptocurrency market, rather than using them for their intended purpose.

Figures 2a and b show the bivariate distribution of the number of DONUT tokens transferred per user, on the Ethereum and on the Gnosis chains

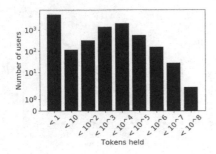

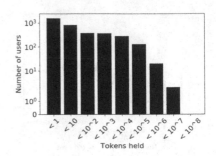

(a) Distribution of the number of DONUTS held per user on the Ethereum chain.

(b) Distribution of the number of DONUTS held per user on the Ethereum chain.

Fig. 3. Distribution of DONUTS token held.

respectively. In both Figures, users are mainly distributed over two separate lines. The vertical line, in correspondence with the number of tokens sent equal to 0, shows the users that only received tokens without ever spending them. On the diagonal line, instead, we find the users that tend to spend the majority of the tokens acquired. This effect can be caused by redditors sending DONUTs to acquire the additional perks discussed in Sect. 3.2, or investors that acquired and sold tokens to increase their wealth. The address that traded the most tokens on the Ethereum chain is the Uniswap DONUT-WETH liquidity pool, with more than 1 billion tokens received and sent. Among the others, we find the genesis address, which is the only address able to mint new tokens, and therefore it has more tokens sent than tokens received. Concerning the Gnosis chain, we find one Uniswap liquidity pool, the contract of Omnibridge, a decentralised service to bridge tokens across multiple blockchains, the treasury fund owned by /r/EthTrader multisignature account, and the genesis address.

We show in Figs. 3a and b the distribution of the number of tokens held by the users on the Ethereum and Gnosis chains. In Ethereum, we can see that the majority of the users hold less than 1 token, meaning that they spent almost all tokens acquired. The rest of the users have more frequently a balance between 100 and 10,000 tokens, while only a very small number of users are extremely wealthy, owning more than 10^7 tokens. Also in the Gnosis chain, most users have less than 1 DONUT and there are progressively fewer users the higher the range of wealth considered.

4.2   Token Swaps

Considering the impact of DEXs, in this Section, we focus on the token swaps. For our study, we will focus on the following ERC-20 tokens deployed on the Ethereum blockchain:

– DONUT: the token on which this study is focused;

- WETH: ERC-20 compliant representation of Ether;
- DAI: stablecoin pegged to the United States Dollar (USD);

Concerning the Gnosis chain we will focus our attention on the following ERC-20 tokens:

- DONUT: the token on which this study is focused;
- WXDAI: the analogous of the WETH token in the Ethereum blockchain;
- HONEY: token used to measure the contribution of a user in Honeyswap, one of the most important DEX on the Gnosis chain.
- xMOON: unofficial bridging from the Rinkeby testnet of the MOON community token, distributed on /r/Cryptocurrency.
- xBRICK: unofficial bridging from the Rinkeby testnet of the BRICK community token, distributed on /r/FortniteBR.

All tokens not listed, are grouped together in a single category called *other*.

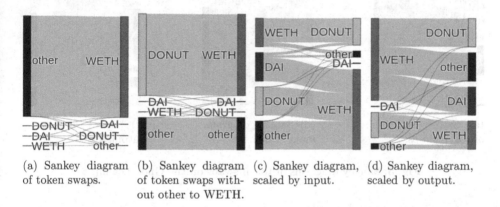

(a) Sankey diagram of token swaps.

(b) Sankey diagram of token swaps without other to WETH.

(c) Sankey diagram, scaled by input.

(d) Sankey diagram, scaled by output.

Fig. 4. Sankey diagrams of token swaps on the Ethereum chain.

Figure 4a shows the Sankey diagram of the tokens swapped in transactions where DONUTs appeared. The Figure shows that the vast majority of the swapped tokens belong to the *other* category, and that they are swapped into WETH tokens. The motivation lies in the fact that most DEXs let users exchange their tokens for WETH tokens and vice-versa, and that WETH can then be turned back into Ether, the liquid currency of the hosting blockchain Ethereum. If we discard the other-WETH swaps, we obtain the results shown in Fig. 4a, in which we can see that the majority of DONUT tokens are swapped for WETH tokens. There is also an important fraction of tokens belonging to the *other* category that are swapped for other non-WETH tokens. By scaling the input of the token swaps, we study what are the most common tokens used as the destination of the swap (see Fig. 4c). The Figure shows that WETH is the most commonly chosen destination token for swaps, thanks to the possibility to have access to a broader swap market and the possibility to convert it to liquid Ether. DONUTs are the second most commonly acquired tokens. Indeed, the majority of WETH and a consistent portion of DAI tokens are used for this goal. This highlights that most DONUTs are acquired through DEXs, instead of being awarded by the Reddit reward system. Figure 4d shows instead the token swaps scaled by the number of tokens obtained as a result of the swap. The Figure shows that WETH is the primary fuel for tokens swaps, covering the majority of swaps involving DONUTS, DAI and *other* tokens. It also shows that a large portion of WETH tokens is obtained by swapping in DONUT tokens. Considering that only a small fraction of WETH is obtained through other tokens, it shows that users heavily prefer to swap their tokens directly into WETH, for easy access to the speculative market.

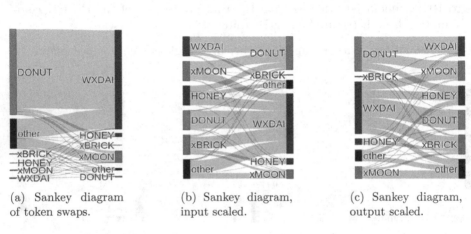

(a) Sankey diagram of token swaps.

(b) Sankey diagram, input scaled.

(c) Sankey diagram, output scaled.

Fig. 5. Sankey diagrams of token swaps on the Gnosis chain.

Figure 5a shows the Sankey diagram of the token swaps on the Gnosis chain. Contrarily to what we observed in Fig. 4a, on the Gnosis chain the DONUT tokens swapped outnumber the *other* tokens swap. On the other hand, similarly to Ethereum, most of the tokens are swapped for WXDAI, the homologous of WETH on the Gnosis chain. A small share of DONUTs is swapped either for HONEY or xMOON. In the first case, this phenomenon indicates a different swapping strategy that entails a token specifically designed for exchanges, and in the second case, an interest in the side projects of the RCPs. By scaling the amount of swapped tokens by the input, in Fig. 5b, we show that in most cases, the majority of the tokens are swapped for WXDAI tokens, because of their importance on the Gnosis chain. Half of the xMOON tokens are swapped for DONUT tokens, which highlights further the importance of the two related projects, /r/Cryptocurrency and /r/EthTrader respectively. On the other hand, the same effect is not as much present as for the xBRICK token, mainly swapped for WXDAI, and only in small quantities swapped for HONEY and xMOON. This is mostly due to the fact that the two aforementioned subreddits share some common topics, therefore are more likely populated by like-minded users who have communal interests. By scaling the amount of swapped tokens by the output, Fig. 5c highlights the versatility of the WXDAI token, which is used as an input token in plenty of swaps. Furthermore, a big portion of tokens tagged as *other* is obtained by swapping in xMOON tokens highlighting their usage outside the common swapping scheme involving WXDAI.

To summarise, these analyses uncovered a significant presence of DEXs, which dominate the DONUT token trading activity on both analysed chains. The phenomenon identified can be seen as a potential problem in the application of ERC-20 standard for community tokens. Indeed, the tokens earned by content creators are easily traded on DEXs for other tokens, which can then be used for investments or speculative purposes. Moreover, while the token should measure community contribution and engagement, it must be noted that, through DEXs, DONUTS can be easily bought. The enormous market provided by Ethereum, its layer-2, side chains, and the bridging services to external blockchain networks, create fertile ground for investors who seek opportunities to generate extreme gains in very short time spans. Even if DONUTs are proposed as community tokens in Reddit their application is completely distorted due to the ERC-20 standard, which makes them easily tradeable on the blockchain.

5   Conclusions and Future Works

Community tokens are tokens that are designed to be awarded to contributors of a community and meant to be spent within the community. In this paper, we analysed the Reddit Community Points, which are Reddit's implementation of community tokens. RCPs were initially proposed for the /r/EthTrader subreddit in the form of an ERC-20 token, called DONUT, now available on the Ethereum and Gnosis chains. Thanks to our analysis, we detected the presence of many DEXs among the addresses more commonly involved. Additional analyses uncover that DEXs are important gateways for having access to countless investment opportunities, highlighting that the DONUT tokens are often used for speculative actions, rather than being used, as intended, within the subreddit ecosystem.

In future works, we plan to investigate more in detail the phenomenon highlighted in this paper by collecting the social activity on the subreddit in order to understand how users collect the community tokens. We also plan to investigate in detail the rewarding system proposed by Reddit and analyse, in particular, whether it is fair, or tends to reward only the same few users. Thanks to the fact that all data is publicly available, we plan to study possible deanonymisation techniques that would allow us to associate Ethereum addresses with Reddit usernames.

References

1. Anderson, K.E.: Ask me anything: what is reddit? Library Hi Tech News (2015)
2. Ba, C.T., Zignani, M., Gaito, S.: Social and rewarding microscopical dynamics in blockchain-based online social networks. In: Proceedings of the Conference on Information Technology for Social Good, pp. 127–132 (2021)
3. Cain, J.A., Imre, I.: Everybody wants some: collection and control of personal information, privacy concerns, and social media use. New Media & Society (2021). https://doi.org/10.1177/14614448211000327
4. Dannen, C.: Introducing Ethereum and Solidity: Foundations of Cryptocurrency and Blockchain Programming for Beginners. 1st Edn., vol. 1. Apress Berkeley, CA (2017). https://doi.org/10.1007/978-1-4842-2535-6
5. Datta, A., Buchegger, S., Vu, L.H., Strufe, T., Rzadca, K.: Decentralized online social networks. In: Furht, B. (eds.) Handbook of Social Network Technologies and Applications, pp. 349–378. Springer, Boston (2010). https://doi.org/10.1007/978-1-4419-7142-5_17
6. El Faqir, Y., Arroyo, J., Hassan, S.: An overview of decentralized autonomous organizations on the blockchain. In: Proceedings of the 16th International Symposium on Open Collaboration, pp. 1–8 (2020)
7. Ferrara, E.: Bots, elections, and social media: a brief overview. Disinformation, Misinformation, and Fake News in Social Media, pp. 95–114 (2020)
8. Fornacciari, P., Mordonini, M., Poggi, A., Sani, L., Tomaiuolo, M.: A holistic system for troll detection on twitter. Comput. Hum. Behav. **89**, 258–268 (2018)
9. Golovchenko, Y.: Fighting propaganda with censorship: a study of the Ukrainian ban on Russian social media. J. Politics **84**(2), 639–654 (2022)
10. Guidi, B.: When blockchain meets online social networks. Pervasive Mob. Comput. **62**, 101131 (2020)
11. Guidi, B., Michienzi, A.: How to reward the web: the social dApp yup. Online Soc. Netw. Media **31**, 100229 (2022)
12. Guidi, B., Michienzi, A., Ricci, L.: Steem blockchain: mining the inner structure of the graph. IEEE Access **8**, 210251–210266 (2020)
13. Guidi, B., Michienzi, A., Ricci, L.: A graph-based socioeconomic analysis of steemit. IEEE Trans. Comput. Soc. Syst. **8**(2), 365–376 (2021)
14. Hassan, S., De Filippi, P.: Decentralized autonomous organization. Internet Policy Rev. **10**(2), 1–10 (2021)
15. Jozani, M., Ayaburi, E., Ko, M., Choo, K.K.R.: Privacy concerns and benefits of engagement with social media-enabled apps: a privacy calculus perspective. Comput. Hum. Behav. **107**, 106260 (2020)
16. Li, C., Palanisamy, B.: Incentivized blockchain-based social media platforms: a case study of steemit. In: Proceedings of the 10th ACM conference on web science, pp. 145–154 (2019)
17. Rathore, S., Loia, V., Park, J.H.: SpamSpotter: an efficient spammer detection framework based on intelligent decision support system on facebook. Appl. Soft Comput. **67**, 920–932 (2018)
18. Shirole, M., Darisi, M., Bhirud, S.: Cryptocurrency token: an overview. IC-BCT **2019**, 133–140 (2020)
19. Wang, Z., Jin, H., Dai, W., Choo, K.-K.R., Zou, D.: Ethereum smart contract security research: survey and future research opportunities. Front. Comp. Sci. **15**(2), 1–18 (2020). https://doi.org/10.1007/s11704-020-9284-9

20. Zheng, Z., Xie, S., Dai, H., Chen, X., Wang, H.: An overview of blockchain technology: architecture, consensus, and future trends. In: 2017 IEEE International Congress on Big Data (BigData congress), pp. 557–564. IEEE (2017)
21. Zichichi, M., Contu, M., Ferretti, S., D'Angelo, G.: LikeStarter: a smart-contract based social DAO for crowdfunding. In: IEEE INFOCOM 2019-IEEE Conference on Computer Communications Workshops (INFOCOM WKSHPS), pp. 313–318. IEEE (2019)

Comparative Analysis of Engagement, Themes, and Causality of Ukraine-Related Debunks and Disinformation

Iknoor Singh$^{(\boxtimes)}$, Kalina Bontcheva , Xingyi Song ,
and Carolina Scarton

Department of Computer Science, University of Sheffield, Sheffield, UK
{i.singh,k.bontcheva,x.song,c.scarton}@sheffield.ac.uk

Abstract. This paper compares quantitatively the spread of Ukraine-related disinformation and its corresponding debunks, first by considering re-tweets, replies, and favourites, which demonstrate that despite platform efforts Ukraine-related disinformation is still spreading wider than its debunks. Next, bidirectional post-hoc analysis is carried out using Granger causality tests, impulse response analysis and forecast error variance decomposition, which demonstrate that the spread of debunks has a positive impact on reducing Ukraine-related disinformation eventually, albeit not instantly. Lastly, the paper investigates the dominant themes in Ukraine-related disinformation and their spatiotemporal distribution. With respect to debunks, we also establish that around 18% of fact-checks are debunking claims which have already been fact-checked in another language. The latter finding highlights an opportunity for better collaboration between fact-checkers, so they can benefit from and amplify each other's debunks through translation, citation, and early publication online.

Keywords: Disinformation · Debunks · Ukraine-related disinformation · Comparative analysis · Social media

1 Introduction

Following on from and interleaved with the COVID-19 infodemic, the war in Ukraine has unleashed a new large stream of mis- and disinformation [1], as evidenced, amongst others, by fact-checkers from the European Digital Media Observatory (EDMO) who found a record-high Ukraine-related disinformation in March 2022[1]. Examples include viral decontextualised videos from past[2] and a popular pro-Kremlin false narrative about the existence of a biolab in Ukraine

---

[1] https://edmo.eu/fact-checking-briefs/.

[2] https://www.politifact.com/factchecks/2022/may/10/facebook-posts/no-not-footage-ukraine-shooting-down-russian-plane/.

F. Hopfgartner et al. (Eds.): SocInfo 2022, LNCS 13618, pp. 128–143, 2022.
https://doi.org/10.1007/978-3-031-19097-1_8

funded by Joe Biden's son[3]. To counter this fast-flowing disinformation, the International Fact-checking Network (IFCN) fact-checkers are working together to maintain and publish a unified database of debunks of Ukraine-related disinformation[4]. In order to measure the effectiveness of these efforts, we carry out a comparative analysis of engagement, themes, and predictive causality of Ukraine-related debunks and disinformation.

The novel contributions of this paper are in answering the following three key research questions through a quantitative analysis of Ukraine-related disinformation and debunks on Twitter:

RQ1 What is the overall engagement of Ukraine-related disinformation and debunks on Twitter (Sect. 4)?

RQ2 Does the spread of debunks have a positive impact in reducing Ukraine-related disinformation (Sect. 5)?

RQ3 What are the underlying themes in Ukraine-related disinformation and their spatiotemporal characteristics on Twitter (Sect. 6)?

In the following sections, we will discuss first related work (Sect. 2) and then detail the data acquisition methodology for this study (Sect. 3).

2   Related Work

Ukraine-related pro-Kremlin disinformation [29] is not new [1,14,15]. For instance, Lange-Ionatamishvili et al. [14] and Mejias and Vokuev [15] studied the spread of disinformation on social media after the 2014 annexation of Crimea by the Russian Federation, while Erlich and Garner [7] investigated if Ukrainian citizens are able to discern between factual information and pro-Kremlin disinformation. Another study [8] investigated the effectiveness of Russian propaganda in swaying the views of its readers. Recently, Park et al. [18] released a Ukraine-related dataset of tweets and carried out an analysis of public reactions to tweets by state-affiliated and independent media. Miller et al. [16] studied the spread of tweets related to hashtags that were trending in February 2022. Nonetheless, these studies do not focus specifically on comparing Ukraine-related disinformation and debunks in terms of engagement, inter-relationship, and topics.

Prior literature on the spread of true and false information is extensive [10,21,28]. Nevertheless, this paper is related to prior work that studied the spread and dynamics of false information and debunks on Twitter [2–5,13,17,19,20,23,26,30]. In particular, Burel et al. [5] compared COVID-related misinformation and fact-checks using impulse response modelling, causal analysis, and spread variance analysis, while Chen et al. [6] investigated the reasons why people share fact-checks and ways to encourage this further. Also, Siwakoti et al. [24] showed that user engagement with fact-checks increased significantly

---

[3] https://www.politifact.com/article/2022/apr/01/facts-behind-russian-right-wing-narratives-claimin/.

[4] https://ukrainefacts.org/.

as a result of the COVID-19 pandemic. However, to the best of our knowledge, no study has examined the predictive causality between Ukraine-related disinformation and debunks, or their spatiotemporal characteristics and top disinformation themes.

Table 1. Top domains of disinformation and debunk links.

Disinformation domains	Debunk domains
facebook.com (30%)	dpa-factchecking.com(25%)
tiktok.com (3%)	euvsdisinfo.eu (25%)
twitter.com (3%)	rumorscanner.com (9%)
oroszhirek.hu (2%)	politifact.com (8%)
sputniknews.com (2%)	factly.in (8%)
nabd.com (2%)	verify-sy.com (6%)
arabic.rt.com (1%)	factcrescendo.com (4%)
fb.watch (1%)	verafiles.org (3%)
de.news-front.info (1%)	factcheck.org (2%)
Other (55%)	Other (10%)

3   Data

The data underpining our analyses spans disinformation and debunks posted between 1 February and 30 April 2022. Specifically, we focus on Ukraine-related debunks and accompanying links to the corresponding disinformation encompassing: *(i)* 110 debunks and 311 links to disinformation published by EUvsDsinfo[5], which primarily fact-checks pro-Kremlin disinformation; *(ii)* 344 debunks indexed by Google in the ClaimReview format[6], which refer to 439 disinformation links. See Appendix A.1 for details on how we collect the disinformation links from debunks. Similar to Burel et al. [5], in addition to the above date restrictions, we also applied keyword-based filtering[7] in order to select only Ukraine-related debunks and disinformation.

In total, this study analyses 454 debunk URLs and 750 links to Ukraine-related disinformation. The latter are provided by the fact-checking organisations themselves within the published debunks (see Appendix A.1), therefore we consider them as accurate. Table 1 shows the top domains that occur within the disinformation and debunk links. The former point either to content on social media platforms or to Kremlin-backed outlets. For debunks, the main domains are EUvsDisinfo (25%) and Dpa-factchecking (25%).

---

[5] https://euvsdisinfo.eu/.

[6] https://www.datacommons.org/factcheck/download.

[7] Where debunked claims were in languages other than English, these were translated automatically with Google Translate first, prior to filtering with the keywords listed here: https://gist.github.com/greenwoodma/430d9443920a589b6802070f2ca54134.

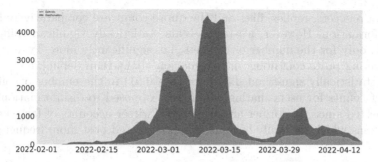

Fig. 1. Stacked plot of a rolling 7-day average of the number of disinformation and debunk tweets.

Table 2. Mean and standard deviation (STD) values of metrics of engagement with disinformation and debunk tweets. * represents a statistical significant difference (p ≤ 0.01)

	Followers	Tweets	Retweets	Replies	Likes	Quote count
Mean - Disinformation	6,814	61,331	15.0*	0.5	4.5	0.2
Mean - Debunks	21,790*	89,098*	1.8	0.4	2.0	0.1
STD - Disinformation	2,04,422	1,22,527	312.3	34.5	631.9	13.9
STD - Debunks	4,55,884	1,55,183	15.0	7.6	28.0	1.3

Next, we use academic research access to the Twitter API[8] to obtain 16,549 unique tweets containing one of the above debunk URLs and another 62,882 unique tweets sharing one of the disinformation links[9]. Retweets are also collected, since we aim to investigate the overall spread of information on Twitter. Hereafter, the tweets containing debunk links are referred to as "debunk tweets" and those containing disinformation links as "disinformation tweets". Figure 1 shows the stacked plot of a rolling 7-day average curve for the spread of disinformation and debunk tweets. It shows that Ukraine-related disinformation spiked in the first half of March 2022, which consequently lead to an increase in published debunks as it is also reported in EDMO's Fact-checking Briefs[10].

4   Comparative Analysis of Engagement

In order to measure the spread of disinformation and debunks through tweets, we first compare the differences in engagement metrics in terms of mean and standard deviation. Table 2 shows the statistics for author's followers, author's tweets, number of retweets, replies, likes and the quote count. We find that the

---

[8] https://developer.twitter.com/en/docs/twitter-api.
[9] The dataset used for analysis received ethical approval from the University of Sheffield Ethics Board. This paper only discusses analysis and results in aggregate data, without providing examples or information about individual users.
[10] https://edmo.eu/fact-checking-briefs.

number of retweets, replies, likes and the quote count are comparatively higher for disinformation. However, a t-test reveals statistically significant difference ($p \leq 0.01$) only for the number of retweets, i.e. significantly more Twitter users are retweeting posts containing disinformation URLs than debunk ones. There is also a statistically significant difference ($p \leq 0.01$) in the number of followers and tweet counts for users sharing debunks as opposed to disinformation. This is as expected since the former are primarily Twitter accounts of fact-checking organisations which naturally have more followers and post more frequently.

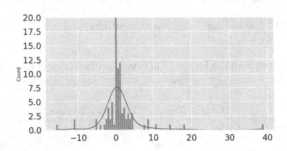

Fig. 2. Average difference in days between the date of publication of disinformation tweets and their corresponding debunk article (Fisher-Pearson coefficient of skewness = 3.37).

Table 3. Top ten cases with country affected by the disinformation and country of the authors of disinformation tweets.

Affected country	Authors' country	Percentage
Ukraine	Russia	9.0
Ukraine	Germany	7.0
Russia	Russia	6.0
Russia	Germany	5.0
Ukraine	United States	4.0
Ukraine	Venezuela	4.0
Ukraine	Mexico	3.0
United States	Mexico	3.0
Other		59.0

Figure 2 shows the histogram and kernel density estimate depicting the average number of days between the date of publication of disinformation tweets and their corresponding debunk articles. In this, for each debunk we compute $\sum_{i=1}^{|N|} (DoP_i - DoP_{debunk})/|N|$, where DoP_{debunk} is the date of publication of a debunk by the fact-checking organisation, DoP_i is the date of publication of a disinformation tweet i and $|N|$ is the total count of disinformation tweets for each debunk. The data is positively skewed, with a Fisher-Pearson coefficient of skewness of 3.37, suggesting some spread of disinformation even after the publication of the corresponding debunk article (see Sect. 5).

Since EUvsDsinfo debunks explicitly list countries where the disinformation is spreading, these can be compared to the country of the authors of those tweets. The latter is derived from the self-declared user location field obtained via the Twitter API[11] (when available). We obtain the location information for authors of 51% of the disinformation-sharing tweets. Unsurprisingly, the biggest proportion (9%) comes from cases where EUvsDisinfo has found the disinformation spreading in Ukraine, while the author's self-declared locations are in Russia (Table 3). Another key observation is the global nature of the disinformation, with spread extending significantly beyond Europe.

Fig. 3. Wordcloud of the most frequent 100 hashtags in disinformation- (left) and debunk-sharing (right) tweets respectively.

Fig. 4. Timeline for a sample of Ukraine-related false narratives that have been debunked multiple times. The y-axis states the false narrative and the x-axis represents the date of publication of its debunks. The language of debunk articles is denoted by different symbols – English: ★; French: ■; Dutch: •; German: ♦

Figure 3 shows the most frequent 100 hashtags in disinformation-sharing vs debunk-sharing tweets. Unsurprisingly Ukraine dominates both, while #FoxNews

---

[11] https://developer.twitter.com/en/docs/twitter-api/data-dictionary/object-model/user. Where needed, Geopy Python library (Ref. https://pypi.org/project/geopy/) is used to extract the country name from the information provided by the API.

is prevalent in tweets sharing disinformation links. This is due to the spread by right-wing American media of a wide-reaching false narrative regarding the presence of U.S.-backed bioweapon labs in Ukraine[12].

We also investigate the presence of identical or highly similar false claims in our dataset that have been debunked multiple times by different fact-checkers. Similar to Singh et al. [23], a state-of-the-art semantic search model[13] is used for this task. Out of the 456 debunks in our dataset (see Sect. 3), 84 of them (18%) were found to be highly similar to false narratives that have already been debunked by another fact-checking organisation. Figure 4 shows some examples of Ukraine-related false narratives that have been debunked multiple times in different languages. This finding demonstrates significant overlap in effort spent by fact-checking organisations in multiple countries, as well as cost- and time-saving opportunities that could be exploited with the help of translation and cross-publishing of debunks.

5   Post-hoc Causality Analysis

We test the bi-directional Granger causality [9] between the disinformation-sharing and debunk-sharing tweets. In other words, we want to investigate whether the spread of debunks has a positive impact on reducing the sharing of Ukraine-related disinformation on Twitter. Although identifying causation relationships between different information types is not trivial, a Granger causality test can be used to evaluate the predictive causality i.e. if the spread of one information type can be used to predict the spread of another. In this, we treat the occurrence of disinformation and debunk tweets as two time series variables and then try to find if one variable can be predicted from the other variable's past values and its own past values.[14] First we build a Vector Regression model (VAR) [22], where a period of three is applied, based on the Akaike's Information Criterion. The Augmented-Dicky Fuller test identifies the data as stationary ($p \leq 0.01$). The general equation of VAR model is

$$disinfo(t) = \sum_{i=1}^{k} \alpha_{1,i} disinfo(t-i) + \sum_{i=1}^{k} \beta_{1,i} debunk(t-i) + \epsilon_1 \qquad (1)$$

$$debunk(t) = \sum_{i=1}^{k} \alpha_{2,i} debunk(t-i) + \sum_{i=1}^{k} \beta_{2,i} disinfo(t-i) + \epsilon_2 \qquad (2)$$

---

[12] https://www.politifact.com/article/2022/mar/11/russia-china-and-tucker-carlson-lack-evidence-ukra/.

[13] The multilingual model available at https://huggingface.co/sentence-transformers/paraphrase-multilingual-mpnet-base-v2, since it performs best according to the leaderboard (Ref. https://www.sbert.net/docs/pretrained_models.html).

[14] The Statsmodel Python library is used to perform the Granger causality test. Ref. https://www.statsmodels.org/.

where $debunk(t)$ and $disinfo(t)$ refers to count of tweets at time t, k is the maximum lag order, $\alpha_{1,i}$ and $\alpha_{2,i}$ are autoregressive coefficients, $\beta_{1,i}$ and $\beta_{2,i}$ are regression coefficients, and ϵ_1 and ϵ_2 are error terms.

The experiments find a Granger causality relation, which shows that debunk spread has predictive causality over disinformation spread ($p \leq 0.01$). In addition, we also observe this weak causation in the opposite direction, i.e. from disinformation to debunks ($p \leq 0.01$). The significant results in both directions imply that changes in the spread of disinformation may induce changes in the spread of debunks and that the spread debunks may likewise cause changes in the disinformation spread. This is similar to the findings of previous work for COVID-19 misinformation [4,5]. In order to further understand the weak causation between Ukraine-related disinformation and debunks, we use the VAR model to perform an impulse response analysis and forecast the error variance decomposition for 14 days periods.

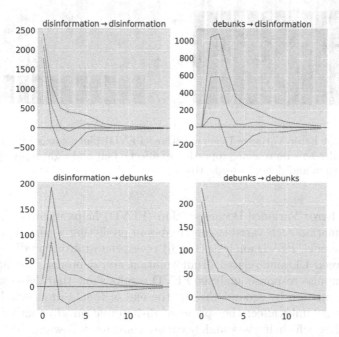

Fig. 5. Impulse Response Analysis (x-axis represents 14 days period and y-axis represents effect of shock). Top left and bottom left shows the effect of disinformation shock on disinformation and debunks respectively. Top right and bottom right shows the effect of debunk shock on disinformation and debunks respectively. By default, asymptotic standard errors are presented at the 95% confidence level.

Impulse response analysis is used to find the effect of shock in one variable to itself and the other variables in the VAR model. The prime reason to investigate this is to check if an increase in the spread of debunks triggers a reduction in disinformation on Twitter. Figure 5 shows that an orthogonal shock[15] from debunks leads to an initial spike in disinformation but there is a downward trend for disinformation afterwards. This suggests that debunks will trigger a reduction in overall disinformation eventually, if not instantly. Similarly, an orthogonal shock from disinformation also triggers an initial spike in debunks (Fig. 5) and an eventual decrease with time, although not instantly. This suggests swift response in debunk publication (mostly from fact-checkers) following a sudden rise in disinformation on social media. Interestingly, we also notice that the shock in disinformation quickly dies as the impact returns to zero with a sharp decrease on the second day, followed by a small post-shock peak during 4–6 day period which finally converges back to zero between 8–10 day period.

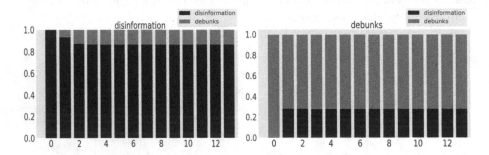

Fig. 6. Forecast Error Variance Decomposition (FEVD) plot (x-axis represents a 14-day period and y-axis represents proportion of affect). Left and right represents FEVD for disinformation and debunks respectively.

Forecast Error Variance Decomposition (FEVD) helps uncover the proportion of information each variable contributes in predicting a particular variable in the VAR model. FEVD analysis (Fig. 6) reveals substantial predictive dependencies between Ukraine-related disinformation and debunks. Similar to what we find in impulse response analysis, FEVD results show that debunks directly affect disinformation by around 15% by the end of the 14-day period. We also observe that debunks affect the spread of disinformation after an initial delay by a day, after which it rises and becomes constant following the third day. On the other hand, we also find that the spread of debunks is also affected by disinformation by around 30%. The results also show that the impact of disinformation on debunks is delayed initially for a day. In other words, this implies that the spread of debunks is not dependent on how Ukraine-related disinformation spreads initially. In summary, our experimental analysis confirms that the spread of debunking tweets does have a positive impact on reducing Ukraine-related disinformation on Twitter.

---

[15] Cholesky decomposition is used for orthogonalisation.

6   Topical Analysis of Ukraine-Related Disinformation

This section investigates the main topics in disinformation and study the engagement around them over time. The debunked claim statements are clustered by applying K-means to embeddings from the semantic search model[16]. The number of clusters is kept at six using the Elbow method and silhouette coefficient score. The model is run for a maximum of 300 iterations with K-means++ used as a method of initialisation. The clustering is applied on debunked claim statements and not on tweets itself. See Appendix A.1 for details on how we collect the debunked claim statements.

The class-based TF-IDF [11] is used to find top words in debunked claim statements in each of the clusters (Table 4). Each cluster has distinct words that separate it from the other five. In order to verify the separation between the clusters, we also plot a heatmap of topic similarity (see Appendix A.2). The results show that except clusters one and two, most of the clusters are distinct in terms of the topics they cover. For instance, cluster four encompasses widespread conspiracies related to the U.S.-backed bioweapon labs in Ukraine and the

Table 4. Top ten words and count of disinformation tweets in each topic cluster. Order of word depicts its importance from left to right.

Topic clusters	Count
0_ukraine_ukrainian_russia_kyiv_neo_coup_nazis_war_crimea_weapons	39,761
1_poland_nato_polish_alliance_west_security_countries_western_europe_russian	10,225
2_putin_biden_know_think_vladimir_lee_answer_prices_says_oil	4,194
3_video_shows_ukraine_ukrainian_proof_jet_marcos_shot_soldiers_fighter	3,793
4_biolabs_ukraine_financed_state_biological_labs_military_biden_victoria_vaccinated	3,132
5_trump_russia_bucha_massacre_billions_evidence_west_100_planted_united	1,777

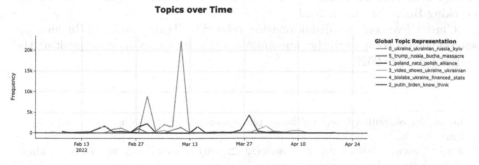

Fig. 7. Temporal spread of disinformation tweets in each topic cluster over time. Legend shows top five words of each cluster from Table 4.

---

[16] We use the BERTTopic [11] Python library for clustering and MPNet [25] as the transformer model. Ref. https://huggingface.co/sentence-transformers/all-mpnet-base-v2.

US planning to send infected migratory birds to infect Russia[17]. Another cluster (one), includes the ongoing false narrative about the NATO country alliance being the real threat to Russia[18]. Table 4 also shows the count of corresponding disinformation tweets (and retweets) in each cluster, identifying that most of the tweets belong to cluster zero and one.

Next, we look at the temporal distribution of the disinformation tweets for each topic cluster. Figure 7 illustrates the line plot for topic prevalence between February and April 2022. For instance, cluster zero includes false claims related to Russia attacking Ukraine, Kyiv, neo-nazism, etc. and has two dominant peaks, one in the first week of March and another one in the second week of March (the tallest one at 10 March 2022). There is also an uptick in February suggesting that the disinformation narratives started spreading even before 24 February and then spiked later in March. Similar results were found in the EDMO's Fact-checking Briefs for February[19] where they noticed a sudden increase in posts about growing tensions between Russia and Ukraine.

Cluster one (disinformation related to NATO and western countries) spiked in the first week of March. It includes a dominant false narrative about NATO attacking countries illegitimately[20].

Cluster two has multiple spikes: one in mid February; another one in mid of March; and the biggest one – at the end of March. It comprises false narratives involving Joe Biden, Vladimir Putin and Russian oil, e.g. that Biden's cancellation of the Keystone pipeline "dramatically increased Americans" dependence on Russian oil.

Cluster three comprises of videos spreading disinformation and their distribution is fairly stable, with only a slight increase in the first and last week of March.

Cluster four contains conspiracies, such as an alleged presence of US biological labs in Ukraine[21] and release of infected migratory birds to infect Russia[22]. Figure 7 shows that these type of conspiratorial narratives spiked during the second week of March. This is also coherent with the findings of EDMO's Fact-checking Briefs for March 2022.

Cluster five contains disinformation related to Trump and the Bucha massacre and has comparatively time-limited span, with only a small peak at the end of February 2022.

---

[17] https://euvsdisinfo.eu/report/the-us-plans-to-send-infected-migratory-birds-to-infect-russia.

[18] https://www.politifact.com/factchecks/2022/feb/28/candace-owens/fact-checking-claims-nato-us-broke-agreement-again/.

[19] https://edmo.eu/fact-checking-briefs.

[20] https://euvsdisinfo.eu/report/nato-is-not-a-defensive-alliance-it-attacks-countries-illegitimately.

[21] https://www.bbc.co.uk/news/60711705.

[22] https://euvsdisinfo.eu/report/the-us-plans-to-send-infected-migratory-birds-to-infect-russia.

7   Limitations and Future Work

Our work should be seen in the light of the following limitations. First, as described in Sect. 3, the study uses only tweets which contain explicit links to known disinformation or debunk articles. While this makes the dataset highly accurate and does not require additional human annotation, it also means that tweets that spread false claims or debunk them without citing a reference link could not be included. Second, this paper only discusses results on aggregate data, without looking at whether the tweets are from real or bot accounts. Lastly, user data, such as their country, is dependent on self-declared information in the user profiles, which is missing for many tweets. Nevertheless, the sample size is sufficiently large and robust to yield useful insights.

In future, we want to analyse the spread of disinformation and debunks before and after the start of the Russia-Ukraine war. We might have different answers for the research questions raised in the paper, which would potentially provide some insights into how an emergency event changes the spreading paradigms of disinformation and debunks. We also want to find ways to automatically detect disinformation tweets which don't explicitly mention links or where the disinformation links mentioned are different from the ones present in our dataset. Lastly, the Granger causality test deals with linear relationship. Hence, in future, we plan to experiment with other non-linear tests like Hiemstra and Jones non-linear Granger causality [12] and Convergent Cross Mapping test [27].

8   Conclusion

This study carried out a comparative analysis of the spread of Ukraine-related false claims and debunks on Twitter between February and April 2022. In particular, our comparative engagement analysis found that tweets spreading disinformation are shared and retweeted significantly more as compared to those containing debunks. With respect to debunks, we also established that around 18% are focused on false claims for which debunks have already been posted in a different country or language. This finding is particularly important, as it points out to two opportunities going forward. Firstly, since many platforms, such as Facebook, already offer machine translation tools to their users, they could us that technology themselves to translate and match debunks automatically, so a false narrative spreading in one language can be flagged as false, based on an authoritative fact-check in another language. Secondly, fact-checkers themselves can benefit from using cross-lingual search and machine translation technologies to find such debunks, which they can then cite as a source or re-publish in translation and thus reduce the time elapsed between a false narrative starting to spread widely online and the time their debunk is published.

Another key finding is that the publication of debunks does ultimately lead to limiting the spread of Ukraine-related disinformation, albeit not immediately. In addition, FEVD results show substantial predictive dependencies between the spread disinformation and debunk tweets. Lastly, our data-driven analysis uncovered also the dominant themes in Ukraine-related disinformation and their temporal intensity. In conclusion, these findings have immediate relevance for a wide range of stakeholders, including digital platforms, fact-checkers, and online information users. The dataset used for analysis is available at https://doi.org/10.5281/zenodo.6992686.

Acknowledgements. This research has been partially supported by a European Union – Horizon 2020 Program, grant no. 825297 (WeVerify), the European Union – Horizon 2020 Program under the scheme "INFRAIA-01-2018-2019 – Integrating Activities for Advanced Communities" and Grant Agreement n.871042 ("SoBigData++: European Integrated Infrastructure for Social Mining and Big Data Analytics" (http://www.sobigdata.eu)).

A Appendix

A.1 Data Collection

As described in Sect. 3, we collect Ukraine-related debunks from EUvsDsinfo and ClaimReview. In order to collect the disinformation links, 1) the debunks indexed in ClaimReview schema has the `itemReviewed`[23] object which includes disinformation links that are being debunked by fact-checking organisation and

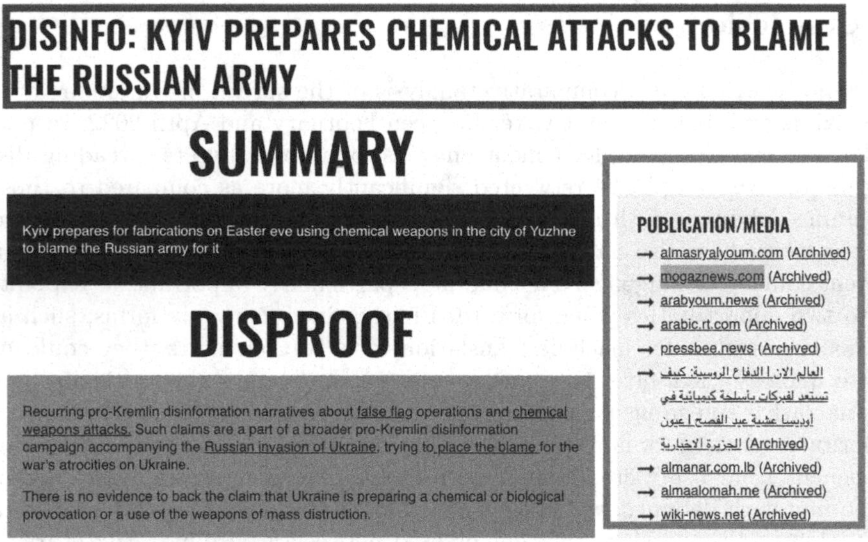

Fig. 8. Screenshot of one of the EUvsDsinfo debunks. Section enclosed in the red box contains disinformation links and the blue box represents the debunked claim statement. (Color figure online)

---

[23] https://schema.org/ClaimReview.

debunked claim statement is present in `claimReviewed` object; 2) the debunks on EUvsDsinfo explicitly mention disinformation links on their website. Figure 8 shows the screenshot of one of the EUvsDsinfo debunks. The section enclosed in the red box contains disinformation links and the blue box represents the debunked claim statement.

A.2 Heatmap

Figure 9 illustrates the heatmap of cluster similarity. The results show that except clusters one and two, most of the clusters are distinct in terms of the topics they cover. This indicates reasonable separation between the clusters found in Sect. 6.

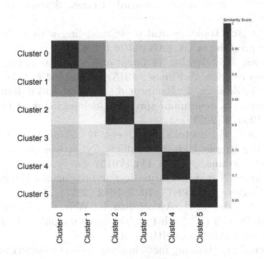

Fig. 9. Heatmap for topic cluster similarity. The description of clusters can be found in Sect. 6.

References

1. Aguerri, J., Santisteban, M., Miró-Llinares, F.: The fight against disinformation and its consequences: measuring the impact of "Russia state-affiliated media" on Twitter. SocArXiv (2022)
2. Allcott, H., Gentzkow, M.: Social media and fake news in the 2016 election. J. Econom. Perspect. **31**(2), 211–36 (2017)
3. Barrera, O., Guriev, S., Henry, E., Zhuravskaya, E.: Facts, alternative facts, and fact checking in times of post-truth politics. J. Public Econ. **182**, 104123 (2020)
4. Burel, G., Farrell, T., Alani, H.: Demographics and topics impact on the co-spread of COVID-19 misinformation and fact-checks on Twitter. Inform. Process. Manage. **58**(6), 102732 (2021)

5. Burel, G., Farrell, T., Mensio, M., Khare, P., Alani, H.: Co-spread of misinformation and fact-checking content during the COVID-19 pandemic. In: International Conference on Social Informatics, pp. 28–42, Springer (2020). https://doi.org/10.1007/978-3-030-60975-7_3

6. Chen, Q., Zhang, Y., Evans, R., Min, C.: Why do citizens share COVID-19 fact-checks posted by Chinese government social media accounts? The elaboration likelihood model. Int. J. Environ. Res. Public Health **18**(19), 10058 (2021)

7. Erlich, A., Garner, C.: Is pro-kremlin disinformation effective? Evidence from Ukraine. Int. J. Press/Polit. 19401612211045221 (2021)

8. Gerber, T.P., Zavisca, J.: Does Russian propaganda work? Wash. Q. **39**(2), 79–98 (2016)

9. Granger, C.W.: Investigating causal relations by econometric models and cross-spectral methods. Econometrica: J. Econom. Soc. 424–438 (1969)

10. Grinberg, N., Joseph, K., Friedland, L., Swire-Thompson, B., Lazer, D.: Fake news on twitter during the 2016 us presidential election. Science **363**(6425), 374–378 (2019)

11. Grootendorst, M.: BERTopic: Neural topic modeling with a class-based TF-IDF procedure. arXiv preprint arXiv:2203.05794 (2022)

12. Hiemstra, C., Jones, J.D.: Testing for linear and nonlinear granger causality in the stock price-volume relation. J. Financ. **49**(5), 1639–1664 (1994)

13. Jiang, M., Gao, Q., Zhuang, J.: Reciprocal spreading and debunking processes of online misinformation: a new rumor spreading-debunking model with a case study. Physica A **565**, 125572 (2021)

14. Lange-Ionatamishvili, E., Svetoka, S., Geers, K.: Strategic communications and social media in the Russia Ukraine conflict. Cyber war in perspective: Russian aggression against Ukraine, pp. 103–111 (2015)

15. Mejias, U.A., Vokuev, N.E.: Disinformation and the media: the case of Russia and Ukraine. Media Culture Soc. **39**(7), 1027–1042 (2017)

16. Miller, C., Inskip, C., Marsh, O., Arcostanzo, F., Weir, D.: Message-based Community Detection on Twitter (2022). https://glavcom.ua/pub/pdf/49/4935/message-based-community-detection-on-twitter.pdf

17. Nyhan, B., Reifler, J.: Estimating fact-checking's effects. American Press Institute, Arlington, VA (2015)

18. Park, C.Y., Mendelsohn, J., Field, A., Tsvetkov, Y.: VoynaSlov: a data set of Russian social media activity during the 2022 Ukraine-Russia War. arXiv preprint arXiv:2205.12382 (2022)

19. Park, S., Park, J.Y., Chin, H., Kang, J.h., Cha, M.: An experimental study to understand user experience and perception bias occurred by fact-checking messages. In: Proceedings of the Web Conference 2021, pp. 2769–2780 (2021)

20. Recuero, R., Soares, F.B., Vinhas, O., Volcan, T., Hüttner, L.R.G., Silva, V.: Bolsonaro and the far right: how disinformation about COVID-19 circulates on Facebook in Brazil. Int. J. Commun. **16**, 24 (2022)

21. Shao, C., Ciampaglia, G.L., Varol, O., Yang, K.C., Flammini, A., Menczer, F.: The spread of low-credibility content by social bots. Nat. Commun. **9**(1), 1–9 (2018)

22. Sims, C.A.: Macroeconomics and reality. Econometrica: J. Econom. Soc. 1–48 (1980)

23. Singh, I., Bontcheva, K., Scarton, C.: The false COVID-19 narratives that keep being debunked: a spatiotemporal analysis. arXiv preprint arXiv:2107.12303 (2021)

24. Siwakoti, S., Yadav, K., Bariletto, N., Zanotti, L., Erdogdu, U., Shapiro, J.N.: How COVID drove the evolution of fact-checking. Harvard Kennedy School Misinformation Review (2021)

25. Song, K., Tan, X., Qin, T., Lu, J., Liu, T.Y.: MPNet: masked and permuted pre-training for language understanding. Adv. Neural Inf. Process. Syst. 16857–16867 (2020)
26. Swire, B., Berinsky, A.J., Lewandowsky, S., Ecker, U.K.: Processing political misinformation: comprehending the Trump phenomenon. Royal Soc. Open Sci. **4**(3), 160802 (2017)
27. Tsonis, A.A., Deyle, E.R., Ye, H., Sugihara, G.: Convergent cross mapping: theory and an example. Adv. Nonlinear Geosci. 587–600 (2018)
28. Vosoughi, S., Roy, D., Aral, S.: The spread of true and false news online. Science **359**(6380), 1146–1151 (2018)
29. Yablokov, I.: Russian disinformation finds fertile ground in the West. Nature Hum. Behav. 1–2 (2022)
30. Zhang, Y., et al.: Investigation of the determinants for misinformation correction effectiveness on social media during COVID-19 pandemic. Inform. Process. Manage. **59**(3), 102935 (2022)

Polarizing Opinion Dynamics
with Confirmation Bias

Tianyi Chen[1], Xu Wang[1], and Charalampos E. Tsourakakis[1,2]([✉])

[1] Boston University, Boston, USA
[2] ISI Foundation, Turin, Italy
{ctony,xuwang,ctsourak}@bu.edu

Abstract. Social media and online networks have enabled discussions between users at a planetary scale on controversial topics. However, instead of seeing users converging to a consensus, they tend to partition into groups holding diametric opinions. In this work we propose an opinion dynamics model that starts from a given graph topology, and updates in each iteration both the opinions of the agents, and the *listening* structure of each agent, assuming there is confirmation bias. We analyze our model, both theoretically and empirically, and prove that it generates a listening structure that is likely to be polarized. We show a novel application of our model, specifically how it can be used to find polarized niches across different Twitter layers. Finally, we evaluate and compare our model to other polarization models on various synthetic datasets, showing that it yields equilibria with unique characteristics, including high polarization and low disagreement.

1 Introduction

Nowadays opinions are increasingly shaped by online interactions that take place on social media platforms, including Facebook, Twitter, Reddit, Instagram among others. Users are exposed to a diversity of opinions at a planetary scale, and to authoritative sources of information. However, instead of observing a convergence of opinions on important social topics, we observe an increasing amount of polarization [24], and the widespread of misinformation [4]. We observe that users cluster into groups with diametrically opposite opinions on numerous important social issues such as gun control, and vaccination against COVID-19. The negative implications of this phenomenon can be devastating, leading to a widening political divide, conflict, and radicalization [8]. Furthermore, polarization facilitates the spread of misinformation [7]. One of the roots of evil behind the polarization phenomenon is a human cognitive bias, *confirmation bias*. Specifically, biased assimilation or confirmation bias is the phenomenon according to which individuals process new information in a biased way towards existing beliefs, or expectations. Lord et al. have shown that two people with initially different opinions/conflicting views can examine the same evidence and find reasons to increase the strength of their existing opinions [25]. The groups of users with homogeneous opinions are also known as echo chambers [10].

F. Hopfgartner et al. (Eds.): SocInfo 2022, LNCS 13618, pp. 144–158, 2022.
https://doi.org/10.1007/978-3-031-19097-1_9

Understanding how polarization and echo chambers naturally emerge on social media, is a subject of paramount importance, and of interest to a diverse group of researchers, in sociology, economics, and computer science. In recent years, numerous polarizing opinion dynamics models [6,12,15,19,22] have been proposed. In this work, we propose a simple model of opinion dynamics that extends the model of opinion dynamics used by Abebe et al. [3], that extends the classic work of Friedkin and Johnsen [13,17]. Our model is iterative (i.e., discrete time), and initially starts with a directed network structure G of n agents with confirmation bias that have an initial opinion on a given topic. We also assume that arcs are weighted and normalized; the weight $W_{u \to v}$ corresponds to the social influence strength of u to v, namely how much v "listens" to u. In each iteration, the agents update their opinion by taking into account their initial opinion, and the opinions of their in-neighbors, and also adapt the *listening structure*. Originally, the listening structure is identical to the input network, but the agents due to their confirmation bias tend to strengthen connections towards neighbors that share the same type of opinion as theirs. We focus on unidimensional opinions, that are normalized in the range of $[-1, 1]$; it is known that despite their unidimensionality, they can capture opinions over a multidimensional set of issues due to the political "left-right" spectrum [9,16]. Our two main contributions are the following:

- We propose a Friedkin-Johnsen type model of opinion dynamics that incorporates confirmation bias (FJCB) to modify in each iteration the *listening structure* of each agent. We analyze the dynamics, by finding the equilibrium opinions and listening structure, and by proving the structural properties of the listening structure.
- We perform several experiments, both on synthetic and real datasets, and compare our method to other polarizing opinion dynamics models with respect to different measures. We show that our method yields listening structures with high polarization, and low opinion disagreement, resembling echo chambers.
- We show a novel application of our model in predicting the ideological community participation of Twitter users in the retweet network (i.e., the graph formed by retweets), using information from the follow network.

Notation. We use the terms agent and node interchangeably. For any agent u, we denote its opinion at time t as $x_u(t)$, and its initial opinion as s_u. A directed edge (v, u) means that node u *listens* to node v. The initial listening structure is the weighted graph $G(V, E, w)$ and the weights of the incoming edges (if there exist any) to any node u sum up to 1. The weight w of the edge (v, u) captures the influence of v on u. The in-neighborhood of a node u at time t is denoted as $N_u^-(t)$. While the weights of the edges may change, $N_u^-(t+1) \subseteq N_u^-(t)$, i.e., no edges are added but some may be deleted. Similarly, the listening structure at time t is $\mathcal{L}(t)$, and initially it is equal to G. The weight of an edge (v, u) at time t is denoted as $W_{v \to u}(t)$. To denote the equilibrium, we use $\star$ as a superscript.

2   Related Work

Opinion dynamics is the study of how agents interact with one another and reach (or perhaps not) consensus. It has been a topic of intense study by multiple disciplines. We discuss two important models that lie close to our work. DeGroot introduced a continuous opinion dynamics model [13]. The model is based on repeated averaging. Specifically an agent updates her opinion to the weighted average of her neighbors' and her own opinion from the previous time step. Friedkin and Johnsen [18] extended the DeGroot model by including in their model that each individual has certain innate beliefs. Other models allow each agent to have a different degree of "stubbornness", see [3]. The stubbornness of the agents is measured by a vector $\alpha \in [0,1]^V$, where value of α_i close to one means that agent i is more resistant towards keeping their own innate opinion. According to this model (**FJ**), the opinion $x_i(t+1)$ of node i at time $t+1$ is equal to

$$x_i(t+1) = \alpha_i s_i + (1 - \alpha_i)\frac{\sum\limits_{j \in N_i} w_{ij}x_j(t)}{deg(i)}. \tag{1}$$

Here, $deg(i) = \sum\limits_{j \in N_i} w_{ij}$ is the weighted degree of node i, and s_i be the innate belief of node i. Recently Auletta et al. [5] extended this model by evolving stubbornness and social relations, and proved such dynamics converges to a consensus with reasonable conditions. The interested reader may refer to the survey by Mossel and Tamuz and references therein for more related work on opinion dynamics [26].

Garimella et al. [20] proposed a pipeline that constructs Twitter network datasets with controversial topics from different domain. The pipeline first builds a conversation graph related to a topic, e.g. Twitter follow graph and retweet graph; Then it splits the graph into two partitions with a graph partitioning algorithm, e.g. METIS [23]; Finally the controversy of this topic is measuresd by how well two partitions are connected.

Polarization and Disagreement. We use the notions of polarization and disagreement as introduced by Musco, Musco, and Tsourakakis [27]. While these notions were introduced for the equilibrium point x^* of a convergent opinion dynamics model, the same notions are applicable to any vector of opinions x in a graph $G(V,E)$. Let $\bar{x}$ be the mean-centered vector, i.e., $\bar{x} = x - \frac{x^T 1}{n}\mathbf{1}$. The disagreement $d_{uv}(x)$ of edge (u,v) is defined as $d_{uv}(x) = w_{uv}(x_u - x_v)^2$, and the total disagreement $D_G(x)$ and polarization $P(x)$ that intuitively captures how agents' opinions deviate from the average opinion are defined respectively as

$$D_G(x) = \sum_{(u,v) \in E} d_{uv}(x), \quad \text{and} \quad P(x) = \bar{x}^T \bar{x}. \tag{2}$$

Polarization Models. In recent years, there has been an increased interest in developing polarization models. Dandekar et al. [12] propose the model Biased

Opinion Formation (**BOF**), and prove that under certain conditions it can explain why extreme polarization occurs. In their model, each agent at time $t + 1$ updates its opinion according to the following equation:

$$x_i(t+1) = \frac{W_{ii}x_i(t) + (x_i(t))^{b_i}s_i(t)}{w_{ii} + (x_i(t))^{b_i}s_i(t) + (1 - x_i(t))^{b_i}(d_i - s_i(t))}. \tag{3}$$

Here, $s_i(t) = \sum_{j \in N_i} w_{ij}x_j(t)$ is the weighted sum of the opinions of i's neighbors, d_i is i's weighted degree and $b_i \geq 0$ is a bias parameter.

Given d topics, Hazla et al. [21] model an agent's opinion $u \in \mathcal{R}^d$ as a vector that lies on a d dimensional Euclidean sphere. Any global intervention v affects the opinion vector of the agent proportional to $\langle u, v \rangle \cdot v$. They show that opinions polarize if there are one or more influencers sending interventions strategically, heuristically, or randomly. Gaitonde et al. [19] further generalize the study by proving the polarization of opinions exhibits with higher opinion dimension and network interactions. Vicario et al. [14] develop two variants of Bounded Confidence Model(BCM), i.e., a class of models where two agents interact only if they are connected and their opinions are close enough. Specifically, when the distance between opinions from two connected agents is larger than a pre-defined tolerance, with certain probability, their first model rewire such connection while the second model push agents' opinions further. Close to this is the ECHO model proposed by Sasahara et al. [29]. Derived from BCM, it simulates the phenomenon of biased assimilation on online social media. Specifically, each agent expresses its opinions by posting *messages*, and receiving information from neighbors through checking *messages* within a sized *screen*. Furthermore, at the end of each iteration, ECHO also rewire the connection between two agents if the distance between their opinions is larger than the tolerance, thus is able to create echo chambers.

3   Proposed Model

Our proposed model is iterative. At round/time 0, each node u holds its original value s_u. Each round consists of two steps during which agents update (i) their expressed opinion, and the (ii) the strength of their connections. For the former step we use a popular variation of the Friedkin-Johnsen model that incorporates stubbornness parameters $\{\alpha_i\}_{i \in V}$ [3]. Equation (4) describes how each node u updates its value from round $t - 1$ to t.

$$x_u(t) = \alpha_u s_u + (1 - \alpha_u) \sum_{v \in N_u^-(t-1)} W_{v \rightarrow u}(t-1)x_v(t-1) \quad \forall u \in V, t \in \mathbb{N} \tag{4}$$

Initially, $x_u(0) = s_u$ for all $u \in V$. Once the agents update their values, they update the strength of their *incoming* connections; an agent can only control how much influence other nodes exert on her, rather than how much influence she can exert on her neighbors. The next step of the proposed method encodes a well-known human bias, the *confirmation bias* (aka biased assimilation) that is the psychological tendency to value more evidence, regardless its validity, that reinforces already held beliefs [28]. We do this as follows: an agent i prefers to increase the (relative) strength of connection $j \to i$ according to the values of its endpoints and a positive parameter η that adjusts the changing scale:

$$W_{i \to j}(t) = \max(0, W_{i \to j}(t-1) + \eta x_i(t) x_j(t)) \qquad \forall (i,j) \in A(G(t-1)) \quad (5)$$

By convention, an arc of weight of zero does not exist, and we delete an arc if its weight become nonpositive. Observe that when $\eta = 0$, edge weight does not change at all. And the edges can quickly got enhanced/eliminated as we increase the value of η, thus reveal community information, or even reshape the graph structure. Once the weights are updated according to Eq. (5), each node updates the weights of its incoming edges according to the following equation:

$$W_{i \to j}(t) = \begin{cases} \frac{W_{i \to j}(t)}{\sum_{k \in N^-(j)} W_{k \to j}(t)} & \text{if } \sum_{k \in N^-(j)} x_k(t) W_{k \to j}(t) \neq 0 \quad \text{(\underline{Case I})} \\ W_{i \to j}(t-1) & \text{if } \sum_{k \in N^-(j)} x_k(t) W_{k \to j}(t) = 0 \quad \text{(\underline{Case II})} \end{cases}$$
$$(6)$$

In Case I, once we normalize according to Eq. (6), the weights of the incoming arcs sum up to one. If the incoming influence is equal to 0, we leave the weights as they were in the previous iteration. This completes one full iteration. The model proceeds to the next iteration, and continues until convergence or until the maximum number of iterations is reached. Under the assumption that an equilibrium point exists, we can find it. This is stated as the next theorem. Understanding the convergence of our dynamics is an interesting open question.

Theorem 1. *Suppose the dynamical system converges to an equilibrium point* (x^*, W^*). *At equilibrium, the opinion of any node* $u \in V(G)$ *satisfies:*

$$x_u^* = \begin{cases} \alpha_u s_u + (1 - \alpha_u) \frac{\sum_{k \to u} x_k^{*2}}{\sum_{k \to u} x_k^*} & \text{if } \sum_{k \in N_u^{-*}} x_k^* \neq 0, \sum_{k \in N_u^{-*}} W_{k \to u}^* x_k^* \neq 0, \\ \alpha_u s_u & N_u^{-*} = \{v : W_{v \to u}^* > 0\} = \emptyset \\ 0 & \text{otherwise} \end{cases}$$
$$(7)$$

Proof. We consider three cases, depending on the listening structure at equilibrium, and the social influence of the in-neighbors of a node.
<u>Case I:</u> Consider a node u at equilibrium whose local listening structure satisfies $\sum_{k \in N_u^{-*}} x_k^* \neq 0$ and $\sum_{k \in N_u^{-*}} W_{k \to u}^* x_k^* \neq 0$. By the definition of an equilibrium we obtain that the following equations are satisfied

$$x_u^* = \alpha_u s_u + (1 - \alpha_u) \sum_{k \to u} W_{k \to u}^* x_k^* \qquad (8)$$

$$W_{v \to u}^* = \frac{W_{v \to u}^* + \eta x_v^* x_u^*}{\sum_{k \to u} (W_{k \to u}^* + \eta x_k^* x_u^*)} = \frac{W_{v \to u}^* + \eta x_v^* x_u^*}{1 + \eta x_u^* \sum_{k \to u} x_k^*} \qquad (9)$$

Simplifying Eq. (9), yields that the edge weight at equilibrium satisfies

$$W_{v \to u}^* \eta x_u^* \sum_{k \to u} x_k^* = \eta x_u^* x_v^* \Rightarrow W_{v \to u}^* = \frac{x_v^*}{\sum_{k \to u} x_k^*}.$$

By substituting this value in Eq. (8), we obtain the following expression:

$$x_u^\star = \alpha_u s_u + (1 - \alpha_u) \sum_{k \to u} W_{k \to u}^\star x_k^\star = \alpha_u s_u + (1 - \alpha_u) \sum_{k \to u} \frac{x_k^\star}{\sum_{k \to u} x_k^\star} x_k^\star \to$$

$$x_u^\star = \alpha_u s_u + (1 - \alpha_u) \frac{\sum_{k \to u} (x_k^\star)^2}{\sum_{k \to u} x_k^\star}.$$

<u>Case II:</u> Suppose there exists a node u at equilibrium such that $\sum_{k \in N_u^-} W_{k \to u} x_k^\star = 0$. This can happen in two cases, depending on whether the node listens to some or none of the rest of the nodes.

<u>Case (a):</u> Node u is not listening to any node at equilibrium, i.e., $N_u^{-\star} = \emptyset$. In this case $x_u^\star = \alpha_u s_u$.

<u>Case (b):</u> Suppose $N_u^{-\star} \neq \emptyset$. Without loss of generality, we can partition the in-neighborhood in three sets $S_{pos}, S_{neutral}, S_{neg}$, depending on whether the nodes have positive, neutral, or negative opinion respectively. Clearly, $S_{pos}, S_{neg} \neq \emptyset$, and

$$\sum_{k \in S_{pos}} W_{k \to u}^\star x_k^\star + \sum_{k \in S_{neg}} W_{k \to u}^\star x_k^\star = 0.$$

Furthermore, node u at equilibrium has to be neutral, i.e., the term $x_u^\star = a_u \cdot s_u$ has to be equal to 0. If not, then $x_u^\star \neq 0$, and this contradicts the equilibrium property of the edge weights from S_{pos}, S_{neg} to u, i.e., $\exists k \in S_{pos}, k' \in S_{neg}$ such that $W_{k \to u}$ will increase, $W_{k \to u}$ will decrease (i.e., if $x_u^\star > 0$) or vice versa if $x_u^\star < 0$.

<u>Case III:</u> If $\sum_{k \in N_u^{-\star}} x_k^\star = 0$ and $\sum_{k \in N_u^-} W_{k \to u} x_k^\star \neq 0$, then with a similar reasoning, we obtain $x_u^\star = 0$. ∎

It is worth mentioning that in case II(b), one can also prove using contradiction that there exist no edges between S_{pos}, S_{neg}. In the following, we prove important structural properties of the equilibrium, that show that our model achieves a certain type of polarization, and exhibits an interesting structure depending on the setting of the various model parameters.

Lemma 1. *Let* $\mathcal{L}_{eq}$ *be the listening structure at equilibrium. Consider a non-neutral node* u *whose local listening structure* $N_u^{-\star}$ *satisfies* $\sum_{k \in N_u^{-\star}} x_k^\star \neq 0$ *and* $\sum_{k \in N_u^{-\star}} W_{k \to u}^\star x_k^\star \neq 0$. *Then, all the nodes* $v \in N_{eq}^-(u)$ *that node* u *listens to, share the same opinion, i.e., they have the same opinion sign.*

Fig. 1. At equilibrium $W_{u_i \to v}^\star = \frac{x_{u_i}^\star}{Z}, i = 1, 2$ where Z is a normalizing constant. Since the edge weights $W_{u_1 \to v}^\star, W_{u_2 \to v}^\star > 0$ are positive, we observe $sgn(x_{u_1}^\star) = sgn(x_{u_2}^\star) = sgn(Z)$. For details, see Lemma 1.

Proof. The statement trivially holds for any node with in-degree 0 or 1. Consider an arbitrary node node v with at least two in-coming neighbors; let $u_1, u_2 \in N^-(v)$ be two arbitrary such in-neighbors of v in $G^\star$ as shown in Fig. 1. At equilibrium the positive edge weights $W^\star_{u_1 \to v}, W^\star_{u_2 \to v}$ satisfy $W^\star_{u_i \to v} = \frac{x^\star_{u_i}}{Z}, i = 1, 2$ where Z is a normalizing constant, as shown in Case I of Theorem 1. Since the edge weights are positive, i.e., $W^\star_{u_1 \to v}, W^\star_{u_2 \to v} > 0$, we obtain $sgn(x^\star_{u_1}) = sgn(x^\star_{u_2}) = sgn(Z)$. Thus, at equilibrium $sgn(x^\star_u) = \sigma \in \{-1, +1\}, \forall u \in N^{-\star}_u$. ∎

From now on, if the in-neighbors of a node u have a negative (positive) opinion, we will refer to the in-neighborhood as negative (positive). Can a node u whose in-neighborhood is negative have a positive opinion $x^\star_u$ at equilibrium? The answer to this question is not immediately clear, even when one considers a "stubborn" node u with $\alpha_u = 1$ with a positive initial opinion s_u. While it is clear that node u will never change opinion, it is not (perhaps) clear why u will be connected to nodes of opposite opinion. Should not the edge weight $W_{v \to u}$ between $v \in N^-_u$ and u decrease gradually according to Eq. (5), and become zero eventually? The answer is no. To see why consider a graph with a single edge $v \to u$, i.e., node u has in-degree 1, and let $x_u > 0 > x_v$. If the edge weight $W_{v \to u}$ is not zeroed-out after the decrease by $\eta x_u x_v$ according to Eq. (5), then after the normalization step in Eq. (6) it remains 1. Notice that in our toy example, the edge weight does not become zero, when the parameter η satisfies $1 + \eta x_u x_v > 0$, or equivalently $\eta < \frac{1}{|x_u||x_v|}$.

The next lemma answers this question more generally. We consider one case for the sign of the in-neighborhood at equilibrium, the other case is symmetric and treated in a similar way. The following lemma is proved in Appendix.

Lemma 2. *Consider a node u with a negative in-neighborhood $N^{-\star}_u$. Then, the opinion of node u at equilibrium can be positive when conditions (i)-(v) hold:*

$$(i) \quad s_u > 0 \qquad and \qquad (ii) \; \frac{s_u}{\sum_{v \in N^{-\star}_u} W^\star_{v \to u} |x^\star_v|} > \frac{1 - \alpha_u}{\alpha_u}$$

$$and \; (iii) \; W^\star_{v \to u} = \frac{1}{|N^{-\star}_u|} \quad \forall v \in N^{-\star}_u$$

$$and \; (iv) \; x^\star_v = c \qquad and \qquad (v) \; \eta < \frac{1}{|N^{-\star}_u| \|x^\star_u\| |x^\star_v|}$$

To summarize our results, the typical case of a node u at equilibrium is to be listening to nodes with the same opinion, unless a set of complicated conditions hold. Furthermore, neutral nodes (as shown in Case II b) can be listening to both negative, and positive opinions. Our experimental results show that almost always on real data, or on data with random opinions, we obtain polarized echo-chambers, unless we create artifacts as described, e.g., in Lemma 2.

4 Experiments

4.1 Experimental Setup

Real-world Datasets. We use five publicly available Twitter datasets [11,20] to evaluate our model. The datasets are summarized in Table 1. Each dataset focuses on a single controversial topic. A *follow* graph and a *retweet* graph are collected based on hashtags related to the topic, and they are converted into undirected graphs, for details see [11,20]. Both graphs are partitioned into two communities using METIS [23], that can thought of as echo chambers with users with diametric opinions (i.e., positive vs negative). For any Twitter user u, given its neighborhood N_u and the community C_u it belongs to, we assign u's *ideological community participation* (or polarity in short) as $sgn(C_u)\frac{|N_u \cap C_u|}{|N_u|}$. We say that a user u is *persistent* if its polarity in the follow layer is equal to its polarity in the retweet layer.

Table 1. Description of Twitter follow and retweet graphs induced by topic hashtags.

Topic	# follows	# retweets	# common nodes	# *persistent* nodes
Russia march [20]	16 471	2 951	482	302
Debate [20]	344 088	44 174	5 015	580
Beefban [20]	6 026	1 978	284	120
Baltimore [20]	28 291	4 505	356	61
Vaxnovax [11]	1 806 164	68 543	17 650	2 753

Competitors. We compare our model to three polarizing opinion dynamics models, the FJ model [18], the ECHO model [29][1], and the BOF model [12]. For ECHO, the numerous parameters of the model (see [29]) are set to the default values, unless specified otherwise.

Machine. All experiments run on a laptop with 3.10 GHz Intel Core i5-7267U CPU and 8 GB of main memory. The code is written in Python 3 and will become publicly available upon publication.

4.2   Synthetic Experiments

Evaluation. In order to understand the emergence of polarized communities we use the stochastic block-model [2]. We construct two equal-sized communities with 100 nodes per each. The probability of an edge between two nodes from the same (different) community (communities) is 0.2(0.05). Metrics including polarization, disagreement (see Eq. (2)), conductance of the nodes with positive opinions, and kurtosis of opinions are reported to show how echo chambers are created by our model. Specifically, given a node subset S, we can convert the graph to undirected and calculate its conductance. Kurtosis is a unitless measure of a distribution's shape, and becomes a smaller value when the distribution has a lower tendency for producing extreme values. Formally, given any distribution D with mean μ, variance σ and random variable $X \sim D$, its kurtosis is defined as $Kurt = E[(\frac{X-\mu}{\sigma})^4]$. A completely bimodal distribution is reflected by a kurtosis value of -2.

---

[1] https://github.com/soramame0518/echo_chamber_model.

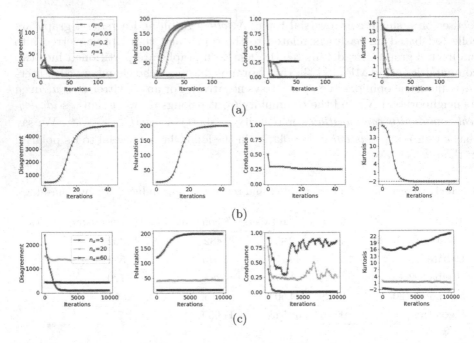

Fig. 2. Disagreement, polarization, conductance, and kurtosis per iteration for models on stochastic block model graphs with $p = 0.2$ and $q = 0.05$ (a): FJCB with different η, note with $\eta = 0$ it becomes FJ, (b): BOF, (c): ECHO with different number of initial stubborn nodes n_α.

Initially, we randomly pick n_α *stubborn nodes* from each community and set their opinions to $+1$ and -1 respectively, and their stubbornness parameter is set to be 1. For FJCB and BOF $n_\alpha = 5$, and for ECHO n_α is ranged between 5, 20 and 60. The initial opinions of the rest of the nodes are set to 0, and their stubbornness parameter to 0.001. Figures 2(a), (b) and (c) plot the four metrics versus the iteration for FJCB, BOF, and ECHO respectively. Note when we set $\eta = 0$, FJCB becomes FJ. Recall the listening structures are directed, but in the case of conductance we consider it to be undirected. For ECHO, we set its confidence distance $\epsilon = 1.01$ in order for the model to work, i.e., opinions can start propagating in the beginning. Some observations follow:

- All methods except FJ can return equally polarized opinions at equilibrium, reaching a value of 200. ECHO requires a large number of stubborn nodes for this to happen (i.e., $n_\alpha = 60$), in contrast to FJCB and BOF. The kurtosis becomes -2, reflecting a completely bimodal distribution.
- FJCB converges after at most 120 iterations, for all η values. With non-zero η values, it disconnects the graph into two components whose nodes have different signs of opinions. This happens, within the first 20 iterations, as the conductance drops to 0, even for small values of η. In all our experiments FJCB reaches an equilibrium. FJ, i.e. FJCB with $\eta = 0$, shows limited

polarization ability as the changes of its metrics are insignificant compared to other methods.

- FJCB shows the emergence of two polarized niches, with high polarization and low disagreement. BOF (by design) does not alter the listening structure of the network, and therefore disagreement remains high. Our model clearly contrasts the initial graph topology, to the final listening structure that is polarized, and is consistent with the creation of echo chambers [1].
- Interestingly, in Fig. 2(a) we observe a rise of disagreement before the final drop. This happens because initially the majority of the nodes are neutral. As their opinions start changing, an increasing number of neighbors produce non-zero disagreement terms, which results in the increase of disagreement. As the method starts converging to echo-chambers, disagreement starts decreasing.
- ECHO does not perform well with respect to creating echo-chambers when there is a small number of stubborn nodes, resulting in an unpredictable performance, as indicated by the fluctuation in the conductance.

Study the Effect of η. We also study the effect of parameter η. Figure 2(a) shows the changes we observe with different η values. Empirically we find larger η leads to faster convergence as FJCB can break connections between agents with opposite opinions with fewer iterations. When η becomes 0, the model becomes to FJ with static network structure and loses the ability to simulate extreme polarization.

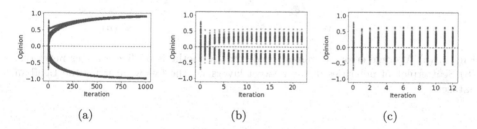

(a)   (b)   (c)

Fig. 3. Scatter plot of agent opinions over time according to the FJCB model with different choice of α values, and initial opinions sampled from $\mathcal{N}(0, 0.3)$. For any non-stubborn agent u, its stubbornness parameter is set to (a) $\alpha_u = 0.001$. (b) α_u sampled from the half-normal distribution, and then normalized to be in the range of $(0, 1)$. (c) α_u sampled uniformly at random from $(0, 1)$.

Effect of α Values. What is the effect of the stubbornness parameters $\{\alpha_u\}_{u \in V}$ on the final opinions? Our results are shown in Fig. 3.

We use again the stochastic block model with $n_\alpha = 1$. Additionally, we sample for every non-stubborn node an initial opinion from the normal distribution $N(\mu = 0, \sigma^2 = 0.3^2)$, and adjust the signs according to the block structure, i.e., nodes within the same block have the same opinion, but opposite across blocks.

We then assign stubbornness parameters to the non-stubborn nodes in different ways, and plot the polarity vs. the iteration. For Fig. 3(a) we set all stubbornness parameters to be 0.001. We see that at equilibrium the non-stubborn nodes have converged to the sign of the stubborn node from their own block. For Fig. 3(b), the stubbornness parameters are sampled from the half-normal distribution, and then normalized to be in the range of $(0, 1)$. We observe that due to the presence of fairly stubborn nodes, they do not converge to ± 1 as in Fig. 3(a), but still the resulting distribution is bimodal, and polarized. Finally, for Fig. 3(c) we sample the stubbornness parameters from the uniform distribution in $(0, 1)$. We observe the same behavior as in (b), with less polarization due to the presence of more stubborn nodes.

4.3   Predicting Echo Chamber Participation

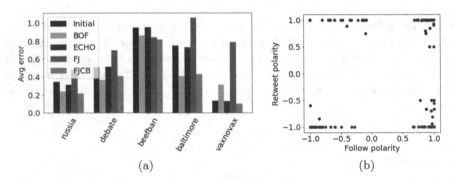

(a)   (b)

Fig. 4. (a) Average error of opinion predicted by methods on five Twitter networks. (b) Scatterplot of polarities of the retweet layers vs. the follow layer for the Beefban dataset.

Polarized Niches Across Twitter Layers. In this application, we are interested in understanding how the communities in the *follow* layer of Twitter can predict the structure of echo-chambers in the *retweet* layer. As mentioned in Sect. 4.1, for any node u we define its polarity in a given Twitter layer as $sgn(C_u)\frac{|\{N_u \cap C_u\}|}{|N_u|}$. Notice that the sign function preserves the polarity of the node with respect to its community C_u, whereas the second term $\frac{|\{N_u \cap C_u\}|}{|N_u|}$ measures the cohesiveness of the node within its community; in the extreme case where $N_u \subseteq C_u$ the cohesiveness is equal to 1. We show here that we can accurately predict the polarities in the *retweet* layer for the non-persistent users, if we have the *follow* graph and all persistent users. As a baseline, we use the method *Initial* that naively predicts the polarity of a node in the *retweet* layer to be equal to the polarity in the *follow* layer.

On all Twitter datasets, we apply FJCB, FJ, BOF, ECHO. We run these models as follows: we consider the polarities in the *follow* layer as the initial opinions of the agents, and we use the opinions at equilibrium as our predictor for the non-persistent nodes. The follow graph is used as the initial *listening structure*. In both FJCB, FJ and BOF, the stubbornness parameters for persistent users are set to 1, and 0.001 for the rest. We also fix the opinions of persistent users in ECHO throughout the iterations. In Fig. 4, we report the average error in the ℓ_1 norm, i.e., the average difference between the predicted opinions and the *retweet* polarities of all users. We observe FJCB has comparable performance to BOF, and both models outperform the *Initial* baseline, but not always. The performance of ECHO is close to *Initial*. FJ has the worst performance over four dataset as it tends to give highly biased predictions, see Fig. 5 in Appendix for an example. FJCB is capable of predicting the *retweet* polarities on vaxnovax dataset with less than 0.1 average error. By further investigation, we find the retweet network of this topic is composed of two almost disconnected communities, making its polarities highly concentrated to 1 and -1. All methods cannot accurately predict the *retweet* polarities on Beefban dataset, as the partitions of its follow and retweet graphs are pretty much orthogonal. In Fig. 4(b), we see blocks of users on all four corners, since a large number of users belong to different communities on two layers.

Interpretation. Given a topic, why models of opinion dynamics can predict the structure of the *retweet* layer with the *follow* layer? In general, *follow* is a long-term connection that can exist due to various reasons, including friendship or interest of an agent in *any* posted content by the other agent. Such a relationship describes a user's community belonging and stance comprehensively from a high level. On the other hand, retweets without quote usually indicate endorsement [20]. In our Twitter datasets, the retweet connections can be considered as users' agreements with respect to a specific topic. Therefore, it is reasonable to regard users' *follow* polarities as their initial opinions, and the *retweet* polarities as their final opinions after all the propagation of information.

5   Conclusion

In this work, we propose FJCB, a Friedkin-Johnsen (FJ) opinion dynamics model that in addition to the classic FJ model incorporates confirmation bias. The model iteratively updates both the opinions of the agents and the listening structure, i.e., to whom each agent listens. We analyze the dynamics, and show that at equilibrium the listening structure is in principle polarized, but it also exhibits interesting structure due to the existence of neutral nodes. We evaluate our model both on synthetic and real data, showing the effect of the various parameters, and its applicability to predicting the echo chamber community participation. An interesting open direction is to prove the convergence of our dynamics, and explore more properties of the equilibrium.

A   Appendix

A.1   Proof of Lemma 2

Proof. Consider the opinion $x_u^\star$ of node u at equilibrium with a negative in-neighborhood, it has to satisfy Eq. (4), i.e.,

$$x_u^\star = \alpha_u s_u + (1 - \alpha_u) \sum_{v \to u} W_{v \to u}^\star x_v^\star.$$

When $x_u^\star > 0$, it is necessary that $s_u > 0$, otherwise $x_u^\star < 0$ since the second term in the summation is negative. By rearranging the inequality $\alpha_u s_u + (1 - \alpha_u) \sum_{v \to u} W_{v \to u}^\star x_v^\star > 0$ we obtain $\frac{s_u}{\sum_{v \to u} W_{v \to u} |x_v^\star|} > \frac{1 - \alpha_u}{\alpha_u}$. Further-more, $W_{v \to u} = \frac{1}{|N_u^{-\star}|}$ for all in-neighbors $v \in N_u^{-\star}$. To see why, for the sake of contradiction, assume without loss of generality[2] that there exists an arc $v \to u$ such that $W_{v \to u}^\star < \frac{1}{|N_u^{-\star}|}$. Observe that each arc weight is updated in every iter-ation according to Eqs. (5) and (6). It is straight-forward to check that in that case $W_{v \to u}^\star$ will decrease in an iteration, contradicting its equilibrium property. Furthermore, in order for all the incoming arcs to u have the same weight, the update term $\eta x_v^\star x_u^\star$ must be equal for all $v \in N_u^{-\star}$, and it must not zero-out the weight. These two facts imply that $x_v^\star = x$ for some value x for all $v \in N_u^{-\star}$, and $\frac{1}{|N_u^{-\star}|} - \eta x_v^\star x_u > 0$ which implies the last condition.   ∎

A.2   Example of Section 4.3

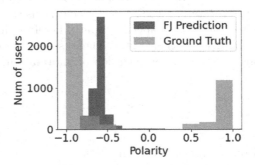

Fig. 5. Histogram of user retweet polarity ground truth and the prediction by FJ model on debate dataset.

---

[2] The sum of the arcs is 1, so if they are not all equal there exists an arc less than the average $\frac{1}{|N_u^{-\star}|}$.

References

1. Concept of echo chamber. https://en.wikipedia.org/wiki/Echo_chamber_(media)
2. Abbe, E., Bandeira, A.S., Hall, G.: Exact recovery in the stochastic block model. IEEE Trans. Inf. Theory **62**(1), 471–487 (2015)
3. Abebe, R., Kleinberg, J., Parkes, D., Tsourakakis, C.E.: Opinion dynamics with varying susceptibility to persuasion. In: Proceedings of the 24th ACM SIGKDD International Conference on Knowledge Discovery & Data Mining, pp. 1089–1098 (2018)
4. Allcott, H., Gentzkow, M.: Social media and fake news in the 2016 election. J. Econom. Perspect. **31**(2), 211–36 (2017)
5. Auletta, V., Fanelli, A., Ferraioli, D.: Consensus in opinion formation processes in fully evolving environments. In: Proceedings of the AAAI Conference on Artificial Intelligence, vol. 33(01), pp. 6022–6029 (2019)
6. Baumann, F., Lorenz-Spreen, P., Sokolov, I.M., Starnini, M.: Modeling echo chambers and polarization dynamics in social networks. Phys. Rev. Lett. **124**(4), 048301 (2020)
7. Bessi, A., et al.: Viral misinformation: the role of homophily and polarization. In: Proceedings of the 24th International Conference on World Wide Web, pp. 355–356 (2015)
8. Boxell, L., Gentzkow, M., Shapiro, J.M.: Cross-country trends in affective polarization. Technical report, National Bureau of Economic Research (2020)
9. Brandts, J., Giritligil, A.E., Weber, R.A.: An experimental study of persuasion bias and social influence in networks. Eur. Econ. Rev. **80**, 214–229 (2015)
10. Cinelli, M., De Francisci Morales, G., Galeazzi, A., Quattrociocchi, W., Starnini, M.: The echo chamber effect on social media. In: Proceedings of the National Academy of Sciences, vol. 118(9), p. e2023301118 (2021)
11. Cossard, A., De Francisci Morales, G., Kalimeri, K., Mejova, Y., Paolotti, D., Starnini, M.: Falling into the echo chamber: the Italian vaccination debate on twitter. In: Proceedings of the International AAAI Conference on Web and Social Media, vol. 14(1), pp. 130–140, May 2020
12. Dandekar, P., Goel, A., Lee, D.T.: Biased assimilation, homophily, and the dynamics of polarization. Proc. Natl. Acad. Sci. **110**(15), 5791–5796 (2013)
13. DeGroot, M.H.: Reaching a consensus. J. Am. Stat. Assoc. **69**(345), 118–121 (1974)
14. Del Vicario, M., Scala, A., Caldarelli, G., Stanley, H., Quattrociocchi, W.: Modeling confirmation bias and polarization. Sci. Rep. **7**, 06 (2016)
15. Del Vicario, M., Scala, A., Caldarelli, G., Stanley, H.E., Quattrociocchi, W.: Modeling confirmation bias and polarization. Sci. Rep. **7**(1), 1–9 (2017)
16. DeMarzo, P.M., Vayanos, D., Zwiebel, J.: Persuasion bias, social influence, and unidimensional opinions. Q. J. Econ. **118**(3), 909–968 (2003)
17. Friedkin, N.E., Johnsen, E.C.: Social influence and opinions. J. Math. Sociol. **15**(3–4), 193–206 (1990)
18. Friedkin, N.E., Johnsen, E.C.: Social positions in influence networks. Soc. Netw. **19**(3), 209–222 (1997)
19. Gaitonde, J., Kleinberg, J., Tardos, É.: Polarization in geometric opinion dynamics. In: Proceedings of the 22nd ACM Conference on Economics and Computation, pp. 499–519 (2021)
20. Garimella, K., Morales, G.D.F., Gionis, A., Mathioudakis, M.: Quantifying controversy on social media. Trans. Soc. Comput. **1**(1), 1–27 (2018)

21. Hazla, J., Jin, Y., Mossel, E., Ramnarayan, G.: A geometric model of opinion polarization. CoRR, abs/1910.05274 (2019)
22. Hk, J., Jin, Y., Mossel, E., Ramnarayan, G., et al.: A geometric model of opinion polarization. Technical report (2021)
23. Karypis, G., Kumar, V.: A fast and high quality multilevel scheme for partitioning irregular graphs. SIAM J. Sci. Comput. **20**, 01 (1999)
24. E. Klein. Why we're polarized. Simon and Schuster, 2020
25. Lord, C.G., Ross, L., Lepper, M.R.: Biased assimilation and attitude polarization: The effects of prior theories on subsequently considered evidence. J. Pers. Soc. Psychol. **37**(11), 2098 (1979)
26. Mossel, E., Tamuz, O., et al.: Opinion exchange dynamics. Probab. Surv. **14**, 155–204 (2017)
27. Musco, C., Musco, C., Tsourakakis, C.E.: Minimizing polarization and disagreement in social networks. In: Proceedings of the 2018 World Wide Web Conference, pp. 369–378 (2018)
28. Nickerson, R.S.: Confirmation bias: a ubiquitous phenomenon in many guises. Rev. Gen. Psychol. **2**(2), 175–220 (1998)
29. Sasahara, K., Chen, W., Peng, H., Ciampaglia, G., Flammini, A., Menczer, F.: Social influence and unfollowing accelerate the emergence of echo chambers. J. Comput. Soc. Sci. **4**, 1–22 (2021)

Harnessing Unsupervised Word Translation to Address Resource Inequality for Peace and Health

Ashiqur R. KhudaBukhsh[1]([✉]) [iD], Shriphani Palakodety[2] [iD],
and Tom M. Mitchell[3] [iD]

[1] Rochester Institute of Technology, Rochester, NY 14623, USA
axkvse@rit.edu
[2] Onai, San Jose, CA 95123, USA
spalakod@onai.com
[3] Carnegie Mellon University, Pittsburgh, PA 15213, USA
tom.mitchell@cs.cmu.edu

Abstract. Research geared toward human well-being in developing nations often concentrates on web content written in a world language (e.g., English) and ignores a significant chunk of content written in a poorly resourced yet highly prevalent first language of the region in concern (e.g., Hindi). Such omissions are common due to the sheer mismatch between linguistic resources offered in a world language and its low-resource counterpart. However, during a global pandemic or an imminent war, demand for linguistic resources might get recalibrated. In this work, we focus on the high-resource and low-resource language pair $\langle en, hi_e \rangle$ (English, and Romanized Hindi) and present a cross-lingual sampling method that takes example documents in English, and retrieves similar content written in Romanized Hindi, the most popular form of Hindi observed in social media. At the core of our technique is a novel finding that a surprisingly simple constrained nearest-neighbor sampling in polyglot Skip-gram word embedding space can retrieve substantial bilingual lexicons, even from harsh social media data sets. Our cross-lingual sampling method obtains substantial performance improvement in the important domains of detecting peace-seeking, hostility-diffusing *hope speech* in the context of the 2019 India-Pakistan conflict, and in detecting comments encouraging compliance with COVID-19 guidelines.

Keywords: Unsupervised word translation · Low-resource languages · *Hope speech* detection

1 Introduction

Research geared toward human well-being and sustainability challenges in developing nations such as India often focus on content produced in English [11, 22, 30, 33]. Such omissions are common due to the stark contrast between linguistic

---

A.R. KhudaBukhsh and S. Palakodety—Equal contribution first authors.

F. Hopfgartner et al. (Eds.): SocInfo 2022, LNCS 13618, pp. 159–180, 2022.
https://doi.org/10.1007/978-3-031-19097-1_10

resources available in a world language such as English (denoted by *en*) and resources available for a highly prevalent yet poorly resourced language such as Romanized Hindi (Hindi expressed using Roman script; denoted by hi_e).

With a combined language base of more than 500 million speakers of Hindi in India and Pakistan, and a considerable fraction using hi_e on the web [8], extending linguistic resources to hi_e has compelling benefits. To this end, recent work focused on *extending linguistic resources in English to its low-resource counterpart for applications critical for peace and human well-being* [11]. Two important tasks were considered: (1) detecting peace-seeking, hostility-diffusing *hope speech* by [22] in the context of heated political discussions between nuclear adversaries; and (2) detecting user-generated web-content encouraging COVID-19 health guidelines compliance. On these two tasks, the previously proposed cross-lingual sampling method demonstrated considerable efficacy in detecting content in hi_e [11].

In prior art, [11] accomplished cross-lingual sampling through code switching - a linguistic phenomenon commonly encountered in multilingual societies. Code switching is the seamless alteration between multiple languages within the same document boundary [9]. In this work, we show that while code switching can present an interesting path to exploit semantic parallelism, unsupervised single word translations can form the basis of substantially superior cross-lingual sampling methods.

Our methodological contributions are two-fold:

1. We first present a surprisingly simple constrained nearest neighbor sampling technique in the polyglot word embedding space that performs unsupervised single word translation, aka bilingual lexicon induction, in harsh $en\text{-}hi_e$ social media data.
2. We leverage this single world translation technique to further develop an unsupervised cross-lingual sampling method that obtains substantial improvement over the state of the art [11] on the aforementioned two tasks. Our contributions have high societal impact given the geopolitical history and severity of COVID-19 in the area.

To summarize, our contributions are the following:

• **Methods:** We introduce (1) a novel single word translation method and (2) leverage it to construct a new cross-lingual sampling algorithm.

• **Resource:** We release the resulting lexicon of 1,100 word pairs from our single word translation method[1].

• **Embedding space:** We demonstrate that the polyglot word embedding space captures a rich semantic representation of words such that a constrained nearest neighbor sampling can perform unsupervised word translation. We investigate this novel observation and possible causes.

• **Human well-being:** Finally, our main contribution is an end-to-end unsupervised system to perform cross-lingual sampling for two critical humanitarian domains: peace-mediation between nuclear adversaries, and compliance to

---

[1] Resources and additional details are available at: https://www.cs.cmu.edu/~akhudabu/SocInfo2022.html.

COVID-19 health guidelines. On these two tasks, we outperform the state of the art by 45% and 174%, respectively.

2   Problem Definition, Background

2.1   Low-Resource Language

A low-resource or under-resourced language is defined as a language that lacks computational resources such as large corpora (monolingual or parallel) and annotated resources typically needed for NLP methods (e.g., parsers, Named Entity Recognition taggers etc.) [5]. Examples of low-resource language include Romanized Hindi, or Bengali.

2.2   Domains

We consider the following two humanitarian domains.
• *Hope speech*: Introduced in [22] in the context of heated political discussions between two nuclear adversaries at the brink of a full-fledged war, this work advocates the importance of detecting hostility-diffusing, peace-seeking *hope speech*. India and Pakistan have a long history of conflicts with four major wars and many skirmishes; a recent study reported a grim forecast of 100 million deaths should there be a full-fledged war between these two nuclear powers [32]. In [22], *hope speech* is defined as content that contains a unifying message focusing on war's futility, the importance of peace, and the human and economic costs involved, or expresses criticism of either the author's own nation's entities or policies, or the actions or entities of the two involved countries (for a precise definition, see [22]). This work is a part of the recent trend of *counter speech* research [2,3,16,24,28,34].
• **COVID-19 health guidelines compliance:** Introduced in [11], this task detects comments exhibiting compliance to the following five CDC-recommended guidelines:[2] (1) maintaining social distancing; (2) avoiding public gatherings; (3) staying home when sick; (4) covering coughs and sneezes; and (5) washing hands regularly.

2.3   Cross-lingual Sampling

Introduced in [11], the cross lingual sampling task retrieves documents in a target language semantically similar to documents in the source language. For instance, given *hope speech* comments or comments encouraging COVID-19 guideline compliance in *en*, we return semantically similar comments authored in hi_e. The two tasks considered are highly challenging given that a random sampling would yield 1.8% *hope speech* and 2.88% comments encouraging COVID-19 guideline compliance [11].

---

[2] https://www.cdc.gov/coronavirus/2019-ncov/prevent-getting-sick/prevention.html.

3   Data

We use three Indian social media data sets:

- $\mathcal{D}^{hope}$ consists of 2.04 million comments posted by 791,289 users on 2,890 YouTube videos relevant to the 2019 India-Pakistan conflict [22]. The en and hi_e subsets denoted as $\mathcal{D}^{hope}_{en}$ and $\mathcal{D}^{hope}_{hi_e}$, consist of 921,235 and 1,033,908 comments respectively.
- $\mathcal{D}^{election}$ consists of 6.18 million comments on 130,067 videos by 1,518,077 users posted in a 100 day period leading up to the 2019 Indian General Election [23].
- $\mathcal{D}^{covid}$ consists of 3,144,988 comments on 44,888 videos from fourteen Indian news outlets (see, Appendix for details) posted between 30th January, 2020 and 10th April, 2020 [11]. The en and hi_e subsets denoted as $\mathcal{D}^{covid}_{en}$ and $\mathcal{D}^{covid}_{hi_e}$, consist of 771,035 and 1,720,703 comments respectively.

Data Set Challenges: Typical to most noisy, short social media texts generated in linguistically diverse regions, the data sets we consider exhibit a considerable presence of code switching, and grammar and spelling disfluencies [29]. Furthermore, due to a strong presence of content contributors who do not speak English as their first language, varying levels of English proficiency in the corpus with a substantial incidence of phonetic spelling errors were reported. For example, 32% of times, the word `liar` was misspelled as `lier`, or consider the following example comment from $\mathcal{D}^{hope}$ – [pak pm godblashu my ind pailat thanksh you cantri] that possibly intended to express *Pak PM God bless you; my Ind pilot, thank you country*. Second, since hi_e does not have any standard spelling rules [8] (e.g., the word nuksaan meaning damage is spelled in the corpus as nuksaan, nuqsaan and nuksan), a high level of spelling variations added to the challenges. Finally, we observe that unfamiliar words induce extremely challenging spelling variations such has korona bairesh (possibly intended to express *corona virus*) and seni tiger (possibly intended to express *sanitizer*).

4   Related Work

Bilingual lexicon induction aka single word translation has a rich line of prior literature (e.g., [7,13,18,31,35]). Modern methods leverage several advances in word-embeddings [1,4,13,17,25]. While this list is far from exhaustive, several of these focus on alleviating resource requirements like seed lexicon [1], or parallel data [13].

Our work contrasts with the literature in the following key ways. Unlike previous work, we embrace the challenge of learning bilingual lexicons from harsh, social media data. Our method ***does not require clean, monolingual corpora***; we learn a single Skip-gram embedding on the full bilingual corpus and retrieve the lexicon using only constrained nearest neighbor sampling ***without any explicit attempt to align***. Our unsupervised method is particularly well-suited for noisy language expression typical of informal social media settings (e.g., hi_e) where procuring clean, monolingual (let alone parallel) data could be difficult. Recent works in unsupervised machine translation [13,14] utilize monolingual language models and alignment steps to perform translation. Our work discards the individual monolingual models and the alignment steps, and instead, uses just a single polyglot Skip-gram model and a mining step. To the best of our knowledge, no other current method can perform single word translation without monolingual corpora. In addition, our motivations are not purely performance-driven – this paper explores the extent of multilingual information embedded in polyglot Skip-gram models. While polyglot word-embeddings and polyglot training in particular have received attention recently for demonstrating performance improvements across a variety of NLP tasks [11, 19–22], to the best of our knowledge, no previous work has explored their effectiveness in performing unsupervised word translation.

Our work is related to [11] in our shared motivation to perform cross-lingual sampling for two important domains of human well-being and differs in the technique in that we remove the explicit dependence on code switching, directly obtain a word-translation from the corpus, and improve upon the performance by up to 174% on the aforementioned tasks.

5   Method

5.1   Unsupervised Word Translation

Skip-Gram: The Skip-gram objective predicts an input word's context [17]. Nearest neighbor sampling in the resulting embedding space yields (syntactically or semantically) similar words; subtle semantic relationships like word-associations (e.g., $big:bigger::quick:quicker$ or $France:Paris::Italy:Rome$) are also revealed. Prior research reported that *two separate* Skip-gram models trained on two distinct monolingual corpora exhibit isomorphism [18] which forms the basis of supervised lexicon induction.

Polyglot Training: In this scheme, a single Skip-gram model is trained on a multi-lingual corpus. Naive nearest neighbor sampling in a polyglot embedding space shows identical behavior as observed in embeddings trained on monolingual corpora. For example, Fig. 1 shows that sampling a word's nearest neighbors in a polyglot embedding space trained on a bilingual corpus yields semantically similar words, misspellings, and spelling variations, all in the same language of the probe word.

We now introduce a surprisingly simple constrained nearest neighbor sampling method that allows us to perform unsupervised word translation that requires: (1) no seed lexicon; (2) no parallel data; (3) no explicit alignment; and even (4) *no monolingual corpora*. Our nearest neighbor sampling technique has a simple constraint: the nearest neighbor search has to be restricted to words in the corpus written in the *target language* (e.g., for translation direction $en \rightarrow hi_e$ the source language is en and the target language is hi_e).

When we perform nearest neighbor sampling with this additional constraint, surprisingly, we find that the nearest neighbor of *religion* is *mazhab*! Our method

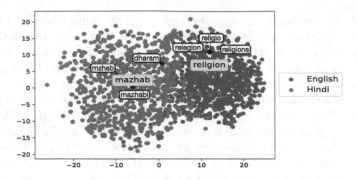

Fig. 1. A t-SNE [15] 2D visualization of Skip-gram polyglot embeddings trained on (a) a data set of 2.04 million YouTube comments relevant to the 2019 India-Pakistan conflict [22] . Three nearest neighbors (using cosine distance) of the Hindi word *mazhab* "religion" and the English word *religion* are highlighted. These results indicate that naive nearest neighbor sampling of a word yields other words with similar meaning in the same language.

involves no monolingual corpora and no explicit attempt to align multiple embedding spaces; a single Skip-gram model is trained on a bilingual corpus and word translation is performed using this simple constrained nearest neighbor sampling.

Formally, in a bilingual corpus $\mathcal{D}$ of two languages $\mathcal{L}_{source}$ and $\mathcal{L}_{target}$, let $\mathcal{V}_{source}$ and $\mathcal{V}_{target}$ denote the vocabularies of the two languages, respectively. The translation scheme $\mathcal{L}_{source} \rightarrow \mathcal{L}_{target}$ takes a word $w_{source} \in \mathcal{V}_{source}$ as input and outputs a single word translation, w_{target}, such that $w_{target} \in \mathcal{V}_{target}$ and $\forall w \in \mathcal{V}_{target}, dist(w_{source}, w) \geq dist(w_{source}, w_{target})$. Following [17], we take cosine distance as our distance metric ($dist(.)$). Since we are operating on a single multilingual, noisy, social media corpus and hi_e does not have any standard spelling rules (e.g., the word *amaan* meaning peace in Hindi can be spelled as *aman* or *amun*), we need to construct $\mathcal{V}_{source}$ and $\mathcal{V}_{target}$ from the data itself. For this, we use an off-the-shelf, unsupervised algorithm from [11].

5.2   Cross-lingual Sampling

Introduced in [11], the cross lingual sampling task retrieves documents in a target language semantically similar to documents in the source language. For instance, given *hope speech* comments or comments encouraging COVID-19 guideline compliance in *en*, we return semantically similar comments authored in hi_e.

Our proposed method first utilizes the unsupervised word translation scheme introduced in Sect. 5.1 to obtain a document embedding of the source document S_{source} in the target language, $\mathcal{L}_{target}$ using `translateEmbedding` (Algorithm 1). Essentially, a noisy single word translation to $\mathcal{L}_{target}$ for each word in S_{source} is obtained, and the word embeddings of this translated document are averaged to obtain a document embedding in $\mathcal{L}_{target}$. Next, we conduct nearest neighbor sampling in the $\mathcal{L}_{target}$ document embedding space returning documents authored

---

Algorithm 1: `translateEmbedding`($\mathcal{S}_{source}$)

Input: A document $\mathcal{S}_{source}$ denoted by $[w_1,\ldots,w_k]$
Output: A document embedding of $\mathcal{S}_{source}$ translated into $\mathcal{L}_{target}$
Dependency: $topTranslations(w_i, N)^{\mathcal{L}_{target}}$ returns N nearest neighbors of $embedding(w_i)$
from $\mathcal{V}_{target}$ using the method described in Sect. 5.1
Initialization: $\mathcal{E} \leftarrow \{\}$
Main loop:
foreach word $w_i \in \mathcal{S}_{source}$ **do**
    if $\mathcal{L}(w_i) = \mathcal{L}_{target}$ **then**
        $\mathcal{E} \leftarrow \mathcal{E} \cup \{embedding(w_i)\}$
    else
        $\mathcal{T} \leftarrow topTranslations(w_i, N)^{\mathcal{L}_{target}}$
        $\mathcal{C} \leftarrow \{\}$
        foreach word $w_t \in \mathcal{T}$ **do**
            if $w_i \in topTranslations(w_t, N)^{\mathcal{L}_{source}}$ **then**
                $\mathcal{C} \leftarrow \mathcal{C} \cup \{w_t\}$
            end
        end
        if $\mathcal{C} \neq \{\}$ **then**
            randomly select w from $\mathcal{C}$
            $\mathcal{E} \leftarrow \mathcal{E} \cup \{embedding(w)\}$
        end
    end
end
Output: Average of $\mathcal{E}$

---

in $\mathcal{L}_{target}$ that are semantically similar to $\mathcal{S}_{source}$ using `NN-Sample` (Algorithm 2; introduced in [11]). The complete pipeline is illustrated in the Appendix.

Our `translateEmbedding` algorithm is inspired by [31] with the following modifications. Performing a naive translation using our translation scheme runs into the well-studied hubness problem observed in high-dimensional spaces [6, 10,26]. Essentially, the hubness problem arises when a small subset of words are "universal" neighbors and hence attract several many-to-one mappings. Existing strategies like mutual nearest neighbor [6] and a more involved method of Cross-Domain Similarity Local Scaling [13] have been previously proposed to address this issue. We employ a simple mutual nearest neighbor technique, i.e., a source word's top translations should include only those target words that include the source word when translated back.

As we will find later in Sect. 6.1, our unsupervised translation scheme finds several synonyms in its top choices (e.g., religion has mazhab, dharam and jaat in its top translated choices). Also, since hi_e does not have standard spelling rules, the translations often contained prevalent spelling variations of the same word (e.g., aman, amaan, jung, jang). Moreover, our retrieved dictionaries are noisy with substantially better p@10 than p@1 performance. To account for this noise in translation and to induce more diversity, for each word, we randomly sample a mutually nearest neighbor.

The only configurable parameter of Algorithm 1, N, is set to 10. For fair comparison, hyperparameter *size* in Algorithm 2 is set to 5 following [11].

Algorithm 2: NN-Sample($\mathcal{S}, \mathcal{U}$)

Input: $\mathcal{S}$ is a collection of example documents authored in $\mathcal{L}_{target}$,
    $\mathcal{U}$ is the sample pool authored in $\mathcal{L}_{target}$
Output: $\mathcal{A} \subseteq \mathcal{U}$ where $\mathcal{A}$ contains documents semantically similar to $\mathcal{S}$
Initialization: $\mathcal{A} \leftarrow \{\}$
Main loop:
foreach document $c \in \mathcal{S}$ **do**
    $count \leftarrow 0$
    $dist \leftarrow 0$
    while $count \leq size$ **do**
        $neighbor \leftarrow getNearestNeighbor(c, dist)$
        $dist \leftarrow cosineDistance(c, neighbor)$
        if $neighbor \notin \mathcal{A} \cup \mathcal{S}$ **then**
            $\mathcal{A} \leftarrow \mathcal{A} \cup \{neighbor\}$
            $count \leftarrow count + 1$
        end
    end
end
Output: $\mathcal{A}$

5.3   Design Considerations, Baselines

Decoupled Design: Note that, the cross-lingual sampling technique discussed here is in no way tied to the unsupervised word-translation technique and a superior word-translation technique can be easily used as a drop-in replacement for our sampler.

Baseline for Unsupervised Word Translation: We do not compare our unsupervised word translation method's performance with any other baseline for the following reasons. First, as explained above, our decoupled design allows any other more powerful word translation method (supervised or unsupervised) to replace our unsupervised method without disturbing the workflow of our pipeline. Our primary goal is cross-lingual sampling, and we do compare with the SOTA on that task. Second, while bilingual lexicon induction (aka unsupervised word translation) is a well-studied research sub-field for years [27], to our knowledge, no other method satisfies the following criteria: (1) word translation **without explicit alignment**; (2) word translation using harsh, social media data; (3) word translation without parallel data; (4) word translation without clean, monolingual corpora; and (5) end-to-end unsupervised word translation without seed lexicon. Finally, our unsupervised word translation method points to a semantic richness aspect of the polyglot word embedding never discovered or explored before. That said, if the reviewers recommend us any lexicon induction algorithm that satisfies all the above criteria, if accepted, we would be happy to incorporate that to the final version.

Baseline for Cross-Lingual Sampling: We choose two baselines for cross-lingual sampling – the state of the art and the random baseline presented in [11]. We do not compare against a supervised solution, say, a Hindi *hope speech classifier* because none exists. Furthermore, the goal of a sampling method for rare positives is to mine enough positives to lend balance to a training data set to make supervised solutions feasible. Hence, our unsupervised cross-lingual sampling method is a critical first step to supervised solutions for rare positives.

Thus a supervised solution is in no way a direct competitor of an end-to-end unsupervised sampling algorithm.

Generalizability: *Does this method generalize to other language pairs?* We acknowledge that generalizability of solutions are important and point out that our method *generalizes* to (1) three different corpora, all introduced in earlier papers; (2) two cross-lingual sampling tasks, both introduced in earlier papers; and (3) the Appendix contains $\langle en, es \rangle$ and $\langle en, de \rangle$ results. That said, we reiterate that our method addresses a language spoken by more than 500 million people; and considers two tasks – one on a global pandemic and the other on promoting peace between nuclear adversaries with a history of four wars.

6   Results

Table 1. Word translation performance on social media data. For each training corpus and translation direction, 500 source words are selected from $\mathcal{V}_{source}^{0-5}$ and are mapped to target words in $\mathcal{V}_{target}$ that are present in the corpus for at least 100 or more times. p@K indicates top-K accuracy.

| Measure | $hi_e \to en$ | $en \to hi_e$ | $hi_e \to en$ | $en \to hi_e$ | $hi_e \to en$ | $en \to hi_e$ |
	$\mathcal{D}^{hope}$	$\mathcal{D}^{hope}$	$\mathcal{D}^{election}$	$\mathcal{D}^{election}$	$\mathcal{D}^{covid}$	$\mathcal{D}^{covid}$
p@1	0.18	0.10	0.21	0.24	0.29	0.31
p@5	0.39	0.27	0.44	0.50	0.54	0.53
p@10	0.47	0.38	0.52	0.61	0.63	0.63

6.1   Unsupervised Word Translation

Table 2. A random sample of word pairs translated by our algorithm. The Appendix contains more examples.

$\mathcal{D}^{hope}$	$\mathcal{D}^{election}$	$\mathcal{D}^{covid}$
aatankvadi terrorist	deshbhakti patriotism	ilaz treatment
bahaduri bravery	turant immediately	joota shoe
musalmano muslims	patrakaar journalist	kahani story
andha blind	angrezo britishers	jukam cold
nuksan damage	berojgari unemployment	saf clean
faida benefit	ummeed expectation	hathon hands
dino days	nokri jobs	bachhc kids
bharosa trust	bikash devlopment	mudde issues
tarakki progress	gareebi poverty	marij patient
gayab vanish	shi ryt	sankramit infected

Table 1 summarizes our unsupervised world translation performance across three Indian social media data sets. Following standard practice [13,31], we report p@1, p@5 and p@10 performance. p@K is defined as the top-K accuracy [18], i.e., an accurate translation of the source word is present in the retrieved top K target words. It is common practice to restrict the vocabularies for the source words (and target words) based on some prevalence criterion [13]. We denote the top 5% of words by frequency in the vocabulary as $\mathcal{V}^{0-5}$. We restrict $\mathcal{V}_{source}$ to $\mathcal{V}^{0-5}_{source}$ and $\mathcal{V}_{target}$ to words that have appeared at least 100 times in the corpus (Appendix contains hyperparameter sensitivity analysis).

As shown in Table 1, we observe that substantial bilingual lexicons can be retrieved using our unsupervised method. Even on multilingual, challenging social media data sets, a p@5 performance as high as 0.5 was achieved on multiple occasions. We will release this bilingual lexicon (consensus label by two annotators, Appendix contains annotator details) of 1,100 unique word pairs as a resource. Table 2 lists a few randomly chosen examples of successfully translated word pairs across our three data sets. Investigation of the discovered word-pairs reveals that our scheme can capture nouns, adjective, adverbs, loan-words. Appendix contains a detailed description.

6.2   Ablation Analysis

We now summarize the findings from our ablation studies to understand this phenomenon (Appendix contains details).

Disabling Numbers: In prior literature, [1] showed that digits can be used as seed lexicons to align monolingual embeddings. Although our method doesn't make any explicit attempt to align, phrases like 2019 election (2019 chunao), 1971 war (1971 jung) can appear in both languages and hence can serve as signals. We replaced all numbers with a specific randomly chosen string that does not occur in the original corpus and evaluated the retrieval performance of our previously successful p@1 translations. We observed a performance dip of 28% which indicates that numeric literals may contribute to this phenomenon.

Loanwords: We observe that in most cases, in successfully translated word pairs (e.g., ⟨madad, help⟩, ⟨ilaj, treatment⟩), at least one of the words is borrowed and used in the other language (e.g., humein help chahiye "we need help"). These loanwords thus result in similar contexts for word pairs from different languages - which are possibly reflected in the obtained word embeddings facilitating translation. We perform a frequency preserving loanword exchange (see, Appendix) to modify the corpus where translated word pairs are interchanged to diminish the extent of borrowing of these loanwords (e.g., phrases like humein help chahiye is rewritten as humein madad chahiye). We observe that the p@1 performance dipped by 33% after this corpus modification indicating that loanwords are possibly major contributors to this phenomenon.

6.3   Cross-lingual Sampling

We now present our cross-lingual sampling results on two tasks described in Sect. 2.2. We include the best-performing methods presented in [11] and their baselines (random sampling) for performance comparison. We used two annotators fluent in Hindi, Urdu and English. For human evaluation of cross-lingual

Table 3. Random sample of hi_e hope speech obtained through our method.

Sampled hope speech	Loose translation
kaash dono mulko me dosti ho jaye dono mil kr **Europe** ke desho ki tra **developed** ho skte hai **piece** love	I wish two countries make friendship and together prosper and develop like European countries; peace, love.
kaash dono desho mein shanti k rishte kayam ho sake	I wish both countries can forge a relationship of peace.
jung talti rhe to bahtar he ap or ham sabhi k anagan me shama jalti rhe to bahatr he jung to khud hi ek masla he jung kiya maslo ka hal de gi	It is better if war is avoided. All of us should prosper. War in itself is a problem, how can it be a solution?

Table 4. Random sample of hi_e comments expressing compliance to COVID-19 health guidelines obtained through our method.

Sampled comments expressing compliance to COVID-19 health guidelines	Loose translation
koi surakshit nhi **please** sab ghar pe raho dosto	Nobody is safe. Friends, please stay at home.
agr **friends corona virus** se bachna h to chikte ya khaste vaqt muh par rumal rakho or bar bar muh aakh or nak par hth mtt lgao or sabun se achi trah hth dho ...	Friends, if you wish to stay safe from corona virus, please cover your face while coughing and sneezing with a handkerchief; do not touch your face or nose frequently; and wash your hands rigorously with soap.
bhai yo ap sab se vinti hai ki **please** surakshit rahai or bahar na jaye sirf sman lene hi bhahar jaye jai hind	Brothers, my request to all of you is to stay safe, only leave home for groceries. Hail India!

methods, the minimum Fleiss' κ measure was high (0.88) indicating strong interrater agreement. After independent labeling, differences were resolved through a follow-up adjudication process.

Table 5 compares the performance of our sampling method against existing approaches. To explore the influence of different design choices for Algorithm 1, we present ablation studies after disabling random sampling from top choices and back-translation to address the hubness problem. We notice that strictly limiting ourselves to the top translation choice and not accounting for hubness yields substantially worse performance. Allowing more diversity through randomly selecting one of the top translation choices improves performance somewhat, however, the hubness problem appears to be the primary performance bottleneck. Our final algorithm as described in Algorithm 1 achieves the best performance. On a highly challenging task of mining rare positives (random sampling yields 1.8% hope speech), we obtained a 45% improvement over the previously reported best

Table 5. Sampling performance. Percentage of samples output by the algorithm that are judged correct by human. Results marked with symbol † are obtained from [11].

Method	Hope speech	Covid compliance
Random baseline reported in [11]†	1.8%	2.88%
Best result reported in [11]†	31.68%	14.88%
Only top translation choice without back-translation	23.08%	13.12%
Without back-translation	25.36%	19.84%
Method described in Algorithm 1	**46.04%**	**40.8%**

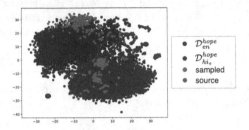

Fig. 2. A t-SNE [15] 2D visualization showing the sampling results against the document embedding space.

result. Our improvement over the state of the art in detecting content expressing compliance to COVID-19 health guidelines is even more pronounced. We obtain a performance gain of 174% over the state of the art on this task.

Table 3 and 4 list a random sample of hi_e documents obtained using our cross-lingual sampling method. We notice that the comments are mostly written in hi_e. A 2D visualization of the obtained *hope speech* comments indicate (see, Fig. 2) that our method retrieved comments reasonably distributed across the Hindi region.

7   Conclusions and Future Work

In this paper, we explore cross-lingual sampling in two important humanitarian domains: *hope speech detection* and detecting content that expresses compliance to COVID-19 health guidelines. Our work introduces a technique to perform unsupervised word translation and requires no monolingual corpora or monolingual language models. Our method improves upon the current SOTA that utilizes code switching. The *en-hi_e* setting is a common occurrence in several corpora sourced in the Indian subcontinent. The (relatively) poorly resourced hi_e, and consequently the difficulty in obtaining monolingual corpora in this language pair make our observations and methods particularly well-suited for this setting. We conduct detailed ablation studies of this phenomenon. Future directions include exploring the presence of this phenomenon in settings like contextual embeddings, and alternate models such as the highly successful transformer based methods.

A   Appendix

A.1   Ethics Statement

While the setting discussed in the paper involves humanitarian tasks, the techniques can be trivially adapted to conduct cross-lingual sampling and surfacing of content like *hate speech*, or detection of *hope speech* with the explicit object to censor it. In many recent conflicts in the Indian subcontinent, such systems can have adverse social effects and thus particular care is needed before these systems are deployed. Next, language-specific features can sometimes cause syntactically similar but semantically opposite content to be surfaced underscoring the need for a human-in-the-loop setting before such systems are deployed for social media content moderation tasks. Finally, in this work, care is taken to ensure that no particular community is the target of the sampled content. NLP methods can be utilized to selectively conduct cross lingual sampling to discover content against disenfranchised communities - it is imperative for the system designers to ensure that unwittingly or otherwise, communities at large are not targeted by system deployments.

A.2   News Networks

See Table 10.

A.3   Analyzing Other Language Pairs

We were curious to learn if our approach works with other language pairs. On two European language pairs, $\langle en, es \rangle$ and $\langle en, de \rangle$, we observed that our simple approach of constrained nearest neighbor sampling retrieves reasonable bilingual lexicons even when trained on a single, multilingual corpus (synthetically induced) without any explicit attempt to align.

Data Sets: We conduct experiments using Europarl [12] and Wikipedia data sets. We synthetically induce a multilingual corpus by combining two monolingual corpora and then randomly shuffling at the sentence level. Table 6 summarizes our results. We find that our overall performance improved with Wikipedia data especially for $de \rightarrow en$ and $es \rightarrow en$. [13] also reported a performance boost with Wikipedia data.

Our primary takeaways are:

• **Source word frequency:** Our experiments with Indian social media data sets indicate that our method performs better when we restrict ourselves to high-frequency source words. A fine-grained look at the performance based on the frequency of the source word reveals that we perform substantially better on high-frequency words belonging to $\mathcal{V}_{source}^{0-5}$ (e.g., $en \rightarrow es$ performance jumps from 0.25 to 0.61 when we consider words in $\mathcal{V}_{source}^{0-5}$).

• **Topical cohesion:** When we sample the *en* part of the corpus from Europarl and the *es* (or *de*) part from Wikipedia, we remove the topical cohesion between the *en* and *es* (*de*) components. We observe that performance dips slightly.

A.4 $\mathcal{D}^{covid}$ Data Set Visualization

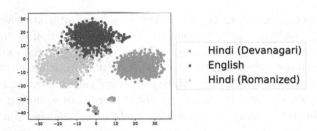

Fig. 3. A 2D visualization of $\mathcal{D}^{covid}$. Apart from English and Romanized Hindi, Hindi in Devanagari also has substantial presence in the corpus.

Figure 3 presents a 2D visualization of the word embeddings obtained using the language-identifier we considered [11]. The visualization indicates that apart from Romanized Hindi and English, our data set also demonstrates substantial presence of Hindi written in Devanagari script further establishing the challenges associated to our task. The size of the estimated vocabularies is presented in Table 9 (Table 11).

A.5 Annotation

We used two annotators fluent in Hindi, Urdu and English. For word translations, consensus labels were used. For *hope speech* annotation, the minimum Fleiss' κ measure was high (0.88) indicating strong inter-rater agreement. After independent labeling, differences were resolved through discussion.

A.6 System Pipeline

See Fig. 4.

Table 6. Performance comparison on Europarl [12] and Wikipedia. $\mathcal{V}_{target}$ is restricted to words that appeared more than 100 times in the corpus.

Data set	Measure	$en \rightarrow es$	$es \rightarrow en$	$en \rightarrow de$	$de \rightarrow en$
Europarl	p@1	0.25	0.25	0.19	0.16
	p@5	0.37	0.39	0.30	0.18
	p@10	0.39	0.44	0.33	0.19
Wikipedia	p@1	0.24	0.34	0.16	0.34
	p@5	0.40	0.50	0.31	0.46
	p@10	0.48	0.56	0.38	0.50

Table 7. Word translation performance on social media data. Each cell summarizes the $p@K$ performance for a given translation direction on a data set as $a/b/c$, where a (top) is the performance observed when the source vocabulary is restricted to $\mathcal{V}^{0-5}_{source}$ (color coded with blue); b (middle) is the performance observed when the source vocabulary is restricted to $\mathcal{V}^{5-10}_{source}$ (color coded with red); c (bottom) is the performance observed when the source vocabulary is restricted to $\mathcal{V}^{10-100}_{source}$ (color coded with gray). 500 source words are randomly selected from $\mathcal{V}^{0-5}_{source}$; from $\mathcal{V}^{5-10}_{source}$ and $\mathcal{V}^{10-100}_{source}$, 100 source words are randomly selected. The selected words are mapped to target words in $\mathcal{V}_{target}$ that are present in the corpus for at least 100 or more times. $p@K$ indicates top-K accuracy.

Measure	$\mathcal{V}_{source}$	$hi_e \to en$ $\mathcal{D}^{hope}$	$en \to hi_e$ $\mathcal{D}^{hope}$	$hi_e \to en$ $\mathcal{D}^{election}$	$en \to hi_e$ $\mathcal{D}^{election}$	$hi_e \to en$ $\mathcal{D}^{covid}$	$en \to hi_e$ $\mathcal{D}^{covid}$
p@1	$\mathcal{V}^{0-5}_{source}$	0.18	0.10	0.21	0.24	0.29	0.31
	$\mathcal{V}^{5-10}_{source}$	0.11	0.02	0.22	0.19	0.27	0.16
	$\mathcal{V}^{10-100}_{source}$	0.09	0.02	0.06	0.11	0.07	0.05
p@5	$\mathcal{V}^{0-5}_{source}$	0.39	0.27	0.44	0.50	0.54	0.53
	$\mathcal{V}^{5-10}_{source}$	0.26	0.15	0.43	0.33	0.45	0.43
	$\mathcal{V}^{10-100}_{source}$	0.20	0.07	0.18	0.21	0.23	0.11
p@10	$\mathcal{V}^{0-5}_{source}$	0.47	0.38	0.52	0.61	0.63	0.63
	$\mathcal{V}^{5-10}_{source}$	0.35	0.20	0.48	0.46	0.50	0.53
	$\mathcal{V}^{10-100}$	0.22	0.10	0.22	0.26	0.26	0.13

Table 8. Performance summary of our approach with training data set Europarl [12]; test data set (denoted by $\mathcal{D}_{test}$) introduced in [13]. $\mathcal{V}_{target}$ is restricted to words that appeared more than 100 times in the training data set. Each cell summarizes the $p@K$ performance for a given translation direction as $a/b/c/d$, where a (top) is the overall performance observed on $\mathcal{D}_{test}$; b is the performance observed on $\mathcal{V}^{0-5}_{source} \cap \mathcal{D}_{test}$ (color coded with blue); c is the performance observed on $\mathcal{V}^{5-10}_{source} \cap \mathcal{D}_{test}$ (color coded with red); d (bottom) is the performance observed on $\mathcal{V}^{10-100}_{source} \cap \mathcal{D}_{test}$ (color coded with gray).

Data set	Measure	$en \to es$	$es \to en$	$en \to de$	$de \to en$
Europarl	p@1	0.25	0.25	0.19	0.16
		0.61	0.26	0.43	0.15
		0.50	0.28	0.39	0.12
		0.17	0.24	0.13	0.22
	p@5	0.37	0.39	0.30	0.18
		0.79	0.58	0.68	0.38
		0.70	0.52	0.65	0.34
		0.26	0.33	0.19	0.28
	p@10	0.39	0.44	0.33	0.19
		0.83	0.66	0.73	0.50
		0.76	0.59	0.70	0.43
		0.28	0.37	0.22	0.31

A.7   Hyperparameters

Our preprocessing steps and hyperparameters to train embeddings are identical to previous literature [11]. All the models discussed in this paper are obtained

Table 9. Size of the estimated vocabularies using language identifier presented in [11] on our data sets. Spelling variations in Romanized Hindi possibly contributed to a large size of Romanized Hindi vocabulary.

Corpus	$\mathcal{V}$ for en	$\mathcal{V}$ for hi_e	$\mathcal{V}$ for hi_e
$\mathcal{D}^{hope}$	38,516	71,677	23,560
$\mathcal{D}^{election}$	55,164	109,341	45,467
$\mathcal{D}^{covid}$	46,504	109,809	59,219

Table 10. National channels.

IndiaTV, NDTV India, Republic World, The Times of India, Zee News, Aaj Tak, ABP NEWS, CNN-News18, News18 India, NDTV, TIMES NOW, India Today, The Economic Times, Hindustan Times

by training Fasttext [4] Skip-gram models with the following parameters unless stated otherwise:

– Dimension: 100
– Minimum subword unit length: 2
– Maximum subword unit length: 4
– Epochs: 5
– Context window: 5
– Number of negatives sampled: 5

A.8   Hyperparameter Sensitivity Analysis

Recall that, we restricted $\mathcal{V}_{source}$ and $\mathcal{V}_{target}$ to prevalence criteria that (1) $\mathcal{V}_{source}$ is restricted to $\mathcal{V}_{source}^{0-5}$ (2) $\mathcal{V}_{target}$ contains words that have appeared at least 100 or more times in the corpus. In Table 7, we relax the prevalence criterion on $\mathcal{V}_{source}$ and observe that as we move towards more infrequent words, the translation performance degrades. The performance drop is more visible with $\mathcal{V}_{source}^{10-100}$. Our annotators informed that poor quality of spelling and increased

Table 11. Evaluating the importance of topical cohesion. Blue, red and gray denote Europarl, Wikipedia and a mixed corpus where English is sampled from Europarl and the other language (Spanish or German) is sampled from Wikipedia, respectively. Results indicate that lack of topical cohesion affects performance. However, in spite of reduced topical cohesion, our method still retrieves bilingual lexicons of reasonable size.

Measure	$en \rightarrow es$			$es \rightarrow en$			$en \rightarrow de$			$de \rightarrow en$		
p@1	0.25	0.24	0.14	0.25	0.34	0.21	0.19	0.16	0.10	0.16	0.34	0.27
p@5	0.37	0.40	0.25	0.39	0.50	0.24	0.30	0.31	0.17	0.18	0.46	0.28
p@10	0.39	0.48	0.30	0.44	0.56	0.26	0.33	0.38	0.20	0.19	0.50	0.30

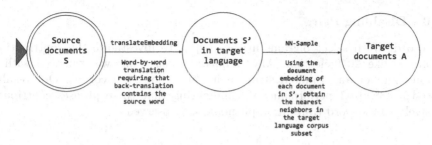

Fig. 4. The full pipeline. We start with a set of source documents, and run translateEmbedding on each and then $NN - Sample$ to return target language documents similar to the original.

prevalence of contraction made the annotation task particularly challenging for rare words.

We next analyze the effect of the frequency threshold of 100 on $\mathcal{V}_{target}$. In order to reduce annotation burden, we only focused on the subset of words with perfect translation (i.e., p@1 performance 100%). When we relax the frequency threshold to 10, our p@1, p@5 and p@10 numbers are respectively, 0.38, 0.84, 0.91, respectively. Hence, although for 91% or the source words we found a translation within the top 10 translations, our p@1 performance took a considerable hit. Our annotators reported that with a lowered frequency threshold, the retrieved translations contained higher degree of misspellings. Our conclusion from this experiment is 100 is a reasonable threshold given the noisy nature of our corpora.

We conducted a similar analysis on our word translation tasks using European language pairs. As shown in Table 8, when English is the source language, our translation performance on frequent words is substantially better than rare words. However, when English is the target language, we did not observe any similar trend, the performance was roughly equal across the entire spectrum of words ranked by frequency. With Wikipedia corpus (not shown in the Table), we observed qualitatively similar trends.

A.9 Extended Examples of Lexicons

Table 12 lists an extended bilingual lexicon containing 90 words pairs (30 from each corpus) obtained using our method. We will release the complete lexicon of 1,100 word pairs upon acceptance.

A.10   Disabling Pair

We also disabled select bigrams in the corpus to investigate the contribution of phrases like 2019 election. Any $\langle number, string \rangle$ pair, was replaced with a random number and random string pair throughout the corpus. Our results showed a 48% p@1 performance dip indicating that these phrases contribute massively to the word translation phenomenon observed.

A.11   Loanword

We now slightly abuse the definition of a loanword and consider a word is a loanword if it appears in a context of words written in a different language, and define a simple measure to quantify to what extent this occurs in a two-language setting. Let c denote the context (single word left and right) of a word w. We first count the instances where the language labels of c and w agree, i.e., $\mathcal{L}(w) = \mathcal{L}(c)$ (e.g., help is not a loanword in the following phrase: please help us). Let this number be denoted as $\mathcal{N}_{not\text{-}borrowed}$. Similarly, we count the instances when c and w have different language labels, i.e., $\mathcal{L}(w) \neq \mathcal{L}(c)$. This scenario would arise when a word is borrowed from a different language (e.g., help is a loanword in humein help chahiye). In our scheme, the Loan Word Index (LWI) of a word w is defined as $LWI(w) = \frac{N_{borrowed}}{N_{borrowed} + N_{not\text{-}borrowed}}$. A high LWI indicates substantial lexical borrowing of the word outside its language. For a word pair $\langle w_{source}, w_{target} \rangle$, we define $LWI(.)$ as the maximum of their individual LWIs. For example, if the LWI is high for the pair $\langle help, madad \rangle$, it indicates that at least one of these words was substantially borrowed. Our hypothesis is that successfully translated word pairs would have a high LWI indicating at least one of the pair was used as a loanword facilitating translation. The average Loan Word Index of all successfully translated word pairs in our test data sets across all three corpora is 0.15. Compared to this, randomly generated word pairings have an average Loan Word Index of 0.09. We next performed a frequency preserving loan word exchange to modify the corpus where translated word pairs are interchanged to diminish the extent to which words are borrowed (e.g., phrases like humein help chahiye is rewritten as humein madad chahiye). Frequency is preserved by interchanging both words in a successfully translated word pair as many times as the least borrowed word is borrowed. In our example if madad was borrowed 10 times, and help 15 times, we alter 10 instances where madad is borrowed with help, and 10 instances where help is borrowed with madad. We thus preserve word frequencies while diminishing the loanword phenomenon. We observed that the retrieval performance of our p@1 set dipped by 33% after this corpus modification indicating that frequent borrowing of words possibly positively contributed to our method's translation performance.

A.12   Analysis of Discovered Words

In our translation scheme, we found that translations for nouns, adjectives and adverbs were successfully discovered (see Table 2). Preserving plurality (hazaron thousands, musalmano muslims, naare slogans) on most occasions, translating numerals (char 4, eik one) were among some surprising observations considering the noisy social media setting. For a given source word, multiple valid synonymous target words were often among the top translations produced by our method (e.g., aman and shanti for peace; dharam, mazhab and jaat for religion). Stylistic choices like contraction were reflected in the translation (e.g., kyki (*kyuki*) mapped to bcz (*because*), and shi (*sahi*) mapped to ryt (*right*)). Verbs are conjugated differently in Hindi and English and word-for-word translations don't typically exist - for instance help him translates to uska "him" madad "help" karo "do", thus words like karo were rarely successfully translated.

Polysemy: During single word translation, without context, resolving polysemous words to their true meanings w.r.t. the context is not possible. However, we noticed that in a few instances top translation choices of polysemous source words include valid translations of their different meanings. For example, the word cold can mean both low temperature or a common viral infection. In $\mathcal{D}^{covid}$, both these meanings were captured in the top translations.

Nativization of Loanwords: Lexical borrowing across language pairs in the context of loanwords (or borrowed words) has been studied in linguistics and computational linguistics. Borrowed words, also known as loanwords, are lexical items borrowed from a donor language. For example, the English word avatar or yoga is borrowed from Hindi, while botal (bottle) and astabal (stable) are Hindi words borrowed from English. We noticed nativized loanwords, i.e., borrowed words that underwent phonological repairs to adapt to a foreign language, translate back to their English donor counterpart (e.g., rashan and angrezi translate to donor words ration and English, respectively).

A.13   Topical Cohesion

We break topical cohesion by sampling *en* and *es* (*de*) from Europarl and Wikipedia respectively. Our results show that bilingual lexicons are still retrieved albeit with marginally lower performance. We conclude that topical cohesion possibly helps but may not be a prerequisite for retrieving a reasonably sized bilingual lexicon.

Table 12. A random sample of translated word pairs from our corpora.

$\mathcal{D}^{hope}$	$\mathcal{D}^{election}$	$\mathcal{D}^{covid}$
aatankvadi terrorist	deshbhakti patriotism	ilaz treatment
bahaduri bravery	turant immediately	joota shoe
musalmano muslims	patrakaar journalist	kahani story
andha blind	angrezo britishers	jukam cold
nuksan damage	berojgari unemployment	saf clean
faida benefit	ummeed expectation	hathon hands
dino days	nokri jobs	bachhe kids
bharosa trust	bikash devlopment	mudde issues
tarakki progress	gareebi poverty	marij patient
gayab vanish	shi ryt	sankramit infected
kyki bcz	bazar market	hoshiyar smart
jahannam hell	masoom innocent	khubsurat beautiful
tel oil	sanghatan organization	dange riots
darr fear	chhavi image	bilkul absolutely
halat condition	mahina month	arakshan reservation
intzaar wait	qatal murder	palan obey
sipahi soldier	hinsak violent	maut death
peety drinking	bohot very	sadasya member
gau cows	garibon poors	achanak suddenly
jawab answer	blot dhabba	dost friend
alag separate	chokidaar watchman	hinsa violence
pahele first	shabd word	behad extremely
farq difference	fela spread	bukhar fever
banana make	peshaab urine	bhedbhav discrimination
sahi right	niyam regulations	vakeel lawyer
panah shelter	mouka chance	taqat strength
khao eat	pehla 1st	aurat woman
sadak road	bahas debate	unpadh uneducated
shukar thanks	akhri last	sabkuch everything
dhyan focus	gotala scam	sanskriti culture

References

1. Artetxe, M., Labaka, G., Agirre, E.: Learning bilingual word embeddings with (almost) no bilingual data. In: ACL 2017, pp. 451–462 (2017). https://doi.org/10.18653/v1/P17-1042
2. Benesch, S.: Defining and diminishing hate speech. State World's Minorities Indigenous Peoples **2014**, 18–25 (2014)

3. Benesch, S., Ruths, D., Dillon, K.P., Saleem, H.M., Wright, L.: Counterspeech on twitter: A field study. A report for Public Safety Canada under the Kanishka Project (2016)
4. Bojanowski, P., Grave, E., Joulin, A., Mikolov, T.: Enriching word vectors with subword information. TACL **5**, 135–146 (2017)
5. Cieri, C., Maxwell, M., Strassel, S., Tracey, J.: Selection criteria for low resource language programs. In: LREC, pp. 4543–4549 (2016)
6. Dinu, G., Lazaridou, A., Baroni, M.: Improving zero-shot learning by mitigating the hubness problem. arXiv preprint arXiv:1412.6568 (2014)
7. Dou, Z.Y., Zhou, Z.H., Huang, S.: Unsupervised bilingual lexicon induction via latent variable models. In: EMNLP 2018, pp. 621–626 (2018)
8. Gella, S., Bali, K., Choudhury, M.: "ye word kis lang ka hai bhai?" testing the limits of word level language identification. In: ICNLP-2014, pp. 368–377 (2014)
9. Gumperz, J.J.: Discourse Strategies, vol. 1. Cambridge University Press, Cambridge (1982)
10. Jegou, H., Schmid, C., Harzallah, H., Verbeek, J.: Accurate image search using the contextual dissimilarity measure. PAMI 2008 **32**(1), 2–11 (2008)
11. KhudaBukhsh, A.R., Palakodety, S., Carbonell, J.G.: Harnessing code switching to transcend the linguistic barrier. In: IJCAI-PRICAI, pp. 4366–4374 (2020)
12. Koehn, P.: Europarl: a parallel corpus for statistical machine translation. In: MT summit, vol. 5, pp. 79–86 (2005)
13. Lample, G., Conneau, A., Ranzato, M., Denoyer, L., Jégou, H.: Word translation without parallel data. In: 6th International Conference on Learning Representations, ICLR 2018. OpenReview.net (2018). https://openreview.net/forum?id=H196sainb
14. Lample, G., Ott, M., Conneau, A., Denoyer, L., Ranzato, M.: Phrase-based & neural unsupervised machine translation. In: EMNLP-2018, pp. 5039–5049 (2018). https://doi.org/10.18653/v1/D18-1549, https://www.aclweb.org/anthology/D18-1549
15. Van der Maaten, L., Hinton, G.: Visualizing data using t-SNE. J. Mach. Learn. Res. **9**(11) (2008)
16. Mathew, B., et al.: Thou shalt not hate: countering online hate speech. In: Proceedings of the Thirteenth International Conference on Web and Social Media, ICWSM 2019, pp. 369–380. AAAI Press (2019)
17. Mikolov, T., Chen, K., Corrado, G., Dean, J.: Efficient estimation of word representations in vector space. arXiv preprint arXiv:1301.3781 (2013)
18. Mikolov, T., Le, Q.V., Sutskever, I.: Exploiting similarities among languages for machine translation. arXiv preprint arXiv:1309.4168 (2013)
19. Mulcaire, P., Kasai, J., Smith, N.A.: Low-resource parsing with crosslingual contextualized representations. In: CoNLL, pp. 304–315 (2019)
20. Mulcaire, P., Kasai, J., Smith, N.A.: Polyglot contextual representations improve crosslingual transfer. In: NAACL-HLT-2019, pp. 3912–3918 (2019). https://doi.org/10.18653/v1/N19-1392
21. Mulcaire, P., Swayamdipta, S., Smith, N.A.: Polyglot semantic role labeling. In: ACL-2018, pp. 667–672 (2018). https://doi.org/10.18653/v1/P18-2106, https://www.aclweb.org/anthology/P18-2106
22. Palakodety, S., KhudaBukhsh, A.R., Carbonell, J.G.: Hope speech detection: a computational analysis of the voice of peace. In: ECAI-2020, pp. 1881–1889 (2020)
23. Palakodety, S., KhudaBukhsh, A.R., Carbonell, J.G.: Mining insights from large-scale corpora using fine-tuned language models. In: ECAI-20, pp. 1890–1897 (2020)

24. Palakodety, S., KhudaBukhsh, A.R., Carbonell, J.G.: Voice for the voiceless: active sampling to detect comments supporting the Rohingyas. In: AAAI-20, pp. 454–462 (2020)
25. Pennington, J., Socher, R., Manning, C.D.: GLOVE: global vectors for word representation. In: Proceedings of the EMNLP, pp. 1532–1543 (2014)
26. Radovanović, M., Nanopoulos, A., Ivanović, M.: Hubs in space: popular nearest neighbors in high-dimensional data. JMLR **11**(Sep), 2487–2531 (2010)
27. Ruder, S., Vulić, I., Søgaard, A.: A survey of cross-lingual word embedding models. J. Artif. Intell. Res. **65**, 569–631 (2019)
28. Saha, P., Singh, K., Kumar, A., Mathew, B., Mukherjee, A.: CounterGeDi: a controllable approach to generate polite, detoxified and emotional counter speech. In: Proceedings of the Thirty-First International Joint Conference on Artificial Intelligence, IJCAI 2022, pp. 5157–5163. ijcai.org (2022)
29. Sarkar, R., Mahinder, S., KhudaBukhsh, A.: The non-native speaker aspect: Indian English in social media. In: Proceedings of the Sixth Workshop on Noisy User-generated Text (W-NUT 2020), pp. 61–70. Association for Computational Linguistics, Online (2020)
30. Sarkar, R., Mahinder, S., Sarkar, H., KhudaBukhsh, A.: Social media attributions in the context of water crisis. In: EMNLP, pp. 1402–1412. Online (2020). https://doi.org/10.18653/v1/2020.emnlp-main.109, https://www.aclweb.org/anthology/2020.emnlp-main.109
31. Smith, S.L., Turban, D.H., Hamblin, S., Hammerla, N.Y.: Offline bilingual word vectors, orthogonal transformations and the inverted softmax. arXiv preprint arXiv:1702.03859 (2017)
32. Toon, O.B., et al.: Rapidly expanding nuclear arsenals in Pakistan and India portend regional and global catastrophe. Sci. Adv. **5**(10), eaay5478 (2019)
33. Tyagi, A., Field, A., Lathwal, P., Tsvetkov, Y., Carley, K.M.: A computational analysis of polarization on Indian and Pakistani social media. In: SocInfo 2020. Lecture Notes in Computer Science, vol. 12467, pp. 364–379 (2020). https://doi.org/10.1007/978-3-030-60975-7_27, https://doi.org/10.1007/978-3-030-60975-7_27
34. Yoo, C.H., Palakodety, S., Sarkar, R., KhudaBukhsh, A.: Empathy and hope: resource transfer to model inter-country social media dynamics. In: Proceedings of the 1st Workshop on NLP for Positive Impact, pp. 125–134. Association for Computational Linguistics, Online (2021)
35. Zhang, M., Liu, Y., Luan, H., Sun, M.: Adversarial training for unsupervised bilingual lexicon induction. In: ACL-2017, pp. 1959–1970 (2017)

More of the Same? A Study of Images Shared on Mastodon's Federated Timeline

Gabriel P. Nobre[1]([⊠]), Carlos H. G. Ferreira[1,2], and Jussara M. Almeida[1]

[1] Universidade Federal de Minas Gerais, Belo Horizonte, Brazil
{gabrielnobre,jussara}@dcc.ufmg.br, chgferreira@ufop.edu.br
[2] Universidade Federal de Ouro Preto, João Monlevade, Brazil

Abstract. We offer a first analysis of image content sharing on the Mastodon platform, one of the currently most popular decentralized online social networks. Our study relies on a dataset of toots gathered from a federated timeline (hosted in mastodon.social), consisting of over 1 million images shared by more than 100 thousand users. We focus on two key aspects: (i) profiling image content in terms of presence of explicit content (e.g., violence) and (ii) exploring potential channels between Mastodon instances as well as between Mastodon and the rest of the Web. Our main results offer evidence of a large amount of explicit content shared in the environment as well as the frequent presence of such content on the Web. In addition, we estimate a consistent flow of images (including explicit content) from other Web platforms (e.g., Twitter, Reddit, Facebook) to Mastodon. Finally, we also observed several image co-sharing user communities, ultimately bridging instance boundaries.

Keywords: Mastodon · Decentralized online social networks · Information dissemination · Images

1 Introduction

The concept of *decentralized web* emerged in recent years often promoted by the recently deployed decentralized social media (e.g. Mastodon[1], Pleroma[2]) in opposition to traditional social media (e.g. Facebook, Twitter, Instagram). Its core characteristic consists in a decentralized hosting infrastructure, also known as the *fediverse*, composed of independent instances which ultimately leads to loose content moderation and disfavors governmental regulation [3,7,31]. Yet, the increased popularity of various fediverse applications with already millions of users and thousands of instances[3], along with recent concerns about the large volume of toxic content (i.e., hate speech, disinformation) sharing on the environment [5,30] leads to a key question: *to which extent is this new environment*

---

[1] https://mastodon.social.
[2] https://pleroma.social.
[3] https://the-federation.info.

F. Hopfgartner et al. (Eds.): SocInfo 2022, LNCS 13618, pp. 181–195, 2022.
https://doi.org/10.1007/978-3-031-19097-1_11

detached from the other traditional Web applications with respect to content sharing?

The few prior studies of the fediverse, notably Pleroma and Mastodon, investigated the spread of toxic content [5,30], often by analyzing explicit follow links established between users [7,8,28] and alternative content moderation policies [5]. Such studies focused mostly on the textual content shared by users (called toots on Mastodon), disregarding content spread in other media types. Yet, rich media may also be popular means to spread information in such environments (and this is the case of Mastodon, as we show in Sect. 4). Images are of particular interest given their reported capacity to attract and generate more user engagement, compared to only textual content [16].

Moreover, prior work mostly analyzed the fediverse as independent from the rest of the (often centralized) Web platforms. This approach may suggest some sort of detachment between the two environments. Is that really the case? To which extent the information shared on both environments is indeed different? To our knowledge, this question remains open as no prior work looked into the connections between the fediverse and other Web applications notably with respect to content sharing.

In this work we take a step towards addressing those open questions. We do so by gathering a dataset of *images* shared in the *federated* timeline of *mastodon.social*, the current largest Mastodon's instance[4]. This is a public timeline, from where any mastodon.social user sees all public posts from instances that this server knows about. It is sorted based solely on the posting date and it is not affected by ads or any other algorithm. Our dataset covers a 2-month period (from March 27th to May 28th 2022) and, consists of 4.6 M toots in total originated from 4,3 k instances (in addition to mastodon.social). Over 900 k collected toots contain images that, in its turn, represent above 90% of the non-text media in our dataset (others are audios, videos and gifs).

Our study is driven by two goals: (1) analyzing the content shared in and visible to *mastodon.social* users, notably with respect to the presence of potentially toxic *image* content, and (2) investigating potential channels of information flow both across Mastodon's instances and between Mastodon and other Web platforms. Specifically, we tackle the following research questions (RQs):

- **RQ1:** What is the profile of the images shared in Mastodon's timeline with respect to explicit content?
- **RQ2:** What is the interplay between different Mastodon's instances as well Mastodon and the rest of the Web with respect to image sharing?

Towards answering these questions, we focus on the 30 k most shared images, which account for 7% of all image shares in our data. We use Google's Cloud Vision API[5] to profile the images's content in terms of presence of various types of unsafe-search content (e.g., violence, racy and adult content). We also submit

---

[4] https://instances.social.
[5] https://cloud.google.com/vision.

the selected images to Google Image Web Search[6] to gather evidence of their presence in other Web applications, notably (traditional) social networks such as Twitter and Facebook. Whenever possible, we also gather estimates of first sharing times on each application so as to extrapolate on potential directions of information flow between Mastodon and the Web. Finally, we analyze the formation of implicit (i.e., latent) user connections to promote content dissemination across Mastodon. Specifically, we build an *image co-sharing network* [19,20] which connects users who share the same images in order to identify high-level user *communities*. We characterize the identified communities in terms of content properties and instance reach. Notably, we investigate whether these communities cross instance boundaries, which ultimately may disfavor content moderation.

The rest of this paper is organized as follows. We briefly discuss related work in Sect. 2 and present our methodology to tackle our RQs in Sect. 3. Main results are discussed in Sect. 4 while conclusions are offered in Sect. 5.

2   Related Work

Prior work related to our present effort are grouped into: i) studies on information dissemination in online social networks in general and ii) studies on decentralized online social networks. A brief review of them is presented next.

Information spread in online social networks has been the focus of research for a while [14,17] and yet remains a trendy topic [10,12,23,25] mostly driven by the increasing use of these applications to spread toxic [10] and misinformation content [23–25]. Prior work in this area often made use of network analyses to characterize the information dissemination process [23] on various platforms including Twitter [10,15,24,26], Facebook [2] and Instagram [11,12]. They also often explored the user follow network [18] though some authors have explored other metadata as well [26]. In a nutshell, these studies are often driven by the goals of identifying the most influential users [1,18] as well as higher level groupings (e.g. user communities) with key roles in the information dissemination [2,12].

In the specific case of decentralized online social networks, the literature is somewhat scarce as the environment itself is still in its infancy. A number of recent studies offered some high-level overview of existing applications, notably Mastodon [7,22,28,31]. For example, the authors of [28,31] discussed characteristics and comparisons between Mastodon and traditional social networks (e.g., Twitter), whereas the robustness of the environment to outages in some instances was analyzed in [22]. Others have explored the user follow network to investigate topological properties of the network of instances in Mastodon. [7–9,28,29]. In that direction, researchers have characterized the interactions of users with other instances from the perspective of information production and consumption [9], detecting the existence of bridges between instances [7,8,29], which facilitate information flow across Mastodon's instance boundaries. Yet, it has also been

---

[6] https://images.google.com.

observed that users tend to stay strongly bounded inside their own instances [29]. In [7], the authors analyzed how the structural features of the Mastodon network of instances evolved over time, finding that most instances did not change their position with respect to network centrality. Some other studies have analyzed the content shared on decentralized social networks (Mastodon an Pleroma), often with respect to the presence of toxic and sensitive content [28] as well as the effectiveness of content moderation [5] or instance rejection policies [13]. Yet, all these studies focused primarily on textual content.

Comparatively, our work offers a complementary view of information spread on Mastodon. Unlike all prior studies, we here analyze information conveyed in *images*, a rich media type that is known to generate much more user engagement, with particular focus on the presence of explicit (and to some extent toxic) content. Also, like some prior work, we also investigate the relationships among instances but focusing on a different (latent/implicit) network that emerges from user sharing patterns. Moreover, we take a step further and offer a first look into the connections between Mastodon and other (traditional) Web applications, hinting at potential channels that bridge these platforms.

3   Methodology

In this section we describe the methodology followed in this work. We first report how we performed the data collection from Mastodon in Sect. 3.1 and then detail how we executed the image profiling with respect to explicit content in Sect. 3.2. Finally, we describe our network model and how we performed the network analysis in Sect. 3.3.

3.1   Toots and Images Collection

The first step in our methodology is to perform the toot collection from Mastodon. In order to do so, we use the Mastodon API[7]. This is a facility created by Mastodon to enable server instances and also, in our case, fetch metadata about the content that is shared in the social media. In this metadata, for each user toot, we have information about the user account, instance, publishing date and multimedia content.

We focused our data collection in the federated timeline of the mastodon.social server, a general purpose instance with the current largest user base. The federated timeline[8] is different from traditional social media timelines, where often a user sees what it directly follows. In this case, if a user from an instance follows a new server, any other user in this given user's instance is now a potential audience in the federated timeline. Not all content from this new instance is shared there, but only the toots that the poster flagged as public. Furthermore, some servers allow the federated timeline to be public, meaning that even a person without a user account can access it.

---

[7] https://docs.joinmastodon.org/client/intro.
[8] https://docs.joinmastodon.org/user/network/.

Next, we proceed to download and store all available images from the toots that we collected. In detail, it was executed by using the provided Uniform Resource Locator (URL) in the images' metadata that often reached servers external to Mastodon. This was a necessary step so we could perform the detection of near-duplicate images to further select the most shared ones as well as identify co-sharing activity. To achieve it, we executed the Perceptual Hash (pHash) [27], which works by calculating a hash value given color variations in images, overcoming resizing and small modifications. Hence, we executed this algorithm on each image file and grouped the ones with same hash.

3.2 Explicit Profiling and Web Search

The next step in our methodology is to perform the explicit content profiling over the shared images. To achieve this, we make use of the SafeSearch[9] functionality available in Google's Cloud Vision API. In summary, this tool evaluates the input image using pre-computed models in the form of a likelihood profiling (very unlikely, unlikely, possible, likely, and very likely) of the five categories (adult, spoof, medical, violence, and racy). Among other features, these categories evaluates the likelihood that an image shows adult content (e.g., nudity or sexual activity), has been altered to be funny or offensive, or contains violent content. Hence, we proceeded to flag an image as *explicit* if the tool reported at least *possible* likelihood for one of the mentioned categories.

In addition, we search the Web using Google Image Search to determine both the hosting domain of the image and the date it was originally published. After providing an image file as an input, this tool will output the URLs where the image was indexed and, in some cases, the date of indexing. In the case of more than one date being available on the first page of results, we considered the minimum indexing date[10]. This result allows us to estimate whether an image was first published in Mastodon or in the Web, and illustrate how the interaction occurs between these entities in terms of content sharing. We note that the used Mastodon's publishing date is also an estimate, as it is nearly unfeasible to crawl its entire database to determine the original source of an image.

3.3 Network of Image Co-sharing Users

The final step in our methodology begins with the network modelling of user co-sharing activities in Mastodon. Hence, we established the following network represented as a graph $G(V, E)$. In this graph, each vertex v in V represents an user and each undirected and weighted edge $e = (v_i, v_j)$ in E quantifies the observed image co-sharing activity of two users v_i and v_j. Furthermore, we highlight that the users v_i and v_j have no pre-defined membership instances, in a way that they could be hosted in the same Mastodon instance or in different

---

[9] https://cloud.google.com/vision/docs/detecting-safe-search.

[10] With this measurement, the Mastodon-to-Web information flow is probably overestimated.

instances. Additionally, the edge weight w_{ij} consists of the detected amount of images co-shared in common between users v_i and v_j.

With the constructed graph $G(V, E)$ we start its characterization by computing network metrics that will help us understand how is this network structured as well as what it represents in terms of user image co-sharing activities. For instance, we make use of traditional network metrics as evaluating the connected components, the average degree of the nodes, the average weight of the edges, and the average clustering coefficient. The clustering coefficient, in its turn, computes how well connected the neighbours of a given node of a graph are and yields a value from 0 (loosely connected) to 1 (fully connected) [4].

Next, as a final procedure, we perform the community identification in $G(V, E)$. The current literature describes diversified methods to achieve this task and, in our case, we decided to execute the Louvain algorithm [6]. This algorithm is commonly used for community extraction in social media networks and is also used in diverse domains [21]. It works iteratively by optimizing the modularity metric that quantifies the quality of the observed communities, ranging from -0.5 to 1. The modularity Q is defined as:

$$Q = \frac{1}{2m} \sum_{ij} \left[A_{ij} - \frac{k_i k_j}{2m} \right] \delta(c_i, c_j), \tag{1}$$

where m is the sum of all of the edge weights; A_{ij} is the weight of edge (v_i, v_j); $k_i(k_j)$ is the sum of the weights of the edges attached to $v_i(v_j)$; $c_i(c_j)$ is the community assigned to $v_i(v_j)$; and $\delta(c_i, c_j) = 1$ if $c_i = c_j$ or 0 otherwise. By the end of the process, each node is assigned to a community whereas the set of partitions represent an optimal modularity value.

Finally, with the set of communities, we can determine whether there are communities in which its users cross instance boundaries as well as whether these communities are responsible for sharing explicit content.

4   Results

Now we present our results in this section. We start by presenting the dataset collection results as well as an overview of the images shared in the period under analysis in Sect. 4.1. Next, we present the explicit image profiling and Mastodon-Web interaction results in Sects. 4.2 and 4.3, respectively. Finally, we present a characterization for the Mastodon's image co-sharing communities in Sect. 4.4.

4.1   Dataset and Image Results

Our data gathering[11] consists of the toots shared in the mastodon.social's federated timeline from March 27th to May 28th 2022. Next, we summarize our dataset in Table 1.

---

[11] We make our (anonymized) data available at https://zenodo.org/record/6977415#. YvdJ_ExByXI.

Table 1. Overview of our dataset

Number of toots	4,628,113
Number of active users	103,477
Average number of toots per user	44.73
Number of instances	4,354
Average number of toots per instance	1,062.96
Average number of users per instance	23.77
Total number of media	1,195,558
Number of toots with media	1,003,636
Number of images	1,109,654
Number of audios, videos, gifs	85,904
Number of toots with images	924,975
Number of unique images	919,497
Number of replicated images	58,103
Average number of shares of replicated images	3.01
Maximum number of shares of a replicated image	1,265

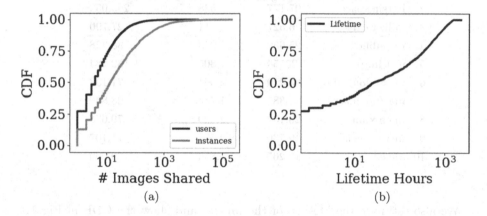

Fig. 1. (a) Image sharing activity. (b) Image lifetime span. (Color figure online)

We first take a look at the overall high-level numbers of the dataset in Table 1. We observe that the dataset contains over 4.6 M toots shared by 103,477 unique users, yielding an average of 44.73 toots per user. Moreover, we note that we identified toots from 4,354 unique instances, from which we had, on average, 23.77 users sharing 1,062.96 toots. Also in Table 1, we outline the total number of 1.2M multi-media identified, where we highlight that, from all media types, around 93% of the total non-text content were indeed images.

Now we focus on the numbers related to the images, available in Table 1. First, we notice that about 1 in 5 toots contains at least one image file, highlighting that this type of media is widely popular in Mastodon. In addition, we note that the average user shared about 9 images during the analysis period, and this value raises to 212.44 for the average instance. In Fig. 1a we also see the Cumulative Distributive Function (CDF) for the number of images shared by users (blue lines) and instances (orange lines). Not only do we find that about 25% of users and 12% of instances have shared at least one image, but also that the top 25% of both entities have shared more than 100 images during this period. This observation also underlines how popular the images are in this environment.

Before performing the identification of near-duplicates images, we downloaded all available images (93.5% of the total). We then determined that approximately 58k images were replicated at least once, as shown in Table 1. For each replicated image, an average of 3 replicates were observed. This observation serves as evidence that several images were indeed shared multiple times in this environment, up to a maximum number of 1,265.

Table 2. Top-10 image sharing mastodon instances

#	Instance name	# of Images	# of Active users	# of Toots
1	mastodon.social	204,056	33,848	680,073
2	botsin.space	97,177	538	293,052
3	milker.cafe	26,527	11	27,790
4	respublicae.eu	25,659	273	38,328
5	mstdn.jp	23554	805	182,484
6	mastodon.online	23,419	2,961	71,133
7	mastodon.art	22,387	1,736	28,890
8	m.cmx.im	20,132	2,529	70,688
9	mstdn.social	19,730	2,571	71,107
10	alive.bar	16,265	1,854	69,009

We also estimate the lifetime of the images and show the CDF in Fig. 1b, which is shown in the blue lines. It is calculated by taking all the image replicates and subtracting the last date of occurrence from the first of occurrence. We find that about 25% of the images have a lifetime of less than 1 h, which is a fairly fast lifetime. For the remaining 75%, the lifetime ranges from 1 to about 1500 h hours. This indicates that a relevant fraction of the images (about 50%) remain in the environment for more than one day.

Additionally, to better understand the source of images in the federated timeline, we show in Table 2 the top-10 instances that shared more images, in parallel with the number of active users and toots shared. From these results, we can see that the mastodon.social instance has shared more images by far, while having the largest number of active users. However, we next note that the number of active users alone does not tell us much about the number of images shared. For example, milker.cafe, with only 11 active users, shared over 27 k images, with a

Table 3. Summary of explicit profiling

Likelihood	Very likely	Unlikely	Possible	Likely	Very likely
Racy	15,542	5,544	2,402	1,180	5,331
Adult	20,849	4,491	1,269	844	2,546
Spoof	21,223	5,622	1,045	1,060	1,049
Medical	17,725	11,145	834	210	85
Violence	15,335	13,844	709	99	12

ratio of almost 1:1 to the number of toots. For the remaining instances, a wide range of image sharing activities can be observed, both in terms of the number of images shared and active users and the number of toots. These last observations ultimately indicate that it is unfeasible to fit all instances and users into a single image sharing profile.

4.2   Explicit Profiling Results

As for our next results, we summarize the image profiling on explicit content for the top-30 k shared images in Table 3. We observe that we have diverse numbers of images that display explicit content for all categories. This occurs more frequently on the racy, adult, and spoof categories, in which we have about 30%, 15% and 10% of the images, respectively, with likelihood equal to or stronger than *possible*. Whereas for medical and violence categories, we observe values of about 3% and 2%, respectively. In general terms, we observe that 11,708 images (39%) have a likelihood stronger than possible to display explicit content in at least one of the categories. This observation suggests that moderation is necessary in the Mastodon environment as images, while being a popular media format, indeed display a consistent level of explicit content.

4.3   Mastodon-Web Interaction

We now present the results for the Web search of the top-30k shared images in Mastodon. Based on these results, we estimated the interval of appearance on the Web and Mastodon expressed by the difference of the minimum date in the Web and first observed occurrence in Mastodon. In summary, we found Web results for 29,993 of the images and we were able to estimate dates for 15,354 of them. We display a CDF of these time interval in the blue line in Fig. 2a. First, we note that the vast majority of the interval are positive, and it is an indicating that, for around 94% of the calculated intervals, the image flow is actually from the Web to Mastodon. However, we still have 6% of the images with negative time intervals, indicating information flow from Mastodon to the Web.

Next, we deep dive into the Web domains obtained by the search results to have an overview of what are those more strongly connected to Mastodon. We illustrate such interactions in the graph displayed in Fig. 2b, where we display in

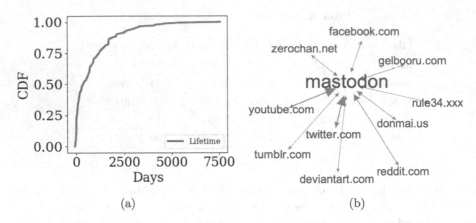

(a)   (b)

Fig. 2. (a) Interval from Web to Mastodon. (b) Mastodon-Web interaction. (Color figure online)

Table 4. Top-10 mastodon-web interactions

#	Web domain	Web links (†)	To the web (†)	From the web (†)
1	twitter.com	2985 (1095)	405 (111)	1339 (614)
2	youtube.com	2069 (922)	74 (25)	1374 (616)
3	reddit.com	1224 (848)	71 (36)	652 (473)
4	gelbooru.com	642 (638)	2 (2)	430 (428)
5	donmai.us	635 (610)	2 (2)	418 (397)
6	facebook.com	236 (128)	9 (3)	141 (73)
7	zerochan.net	224 (215)	1 (1)	167 (159)
8	deviantart.com	167 (142)	5 (5)	113 (91)
9	tumblr.com	156 (92)	6 (4)	99 (56)
10	rule34.xxx	153 (152)	2 (2)	66 (66)

†: Refers to images with possible explicit content.

blue the top-10 Web domains with the largest amount of estimated image flow. In this graph, the edges are weighted and their thickness represent the volume of images flowing. The arrow direction, in its turn, represent if this amount of images is going to the Web domains from Mastodon or the contrary. From observing the graph, we note that several domains interact with Mastodon, but specially domains from social media as Twitter, YouTube, Reddit, and Facebook.

We now present an overview of the amount of images shared in Mastodon and found in the Web in Table 4. The table displays the Web domains (column 2) found in the Web after we searched for the top-30 k most shared ones, ordered (column 1) by the number of links found to a specific domain (column 3). Again, as it was displayed in Fig. 2b, we note that the highest volume of content exchange occurs with other social media domains, specially Twitter. Next, we

also display the amount of the estimated flow, as if the images were alter transferred to (column 4) or originated from the Web (column 5). Specifically, we
note that the amount of content being transferred from the Web is much higher
than the amount of content being transferred to the Web. This observation is
also true for content flagged as explicit.

4.4 Image Co-sharing Communities

Finally, we now proceed to present our analysis after we constructed the image
sharing network by connecting users that co-shared images in common. We first
evaluate the general properties of this network as per the results in Table 5. In
this table, we observe that we have 8,714 users users interconnected via more
than 26 k edges, resulting in an average node degree of 6.18 and with an corresponding average edge weight of 1.66. This network consists in around 8% of the
total active users that are connected in over 1k separate connected components.
However, we highlight that the largest connected components holds 74% of the
total network users. We also display in Table 5 the results for the extracted communities. We observed a total of 1,059 communities, a fairly high number, but
we note that the largest connected component alone includes 49 communities.
Regarding the quality of the communities, we obtained a modularity result of
0.79. By considering this modularity result along with the average clustering
coefficient result of 0.31, we identify the formation of well delimited communities but with somewhat loose connections amongst its own members. This is an
indication that the communities tend not to share images in common, hence well
defined, while its own users tend to share diverse images and not often forming
cliques.

Next, we investigate in Fig. 3a if the identified communities do cross
Mastodon instance's. In this figure we have blue dots representing each community and on the x-axis we have the community size and on the y-axis the
number of instances from which its members belong to. Additionally, the red
line represents the values where the sizes of the communities are equal to the
number of instances for its members or, simply, a 1 to 1 ratio. From these results
we note that the vast majority of the observed communities in the network of
image co-share in Mastodon cross multiple instances even while having hundreds
of users.

Finally, we display the identified amount of explicit images that the communities shared in Fig. 3b. In this figure, we again have blue dots representing
the communities and on the x-axis the communities sizes. This time, we have
the number of explicit images shared by each community on the y-axis. From
this figure, we observe that essentially almost every community shared at least
one explicit image. More specifically, we note that several communities shared
hundreds of explicit images, which is even more common, and expected, for the
largest communities.

Table 5. Image co-sharing network properties

Number of nodes	8,714
Number of edges	26,930
Average node degree	6.18
Average edge weight	1.66
Number of connected components	1,059
Largest connected component size	6,454
Average clustering coefficient	0.31
Number of communities	1,059
Modularity	0.79

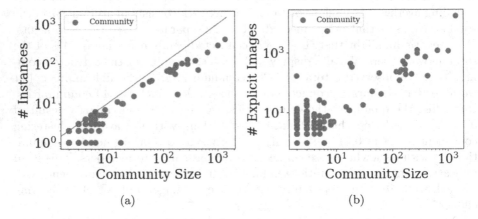

(a)   (b)

Fig. 3. (a) Cross-instance communities. (b) Explicit image activity. (Color figure online)

5   Conclusion and Future Work

This work took a first look at the images shared on Mastodon. We collected over 1M images shared over a 2-month period to analyze both their profile in terms of explicit content and information dissemination between Mastodon and the Web, as well as between instances of the platform. First, we detected that a relevant number of images contained explicit content, notably racy, adult, and spoof. Second, we estimated that the vast majority of those images (approximately 94%) originated from the Web, specially domains from other social media such as Twitter, YouTube, Reddit, and Facebook. These findings suggest little detachment between fediverse and the rest of Web, notably the mentioned centralized platforms, with respect to content sharing, it being explicit or not.

Finally, we built an underlying image co-sharing network to characterize the flow of information between Mastodon instances, an important aspect to evaluate when considering explicit content moderation. From this analysis, we observed the occurrence of several large communities that indicate consistent image co-sharing activities of users from multiple different instances. These communities may represent an underlying challenge for explicit content moderation as traditional[12] individual and instance-wide moderation might not be enough to mitigate this type of content.

We note that our dataset is limited by the public federated timeline, which consists of one of the possible views of Mastodon. Therefore, our dataset does not encompasses the whole content shared in this environment. In addition, we can only estimate the flow of information between Mastodon and the Web, as we are limited by the search tool we used.

In future work, we plan to include more media types in our research, including text, video, and audio content. Additionally, we will investigate temporal aspects of the information dissemination network as well as identify its core structures. Finally, we will further investigate the role that different levels of users aggregation (individuals, instances, and communities) play in terms of explicit content sharing.

References

1. Al-Garadi, M.A., et al.: Analysis of online social network connections for identification of influential users: Survey and open research issues. ACM Comput. Surv. **51**(1), 1–37 (2018)
2. Asim, Y., Malik, A.K., Raza, B., Shahid, A.R.: A trust model for analysis of trust, influence and their relationship in social network communities. Telematics Inform. **36**, 94–116 (2019)
3. Bailey, R., Misra, P.: Interoperability of social media: an appraisal of the regulatory and technical ecosystem. Available at SSRN (2022)
4. Barabási, A.L.: Network science. Philos. Trans. R. Soc. A Math. Phys. Eng. Sci. **371**, 20120375 (2013). https://doi.org/10.1098/rsta.2012.0375
5. Zia, B., et al.: Toxicity in the decentralized web and the potential for model sharing. In: ACM on Measurement and Analysis of Computing Systems (2022)
6. Blondel, V.D., Guillaume, J.L., Lambiotte, R., Lefebvre, E.: Fast unfolding of communities in large networks. J. Stat. Mech. Theory Exp. **2008**(10), P10008 (2008)
7. La Cava, L., Greco, S., Tagarelli, A.: Understanding the growth of the Fediverse through the lens of Mastodon. Appl. Netw. Sci. **6**(1), 1–35 (2021). https://doi.org/10.1007/s41109-021-00392-5
8. Cava, L.L., Greco, S., Tagarelli, A.: Information consumption and boundary spanning in decentralized online social networks: the case of mastodon users. Online Soc. Netw. Media **30**, 100220 (2022)
9. Cava, L.L., Greco, S., Tagarelli, A.: Network analysis of the information consumption-production dichotomy in mastodon user behaviors. In: Proceedings of the International AAAI Conference on Web and Social Media, pp. 1378–1382 (2022)
10. d'Sa, A.G., Illina, I., Fohr, D.: Bert and fastText embeddings for automatic detection of toxic speech. In: International Multi Conference on: Organization of Knowledge and Advanced Technologies (OCTA) (2020)

---

[12] https://docs.joinmastodon.org/admin/moderation/.

11. Ferreira, C.H., et al.: On the dynamics of political discussions on instagram: a network perspective. Online Soc. Netw. Media **25**, 100155 (2021)
12. Gomes Ferreira, C.H., et al.: Unveiling community dynamics on instagram political network. In: 12th ACM Conference on Web Science, pp. 231–240 (2020)
13. Hassan, A.I., et al.: Exploring content moderation in the decentralised web: the pleroma case. In: 17th International Conference on Emerging Networking Experiments and Technologies (2021)
14. Hou, Q., Han, M., Cai, Z.: Survey on data analysis in social media: a practical application aspect. Big Data Mining Anal. **3**(4), 259–279 (2020)
15. Li, C.T., Lin, Y.J., Yeh, M.Y.: The roles of network communities in social information diffusion. In: IEEE International Conference on Big Data (Big Data), pp. 391–400 (2015)
16. Li, Y., Xie, Y.: Is a picture worth a thousand words? an empirical study of image content and social media engagement. J. Mark. Res. **57**(1), 1–19 (2020)
17. Meel, P., Vishwakarma, D.K.: Fake news, rumor, information pollution in social media and web: a contemporary survey of state-of-the-arts, challenges and opportunities. Expert Syst. Appl. **153**, 112986 (2020)
18. Münch, F.V., Thies, B., Puschmann, C., Bruns, A.: Walking through twitter: sampling a language-based follow network of influential twitter accounts. Social Media + Society **7**(1) (2021). https://doi.org/10.1177/2056305120984475
19. Nobre, G.P., Ferreira, C.H.G., Almeida, J.M.: Beyond groups: uncovering dynamic communities on the whatsapp network of information dissemination. In: Aref, S., et al. (eds.) SocInfo 2020. LNCS, vol. 12467, pp. 252–266. Springer, Cham (2020). https://doi.org/10.1007/978-3-030-60975-7_19
20. Nobre, G.P., Ferreira, C.H., Almeida, J.M.: A hierarchical network-oriented analysis of user participation in misinformation spread on WhatsApp. Inf. Process. Manage. **59**(1), 102757 (2022)
21. Papadopoulos, S., Kompatsiaris, I., Vakali, A., Spyridonos, P.: Community detection in social media. Data Min. Knowl. Disc. **24**, 515–554 (2012). https://doi.org/10.1007/s10618-011-0224-z
22. Raman, A., Joglekar, S., Cristofaro, E.D., Sastry, N., Tyson, G.: Challenges in the decentralised web: the mastodon case. In: IMC 2019, pp. 217–229 (2019)
23. Resende, G., et al.: (Mis) information dissemination in WhatsApp: gathering, analyzing and countermeasures. In: The Web Conference, pp. 818–828 (2019)
24. Vosoughi, S., Roy, D., Aral, S.: The spread of true and false news online. Science **359**(6380), 1146–1151 (2018)
25. Wu, L., Morstatter, F., Carley, K.M., Liu, H.: Misinformation in social media: definition, manipulation, and detection. ACM SIGKDD Explor. Newsl. **21**(2), 80–90 (2019)
26. Xu, S., Zhou, A.: Hashtag homophily in twitter network: examining a controversial cause-related marketing campaign. Comput. Hum. Behav. **102**, 87–96 (2020)
27. Zauner, C., Steinebach, M., Hermann, E.: Rihamark: perceptual image hash benchmarking. In: Media watermarking, security, and forensics III (2011)
28. Zignani, M., Gaito, S., Rossi, G.P.: Follow the "mastodon": structure and evolution of a decentralized online social network. In: International AAAI Conference on Web and Social Media, pp. 541–550 (2018)
29. Zignani, M., Quadri, C., Gaito, S., Cherifi, H., Rossi, G.P.: The footprints of a "mastodon": how a decentralized architecture influences online social relationships. In: IEEE Conference on Computer Communications Workshops (2019)

30. Zignani, M., Quadri, C., Galdeman, A., Gaito, S., Rossi, G.P.: Mastodon content warnings: inappropriate contents in a microblogging platform. In: International AAAI Conference on Web and Social Media, pp. 639–645 (2019)
31. Zulli, D., Liu, M., Gehl, R.: Rethinking the "social" in "social media": insights into topology, abstraction, and scale on the mastodon social network. New Media Soc. **22**(7), 1188–1205 (2020)

Measuring COVID-19 Vaccine Hesitancy: Consistency of Social Media with Surveys

Ninghan Chen[1], Xihui Chen[1(✉)], Jun Pang[1], Liyousew G. Borga[2], Conchita D'Ambrosio[2], and Claus Vögele[2]

[1] Department of Computer Science, University of Luxembourg, Esch-sur-Alzette, Luxembourg
{ninghan.chen,xihui.chen,jun.pang}@uni.lu
[2] Department of Behavioural and Cognitive Sciences, University of Luxembourg, Esch-sur-Alzette, Luxembourg
{liyousew.borga,conchita.dambrosio,claus.voegele}@uni.lu

Abstract. We validate whether social media data can be used to complement social surveys to monitor the public's COVID-19 vaccine hesitancy. Taking advantage of recent artificial intelligence advances, we propose a framework to estimate individuals' vaccine hesitancy from their social media posts. With 745,661 vaccine-related tweets originating from three Western European countries, we compare vaccine hesitancy levels measured with our framework against that collected from multiple consecutive waves of surveys. We successfully validate that Twitter, one popular social media platform, can be used as a data source to calculate consistent public acceptance of COVID-19 vaccines with surveys at both country and region levels. In addition, this consistency persists over time although it varies among socio-demographic sub-populations. Our findings establish the power of social media in complementing social surveys to capture the continuously changing vaccine hesitancy in a global health crisis similar to the COVID-19 pandemic.

Keywords: Twitter · Surveys · COVID-19 vaccine hesitancy

1 Introduction

The last two and half years have seen the impacts of the unprecedented global COVID-19 pandemic on public health and the economy. Thanks to the successful vaccination program, our societies are gradually reopening and going back to the pre-pandemic states. So far, 68.1% of worldwide populations have been fully vaccinated. This milestone cannot be achieved without fast and accurate understanding of the opinions and responses of general populations towards COVID-19 vaccines and their changes over time. For instance, it allows for identifying the right intervention time and evaluating the effectiveness of deployed measures.

Social media has shown its strengths in complementing conventional surveys to study vaccine hesitancy [27]. Social media overcomes the decreasing response

© The Author(s), under exclusive license to Springer Nature Switzerland AG 2022
F. Hopfgartner et al. (Eds.): SocInfo 2022, LNCS 13618, pp. 196–210, 2022.
https://doi.org/10.1007/978-3-031-19097-1_12

rates of surveys and provides a cost-effective way to reach a significantly larger population [14]. In addition, it allows for capturing the evolution of public opinions over time, especially, in case of emergent incidents such as a sudden outburst of misinformation when there is no sufficient time for conducting surveys. In spite of these advantages, the results derived from social media are often questioned mainly because of three inherent sources of errors: *measurements*, *coding* and *missingness* [4,22]. Measurement errors are incurred by the fact that social media users may not express their real attitudes in their posts while coding errors come from the deficiency of methods in capturing public opinions. Missingness is caused by non-representative social media users, namely, not all people express their opinions online. For instance, Twitter is more favourable to young users while Facebook attracts the elders [33].

We aim to address these challenges confronted in measuring the levels of public vaccine hesitancy with Twitter, one of the most widely used sources of social media data [10,27,34]. Unlike existing works examining correlated factors [27], our purpose is to exemplify that with properly designed methods, individuals' vaccine hesitancy can be *accurately* measured from social media and the estimation is consistent with surveys *continuously over time* and *across countries and regions*. To the best of our knowledge, this is the first attempt to study the temporal consistency of social media with surveys regarding vaccine hesitancy.

We perform a cross-validation by making use of the social survey of multiple waves we conducted and the collected 745,661 tweets related to COVID-19 vaccines from three Western European countries. We take advantage of recent advances in natural language processing techniques, and quantify individuals' vaccine hesitancy based on their attitudes expressed in textual posts. In order to overcome the missingness errors caused by non-representative Twitter users, we show that with three socio-demographic attributes, i.e., gender, age and political ideology, the demographic selection bias can be effectively corrected. When designing our framework, we consider its applicability in a global pandemic like COVID-19 and ensure it can be used in multilingual environments.

With comprehensive analysis, we successfully validate that Twitter is able to give close estimation of vaccine hesitancy to surveys. This closeness persists at a similar level across geographical regions and over time. The large Pearson correlation coefficients indicate at least a strong correlation between the results from surveys and Twitter. We also show that the consistency varies among different socio-demographic groups. Our research re-established the power of Twitter to act as a complementary source to continuously monitor public vaccine hesitancy in COVID-19 and future health crises of similar types.

2 Related Work

Since the outbreak of the COVID-19 pandemic, great efforts have been devoted to studying the potential of social media in understanding the public's hesitancy in the fast developed vaccines [2,10,36,39], based on the pre-pandemic success in studying public opinions [23,27,30,34]. For instance, Cascini et al. [10] reviewed the literature during the COVID-19 pandemic about how diffused information on social media impacts vaccination attitudes. In general, previous works aim to study the correlation of social media users' online activities, e.g., information perception, to vaccine hesitancy. According to sources of online digital traces, the related work falls into two categories. The first category makes use of questionnaires or public polls to collect participants' usage habits of various social media platforms as well as their vaccination attitudes. For instance, with a survey of 504 participants, Alfatease et al. [2] observed the dependence between social media usage and willingness to accept vaccination in Saudi Arabia. Wilson et al. [39] revealed the correlation between online disinformation campaign and activity organisation on social media to vaccine hesitancy. The second category leverages tools such as stance detection to infer various features of online activities from social media data of various formats including hashtags, hyperlinks and textual posts. For instance, Shaaban et al. [36] studied vaccine acceptance with positions and tones of comments on various social media platforms. Lyu et al. [25] inferred user demographics as well as vaccine attitudes through a text-based machine learning approach, and analysed vaccine acceptance among people with different demographic characteristics.

Three characteristics have been well accepted as the advantages of social media over surveys, i.e., *volume, velocity* and *variety* [32] and promoted social media data as a complementary or alternative source of public opinions. However, the inherent limits such as the bias of population coverage and accuracy of extracted opinions, inevitably cause doubts about claims drawn from social media [35]. Several attempts have been conducted to study the reliability of social media data in studying public opinions by comparison to surveys [3,15,27,34]. Davis et al. [15] compared the sentiments of tweets to the polls about public opinions of the Obamacare act and showed the comparability of Twitter public opinions with survey results. Scarborough [34] illustrated the correlation of tweet sentiments to gender attitudes. Amaya et al. [3] evaluated three types of errors that generate the difference between social media and public polls.

Identified Challenges. Few existing works study how and whether individuals' vaccine hesitancy can be directly estimated with digital traces on social media, and whether the estimation is consistent with surveys, especially over time. Although a number of factors have been revealed to be correlated, they can only be interpreted as indicators but not a precise estimation. Without a proper cross-validation, it is unclear whether social media can be used for real-time vaccine hesitancy monitoring as suggested [31]. The work most related to this paper is [18], which compares existing selection bias correction methods with demographic attributes extracted with machining learning models. Different from our paper, it aims at public health status and does not study the consistency of the predictability of online discourses over time.

3   Survey and Twitter Data

Survey. We conducted a survey of people over 18 years of age in 6 European countries, ensuring in each country that the sample was representative in terms of gender, region and age. Information on the status of respondents in the pandemic was collected in order to study the impact of the COVID-19 pandemic [8].

Table 1. Statistics of survey participants and Twitter users.

	#Survey participants	#Twitter users	#Tweets
Luxembourg	474	1,764	28,148
Germany	501	13,390	270,695
France	711	26,562	446,818

We select three adjacent countries, i.e., Germany, France and Luxembourg, as our research objects because of their synchronised vaccination policies and close economic connections. Moreover, the diverse origins of the people are also representative for the worldwide populations. Respondents were invited to fill in online questionnaires including questions about their living conditions, mental health and opinions about vaccination. Meanwhile, socio-demographic characteristics such as age, gender, education and income are also collected. Our survey is conducted in multiple waves at intervals of approximately 4 months. During the waves in June and October of 2021, and March 2022, we consecutively asked about individuals' vaccination attitudes through the following question:

> *Have you been vaccinated against COVID-19?*
> ① *Yes*
> ② *No, but I plan to*
> ③ *No and I do not plan to*

More than 8,000 individuals participated in the first wave. However, only part of them participated consistently in the following waves. As one of our purposes is to test whether Twitter can capture the changes in individuals' vaccination attitudes over time, we only keep the participants that responded in all the three waves. Table 1 shows the statistics of our survey data.

Vaccine Hesitancy Evaluation. The vaccine hesitancy is calculated as the proportion of the participants marking the third option. Let $N_i^{\ell,t}$ ($i \in \{1, 2, 3\}$) be the number of respondents from a given region/country ℓ ticking the i-th option, in a given survey wave t. As the first two options indicate acceptance of COVID-19 vaccines, the vaccine hesitancy of a region ℓ in the survey wave t, denoted by VH_ℓ^t, is calculated as: $VH_\ell^t = \frac{N_3^{\ell,t}}{N_1^{\ell,t} + N_2^{\ell,t} + N_3^{\ell,t}}$.

Twitter Data. We constructed a dataset of Twitter users located in our targeted countries who actively participated in vaccine-related discussions in the periods corresponding to the selected three survey waves. Their tweets are also needed to infer their vaccine hesitancy. As we will see later in Sect. 4.1, in order to employ the vaccination attitude learning model [13], we crawled their social connections as well. Instead of directly crawling tweets worldwide, for the purpose of efficiency, we referred to a publicly available Twitter dataset [11] to obtain the preliminary set of users. The dataset consists of the IDs of 2,198,090 tweets related to vaccination originating from four European countries, i.e., Germany, France, Belgium and Luxembourg generated up to March 2021. Among these tweets, about 17,934 are annotated with the vaccination attitudes expressed, i.e., *positive*, *negative* and *neutral*. We obtained the tweets according to the published tweet IDs with the official Twitter API. From the associated metadata of every downloaded tweet, we derive the IDs of the originating user and his/her location. The geographic information of a tweet is either self-provided by the originator or attached by the device's positioning services such as GPS. We adopted ArcGis, the same approach used in previous works [20], to regularise the locations whenever they are ambiguous into the form of countries and regions. When a user posted multiple tweets with different regions, we select the most frequently used one as the user's location. We only kept the 49,791 users located in Luxembourg, Germany and France. We further downloaded the following relations of each user and constructed a social network represented as a directed graph. A vertex represents a Twitter user while an edge from vertex v to vertex v' indicates that the user corresponding to v follows the user represented by v'.

With the identified Twitter users, we downloaded their tweets posted in the three months when the targeted survey waves were conducted. We used the same keywords as [11] to filter the tweets related to COVID-19 vaccines. We only kept users that posted at least 5 tweets in every targeted month to ensure the reliability of vaccination attitudes calculation. Note that we do *not* consider retweets because compared to quoted and original tweets, they are more likely to carry the intentions of their originating users. As Twitter contains accounts maintained by organisations such as newsagents and healthcare departments, we removed such organisation accounts to ensure that vaccination attitudes belong to the general population. We applied the pre-trained model in [38] to identify such accounts. In total, we removed 5,070 organisation accounts. In the end, we have 1,764 Twitter users from Luxembourg, 13,390 from Germany and 26,562 from France, which are almost 30 times as many as the survey respondents. The IDs of our collected tweets are available at https://anonymous.4open.science/r/country_3_vax_data-43F5/.

4   Measuring Vaccine Hesitancy with Twitter

We select Twitter as the source of vaccination attitudes by assuming Twitter users tend to express their real opinions about COVID-19 vaccines. In other words, we hypothesise the *measurement* error is acceptable when Twitter data is used. In this section, we describe how we handle the other two inherent errors with three sequential steps. The first step targets at reducing the coding error by proposing a measurement of vaccine hesitancy while the other two steps are to correct the missingness error. Note that our aim is not to eliminate the errors but to mitigate the impact of these errors. We adopt widely accepted methodologies to avoid statistic manipulation and thus ensure the generality of our framework.

4.1   Measuring Individual Vaccine Hesitancy

A significant amount of research has been devoted in understanding public opinions from social media posts, varying from word-level [6,19] to data-driven approaches [28,41]. We use one recent deep learning model which is specifically designed to infer COVID-19 vaccination attitudes expressed in tweets and over-whelms existing models in classification accuracy [13]. Another reason for our selection is its power of dealing with multilingualism which is essential for the global demands of vaccination attitude monitoring. Intuitively, the model uses RoBERTa [29], the most popular pre-trained embedding method, to calculate the representation of tweets, and leverages social connections to integrate the recent tweets of each user's friends with a variant of H2GCN [42]. The model takes the text representation of a tweet under analysis and the integrated embedding of the recent discourse of the originating user's friends as input and output the possibility that the tweet is classified into attitudes corresponding to *vaccine support*, *anti-vaccine*, and *neutral*. We retrain this model with the release annotations [11], our constructed social network and collected tweets. The resulted model achieves an accuracy of 0.80 and Marco F1-score of 0.79.

Vaccine Hesitancy Calculation. To estimate an individual user's vaccine hesitancy, we leverage the vaccination attitudes expressed in his/her tweets. Inspired by the measurements in [7,12] which are originally proposed to evaluate subjective well-being, we construct the measurement of vaccine hesitancy. Intuitively, users who post more tweets supporting vaccination are considered more acceptable of COVID-19 vaccines and thus more likely to get vaccinated. Formally, let $N_s(u)$, $N_a(u)$ and $N_{neu}(u)$ be the numbers of tweets of user u posted in a given period t (i.e., June and October 2020, and March 2022 in our analysis), indicating his supportive, anti-vaccine and neutral stance about COVID-19 vaccination, respectively. The vaccine hesitancy of u, denoted by $VH^t(u)$, is calculated as:

$$VH^t(u) = 1 - \frac{VA^t(u)+1}{2}, \text{ where } VA^t(u) = \frac{N_s(u)-N_a(u)}{N_s(u)+N_a(u)} \cdot \left(\frac{N_s(u)+N_a(u)}{N_s(u)+N_a(u)+N_{neu}(u)}\right)^{\frac{1}{2}}.$$
(1)

Note that $VA^t(u)$ is extended by Chen et al. [12] from [7] with *neutral* messages considered by adding a scaling factor. It actually measures the vaccination acceptance of user u and is between -1 and 1. We first normalise it to the domain between 0 to 1 and then compute the complement as the level of vaccine hesitancy. As a result, a user's vaccine hesitancy of 1 indicates total opposition against vaccination and 0 means complete belief in COVID-19 vaccines.

4.2   Inferring Socio-demographic Profiles

The missingness error is related to the socio-demographic selection bias which is a well-recognised inherent limit of social media [33]. One way to correct such bias is to adjust each individual's vaccine hesitancy level by multiplying a factor that is calculated according to the difference between the distributions of social media users and the general population. Despite the large number of out-of-box methods inferring various demographic attributes such as education [18] and income [26], few can be used in our analysis due to their limitation in dealing with multilingual texts. Existing methods, especially the ones based on machine/deep learning, can be extended to multilingual data with well-annotated multilingual data for training and testing. However, due to the privacy protection regulations such as GDPR, it is challenging to collect people's social media accounts and their corresponding socio-demographic information.

In order to ensure our framework applicable globally, we need to select the demographic attributes that can be inferred with multilingual data and effectively mitigate socio-demographic selection bias. Considering these two requirements, we select three socio-demographic attributes, i.e., age, gender and political ideology. We detail the models adopted or extended to infer these three attributes.

Age and Gender. We use the multi-modal deep neural model M3 [38] to infer the age and gender of Twitter users. These two attributes are simultaneously inferred by M3 with users' account name, screen name, self-descriptive description and profile image. A user's age falls into one of the three ranges: 19–29, 30–39 and ≥ 40. Multilingual textual inputs are first translated into English word by word, and the 3,000 most frequent characters are selected to calculate users' embedding. Although the performance of the M3 model has been confirmed by previous studies [17,41], we still construct a sample dataset to test its performance on our collected Twitter data. This sample dataset consists of 100 randomly selected users, whose ages and genders are manually annotated by two annotators. The annotated labels are highly agreed between the two annotators with large Cohen's Kappa coefficients ($k = 0.95$ for gender and $k = 0.81$ for age). When tested on our sample dataset, the M3 model achieves a Macro F1 score of 0.92 and an accuracy of 0.91 for age classification. For gender classification the Macro F1 score is 0.78 and the accuracy is 0.75.

Political Ideology. We infer Twitter users' political ideology by the Multi-task Multi-relational Embedding model (TIMME) [40]. TIMME utilises the heterogeneous types of relationships between Twitter users including 'following', 'retweet', 'mention' and 'like' in conjunction with tweets to infer users' bipolar political ideologies, i.e., left and right. As TIMME is designed for English-only data, we have to re-train it on a multilingual dataset. One distinguishing feature of TIMME is that it can be trained only with a sparsely annotated training set. This allows us to prepare a new training set of a relatively small size from our collected Twitter data with the public Twitter parliamentarians dataset [37]. The dataset [37] contains manually verified parliamentarians from 26 countries, including France, Germany, and Luxembourg, with their names, political ideology, and Twitter IDs. The political ideology is evaluated in a scale from 0 to 10. We manually update the list of parliamentarians of the three countries by i) adding new politicians who joined after the data release, and ii) updating the obsolete Twitter IDs. In total, we constructed a training dataset of 1,021 parliamentarians. We encode the political ideology scores into left, centre and right. Specifically, a score smaller than 4 is encoded as left while a score larger than 6 is encoded as right. A score between 4 and 6 belongs to centre.

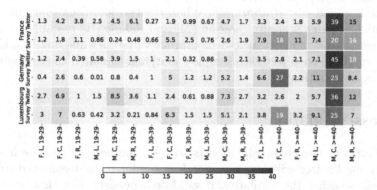

Fig. 1. Population distribution according to age, gender (F: female, M: male) and political ideology (L: left, C: centre, R: right).

We conduct two extensions to TIMME. First, we extend TIMME to a triple classification model (with '*centre*' added) by replacing the binary cross-entropy loss function with a categorical cross-entropy loss function. Second, to enable TIMME to handle multilingual texts, we replace the word-level embedding with RoBERTa [29]. We train the extended TIMME model with the parliamentarian dataset and achieve an accuracy of 0.77 and Marco F1-score of 0.78.

Socio-demographic Selection Bias in our Twitter Data. Figure 1 presents the socio-demographic distributions of the survey participants and our collected Twitter users in the three targeted countries. A significant difference between the two distributions in every country is observed. Moreover, the difference varies from one country to another. When measured by KL-Divergence, we have the distances of 0.52, 0.29 and 0.38 in France, Germany and Luxembourg. This shows the non-representation of Twitter users and the necessity of correction.

4.3 Correcting Socio-demographic Selection Bias

The general idea of socio-demographic correction is to re-weigh non-representative samples' vaccine hesitancy with scalars calculated according to their percentage differences from the representative population. Let ϕ_u be the socio-demographic attributes of user u in the form of age, gender and political ideology. Suppose $\Pr_\ell^S(\phi_u)$ ($\Pr_\ell^T(\phi_u)$) be the percentage of survey participants

(Twitter users) with the same demographic attribute as u in region ℓ. We use $\mathcal{U}^\ell$ to denote the set of users located in the given region ℓ. Thus, the corrected average vaccine hesitancy of region ℓ in time period t is

$$\widehat{VH}_\ell^t = \frac{1}{|\mathcal{U}^\ell|} \sum_{u \in \mathcal{U}^\ell} VH^t(u) \cdot \frac{\Pr_\ell^S(\phi_u)}{\Pr_\ell^T(\phi_u)}. \tag{2}$$

According to the availability of the joint distributions (i.e., $\Pr_\ell^S$ and $\Pr_\ell^T$), we can use different implementations. When the joint distributions are available, the correction is called *post-stratification*. When the two joint distributions are not both available, *naive post-stratification* [24] and *Raking* [16] are applicable. The former assumes independent socio-demographic variables while Raking adopts an iterative approach to adjust each sample's marginal to match the representative population distribution.

5   Cross-Validation

Our objective of the cross-validation is to test whether the vaccine hesitancy inferred from Twitter with our framework is similar to that collected from the survey and whether the similarity, if validated, persists over time and across regions/countries. As vaccine hesitancy varies among countries and regions [21], we study both the country- and region-level vaccine hesitancy. Note that we use post-stratification as the correction method because of the availability of the joint distributions of the three selected socio-demographic attributes.

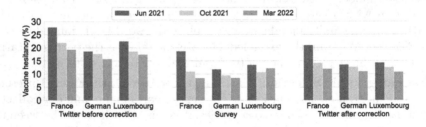

Fig. 2. Vaccine hesitancy across countries.

5.1   Vaccine Hesitancy Across Countries

In Fig. 2, we show the average vaccine hesitancy in Germany, France and Luxembourg in the three survey waves calculated with Twitter data and surveys. In general, Twitter users are more negative about vaccination. In addition, we have three other observations. First, we observe similar changes of vaccine hesitancy over time. This complies with the latest updates derived from surveys/polls around the world which indicate a decreasing trend of vaccine hesitancy [5,9].

This trend presents in all the three countries even without the socio-demographic selection bias correction. Special attention should be paid to the survey of Luxembourg in the last wave. The vaccine hesitancy increased by about 0.015 compared to the second wave. With a manual check, we notice that about 8 participants changed their choice from '*No but I plan to*' to the third option '*No and I do not plan to*'. This increase is actually not consistent with the continuous increase of vaccinated population since October 2021 and may be caused by the relatively smaller number of respondents in Luxembourg. Second, when ordered by their vaccine hesitancy, the countries have similar rankings. Residents in France are relatively more reluctant to get vaccinated compared to the other two countries and people in Germany are more favourable to vaccination. Our third observation is that without bias correction, the vaccine hesitancy calculated with Twitter data is rather different from the survey while correcting selection bias can significantly reduce the difference and ensure a similar estimation. Without the bias correction, the average vaccine hesitancy differences of the three countries are 0.083, 0.089 and 0.077 in the three waves, respectively. The differences drop by more than 70% to 0.019, 0.027 and 0.024 after correction.

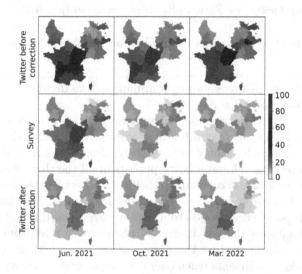

Fig. 3. Vaccine hesitancy across regions from Twitter and survey.

5.2   Vaccine Hesitancy Across Regions

We obtain the regions according to the administrative divisions of the three countries. As the distribution of our survey respondents is not uniform across regions, to ensure the reliability of the vaccination reluctance calculated from our survey, we remove those regions with fewer than 11 participants. In total, we obtain 24 regions including 8 administrative regions of France and 13 states of Germany.

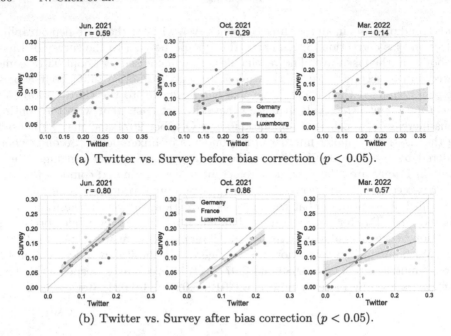

(a) Twitter vs. Survey before bias correction ($p < 0.05$).

(b) Twitter vs. Survey after bias correction ($p < 0.05$).

Fig. 4. Region-level correlations of vaccine hesitancy between Twitter and survey.

Due to the small size of Luxembourg communities, we divide Luxembourg into three regions: north, south and central.

Figure 3 illustrates the region-level vaccine hesitancy in the three survey waves. We can clearly see that after bias correction, Twitter data can reflect similar levels of vaccine hesitancy to the surveys despite the relatively big differences in certain regions. This similarity persists in all the three waves. In Fig. 4, we further show the Pearson correlation coefficient r between the hesitancy levels calculated from Twitter and surveys before and after the socio-demographic bias correction. Each point corresponds to a region with a coordinate (x, y) where x is the vaccine hesitancy derived from Twitter and y is that from the surveys. The orange line is composed by the points where $x = y$. After correction, the Pearson correlation coefficients reach over 0.80 in the first two waves, which indicates a *very strong* correlation according to the well-accepted standard [1]. In the third wave, the correlation strength decreases to 0.57 which is still interpreted as *strong*. After a closer look, we observe that the points that are relatively far from the orange line mainly belong to France and Twitter users acted more negatively about COVID-19 vaccines. We check the news in March 2022 and find that this is the period when the Omicron variants were transmitted fast in eastern France regions. This also implies that Twitter can capture the changes of vaccination attitudes faster than survey in emergent incidents.

We further check whether the above identified correlation persists in various socio-demographic sub-populations. We divide the survey respondents and Twitter users into 18 groups according to their age, gender and political ideology. Then we calculate the region-level vaccination reluctance rates for each group, and compute the Pearson correlation between the reluctance rates of each Twitter group and the corresponding survey group. Figure 5 depicts the results. The general observation is that the correlation indeed varies among different demographic groups. The correlation increases for groups with larger ages but remains almost the same regardless of gender and political ideology. This implies that younger people may actively participate in discussion about vaccines, but they are less willing to express their real intention of vaccination on Twitter. In addition, the correlation decreases with time, which implies when a high-level vaccination rate is reached, the topics on Twitter about COVID-19 vaccines become less relevant to users' intention of vaccination.

6   Discussion and Conclusion

We have proposed a framework to directly estimate public vaccine hesitancy from Twitter. Our framework addressed the widely recognised inherent errors when analysing social media data with a quantitative measurement of vaccine hesitancy and an adapted method correcting socio-demographic selection bias. With our multi-wave surveys and collection of tweets, we conducted the first attempt to validate the consistency between Twitter and surveys regarding monitoring COVID-19 vaccine hesitancy both across regions and over time. Through comprehensive cross-validation, we have shown that Twitter can capture the public vaccine hesitancy and generate at least strongly correlated estimation with that inferred by surveys. Moreover, this correlation is consistent over time on levels of both countries and regions although it varies among different socio-demographic sub-populations. Last but not least, we considered the global demands of vaccination attitude monitoring and empower our framework to deal with multilingual texts. With this paper, we re-established the power of social media in complementing social surveys to continuously capture the fast evolution of vaccine hesitancy in public health crises like COVID-19. Moreover, our work can encourage social scientists to use social media in studies, especially for the topics which are hard to formulate in questionnaires e.g., influences of social interactions on vaccine hesitancy.

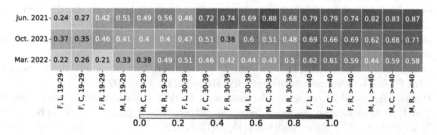

Fig. 5. Pearson correlations (r) between Twitter and survey across 24 regions by Age, gender (F: female, M: male) and political ideology (L: left, C: centre, R: right).

We have a few limitations that will be addressed in future. First, our cross-validation is conducted in Western Europe. Similar studies in other areas can further validate the generality of our framework and our findings. Second, with vaccine hesitancy consistency validated, it will be helpful to examine whether existing social findings such as correlated factors can also be confirmed on social media data. Third, we only tested three socio-demographic attributes. In spite of their effectiveness in bias correction, other socio-demographic attributes can also be tested and added to the bias correction if they can lead to better performance, especially with new progress in artificial intelligence.

Acknowledgement. This research was funded in whole, or in part, by the Luxembourg National Research Fund (FNR), grant reference PRIDE17/12252781 (DRVIVEN), C21/IS/16281848 (HETERS) and 14840950 (COME-HERE). The research is also supported by André Losch Fondation, Art2Cure, Cargolux, and CINVEN Foundation.

Ethical Consideration. This work is solely grounded in public data and does not involve any private information from individuals. The research process was established in full compliance with FAIR data principles, Twitter Developer Agreement & Policy and relevant policies. The survey is also approved by the Ethics Review Panel of our institution.

References

1. Akoglu, H.: User's guide to correlation coefficients. Turk. J. Emerg. Med. **18**(3), 91–93 (2018)
2. Alfatease, A., Alqahtani, A.M., Orayj, K., Alshahrani, S.M.: The impact of social media on the acceptance of the COVID-19 vaccine: a cross-sectional study from Saudi Arabia. Patient Prefer. Adherence **15**, 2673–2681 (2021)
3. Amaya, A., Bach, R., Kreuter, F., Keusch, F.: Measuring the Strength of Attitudes in Social Media Data, chap. 5, pp. 163–192. John Wiley & Sons Ltd. (2020)
4. Baker, R.: Big Data, chap. 3, pp. 47–69. John Wiley & Sons Ltd. (2017)
5. Bartoš, V., Bauer, M., Cahlíková, J., Chytilová, J.: Communicating doctors' consensus persistently increases COVID-19 vaccinations. Nature **606**(7914), 542–549 (2022)
6. Bi, D., Kong, J., Zhang, X., Yang, J.: Analysis on health information acquisition of social network users by opinion mining: case analysis based on the discussion on COVID-19 vaccinations. J. Healthc. Eng. **2021**, 2122095 (2021)
7. Bollen, J., Gonçalves, B., Ruan, G., Mao, H.: Happiness is assortative in online social networks. Artif. Life **17**(3), 237–251 (2011)
8. Borga, L.G., Clark, A.E., D'Ambrosio, C., Lepinteur, A.: Characteristics associated with COVID-19 vaccine hesitancy. Sci. Rep. **12**(1), 1–9 (2022)
9. Burger, R., et al.: Longitudinal changes in COVID-19 vaccination intent among South African adults: evidence from the NIDS-CRAM panel survey, February to May 2021. BMC Public Health **22**(1), 1–10 (2022)
10. Cascini, F., et al.: Social media and attitudes towards COVID-19 vaccination: a systematic review of the literature. eClinicalMedicine **48**, 101454 (2022)

11. Chen, N., Chen, X., Pang, J.: A multilingual dataset of COVID-19 vaccination attitudes on Twitter. Data Brief **44**, article 108503 (2022)
12. Chen, N., Chen, X., Zhong, Z., Pang, J.: The burden of being a bridge: analysing subjective well-being of Twitter users during the COVID-19 pandemic. In: Proceedings 2022 European Conference on Machine Learning and 26th Principles and Practice of Knowledge Discovery in Databases (ECML/PKDD). Lecture Notes in Computer Science. Springer (2022)
13. Chen, N., Chen, X., Zhong, Z., Pang, J.: "Double vaccinated, 5G boosted!": learning attitudes towards COVID-19 vaccination from social media (2022). https://doi.org/10.48550/ARXIV.2206.13456
14. Chen, N., Chen, X., Zhong, Z., Pang, J.: Exploring spillover effects for COVID-19 cascade prediction. Entropy **24**(2), 222 (2022)
15. Davis, M.A., Zheng, K., Liu, Y., Levy, H.: Public response to obamacare on Twitter. J. Med. Internet Res. **19**(5), e167 (2017)
16. Deville, J.C., Särndal, C.E., Sautory, O.: Generalized raking procedures in survey sampling. J. Am. Stat. Assoc. **88**(423), 1013–1020 (1993)
17. Duong, V., Luo, J., Pham, P., Yang, T., Wang, Y.: The ivory tower lost: how college students respond differently than the general public to the COVID-19 pandemic. In: Proceedings of the 2020 IEEE/ACM International Conference on Advances in Social Networks Analysis and Mining (ASONAM), pp. 126–130. IEEE (2020)
18. Giorgi, S., et al.: Correcting sociodemographic selection biases for population prediction from social media. In: Proceedings of the 2022 International AAAI Conference on Web and Social Media (ICWSM), vol. 16(1), pp. 228–240 (2022)
19. Gori, D., et al.: Mis-tweeting communication: a vaccine hesitancy analysis among Twitter users in Italy. Acta Bio Medica: Atenei Parmensis **92**(S6) (2021)
20. Hecht, B.J., Hong, L., Suh, B., Chi, E.H.: Tweets from Justin Bieber's heart: the dynamics of the location field in user profiles. In: Proceedings of the 2011 International Conference on Human Factors in Computing Systems (CHI), pp. 237–246. ACM (2011)
21. Hou, Z., et al.: Assessing COVID-19 vaccine hesitancy, confidence, and public engagement: a global social listening study. J. Med. Internet Res. **23**(6), e27632 (2021)
22. Hsieh, Y.P., Murphy, J.: Total Twitter Error, chap. 2, pp. 23–46. John Wiley & Sons Ltd. (2017)
23. Jaidka, K., Giorgi, S., Schwartz, H.A., Kern, M.L., Ungar, L.H., Eichstaedt, J.C.: Estimating geographic subjective well-being from Twitter: a comparison of dictionary and data-driven language methods. Proc. Natl. Acad. Sci. **117**(19), 10165–10171 (2020)
24. Leemann, L., Wasserfallen, F.: Extending the use and prediction precision of subnational public opinion estimation. Am. J. Polit. Sci. **61**(4), 1003–1022 (2017)
25. Lyu, H., et al.: Social media study of public opinions on potential COVID-19 vaccines: informing dissent, disparities, and dissemination. Intell. Med. **2**(1), 1–12 (2022)
26. Matz, S.C., Menges, J.I., Stillwell, D.J., Schwartz, H.A.: Predicting individual-level income from Facebook profiles. PLoS ONE **14**(3), e0214369 (2019)
27. Nowak, S.A., Chen, C., Parker, A.M., Gidengil, C.A., Matthews, L.J.: Comparing covariation among vaccine hesitancy and broader beliefs within Twitter and survey data. PLOS ONE **15**(10), 1–16 (2020)
28. Nyawa, S., Tchuente, D., Fosso-Wamba, S.: COVID-19 vaccine hesitancy: a social media analysis using deep learning. Ann. Oper. Res. **16**, 1–39 (2022)

29. Ou, X., Li, H.: Ynu_oxz @ haspeede 2 and AMI : XLM-RoBERTa with ordered neurons LSTM for classification task at EVALITA 2020. In: Proceedings of the 2020 Evaluation Campaign of Natural Language Processing and Speech Tools for Italian (EVALITA), vol. 2765. CEUR-WS.org (2020)

30. Piedrahita-Valdés, H., et al.: Vaccine hesitancy on social media: sentiment analysis from June 2011 to April 2019. Vaccines **9**(1), 28 (2021)

31. Puri, N., Coomes, E.A., Haghbayan, H., Gunaratne, K.: Social media and vaccine hesitancy: new updates for the era of COVID-19 and globalized infectious diseases. Huamn Vacc. Immunotherapeut. **16**(11), 2586–2593 (2020)

32. Reveilhac, M., Steinmetz, S., Morselli, D.: A systematic literature review of how and whether social media data can complement traditional survey data to study public opinion. Multimedia Tools Appl. **81**(7), 10107–10142 (2022). https://doi. org/10.1007/s11042-022-12101-0

33. Ribeiro, F.N., Benevenuto, F., Zagheni, E.: How biased is the population of Facebook users? Comparing the demographics of Facebook users with census data to generate correction factors. In: Proceedings of the 2020 ACM Conference on Web Science (WebSci), pp. 325–334. ACM (2020)

34. Scarborough, W.J.: Feminist Twitter and gender attitudes: opportunities and limitations to using Twitter in the study of public opinion. Socius **4**, 2378023118780760 (2018)

35. Schober, M.F., Pasek, J., Guggenheim, L., Lampe, C., Conrad, F.G.: Social media analyses for social measurement. Public Opin. Q. **80**(1), 180–211 (2016)

36. Shaaban, R., Ghazy, R.M., Elsherif, F., et al.: COVID-19 vaccine acceptance among social media users: a content analysis, multi-continent study. Int. J. Environ. Res. Public Health **19**(9), 5737 (2022)

37. van Vliet, L., Törnberg, P., Uitermark, J.: The Twitter parliamentarian database: analyzing Twitter politics across 26 countries. PLoS ONE **15**(9), e0237073 (2020)

38. Wang, Z., et al.: Demographic inference and representative population estimates from multilingual social media data. In: Proceedings of the 2019 World Wide Web Conference (WWW), pp. 2056–2067. ACM (2019)

39. Wilson, S.L., Wiysonge, C.: Social media and vaccine hesitancy. BMJ Global Health **5**(10), e004206 (2020)

40. Xiao, Z., Song, W., Xu, H., Ren, Z., Sun, Y.: TIMME: Twitter ideology-detection via multi-task multi-relational embedding. In: Proceedings of the 2020 ACM SIGKDD International Conference on Knowledge Discovery & Data Mining (KDD), pp. 2258–2268. ACM (2020)

41. Zhang, C., Xu, S., Li, Z., Liu, G., Dai, D., Dong, C., et al.: The evolution and disparities of online attitudes toward COVID-19 vaccines: year-long longitudinal and cross-sectional study. J. Med. Internet Res. **24**(1), e32394 (2022)

42. Zhu, J., Yan, Y., Zhao, L., Heimann, M., Akoglu, L., Koutra, D.: Beyond homophily in graph neural networks: current limitations and effective designs. In: Proceedings of the 2020 Annual Conference on Neural Information Processing Systems (NeurIPS), vol. 33, pp. 7793–7804. NeurIPS (2020)

A Quantitative Field Study
of a Persuasive Security Technology
in the Wild

John Paul Vargheese[1]($\boxtimes$), Matthew Collinson[2], and Judith Masthoff[3]

[1] Edinburgh Napier University, Edinburgh, UK
jpvargheese@acm.org
[2] University of Aberdeen, Aberdeen, UK
matthew.collinson@abdn.ac.uk
[3] Utrecht University, Utrecht, The Netherlands
j.f.m.masthoff@uu.nl

Abstract. Persuasive techniques and persuasive technologies have been suggested as a means to improve user cybersecurity behaviour, but there have been few quantitative studies in this area. In this paper, we present a large scale evaluation of persuasive messages designed to encourage University staff to complete security training. Persuasive messages were based on Cialdini's principles of persuasion, randomly assigned, and transmitted by email. The training was real, and the messages sent constituted the real campaign to motivate users during the study period. We observed statistically significant variations, but with mild effect sizes, in participant responses to the persuasive messages. 'Unity' persuasive messages that had increased emphasis on the collaborative role of individual users as part of an organisation-wide team effort towards cybersecurity were more effective compared to 'Authority' messages that had increased emphasis on a mandatory obligation of users imposed by a hierarchical authority. Participant and organisational factors also appear to impact upon participant responses. The study suggests that the use of messages emphasising different principles of persuasion may have different levels of effectiveness in encouraging users to take particular security actions. In particular, it suggests that the use of social capital, in the form of increased emphasis of 'unity', may be more effective than increased emphasis of 'authority'. These findings motivate further studies of how the use of Social capital may be beneficial for encouraging individuals to adopt similar positive security behaviours.

Keywords: Cybersecurity · Behaviour change · Persuasive technology · Actual effectiveness · Quantitative field study

© The Author(s), under exclusive license to Springer Nature Switzerland AG 2022
F. Hopfgartner et al. (Eds.): SocInfo 2022, LNCS 13618, pp. 211–232, 2022.
https://doi.org/10.1007/978-3-031-19097-1_13

1   Introduction

Organisations are increasingly at risk to cyberattacks designed to manipulate users' behaviour to create and exploit cybersecurity vulnerabilities [4,17,101]. This often involves attackers imitating legitimate channels of communications to prompt and trigger insecure behaviour amongst users that can result in their and or an entire organisation's security being compromised [6,28,44,45,68,81]. To address the increasing risk posed by cyberthreats, many organisations invest in and apply technical solutions such as firewalls, anti-virus software, and other tools for monitoring IT systems to maintain security [34,43,53,70,74,86,98]. Despite these efforts, recent studies have emphasised that technical approaches alone are not sufficient [49,50,54,78,96] and organisations continue to be susceptible to cyberattacks [52,71]. This has led to increasing calls for organisations to address individual and organisational factors to maintain their security [74,102]. To achieve this, organisations design security policies to manage users' behaviour and encourage safe and secure usage of their IT systems [16,34,51,59,74,86,87,98]. However, this approach is also insufficient as users' do not always comply with security policies [47,52,62,74,85,87–89,96]. Furthermore, studies investigating causes of insecure behaviour indicate that these are not always related to users' non-compliance with security policies but often overlap with other individual personal and organisational factors [8,13,29,36]. Consequently, users' behaviour continues to be frequently reported as a significant cause of security breaches [26] and there is an increasing need for organisations to discover effective ways to encourage safe and secure behaviour amongst users [12,13,63].

The user's environment, including technological environment and social environment, is composed by factors that influence their behaviour. This suggests the need to bring insights from psychology, including social psychology, to the problem in order to design behaviour change interventions that will address user security behaviours [32,33]. At the same time, technology offers a potential mode for delivering behavioural interventions. If an intervention can be automated, this can allow it to scale-up to larger user bases where other types of intervention may be infeasible. Further, it may be that the most appropriate way to intervene is via technology, for example at the moment that the user's vulnerability is being exploited, or by changing the technological environment. Existing security technologies and management strategies already take advantage of these two benefits of technology, but, perhaps, not always in an optimal fashion.

The field of *persuasive technology* (or the roughly synonymous term *digital behaviour intervention*) is concerned with the study and introduction of technologies that change behaviour, specifically without coercion, with applications across a number of areas. A number of authors from the security domain have suggested that persuasive technologies, and persuasive techniques, may have an important role to play in security [5,8,22,42,100]. While the underlying technology substrate may sometimes be commonplace (for example email in this study), persuasive technology researchers draw upon insights from psychology in designing interventions on top of that substrate, and use rigorous scientific methods for analysis and evaluation [25,64,91].

One proposed behaviour change approach, much studied in recent years, includes applying behavioural *nudges*, in which re-design of an individual's decision environment ('choice architecture') guides them to make certain choices rather than others. Often the nudge is in a form such that the individual is not explicitly aware of it. Examples of this approach are the MINDSPACE framework [35], and the SCENE framework [30] tailored for cybersecurity. Applications of nudging to cybersecurity include encouraging safer mobile device usage [9,23,92,94], improving password management [55,77], quantitative access control [69], increasing awareness and improving decision making related to social media disclosures and general privacy concerns [2,99].

An alternative approach involves applying *explicit* persuasive messages. This approach is commonly applied within the persuasive technology domain, and has been demonstrated to be effective for changing individuals behaviour across a range of domains by encouraging healthy eating, increasing physical activity, participating in health and wellbeing activities and sustainable ecological behaviour [48,73]. However, study of the use of explicit persuasive messages, such as those based on Cialdini's well-known principles of persuasion [24], together with measures of actual effectiveness, rather than perceived effectiveness, and particularly in-the-wild, has been limited within the context of encouraging users to engage with information security. An exception is a major study of the effectiveness of the 'social proof' persuasive strategy [33].

In this paper, we present results from a large-scale, quantitative, empirical field study of persuasive messaging for encouraging staff in an organisation (a university) to participate in information security awareness (ISA) training. This study was conducted by incorporating explicit persuasive messages based on random assignment of Cialdini's [24] principles of persuasion within an existing corporate communications infrastructure. Evaluation studies of persuasive messages, widely reported in the persuasive technology literature, often involve the use of *perceived effectiveness* as an outcome measure, based on participant self reporting measures [73]. For this study, we used *actual effectiveness* as an outcome measure based on the direct observable behaviour of participants in response to the persuasive messages applied during the study. This provided us with a more objective measure of the persuasive messages' effectiveness in a real non controlled environment. Our results indicate that there are significant differences in the effectiveness of the persuasive messages used in the study and the role of individual and organisational factors. We also discovered that persuasive messages that included reference to the collaborative role of staff to safeguard the university from potential cyberthreats (aligned with the 'unity' persuasive strategy [24]) were more effective compared to those which emphasised the authority imposed, mandatory requirement for all members of staff to complete their training (aligned with the 'authority' persuasive strategy [24]).

In Sect. 2 of this paper we provide an overview of behaviour change and persuasive techniques, followed by a brief review of behaviour change interventions within a cybersecurity context. In Sect. 3 we describe our methodology, study procedure and present our research question and hypothesis. We present the results of our study in Sect. 4. The limitations of the study are discussed in Sect. 5 and in Sect. 6 we review and discuss key findings and outline our plans for future work.

2   Related Work

Interventions capable of changing individual behaviour are increasingly in demand, because of the impact of the negative consequences that may arise from an individual's actions and decisions. For example, poor diet, lack of exercise and smoking, may result in severe health problems. Similarly, insecure usage of IT systems such as clicking on a link within a phishing email and sharing passwords may compromise security. Behaviour change interventions aim to motivate and encourage individuals towards improving their behaviour, in addition to deterring behaviours that can lead to negative and undesirable consequences [73].

2.1   Behaviour Change and Persuasive Techniques

In broad terms, human behaviour may occur as a result of either automatic, indirect (also referred to as System 1) processing and/or reflective, direct (System 2) processing of cues within the context of a given scenario or environment [19,39,76,90]. Many behaviour change interventions and persuasive technology design frameworks incorporate a model of behaviour that may be used to elicit behavioural determinants or factors that may influence and change an individual's behaviour for a given scenario [41,65,72]. Upon establishing how certain behaviours occur and why, it is possible to begin considering what specific techniques may be applied to bring about a desired outcome. However, it is often difficult for intervention designers to establish a suitable theoretical foundation, that provides a testable hypothesis for how and why a particular behavioural change or persuasive technique may influence and determine an individual's behaviour [7,66]. This is often due to the diversity and interrelated aspect of behavioural determinants that may lead to an intervention's means of achieving the intended outcome [31].

Within the Persuasive Technology domain, a common approach towards designing behaviour change interventions involves applying persuasive messages based on principles of persuasion as defined by Cialdini [24]. Such persuasive messages may be designed to bring about changes in behaviour using either 'System 1' or 'System 2' processing, but in the case of the latter, these are intended to trigger a willing change in beliefs and attitudes that may result in a change of behaviour [20,40,84]. Table 1 lists Cialdini's principles and how these may be applied to develop persuasive messages for behaviour change.

An alternative approach that incorporates both the MINDSPACE [35] framework and Cialdini's [24] principles of persuasion is the Behaviour Change Wheel (BCW) [65]. BCW incorporates the Capability, Opportunity, Behaviour

Table 1. Cialdini's principles of persuasion and how these may be applied within persuasive strategies to change behaviour [24]

Principle of persuasion	Potential strategy approach and impact on behaviour
Reciprocity	We are likely to respond in kind as the receiving party in an exchange out of a sense of obligation to do so
Commitment and Consistency	We aim to be consistent in our actions and decision to avoid complexity arising from inconsistencies in our behaviour
Social proof	Our actions beliefs and behaviours may be strongly influenced by what we observe in others as correct and/or appropriate
Liking	We may be significantly influenced by what is attractive and appealing to us
Authority	We will often accept the beliefs and attitudes of those we consider to be within a position of expertise
Scarcity	We are strongly influenced to avoid loss
Unity	Reference to shared identities we define ourselves as a member of together with others can strongly influence our behaviour

(COM-B) model which is based upon a systematic analysis of 19 frameworks of behaviour change [65]. The COM-B model may be used to perform a "behavioural diagnosis" based upon how the three components of this model interact to form behaviour which also has an effect and impact on these components [67]. BCW may be used to link the findings from this analysis to specific intervention types and policies that support their implementation [65,67]. In the next Section, we discuss examples of behaviour change techniques within the security domain.

2.2 Behaviour Change for Cybersecurity

As discussed by Briggs et al. [15], protection motivation theory (PMT) [79] has been applied to a range of studies [21,60,82] investigating users' behaviour within a cybersecurity context. In summary, PMT suggests that individuals will perform protective actions based on a prior assessment of a potential threat (threat appraisal) and their ability to engage in recommended preventative measures (response efficacy and coping appraisal) [79].

Nudges have been suggested as a suitable approach towards changing users' behaviour by aiding decision making related to application privacy settings, in order to avoid unintended disclosure of personal information [1,2,9,10,30]. Users' are often willing to accept a trade-off for security and privacy settings due to what has been described as "Psychological distortions" driven by heuristics, cognitive and behavioural biases such as hyperbolic discounting, lack of self control and immediate gain; that may lead to insecure behaviours [1,2,29]. Nudges may be applied to address these issues by taking advantage of how users' may be influenced by such 'System 1' and/or automatic cues, to change their behaviour.

For example, Choe et al. investigated positive and negative framing effects via a visual representation of a mobile application's privacy ratings [23]. Results from this study indicate that this is an effective means for increasing users' understanding of the potential risks of installing privacy-invasive mobile applications and how this may discourage users to do so [23]. Van Brugeen et al. investigated how messages based on incentives, morality and deterrence may be used for encouraging users to lock their smartphones [94]. Results of this study indicate that messages based on morality are most effective over time, while those based on deterrence are more immediately effective [94]. Nudges incorporated within personal firewall warning messages have also been demonstrated to be effective with increasing users' risk perception and understanding of the possible negative consequences of their actions in addition to encouraging safer behaviours after receiving such warnings [75].

Kankane et al. conducted a study investigating the effects of five different messages based on incentive, norm, default, salience and ego nudges that may be used to influence users' password management behaviour [55]. Results indicate that the salience nudge was most effective for reducing participants' perceived level of comfort with accepting an auto-generated password and the default nudge was the least effective.

Nudges have also been demonstrated to be effective for improving users' decision making related to selecting wireless network connections. Nudges investigated included using colour coding, order of presentation and a combination of both nudges, to encourage users to select secure rather than less secure wireless network connections. Results indicate that colour coding was more effective compared to ordering, although the combination of both was the most effective for encouraging users to select secure over less secure networks [92].

2.3   Motivation for Study

To develop effective behaviour change interventions to improve cybersecurity, it is necessary to conduct evaluations studies using direct behavioural measurements (actual effectiveness) that provide evidence of how such interventions may change users' behaviour [38,95]. The study presented in this paper investigates the actual effectiveness of persuasive messages designed to encourage university staff to complete ISA training. For ISA training to be effective, user participation is essential [3] and lack of motivation amongst users' to do so may hinder its overall effectiveness [93].

Understanding of actual effectiveness of behavioural interventions calls for repeated laboratory studies (to get insight into 'efficacy' with significant control over variables under ideal conditions), repeated field studies (to understand 'effectiveness' of interventions where variables are less controlled), and an understanding of the causal mechanisms behind the effectiveness of the intervention (to understand the limits of the transport of results from one field to another)

[18,46]. For our contribution, we conducted one, quite large, field study, focusing on comparisons of a small number of interventions of similar type (explicit persuasive messages) in order to have a reasonable experimental design.

For this study, we had available an existing corporate communications infrastructure, using email, but importantly also access to the underlying organisational structure, for example, the communications team, and sign-off from senior management and the IT department. With the constraints of this real-world context, not all forms and strengths of persuasive message would have been appropriate, or possible, to trial.

3 Methodology

The study was conducted at a university with participants consisting of members of staff only. The university requires staff to complete a range of training courses such as health and safety, equality and diversity and ISA training. The usual procedure for delivering such training involves emailing members of staff a notification that such training is available, required to be completed, and how to access it. Training is usually provided by a web service. Over a period of time, the completion rate for the training is monitored and reminder emails sent to those members of staff who have not yet completed it.

The study procedure for our research followed a similar process, incorporating different types of persuasive messages within notification and reminder emails. We describe each stage of the study procedure in the following sections and an overview of the whole process is presented in Fig. 1.

3.1 Study Procedure

Following current practice at the university, all members of staff received a notification email sent on behalf of a senior member of the management. The email included one of four types of persuasive messages (authority, commitment, reciprocity and unity) which were randomly assigned to participants.

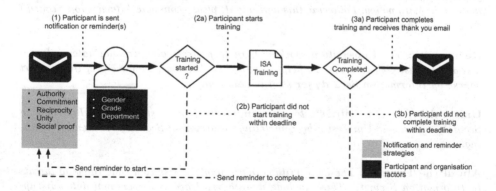

Fig. 1. Study procedure

Two weeks after the original notification emails were sent, reminder emails were sent to members of staff who were yet to start the training. Reminder to start (RTS) emails included a slightly modified and reduced version of the type of persuasive message used in the original notification. This was intended to reduce any possible effect of participants feeling manipulated as discussed in related work concerning repeated use of persuasive messages [97].

Four weeks after the original notification emails were sent, all staff who had not yet completed the training received a reminder to complete (RTC) email. This email was sent irrespective of whether any RTS email had been sent and all RTC emails contained the same Social proof strategy. This strategy aims to influence an individual's behaviour by referring to the behaviour of others in a social context, to encourage an individual to perform the same behaviour [24]. We therefore considered Social proof to be appropriate for RTC emails because this stage of the study provided suitable context for encouraging members of staff to complete the training by referring to those who had already done so.

3.2   Persuasive Messages for Notification and Reminder Emails

Each category of persuasive message used in the study was created using Cialdini's principles of persuasion [24]. We choose not to use scarcity and liking as we believed these would not be suitable for the application context and goal of persuasion (starting and completing ISA training). Each notification email consisted of three sections and was addressed to each member of staff. The first section included one of the following persuasive messages, a generic motivation statement about the training (regardless of which persuasive message participants received) and instructions on how to access the training:

Authority: *The University requires you to complete mandatory Information Security Awareness training. We know that use of our IT systems is crucial to protecting our networks and data.*

Commitment: *You have been issued with a personal IT account. In using this account, you have agreed to usage conditions including compliance with the University's Information Security policy. Following this agreement, please complete Information Security Awareness training.*

Reciprocity: *The University is working hard to protect your personal data and user account against Cyberattacks. To help us with this challenge, we have prepared a short course on Information Security for staff to complete.*

Unity: *All of us can contribute to maintaining the highest standards of Information Security within our University by completing Information Security Awareness Training.*

About the Training: *The University is increasingly at risk to a wide range of threats to Information Security. These include unauthorised access to personal data, disruption to the University network and criminal and fraudulent attacks targeting users. To* *ensure the University is protected against these threats, it is essential that all users are aware of the risks to Information Security and can respond appropriately.*

RTS emails consisted of two sections, a slightly reduced and modified persuasive messages of the same category as the prior notification received and access instructions. The RTS strategies are listed as follows:

Authority: *The Information Security Awareness training has been available since the <date-prior-email-received>. All members of staff should complete this training to ensure access to the University's IT Systems is both safe and secure.*

Commitment: *As part of your agreement with the University regarding safe usage of our IT systems, please start your Information Security Awareness training.*

Reciprocity: *We want to ensure that the user account we have provided for you to carry out your duties is both protected and secure. Please start your Information Security Awareness training.*

Unity: *Please start your Information Security and Awareness training and join your fellow colleagues helping to protect and secure our IT Systems.*

Staff members who did not complete the training received the following RTC email, regardless of any category of persuasive message previously received:

Social Proof: *Please join your fellow colleagues by completing your Information Security Awareness training.*

All emails included a standard disclaimer that provided information concerning how data acquired, based on participants' responses to each email received, would be used for research purposes. Further information included details for how participants could have their data removed from our analysis[1]. A link to the research project website was included, that provided more specific details about the research study, with the exception of how different persuasive messages were being used. This was intended as a means to reduce any possibility of priming participant responses, based on revealing the objectives of the research study. Therefore, at the end of the study period, for all participants who did not request for their data to be withdrawn from our analysis, an email was sent stating that further information about the study was available via the research project website, which stated that a range of different persuasive messages has been used in addition to further information about the objectives of the research study. Participants could still withdraw at this stage.

---

[1] Permission for using opt-out rather than opt-in consent was granted by the university ethics committee, and the emails made it very clear that participation in the study would not impact on work.

3.3 Research Question and Hypothesis

The aim of this study was to gather empirical evidence of the actual effectiveness of persuasive messages for encouraging university staff to complete ISA training. As discussed in Sect. 3, the study procedure followed common practice for encouraging university staff to undertake training courses though the use of notification and reminder emails. This provided a means to investigate the actual effectiveness of the persuasive messages by measuring the distribution of participants' responses throughout the study. Where significant variations in the distribution of participant responses are present, this would suggest that the persuasive messages are not equally effective. This would indicate that at least one persuasive messages was significantly more effective than another. Therefore our research question is as follows:

RQ1 Is the distribution of participant responses the same for all persuasive messages?

To develop a testable hypothesis for RQ1, we categorised participants' responses for those who completed the training as an ordinal dependent variable based on different periods of the study: notification to RTS, RTS to RTC, and RTC to end of study period. A further category for participants who did not complete the training within the study period was also included. This was necessary to ensure the dependent variable was a sufficient measure of actual effectiveness by incorporating all possible participant responses to the persuasive messages during the study. We refer to this measure as *response categories*. Significant variations present in the distribution of response categories would suggest that at least one persuasive message is more effective than another. Therefore our hypothesis for the study is as follows:

H^0 There is no significant variation in the distribution of response categories for all persuasive messages

H^1 There is a significant variation in the distribution of response categories for all persuasive messages

3.4 Confounding Variables

Additional participant data acquired for our analysis included gender, grade[2] and which school of the university participants were associated with. To ensure participants' anonymity was preserved, individual grades of participants were banded into three groups. Grades one to four were grouped into a single band as grade one, grades five to seven were grouped into grade two and all remaining higher grades (eight and nine) grouped into grade three. Grade provides an indication of seniority within the university and also corresponds to participants' age. As such it is possible that participants' grade may have an impact on the distribution of participant responses during the study. We refer to organisational units of the university as 'school' whose disciplines were also anonymised to further ensure participant's anonymity was preserved. As with grade, it is

---

[2] Grade refers to an ordered grouping of roles within the organisation.

possible that participants' responses may vary based upon which school they are associated with. Although we are required to preserve the anonoymity of Schools, we are interested in discovering whether there are any variations in the distribution of participant responses based on School. Due to this study being run in the wild, we could not ensure equal distribution of persuasive messages based on either participant or organisational factors. Therefore our analysis of the results follows the use of non-parametric statistics as these are suitable in cases where the distribution of the dependent variable is not equally distributed amongst the independent variables [83]. In the next section, we report the main findings of this study and an exploratory analysis investigating whether there are any significant variations in the distribution of response categories and participant and organisational factors(gender, grade and school) is presented in Appendix A.

4   Results

The study was conducted with 1592 participants[3]. The sample included (58%) female, (42%) male, (29%) within grade 1, (52%) within grade 2 and (20%) within grade 3. The distribution of participants across individual Schools is shown in Appendix A, in Table 5, together with results from our exploratory analysis of participant and organisational factors as discussed in Sect. 3.4. We conducted a χ^2 test to discover whether there was a significant imbalance of persuasive messages across participant and organisational factors, for each factor. This is considered suitable to discover whether there is a significant difference in the frequencies of two or more independent groups (persuasive messages, participant and organisational factors) [83]. Results from these tests indicate that there is no significant difference between the frequencies of persuasive messages received based on participants gender ($\chi^2(3) = 5.559, p = .013$), grade ($\chi^2(6) = 12.591, p = .05$) and school ($\chi^2(36) = 32.683, p = .627$).

Table 2 list the distribution of response categories for all persuasive messages. To discover whether there was any significant variation in the distribution of response categories for all persuasive messages, we conducted a Kruskal Wallis test, which is suitable for identifying whether there is a significant difference between two or more groups of an independent variable (persuasive messages) which are not equally distributed using an ordinal dependent variable (response categories) [83]. Results from this test indicate that there is a significant difference in the distribution of response categories for all persuasive messages: ($H(3) = 8.94, p = .03$). These results provide support for H^1 by indicating that there is a significant variation in the distribution of response categories for all persuasive messages. Therefore, we address **RQ1** by concluding that the distribution of participant responses is not the same for all persuasive messages. This

---

[3] This is after the exclusion of staff who opted-out, staff who were excluded as their anonymity could not be guaranteed, and cases where the data showed anomalies such as training being completed before the notifications were sent, e.g. IT staff testing access to the training.

suggests that the persuasive messages are not equally effective and at least one persuasive message is more effective than another.

Following these results, we conducted a post hoc Dunn's test, to discover whether there were any specific significant variations in response categories between the persuasive messages using a Bonferroni correction to control for type 1 errors [37]. We discovered a significant variation in the distribution of response categories between the Unity and Authority persuasive messages ($p = .03, r = .1$). Participants who received the unity persuasive message completed the training earlier, with fewer not completing the training compared to those who received authority. No other significant variation in the distribution of response categories was discovered for any other pairwise comparison of persuasive messages. Therefore, we conclude that the unity persuasive message was more effective compared to the authority persuasive message only. We note that despite a significant variation in the distribution of response categories between the unity and authority persuasive message, the effect size is small [27].

Table 2. Distribution of response categories for each persuasive message

	Persuasive message				
Study period	Authority	Commitment	Reciprocity	Unity	Total
Notification to RTS	164	172	136	157	629
RTS to RTC	86	85	90	86	347
RTC to End	82	71	58	67	278
Not completed	112	85	83	58	338
Total	444	413	367	368	1592

5   Study Limitations

As part of the conditions for ethical approval to perform this study, it was necessary to acquire informed consent by participants using a disclaimer included within the emails sent to participants during the study. Consequently, it is possible that participants may have responded differently if they were not informed about the study in progress. To minimise this effect, participants were only informed that a study on the use of persuasive messages was being conducted but not that different message strategies had been used throughout. This information was later released on the project website and participants who did not opt out of the study, regardless of whether they completed the training or when, received this information as part of the thank you email.

Another condition as part of our ethical approval included the need to mention within the disclaimer, that regardless of whether participants choose to opt out of the study or not, that it was mandatory for members of staff to undertake training as part of university policy. This may also have influenced the participants in addition to type of persuasive message received and as such, each email contained some aspect of the authority principal.

The live nature and environment for this field study limited the way in which the study could be run, and this limits the conclusions that can be drawn. For example, no control or neutral (no persuasive message applied) condition could be applied to participants. This was necessary as part of the conditions for ethical approval to perform the study and to fulfil the university requirement that all members of staff complete the training. It was considered that participants who did not receive a persuasive message containing at least one persuasive principle may be less likely to complete the training compared to those who did receive a persuasive message containing at least one persuasive principle. For a second example, while messages were intended to emphasise one persuasive principle or other, they (through the message itself or source and channel) often contained other factors that could influence behaviour (e.g. other principles). For example, all messages were known to come from an authoritative source (the university). We therefore cannot conclude in all certainty that the effectiveness of a message was a result of its privileged persuasive principle, rather than the result of some other factor.

6   Conclusions and Discussion

This paper presents a study of the relative effectiveness of four persuasive messages for encouraging users to complete ISA training. This study is one of very few which was performed in the wild and measured the actual effectiveness rather than perceived effectiveness of persuasive messages. We observed that there was a significant variation in participants responses to the persuasive messages. This suggests that some persuasive messages differ in effectiveness. There was a significant difference between the responses to the unity and authority persuasive messages, but the effect size associated with the significant variation in participant responses between the two was small. This is perhaps because the different messages had mild variations of emphasis of different persuasive principles, rather than using completely different principles. As discussed in Sect. 3.2, only the first section of each email contained one of the persuasive messages with the remaining content being identical for all emails. Furthermore, as discussed in Sect. 5, each email included some aspect of the authority principle within the disclaimer which may have influenced participants. However, this means that such small changes of emphasis may not make a practical difference.

Our results concerning the unity persuasive message would appear to support claims that individuals may alter their behaviours (within the context of cybersecurity related behaviours) to match others whom they identify as being a part of the same group (in the case of our study, members of staff at the University) [11]. It is possible that the unity persuasive message triggers social capital as the motivation for participants to complete their training, through this message's emphasis on shared collaboration towards a common beneficial goal. As discussed by Sasse et al. [58] individuals within an organisation are, to a certain degree, "emotionally attached" to the organisations they are apart of [61, 80] and may be motivated and capable of performing protective behaviours

[14,56,57], which is the overall objective for engaging with ISA training. Herath et al. suggests that motivation to perform security related behaviours (in the case of our study engaging with ISA training) may be influenced by users' "closeness" to organisation they are a part of [50]. At the same time it is possible that the authority message constrains and/or weakens social capital as a motivator by implying that although completing the training is important, this is nevertheless a mandatory (enforced) request. Further studies are required to clarify this.

In future work, we plan to investigate the perceived effectiveness of the persuasive messages using a scenario based approach that provides a greater means to measure specific individual and organisational factors, compared to a field study in the wild. We intend to discover whether the results from such a study would yield similar results with respect to the variations in participant responses to the unity and authority message and to what extent more specific measures of participant and organisational factors may influence participants' susceptibility to the persuasive messages.

Acknowledgements. This research was supported by the UKRI EPSRC award: EP/P011829/1.

A   Exploratory Analysis

This section reports results from an exploratory analysis of participant and organisational factors captured during the study. The aim of this analysis was to discover whether there are significant variations in the distribution of response categories for each factor. Our research questions and hypothesis are:

RQ2 Is the distribution of participant responses the same for all participant and organisational factors?

H^0 There is no significant variation in the distribution of response categories for all participant and organisational factors.
H^1 There is a significant variation in the distribution of response categories for all participant and organisational factors.

We expanded *RQ2* to *RQ2a*, *RQ2b* and *RQ2c* to account for gender, grade and School respectively.

A.1   Analysis of Gender and Participant Responses

Table 3. Distribution of response categories by gender

Study period	Female	Male	Total
Notification to RTS	385	244	629
RTS to RTC	192	155	347
RTC to End	161	117	278
Not completed within study period	181	157	338
Total	919	673	1592

Table 3 shows the distribution of response categories by gender. To discover whether there is a significant variation in the distribution of response categories by participant gender, we conducted a Mann-Whitney U test, which is suitable for identifying whether there is a significant variation in the distribution of an dependent variable (response categories) between two independent groups (male and female). Results from this test indicates that there is an overall significant difference *between female and male* participants ($U(Female = 919, Male = 673) = 328527, two tailed, p = .03, r = .1$). It appears that female participants completing the training earlier with fewer not completing the training compared to male participants. We therefore address **RQ2a** by concluding that there was an overall impact of gender on participant responses during the study. We note that despite discovering a significant variation in the distribution of response categories between female and male participants, the effect size is small [27].

A.2   Analysis of Grade and Participant Responses

Table 4 shows the distribution of response categories by participant grade. To discover whether was any significant variation in the distribution of response categories by grade, we conducted a Kruskal Wallis test as discussed in Sect. 4. Results from this test indicate that there is an overall significant variation in the distribution of response categories *between grades* ($H(2) = 10, p = 0.007$). Following these results, we conducted a post-hoc Dunn's test to discover whether there were any specific significant variations in response categories *between grades*. Pairwise comparisons using Bonferroni adjusted p-values reveal a significant difference *between Grades 1 and 3* ($p = .01, r = -.1$) and *between Grades 2 and 3* ($p = .03, r = -.1$). It appears that participants within lower grades completed the training earlier, with fewer participants not completing the training, with the greatest difference being *between Grades 1 and 3* compared to *between Grades 2 and 3*, although we note that effect sizes for these observations are small [27]. We therefore address **RQ2b** by concluding that there was an overall impact of grade on participant responses during the study. Results from our post-hoc analysis suggests participants in lower grades completed the training earlier with fewer participants not completing the training, compared to those in higher grades.

Table 4. Distribution of response categories by grade

Study period	Grade 1	Grade 2	Grade 3	Total
Notification to RTS	198	328	103	629
RTS to RTC	92	188	67	347
RTC to End	73	146	59	278
Not completed within study period	91	165	82	338
Total	454	827	311	1592

A.3   Analysis of School and Participant Responses

Table 5. Distribution of response categories by School

Study period	School													**Total**
	1	2	3	4	5	6	7	8	9	10	11	12	13	
Notification to RTS	191	6	12	94	4	196	34	28	10	9	25	10	10	629
RTS to RTC	100	7	17	48	5	82	24	24	8	8	10	9	5	347
RTC to End	79	4	11	62	6	59	16	10	6	7	12	5	1	278
Not completed within study period	75	9	19	32	12	77	15	23	15	22	19	5	15	338
Total	445	26	59	236	27	414	89	85	39	46	66	29	31	1592

Table 5 shows the distribution of response categories by School. We repeat our approach for analysis grade in our analysis of School using a Kruskal Wallis test. Results indicate a significant variation in the distribution of response categories *between* Schools ($H(12) = 64.1, p < .01$). Table 6 lists all significant pairwise comparisons between Schools, with Bonferroni corrected p values.

For each significant comparison, it appears that participants in Schools 1, 4, 6 and 7 completed the training earlier, with fewer participants not completing the training, compared to Schools 3, 5 and 10, respectively for each comparison listed. Effect sizes for these observations are small. We address **RQ2c** by concluding that there was an overall impact of school on participant responses during the study. Due to the needs to preserve the anonymity of schools within the university, our conclusions as to the specific pairwise differences between schools are limited. Further studies are required to investigate what properties of the schools may lead to such results.

Table 6. Post-hoc pairwise comparison of response categories by School with Bonferroni adjusted p values (non significant results have been excluded)

Pairwise comparison		n	z	p	r
School 1	School 5	472	−3.70	.02	−.2
School 6	Schooll 10	460	−4.69	<.001	−.2
School 1	School 10	491	−4.38	<.001	−.2
School 4	School 10	282	−3.91	.01	−.2
School 7	School 10	135	−3.44	.04	−.2
School 1	School 3	504	−3.42	.04	−.2
School 6	School 3	473	−3.76	.01	−.2
School 6	School 5	441	−3.94	.01	−.2

References

1. Acquisti, A.: Privacy in electronic commerce and the economics of immediate gratification. In: Proceedings of 5th ACM Conference on Electronic Commerce, pp. 21–29 (2004)
2. Acquisti, A.: Nudging privacy: the behavioral economics of personal information. IEEE Secur. Priv. **7**(6), 82–85 (2009)
3. Albrechtsen, E., Hovden, J.: Improving information security awareness and behaviour through dialogue, participation and collective reflection. an intervention study. Comput. Secur. **29**(4), 432–445 (2010)
4. Anderson, R.J.: Security Engineering: A Guide to Building Dependable Distributed Systems. 2nd edn, Wiley, Hoboken (2008)
5. Ashenden, D., Lawrence, D.: Can we sell security like soap?: A new approach to behaviour change. In: Proceedings of 2013 New Security Paradigms Workshop, ACM (2013)
6. Atkins, B., Huang, W.: A study of social engineering in online frauds. Open J. Soc. Sci. **1**(03), 23 (2013)
7. Atkins, L., et al.: A guide to using the theoretical domains framework of behaviour change to investigate implementation problems. Implementation Sci. **12**(1), 77 (2017)
8. Bada, M., Sasse, A., Nurse, J.R.: Cyber security awareness campaigns: why do they fail to change behaviour? In: international conference on Cyber Security for Sustainable Society (2015)
9. Balebako, R., et al.: Nuding users towards privacy on mobile phones. In: Procs of PINC2011: 2nd International Workshop on Persuasion, Influence, Nudge & Coercion through Mobile Devices, vol. 8 (2011)
10. Balebako, R., Marsh, A., Lin, J., Hong, J.I., Cranor, L.F.: The privacy and security behaviors of smartphone app developers. NDSS Symposium (2014)
11. Benson, V., McAlaney, J., Frumkin, L.A.: Emerging threats for the human element and countermeasures in current cyber security landscape. In: Psychological and Behavioral Examinations in Cyber Security, pp. 266–271. IGI Global (2018)
12. Blythe, J.: Cyber security in the workplace: understanding and promoting behaviour change. In: Bottoni, P., Matera, M. (eds.) Proceedings of the CHItaly

2013 Doctoral Consortium co-located with the 10th International Conference of the Italian SIGCHI Chapter (CHItaly 2013), Trento, Italy, 16 September 2013. CEUR Workshop Proceedings, vol. 1065, pp. 92–101. CEUR-WS.org (2013)

13. Blythe, J., Coventry, L., Little, L.: Unpacking security policy compliance: The motivators and barriers of employees' security behaviors. In: S.O.U.P.S. 2015, pp. 103–122 (2015)

14. Blythe, J., Koppel, R., Smith, S.W.: Circumvention of security: good users do bad things. IEEE Secur. Priv. **11**(5), 80–83 (2013)

15. Briggs, P., Jeske, D., Coventry, L.: Behavior change interventions for cybersecurity. In: Behavior Change Research and Theory, pp. 115–136. Elsevier (2017)

16. Bulgurcu, B., Cavusoglu, H., Benbasat, I.: Information security policy compliance: an empirical study of rationality-based beliefs and information security awareness. MIS quart. **34**(3), 523–548 (2010)

17. Button, M., Nicholls, C.M., Kerr, J., Owen, R.: Online frauds: learning from victims why they fall for these scams. Aust. NZ J. Criminol. **47**(3), 391–408 (2014)

18. Cartwright, N.: Evidence-based policy: what's to be done about relevance? Philos. Stud. **143**(1), 127–136 (2009)

19. Chaiken, S., Trope, Y.: Dual-Process theories in Social Psychology. Guilford, New York (1999)

20. Chatterjee, S., Price, A.: Healthy living with persuasive technologies: framework, issues, and challenges. J. Am. Med. Inf. Assoc. **16**(2), 171–178 (2009)

21. Chenoweth, T., Minch, R., Gattiker, T.: Application of protection motivation theory to adoption of protective technologies. In: 2009 42nd Hawaii International Conference on System Sciences, pp. 1–10. IEEE (2009)

22. Chiasson, S., Stobert, E., Forget, A., Biddle, R., Van Oorschot, P.: Persuasive cued click-points: design, implementation, and evaluation of a knowledge-based authentication mechanism. IEEE Trans. Dependable Secure Comput. **9**(2), 222–235 (2012)

23. Choe, E.K., Jung, J., Lee, B., Fisher, K.: Nudging people away from privacy-invasive mobile apps through visual framing. In: Kotzé, P., Marsden, G., Lindgaard, G., Wesson, J., Winckler, M. (eds.) INTERACT 2013. LNCS, vol. 8119, pp. 74–91. Springer, Heidelberg (2013). https://doi.org/10.1007/978-3-642-40477-1_5

24. Cialdini, R.: Pre-Suasion: A Revolutionary way to Influence and Persuade. Simon & Schuster, New York (2016)

25. Ciocarlan, A., Masthoff, J., Oren, N.: Kindness is contagious: study into exploring engagement and adapting persuasive games for wellbeing. In: Proceedings of 26th Conference on U.M.A.P, pp. 311–319. ACM (2018)

26. Coffey, J.W.: Ameliorating sources of human error in cybersecurity: technological and human-centered approaches. In: The 8th International Multi-Conference on Complexity, Informatics and Cybernetics, Pensacola, pp. 85–88 (2017)

27. Cohen, J.: Statistical power analysis. Curr. Dir. Psychol. Sci. **1**(3), 98–101 (1992)

28. Corradini, I.: Building a Cybersecurity Culture in Organizations. SSDC, vol. 284. Springer, Cham (2020). https://doi.org/10.1007/978-3-030-43999-6

29. Coventry, L., Briggs, P., Blythe, J., Tran, M.: Using behavioural insights to improve the public's use of cyber security best practices (2014), uK GOV. Off. for Sci, Ref: GS/14/835

30. Coventry, L., Briggs, P., Jeske, D., van Moorsel, A.: SCENE: a structured means for creating and evaluating behavioral nudges in a cyber security environment.

In: Marcus, A. (ed.) DUXU 2014. LNCS, vol. 8517, pp. 229–239. Springer, Cham (2014). https://doi.org/10.1007/978-3-319-07668-3_23

31. Craig, P., Dieppe, P., Macintyre, S., Michie, S., Nazareth, I., Petticrew, M.: Developing and evaluating complex interventions: the new medical research council guidance. Int. J. Nurs. Stud. **50**(5), 587–592 (2013)

32. Das, S., Kim, H., Dabbish, L., Hong, J.: The effect of social influence on security sensitivity. In: S.O.U.P.S. 2014. USENIX Association (2014)

33. Das, S., Kramer, A.D., Dabbish, L.A., Hong, J.I.: Increasing security sensitivity with social proof: a large-scale experimental confirmation. In: Proceedings of the 2014 ACM SIGSAC Conference on Computer and Communications Security, pp. 739–749. ACM, New York (2014)

34. Dhillon, G., Backhouse, J.: Current directions in is security research: towards socio-organizational perspectives. I.S. J. **11**(2), 127–153 (2001)

35. Dolan, P., Hallsworth, M., Halpern, D., King, D., Metcalfe, R., Vlaev, I.: Influencing behaviour: the mindspace way. J. Econ. Psychol. **33**(1), 264–277 (2012)

36. Douligers, C., Raghimi, O., Lourenco Barros, M., Marinos, L.: Enisa main incidents in the EU. Technical Report, European Union Agency for Cybersecurity (2020)

37. Dunn, O.J.: Multiple comparisons among means. J. Am. Stat. Assoc. **56**(293), 52–64 (1961)

38. ENISA: cybersecurity culture guidelines: behavioural aspects of cybersecurity. Technical Report, European Union Agency for Network and Information Security (2019)

39. Evans, J.S.B.: Dual-processing accounts of reasoning, judgment, and social cognition. Annu. Rev. Psychol. **59**, 255–278 (2008)

40. Fogg, B.: Persuasive Technology: Using Computers to Change What We Think and Do. Morgan Kaufmann, Burlington (2003)

41. Fogg, B.J.: Creating persuasive technologies: an eight-step design process. In: Proceedings of the 4th International Conference on Persuasive Technology, p. 44. ACM (2009)

42. Forget, A., Chiasson, S., Biddle, R.: Persuasion as education for computer security. In: Bastiaens, T., Carliner, S. (eds.) Proceedings of E-Learn 2007-World Conference on E-Learning in Corporate, Government, Healthcare, and Higher Education, pp. 822–829 (2007)

43. Gallegos-Segovia, P.L., Bravo-Torres, J.F., Larios-Rosillo, V.M., Vintimilla-Tapia, P.E., Yuquilima-Albarado, I.F., Jara-Saltos, J.D.: Social engineering as an attack vector for ransomware. In: 2017 CHILEAN Conference on Electrical, Electronics Engineering, Information and Communication Technologies (CHILECON), pp. 1–6. IEEE (2017)

44. Gordon, S., Ford, R.: On the definition and classification of cybercrime. J. Comput. Virol. **2**(1), 13–20 (2006)

45. Greitzer, F.L., Strozer, J.R., Cohen, S., Moore, A.P., Mundie, D., Cowley, J.: Analysis of unintentional insider threats deriving from social engineering exploits. In: Security and Privacy Workshops (SPW), 2014 IEEE, pp. 236–250. IEEE (2014)

46. Grüne-Yanoff, T.: Why behavioural policy needs mechanistic evidence. Econ. Philos. **32**(3), 463–483 (2016)

47. Guo, K.H., Yuan, Y., Archer, N.P., Connelly, C.E.: Understanding nonmalicious security violations in the workplace: a composite behavior model. J. Manag. I.S. **28**(2), 203–236 (2011)

48. Hamari, J., Koivisto, J., Pakkanen, T.: Do persuasive technologies persuade? - A review of empirical studies. In: Spagnolli, A., Chittaro, L., Gamberini, L. (eds.) PERSUASIVE 2014. LNCS, vol. 8462, pp. 118–136. Springer, Cham (2014). https://doi.org/10.1007/978-3-319-07127-5_11
49. Herath, T., Rao, H.R.: Encouraging information security behaviors in organizations: role of penalties, pressures and perceived effectiveness. Decis. Support Syst. **47**(2), 154–165 (2009)
50. Herath, T., Rao, H.R.: Protection motivation and deterrence: a framework for security policy compliance in organisations. Eur. J. I.S. **18**(2), 106–125 (2009)
51. Hu, Q., Xu, Z., Dinev, T., Ling, H.: Does deterrence work in reducing information security policy abuse by employees? Comm. ACM **54**(6), 54–60 (2011)
52. Ifinedo, P.: Understanding information systems security policy compliance: an integration of the theory of planned behavior and the protection motivation theory. Comput. Secur. **31**(1), 83–95 (2012)
53. Ifinedo, P.: Information systems security policy compliance: an empirical study of the effects of socialisation, influence, and cognition. Inf. Manage. **51**(1), 69–79 (2014)
54. Jeong, J., Mihelcic, J., Oliver, G., Rudolph, C.: Towards an improved understanding of human factors in cybersecurity. In: 2019 IEEE 5th International Conference on Collaboration and Internet Computing (CIC), pp. 338–345. IEEE (2019)
55. Kankane, S., DiRusso, C., Buckley, C.: Can we nudge users toward better password management?: An initial study. In: Extended Abstracts of the 2018 CHI Conf. on Human Factors in Computing Systems, p. LBW593. ACM (2018)
56. Kirlappos, I., Beautement, A., Sasse, M.A.: "Comply or Die" is dead: long live security-aware principal agents. In: Adams, A.A., Brenner, M., Smith, M. (eds.) FC 2013. LNCS, vol. 7862, pp. 70–82. Springer, Heidelberg (2013). https://doi.org/10.1007/978-3-642-41320-9_5
57. Kirlappos, I., Parkin, S., Sasse, M.A.: Learning from "shadow security": why understanding non-compliance provides the basis for effective security. In: Workshop on Usable Security (2014)
58. Kirlappos, I., Sasse, M.A.: Fixing security together: leveraging trust relationships to improve security in organizations. In: Proceedings of the NDSS Symposium 2015. Internet Society (2015)
59. Knapp, K.J., Marshall, T.E., Kelly Rainer, R., Nelson Ford, F.: Information security: management's effect on culture and policy. Inf. Manage. Comput. Secur. **14**(1), 24–36 (2006)
60. LeFebvre, R.: The human element in cyber security: a study on student motivation to act. In: Proceedings of the 2012 Information Security Curriculum Development Conference, pp. 1–8. ACM (2012)
61. Love, L.F., Singh, P.: Workplace branding: leveraging human resources management practices for competitive advantage through "best employer" surveys. J. Bus. Psychol. **26**(2), 175 (2011)
62. Maalem Lahcen, R.A., Caulkins, B., Mohapatra, R., Kumar, M.: Review and insight on the behavioral aspects of cybersecurity. Cybersecurity **3**(1), 1–18 (2020). https://doi.org/10.1186/s42400-020-00050-w
63. Malkin, N., Mathur, A., Harbach, M., Egelman, S.: Personalized security messaging: nudges for compliance with browser warnings. In: 2nd European Workshop on Usable Security. Internet Society (2017)
64. Masthoff, J., Grasso, F., Ham, J.: Preface to the special issue on personalization and behavior change. User Model. User-Adap. Inter. **24**(5), 345–350 (2014). https://doi.org/10.1007/s11257-014-9151-1

65. Michie, S., Atkins, L., West, R.: The Behaviour Change Wheel. A guide to Designing Interventions. 1st ed. Silverback, Great Britain (2014)
66. Michie, S., Johnston, M., Francis, J., Hardeman, W., Eccles, M.: From theory to intervention: mapping theoretically derived behavioural determinants to behaviour change techniques. Appl. Psychol. 57(4), 660–680 (2008)
67. Michie, S., Van Stralen, M.M., West, R.: The behaviour change wheel: a new method for characterising and designing behaviour change interventions. Implementation Sci. 6(1), 42 (2011)
68. Mitnick, K.D., Simon, W.L.: The Art of Intrusion: The Real Stories behind the Exploits of Hackers, Intruders and Deceivers. Wiley, Hoboken (2009)
69. Morisset, C., Groß, T., van Moorsel, A., Yevseyeva, I.: Nudging for quantitative access control systems. In: Tryfonas, T., Askoxylakis, I. (eds.) HAS 2014. LNCS, vol. 8533, pp. 340–351. Springer, Cham (2014). https://doi.org/10.1007/978-3-319-07620-1_30
70. Mouton, F., Leenen, L., Venter, H.S.: Social engineering attack examples, templates and scenarios. Comput. Secur. 59, 186–209 (2016)
71. Ng, B.Y., Kankanhalli, A., Xu, Y.C.: Studying users' computer security behavior: a health belief perspective. Decis. Support Syst. 46(4), 815–825 (2009)
72. Oinas-Kukkonen, H., Harjumaa, M.: Persuasive systems design: key issues, process model and system features. In: Routledge Handbook of Policy Design, pp. 105–123. Routledge (2018)
73. Orji, R., Moffatt, K.: Persuasive technology for health and wellness: state-of-the-art and emerging trends. Health Inf. J. 24(1), 66–91 (2018)
74. Pahnila, S., Siponen, M., Mahmood, A.: Employees' behavior towards is security policy compliance. In: 40Th Annual Hawaii International Conference on System Sciences, HICSS 2007. pp. 156b–156b. IEEE (2007)
75. Raja, F., Hawkey, K., Hsu, S., Wang, K.L.C., Beznosov, K.: A brick wall, a locked door, and a bandit: a physical security metaphor for firewall warnings. In: S.O.U.P.S. 2011, p. 1. ACM (2011)
76. Rangel, A., Camerer, C., Montague, P.R.: A framework for studying the neurobiology of value-based decision making. Nat. Rev. Neurosci. 9(7), 545 (2008)
77. Renaud, K., Zimmerman, V.: Nudging folks towards stronger password choices: providing certainty is the key. Behav. Public Policy 3(2), 1–31 (2018)
78. Rhodes, K.: Operations security awareness: the mind has no firewall. Comput. Secur. J. 17(3), 1–12 (2001)
79. Rogers, R.W., Prentice-Dunn, S.: Protection motivation theory. Handbook of Health Behaviour Research 1 : Personal and Social Determinants, pp. 113–132 (1997)
80. Rousseau, D.M.: Psychological and implied contracts in organizations. Empl. Responsibilities Rights J. 2(2), 121–139 (1989)
81. Schneier, B.: Secrets & Lies: Digital Security in a Networked World, 1st edn. Wiley, New York (2000)
82. Shillair, R., Cotten, S.R., Tsai, H.Y.S., Alhabash, S., LaRose, R., Rifon, N.J.: Online safety begins with you and me: convincing internet users to protect themselves. Comput. Hum. Behav. 48, 199–207 (2015)
83. Siegel, S., Castellan, N.J.: Nonparametric Statistics for the Behavioral Sciences, 2nd edn. McGraw-Hill, New York (1988)
84. Simons, H.W., Jones, J.: Persuasion in Society. Taylor & Francis, New York (2011)
85. Siponen, M., Willison, R.: Information security management standards: problems and solutions. Inf. Manage. 46(5), 267–270 (2009)

86. Siponen, M.T.: Analysis of modern is security development approaches: towards the next generation of social and adaptable ISS methods. Inf. Organ. **15**(4), 339–375 (2005)
87. Son, J.Y.: Out of fear or desire? toward a better understanding of employees' motivation to follow is security policies. Inf. Manage. **48**(7), 296–302 (2011)
88. Spears, J.L., Barki, H.: User participation in information systems security risk management. MIS Quart. **34**, 503–522 (2010)
89. Stanton, J.M., Stam, K.R., Mastrangelo, P., Jolton, J.: Analysis of end user security behaviors. Comput. Secur. **24**(2), 124–133 (2005)
90. Strack, F., Deutsch, R.: Reflective and impulsive determinants of social behavior. Pers. Soc Psychol. Rev. **8**(3), 220–247 (2004)
91. Josekutty Thomas, R., Masthoff, J., Oren, N.: Adapting healthy eating messages to personality. In: de Vries, P.W., Oinas-Kukkonen, H., Siemons, L., Beerlage-de Jong, N., van Gemert-Pijnen, L. (eds.) PERSUASIVE 2017. LNCS, vol. 10171, pp. 119–132. Springer, Cham (2017). https://doi.org/10.1007/978-3-319-55134-0_10
92. Turland, J., Coventry, L., Jeske, D., Briggs, P., van Moorsel, A.: Nudging towards security: developing an application for wireless network selection for android phones. In: Proceedings of 2015 British HCI Conference, pp. 193–201. ACM (2015)
93. Valentine, J.A.: Enhancing the employee security awareness model. Comput. Fraud Secur. **2006**(6), 17–19 (2006)
94. Van Bruggen, D., Liu, S., Kajzer, M., Striegel, A., Crowell, C.R., D'Arcy, J.: Modifying smartphone user locking behavior. In: S.O.U.P.S. 2013, p. 10. ACM (2013)
95. Van Steen, T., Norris, E., Atha, K., Joinson, A.: What (if any) behaviour change techniques do government-led cybersecurity awareness campaigns use? J. Cybersecurity **6**(1), tyaa019 (2020)
96. Vance, A., Siponen, M., Pahnila, S.: Motivating is security compliance: insights from habit and protection motivation theory. Inf. Manage. **49**(3–4), 190–198 (2012)
97. Vargheese, J.P., Sripada, S., Masthoff, J., Oren, N., Dennis, M.: A dynamic persuasive dialogue model for encouraging social interaction for older adults. In: I.V.A, pp. 464–465. Springer (2013)
98. Villarroel, R., Fernández-Medina, E., Piattini, M.: Secure information systems development-a survey and comparison. Comput. Secur. **24**(4), 308–321 (2005)
99. Wang, Y., Leon, P.G., Scott, K., Chen, X., Acquisti, A., Cranor, L.F.: Privacy nudges for social media: an exploratory Facebook study. In: Proceedings of the 22nd International Conference on World Wide Web, pp. 763–770. ACM (2013)
100. Weirich, D., Sasse, M.A.: Pretty good persuasion: a first step towards effective password security in the real world. In: Proceedings of 2001 Workshop on New Security Paradigms, pp. 137–143 (2001)
101. Williams, E.J., Beardmore, A., Joinson, A.N.: Individual differences in susceptibility to online influence: a theoretical review. Comput. Hum. Beh. **72**, 412–421 (2017)
102. Zimmermann, V., Renaud, K.: Moving from a "human-as-problem" to a "human-as-solution" cybersecurity mindset. Int. J. Hum.-Comput. Stud. **131**, 169–187 (2019)

XAI Analysis of Online Activism to Capture Integration in Irish Society Through Twitter

Arjumand Younus[1(✉)], M. Atif Qureshi[1,2], Mingyeong Jeon[1,2], Arefeh Kazemi[3], and Simon Caton[3]

[1] eXplainable Analytics Group, Faculty of Business, Technological University Dublin, Dublin, Ireland
{arjumand.younus,muhammadatif.qureshi,mingyeong.jeon}@tudublin.ie
[2] ADAPT Centre, Dublin, Ireland
[3] School of Computer Science, University College Dublin, Dublin, Ireland
{arefeh.kazemi,simon.caton}@ucd.ie

Abstract. Online activism over Twitter has assumed a multidimensional nature, especially in societies with abundant multicultural identities. In this paper, we pursue a case study of Ireland's Twitter landscape and specifically migrant and native activists on this platform. We aim to capture the level to which immigrants are integrated into Irish society and study the similarities and differences between their characteristic patterns by delving into the features that play a significant role in classifying a Twitterer as a migrant or a native. A study such as ours can provide a window into the level of integration and harmony in society.

Keywords: Integration · Explainable artificial intelligence · Society · Twitter metadata · Textual

1 Introduction

Twitter has assumed a multi-faceted role as a communications platform while also becoming a platform for knowledge sharing, activism, journalism etc. Many researchers have used Twitter data to analyse social phenomena, opening research pathways toward data science for social good initiatives. One prominent area is that of migration studies, with many works relying on geo-tagged location data within tweets to make inferences about migration patterns [19, 22], and mobility flows. However, we argue for a more nuanced approach to studying how immigrants have integrated into their migrated society. In this paper, we take up Ireland as a case study and utilise Twitter data from within Ireland to perform an analysis of migrants' integration into Irish society.

This publication has emanated from research conducted with the support of Irish Research Council under award no. GOIPG/2021/1354 & COALESCE/2021/112 and with the financial support of Science Foundation Ireland under grant no. 13/RC/2106_P2 at the ADAPT SFI Research Centre.

Ireland has recently grown into a multicultural society [13] with an increase in migration of foreign working professionals, international students and asylum seekers and refugees. Due to its welcoming policies confirming diversity and inclusion, Ireland has embraced these communities as their own [17]. However, the transformation has caused a plethora of online activism from migrant communities of Ireland and the native population of Ireland. Much of this online activism is displayed on popular social networks, such as Twitter [24]. On one end, there are activists from migrant communities, and on the other, there are those from the natives, both advocating for various social causes. There are, however, similarities and dissimilarities in the causes these activists support concerning society and the overall transformation. There is a lack of objective reasoning into the different communication patterns and causes advocated by local activists and migrant ones, and this work aims to present a computational methodology to fill that gap.

In an attempt to study the various aspects of migrants' integration in Irish society, we analyse different aspects of Twitter activity (of natives and migrants) by means of Twitter metadata and the textual content of tweets. Learning user representations via the textual content they generate has gained tremendous attention due to its usefulness in solving various user classification tasks such as hate speech detection, mental illness prediction, and fake news detection [16]. We embrace a different approach, mainly relying on unsupervised learning methods for extraction of different aspects of Twitter activity, followed by usage of these features in explainable artificial intelligence based classification models [3]. We fundamentally frame the task around the prediction of whether or not a given Twitter activist is a migrant or native, along with the most informative and distinguishing features. This classification model and associated feature analysis, in turn, helps us identify the features that make sense to determine migrants' integration into society.

Our main contributions in this work are summarized as follows

- A best-of-both worlds approach is adopted by making use of rich Twitter communication patterns (such as mentions, retweets, and quotes) together with textual contents' overlap within a tabular data representation for migrant and native communities of Ireland.
- Use of two well-known explainable artificial intelligence approaches to provide a glimpse into the most discriminating features of migrants and natives, thereby providing a basic mechanism from where one can begin to assess the level of migrants' integration in society.
- A curated, custom dataset has been made publicly available to the research community to enable further development of migration studies using textual data.

The remainder of this paper is organised as follows. In Sect. 2, we discuss related work while attempting to cover migration studies along with works on user representations using social media data. Furthermore, we also present a brief explanation of the research gap and position our work concerning how it attempts to fill this gap. In Sect. 3, we present details of our collected data and methodology. In Sect. 4, we present our findings along with a discussion around the implications of these findings. In Sect. 5, we conclude with a brief overview of future work.

2 Related Work

In any society where multicultural identities are present, there remains a boundary between natives and migrants in various aspects. More specifically, over the years, in cases of increased migration to European Union countries, there remains a certain level of scepticism on policies proposed for integrating migrants into society [15]. The general consensus, however, is that the policies have been ineffective in achieving the said goals. The general problem with this consensus is that there has been limited quantitative analysis of migrants' lived experiences. We aim to fill this gap using social media data for this analysis.

In studies that leverage social media, we can easily distinguish studies that investigate more large-scale macro-level events, such as political campaigning (e.g. [10]), riots and civil unrest (e.g. [7]), event detection (e.g. [1,18]), and large-scale news events like COVID-19 (e.g. [23]). Here, researchers often use social media as a lens to understand the perceptions and viewpoints of a subset of society or seek to identify key events that occur during the period(s) of observation. In these cases, it is generally easy to think about how to access and curate a meaningful and large corpus of text content. This is, however, not quite the case for studying immigrants: they are, as a hard-to-reach and arguably marginalised group, hard(er) to locate and study with social media. In fact, when it comes to marginalised groups, there is a general observation that researchers lack robust methodological guidelines [2].

There has been a lot of work (e.g. [6,8,28,31]) studying hate, toxicity, and cyberbullying, which is often directed towards immigrants and marginalised groups via social media. Though useful from a methods perspective, these studies often have a strong content bias towards content stemming from North America and the United Kingdom [21]. [9] outlines how social media can be used to specifically study marginalised groups and discusses a number of the associated challenges. The key here is to ensure that corpus is representative and not just an echo-chamber of a few (obvious) selected topics.

The literature has a number of consistent strategies for curating data samples for studying marginalised communities. One common method is to select key users and extract their tweet history (e.g. [30]), using a set of seed users and sample from "key" related users (e.g. [11,27,30]), focusing around specific hashtags (e.g. [2,27]), based on specific locations (e.g. [26])[1], and using online repositories of Twitter archives for key public figures (e.g. [11]). Other exploratory data analysis techniques can also be used for vernacular discovery to identify specific keywords for content search. This, as noted by [30], is useful in identifying specific sociolinguistic variations of language, slang, shorthand etc. However, as noted by [4,30], researcher training in the area of study (to generate domain

---

[1] It should be noted that geo-location data can be unreliable.

knowledge) is critical. An alternative method to determine a (starting) vocabulary set, as introduced by [5], is to collect anonymised data from relevant Web forums, blogs and microblogs, and ask human annotators to identify whether the content contains specific references of use.

Our work adopts the approach of selecting a manually curated set of users as proposed in [30] with the "activism" of a user being the key focus. To the best of our knowledge, our work provides a novel direction in studying a diverse range of topics emanating from marginalised communities versus privileged ones, with previous such studies limiting their study around an event, hashtag or group of similar users [11, 26, 27].

3   Dataset and Methodology

Our model of choice is TabNet on account of its support for multiple modalities together with the features it offers for explaining its outcomes. Explainability offers deeper insights for a task such as the one addressed in this paper of determining the levels to which migrants feel included in or excluded from society.

In this section, we first delve into the details of our dataset, followed by an explanation of the features used to make the predictions of whether a particular Twitterer from within our dataset is a migrant or a native.

Table 1. Characteristics of Curated Twitter Activists' Dataset from Both Communities

Type	Mean Tweets	Mean followers	Mean following
Migrants	2506	4184	1793
Natives	3053	12116	3289

3.1   Dataset: Activists from Both Communities

For the dataset creation, we manually curate a list of Twitter activists from within migrant and native communities of Ireland, with the criteria that the Twitterer must have had tweeted/retweeted four or more tweets on a social justice issue within Ireland. The curation is performed by one of the authors, familiar with Ireland's social justice landscape, and can distinguish between a native/local and a migrant. The data curation involves the following steps as an inclusion/differentiation criteria of natives vs migrants for our Irish Twitter dataset:

- Irish surname check done by means of https://www.duchas.ie/en/nom
- Reading Twitter biography field and checking for Irish terms in addition to flags of various countries[2]

---

[2] It has been observed that migrants within Ireland usually insert a flag representing Ireland and their country of origin.

– Reading last 20–100 tweets of an activist to determine whether or not there's any explicit mention of belonging from any country.

The above process yielded a total of 66 natives and 66 migrant activists. Despite the sample not being large, it serves as a fair representation of the Irish Twitter landscape, and Table 1 shows the characteristics of the selected activists. For each user in the curated list, we extract tweets and Twitter metadata associated with these tweets. Using Twitter API's academic research product track, the last 3200 tweets of the Twitterers in our list were crawled[3].

3.2   Twitter Metadata Features to Study Integration

As has been observed in research on Twitter communication patterns [12,33], the various forms of communication on Twitter, such as mentions, retweets, and the newly introduced feature quoted tweets, give an insight into significant aspects of a user. Regarding migrants and natives, these Twitter features specifically can help determine social bonding factors [29] between these two, which is why the following features are used in our prediction framework.

– Follower Following Ratio: The ratio between the Twitter followers and those a certain user follows serves as an important indication of online popularity. To illustrate the results in the next section, we use the notation *followerfollowingratio* for this particular feature.
– Mentions Percentage: The percentage of mentions within the last 3200 tweets of a user; this can be extracted from Twitter metadata's *replied_to* feature. To illustrate the results in the next section, we use the notation *mentionspercentage* for this particular feature.
– Retweets Percentage: The percentage of retweets within the last 3200 tweets of a user; this can be extracted from Twitter metadata's *retweeted* feature. To illustrate the results in the next section, we use the notation *retweetedpercentage* for this particular feature.
– Quoted Percentage: The percentage of quoted tweets within the last 3200 tweets of a user; this can be extracted from Twitter metadata's *quoted* feature. To illustrate the results in the next section, we use the notation *quotedpercentage* for this particular feature.

3.3   Textual Features to Study Integration

Two types of features were used as the textual features, i.e., based on word embeddings and topic models. Both are textual modelling techniques well-known in the literature for making inferences concerning various classes of users (we covered some of these in Sect. 2). These techniques are able to coherently capture similar and dissimilar topics from a huge body of text which in our case is all the

---

[3] Note that an anonymised version of this dataset has been released for public download at https://github.com/arjumandyounus/ineire_tweetsdataset.

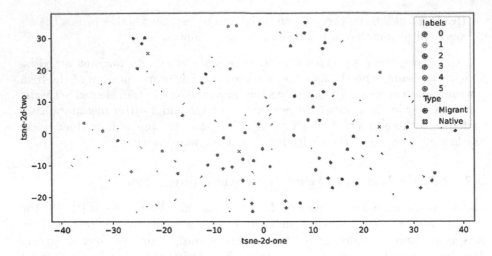

Fig. 1. TSNE visualisation of clusters obtained from KMeans over user Tweet embeddings.

tweets by migrants and activists. A particularly challenging aspect, however, in the kind of task we have proposed is the different means by which accumulation of topics for a particular user can be done on account of a user being very diverse in tweeting habits and topical interests. We solve this challenge by taking Twitterer's most frequent words in word embeddings and the most frequent topics in the case of topic models.

For the word embedding based ones, we combine all tweet tokens of a user into a single document, thereby treating the user as a document. This is followed by a reduction process where each user document is then reduced to top-20 most frequent tokens. These tokens corresponding to each user are trained with a word2vec model [25] to obtain word embeddings and finally, KMeans clustering [14] is applied over all users[4]. The label of the cluster to which each user belongs is used as a feature in the model. Figure 1 shows the results of the KMeans clustering via tsne dimensionality reduction over the word embeddings of migrants and activists in our dataset. To illustrate the results in the next section, we use the notation *labels* for this feature.

For the topic modelling features, we first apply the Gibbs Sampling Dirichlet Multinomial Mixture model (i.e., GSDMM) [32] for short text clustering to all the tweets of each user. Our choice of this alternative compared to the traditional Latent Dirichlet Allocation model is motivated by its strength in modelling via collapsed Gibbs sampling of one topic per document, making it more suited to short texts such as tweets. The application of GSDMM yields a collection of topics equivalent to the number of tweets by each user, and from this collection, we derive the top-4 topics for each user. We also derive the top-4 topics for the migrants and natives in our sample. For each user, we then compute the Jaccard

---

[4] An empirical analysis led to a stable number of 6 clusters.

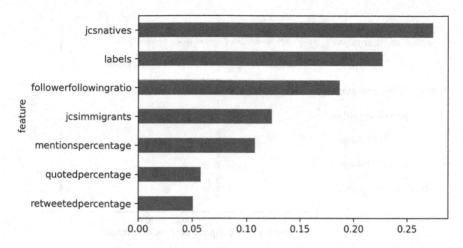

Fig. 2. Features' importance for TabNet

similarity score across the top-4 topics for migrants and natives; this score is then converted into a categorical feature whereby a score greater than 0.5 across migrants' top-4 topics is assigned a category *"SimilarToMigrants"* and a score less than or equal to 0.5 is assigned a category *"DisSimilarToMigrants"*. Note that a similar categorical assignment is performed with topics within tweets by natives. To illustrate the results in the next section, we use the notation *jcsimmigrants* and *jcsnatives* for these topic model based features.

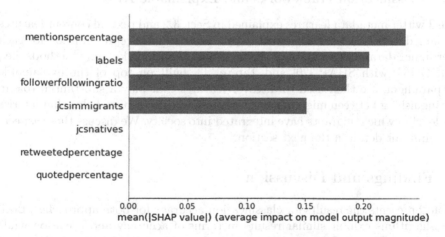

Fig. 3. Features' importance for XGBoost

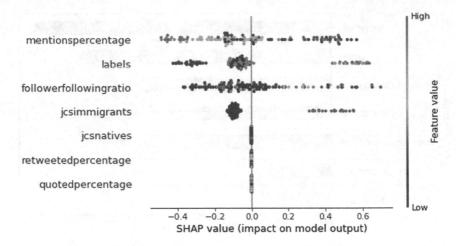

Fig. 4. SHAP Summary Plot for Tree Explainer of XGBoost

Table 2. Classification results across prediction task of Twitter activist being migrant or native

Classification approach	Accuracy	Precision
TabNet	0.85	0.78
XGBoost	0.87	0.80

3.4   Classification Frameworks and Explainable AI

The Twitter metadata features explained in Sect. 3.2 and textual content features explained in Sect. 3.3 are combined to produce a tabular representation for each user in our dataset. Two state-of-the-art tabular machine learning methods, i.e., XGBOOST with SHAP [20] and TabNet [3] built on top of the explainable AI paradigm, are then used to discover features that play a substantial role in distinguishing between migrants and natives; and this, in turn, helps characterise the level to which migrants have integrated into society. We discuss these aspects in significant detail in the next section.

4   Findings and Discussion

Table 2 presents the results for classification accuracy for both approaches. Both the algorithms exhibit similar results in terms of accuracy and precision while showing variations in feature importance (refer to Fig. 2 and Fig. 3). With respect to feature importance and associated explanations however an interesting pattern is observed from the features *labels* and *followerfollowingratio* whereby both play a significant role within both classification methods. A deeper analysis via SHAP values however reveals the stability of *labels* feature over other Twitter metadata features. SHapley Additive exPlanations (SHAP values) quantify

Table 3. Description of topics in top six clusters

Cluster Number (No. of Tweets Inside)	Top four words
Number 5 (80201)	Covid cases hospital people
Number 7 (45319)	People today Ireland Government
Number 8 (44564)	Work stamp people visa
Number 9 (40977)	Dublin great day weather
Number 1 (40192)	Black garda race need
Number 2 (37319)	Women trans Ireland rights

the contribution of each feature corresponding to the predictions made by a given machine learning model, and thereby gives deeper insights into local interpretability of a predictive model. The insights derived from the SHAP summary plot of Fig. 4 point to the observation that the *labels* feature derived from word embeddings of textual content within migrants' and natives' tweets leads to stable predictions, and a coherent level of linearity. This points to a significant aspect with respect to migrants' integration into society where the topics and interests of both communities are defining factors. As an example we revisit the tsne visualisation of Fig. 1 whereby labels 0 and 2 in particular show a distinct pattern of differences in content posted by migrants and natives on Twitter; *label 0* is derived from words textit "stereotype, racism, black, twitter" while *label 4* is derived from words textit "savenmh, abortion, women, repealed" whereby migrants have a large proportion of belonging to *label 0* while natives have a large proportion of belonging to *label 4*. From this pattern, there is a clear demarcation of interests and concerns of both communities depicting a probable lack of migrant integration into Irish society specially given the fact that *"savenmh"* made headlines for many weeks.

To dig deeper into the differences in topical interests of migrants and natives, we show the top four words within the top six topics obtained via GSDMM in Table 3. The topics are in descending order by the number of documents/tweets in each topic. As with the labels obtained from word embeddings, there is an apparent topical difference, particularly in Clusters 2, 8, and 9 whereby most tweets in Cluster 8 and 9 are those from migrant activists, while most in Cluster 2 are those from native activists.

Our research confirms the following findings

- The topical distribution of tweets by migrants and natives shows significant differences in terms of ideas and interests.
- Natives exhibit a higher degree of content-based homophily in their interactions as compared to migrants specifically in relation to friends.

5   Conclusion

This paper presents an analysis via explainable artificial intelligence of features that play a critical role in distinguishing between migrant and native activists on Twitter. Both Twitter metadata and textual contents of tweets were used as features in two state-of-the-art machine learning classification models; and labels derived by application of KMeans clustering over word embeddings are determined to be stable features for the prediction task of migrant activists vs native activists. This essentially points towards a lack of migrants' integration into Irish society in terms of the concerns and interests of the two different communities, where the identification of concerns and interests was captured using gathered topics embodied in word embeddings. The work in this paper can serve as a first step in utilising advanced textual features in solving the societal challenge of assessing migrants' integration into society. In future work, we aim to incorporate mention and retweet networks into the model separately while also incorporating a detailed analysis of conversation threads by both natives and migrants. To summarise, an analysis such as ours can aid policymakers in gaining deeper insights into the causes behind societal conflicts introduced by inward migration into their countries; it also has significant implications from a European Union perspective.

References

1. Aiello, L.M., Petkos, G., et al.: Sensing trending topics in Twitter. IEEE Trans. Multimedia **15**(6), 1268–1282 (2013)
2. Arastoopour Irgens, G.: Using knowledgeable agents of the digital and data feminism to uncover social identities in the# blackgirlmagic twitter community. Learn. Media Technol. **47**(1), 79–94 (2022)
3. Arık, S.O., Pfister, T.: Tabnet: Attentive interpretable tabular learning. In: AAAI, vol. 35, pp. 6679–6687 (2021)
4. Bunting, A.M., Frank, D., Arshonsky, J., Bragg, M.A., Friedman, S.R., Krawczyk, N.: Socially-supportive norms and mutual aid of people who use opioids: An analysis of reddit during the initial Covid-19 pandemic. Drug Alcohol Depend. **222**, 108672 (2021)
5. Burnap, P., Colombo, G., Amery, R., Hodorog, A., Scourfield, J.: Multi-class machine classification of suicide-related communication on twitter. Online Soc. Netw. Media **2**, 32–44 (2017)
6. Burnap, P., Williams, M.L.: Cyber hate speech on twitter: an application of machine classification and statistical modeling for policy and decision making. Policy Internet **7**(2), 223–242 (2015)
7. Burnap, P., et al.: Tweeting the terror: modelling the social media reaction to the woolwich terrorist attack. Soc. Netw. Anal. Min. **4**(1), 1–14 (2014)
8. Calvete, E., Orue, I., Gámez-Guadix, M.: Cyberbullying victimization and depression in adolescents: the mediating role of body image and cognitive schemas in a one-year prospective study. Eur. J. Crim. Policy Res. **22**(2), 271–284 (2016)
9. Caton, S.: Using social media and text analytics to investigate marginal phenomena. Eurofound working paper WPEF21052 (2022)
10. Caton, S., Hall, M., Weinhardt, C.: How do politicians use Facebook? an applied social observatory. Big Data Soc. **2**(2), 2053951715612822 (2015)
11. Coe, K., Griffin, R.A.: Marginalized identity invocation online: the case of president Donald trump on twitter. Soc. Media Soc. **6**(1), 2056305120913979 (2020)

12. Fan, Y., Zhang, Y., Ye, Y., Li, X.: Automatic opioid user detection from twitter: transductive ensemble built on different meta-graph based similarities over heterogeneous information network. In: IJCAI, pp. 3357–3363 (2018)
13. Fanning, B.: Multiculturalism in Ireland. In: Racism and Social Change in the Republic of Ireland, pp. 178–198. Manchester University Press (2018)
14. Forgy, E.W.: Cluster analysis of multivariate data: efficiency versus interpretability of classifications. Biometrics **21**, 768–769 (1965)
15. Gońda, M., Lesińska, M., Pachocka, M.: Relations Between Immigration and Integration Policies in Postwar Europe, pp. 24–45 (2020)
16. Islam, T., Goldwasser, D.: Analysis of twitter users' lifestyle choices using joint embedding model. In: Proceedings of the International AAAI Conference on Web and Social Media, vol. 15, pp. 242–253 (2021)
17. Trinity College Dublin: Equality, diversity and inclusion strategy (2022). https://www.justice.ie/en/JELR/Pages/DoJ_EDI_Strategy
18. Kilroy, D., Caton, S., Healy, G.: Finding short lived events on social media. In: 28th AIAI Irish Conference on Artificial Intelligence and Cognitive Science (AICS) (2020)
19. Kim, J., Sîrbu, A., Giannotti, F., Gabrielli, L.: Digital footprints of international migration on twitter. In: International Symposium on Intelligent Data Analysis. pp. 274–286. Springer (2020)
20. Lundberg, S.M., Lee, S.I.: A unified approach to interpreting model predictions. In: Advances in Neural Information Processing Systems, vol. 30 (2017)
21. Matamoros-Fernández, A., Farkas, J.: Racism, hate speech, and social media: a systematic review and critique. Televis. New Media **22**(2), 205–224 (2021)
22. Mazzoli, M., et al.: Migrant mobility flows characterized with digital data. PLoS ONE **15**(3), e0230264 (2020)
23. de Melo, T., Figueiredo, C.M.: A first public dataset from Brazilian twitter and news on Covid-19 in Portuguese. Data Brief **32**, 106179 (2020)
24. Michael, L.: Reports of racism in Ireland (2020). https://inar.ie/wp-content/uploads/2020/03/2019_iReport_Final.pdf
25. Mikolov, T., Sutskever, I., Chen, K., Corrado, G.S., Dean, J.: Distributed representations of words and phrases and their compositionality. In: Advances in Neural Information Processing Systems, vol. 26 (2013)
26. Murthy, D., Gross, A., Pensavalle, A.: Urban social media demographics: an exploration of twitter use in major American cities. J. Comput.-Mediat. Commun. **21**(1), 33–49 (2016)
27. Nartey, M.: Centering marginalized voices: a discourse analytic study of the black lives matter movement on twitter. Crit. Discour. Stud. **9**(2), 1–16 (2021)
28. Naseem, U., Razzak, I., Eklund, P.W.: A survey of pre-processing techniques to improve short-text quality: a case study on hate speech detection on twitter. Multim. Tools Appl. **80**(28), 35239–35266 (2021)
29. Norris, P.: The bridging and bonding role of online communities. Press Polit. **7**, 3–14 (2002)
30. Patton, D.U., Lane, J., Leonard, P., Macbeth, J., Smith Lee, J.R.: Gang violence on the digital street: case study of a south side Chicago gang member's twitter communication. New Media Soc. **19**(7), 1000–1018 (2017)
31. Poletto, F., Basile, V., Sanguinetti, M., Bosco, C., Patti, V.: Resources and benchmark corpora for hate speech detection: a systematic review. Lang. Resour. Eval. **55**(2), 477–523 (2020). https://doi.org/10.1007/s10579-020-09502-8

32. Yin, J., Wang, J.: A dirichlet multinomial mixture model-based approach for short text clustering. In: Proceedings of the 20th ACM SIGKDD International Conference on Knowledge Discovery and Data Mining, pp. 233–242 (2014)
33. Younus, Arjumand: Use of microblog behavior data in a language modeling framework to enhance web search personalization. In: Ma, S., et al. (eds.) AIRS 2016. LNCS, vol. 9994, pp. 171–183. Springer, Cham (2016). https://doi.org/10.1007/978-3-319-48051-0_13

Reliability of News and Toxicity in Twitter Conversations

Alessandro Quattrociocchi, Gabriele Etta, Michele Avalle, Matteo Cinelli(✉),
and Walter Quattrociocchi(iD)

Department of Computer Science Sapienza, University of Rome,
Viale Regina Elena 295, 00168 Rome, Italy
{etta,avalle}@di.uniroma1.it,
{matteo.cinelli,walter.quattrociocchi}@uniroma1.it

Abstract. Social media platforms like Twitter play a pivotal role in public debates. Recent studies showed that users online tend to join groups of like-minded peers, called echo chambers, in which they frame and reinforce a shared narrative. Such a polarized configuration may trigger heated debates and foment misinformation spreading. In this work, we explore the interplay between the systematic spreading of misinformation and the emergence of toxic conversations. We perform a thorough quantitative analysis on 3.3 M comments by more than 1 M unique users from 25 K conversations involving 60 news outlets active on Twitter from January 2020 to April 2022. By tagging the news triggering the conversation with a specific reliability score provided by an independent fact-checking organization (NewsGuard), we perform a network-based analysis of the structure of toxic conversations on Twitter. We find that users using toxic language are few and evenly distributed over the entire reliability score range, showing no significant evidence for the interplay between toxic speech and misinformation spreading.

Keywords: Twitter conversations · Reliability of news · Toxic speech · Hate speech

1 Introduction

The advent of social media such as Twitter has dramatically changed how information is produced and acquired by online users. Despite the benefits of being connected, the disintermediated access to a massive wealth of information through social media platforms has exacerbated harmful dynamics such as misinformation spreading and toxic interactions among people, which pose a severe threat to our social fabric. As a remarkable testimony of these widespread concerns, in his recent speech at Stanford University, former US President Barack Obama expressed his worries about "democratic backsliding", blaming social

100683EPID Project "Global Health Security Academic Research Coalition" SCH-00001-3391.

F. Hopfgartner et al. (Eds.): SocInfo 2022, LNCS 13618, pp. 245–256, 2022.
https://doi.org/10.1007/978-3-031-19097-1_15

media for fostering misinformation spreading, distrust and conspiracy think-ing [30]. Thanks to unprecedented availability of data in the last few years, a substantial research effort has been put into addressing these and related prob-lems to gain a quantitative understanding of online human behavior [7,15,27,41]. It has been shown that users online tend to acquire information adhering to their system of beliefs [6], and ignore dissenting information [45] to form polarized groups around a shared narrative [14] (echo chambers). This polarization effect shapes the dynamics of social interactions online [3,14,43]. It may trigger massive propagation of misinformation through the so-called cascades [40] as well as the escalation towards noxious tones in public debates. The spread of low-quality information is sometimes carried out by groups of coordinated or automated accounts that pollute and tamper with our social environments by injecting and sharing a large number of targeted messages [20], i.e., what Facebook calls "coordinated inauthentic behavior". In a recent study, the authors characterized how such techniques effectively manipulate online debates [9]. Although some studies focused on the interplay between false and accurate information and the structural properties of cascades [25,41], the critical point to understand is how data fits into a larger disinformation campaign [35] and how it may even-tually influence online social dynamics. A recent study addressed the interplay between the reliability of content and the hate-speech dynamics on YouTube finding users loyal to reliable sources use, on average, a more toxic language than their counterpart [11]. Another study [8] shows how correlations feature between personality and communication style combined with data from Twitter can improve the prediction of the users who endorsed annotated articles from an Italian newspaper. However, the detection and contrast of hate speech are com-plex issues. There are still ambiguities in the very definition of hate speech, with academic and relevant stakeholders providing their interpretations [34] including social media companies such as Facebook, Twitter, and YouTube declaring dif-ferent community standards. In this work, we explore the interplay between the reliability of news, as identified by the independent fact-checking organization NewsGuard, and the toxicity of online discussions happening under the tweets of such news outlets. In more detail, we characterize the structural features of such discussion using network-based metrics and quantify how structural fea-tures correlate with the reliability of news outlets and the use of toxic language. To this aim, we collected 3.3 M tweets from January 2020 to April 2022 by 1 M users, reconstructed the cascades of comments and analyzed the evolution of the conversation sentiment. We find that users using toxic language are few and evenly distributed over the entire reliability score range, showing no significant evidence for the interplay between language toxicity and misinformation.

2   Related Works

The spreading of misinformation and the presence of toxicity in online debates are two of the most harmful phenomena affecting the infosphere. According to the literature, both can be associated with a polarized environment in which strongly diverging opinions coexist [14,16,24,37]. Nonetheless, only a few studies attempted to examine the relationship between the two. In what follows, we provide an overview of the key findings of misinformation spreading and hate speech online. The spread of misinformation on online social media has been extensively studied in recent years, also developing frameworks to identify users prone to spread fake content [19]. The dynamics seem to be driven by a complex interplay of cognitive and social factors and the configuration of social media platforms. Indeed, feed algorithms may foster selective exposure to consonant content [10] and when combined with the natural tendency of users to ignore dissenting information while acquiring that adhering to their preexisting system of beliefs (*confirmation bias*) [6,45], may lead to the formation of groups of people highly polarized around shared narratives, i.e., echo chambers [14]. An echo chamber can act as a reinforcing mechanism moving a group towards even more extreme positions. For instance, extreme variations of misinformation like conspiracy theories contribute to creating polarized environments and thriving in them [36]. As a result, this polarization effect - which may vary in extent depending on the network structure of the platform and the presence of news feed algorithms [10], but it is nonetheless ubiquitous - in turn shapes the online social dynamics [3,4,18] and may trigger misinformation cascades [40]. Cascades have been regarded as one of the most promising ways to characterize the spreading of misinformation, as they highlight the link between the diffusion process of some content and the structure of conversation around it. By studying their structural properties, one can examine the paths taken by different contents through the network, as well as the interaction patterns between users and information. However, when trying to discriminate between the diffusion of reliable and unreliable information results relying *only* on structural differences in propagation cascades should be taken with some caution. In [12] the authors devised a classifier based on the structural features of the cascades to find that conspiracy and science content propagate almost indistinguishably, thus pointing out the need to integrate content-related features to obtain more robust results. Conversely, a recent study [41] analyzing cascades on Twitter found that false news spread "farther, faster, deeper and more broadly than the truth." A subsequent more in-depth statistical analysis [25] questions those results by showing that the reported structural differences between diffusion paths of true and false news on Twitter are almost entirely explainable because false-news cascades are larger and vanish when comparing only cascades of similar size. The study of online conversation toxicity is strongly related to hate speech. A wide strand of literature focuses on the automatic detection of toxic and hateful speech online by developing new machine learning [13,29,42] and deep learning models [2,5] for automatic detection through text. The task is very challenging since the notion of toxicity and hate are themselves changeable, and the use of certain words may be considered toxic only concerning some targets of hate or within specific communities. For this reason, several studies focused on detecting and characterizing the use of toxic language within online communities [17,24,26,28] also trying to outline the behavioral features of their users [32]. At the community level, there is evidence that when the use of toxic language characterizes inter-community interactions, users tend to increase the level of segregation, thus strengthening the echo chamber effect, and that after being banned, hate communities promptly re-adapt to appear again in different environments with the consequent proliferation of toxicity and hate in unmoderated social media platforms (e.g., Gab). At the individual level, users employing toxic language differ from others regarding their activity patterns, word usage, and network structure. Considering online conversations, some researchers tried to exploit the structure of conversation to predict the occurrence of toxic comments [44] or used generative discussion threads models to outline structural features of online conversations [1]. Another study [33] highlights how the structural characteristics of the conversation tree might predict toxic conversations and the following toxic comment, considering both conversations and users' follower-following relationships. They study three different conversation levels, i.e., individuals, dyads, and groups, showing a lower content of toxicity across the individual level and that users without social relationships tend to be more toxic at the dyad level. Additionally, their findings exhibit larger, wider, and deeper reply trees at the group level. However, less attention has been paid to the structure of the conversation, the social relationships among the conversation participants and the reliability score of the news.

3   Preliminaries and Definitions

3.1   Data Collection and Toxicity Evaluation

The following section describes the data collection and data wrangling processes. We start by collecting a list of news outlets provided by NewsGuard [38], keeping only those US outlets that existed on Twitter. NewsGuard is an organization run by a team of journalists who analyzes the factuality of news outlets based on nine journalistic criteria [39] ranging from the reiterated publishing of false content to the use of clickbait titles. According to these criteria, NewsGuard computes a score for each news outlet that ranges from 0 – indicating a non-factual website – to 100 – indicating a website with complete factuality. NewsGuard sets its credibility threshold at 60: any website receiving a score lower than this threshold is categorized as non-factual. Otherwise, it is referred to as a trusted news outlet. We divided the score range in 5 intervals, i.e., $[0, 20)$, $[20, 40)$, $[40, 60)$, $[60, 80)$, $[80, 100]$, and we collected Twitter data from news outlets belonging to such categories. We retrieved $25, 338$ English tweets produced by 60 US news outlets and conversations (i.e., the comments) generated by such tweets. Data were collected using the Twitter Academic API. The $25, 338$ tweets (i.e., conversation roots) are characterized by having more than 20 comments each, thus resulting in an overall number of comments that is about 3.3 M of comments posted by 1 M unique users in a time window that ranges from 2020/01/01 to 2022/04/10. Each reliability interval set of news outlets was chosen to balance the overall number of posts and comments per category. The unbalance in terms of popularity and numerosity of news outlets per category justifies the heterogeneity in the number of comments across categories. An overview of the data is provided in Table 1.

Table 1. Number of news outlets collected from NewsGuard with a correspondence on Twitter, divided by score interval.

Labels	Scores	News outlets	Conversations	Comments
Very low	0–20	9	7164	499854
Low	20–40	10	1457	76486
Mixed	40–60	12	7292	474379
High	60–80	23	6191	1891537
Very high	80–100	6	3234	380920
Total		**60**	**25338**	**3323176**

To quantify the level of toxic content in the comments set, we employed Google Perspective API [22], which provides machine learning models to quantify the toxicity of a text. In particular, the API provides a score [23] between 0 (no toxicity) and 1 (high toxicity) that quantifies the Toxicity (i.e., the presence of rude, disrespectful, or unreasonable speech that is likely to make people leave a discussion) of text. According to the literature [33], an appropriate threshold for identifying a toxic comment corresponds to a Toxicity score greater or equal to 0.6. Overall, the percentage of toxic comments is about 7% of the total.

3.2 Conversation Reconstruction Algorithm

The Twitter endpoint, queried on a *conversation_id*, returns fields related to the user and the post, such as the *post_id*, *reply_id*, *type*, *timestamp*, *author_id* and *in_reply_to_user_id*. We modeled a conversation as a rooted tree, where the first node is the root, identified by the *conversation_id* identifier and the other nodes are the replies. Replies can either target the root node, i.e., the user replied to the root, or they can be nested, i.e., a user participates in other user's conversations. Therefore, each node is a *child* node whenever it is a reply to an existing *parent* node. Due to moderation efforts or users' decisions, replies can be deleted, causing a break in the discussion tree that becomes separated into multiple components. In order to reconstruct a connected discussion tree, we implement a procedure that iterates over the nodes in the tree (i.e., the replies), searches for their parent node and, in the case of *orphan* nodes (i.e., nodes that do not have a *parent*), reconnects them to the root node.

3.3 Cascade Metrics

A tree graph can be defined as a pair $T = (V, E)$, where $V = \{1, \ldots, n\}$ represents the set of nodes and $E = \{1, \ldots, m\}$ the set of links. In this paper, we consider directed trees, with n nodes and $m = n - 1$ links, rooted in a node corresponding to the tweet that generated the conversation.

Size. The size is the number of nodes in the tree, denoted as $n = |V|$, where $|\cdot|$ is the cardinality of the set V. In our case study, the size is the total number of replies in the conversation tree, assuming that a user can post multiple replies and interact with different users within the conversation.

Depth. The depth $D(T)$ is the distance d of the deepest node in the conversation, which also coincides with the diameter of the tree, i.e., the longest shortest path between the root node and any other node in the graph. The depth can be expressed as follows: $D(T) = max \; (d_{rj}) \; \forall j$, $j \neq r$ where r is the root node.

Wiener Index. The Wiener index measures the structural complexity of the tree and its potential virality [21] and is defined as the average shortest path between each pair of nodes i, j. In the case of a directed tree, the Wiener index can be defined as:

$$W(T) = \frac{2}{n(n-1)} \sum_i \sum_{j>i} d_{ij} \tag{1}$$

where $\frac{2}{n(n-1)}$ is a normalization factor to account for all paths among couples of nodes. The Wiener index ranges between $[1, \infty)$ and, in general, it is minimized for broadcast structures and maximized for low branching structures [21].

Toxicity Ratio. The toxicity ratio is the average number of toxic comments in the conversation tree T, considering the number of toxic replies out of the total number in the conversation. The toxicity ratio can be defined as

$$TR(T) = \frac{card\{V \mid s > 0.6\}}{card\{V\}}, \tag{2}$$

where s is the toxicity score of the comment $v \in V$ and 0.6 is the toxicity threshold value, such that a comment that satisfies the equation $s > t$ is considered toxic.

Average Toxicity Distance. The average toxicity distance is the average normalized distance of toxic comments from the root, defined as

$$TD(T) = \frac{1}{card\{V \mid s > 0.6\}} \sum_j \frac{d_{rj}}{D(T)}. \tag{3}$$

TD(T) is bounded in $(0, 1]$ and low values of this quantity imply that toxic comments are, on average, located close to the root.

Assortativity. The assortativity coefficient r measures the extent to which similar nodes tend to be connected with each other [31]. Being the analog of Pearson's correlation, it varies in the range $[-1, 1]$ with negative values indicating disassortativity (i.e., nodes with different features tend to be interconnected more than expected at random) and positive values indicating assortativity (i.e., nodes with similar features tend to be interconnected more than expected at random). Assortativity values close to zero are related to a distribution of node features close to random. We consider as node feature their toxicity score and to compute the assortativity coefficient, we ignore the direction of the links obtaining the following equation:

$$r(T) = \frac{\sum_{ij}(a_{ij} - \frac{k_i k_j}{2m})x_i x_j}{\sum_{ij}(a_{ij}x_i^2 - \frac{k_i k_j}{2m}x_i x_j)}, \tag{4}$$

where a_{ij} is the element the adjacency matrix $A = (a_{ij})_{i,j \in V}$ in which $a_{ij} = 1$ ($a_{ij} = 0$) indicates the presence (absence) of a link between nodes i and j, $k_i = \sum_{j=1}^{n} a_{ij}$ is the node degree, and x_i is the feature assigned to node i.

4 Experimental Results

4.1 Reliability and Conversations Structure

As the first step of our analysis, we assess the structural properties of Twitter conversations for different levels of reliability score. In Fig. 1 we show the Complementary Cumulative Distribution Function (CCDF) of different metrics: size, number of unique users, depth and Wiener Index. For each panel, the outer plot shows a fined-grained grouping of the CCDFs into five classes according to their respective reliability score as explained in Sect. 3.1. The inner panels describe the metrics, exploiting a binary flag of each news outlet: Questionable and Reliable. The x-axis of each panel reports the values of the measurements, while the y-axis represents the probability values of each observation.

Panel A of Fig. 1 shows the CCDF of the trees' size for conversations occurring under the five classes of news outlets. We notice that the metrics considered are characterized by heavy-tailed distributions, showing a significant difference in the tree size and the number of users (panel B) between outlets with Very Low, Low and Mixed scores with respect to outlets labeled as High and Very High. Furthermore, the similarities between panels A and B suggest that users tend to comment on posts only a few times, making the number of replies close to that of unique users. A similar situation can be observed in insets. From panels C and D of Fig. 1 we notice that conversations occurring under tweets by all kinds of outlets except low-reliability ones display similar distributions of depth and Wiener index. When dividing the outlets into two categories, the similarity holds only in the case of structural complexity. The deviations in the distributions related to news outlets belonging to the low class [20,40) can be traced back to the under-sampling of the number of comments for such a category.

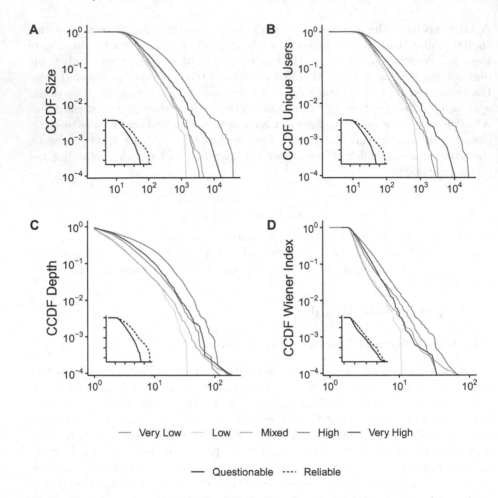

Fig. 1. Complementary cumulative distribution functions of the structural measures of conversation trees. Outer panels show the CCDFs of the five classes (Very Low: [0, 20], Low: (20, 40], Mixed (40, 60], High(60, 80], Very High:(80, 100]), instead the inner plots show CCDFs of the two classes (Questionable:[0, 60], Reliable:(60, 100]). Panel A: CCDF of the tree size, i.e., the number of nodes in the reply tree. Panel B: CCDF of the number of unique users in the conversation. Panel C: CCDF of the tree depth, i.e., the length of the deepest node from the root or the tree's diameter. Panel D: CCDF of Wiener index that measures the complexity of the structure of each conversation tree.

4.2   Reliability and Conversations Toxicity

As a further step, we focus on whether misinformation can be associated with the presence of toxic speech. In Fig. 2 we show the distribution of the toxicity ratio, i.e., the proportion of toxic comments, for conversations occurring below different categories of news outlets. We find that strongly toxic conversations are few (outliers in the distributions) and evenly distributed over the entire reliability score range, thus providing weak evidence for the interplay between toxicity and misinformation.

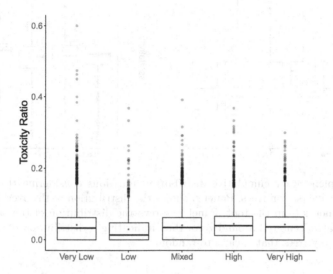

Fig. 2. Distribution of the toxicity ratio, i.e., the fraction of the number of toxic nodes in the tree with respect to the tree size. Comments toxicity is evaluated by means of the Google Perspective API, which returns a value between [0,1], where 0 means no toxicity and 1 indicates a maximum level of toxicity. A comment is considered toxic if it exceeds a toxicity threshold $t = 0.6$.

4.3   Patterns of Toxic Conversations

As a final assessment, we characterize toxic conversations by looking for patterns of toxic comments within conversation trees. To this aim, we analyze whether negative comments tend to occur at the early stage of the conversation and if they tend to cluster in certain areas of the tree. The first analysis is conducted using the average toxicity distance that measures the average distance of toxic comments from the root node. We observe that most toxic comments are located at a short relative distance from the root, except for a few cases whereas toxic replies occur far from the source node. The second analysis exploits the assortativity coefficient to understand if similarly toxic comments tend to be more interconnected than expected at random. We find that the median assortativity coefficient is around zero, despite the presence of some outliers, thus indicating the absence of specific toxicity patterns in reply trees (Fig. 3).

A

B

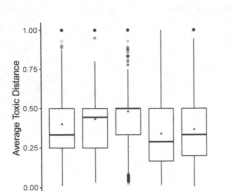
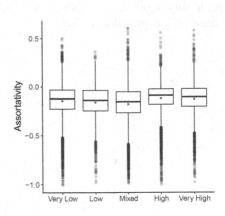

Fig. 3. Complementary cumulative distribution functions considering the structural measures of conversation trees. Panel A shows the distribution of the average distance of toxic comments from the root. Panel B shows the distribution of the assortativity coefficient that is centered around zero, thus indicating a distribution of the toxicity score along reply trees that is close to random.

5   Conclusions

In this work, we studied the interplay between two antisocial behaviors: the systematic spreading of misinformation and the production of toxic speech. We analyze several Twitter conversations happening in correspondence with tweets by news outlets categorized based on their reliability during a time window of about two years. Despite a few differences in structural features of conversation trees, we do not find any relevant association between the reliability of news outlets and the presence of toxicity within discussion trees stemming from their tweets. This result suggests that the consumption of misinformation does not imply exposure to toxicity and hate more than the consumption of fact-checked news. Studying the co-occurrence of such phenomena is useful for disentangling their effect on society and understanding the extent to which policy efforts to contrast one phenomenon could effectively reduce the other. The next envisioned step in this stream is to explore the interplay of misinformation and toxic conversation on different platforms and how users react to strong moderation policies.

References

1. Aragón, P., Gómez, V., García, D., Kaltenbrunner, A.: Generative models of online discussion threads: state of the art and research challenges. J. Internet Serv. Appl. **8**(1), 1–17 (2017). https://doi.org/10.1186/s13174-017-0066-z
2. Badjatiya, P., Gupta, S., Gupta, M., Varma, V.: Deep learning for hate speech detection in tweets. In: Proceedings of the 26th International Conference on World Wide Web Companion, pp. 759–760 (2017)

3. Bail, C.A., et al.: Exposure to opposing views on social media can increase political polarization. Proc. Nat. Acad. Sci. **115**(37), 9216–9221 (2018)
4. Barberá, P.: Social media, echo chambers, and political polarization. Soc. Media Democracy State Field prospects Reform **34** (2020)
5. Basile, V., et al.: Semeval-2019 task 5: multilingual detection of hate speech against immigrants and women in twitter. In: Proceedings of the 13th International Workshop on Semantic Evaluation, pp. 54–63 (2019)
6. Bessi, A., Coletto, M., Davidescu, G.A., Scala, A., Caldarelli, G., Quattrociocchi, W.: Science vs conspiracy: collective narratives in the age of misinformation. PLoS ONE **10**(2), e0118093 (2015)
7. Briand, S.C., et al.: Infodemics: a new challenge for public health. Cell **184**(25), 6010–6014 (2021)
8. Celli, F., Ghosh, A., Alam, F., Riccardi, G.: In the mood for sharing contents: emotions, personality and interaction styles in the diffusion of news. Inf. Process. Manag. **52**(1), 93–98 (2016)
9. Cinelli, M., Cresci, S., Quattrociocchi, W., Tesconi, M., Zola, P.: Coordinated inauthentic behavior and information spreading on twitter. Decis. Support Syst. **160**, 113819 (2022)
10. Cinelli, M., De Francisci Morales, G., Galeazzi, A., Quattrociocchi, W., Starnini, M.: The echo chamber effect on social media. Proc. Nat. Acad. Sci. **118**(9), e2023301118 (2021)
11. Cinelli, M., Pelicon, A., Mozetič, I., Quattrociocchi, W., Novak, P.K., Zollo, F.: Dynamics of online hate and misinformation. Sci. Rep. **11**(1), 1–12 (2021)
12. Conti, M., Lain, D., Lazzeretti, R., Lovisotto, G., Quattrociocchi, W.: It's always April fools' day!: On the difficulty of social network misinformation classification via propagation features. In: 2017 IEEE Workshop on Information Forensics and Security (WIFS), pp. 1–6 (2017)
13. Davidson, T., Warmsley, D., Macy, M., Weber, I.: Automated hate speech detection and the problem of offensive language. In: Proceedings of the International AAAI Conference on Web and Social Media, vol. 11, pp. 512–515 (2017)
14. Del Vicario, M., et al.: The spreading of misinformation online. Proc. Nat. Acad. Sci. **113**(3), 554–559 (2016)
15. Del Vicario, M., et al.: Echo chambers: emotional contagion and group polarization on Facebook. Sci. Rep. **6**(1), 1–12 (2016)
16. Etta, G., Cinelli, M., Galeazzi, A., Valensise, C.M., Quattrociocchi, W., Conti, M.: Comparing the impact of social media regulations on news consumption. IEEE Trans. Comput. Soc. Syst. 1–11 (2022). https://doi.org/10.1109/TCSS.2022.3171391
17. Evkoski, B., Pelicon, A., Mozetič, I., Ljubešić, N., Kralj Novak, P.: Retweet communities reveal the main sources of hate speech. PLoS ONE **17**(3), e0265602 (2022)
18. Garimella, K.: Polarization on social media (2018)
19. Giachanou, A., Ríssola, E.A., Ghanem, B., Crestani, F., Rosso, P.: The role of personality and linguistic patterns in discriminating between fake news spreaders and fact checkers. In: Métais, E., Meziane, F., Horacek, H., Cimiano, P. (eds.) NLDB 2020. LNCS, vol. 12089, pp. 181–192. Springer, Cham (2020). https://doi.org/10.1007/978-3-030-51310-8_17
20. Gleicher, N.: Taking down more coordinated inauthentic behavior: what we've found so far. Facebook Newsroom (2018)
21. Goel, S., Anderson, A., Hofman, J., Watts, D.J.: The structural virality of online diffusion. Manag. Sci. **62**(1), 180–196 (2016)

22. Jigsaw, G.: Perspective API. https://perspectiveapi.com/
23. Jigsaw, G.: Perspective api - attributes & languages. https://developers.perspectiveapi.com/s/about-the-api-attributes-and-languages
24. Johnson, N.F., et al.: Hidden resilience and adaptive dynamics of the global online hate ecology. Nature **573**(7773), 261–265 (2019)
25. Juul, J.L., Ugander, J.: Comparing information diffusion mechanisms by matching on cascade size. Proc. Nat. Acad. Sci. **118**(46), e2100786118 (2021)
26. Kumar, S., Hamilton, W.L., Leskovec, J., Jurafsky, D.: Community interaction and conflict on the web. In: Proceedings of the 2018 World Wide Web Conference, pp. 933–943 (2018)
27. Lazer, D., et al.: Computational social science. Science **323**(5915), 721–723 (2009)
28. Mathew, B., Illendula, A., Saha, P., Sarkar, S., Goyal, P., Mukherjee, A.: Hate begets hate: A temporal study of hate speech. Proc. ACM on Hum.-Comput. Interact. **4**(CSCW2), 1–24 (2020)
29. Mondal, M., Silva, L.A., Benevenuto, F.: A measurement study of hate speech in social media. In: Proceedings of the 28th ACM Conference on Hypertext and Social Media, pp. 85–94 (2017)
30. Myers, S.L.: Obama calls for more regulatory oversight of social media giants, May 2022. https://www.nytimes.com/2022/04/21/technology/obama-stanford-tech-regulation.html
31. Newman, M.E.: Mixing patterns in networks. Phys. Rev. E **67**(2), 026126 (2003)
32. Ribeiro, M.H., Calais, P.H., Santos, Y.A., Almeida, V.A., Meira Jr, W.: Characterizing and detecting hateful users on twitter. In: Twelfth International AAAI Conference on Web and Social Media (2018)
33. Saveski, M., Roy, B., Roy, D.: The structure of toxic conversations on twitter. In: Proceedings of the Web Conference 2021, pp. 1086–1097 (2021)
34. Siegel, A.A.: Online hate speech. Soc. Media Democracy Stat. Field Prospects Reform 56–88 (2020)
35. Starbird, K.: Disinformation's spread: bots, trolls and all of us. Nature **571**(7766), 449 (2019)
36. Sunstein, C.R.: # republic. In: # Republic. Princeton University Press, Princeton (2018)
37. Tahmasbi, F., et al.: "go eat a bat, chang!": On the emergence of sinophobic behavior on web communities in the face of covid-19. In: Proceedings of the Web Conference 2021, pp. 1122–1133 (2021)
38. Technologies, N.: Newsguard. https://www.newsguardtech.com/
39. Technologies, N.: Rating process and criteria. https://www.newsguardtech.com/ratings/rating-process-criteria/
40. Vicario, M.D., Quattrociocchi, W., Scala, A., Zollo, F.: Polarization and fake news: early warning of potential misinformation targets. ACM Trans. Web (TWEB) **13**(2), 1–22 (2019)
41. Vosoughi, S., Roy, D., Aral, S.: The spread of true and false news online. Science **359**(6380), 1146–1151 (2018)
42. Wulczyn, E., Thain, N., Dixon, L.: Ex machina: personal attacks seen at scale. In: Proceedings of the 26th International Conference on World Wide Web, pp. 1391–1399 (2017)
43. Yardi, S., Boyd, D.: Dynamic debates: an analysis of group polarization over time on twitter. Bull. Sci. Technol. Soc. **30**(5), 316–327 (2010)
44. Zhang, J., et al.: Conversations gone awry: Detecting early signs of conversational failure. arXiv preprint arXiv:1805.05345 (2018)
45. Zollo, F., et al.: Debunking in a world of tribes. PLoS ONE **12**(7), e0181821 (2017)

Characterizing Early Electoral Advertisements on Twitter: A Brazilian Case Study

Josemar Caetano[1]([✉]), Samuel Guimarães[1], Marcelo M. R. Araújo[1], Márcio Silva[1,2], Júlio C. S. Reis[3], Ana P. C. Silva[1], Fabrício Benevenuto[1], and Jussara M. Almeida[1]

[1] Department of Computer Science, Universidade Federal de Minas Gerais, Belo Horizonte, Brazil
{josemarcaetano,samuelsg,marceloaraujo,ana.coutosilva, fabricio,jussara}@dcc.ufmg.br
[2] College of Computer Science, Universidade Federal do Mato Grosso do Sul, Campo Grande, Brazil
marcio@facom.ufms.br
[3] Department of Informatics, Universidade Federal de Viçosa, Viçosa, Brazil
jreis@ufv.br

Abstract. Some countries impose strict regulations regarding the distribution of electoral advertising during election periods. This is the case of Brazil, where electoral ads distributed *before* a predetermined period (called *early ad*) are prohibited by law. Whereas the enforcement of such regulation on traditional mass media technologies (e.g., radio and TV) is common practice in the country, the same is a very challenging task for content shared on social media platforms, mostly due to the lack of proper tools to automatically identify content containing (early) electoral ads. This study aims to develop fundamental knowledge about characteristics of textual content containing early ads shared on Twitter, so as to drive the future design of effective detection tools. We offer a broad characterization of the textual content associated with a set of early electoral ads shared on Twitter in pre-election periods of three recent elections in Brazil, comparing their textual properties with those of other (non ads) tweets. Our main findings are that ads tend to have a negative or neutral sentiment, a certain syntactic structure, while most tend to explicitly mention a candidate or party to be chosen or avoided.

Keywords: Electoral advertising · Social media · Twitter · Textual analysis

1 Introduction

Online social networks have now become an essential communication tool between voters and their candidates. However, this communication can be distorted when online profiles of political candidates become real platforms during

---

J. Caetano and S. Guimarães—These authors contributed equally to this work.

F. Hopfgartner et al. (Eds.): SocInfo 2022, LNCS 13618, pp. 257–272, 2022.
https://doi.org/10.1007/978-3-031-19097-1_16

electoral periods. Although allowed, elections have clear rules regarding the correct use of these platforms as campaign tools in some countries. This is the case in Brazil, where it is prohibited by current electoral legislation to carry out political advertisements during determined pre-election periods (here referred to as *early electoral ads*) [20]. Such legislation is enforced by the Brazilian Superior Electoral Court as a means to balance the competition between candidates. Similar legislations exist in other countries such as France[1] and Portugal[2].

In such a scenario, monitoring the compliance with the electoral legislation when it comes to broadcasts on traditional mass media platforms, such as radio and television, is a common practice by law enforcing agencies, notably the Brazilian Superior Electoral Court (TSE). However, such monitoring becomes quite challenging when it comes to online social media platforms due to the large volume of information shared on a daily basis. Indeed, prior studies have already shown evidence of the (mis)use of these platforms to disseminate electoral ads [3,23], notably before the electoral period established by law [20]. Fighting such practice is currently hampered by the absence of automatic tools and methods for detecting electoral ads, raising concerns about how to effectively mitigate the problem [17,21]. Detecting such content is challenging as what indeed constitutes electoral ads has a high degree of subjectivity. For example, an early ad may not explicitly include the name of a politician or political party, as one may be inferred from its content. Thus, the design of effective detection methods needs to be based on a broad and fundamental knowledge about the outstanding characteristics of this type of content. Yet, such knowledge is still very limited in the available literature [16], mainly with respect to ads written in Portuguese.

In this paper, we aim to contribute to this knowledge by presenting a characterization of early electoral ads identified in public data collected from Twitter. Our interest in Twitter is justified by the lack of prior studies on this type of content gathered from this platform, despite the large presence of political actors and political debate on it [12,23]. Our study focuses on the Brazilian scenario, motivated by the current political scenario in the country[3], being thus constrained to tweets written in Portuguese. It is driven by two questions: (i) *What are key properties of the textual content associated with early electoral ads shared on Twitter in different pre-election periods?* and (ii) *What are the (textual) differences between messages (tweets) containing early electoral ads and the other?*

To answer these questions, our study covered data (tweets) collected from three different periods, associated with different elections in Brazil (i.e., 2016, 2018 and 2020). For each period, we analyze several textual characteristics, including attributes associated with semantic and syntactic properties, searching for similarities and differences between tweets containing early electoral ads and the other tweets.

Our results show that early ads typically have a negative or neutral sentiment, with neutral sentiment increasing over the years and have a recurring pattern

---

[1] https://www.elections.interieur.gouv.fr/en/how-to-vote.

[2] https://www.portaldoeleitor.pt/Paginas/PerguntasFrequentes.aspx.

[3] General elections are scheduled to take place on October 2022 in Brazil.

regarding the use of *hashtags* and *links*, in addition to mentions of other profiles. Such patters were consistently observed across all three periods analyzed, while differences found are generally related to the specific electoral context. Moreover, early ads often make more references to syntactic attributes, such as pronouns and prepositions. Regarding semantic attributes, we highlight attributes related to decisions (*vote*, *elect*) and space (*city*, *near*). Finally, around half of electoral ads refer to some entity (parties, places, people) or other profiles on Twitter.

The rest of this paper is as follows. Section 2 briefly reviews related work. The methodology we adopt in our study as well as our main results are discussed in Sects. 3 and 4. Finally, conclusions are offered in Sect. 5.

2   Related Work

A number of prior studies have focused on analyzing political discourse in social media [2,4–6,8,9,11,14,16,17]. For instance, the authors in [2] selected a set of *hashtags* to characterize tweets with political content. Their results show that the network of political retweets exhibits a highly segregated partisan structure, with extremely limited connectivity between left and right-leaning users. Similarly, Grimaldi *et al.* [4] analyzed *tweets* and content from traditional media (e.g., newspapers and television programs) about the 2019 Spanish election to conclude that the former could be used to analyze political discourse and clarify the impact of candidate messages to future voters. In [11], in turn, *tweets* from Brazilian congressmen were used to automatically detect political messages, estimating the prevalence of political content on the platform.

Some prior work aimed at assessing how posts in social media can influence public opinion. For example, the authors in [5,14] analyzed how Russian ads on Facebook and Twitter, respectively, influenced the 2016 US presidential election. Other efforts addressed the monitoring of political campaigns on Facebook [8], the characterization of interactions between users in the context of specific social and political movements [1,6] and the correlations between online activities and opinions or voting intentions for specific candidates [9].

Regarding the characterization of electoral ads on social media, focus of our present effort, two prior studies, more closely related to ours, can be cited. Silva et al. [16] labeled ads from Facebook's public Brazilian ad library to train a classifier to detect electoral ads, while Sosnovik *et al.* [17] used ads on Facebook to demonstrate the complexity of the task of identifying this type of content. To the best of our knowledge, our investigation is the first to focus on providing a deep characterization of textual properties of early electoral ads identified in Portuguese-language tweets. Such analysis is particularly compelling given our focus on early electoral ads, which violates current Brazilian legislation.

3   Dataset

Our data collection focuses on gathering a corpus of Portuguese-language tweets published in three periods of time, associated with different elections in Brazil

(2016, 2018 and 2020). To that end, we used the Twitter API Search[4] to collect tweets based on specific keywords related to early electoral ads. We built a list of such keywords that include terms indicating implicit or explicit vote requests, originally suggested by a domain expert and further refined to include other terms based on early observations. Examples of keywords are (in English): *'Vote for me'*, *'Vote for the candidate'*, *'Vote for president'*, *'I want to be your candidate'* and *'If I am elected'*. To filter tweets related to different types of events in which public voting happens (e.g. TV reality shows), we built a blacklist including terms such as *'MasterChef'*, *'bts'*, and *'kpop'*[5].

We then manually assigned a label – electoral ad or not – to each tweet. The annotation process was carried out by three volunteers, following the guidelines provided by domain experts in how to accurately classify this type of content.

Tweets containing requests to vote for oneself, requests to vote for someone else, as well as propaganda against an opponent or a rival party were labeled as *electoral ads* Tweets with content referring to elections but without (implicit or explicit) requests for votes, without personal attacks or praise to specific politicians or political parties and tweets with non-political content or with references to political issues from other countries were labeled as *non electoral ads.*

We assessed labeling reliability using the percentage of agreement between volunteers and the Cohen's Kappa coefficient (κ) [7]. In general, there was an agreement between pairs of volunteers greater than 75%, with κ ranging between 0.48 and 0.58 (depending on the pair of volunteers). The total agreement between the three volunteers showed a Fleiss' Kappa κ of 0.53. According to [7], such value suggests a "moderate" agreement, which is acceptable considering that in many messages electoral advertisement does not appear explicitly, leaving room for multiple interpretations. One such example is: "Don't VOTE for those who approved this nonsense! LINK", which makes reference to a politician indirectly. Moreover, as discussed in [17], ads related to societal and humanitarian issues, such as electoral ads, are intrinsically hard to label. Thus, we argue that the agreement observed between our volunteers is acceptable.

The final label of each message (electoral ad or non-ad) was given by the majority of the three volunteers. All tweets labeled as electoral ads were posts *before* the period allowed by the Brazilian legislation started, being thus *early* electoral ads. Yet, for the sake of simplicity, we refer to them as simply electoral ads from now on. Table 1 presents a brief description of the data collected[6], including collection period, as well as numbers and percentages of messages containing electoral ad and non-electoral ad.

4   Analyses and Results

Our present study is guided by the following driving question: "*What are the textual properties of early electoral advertisements on Twitter?*". Towards answering

---

[4] https://developer.twitter.com/en/docs/twitter-api/v1/tweets/search/api-reference/get-search-tweets.

[5] The complete blacklist is available at: bit.ly/3phAkkm.

[6] The anonymized data can be made available upon request by email to the authors.

Table 1. Tweets labeled as Electoral Ad (EA) and Non-Electoral Ad (NEA).

Dataset	Period	#EA	#NEA	#Messages
Twitter 2016	Jan 1, 16 - Aug 15, 2016	147 (22,21%)	515 (77,79%)	662
Twitter 2018	Jan 1, 18 - Aug 15, 2018	188 (37,38%)	315 (62,62%)	503
Twitter 2020	Jan 1, 20 - Sep 25, 2020	786 (45,15%)	955 (54,85%)	1741

such question, we analyzed attributes of the (textual) content associated with messages labeled as early electoral ads in our dataset. Specifically, we character-ize the data described in column 2 (#Electoral Ads) of Table 1.

The analyzed attributes are associated with four dimensions: (i) sentiment; (ii) most common syntactic structures (e.g., phrases and sentences); (iii) psy-cholinguistic attributes; and (iv) named entities. These four dimensions comple-ment each other as follows. Sentiment analysis allows us to verify the tone of the ads, revealing whether the discourse used tends to be more positive, negative or neutral. The analyses of the most common syntactic structures offer evidence of the most characteristic patterns of sentences (e.g., voting requests) used in electoral ads. Taking a step further, the analysis of psycholinguistic attributes associated with the words used allows us to offer a finer characterization of the content. Finally, the analysis of entities allows us to assess the presence of ref-erences to organizations, places, people and profiles on Twitter, revealing how the political context of each election may affect the textual patterns used in the advertisements.

In the following, we present and discuss our characterization results in each aforementioned dimension. For each analysis, we describe the methodology used, followed by the main observations.

4.1 Sentiment Analysis

We start by analyzing the sentiment expressed in the electoral ads present in our dataset for the three periods studied. To that end, we used the SentiStrength [19] tool, which is widely used for this task [13]. SentiStrength provides an integer score ranging from -4 to $+4$, from strongly negative to strongly positive, with 0 indicating neutral sentiment. To facilitate the interpretation, we chose to dis-cretize the values into the following classes: very negative (-4 and -3), negative (-1 and -2), neutral (0), positive (1 and 2) and very positive (3 and 4). Figure 1 shows the histogram with the percentage of messages in each class (with the cor-responding confidence intervals for sample proportions [10]), for each of the three periods analyzed.

As shown in the Fig. 1a, negative and neutral sentiments are much more fre-quent in the electoral ads shared in the three analyzed periods, with a tendency of decreasing negative sentiments and increasing neutral sentiment in the most recent elections (2018 and 2020). Despite the growth of neutral sentiments, nega-tive ads are the majority, with more than 50% of all messages with this sentiment

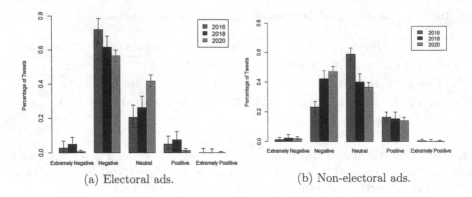

(a) Electoral ads.   (b) Non-electoral ads.

Fig. 1. Sentiment analysis.

in the three periods. Examples of electoral ads with negative, neutral and positive sentiment are, respectively, *"NAME OF CANDIDATE is f*cking fake, DO NOT VOTE FOR HIM LINK"*, *"Let's change everybody. Vote for those who have NEVER been elected. LINK"* and *"Pay attention, in the next elections do not re-elect anyone, renew. Vote for who wants the best for Brazil. LINK"*.

Figure 1b, shows different patterns for non-electoral ads. Notably, on average, we note an opposite tendency of increasing volume of negative tweets in the most recent years as well as decreasing neutral tweets. Finally, although extreme positive and negative sentiments were rarely observed in both ads and non-ads, we observe a much smaller fraction of positive tweets for electoral ads than for non-electoral ads.

4.2   Most Common Textual Structures

In this section, we focus on identifying the phrases (i.e., sequences of words) that occur most frequently in electoral advertisements for each analyzed period. To that end, we used the word trees, which offers an intuitive visualization of the structure of these sentences [22]. In this technique, firstly, a word is selected that will be considered as the root of the tree and, in a recursive process, subsequent words that have higher frequency are interconnected by branches. As result, a tree describing the set of most frequent phrases starting from the root is built.

Aiming at identifying the most relevant textual structures and characteristics of electoral ads, we selected as root the word "vote", which was the most characteristic (most frequent) of electoral ads in all periods analyzed. Due to space constraints and to improve readability, Fig. 2 shows only one tree, i.e., the one built for electoral ads in 2016. The trees for electoral ads in the other two periods as well as all three tree for non-electoral ads are presented in Appendix A (Fig. 5a, b, 6a, b, and c).

As illustrated in Fig. 2, the most frequent sentences in electoral ads begin with "Vote for those who", suggesting a tendency of explicitly recommending candidates to be voted on, as well as candidates to be avoided. The same was

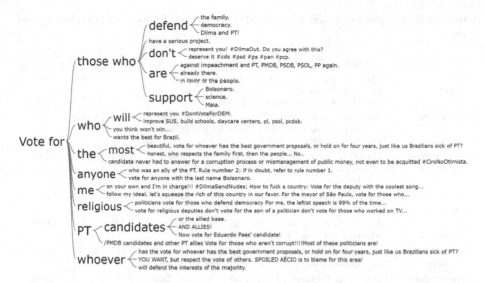

Fig. 2. Reduced word tree with common sentences in electoral ads in 2016.

observed in all three periods analyzed (see figures in Appendix A). An example of a request against voting for someone is "Don't vote for those who use *fundão*"[7], represented with the omission of the word "no" in the 2020 tree. Also, both in 2016 and in 2018 , there were citations to the Worker's Party (PT) and requests for political renewal, through the use of sentences such as "do not vote for those who have a mandate" and "do not vote for the PT candidate(s)". References to a candidate's positioning with respect to some political or ideological aspect are also often used in electoral ads. Examples are phrases such as "vote for those who defend", with family and crooks being used for positive and negative electoral advertisements, respectively.

For illustration purposes, Table 2 shows examples of the most common phrases in our set of electoral ads, with the frequency of ads that used each phrase for each period analyzed. This set was built by taking the union of the top-5 most common phrases in each period. In general, we do observe specific patterns of requesting votes and recommending candidates to avoid in each election, with the particular context of each period driving the discourse. For example, political parties were cited more often in 2016. In 2018, in turn, corruption and the Lava Jato operation[8] were topics of great social mobilization and, as such, were often used in requests to avoid particular candidates. Finally, in the 2020 election, electoral ads are often against specific candidates. Notably, the increased political polarization in the country at the time can be noted by most

---

[7] *Fundão* refers to the use of public funding in electoral campaigns.

[8] Lava Jato (*Car wash* in English) operation was a major criminal investigation by the Federal Police, which led to a major political and economical crisis in the country.

Table 2. Most common phrases in electoral ads and their frequencies in each analyzed period.

Common phrase	Example ad (Translated to English)	2016	2018	2020
vote for candidate	They got together and fucked Rio de Janeiro. 3 in 1 -3 PMDB and 1PT. In 2016 do not vote for the candidate that they support. LINK	5,44%	10,64%	2,80%
vote for those whom you	Are you a public servant? Vote for those who value you professionally, not for those who use your profession politically. LINK	6,12%	4,26%	5,73%
vote for those who defend	My whole family will vote for ARROBA. Vote for who defends the homeland and will NOT let HASHTAGs be stolen	7,48%	3,19%	2,93%
vote for those who use	Don't vote for those who use religion to get elected!	0,00%	1,60%	10,43%
vote for those who do not	This Party is a scammer. Do not vote for those who do not respect the poll results. LINK	5,44%	2,66%	3,69%
vote for those who have	Do not vote for those who have a mandate. Total disappointment, they do not represent us. LINK	4,08%	2,66%	2,93%
vote for those who support	Don't vote for those who support Bolsonaro. Don't vote for evangelicals.	2,72%	1,06%	5,09%
vote for those who are	Think about it, in the next elections vote for those who are pro-employment and company, never for someone pro-State, remember Dilma!	1,36%	3,72%	1,78%
vote for candidates	Don't re-elect anyone! Do not vote for PMDB candidates, don't vote for those who were against UBER. LINK	4,76%	0,00%	1,27%
vote for those who are using	Do not vote for anyone using the LINK party fund	0,00%	0,00%	3,05%

electoral ads containing negative content against one of the two main candidates from the right-wing (Jair Bolsonaro) and left-wing (PT candidate).

For non-electoral ads, in all three years, the word "vote" is associated with generic voting advices (e.g. "vote for whoever you want") as well as intentions to vote to eliminate participants on reality shows (e.g. Big Brother Brazil), as shown in Appendix A.

4.3   Psycholinguistic Attributes

In this section, we delve deeper into the properties of the electoral and non-electoral ads using *Linguistic Inquiry and Word Count* (LIWC) [18], a lexicon system that categorizes text into psycholinguistic properties. Words of the target language are organized as a hierarchy of categories and subcategories that form the set of LIWC attributes. We apply LIWC to each advertisement to quantify the fraction of words that falls into each LIWC attribute. By analyzing these fractions, we can have a more in-depth view of the narrative behind electoral and non-electoral ads.

For each pre-election period, we first analyzed each tweet separately, to obtain the frequency of words characteristic of each LIWC attribute. We then aggregated the frequencies for all tweets from each period, to obtain average values. As the same word can belong to different LIWC attributes, the frequencies sum can exceed 100%.

Figure 3 shows the average frequency distribution of the 14 most frequent LIWC attributes presented in the analyzed tweets and their confidence intervals as well.[9] The attributes are ordered on the x-axis by the average occurrence in all tweets. The 14-attribute set was built by the union of the 10 most frequent attributes in each period. There is a large overlap between the most frequent attributes from the analyzed periods, revealing a common syntactic-semantic structure of the electoral and non-electoral tweets. Our analysis also captures some important period differences, such as changes on the ranking of the attributes. For instance, the attribute *regular verbs* and the attribute *personal pronouns* have their order reversed from 2018 to 2020. We do not observe a clear distinction between psycholinguistic attributes on electoral and non-electoral ads. Moreover, the most frequent attributes are associated with syntactic properties (e.g., prepositions and pronouns). In general, the frequencies' differences from the analyzed periods are quite subtle (on average $\leq 1\%$). The largest difference (2.45%) we found regards the increasing trend in the use of impersonal pronouns (e.g., that, those) between 2016 and 2020.

Figure 3 also reveals the presence of attributes such as *insight*, *space*, and *inclusion* in the tweets, all of them associated with semantic properties. The *insight* attribute is a cognitive process characterized by words related to decisions such as "vote", "elect", "choose" and "represent". These words often occur in ads that use warnings and imperative verbs to encourage some particular choice of vote. The *space* attribute associates to notions of position, being represented by words such as "city", "involved", "near" and "outside". Finally, the *inclusion* attribute encompasses words that describe situations or actions that involve a group or that assemble something together, such as "involved", "we will stay", and "disclose".

4.4   Entity Analysis

Our last analysis characterizes the tweets in terms of the frequency of references to entities. To that end, we used the technique of recognition of mentioned entities (*named-entity recognition*) [15], available in the library *Spacy*.[10] In this technique, entities are categorized in terms of the domain to which they apply. Given an input text, a list of entities identified in the input with their respective categories is produced.

We considered 3 categories: LOC for physical places such as cities or states, ORG for organizations such as parties and government bodies, and PER for real people or characters, such as candidates or some mascot. After preliminary analysis, we observed that some entities were inaccurately categorized by the tool. For instance, some government bodies have been categorized as LOC, rather

---

[9] We translated into Portuguese attribute names.

[10] The model *pt_core_news_lg* used is in https://github.com/explosion/spaCy.

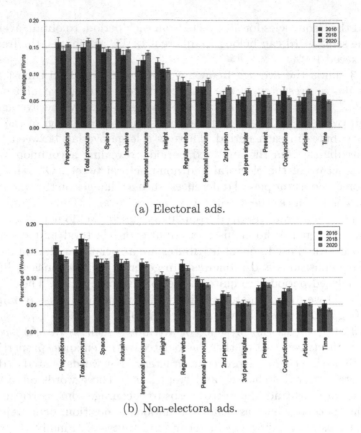

(a) Electoral ads.

(b) Non-electoral ads.

Fig. 3. Psycholinguistic attributes (LIWC).

than ORG. We then manually evaluated the categorization and corrected any inaccuracies. Moreover, we included some citations to profiles on Twitter in the list of entities, which were associated with a new category, named as AT. We then performed two analyzes. First, we examined the percentages of tweets that referenced some entity and, later, we verified the distribution of the mentioned categories in each period.

In the three analyzed periods, around half of the electoral ads refer to some entity or profile on Twitter, with 2018 having a slightly higher percentage (more than 60%). This result suggests two patterns of advertisements: (i) those that make explicit reference to candidates and parties, and (ii) those without explicit mentions, but that implicitly suggest a candidate or party (to vote or not) when describing their ideas and/or or opinions. For illustration purposes, the top-5 most cited entities in each period are: PT, Brasil, Dilma, Bolsonaro and PMDB (2016); Brazil, PT, Bolsonaro, Temer and Lula (2018); Bolsonaro, Brazil, Fundão, PT and Rodrigo Maia (2020). There is a great relationship between the frequent entities and the political context of each election, and these facts are possibly useful to explain part of the results identified.

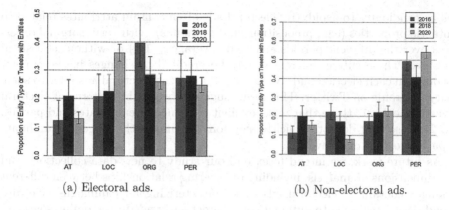

(a) Electoral ads.   (b) Non-electoral ads.

Fig. 4. Distribution of entity categories.

Focusing on electoral ads with explicit references to entities, Fig. 4a shows that organizations (ORG), which include political parties and government bodies, and persons (PER) tend to be the most cited entities overall. Locations (LOC) and profiles (AT) come next. Furthermore, organizations were the most cited entities in the advertisements shared in 2016, with a much higher frequency compared to the other categories. Examples of organizations often cited in the 2016 advertisements are PT and PMDB, two most prominent parties in that year's elections. In 2018, organizations and people started to have closer proportions, with a significant increase in citations to Twitter profiles (AT). For instance, PT, Bolsonaro and Temer were entities frequently mentioned in advertisements in 2018. Finally, places, such as Brazil and São Paulo, are the entities most frequently mentioned in advertisements in 2020. Once again, these differences may be the result of contextual aspects related to the elections in each period. For example, during the 2018 presidential elections, the names of the main candidates and political parties gained prominence. In the 2020 municipal elections, mentions of specific locations gain greater visibility.

Figure 4b shows that non-electoral ads generally have less organizations (ORG), locations (LOC) and Twitter profiles (AT) than electoral ads. However, they have more words related to political parties and government bodies, and persons (PER) than electoral ads.

5   Conclusions and Future Work

In this work, we analyze data from early electoral advertisements shared on Twitter during the last three Brazilian elections of 2016, 2018 and 2020. Our results revealed that: (i) the most frequent sentiments are negative and neutral, with a tendency of increasing neutral sentiment over the three elections; (ii) it is common for advertisements to explore links and hashtags as a strategy to request votes; (iii) there is a tendency to explicitly recommend candidates to vote on as well as candidates to avoid; (iv) electoral ads often contain attributes related to syntactic properties (e.g., prepositions and pronouns), with very marginal differences over the different periods analyzed (average $\leq 1\%$) or without statistical relevance. These subtle differences may be credited to changes in the current discourse in each election and; (v) half of all analyzed electoral ads refer to some entity or profile on Twitter. This result suggests two main patterns of electoral advertisements: 1) those that make explicit reference to candidates and parties, and 2) those that do not explicitly mention, but implicitly suggest a candidate or party (to vote or to avoid).

As future work, we intend to extend our study to new data collections and new dimensions of analysis, including uncovering relationships between different messages containing electoral ads and characterizing ad campaigns. We also intend design methods to automatically detect early ads in the online space.

Acknowledgements. This work was partially supported by research grants from Ministério Público de Minas Gerais (MPMG), project Analytical Capabilities, CNPq, FAPEMIG, and FAPESP.

A   Additional Figures

This appendix contains all of the supplementary figures used throughout the paper.

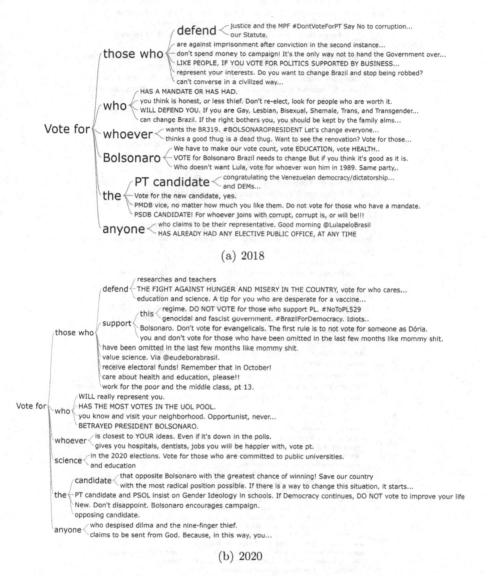

(a) 2018

(b) 2020

Fig. 5. Reduced word trees that shows the most common phrases in electoral ads in 2018 and 2020 election.

Vote for — who —
- you want to eliminate from the house!
- should be eliminated. The game is turning #StayJuliana
- put the nail in the socket. @Lucio_maia
- deserves to Win A PENALTY TODAY IN THE HARDEST GAME OF MY CAREER
- did it well – and who was wrong badly – on the red carpets - ...

me —
- in the best of his world https://t.co/gMZ7cSXsPL ‹‹ VOTE FOR ME ›› GM Noel
- Have you voted yet?! So share with your friends!!! Meliuz challenge!
- and don't WORRY - FALCON LINK via @YouTube Beloved...

whoever —
- he wants. Whoever votes for me will get thousands of kisses ????
- sings it What makes me tired is that...

who —
- are committed to Cassi associates. Vote Plate 2 - Together for Cassi! https://t.
- vote for those who actually performed and have DJ AWARD...
- don't buy votes. The one out was Emily. NOW IS THE FINAL and it will last...
- work for national metal! LINK IN COMMENTS. vote. Be a citizen... https://t.
- who committed Valença ONLINE, vote consciously..

those — who —
- understand and have the face of FLAMENGO. A president who..
- actually performed and have... https://t.co
- accuse the press of being grêmio.
- ask to vote Ted kk?kkkk flw Vote for who would be ideal defender...

(a) 2016

Vote for — who —
- want to win #DancingBrasil...
- you — THINK will win! The match will be this Wednesday (24), at 20h in Vila Capanema.
- 'd bet 50 cents, not who you're rooting for In an interview with GLobo News...
- should play for Corinthians in the Paulistão final
- is best for each position. In goal, which player has the advantage? - Do not Vote...
- fits what you think. Simple. If it's Lula or Bolsonaro ok... but take the trouble to question.
- goes to the sessions of Tan Tan Xxx....

whoever —
- you want to LEAVE!
- she decides. It's appealing with everything. I'm really nervous with Pirates of...
- voted for her ATA One of my grandfather's geniuses...

the —
- of your choice! Every time someone wants to defend the bakery for you.
- IMITATION!!!: Via @YouTube THE 3 SELECTED FOR THE @Warriors_mobile QUIZ
- shortest candidate. Of the evils, the lesser. This Centrão selling his political support
- friendly candidate without first looking at the party.
- funniest candidate in the show!

those —
- who come from SP because they are the enlightened ones, today Santos FC...
- in power. #SHARE!!! Vote for the candidate who requires the Bandeirantes track to..
- being investigated, don't give them the much dreamed privileged forum!!!

me —
- for something :') Who is the boss of politicians??? Your VOTE. Don't vote for those in power.
- I'm 3! https://t.co/yTNexNyOOj I give a cookie to whoever votes for me

(b) 2018

Vote for —

those who —
- are friends with the corrupt.
- don't go to the debates. Don't hand over your country to anyone to administer.
- represent you! If you haven't voted yet, go to the SantanderPrevi website and...!
- vote consciously, vote for the Adidas ticket! #Habblet

you —
- want to leave the house. Manu makes me proud...
- guess will win in the tweet below! @HotancoldDZ and @YooonaTV вᴿ.
- you think will come out on top in the tweet below! Participate with #InvitationalNaOnFire.

who —
- played the most at at Corinthians | Globoesporte
- should be the first-choice goalkeeper of Galo.
- will value you and return the cooperative to the cooperative...
- he wants... DIRTY game....prior wants babu

whoever —
- YOU WANT to stay and then eliminate them both at once!
- wins the poll) | @ATEZOfficial CHICKEN RUN...
- we want her to vote for. My expectation is to really allow us ...
- wants to and leave others alone, peace. Dida or Viafara? Marine or Baby? Pet or Escudero?

the —
- candidate who promises the least. You will be less disappointed." BERNARD BARUCH
- DANCE CANDIDATE.. #ForaGustavoOliveira #forabap #ForaXTudo
- most heroic, vote! Vote for who you want to win and if you didn't vote, hope to give what you want!
- DOUBLE #FUTIRÃO #PRIBU And these are the 4 participants of the glass house, I posted...
- vote for the best point guard and RT for more fans to vote. #WEGHARD
- again because I launched FIFTY DAYS OF CARNIVAL Good Morning!

me —
- for President. Jake Purring 777 Say yes, to otaku culture. Anyone who doesn't vote for me I'll hang..
- vote for me! (•'◡'•) Every time you vote (you can vote every 12 hours!

(c) 2020

Fig. 6. Reduced word trees that show most common phrases in non electoral ads for all electoral periods.

References

1. Caetano, J.A., Almeida, J., Marques-Neto, H.T.: Characterizing politically engaged users' behavior during the 2016 us presidential campaign. In: 2018 IEEE/ACM International Conference on Advances in Social Networks Analysis and Mining (ASONAM), pp. 523–530 (2018). https://doi.org/10.1109/ASONAM.2018.8508459
2. Conover, M., Ratkiewicz, J., Francisco, M., Gonçalves, B., Menczer, F., Flammini, A.: Political Polarization on Twitter. In: Proceedings of the ICWSM (2011)
3. Edelson, L., Lauinger, T., McCoy, D.: A Security Analysis of the Facebook Ad Library. In: 2020 IEEE Symposium on Security and Privacy (SP), pp. 661–678. IEEE (2020)
4. Grimaldi, D.: Can we analyse political discourse using twitter? evidence from Spanish 2019 presidential election. SNAM 9(1), 1–9 (2019)
5. Grinberg, N., Joseph, K., Friedland, L., Swire-Thompson, B., Lazer, D.: Fake news on twitter during the 2016 us presidential election. Science 363(6425), 374–378 (2019)
6. Kou, Y., Kow, Y.M., Gui, X., Cheng, W.: One social movement, two social media sites: a comparative study of public discourses. CSCW 26(4), 807–836 (2017)
7. Landis, J.R., Koch, G.G.: The measurement of observer agreement for categorical data. 33(1), 159–174 (1977)
8. Le Pochat, V., Edelson, L., Van Goethem, T., Joosen, W., McCoy, D., Lauinger, T.: an audit of facebook's political ad policy enforcement. In: Proceedings of the 31st USENIX Security Symposium. USENIX Association (2022)
9. Maruyama, M.T., Robertson, S.P., Douglas, S.K., Semaan, B.C., Faucett, H.A.: Hybrid media consumption: how tweeting during a televised political debate influences the vote decision. In: Proceedings of the CSCW, pp. 1422–1432 (2014)
10. Newcombe, R.G.: Interval estimation for the difference between independent proportions: comparison of eleven methods. Stat. Med. 17(8), 873–890 (1998)
11. Oliveira, L.S.D., Vaz-de Melo, P.O., Amaral, M.S., Pinho, J.A.G.: Do politicians talk about politics? assessing online communication patterns of Brazilian politicians. ACM Trans. Soc. Comput. 3(4), 1–28 (2020)
12. Post, T.W.: Pro-trump youth group enlists teens in secretive campaign likened to a 'troll farm', prompting rebuke by facebook and twitter. https://www.washingtonpost.com/politics/turning-point-teens-disinformation-trump/2020/09/15/c84091ae-f20a-11ea-b796-2dd09962649c_story.html (2021). Accessed 16 Dec 2021
13. Reis, J.C., Correia, A., Murai, F., Veloso, A., Benevenuto, F.: Supervised learning for fake news detection. IEEE Intell. Syst. 34(2), 76–81 (2019)
14. Ribeiro, F.N., et al.: On microtargeting socially divisive ads: a case study of Russia-linked ad campaigns on facebook. In: Proceedings of the FAT (2019)
15. Sang, E.T.K., De Meulder, F.: Introduction to the CoNLL-2003 shared task: language-independent named entity recognition. In: Proceedings of the CoNLL, pp. 142–145. Morgan Kaufman Publishers (2003)
16. Silva, M., de Oliveira, L.S., Andreou, A., de Melo, P.O.V., Goga, O., Benevenuto, F.: Facebook ads monitor: an independent auditing system for political ads on facebook. In: Proceedings of the WebConference (WWW) (2020)
17. Sosnovik, V., Goga, O.: Understanding the complexity of detecting political Ads. In: Proceedings of the WebConference (WWW) (2021)

18. Tausczik, Y.R., Pennebaker, J.W.: The psychological meaning of words: LIWC and computerized text analysis methods. J. Lang. Soc. Psychol. **29**(1), 24–54 (2010)
19. Thelwall, M., Buckley, K., Paltoglou, G., Cai, D., Kappas, A.: Sentiment strength detection in short informal text. JASIST **61**(12), 2544–2558 (2010)
20. Lei Eleitoral N° 13.488, 6 de Outubro, 2017. https://www.tse.jus.br/legislacao/codigo-eleitoral/leis-ordinarias/lei-no-13-488-de-6-de-outubro-de-2017   (2017). Accessed 14 Oct 2019
21. Brazil's electoral justice permanent program on countering disinformation - strategic plan - elections 2022. https://international.tse.jus.br/en/misinformation-and-fake-news/brazil-electoral-justice-permanent-program-on-countering-disinformation (2022). Accessed 30 June 2022
22. Wattenberg, M., Viégas, F.B.: The word tree, an interactive visual concordance. IEEE TVCG **14**(6), 1221–1228 (2008)
23. Weismueller, J., Harrigan, P., Coussement, K., Tessitore, T.: What makes people share political content on social media? the role of emotion, authority and ideology. Comput. Hum. Behav. **129**, 107150 (2022)

Mental Health Issues During COVID-19: A Data Exploration

Salwa M. Althobaity$^{(\boxtimes)}$ and Joemon M. Jose

School of Computing Science, University of Glasgow, Glasgow G12 8RZ, UK
smthobaity@uqu.edu.sa, joemon.jose@glasgow.ac.uk

Abstract. The emergence of COVID-19 and its associated containment strategies, such as lockdowns and social distancing, are expected to impact mental health, which could be more severe among people with pre-existing mental health disorders. In this research, we aim to better understand the changes in mental health during the COVID-19 pandemic by analysing data from mental health-related communities. We have collected data from the 15th of February 2020 to the 15th of July 2020 and analysed these data using interaction, linguistic structure, and interpersonal awareness measures. Our findings show that early in the lockdown, individuals showed selflessness, solidarity, and low rates of seeking help, but they also showed a negative mental health state. Moreover, considering the importance of social support in mental illness, we also aim to explore what derives social support in mental health communities. We found that receiving high social support was hindered by the use more swearing and negative emotional or self-referent words. Furthermore, not receiving social support may push actual help seekers to repeat their posts, which may be considered spamming in Reddit forums. Hence, we investigated the characteristics of duplicate posts authored by real help seekers to build a spam classifier. Our investigation showed that actual help seekers tend to show different levels of mental health when they repeat their posts for seeking immediate help.

Keywords: Social media · Data analytics · COVID-19 · Mental health

1 Introduction

COVID-19 became a pandemic by the beginning of 2020. World Health Organization and respective governments suggested containment strategies to slow down the spread of this disease, such as international travelling restrictions, isolating infected cases, quarantine, and social distancing [22]. In many western countries, stay-at-home orders have been enforced to prevent the spread of this disease. Despite the significant role of these interventions in protecting health, they can lead to negative consequences, such as restricted access to services, loneliness, loss of earnings, and inactivity [21]. These consequences, along with the uncertainty and unpredictability of the crisis, adversely influence the mental health of the entire population, particularly people with pre-existing psychiatric morbidity [15]. However, [17], investigating the existing observational studies about COVID-19 and its effect on mental health, stated that few studies focus on COVID-19's impact on mental health. Most of these studies have been carried out at the early stages of the COVID-19 outbreak and used online surveys, cross-sectional self-rated surveys, or questionnaires as research instruments. Since these studies are self-reported data, the results can be biased. Moreover, focusing only on the early stages of the pandemic may not reveal accurate results about the effect of COVID-19 on mental health [21]. Therefore, to mitigate these limitations, there is a need to analyse data spanning over a long time and employ different analysis methods to better understand mental health changes in COIVD-19.

Social media collect and disseminate users' feelings, opinions, and behaviours. It can provide evidence of the implications of events on individuals' lives in the form of their online engagement or linguistic expression style [8]. Of these social media sites, Reddit stands out because of its semi-anonymous feature, which promotes honesty in self-disclosure [9]. Additionally, Reddit has mental-health-focused subreddits that allow more targeted analysis [3]. Applying computational methods and text analysis to data from social media has been growing since 2013 to define mental-health-related behaviour and predict mental health conditions [5]. Weaving together the unique characteristics of Reddit as a data source and the association between users' behaviour, linguistic style and mental health state, we aim to understand mental health changes during COVID-19.

Social support is essential for mental disorders, and its role in improving perceived self-efficacy has been identified [9]. However, not having this kind of support may push help seekers to repost their content; however, it is treated by Reddit as spam [18]. Hence, based on content analysis, we investigated factors that derive social support and detect duplicate posts that genuine help seekers author. Given the above discussion, our aim is to develop data analytic approaches to understand mental health issues during COVID-19. For this purpose, we have identified the following research questions:

1. How did mental health issues materialise during COVID-19 crisis? This research question is broken-down into the following sub-questions:
   - What is the general picture of changes in mental health status before, during and after lockdown?
   - Did users who posted and commented before, during and after lockdown show different levels of mental health status?
   - Were users with different mental health conditions (posting in different mental health subreddits) affected differently by COVID-19?
2. What are the factors which derive social support?
3. How can we distinguish duplicate posts authored by an actual help seeker from those written by a spammer?

2   Related Work

Although very few self-reported studies analyzed the effect of COVID-19 on mental health [17], some researchers analyzed online behaviour and social media content. Jacobson [12] aimed to study whether stay-at-home orders implemented in the U.S. caused changes in mental health status. They analyzed shifts in the frequency of mental-health-related search queries on Google after the order issuance. The result showed a dramatic increase in such queries before issuing the order, and the growth plateaued when it came into effect. However, this result only showed the short-term impact of the stay-at-home order on mental health. Li [14] explored the impact of declaring COVID-19 as an epidemic on mental health. They sampled posts of 17,865 active users on a Chinese social site and analyzed them by measuring psycholinguistic attributes. Their results showed that the mental health status was negatively affected after the declaration by increasing negative emotions and sensitivity to social risks. Biester [3] examined the variation between pre-COVID-19 and post-COVID-19 regarding users' online activity and discussion content within Anxiety, Depression, and Suicide-Watch subreddits. They found that users in the anxiety subreddit were more active post-COVID-19, whereas users in Depression and SuicideWatch subreddits showed less activity at the beginning of the post-COVID-19 period. Users in all subreddits discussed anxiety, family, and health more than work and school. Although this study showed exciting findings, it analyzed only three mental-health-related subreddits. Also, it is considered post-COVID-19 as one event, whereas lockdown was issued and then eased in this period, which may cause changes in mental health states.

De Choudhury and De [9] in their study of self-discourse and social support on Reddit, explored factors that derive social support, represented in comments or karma, based on post content. They used negative binomial regression as a prediction model. Their results showed that short posts with more positive emotional words and fewer swear words received more karma, whereas question-centric posts or posts with more negative emotional words received more comments. According to Zeileis et al. [23], although negative binomial regression is appropriate for over-dispersed data, using zero-augmented models is better when data exhibits an excess number of zeros.

Others investigated duplicate posts on social media for different objectives. One of these studies considered duplicate posts an irritating issue and proposed an algorithm to restrict duplicate content [11]. Albrektsson [1] aimed to explore the effectiveness of using similarity measures in detecting identical or near-identical messages that have been authored by multiple accounts but are managed by one user. He found that cosine similarity achieves better performance than whole message comparison, word-by-word comparison, and fingerprinting. However, none of these studies examined the case when one account repeated the content of its posts as spam or was motivated by seeking immediate help.

3 Data Collection

Data scraped from six public content subreddits (Alcoholism, Anxiety, Bipo-larReddit, Depression, Schizophrenia, and SuicideWatch) that have been proved to contain mental-health-focused discourse [16]. We collected posts made from the 15th of February 2020 00:00 AM UTC to the 15th of July 2020 11:59 PM UTC using Push-shift Reddit API [2]. We collected the following information for each post: post ID, title, author, body or content, timestamp of sharing the post, upvote ratio, score (which is the difference between upvote and downvote), number of top-level comments (comments on the post), number of overall comments (comments on the post and comments on comments which resulted in tree conversations), and all comments made on the post. The final dataset contained 118,621 posts with 4.29 average words per post and 134,582 unique users. Of these individual users, 23.28% only made posts, 45.45% made comments, and 31.26% posted and commented. Basic descriptive statistics of the dataset is shown in Table 1. In addition, we collected repeated posts and their duplicates.

Table 1. Basic descriptive statistics of the dataset by subreddit

	Anxiety	Alcoholism	SuicideWatch	Bipolarreddit	Depression	Schizophrenia
Number of posts	23877	2127	30882	2921	54695	4119
Mean length of posts (words)	876.99	1070.69	917.18	885.38	922.24	686.38
Number of users who only post	7093	577	9149	343	17106	432
Number of users who only comment	18830	2374	14875	3276	26055	1859
Number of users who post and comment	9648	1171	11566	1295	18543	1527
Average posts per user	1.43	1.22	1.49	1.78	1.53	2.1
Average comments per user	4.55	4.55	4.89	6.54	3.94	8.55
Average comments per post	5.42	7.58	4.18	10.24	3.21	7.03

We separated the data into three time periods: before lockdown, during the lockdown, and after the lockdown. The identification of these periods depended on the announcements of the beginning and end of the stay-at-home orders in the United States, where most Reddit users reside [3]. According to [19], the US states differed in the timing of announcing the orders. The first order was announced on the 19th of March in California, and by the beginning of May, it had eased restrictions in more than half of the states [19]. Therefore, the data was divided as follows: (i) **Before lockdown:** from the 15th of February to the 18th of March; (ii) **During lockdown:** from the 18th of March to the 2nd of May; (iii) **After lockdown:** from the 2nd of May to the 15th of July.

4 Research Methodology

Our approach is a data centric method. We collected data and analysed its characteristics. In this section, we first introduce the research questions we were investigating, and measures used.

4.1 Measures

As in [10], linguistic structure and interpersonal awareness measures are used for studying changes in mental health status.

Linguistic Structure Measure. We examined the linguistic structure of the posts and comments to understand the users' cognitive state. This measure measures the percentage of verbs, adverbs, and negative and positive emotional words. Another variable in this measure is the Automated Readability Index, which estimates the comprehensibility of a text. These variables characterise the text and indicate the writers' psycho-logical state [10].

Interpersonal Awareness Measure. The interpersonal awareness measure is concerned with gauging attention to the self and social awareness and interactivity, which indicates psychological well-being. Calculating the percentage of first-person-singular (I, me, my), first-person-plural (we, our, us), second-person (you, your), and third-person pronouns (they, their, she) in a text, interpersonal awareness are calculated [10].

Interaction Measure. This measure gauges the extent of requests for help, access to social support, and the verbosity of posts [10].

4.2 Research Questions

Our research questions driving our data exploration is given below:

RQ 1.1 What is the General Picture of Changes in Mental Health Status Before, During and After Lock-Down?

The aim was to explore the general picture of mental health during the pandemic by analysing all posts and comments in the dataset. Our goal was to identify any changes in mental health over a period, and hence we segmented the data into two-week groups, which resulted in 11 groups. Subsequently, we computed each group's readability index, interaction, interpersonal awareness, and linguistic structure measures.

RQ 1.2 Did Users who Posted and Commented Before, During and After Lockdown Show Different Levels of Mental Health Status?

First, the IDs of users who posted and commented in the three periods were extracted. After that, for each user, all their posts and comments were grouped into before, during and after lockdown periods. Then, we calculated the interaction, interpersonal awareness, and linguistic structure measures. Regarding interaction measure, we calculated the number of comments the user authored and received to measure their social engagement and access to support [10]. We conducted the Friedman test to examine if there was a significant change in users' mental health over time during the crisis [13].

RQ 1.3 Were Users with Different Mental Health Conditions (Posting in Various Mental Health Subreddits) Affected Differently by COVID-19?

We grouped the posts of each subreddit on a two-week basis to explore if users with different mental health conditions experienced significant differences in mental health states during COVID-19. As a result, each subreddit had 11 groups of posts. After that, we calculated each group's interaction, interpersonal awareness, and linguistic structure measures. To examine if there was a significant difference in the measurements between Anxiety, Alcoholism, BipolarReddit, Depression, Schizophrenia, and SuicideWatch subreddits, we conducted the Kruskal-Wallis test [13].

4.3 Data Exploration and Social Support

This section will explore the data captured and investigate some predictive models. Social support in the Reddit community is provided by voting or commenting on users' posts, through which commenters can offer their advice, information or feedback about others' concerns.

Exploring which posts derive large numbers of comments in mental health communities can be done as a prediction task, and since the dependent variable 'number of comments' is counted, the prediction task is considered a regression problem. Hence for the regression problem, our response variable is the number of comments. So, we will investigate the research question (RQ2):

RQ 2. What Are the Factors which Derive Social Support?

Our predictive variables are specific post attributes, and semantic categories of terms were used as features to estimate the degree of social support. These features are illustrated in Table 2.

Table 2. List of features used in the prediction task

Type	Feature					Description
LIWC semantic categories of words	First-person pronouns (i, we)	Quantifiers	Insight	Sexual	Work	Fraction of words in each category based on LIWC
	Second-person pronouns (you)	Positive emotion	Cause	Ingestion	Leisure	
	Third-person pronouns (they, she, he)	Negative emotion	Discrepancy	Achievement	Home	
	Preposition	Anxiety	Tentative	Risk	Money	
	Adverb	Anger	Certainty	Past focus	Death	
	Conjunction	Sadness	See	Present focus	Swear	
	Negation	Family	Hear	Future focus		
	Verb	Friend	Feel	Motion		
	Interrogatives	Female	Body	Space		
	Number	Male	Health	Time		
Post attributes	Post length					Length of a post in words
	Title length					Length of title in words
	Link flair text					Binary feature, whether the post is tagged or not
	Day					Day of posting a post
	Hour					Hour of posting a post
	Subreddit					Categorical feature (Anxiety, Alcoholism, BipolarReddit, Depression, Schizophrenia, SuicideWatch)

However, the choice of the appropriate regression model depends on whether the count data is over-dispersed and exhibits excess zeros [23]. As shown in Fig. 1 below, the number of comments in our dataset exhibited over-dispersion and excess zeros. Furthermore, social support through comments occurred at different levels, and there were a large number of posts which did not receive any comments at all. Several regression models can handle this problem. For example, Negative binomial regression can be used to model over-dispersed count data. Also, the Hurdle model and Zero-inflated model are capable of modelling count variables which are over-dispersed and have large numbers of zeros [23].

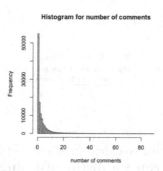

Fig. 1. Frequency distribution for number of comments

4.4 Characteristics of Duplicate Posts Authored by Actual Help Seekers

Spam is defined as "repeated, unwanted, and/or unsolicited actions". Repeated content is considered spam since it may irritate the Reddit audience and negatively affect Reddit communities [18]. However, we argue that duplicating a post could be interpreted from a different point of view: an anxious user may need immediate help, and when their post does not receive any comments, they are more likely to repeat the post. Table 3 provides examples of users duplicating their initial posts to seek help.

We analyzed emotional content and verified that users showed different levels of emotion in their duplicate posts. The first user explicitly asked for immediate help in the title and showed anxiety by writing 'Help me, please', whereas the second user added the word 'serious' in the title and showed negative emotion when he wrote, 'hurting myself'. Genuine help seekers tended to express different levels of emotion and mental health states in their duplicate posts.

Table 3. Examples of duplicate posts authored by actual help seekers. Underlined words show the difference between the main and duplicate posts.

Main post	Duplicate post
Title	
How does it feel to have Anhedonia?	Help me, please! I really need to understand this!
Body	
Hello everyone! What's up? I hope you're all having a nice day. I want to share a little bit of my story and hopefully I'll get some answers about the things that's been rounding my head lately	Hello everyone! What's up? I hope you're all having a nice day. I want to share a little bit of my story and hopefully I'll get some answers about the things that's been rounding my head lately....
Title	
Young doctor (29yo) with suicide thoughts	[serious] Young doctor (29yo) and suicide thoughts
Body	
First, thank you for opening the post. I'm sharing a bit of my story to try to prevent bad things to happen to me. Please share your thoughts or advise in life	First, thank you for opening the post. I'm sharing a bit of my story to try to prevent bad things to happen to me or hurting myself. Please share your thoughts or advise in life

Hence, we created a third research question exploring the nature of duplicate posts. **RQ 3. How can we distinguish duplicate posts authored by a genuine help seeker from those authored by a Spammer?** We can answer this research question by developing a classifier to model the characteristics of duplicate posts authored by genuine help seekers to label them as non-spam posts. First, it was necessary to establish the ground truth using duplicate posts. Then, features from the first post and duplicate posts had to be extracted. Finally, classifier models needed to be trained and tested.

Establishing Ground Truth. Due to time constraints, it was impossible to manually label duplicate posts as spam or not spam. Hence, the ground truth was established automatically based on the analysis suggesting that genuine help seekers tended to express different levels of emotion and mental health states in their duplicate posts. We grouped based on the elapsed time between the first and duplicate posts. To illustrate, all posts which were duplicated within 15 min of the time stamp of their first post were grouped in one category. Using this strategy, four groups were created: Group 1) the elapsed time was less than or equal to 15 min; Group 2) the elapsed time was more than 15 min and less than or equal to one hour; Group 3) the elapsed time was more than one hour and less than or equal to six hours, and Group 4) all posts which were duplicated more than six hours after the time stamp of the first post. After that, we calculated the interpersonal awareness and linguistic structure measures for the first posts and duplicates in each group. The Wilcoxon signed-rank test was conducted to examine if there were significant differences in these measures between first and duplicate posts. The results are shown in Table 4:

Table 4. The significant differences between the first post and duplicate posts based on interpersonal awareness and linguistic structure measures. The Wilcoxon signed-rank test statistics and p-values are reported. *** p <.0001; ** p <.001; * p <.01

Measure	Elapsed time	Main post	Duplicate post	Statistic	P-value	Significance code
Third-person pronouns	<=15 m	0.468	0.466	3787.5	0.103	
	(15 m-1 h]	0.698	0.697	1019.5	0.125	
	(1 h-6 h]	0.668	0.664	369	0.379	
	>6 h	0.627	0.618	1951	0.000913	***
Negative emotion						
Anger	<=15 m	1.081	1.083	7916.5	0.312	
	(15 m-1 h]	1.235	1.248	2072.5	0.385	
	(1 h-6 h]	1.299	1.261	811	0.022	*
	>6 h	1.345	1.385	3319	0.966	

Table 4 shows that when the elapsed time was more than one hour, there was a significant difference between main posts and their duplicates in terms of using third-person pronouns and angry words. Since the use of the third-person pronouns and emotional words (anger) indicates mental health well-being, posts in these groups were labelled 'not spam' (from actual help seekers). As a result, the dataset contained 1,126 spam posts and 376 'not spam' posts.

Feature Extraction. To train classifier models, we extracted some features: The first was a binary feature to indicate whether a duplicate post was posted in the same subreddit as the main post. The motivation for this feature was that when a genuine help seeker who posted in SuicideWatch to seek help about suicidal thoughts wants to repost, he is more likely to repost in the same subreddit rather than another subreddit which discusses a different topic. The second feature was concerned with the engagement of the author. It was a binary feature indicating whether an author engaged in the comments of the main and duplicate posts. This feature was motivated by the assumption that an actual help seeker is likelier to engage with commenters who comment on his post and try to help him. Furthermore, the title and body text of the main and duplicate posts were tokenized and vectorized using a TF-IDF vectorizer.

Classification. The classification aimed to detect if a duplicate post was spam or not (from a genuine help seeker). The dataset was divided into training, validation and testing, as shown in Table 5.

Table 5. Summary of the dataset

	Spam	Not spam	Total
Training	622	218	840
Validation	159	52	211
Testing	345	106	451
Total	1126	376	1502

Clearly an imbalance existed in the dataset since 25% of the dataset was not spam; hence, down-sampling was done on training spam posts. After that, three classifiers were trained to classify posts into spam or not spam: Naive Bayes, Logistic regression, and Random Forest.

5   Results and Discussion

In this section, we will answer the research questions.

RQ 1.1 Results: The General Picture of Changes in Mental Health Status Before, During and After Lockdown.
For this, we analyzed the measures for various sections of the datasets. The results are shown in Figs. 2, 3 and 4, in which the x-axis represents the period on which the study is based. The line charts are coloured as follows: blue represents the period before lockdown; red represents the period during lockdown; and green represents the period after lockdown.

Observations. Users showed high rates of asking for help and self-disclosure behaviours during and after lockdown. The first two weeks of lockdown witnessed the most increased support and the lowest rate of asking for help. Users at the beginning of the lockdown switched from focusing on themselves to focusing on others. Subsequently, they showed negative mental health states after showing excessive attention to the self and detachment from society. Users focused less on actions during and for some weeks after the lockdown: an indication of sensitive disclosures, or it may be because users spent their time at home without taking part in much activity, and after the lockdown, they might still have been worried about catching the virus and preferred to stay at home. Although they showed a slight improvement in their emotional states after two weeks of announcing the end of lockdown, it worsened further.

The general picture of mental health during and after lockdown shows a negative mental health state. This finding is consistent with prior research, which found that anxiety and social isolation were associated with stay-at-home orders [21] and consistent with what was noted by the Centers for Disease Control and Prevention [4], that ending the isolation order might result in stress and fear. Moreover, the beginning of lockdown was characterised by attending to others, high levels of social support, and low rates of seeking help. Although the lowest rate of asking for help at the beginning of the stay-at-home order was not predicted, it is consistent with studies showing that delayed depression is typical following a crisis [3], and switching from being self-focused to attending to others has been observed as people's reaction to community-wide events [7].

RQ 1.2 Results: Mental Health States of Users who Posted and Commented Before, During and After Lockdown. The results are shown in Table 6.

Table 6. The significant differences between interaction, interpersonal awareness, and linguistic structure measures of users who posted before, during and after lockdown. The Friedman test statistics, and p-values are reported. The statistical significance and value of pairwise comparisons using the Wilcoxon test with Bonferroni correction are reported only for groups with significant differences. *** p $<$.0001; ** p $<$.001; * p $<$.01

Measure	Before lockdown	During lockdown	After lockdown	Statistic	P-value	Significant difference between groups			
						Group1	Group2	Statistics	Significance code
Interaction									
Number of posts	2.52	2.95	3.45	44.9	1.82e–10	After	Before	259656	***
						After	During	232468	***
						Before	During	160631	***
Number of comments received	12.7	14.4	15.1	6.67	0.0374	Before	During	337686	*
Number of comments authored	7.65	8.1	10.1	9.73	0.00769	After	Before	330377	*
						Before	During	270337	*
Interpersonal awareness									
First-person-singular pronouns	11.2	10.9	11	7.98	0.0185	Before	During	487344	**
Linguistic structure									
Positive emotion	3.25	3.11	3.15	6.93	0.0312	After	Before	399434	*

Observations. Users asked for help more after lockdown and were more likely to be supported during the lock-down than before. Moreover, users showed less self-attentional focus during the lockdown and negative mental health states after lockdown. Users who posted and commented in the three periods showed different levels of mental health states. They showed negative mental health after lockdown. This finding is consistent with what the Centers for Disease Control and Prevention [4] noted: anxiety, stress and fear might result from terminating isolation orders. Moreover, users were also less self-focused during lockdown than before, which could be a sign of better mental health. However, a study on mental health during lockdown found that mental health issues were associated with stay-at-home orders [21]. Our findings could be a result of social support, which was very high at the beginning of lockdown.

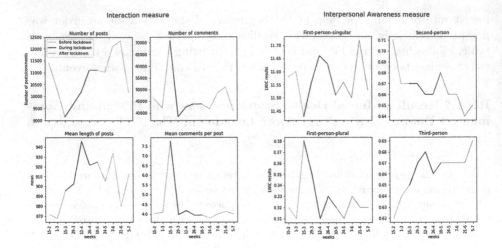

Fig. 2. Interaction measure   **Fig. 3.** Interpersonal awareness

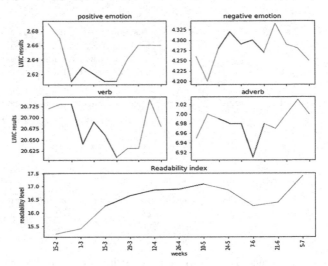

Fig. 4. Linguistic structure measure

RQ 1.3 Results: Mental Health States of Users with Different Mental Health Conditions (Posting in Different Subreddits) in the Time of COVID-19. The results are shown in Table 7.

Table 7. Differences between Alcoholism, Anxiety, BipolarReddit, Depression, Schizophrenia, and SuicideWatch subreddits based on interaction, interpersonal awareness, and linguistic structure measures. The Kruskal-Wallis test statistics and p-values are reported based on the Kruskal-Wallis test. Since most pairs of groups have significant differences, the value of pairwise comparisons using the Wilcoxon test with Bonferroni correction is reported only for groups without significant differences.

Measure	Alcoholism	Anxiety	Bipolar	Depression	Schizophrenia	SuicideWatch	Statistic	P-value	Groups with no significant differences		
									Group1	Group2	Statistic
Interaction											
Number of posts	193	2170	265	4971	374	2806	62.6	3.55e−12			
Mean length of posts	1067	875	885	923	686	918	46.2	8.39e−09	Anxiety	Bipolar	58
									Anxiety	SuicideWatch	19
									Bipolar	Depression	38
									Bipolar	SuicideWatch	42
									Depression	SuicideWatch	68
Number of comments	1465	11765	2717	15968	2631	11747	59.4	1.58e−11	Bipolar	Schizophrenia	81
Mean comments per post	7.67	5.65	10.3	3.21	7.04	4.19	55.1	1.25e−10	Alcoholism	Schizophrenia	80
									Anxiety	SuicideWatch	42
Interpersonal awareness											
First-person-singular pronouns	9.56	10.6	10.4	11.8	9.3	12.4	60.1	1.13e−11	Alcoholism	Schizophrenia	87.5
									Anxiety	Bipolar	79.5
First-person-plural pronouns	0.441	0.336	0.287	0.341	0.353	0.288	34.8	1.65e−06	Anxiety	Bipolar	90
									Anxiety	Depression	51
									Anxiety	Schizophrenia	44
									Bipolar	Depression	31.5
									Bipolar	Schizophrenia	28
									Bipolar	SuicideWatch	54
									Depression	Schizophrenia	46
Second-person pronouns	0.59	0.657	0.657	0.69	0.945	0.612	33	0.0000037	Alcoholism	Anxiety	39
									Alcoholism	Bipolar	39
									Alcoholism	Depression	30
									Alcoholism	SuicideWatch	51.5
									Anxiety	Bipolar	67
									Anxiety	Depression	32.5
									Anxiety	SuicideWatch	92
									Bipolar	Depression	31.5
									Bipolar	SuicideWatch	82
Third-person pronouns	0.403	0.545	0.49	0.682	0.828	0.735	59.4	1.58e−11	Alcoholism	Bipolar	18
									Anxiety	Bipolar	90.5
									Depression	SuicideWatch	19.5
Linguistic structure											
Adverb	6.37	6.8	6.47	7.12	6.29	7.03	57.4	4.26e−11	Alcoholism	Bipolar	33
									Alcoholism	Schizophrenia	78.5
									Bipolar	Schizophrenia	99
Verb	19.2	19.9	19.8	20.8	19.8	21.3	54.5	1.64e−10	Anxiety	Bipolar	82.5
									Anxiety	Schizophrenia	63.5
									Bipolar	Schizophrenia	60.5
Positive emotion	2.35	2.36	2.4	2.79	2.32	2.66	46.1	8.48e−09	Alcoholism	Anxiety	69
									Alcoholism	Bipolar	51.5
									Alcoholism	Schizophrenia	76.5
									Anxiety	Bipolar	52
									Anxiety	Schizophrenia	81.5
									Bipolar	Schizophrenia	86
Negative emotion	3.07	4.7	3.35	4.22	2.96	4.38	60.3	1.07e−11	Alcoholism	Schizophrenia	80.5
Readability	15	15.8	15.5	16.5	17.5	17	11.5	>0.05			

Observations. Users who posted in the Depression subreddit asked for help more than others in the other subreddits; however, they did not receive high levels of support, unlike users who posted in BipolarReddit, who were highly supported. Furthermore, users who posted in the Alcoholism subreddit showed less interaction and more self-disclosure and cognitive complexity, whereas users who posted in the Schizophrenia subreddit showed low self-disclosure and low rates of seeking help. Users in the SuicideWatch and the Depression subreddits showed higher levels of negative emotions, while users in the Schizophrenia and Alcoholism subreddits were less attentive to the self and, therefore, showed better mental states compared with the other subreddits. Users in the SucideWatch and Depression subreddits focused more on actions and used more positive emotional words. Unsurprisingly, users who posted in the SuicideWatch and Depression subreddits used more positive terms than others, an attempt to cope by thinking positively [6]. Users who posted in the Anxiety subreddit showed high levels of negative emotion in their posts compared with others in the other subreddits.

Users who posted in the Anxiety, Depression and SuicideWatch subreddits showed higher levels of adverse mental health than others. Although users who posted in the Alcoholism subreddit showed verbose posts, they and users who posted in the Schizophrenia subreddit showed better mental health, compared with the other subreddits, by showing lower rates of seeking help and less self-attentional focus. This result is consistent with studies which found that anxiety and depressive symptoms were common during the COVID-19 pandemic [6,20].

RQ 2 Results: Factors which Derived Social Support. Since the number of comments in our dataset exhibited overdispersion and excess zeros, zero-augmented models (Hurdle and Zero-inflated) may fit the number of comments better than Negative binomial regression. We fitted negative binomial regression, Hurdle model, and Zero-inflated model to the dataset and compared their performance: comparing the predicted number of zeros to what was observed, log-likelihood and AIC.

Table 8. Results of fitting count regression models in terms of AIC, log-likelihood, expected number of zeros and number of parameters.

Criteria	Negative binomial model	Hurdle model	Zero-inflated model
AIC	572421.6	558050.2	571260
Log-likelihood	−286151	−278906	−285511
Expected number of zeros (Observed = 31584)	37099	31584	37629
Number of estimated parameters	60	119	119

The results in Table 8 showed that the Hurdle model improved the fit by having the lowest values on the log-likelihood and AIC measures. Interestingly, the Hurdle model's expected number of zero counts were equal to the actual number. Therefore, the Hurdle model was the best choice for modelling the number of comments, and it was used to explore factors which derived social support. The result of the two parts of the Hurdle model, zero model and count model are shown in Table 9 and Table 10.

Table 9. Results of the first process in the Hurdle model (zero model). *** p<.0001; ** p<.001; * p<.01

Feature	Coefficients	exp(Coefficients)	Std. Error	Z value	P-value	Significance code
(Intercept)	1.66124	5.27	0.16741	9.923	<2e−16	***
Third-person pronouns (she,he)	4.75637	116.32	2.06688	2.301	0.021378	*
Ingestion	2.32884	10.27	1.04013	2.239	0.025157	*
Negative emotion	1.64184	5.16	0.47847	3.431	0.0006	***
Post length	1.61123	5.01	0.10836	14.869	<2e−16	***
Tentative	1.31143	3.71	0.33665	3.896	9.80e−05	***
Title length	1.29534	3.65	0.08529	15.187	<2e−16	***
Positive emotion	1.22321	3.40	0.27701	4.416	1.01e−05	***
Certainty	1.15721	3.18	0.46957	2.464	0.013725	*
Verb	0.84072	2.32	0.3138	2.679	0.007381	**
Hour	−0.68553	0.50	0.22844	−3.001	0.002692	**
Leisure	−2.41343	0.09	0.75265	−3.207	0.001343	**

Observations. The more the users referred to others in their posts, incorporated negative and positive emotional words, or used tentative language, the more likely they were to receive at least one comment. Moreover, increased post and title length and talking about eating and drinking-related topics increased the chance of having at least one comment. During the COVID-19 period under study, people spent most of their time at home without activities, so topics about eating or drinking may have attracted them to comment. On the other hand, the likelihood of having zero comments increased over time and incorporating leisure words. The more the post contained other-referent words (they, you) and collective attention words (we, us) or sexual terms, the more likely it was to receive a high number of comments. Moreover, having a long title or posting in the BipolarReddit subreddit increased the chance of having more comments. This result is consistent with the results of RQ1.3, which shows that social support in the BipolarReddit community was very high. On the other hand, posts containing swear words, negative emotional words or self-referent words were more likely to receive fewer comments. This result contrasts the study by [9], which found that greater negative emotional words contributed to increased social support. The reason for this may be COVID-19, a socially shared event, so more social support was derived from posts that attended to others and talked about shared issues than posts that were self-focused with negative emotions. It was also observed that the chance of receiving more comments increased over time, whereas the result of the zero model shows that it decreased the possibility of having at least

Table 10. Results of the second process of the Hurdle model (count model). ***
p<.0001; ** p<.001; * p<.01

Feature	Coefficients	exp(Coefficients)	Std. Error	Z value	P-value	Significance code
(Intercept)	5.37491	215.9204386	0.12267	43.817	<2e−16	***
First-person-plural pronouns	6.18663	486.2048319	2.18461	2.832	0.004627	**
Sexual	6.17445	480.3187759	1.57756	3.914	9.08e−05	***
Third-person pronouns (they)	2.94732	19.05481832	1.18177	2.494	0.012632	*
Second-person pronouns	2.77257	15.99970045	0.6593	4.205	2.61e−05	***
Conjunction	1.1961	3.307193683	0.38564	3.102	0.001925	**
Hour	0.7316	2.078403394	0.24104	3.035	0.002403	**
Title length	0.40144	1.493974473	0.0875	4.588	4.48e−06	***
BipolarReddit subreddit	0.37953	1.461597477	0.05846	6.492	8.46e−11	***
Anxiety subreddit	−0.57629	0.561979448	0.04799	−12.009	<2e−16	***
SuicideWatch subreddit	−0.627	0.534191975	0.04598	−13.636	<2e−16	***
Depression subreddit	−0.69477	0.499189248	0.04547	−15.279	<2e−16	***
Verb	−0.84785	0.428334863	0.37541	−2.259	0.023914	*
Adverb	−1.06693	0.344063172	0.33137	−3.22	0.001283	**
Discrepancy	−1.10424	0.331462698	0.51004	−2.165	0.030387	*
First-person-singular pronoun	−1.35502	0.257942136	0.29219	−4.638	3.53e−06	***
Past focus	−1.44729	0.235206836	0.56155	−2.577	0.009957	**
Space	−1.48123	0.227357866	0.407	−3.639	0.000273	***
Work	−1.59082	0.203758461	0.80446	−1.977	0.047986	*
Tentative	−1.75202	0.173423274	0.40728	−4.302	1.69e−05	***
Present focus	−1.92624	0.145694983	0.3668	−5.251	1.51e−07	***
Hear	−2.04256	0.129696263	0.95543	−2.138	0.032529	*
Negative emotion	−2.04521	0.129353023	0.73775	-2.772	0.005567	**
Feel	−2.39195	0.09145118	0.67401	−3.549	0.000387	***
Swear	−3.3853	0.033867481	1.30642	−2.591	0.009562	**
Family	−3.64508	0.02611932	1.58211	−2.304	0.021226	*
Interrogatives	−4.01044	0.018125418	0.598	−6.706	1.99e−11	***
Post length	−4.62064	0.009846492	0.10731	−43.059	<2e−16	***

one comment. This contradictory result could be solved by looking at the distribution of comments over time. Figure 5 shows that from 6:00, the number of comments decreased, which was captured by the zero model, until 14:00, when it began to increase, which was captured by the count model.

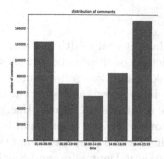

Fig. 5. Distribution of comments over time

RQ 3. Results: Distinguishing Duplicate Posts Authored by an Actual Help Seeker from those Authored by a Spammer. Naive Bayes, Logistic regression, and Random forest were trained to classify duplicate posts into spam or not spam. The performance results on the testing dataset are shown in the following Table 11.

Table 11. Classification results

Model	Accuracy	Precision	Recall	F1 score
Naive bayes	0.698	0.587	0.59	0.589
Logistic regression	0.621	0.576	0.602	0.566
Random forest	0.654	0.593	0.62	0.591

The two classes are essential; it is crucial to label spam duplicates as spam and to label duplicate posts from genuine help seekers as not spam. So, the F1 score is the most critical measure to compare the classifiers. As shown in the table, all the classifiers did not perform well on the testing dataset. As discussed, the imbalance between classes was overcome by down-sampling the majority class; therefore, the low performance of the classifiers may not be due to the imbalance between classes. As mentioned, due to time constraints, we did not investigate each duplicate post in the dataset to label it as spam or not to establish our ground truth. However, we grouped the duplicate posts based on the elapsed time between the duplicate posts and the main posts, and if duplicate posts in group 'A' showed significant differences in the mental health state compared with their first posts, these duplicate posts in this group were labelled as not spam. This was not enough to create confidence in the reliability of the ground truth data, so there could be spam posts found in the group A which, because of our strategy, were labelled as 'not spam'. This will affect the classifier which may not be able to learn the underlying patterns. Therefore, building reliable ground truth is essential as the first step. After that, we can improve the performance by adding additional features to overcome underfitting or eliminating some features to overcome overfitting.

6 Conclusion

This research aimed to explore mental health issues among Reddit users during COVID-19. The general picture of mental health showed that there was high social support, less help-seeking and less self-attentional focus at the beginning of the lockdown; then, later in lockdown and after the ending of lockdown, there was a higher rate of negative mental health states. Users, who posted before, during, and after lockdown, showed less self-attentional focus during the lockdown due to the need to provide high social support during this period. We also found that users who posted in Anxiety, Depression and SuicideWatch subreddits had worse mental health states than those who posted in Alcoholism, BipolarReddit, or Schizophrenia subreddits. Regarding social support, our findings showed that the more individuals referred to others in their posts, used long titles and tentative language, and incorporated negative and positive emotional words, the more likely they were to receive at least one comment. Using more swearing and negative emotional or self-referent words reduced the number of comments received.

Regarding genuine help seekers who authored duplicate posts, we found they tended to show different levels of mental health in the duplicate posts compared with the original posts. However, as our results show, this area needs further work, especially manual labeling of ground truth.

References

1. Albrektsson, F.: Detecting Sockpuppets in Social Media with Plagiarism Detection Algorithms. MS, KTH Royal Institute of Technology (2017)
2. Baumgartner, J., Zannettou, S., Keegan, B., Squire, M., Blackburn, J.: The Pushshift Reddit Dataset. In: AAAI Conference on Web and Social Media. 26 May 2020. vol. 14, pp. 830–839. ICWSM (2020)
3. Biester, L., Matton, K., Rajendran, J., Provost, E.M., Mihalcea, R.: Quantifying the Effects of COVID-19 on Mental Health Support Forums. arXiv preprint arXiv:2009.04008 (2020)
4. Centers for Disease Control and Prevention, 2020. Coping with Stress. https://www.cdc.gov/coronavirus/2019-ncov/daily-life-coping/managing-stress-anxiety.html Accessed 15 Jul 2020
5. Chancellor, S. De Choudhury, M.: Methods in predictive techniques for mental health status on social media: a critical review. NPJ Dig. Med. **3**(1), 1–11 (2020). https://doi.org/10.1038/s41746-020-0233-7
6. Chew, Q.H., Wei, K.C., Vasoo, S., Chua, H.C., Sim, K.: Narrative synthesis of psychological and coping responses towards emerging infectious disease outbreaks in the general population: practical considerations for the COVID-19 pandemic. Singapore Med. J. **61**(7), 350–356 (2020)
7. Chung, C., Pennebaker, J.W.: The psychological functions of function words. In: Fiedler, K. (ed.) 2007, pp. 343–359. Psychology Press, Social Communication, New York (2007)
8. De Choudhury, M., Counts, S., Horvitz, E.: Predicting postpartum changes in emotion and behavior via social media. In: SIGCHI Conference on Human Factors in Computing Systems, pp. 3267–3276 (2013)

9. De Choudhury, M., De, S.: Mental health discourse on reddit: self-disclosure, social support, and anonymity. In: 8th International AAAI Conference on Weblogs and Social Media, 16 May 2014. ICWSM (2014)
10. De Choudhury, M., Kiciman, E., Dredze, M., Coppersmith, G., Kumar, M.: Discovering shifts to suicidal ideation from mental health content in social media. In: Proceedings of the 2016 CHI Conference on Human Factors in Computing Systems, pp. 2098–2110. ACM (2016). https://doi.org/10.1145/2858036.2858207
11. Hridoy, M.N.H., Islam, M.M., Amin, R., Sultana, B.: Duplicate contents restriction algorithm for copied post on online social network. In: Conference on Sustainable Technologies for Industry 4.0 (STI) (2019)
12. Jacobson, N.C., Lekkas, D., Price, G., Heinz, M.V., Song, M., O'Malley, A.J., Barr, P.J.: Flattening the mental health curve: COVID-19 stay-at-home orders are associated with alterations in mental health search behavior in the United States. JMIR Mental Health **7**(6), e19347 (2020)
13. Kassambara, A., Statistical tests. https://www.datanovia.com/en/lessons Accessed 16 Jul 2020
14. Li, S., Wang, Y., Xue, J., Zhao, N., Zhu, T.: The impact of COVID-19 epidemic declaration on psychological consequences: a study on active Weibo users. Int. J. Environ. Res. Public Health **17**(6), 2032 (2020). https://doi.org/10.3390/ijerph17062032
15. Moreno, C., et al.: How mental health care should change as a consequence of the COVID-19 pandemic. Lancet Psychiatry **7**(9), 813–824 (2020). https://doi.org/10.1016/S2215-0366(20)30307-2
16. Pavalanathan, U., De Choudhury, M.: Identity management and mental health discourse in social media. In: Proceedings of the 24th WWW Conference (2015). https://doi.org/10.1145/2740908.2743049
17. Rajkumar, R.P.: COVID-19 and mental health: a review of the existing literature. Asian J. Psychiatry (2020). https://doi.org/10.1016/j.ajp.2020.102066
18. Reddit, What constitutes spam? Am I a spammer? (2020). https://reddit.zendesk.com/hc/en-us/articles/360043504051-What-constitutes-spam-Am-I-a-spammer-Accessed 20 Jul 2020
19. Tolbert, J., Kates, J., Levitt, L.: Lifting social distancing measures in America: state actions & Metrics (2020). https://www.kff.org/policy-watch/lifting-social-distancing-measures-in-america-state-actions-metricsAccessed 29 Jul 2020
20. Torales, J., O'Higgins, M., Castaldelli-Maia, J.M., Ventriglio, A.: The outbreak of COVID-19 coronavirus and its impact on global mental health. Int. J. Soc. Psychiatry **66**(4), 317–320 (2020). https://doi.org/10.1177/0020764020915212
21. Tull, M.T., Edmonds, K.A., Scamaldo, K.M., Richmond, J.R., Rose, J.P., Gratz, K.L.: Psychological outcomes associated with stay-at-home orders and the perceived impact of COVID-19 on daily life. Psychiatry Res. **289**, 113098 (2020). https://doi.org/10.1016/j.psychres.2020.113098
22. World Health Organization, Coronavirus disease 2019 (COVID-19): Situation Report-72. World Health Organization (2020). https://www.who.int/docs/default-source/coronaviruse/situation-reports/20200401-sitrep-72-covid-19.pdf?sfvrsn=3dd8971b_2 Accessed 11 Aug 2020
23. Zeileis, A., Kleiber, C., Jackman, S.: Regression models for count data in R. J. Stat. Softw. **27**(8), 1–25 (2008). https://doi.org/10.18637/jss.v027.i08

On the Presence of Abusive Language in Mis/Disinformation

Breno Matos[(✉)], Rennan C. Lima, Jussara M. Almeida,
Marcos André Gonçalves, and Rodrygo L.T. Santos

Computer Science Department, Universidade Federal de Minas Gerais,
Belo Horizonte, Brazil
{brenomatos,rennancordeiro,jussara,mgoncalv,rodrygo}@dcc.ufmg.br

Abstract. The rise in mis/disinformation and abusive language online is alarming. These problems threaten society, impacting users' mental health and even politics and democracy. Social science studies have already theorized about those problems' mutual spread, for instance, regarding how users interact with mis/disinformation. In this work, we propose to analyze news articles' production patterns instead of the consumption perspective, focusing on the textual news content. We perform a textual analysis of online news and conclude that false news present a higher prevalence of abusive language when compared to real news. The found patterns are consistent across datasets, even when they belong to different topics. To better understand these differences, we analyze psycholinguistic patterns of false and real news writings. Finally, we analyze which news categories are more affected by abusive language.

1 Introduction

Online media outlets are an essential part of the modern Web and play a crucial role in spreading information. However, some non-reliable outlets are associated with significant social contemporary problems – a major one being mis/disinformation spread. Briefly, mis/disinformation can be defined as pieces of false information that try to appear legitimate by claiming to be real [6,29,32]. It has a profound and direct impact on real-world events. For example, it is considered a threat to modern democracy [4,25], due to its negative effects on public opinion. As a specific instance, in the 2016 American presidential election [1], false news were used to manipulate public opinion. Research on this topic is thus necessary to improve Web platforms and combat mis/disinformation spread.

Another alarming problem is the use of abusive language online [15,27,33,34]. We follow previous work [14,19,24], which consider abusive language as one aimed at insulting and slandering its targets. Abusive language is often used to antagonize and provoke. This problem is harmful to society due, for instance, to its impacts on the users' mental health [3]. Abusive language can even incite electoral violence – in Nigeria, during the 2011, 2015, and 2019 presidential elections, abusive language and hate speech was highly disseminated against marginalized social groups [11].

Both abusive language and mis/disinformation are frequently associated with the same social issues. For instance, during the COVID-19 pandemic, we have seen numerous cases of news containing false information or abusive language [21]. Similarly, some social groups and movements are frequently accused of spreading abusive content. For instance, Hannah [13] showed that QAnon, an American conspiracy theory group, has spread mis/disinformation about COVID-19, and Sipka et al. [27] showed that the same group spread hate speech in alternative social networks, such as Parler[1]. For those reasons, we hypothesize that false news are more likely to contain abusive language. Studying this relationship is important to understanding mis/disinformation online and improving detection techniques.

Both, abusive language and mis/disinformation are widely studied topics. By means of social networks posts analysis, many studies focus on social aspects such as how users interact with mis/disinformation. In this paper, we take another perspective by analyzing news articles focusing on the production side instead of the consumption side. Our focus is on the news text itself. To do so, we investigate the presence of abusive language in news text from fact-checking portals. We claim that studying the connection between fake news and abusive language may provide us with a better comprehension of fake news features, facilitating further analyses on the topic. It may also give us insights into which techniques fake news spreaders employ (e.g., more inflammatory discourse) to reach target audiences, intentionally or not.

In more details, we propose here a quantitative analysis of the relationship between abusive language and mis/disinformation in the light of news categories, psycholinguistic attributes, toxicity features and sentiment analysis. We provide the first work that studies this relationship in multiple domains, evidencing consistent dynamics between fake and real news in the used datasets, considering different knowledge fields (e.g., health and celebrities).

Our analyses aim at answering the following research questions: (1) Are false news more associated with abusive language features than real news? (2) What are the news categories with the most significant differences in abusive language-related features between false and real news? (3) What are the main psycholinguistic differences between false and real news? Our investigations concluded that false news present higher averages in abusive language-related features than real ones. Furthermore, psycholinguistic and news theme analysis provided hints regarding how abusive language is used in online mis/disinformation, such as the use of more negative emotion-related words in false news. To allow reproducibility, we release the code used in this paper[2].

We hypothesize that fake news has a strong relationship with abusive language, which is evidenced by our results. Indeed, our studies show that fake news share similar features even when considering different domains. That is, even though we evaluate datasets of news on different themes (e.g., politics, health, celebrities), we see similar patterns when comparing fake and real news

---

[1] https://parler.com/.

[2] https://github.com/brenomatos/abusive-language.

of the same datasets. For instance, fake news presents higher average scores of inflammatory discourse than its real counterparts for all datasets.

This rest of this work is organized as follows. Section 2 covers related work. Section 3 describes our methodology, including the research questions (RQs) we aim to answer. Section 4 discusses our experimental results and the answers to the RQs. Section 5 concludes the paper.

2   Related Work

Several works have explored the online abusive language phenomenon before. For instance, Mathew et al. [16] have shown that hateful content spreads faster and can reach a broader audience on social networks. Moreover, Zannettou et al. [34] explored news content and found that political and divisive events are more related to hateful commenting, which shows that the use of abusive language online is directly related to political polarization. Alternatively, other works also explored online mis/disinformation spread. Blankenship [5] described how mis/disinformation spreads on Twitter. Nan et al. [17] discussed online health mis/disinformation. Furthermore, several works [22,28] agreed that false information spreads faster than genuine content. However, all these works have described the phenomena singly. In contrast, regarding these problems' interplay, other social studies have theorized about their relationship [8,10,20]. Nevertheless, these works did not show quantitative evidence of this relationship. Thus, more studies are needed, and including such analysis can expand our understanding of both problems and, ultimately, improve online debate.

Accordingly, Giachanou and Rosso [12] endorsed the importance of more quantitative studies on both problems. More specifically, the authors presented the evaluation process, datasets, and shared tasks involving mis/disinformation and hateful content online. Also, they mention the importance of textual features to detect such content, which enforces the importance of studying text patterns. Another remarkable work that explored the online abusive language and mis/disinformation dynamics is from Cinelli et al. [7]. In their work, the authors described user behavior, i.e., how humans spread offensive content online, more specifically, in the YouTube video platform, and explored its relationship with the mis/disinformation community. However, the authors focus on online comments written in Italian by YouTube users, which is a narrow sample of such content online. Moreover, the work focuses on users and the social aspect without exploring the original video content. In contrast, we present a deeper analysis in this work. Accordingly, we explore the toxicity of online media outlet news, whose credibility was assessed and disclosed.

3   Methodology

3.1   Research Questions

This paper aims to answer the following research questions:

RQ1: Are false news more associated to abusive language features than real news?

RQ2: What are the news categories with the most significant difference in abusive language-related features between false and real news?

RQ3: What are the main psycholinguistic differences between false and real news?

To address RQ1, we use both Perspective API and sentiment analysis. Perspective is a tool developed by Jigsaw and Google's Counter Abuse Technology team, which evaluates text and returns a score considering various attributes. A score, which ranges from 0 to 1, represents the likelihood that a person would perceive the text evaluated as containing a given attribute. We explore the "Toxicity", "Severe Toxicity", "Identity Attack", "Insult", "Profanity" and "Threat" attributes, which are the ones widely used in the literature. Table 1 presents a concise description of each attribute. More details can be seen in Perspective's documentation[3]. For sentiment analysis, we use a state-of-the-art transformer-based model proposed by Barbieri et al. [2], and trained on 124M tweets from January 2018 to December 2021. The model is open source[4] and can classify an input into three sentiment categories: negative, neutral, and positive. Transformer models have an input length limitation [18], and, for news that surpass this limit, we cap the input to fit the restriction.

Table 1. Perspective attributes description

Attribute name	Description
Toxicity	"A rude, disrespectful, or unreasonable comment that is likely to make people leave a discussion"
Severe toxicity	"A very hateful, aggressive, disrespectful comment or otherwise very likely to make a user leave a discussion or give up on sharing their perspective"
Identity attack	"Negative or hateful comments targeting someone because of their identity"
Insult	"Insulting, inflammatory, or negative comment towards a person or a group of people"
Profanity	"Swear words, curse words, or other obscene or profane language"
Threat	"Describes an intention to inflict pain, injury, or violence against an individual or group"

To address RQ2, we divided the news in different categories, related to their themes, such as politics. This analysis allow us to understand where abusive

---

[3] https://developers.perspectiveapi.com/s/about-the-api-attributes-and-languages.

[4] https://huggingface.co/cardiffnlp/twitter-roberta-base-sentiment-latest.

language is more used to spread mis/disinformation, and, ultimately, better understand the problems' relationship. To do so, we performed news classification using a state-of-the-art contextual language model. Accordingly, we used a large news categories dataset consisting of a set of news' text and its category pairs. The dataset used is called News Category Dataset[5] and contains around 200,000 news headlines published between the year 2012 to 2018 from the Huff-Post[6]. Moreover, each news is assigned to only one of the defined 41 categories, e.g. "POLITICS" and "SPORTS".

We trained a model (using the categories as the label) using all entries from the News Category Dataset. Then, we used this model to predict the news category in all fake news datasets used. After being trained, the model reached 0.586 accuracy, which is a high value considering that there are 41 possible labels. We used the TextClassificationPipeline[7] from HuggingFace. This pipeline consists of a classification layer over a BERT Tiny pre-trained model,[8] which was chosen over vanilla BERT due to resource limitations. This model was trained for three epochs with 256 as the max input size in tokens, with a batch size of 32 entries, which are the best parameters considering the resources of the machine used. Moreover, for the remaining parameters, we used the default ones from HuggingFace's trainer[9].

Once all categories are defined, we explored the news categories that present the highest difference between the means of fake and real news for each of the six Perspective attributes considered in our analyses. To assess statistical significance, we report (for each Perspective attribute) only the news categories with statistically distinct[10] means for fake and real news. This analysis enables us to understand better which news topics are more prevalent in false news and gain deeper insights into their dynamics.

Finally, to address RQ3, we use the Linguistic Inquiry and Word Count (LIWC) [30] lexicon to analyze psycholinguistic attributes of news texts across all datasets. LIWC is a robust tool that allows us to classify words into 73 categories expressing various characteristics (e.g., grammatical classes, cognitive concepts). Since the number of fake and real news for every dataset is different, we compute the overall frequency of each LIWC class separately for fake and real news (divided by dataset); this provides us with a fair comparison between fake and real news. To assess statistical relevance, we report only LIWC classes that pass the Kolmogorov-Smirnov test between fake and real news ($p < 0.05$).

---

[5] https://huggingface.co/datasets/Fraser/news-category-dataset.
[6] https://www.huffpost.com/.
[7] https://huggingface.co/docs/transformers/v4.20.0/en/main_classes/pipelines# transformers.TextClassificationPipeline.
[8] https://huggingface.co/prajjwal1/bert-tiny.
[9] https://huggingface.co/docs/transformers/main_classes/trainer.
[10] We use the Mann-Whitney U test with $p < 0.05$.

3.2 Datasets

We perform a comprehensive analysis on several news datasets: FakeNews-
Net [26], Liar [31], CoAID [9], Celebrity and FakeNewsAMT [23], and the
Fake News Detection Challenge Dataset from KDD 2020[11]. Table 2 describes
the amount of fake and real news on each dataset. FakeNewsNet consists of
news reviewed by Politifact[12], a fact-checker of political news, and Gossipcop[13],
which fact-checks entertainment news. As these websites examine different types
of news, we separate our analyses on this dataset based on the fact-checker. The
remaining datasets are: 1) Liar is an extensive dataset of news also fact-checked
by Politifact; 2) CoAID is a COVID-19 mis/disinformation dataset; 3) KDD
Challenge's dataset consists of multiple news labeled as either fake or real; 4)
Celebrity consists of entertainment news; 5) FakeNewsAMT consists of real news
from various media outlets and fake news generated using Amazon Mechanical
Turk. In total, we analyze 35,210 news articles. Finally, it is worth noting that
we only explored the false and real labels from the datasets, which were the ones
available for all of them. Although this decision removed news partially true or
false from the analysis, it allowed a consistent exploration through all the data.

Table 2. Characterization of each dataset

Dataset	# of Fake	# of Real	Total
FakeNewsNet - Gossipcop	4739	14926	19665
FakeNewsNet - Politifact	373	444	817
KDD Challenge	2008	2970	4979
Liar	2511	2063	4574
CoAID	191	4006	4197
Celebrity	250	249	499
FakeNewsAMT	240	240	480
Total	**10312**	**24898**	**35210**

4 Experimental Results

4.1 RQ1 - Abusive Language Presence on News

Perspective Features. Table 3 shows average values for each attribute, for
each dataset, alongside the difference between average of fake and real news (F -
R columns). For nearly all attributes of all datasets, except Threat for the KDD
Challenge dataset, we observe that false news has comparable or higher means.

---

[11] https://www.microsoft.com/en-us/research/event/kdd-2020-truefact-workshop-
making-a-credible-web-for-tomorrow/shared-tasks/.
[12] www.politifact.com.
[13] www.gossipcop.com.

We observe that Insult, Toxicity, and Inflammatory present a more discernible discrepancy between means of fake and real news. For two datasets (CoAID and Politifact), the Inflammatory attribute means for false news is double the real news' means. These results contribute to the hypothesis that both problems have a strong relationship as they appear in the same contexts.

Amongst politics datasets (i.e., Politifact, Liar, and FakeNewsAMT), Politifact presents higher averages than FakeNewsAMT for all attributes. A similar pattern is observed when comparing Politifact and Liar, except for Threat, Inflammatory, and Identity Attack features.

Furthermore, Gossipcop is the only dataset with higher averages for real news regarding some features: in this case, Severe Toxicity and Threat averages are higher for real news.

Moreover, we also observed that real news from the Liar dataset presented a similar average to its fake counterpart for the Inflammatory attribute. It was also the highest average for the Inflammatory feature compared to real news from other datasets.

Table 3. Means and difference of each attribute, for each dataset, divided into fake and real news

Attribute	Liar			CoAID			Celebrity			FakeNewsAMT		
	Fake	Real	F - R	Fake	Real	F - R	Fake	Real	F - R	Fake	Real	F - R
Toxicity	0.07159	0.05802	0.01357	0.08528	0.02544	0.05984	0.16150	0.11861	0.04289	0.08528	0.02544	0.05984
Severe toxicity	0.00445	0.00327	0.00118	0.00452	0.00161	0.00291	0.01351	0.00861	0.0049	0.00452	0.00161	0.00291
Insult	0.05623	0.04523	0.011	0.06685	0.01985	0.047	0.17499	0.11566	0.05933	0.06685	0.01985	0.047
Profanity	0.01715	0.01373	0.00342	0.02588	0.01046	0.01542	0.06126	0.04127	0.01999	0.02588	0.01046	0.01542
Threat	0.02769	0.02495	0.00274	0.02302	0.0159	0.00712	0.03024	0.02246	0.00778	0.02302	0.01590	0.00712
Inflammatory	0.29252	0.27592	0.0166	0.23519	0.11942	0.11577	0.34951	0.22473	0.12478	0.23519	0.11942	0.11577
Identity attack	0.04491	0.03827	0.00664	0.03765	0.01986	0.01779	0.04892	0.03588	0.01304	0.03765	0.01986	0.01779

Attribute	Politifact			Gossipcop			KDD challenge		
	Fake	Real	F - R	Fake	Real	F - R	Fake	Real	F - R
Toxicity	0.16357	0.08424	0.07933	0.12101	0.10679	0.01422	0.14492	0.12125	0.02367
Severe toxicity	0.01591	0.00458	0.01133	0.00813	0.00827	−0.00014	0.01056	0.00921	0.00135
Insult	0.18027	0.08553	0.09474	0.13444	0.11313	0.02131	0.12098	0.09778	0.0232
Profanity	0.05318	0.02226	0.03092	0.04594	0.04561	0.00033	0.0471	0.04571	0.00139
Threat	0.06001	0.02211	0.0379	0.02506	0.02576	−0.0007	**0.02691**	**0.02668**	0.00023
Inflammatory	0.31794	0.14184	0.1761	0.25519	0.2039	0.05129	0.26023	0.20132	0.05891
Identity attack	0.08199	0.03792	0.04407	0.03904	0.03751	0.00153	0.04429	0.03884	0.00545

Sentiment Analysis. Table 4 presents the total amount of news classified as negative (−), neutral (=), or positive (+) for each dataset. Recall that each dataset has different amounts of fake and real news (see Table 2), so we also report the percentage of news classified as negative (%−) for both fake and real news. We find that all datasets report a higher rate of negative sentiment for false news, which further expands our range of evidence of the use of abusive language in mis/disinformation.

Table 4. Sentiment analysis. Percentages rounded to integer values

	Fake				Real			
	−	=	+	% −	−	=	+	% −
Gossipcop (FNN)	512	3372	870	11%	812	9189	4956	5%
Politifact (FNN)	121	232	20	32%	31	365	50	7%
KDD challenge	278	1354	382	14%	162	1722	1088	5%
Liar	987	1383	141	39%	746	1150	167	36%
CoAID	77	94	20	40%	647	3223	136	16%
Celebrity	35	188	27	14%	4	174	72	2%
FakeNewsAMT	47	147	46	20%	36	157	47	15%

4.2 RQ2 - News Categories Characterization

Table 5 presents the most frequent news classes in each dataset, alongside the number of occurrences Table 5. Table 6 shows results for news categories for which false and real news have statistically different means. We report the difference between the means of the false and real news by Insult, Toxicity, and Inflammatory attributes. POLITICS is a frequent topic, appearing in the list of at least one attribute for all datasets, with false news presenting a higher mean in all cases. CRIME is also a topic with means skewed to false news, appearing in both KDD and Liar datasets. The KDD dataset also has topics related to minorities (WOMEN and BLACK VOICES) in which false news presents higher means than real news. CoAID presents higher means for false news for the SCIENCE category for all Perspective attributes, which is in line with the nature of the dataset (i.e., covid-related mis/disinformation often discredits science). Finally, GREEN, a label that denotes news related to the environment, appears as a topic with averages also skewed to false news in the Politiact dataset, which is also consistent with the dataset's nature, as environmental issues are often polarizing.

4.3 RQ3 - Psycholinguistic Analyses and Differences

Figure 1 shows results for our LIWC analysis across all datasets. We omit results for Liar and FakeNewsAMT, which reported only one and two classes with a statistical difference, respectively. We highlight that all datasets (except CoAID) have more negative emotion-related words (negemo), which is consistent with the results for our RQ2. We hypothesize that CoAID has more negative emotion in fake than real news due to the nature of mis/disinformation related to Covid-19, which often minimizes the effects of the disease. The higher presence of health, risk, and anger-related words in real news in CoAID further supports this hypothesis. For the Politifact dataset, we also highlight that false news has a higher presence of religious (relig), death, family, and anxiety-related (anx) words, which may also be due to the nature of the dataset. Recall that Politifact consists of fact-checked political news, which often tries to incite public backlash and repercussions.

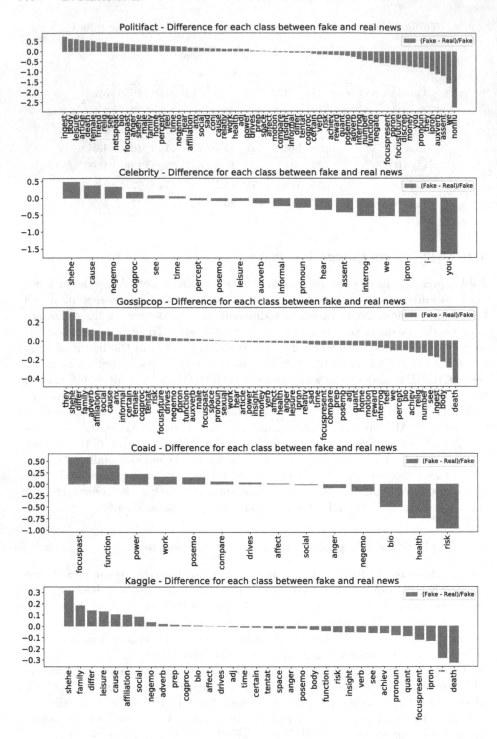

Fig. 1. LIWC results

Table 5. Most frequent categories

Dataset	Categories
Politifact	('POLITICS', 576), ('UNDEFINED', 142), ('BUSINESS', 51), ('TECH', 34), ('SPORTS', 23)
Gossipcop	('ENTERTAINMENT', 13873), ('POLITICS', 995), ('STYLE & BEAUTY', 980), ('QUEER VOICES', 577), ('SPORTS', 430)
KDD challenge	('ENTERTAINMENT', 3352), ('POLITICS', 544), ('STYLE & BEAUTY', 192), ('QUEER VOICES', 151), ('SPORTS', 96)
Liar	('POLITICS', 9336), ('BUSINESS', 1616), ('WELLNESS', 252), ('THE WORLDPOST', 233), ('TRAVEL', 162)
CoAID	('POLITICS', 1830), ('WELLNESS', 1649), ('UNDEFINED', 500), ('IMPACT', 137), ('HEALTHY LIVING', 114)
Celebrity	('ENTERTAINMENT', 423), ('POLITICS', 27), ('STYLE & BEAUTY', 17), ('QUEER VOICES', 14), ('BLACK VOICES', 8)
FakeNewsAMT	('POLITICS', 193), ('SPORTS', 74), ('ENTERTAINMENT', 59), ('TECH', 43), ('BUSINESS', 34)

Table 6. News categories that have means with a statistically significant difference for all datasets

Dataset	Attribute	Categories
Politifact	Insult	('TECH', -0.007), ('GREEN', 0.0764), ('POLITICS', 0.1239)
	Toxicity	('TECH', 0.0049), ('WELLNESS', 0.0111), ('POLITICS', 0.0948), ('GREEN', 0.1043), ('PARENTING', 0.1104)
	Inflammatory	('TECH', −0.0508), ('PARENTING', 0.211), ('POLITICS', 0.2167), ('GREEN', 0.3235)
Gossipcop	Insult	('ENTERTAINMENT', 0.0207), ('POLITICS', 0.0239), ('WEDDINGS', 0.0266), ('MEDIA', 0.0447), ('PARENTS', 0.0514)
	Toxicity	('BUSINESS', −0.0048), ('ENTERTAINMENT', 0.0154), ('DIVORCE', 0.0185), ('WEDDINGS', 0.0218), ('PARENTS', 0.0389)
	Inflammatory	('HOME & LIVING', 0.0396), ('PARENTING', 0.047), ('ENTERTAINMENT', 0.0574), ('COMEDY', 0.1013), ('DIVORCE', 0.1097)
KDD Challenge	Insult	('BUSINESS', −0.0037), ('ENTERTAINMENT', 0.0214), ('POLITICS', 0.0486), ('WEIRD NEWS', 0.0689), ('WOMEN', 0.1104)
	Toxicity	('RELIGION', −0.0409), ('ENTERTAINMENT', 0.0252), ('POLITICS', 0.0309), ('WEIRD NEWS', 0.067)
	Inflammatory	('SPORTS', 0.0971), ('BLACK VOICES', 0.1044), ('POLITICS', 0.1358), ('CRIME', 0.1412), ('PARENTS', 0.1465)
Liar	Insult	('THE WORLDPOST', 0.0072), ('BUSINESS', 0.0082), ('POLITICS', 0.0097), ('SPORTS', 0.0568), ('CRIME', 0.0728)
	Toxicity	('POLITICS', 0.0112), ('THE WORLDPOST', 0.0299), ('SPORTS', 0.0601), ('ENTERTAINMENT', 0.0767), ('CRIME', 0.0911)
	Inflammatory	('WELLNESS', −0.0681), ('BUSINESS', 0.0156), ('POLITICS', 0.0159), ('THE WORLDPOST', 0.077)
CoAID	Insult	('THE WORLDPOST', 0.0402), ('POLITICS', 0.0487), ('SCIENCE', 0.07), ('PARENTING', 0.1141), ('SPORTS', 0.2636)
	Toxicity	('THE WORLDPOST', 0.0729), ('ENTERTAINMENT', 0.0749), ('SCIENCE', 0.0781), ('PARENTING', 0.1185), ('SPORTS', 0.2157)
	Inflammatory	('WELLNESS', 0.05), ('PARENTING', 0.1108), ('POLITICS', 0.1255), ('BUSINESS', 0.1893), ('SCIENCE', 0.204)
Celebrity	Insult	('ENTERTAINMENT', 0.0616)
	Toxicity	('ENTERTAINMENT', 0.0445)
	Inflammatory	('ENTERTAINMENT', 0.1175), ('POLITICS', 0.1648)
FakeNewsAMT	Insult	('POLITICS', 0.0234), ('BUSINESS', 0.0358), ('ENTERTAINMENT', 0.0442), ('SPORTS', 0.0607)
	Toxicity	('POLITICS', 0.0202)
	Inflammatory	('POLITICS', 0.1093)

5   Conclusions

Abusive language online is a widely studied topic, as is false news. However, few studies have tried to quantify the interplay between the two, characterizing false news in light of abusive language features. In this work, we propose a robust analysis of multiple false news datasets. False news reports higher means for features extracted with Perspective API, such as toxicity, inflammatory, and insult. Additionally, we also perform sentiment analysis with a state-of-the-art model, finding that negative sentiment is more prevalent for false news in all datasets. Furthermore, our news classifier allows us to find which topics are more commonplace in false and real news in light of Perspective attributes. Finally, we also analyze LIWC to gather insights into the psycholinguistic characteristics of false news. In future work, we intend to further deepen our analysis by including information on the spread of false news online with engagement signals from social networks, such as likes and shares.

Acknowledgments. This work was partially supported by CNPq, CAPES and Fapemig.

References

1. Allcott, H., Gentzkow, M.: Social media and fake news in the 2016 election. J. Econ. Perspect. **31**(2), 211–36 (2017)
2. Barbieri, F., Camacho-Collados, J., Espinosa Anke, L., Neves, L.: TweetEval: unified benchmark and comparative evaluation for tweet classification. In: Findings of the Association for Computational Linguistics: EMNLP 2020, pp. 1644–1650. Association for Computational Linguistics, Online, November 2020. https://doi.org/10.18653/v1/2020.findings-emnlp.148, https://aclanthology.org/2020.findings-emnlp.148
3. Benesch, S.: Defining and diminishing hate speech. State World's Minorities Indigenous Peoples **2014**, 18–25 (2014)
4. Bessi, A., Ferrara, E.: Social bots distort the 2016 US presidential election online discussion. First Monday **21**(11-7) (2016)
5. Blankenship, M.: How misinformation spreads through twitter (2020)
6. Caramancion, K.M.: Understanding the association of personal outlook in free speech regulation and the risk of being MIS/disinformed. In: 2021 IEEE World AI IoT Congress (AIIoT), pp. 0092–0097 (2021). https://doi.org/10.1109/AIIoT52608.2021.9454212
7. Cinelli, M., Pelicon, A., Mozetič, I., Quattrociocchi, W., Novak, P.K., Zollo, F.: Dynamics of online hate and misinformation. Sci. Rep. **11**(1), 22083 (2021). ISSN 2045-2322, https://doi.org/10.1038/s41598-021-01487-w
8. Claussen, V.: Fighting hate speech and fake news. The network enforcement act (NETZDG) in Germany in the context of European legislation. Rivista di diritto dei media **3**, 1–27 (2018)
9. Cui, L., Lee, D.: CoAID: COVID-19 healthcare misinformation dataset (2020)
10. Darmstadt, A., Prinz, M., Saal, O.: The murder of Keira: misinformation and hate speech as far-right online strategies (2019)

11. Ezeibe, C.: Hate speech and election violence in Nigeria. J. Asian African Stud. **56**(4), 919–935 (2021). https://doi.org/10.1177/0021909620951208
12. Giachanou, A., Rosso, P.: The battle against online harmful information: the cases of fake news and hate speech. In: Proceedings of the 29th ACM International Conference on Information & Knowledge Management, pp. 3503–3504, CIKM 2020. Association for Computing Machinery, New York, NY, USA (2020). ISBN 9781450368599, https://doi.org/10.1145/3340531.3412169
13. Hannah, M.: QAnon and the information dark age. First Monday (2021)
14. Lee, Y., Yoon, S., Jung, K.: Comparative studies of detecting abusive language on Twitter. In: Proceedings of the 2nd Workshop on Abusive Language Online (ALW2), pp. 101–106. Association for Computational Linguistics, Brussels, Belgium, October 2018. https://doi.org/10.18653/v1/W18-5113, https://aclanthology.org/W18-5113
15. Lima, L., Reis, J.C., Melo, P., Murai, F., Benevenuto, F.: Characterizing (un) moderated textual data in social systems. In: ASONAM, pp. 430–434. IEEE (2020)
16. Mathew, B., Dutt, R., Goyal, P., Mukherjee, A.: Spread of hate speech in online social media. In: Proceedings of the 10th ACM Conference on Web Science, WebSci 2019, pp. 173–182. Association for Computing Machinery, New York, NY, USA (2019). ISBN 9781450362023, https://doi.org/10.1145/3292522.3326034
17. Nan, X., Wang, Y., Thier, K.: Health misinformation (2021)
18. Nguyen, D.Q., Vu, T., Nguyen, A.T.: BERTweet: a pre-trained language model for English Tweets. In: Proceedings of the 2020 Conference on Empirical Methods in Natural Language Processing: System Demonstrations, pp. 9–14 (2020)
19. Nobata, C., Tetreault, J., Thomas, A., Mehdad, Y., Chang, Y.: Abusive language detection in online user content. In: Proceedings of the 25th International Conference on World Wide Web, WWW 2016, pp. 145–153. International World Wide Web Conferences Steering Committee, Republic and Canton of Geneva, CHE (2016). ISBN 9781450341431, https://doi.org/10.1145/2872427.2883062
20. Pate, U.A., Ibrahim, A.M.: Fake news, hate speech and Nigeria's struggle for democratic consolidation: a conceptual review. In: Handbook of Research on Politics in the Computer Age, pp. 89–112 (2020)
21. Patwa, P., et al.: Overview of CONSTRAINT 2021 shared tasks: detecting English COVID-19 fake news and Hindi hostile posts. In: Chakraborty, T., Shu, K., Bernard, H.R., Liu, H., Akhtar, M.S. (eds.) CONSTRAINT 2021. CCIS, vol. 1402, pp. 42–53. Springer, Cham (2021). https://doi.org/10.1007/978-3-030-73696-5_5
22. Pennycook, G., Epstein, Z., Mosleh, M., Arechar, A., Eckles, D., Rand, D.: Understanding and reducing the spread of misinformation online. ACR North American Advances (2020)
23. Pérez-Rosas, V., Kleinberg, B., Lefevre, A., Mihalcea, R.: Automatic detection of fake news. In: Proceedings of the 27th International Conference on Computational Linguistics, pp. 3391–3401. Association for Computational Linguistics, Santa Fe, New Mexico, USA, August 2018. https://aclanthology.org/C18-1287
24. Schmidt, A., Wiegand, M.: A survey on hate speech detection using natural language processing. In: Proceedings of the Fifth International Workshop on Natural Language Processing for Social Media, pp. 1–10. Association for Computational Linguistics, Valencia, Spain, April 2017. https://doi.org/10.18653/v1/W17-1101, https://aclanthology.org/W17-1101
25. Shao, C., Ciampaglia, G.L., Varol, O., Yang, K.C., Flammini, A., Menczer, F.: The spread of low-credibility content by social bots. Nat. Commun. **9**(1), 4787 (2018). ISSN 2041-1723, https://doi.org/10.1038/s41467-018-06930-7

26. Shu, K., Mahudeswaran, D., Wang, S., Lee, D., Liu, H.: FakeNewsNet: a data repository with news content, social context, and spatiotemporal information for studying fake news on social media. Big Data **8**(3), 171–188 (2020)
27. Sipka, A., Hannak, A., Urman, A.: Comparing the language of QAnon-related content on Parler, Gab, and Twitter. arXiv preprint arXiv:2111.11118 (2021)
28. Sylvia Chou, W.Y., Gaysynsky, A., Cappella, J.N.: Where we go from here: health misinformation on social media (2020)
29. Tandoc Jr., E.C., Lim, Z.W., Ling, R.: Defining "fake news" a typology of scholarly definitions. Digital Journalism **6**(2), 137–153 (2018)
30. Tausczik, Y.R., Pennebaker, J.W.: The psychological meaning of words: LIWC and computerized text analysis methods. J. Lang. Soc. Psychol. **29**(1), 24–54 (2010)
31. Wang, W.Y.: "Liar, Liar PANTS on Fire": a new benchmark dataset for fake news detection. arXiv preprint arXiv:1705.00648 (2017)
32. Wardle, C., Derakhshan, H.: Information disorder: toward an interdisciplinary framework for research and policymaking (2017)
33. Zannettou, S., et al.: What is Gab: a Bastion of free speech or an alt-right echo chamber (2018)
34. Zannettou, S., Elsherief, M., Belding, E., Nilizadeh, S., Stringhini, G.: Measuring and characterizing hate speech on news websites. In: 12th ACM Conference on Web Science, WebSci 2020, pp. 125–134. Association for Computing Machinery, New York, NY, USA (2020). ISBN 9781450379892, https://doi.org/10.1145/3394231.3397902

Retention and Relapse in Gambling Self-help Communities on Reddit

Niklas Hopfgartner$^{(\boxtimes)}$ ⓘ, Thorsten Ruprechter ⓘ, and Denis Helic ⓘ

Graz University of Technology, Graz, Austria
{n.hopfgartner,ruprechter,dhelic}@tugraz.at

Abstract. Problem gambling endangers the mental health and financial stability of those affected. Individuals who are trying to overcome this problematic behavior often seek support in self-help groups, whether offline or online. Although online gambling self-help groups have become increasingly prominent in recent years, research is still needed to fully understand the social interactions and effectiveness of this medium. In this paper, we analyze behavior of problem gamblers in two gambling self-help communities on Reddit. In particular, following social impact theory, we quantify the strength, frequency, and promptness of users' social interactions and measure their effects on problem gamblers' retention in the community, as well as on their relapse to gambling. Firstly, we find that the magnitude of the community response, and a higher response from users who currently sustain prolonged gambling-free periods are positively associated with retention in the community. Secondly, our relapse analysis indicates that users who engage more strongly in discussions following their own submissions have a lower risk of gambling relapse. We believe that our findings provide useful insights on how to improve support for problem gamblers in online self-help communities.

Keywords: Social impact · Problem gambling · Online self-help groups

1 Introduction

Online and land-based gambling are wide spread forms of recreation and safe for most individuals [6,22]. Nevertheless, a small but significant number of individuals suffer from severe negative consequences of gambling, including financial problems or psychological distress induced by problematic gambling behavior [10,11]. Therefore, preventing and curbing problematic gambling behavior has become a major concern for clinicians, researchers, and policy-makers leading, among others, to the development of so-called responsible gambling tools. Such tools enable gamblers to control and limit their gambling behavior through money and time spending limits, mandatory cooling-off periods, or voluntary self-exclusions [1,2,14,21]. However, money and time limits can be changed after

---

N. Hopfgartner and T. Ruprechter—Contributed equally.

F. Hopfgartner et al. (Eds.): SocInfo 2022, LNCS 13618, pp. 305–319, 2022.
https://doi.org/10.1007/978-3-031-19097-1_19

a certain period, and gamblers might circumvent platform-specific self-exclusions by registering on other gambling platforms. For this reason, problem gamblers usually need additional support during the critical phase of their rehab to help them prevent gambling relapses.

One widely available and cost-effective support measure are self-help groups (e.g., "Gamblers Anonymous"), which provide supportive environments for problem gamblers to receive help and advice for personal problems [27,30]. Besides traditional offline self-help groups, recent studies have also shown that brief motivational treatments via telephone [12,16] as well as online forums and online self-help groups are effective in supporting problem gamblers [13].

Online self-help groups also exist on Reddit, a community-driven discussion platform [29] and one of the most popular websites on the Internet[1]. Reddit aggregates a large amount of so-called *subreddits* (i.e., communities and discussion forums), in which registered users can submit text or media posts (*submissions*) for others to comment on [5]. Due to its anonymity, Reddit allows users to discuss negative feelings as well as personal experiences more openly with like-minded users. However, to successfully provide peer-to-peer support through such an online platform, users need to actively engage with each other [28]. Similar as in offline self-help groups, a person who seeks support (*support seeker*) needs to interact with a person who is willing to provide support (*supporter*).

Research Questions. In this paper, we focus on self-help subreddits related to problem gambling and gambling addiction. Given Reddit's unique characteristics, we address the following research questions in this paper:

- **RQ1:** What factors affect support seeker retention in online self-help groups?
- **RQ2:** What factors affect the risk of relapse for support seekers?

Approach. We address these research questions using a theory-driven approach and derive a set of indicators based on social impact theory [18] to quantify the interaction between support seekers and supporters on Reddit. Specifically, we operationalize (i) supporter strength by the percentage of positive comments and the percentage of comments from players currently in rehab that support seekers' submissions receive, (ii) the social immediacy by the percentage of comments they receive shortly after they post their submissions, and (iii) the interaction magnitude as the number of supporters commenting on their submissions. Furthermore, we apply those indicators to estimate the risk of relapse for individual support seekers using a well-known Cox proportional hazards model.

Results. We find that the number of comments on the support seeker's first submission as well as the percentage of comments by supporters who themselves are currently in rehab have a substantial positive effect on the seeker's retention. For example, each additional comment to the seeker's first submission increases the

---

[1] https://www.similarweb.com/top-websites/.

odds of making another submission by more than 10%. Similarly, a one percent increase of comments made by supporters currently in rehab is associated with almost one percent increase in the odds of seekers making another submission. Further, our results on relapse indicate that user's self-motivation together with positive response from supporters are associated with reduced relapse hazard.

Contributions. As opposed to the study of emotions and sentiment in online gambling communities [17], our work is, to the best of our knowledge, the first to investigate *social interactions* in self-help groups for gambling problems on Reddit. Contextualizing our work within the framework of social impact theory enables us to focus on a specific set of variables to study social interactions in online self-help groups and, in particular, in online gambling self-help groups. We believe that our findings provide actionable insights on how to steer online communities to better support problem gamblers in their efforts to curb their problematic gambling behavior, and hence improve their quality of life. For example, problem gambling subreddits may introduce bots or guidelines that could—based on our results—encourage support seekers to keep reporting their process and supporters to comment on submissions of support seekers. Lastly, we make the Python and R scripts used for this work available online[2].

2 Materials and Methods

2.1 Data

Reddit Communities. Reddit covers a wide variety of topics across hundreds of thousands of active subreddits, where users can consume and contribute content based on their interests [31]. For example, a user interested in video games and American Football might engage with the subreddits */r/gaming* and */r/nfl* (note that the */r/* is a naming convention for communities on Reddit—similar to @ preceding account names on Twitter). Besides these examples of casual discussion topics, some users also use Reddit to get help in challenging times, such as emotional support during the COVID-19 crisis [4,19], community aid for drug addiction, rehab and withdrawal [3,20], or advice for problem gambling [17].

Problem Gambling Subreddits. For problem gambling, there are several subreddits that offer support for affected individuals. In this work, we focus on */r/problemgambling* and */r/GamblingAddiction*, as those are the most prolific subreddits covering this topic. These subreddits act as online self-help groups where support seekers disclose their negative gambling experiences, ask other users for support, or keep a diary about their journey to becoming gambling-free in diary-like submissions. Such diary-like submissions usually include a brief title indicating how many days support seekers have been gambling-free (e.g., "Day 0", "Day 13", "Week 3"), and a text describing their general feelings and state

---

[2] https://gitlab.tugraz.at/3B57777CAD304A73/reddit-gambling.

Fig. 1. Diary-like submission on */r/problemgambling.* A submission on */r/problemgambling*, in which a support seeker (blue) elaborates that they relapsed and have to restart their gambling-free journey, as indicated by "Day 0" in the title. A supporter (gold)—also themselves a problem gambler currently in recovery, as indicated by their gambling-free *flair* ("13 days")—consoles the support seeker via a comment, which the support seeker appreciates by responding positively to that comment. (Color figure online)

of mind. Figure 1 gives an example of such a submission on */r/problemgambling*. In this submission, the support seeker (blue) admits to a relapse, while additionally expressing negative feelings about it. Afterwards, a supporter (gold) adds a comment to the submission, encouraging the support seeker to keep going and that this setback "does not stop the momentum" they "have created in this fight". The supporter also has a so-called *flair* next to their name, showing that the supporter is currently gambling-free for 13 days. Finally, the support seeker greatly appreciates the comment by responding "your words mean more than you can imagine" to the supporter. Overall, this exchange illustrates the dynamics of these problem gambling subreddits, and exemplifies the characteristics of such diary-like submissions that mimic traditional offline self-help groups.

Data Collection and Preprocessing. We use the Pushshift API [5] to retrieve all submissions and comments for */r/problemgambling* and */r/Gambling Addiction* from January 2014 up until December 2020. Afterwards, we extract all submissions resembling diary-like entries that mention temporal progress (e.g., "Day 0", "Week 3", "Month 5") through a regular expression and ignore submissions by accounts that have been deleted since then. For the extracted submissions, we collect the author's username, contribution timestamp, and title.

Furthermore, for all comments to these submissions we collect the user name and flair, timestamp, as well as the text of the comment.

From the collected data, we then compute the following features for each submission: (i) the number of comments (both by the submission seeker as well as supporters), (ii) the percentage of supporters having a flair, (iii) the percentage of comments within one hour of the submission, and (iv) the percentage of positive comments. We calculate sentiment scores (between -1 and 1) of raw comment texts using VADER, and utilize a threshold of greater than 0.05 (less than -0.05) to label comments as positive (negative) [15].

In this work, we only consider submissions by support seekers for which the day they report in their first submission equals "Day 0" or "Day 1". We treat both 0 and 1 as valid first submissions, because that is how support seekers typically document their first day in rehab on the problem gambling subreddits. With this, we ensure our dataset does not include left-censored data (i.e., support seekers starting to report days after the start of their rehab) [9]. Overall, our pre-processed dataset contains 958 support seekers with an average (median) of 5.53 (1) submissions, 5 298 total submissions with an average (median) of 2.36 (1) comments, and 12 506 comments in total.

2.2   Social Impact Indicators on Reddit

In this work, we propose a framework to assess the social impact of the Reddit community on problem gamblers. Social impact (I) is driven by three forces [18]:

$$I \sim S \times i \times N, \tag{1}$$

where S is the strength or power of individuals on the target, i the immediacy or proximity of individuals to the target, and N the number of individuals. We quantify the social impact of the Reddit community by analyzing commenting behavior on the first submission of support seekers signaling the start of their rehab. We operationalize the social impact I by measuring whether support seekers make a second submission in the corresponding problem gambling subreddit (RQ1), and whether they relapse after a certain period of time (RQ2). Furthermore, we quantify the three forces S, i, and N by: the percentage of supporters with a flair and the percentage of positive comments by supporters (S), the percentage of comments within the first hour (i), and the total number of comments on (N) the first submission.

2.3   Retention Analysis

Retention Dataset. To assess the effects of the Reddit community on support seeker retention in online self-help groups, we analyze their first submissions and determine whether they contributed at least another submission within a 30-day observation period. As our measures of social impact include percentage calculations based on the number of received comments (e.g., the percentage of comments by supporters within the first hour), we only analyze submissions with at least one comment. In addition, we remove the top 5% of submissions with the highest number of comments to reduce the impact of outliers. Therefore, we consider only posts with less than 10 comments. We refer to this as the *retention dataset*, which we utilize to predict whether a support seeker will create another submission solely based on social impact features of their first submission. The retention dataset contains the first submission of 782 support seekers, with an average (median) of 3.6 (3) comments per submission.

Approach. We fit a logistic regression to measure the social impact of the Reddit community on the retention of support seekers. A binary variable indicating whether a support seeker makes at least one other submission within 30 days after their first submission forms the dependent variable, and our measures for social impact form the independent variables. Specifically, we fit a logistic regression modeling the probability of the binary retention variable r for user i as $Pr(r_i = 1) = logit^{-1}(\boldsymbol{X}_i\boldsymbol{\beta})$, where $\boldsymbol{X}_i$ is the feature (predictor) vector of user i and $\boldsymbol{\beta}$ is the vector of coefficients. The logistic model for r is then:

$$r \sim n + f + p + h, \tag{2}$$

where n is the number of comments to the support seeker's first submission, f the percentage of comments for the first submission coming from supporters with the gambling-free flair, p the percentage of positive comments for the first submission, and h the percentage of comments posted in one hour after the first submission of a given support seeker.

The coefficients $\boldsymbol{\beta}$ can be interpreted as follows. In logistic regression, logarithm of the odds for retention of user i equals the linear predictor, i.e.,

$$log\left(\frac{Pr(r_i = 1)}{Pr(r_i = 0)}\right) = \boldsymbol{X}_i\boldsymbol{\beta}, \tag{3}$$

and hence increasing the j-th predictor (i.e., X_{ij}) by 1 has the effect of adding the corresponding β_j coefficient to both sizes. Exponentiating both sides multiplies the odds with a factor of e^{β_j}, which is interpreted as the multiplicative factor for the odds corresponding to a unit difference in the j-th predictor.

2.4 Relapse Analysis

Relapse Dataset. To analyze the relapse risk, we begin by aggregating first submissions of relapsed support seekers. For this, we only consider support seekers that contributed at least one other submission within 60 days after their first submission. We then detect whether they relapse or not by examining their self-reported days since the start of their rehab. Specifically, we label an individual as relapsed if they first create one or multiple consecutive diary entries documenting their gambling-free journey (e.g., "Day 0", "Day 5", etc.), before then self-reporting a relapse by creating a post that is again titled "Day 0" (or "Day 1"). If a support seeker relapses, we also record the number of days since their first submission. We refer to this dataset as the *relapse dataset*, as we use it to investigate the factors leading to relapse during gambling addiction rehab. The relapse dataset contains 338 first submissions by users that posted at least twice, with an average (median) of 5.33 (4) comments per submission.

Right-Censored Datasets. Note that through our preprocessing, the retention dataset as well as the relapse dataset are right-censored. A dataset is considered right-censored when records about the investigated event—in our case, the self-reported relapse in the relapse dataset or the second submission in the retention dataset—exist only for parts of the support seekers within the respective observation period [9]. For example, considering the relapse dataset, right-censoring may occur due to three reasons. First, support seekers might not have relapsed by the time the observation period ended and thus no information about this event might exist. Secondly, they could have experienced a relapse during the observation period but might have not reported it. Lastly, a support seeker may have experienced a different event which did not allow them to complete the full observation period (e.g., in the most extreme case, death). Overall, out of our 338 support seekers in the relapse dataset 117 experienced a relapse event during the 60-day observation period.

Approach. The analysis whether (or how long) an individual "survives" an observation period without encountering an event has been termed *survival analysis* in past research [7,8,20,26]. Survival analysis is especially convenient for right-censored data, such as our relapse dataset. In the following, we briefly touch on the aspects and metrics most relevant to survival analysis as performed in this work: The Kaplan–Meier survival estimate as well as the Cox proportional hazards model.

Kaplan–Meier Survival Estimate. To estimate the probability of not relapsing, we use a so-called survival estimate. In particular, the probability that individuals survive to a given time in an observation period can be estimated using the Kaplan–Meier (KM) survival estimate [9]. The KM estimate computes the cumulative survival probability S for each point in time as following:

$$S(t_j) = S(t_{j-1})(1 - \frac{d_j}{n_j}) \qquad S(0) = 1, \quad t_0 = 0 \qquad (4)$$

Equation 4 recursively computes a step survival function S over time, where value of S changes at each event trigger t_j. Events typically refer to "deaths" (i.e., support seeker's relapse). Computation of S in the KM estimate takes into account the number of "alive" individuals (n_j) at t_j as well as the number of events or deaths d_j happening at t_j. In this way, both censored and uncensored individuals contribute to estimating S by providing information for the time they were not exposed to an event (i.e., in our case, relapse). Overall, to estimate the probability of survival at any point during the observation period, the KM

estimate considers, for each individual, the last reported day and whether the event was observed up to that day.

Cox Proportional Hazards Model. To estimate the effect of social impact features on Redditor's relapse into gambling, we utilize a semi-parametric Cox proportional hazards model ("Cox regression"). A Cox regression is a regression model that estimates the probability of an event occurring given a set of features x_i via a hazard function h [7]. This hazard h is derived from the nonparametrically estimated survival probability, i.e., from the *KM* estimator [9]:

$$h(t) = -\frac{d}{dt}[logS(t)] \tag{5}$$

Using this hazard function, we can mathematically express a Cox regression:

$$h(t) = h_0(t) \times \exp(\beta_1 x_1 + \beta_2 x_2 + \cdots + \beta_p x_p) \tag{6}$$

In Eq. 6, the hazard function $h(t)$ describes the probability that an observed individual (i.e., a recovering gambling addict) observes the event (i.e., a relapse) at a given point in time t. Correspondingly, the estimated baseline hazard $h_0(t)$ equals the hazard if all features (x_i) are 0, similar to the intercept in a regular multivariate regression setup but varying with time t. All features x_i are accompanied by a respective coefficient β_i, which describes the effect of the feature x_i on the hazard. Coefficients are usually interpreted in their exponential form e^{β_i}, which is termed "hazard ratio". A hazard ratio (*HR*) greater than 1 signals that as the value of a variable increases, the hazard also increases and thus the estimated length for survival decreases (i.e., the time to relapse shortens). Consequently, a *HR* smaller than 1 corresponds to a decrease in hazard and therefore an increase in survival time when the variable increases, while a *HR* of exactly 1 means that the variable has no effect on the hazard. Altogether, a Cox regression can be understood as a multivariate linear regression with the logarithm of the hazard function as the dependent variable and the features x_i as the independent variables, while *HR* measures the effect sizes of the corresponding x_i.

Using this survival analysis framework, we fit multiple Cox regressions on support seekers' first submissions in the relapse dataset, utilizing the same social impact features as we did in the retention analysis: the percentage of comments by supporters with flair, percentage of comments by supporters with positive sentiment, percentage of comments within one hour after the submission, and total number of comments.

3   Results and Discussion

3.1   Retention

In Fig. 2a we show the exponentiated coefficients reduced by 1, i.e., we show $100(e^{\beta_j} - 1)$, which we interpret as percentage change in the odds corresponding to the j-th predictor. For each coefficient we also show 95% confidence intervals. We can then interpret coefficients with confidence intervals not crossing zero either from above or from below as having a significant positive or negative effect, respectively, on support seeker retention. In our data, we observe that the number of comments a support seeker receives on their first submission, as well as the percentage of comments from supporters with gambling-free flair, both have a significant positive effect on the odds of support seekers making at least one further submission. Numerically, this means that each additional comment increases the odds of a support seeker making a second submission by 10.21%. Similarly, we observe that when the percentage of comments from supporters with flair increases by one (ten) percents, the odds of making a second submission increase by approximately 0.84% (8.4%). Both the percentage of positive supporter comments and the percentage of comments within the first hour are non-significantly associated with the outcome variable as their confidence intervals intersect with zero. The model achieves a Nagelkerke R^2 of 0.033 [24].

In Figs. 2b and 2c we also show the relationship between the percentage of support seekers making another submission and the number of comments, as well as the percentage of supporters commenting with a flair. In both figures, we observe that the more comments support seekers receive, and the higher the percentage of supporters commenting with a flair, the higher the percentage of support seekers making another submission. Altogether, our analysis indicates that two of our conceived social impact features (i.e., number of comments and presence of supporters with flair) have significant effects on support seeker retention, suggesting the relevance of such features.

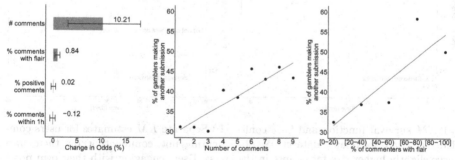

(a) Change in odds in percent with 95% confidence intervals for the predictors of the logistic regression.

(b) Percentage of support seekers making another submission vs. the number of comments.

(c) Percentage of support seekers making another submission vs. the percentage of supporters with a flair.

Fig. 2. Retention analysis using logistic regression. Figure 2(a) shows the change in odds of the independent variables, where a one-unit change in the predictor variable translates into a corresponding percentage change in the odds of making another submission. Both the number of comments, as well as the percentage of supporters with flair have a significant positive effect on the odds of making another submission. Figures 2(b) and 2(c) highlight the positive correlation between the two significant predictor variables and the percentage of gamblers making another submission.

3.2   Relapse

First, we compute the *KM* estimate for the cumulative survival function, which
we plot in Fig. 3a. We observe a monotonically decreasing survival probability, with slightly higher relapse probabilities in the first 10 days. The relapse
probability has another peak around day 50. Using this estimate, we proceed
to fitting several Cox regressions. To that end, we perform multiple univariate
Cox regressions using each social impact feature individually before then fitting
a multivariate regression using all features.

Although the univariate models generally signal a reduction of the hazard by
the social impact features, none of the employed features affect survival significantly ($p > 0.1$, cf. first column in Table 1). Most notably, the *HR*s for percentage
of positive supporter comments and the percentage of supporter comments with
flairs (i.e., also currently recovering gamblers) indicate that interacting with
individuals who are going through the same recovery process as well as receiving positive encouragement prolong survival times for support seekers (*HR* of
0.6817 and 0.8329, resp.). Next, we fit a Cox regression combining all of our

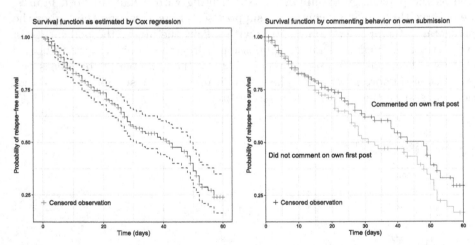

(a) *KM* survival function and 95% confidence intervals for relapse dataset. We observe slightly higher risk for relapse in the
first 10 days and around day 50.

(b) Separate *KM* estimates for users com-
menting/not commenting on their own
post. Users engaging with their own posts
have a higher chance of survival.

Fig. 3. Relapse analysis using *KM* survival function. In Fig. 3(a), the plot for
the *KM* survival curve computed for the relapse dataset depicts a regularly decreasing
survival function, with slightly higher risk for relapse in the first 10 days as well as high
risks of relapse around day 50. In Fig. 3(b), the *KM* estimate is shown for two groups
of individuals: support seekers who commented on their own first submissions (cyan
curve) and those who did not (red curve). The survival curve hints towards support
seekers who show self-motivation to engage with the community being more successful
in surviving until the end of the observation period (logrank test, $p = 0.1$). (Color
figure online)

social impact features. This multivariate model yields similar insignificant *HRs* ($p > 0.3$) for all features and does not numerically differ considerably from the univariate models (cf. second column in Table 1). Altogether, our investigation of the influence of social impact on support seeker survivability does not yield significant results, although a trend in reduction of the hazard is observable for some of the social impact indicators.

Effect of Self-motivation on Survival. Due to the non-significant effect of social impact features on survival, we now extend our analysis to also include self-motivation. For this, we categorize all support seekers in the relapse dataset (338 users) into two groups signaling whether they themselves commented on their first submission or not (189 and 149 users, resp.). We consider this to be an indicator of (self-)motivation to actively engage with others in an online self-help group. The *KM* survival curves for the corresponding two groups (Fig. 3b) hint toward support seekers that are motivated to comment on their own submission having slightly higher chance of survival (logrank test, $p = 0.1$). Moreover, we investigate the difference in effects between the two groups for our social impact features using Cox regression. While we find no significantly different effects for the number of comments ($HR = 1.126$, $p = 0.125$), percentage of comments with flair ($HR = 0.947$, $p = 0.22$), or percentage of comments within one hour after the submission ($HR = 0.072$, $p = 0.51$), we observe a significant difference for the percentage of positive comments ($HR = 0.286$, $p < 0.05$). This suggests that support-seekers that exhibit self-motivation in commenting on their own posts benefit considerably more from receiving positive encouragement than those that do not. Overall, future work attempting relapse analysis in online support groups may also consider such characteristics of self-motivation as relevant factors.

Table 1. Cox regression results. The hazard ratio (HR) computed from the coefficients (β_i) as well as their 95% confidence interval (CI) and p-values (Wald test) for both univariate and multivariate analysis of social impact features.

Covariate	Univariate analysis			Multivariate analysis		
	HR[exp(β_i)]	95% CI	p-value	HR[exp(β_i)]	95% CI	p-value
#comments	0.971	(0.923–1.018)	0.219	0.992	(0.939–1.048)	0.777
% positive comments	0.682	(0.401–1.159)	0.157	0.736	(0.407–1.331)	0.310
% comments with flair	0.833	(0.411–1.687)	0.612	1.040	(0.491–2.205)	0.918
% comments within 1 h	0.959	(0.733–1.124)	0.159	0.970	(0.907–1.037)	0.369

3.3 Limitations

There are several limitations of our analysis. Firstly, Reddit only covers a portion of the population affected by problematic gambling behavior. Most Reddit users are younger than 40, male, and from the United States (75.2%, 62.8%, 50%

of all users, respectively[3]). Thus, we can assume that other demographics are underrepresented in our dataset. Secondly, our investigated sample may be even more biased as we strictly focus on problem gamblers that self-select to actually report on their problems online. Therefore, gamblers without the motivation to actively engage in online discussions of their problems with others are also underrepresented in our sample. Thirdly, although we took care about controlling for several factors such as left- and right-censored data or self-motivation in engaging with the community, we still mainly reported on correlations and predictive effects (as opposed to causal effects) of social impact indicators on retention and relapse of gamblers. We leave the investigation of causality as a promising avenue for future research. On a separate note, Latane [18] mentions multiple limitations of social impact theory. For example, the initial theory does not consider people as active seekers of social impact. In addition, the model does not allow for dynamic components. This is also prevalent in our analysis, as we mostly consider features of user's first posts. Future work could incorporate information from user's later posts to gain further insights about the social impact Reddit's online self-help groups have on problem gamblers.

4   Conclusions

In this work, we propose a framework on how to measure the social impact of the Reddit community on problem gamblers who seek support online. The framework is based on social impact theory and aims to operationalize its factors to analyze social interactions between users in self-help gambling communities on Reddit.

Our results suggest that a higher number of comments from supporters, as well as a higher percentage of supporter comments with gambling-free flair increase the retention of support seekers in online self-help groups on Reddit. We additionally analyze the effect of social impact on relapses of recovering problem gamblers using survival analysis, but obtain mostly statistically non-significant results. The only statistically significant exception is related to support seekers who engage in the discussion with others, e.g., by commenting on their own first submission. For those users, the percentage of positive comments from others has a positive effect reducing the probability of their relapse and indicating that a positive encouragement for motivated support seekers is beneficial.

There are multiple possibilities for extending the work presented in this paper. Firstly, user activity in subreddits other than /r/problemgambling and /r/GamblingAddiction could be taken into account. It might be possible that behavior of recovering addicts as indicated by their Reddit activity is a predictor of their survival probability. For example, if users find an alternative outlet or substitution for their addictive behavior (e.g., video games or sports), they might have higher chances of successfully recovering from their gambling addiction. Secondly, besides parsimonious sentiment measurements it might prove

---

[3] From: statista.com/statistics/1125159/reddit-us-app-users-age, statista.com/statistics/1255182/distribution-of-users-on-reddit-worldwide-gender, statista.com/statistics/325144/reddit-global-active-user-distribution.

feasible to include other indicators of emotion, such as valence, arousal, and dominance [23,25,32]. Furthermore, incorporating word embeddings or other similar text features into such analysis might prove fruitful as well [20].

Overall, our results may help in providing additional support to potential problem gamblers in their strive to change their gambling behavior. For example, senior users and users with a gambling-free flair should be encouraged—either through subreddit rules or by bots—to support newcomers (support seekers) when they post their very first submission. Moreover, we believe that our approach to analyzing social interactions in gambling self-help groups on Reddit through the lenses of social impact theory can be useful for future studies of user interactions in the context of online self-help communities.

Acknowledgements. We thank David Garcia for his helpful feedback and discussion on this topic. The authors also thank the anonymous reviewers for their comments, which improved this work.

References

1. Auer, M., Hopfgartner, N., Griffiths, M.D.: An empirical study of the effect of voluntary limit-setting on gamblers' loyalty using behavioural tracking data. Int. J. Mental Health Addict. **19**, 1939–1950 (2019)
2. Auer, M., Hopfgartner, N., Griffiths, M.D.: The effects of voluntary deposit limit-setting on long-term online gambling expenditure. Cyberpsychol. Behav. Soc. Networking **23**(2), 113–118 (2020)
3. Balsamo, D., Bajardi, P., Panisson, A.: Firsthand opiates abuse on social media: monitoring geospatial patterns of interest through a digital cohort. In: The World Wide Web Conference, pp. 2572–2579 (2019)
4. Basile, V., Cauteruccio, F., Terracina, G.: How dramatic events can affect emotionality in social posting: the impact of Covid-19 on Reddit. Future Internet **13**(2), 29 (2021)
5. Baumgartner, J., Zannettou, S., Keegan, B., Squire, M., Blackburn, J.: The pushshift reddit dataset. In: Proceedings of the International AAAI Conference on Web and Social Media, vol. 14, pp. 830–839 (2020)
6. Bernhard, B.J., Dickens, D.R., Shapiro, P.D.: Gambling alone? A study of solitary and social gambling in America. UNLV Gaming Res. Rev. J. **11**(2), 1 (2007)
7. Bradburn, M.J., Clark, T.G., Love, S.B., Altman, D.G.: Survival analysis part III: multivariate data analysis - choosing a model and assessing its adequacy and fit. Br. J. Cancer **89**(4), 605–611 (2003). https://doi.org/10.1038/sj.bjc.6601120
8. Clark, T.G., Altman, D.G.: Developing a prognostic model in the presence of missing data: an ovarian cancer case study. J. Clin. Epidemiol. **56**(1), 28–37 (2003)
9. Clark, T.G., Bradburn, M.J., Love, S.B., Altman, D.G.: Survival analysis part i: basic concepts and first analyses. Br. J. Cancer **89**(2), 232–238 (2003)
10. Díaz, A., Pérez, L.: Online gambling-related harm: findings from the study on the prevalence, behavior and characteristics of gamblers in Spain. J. Gambl. Stud. **37**(2), 599–607 (2021)
11. Dowling, N.A., Suomi, A., Jackson, A.C., Lavis, T.: Problem gambling family impacts: development of the problem gambling family impact scale. J. Gambl. Stud. **32**(3), 935–955 (2016)

12. Erevik, E.K., Pallesen, S., Mohn, M., Aspeland, T., Vedaa, Ø., Torsheim, T.: The Norwegian remote intervention programme for problem gambling: short-and long-term outcomes. Nordic Stud. Alcohol Drugs **37**(4), 365–383 (2020)
13. Eysenbach, G., Powell, J., Englesakis, M., Rizo, C., Stern, A.: Health related virtual communities and electronic support groups: systematic review of the effects of online peer to peer interactions. BMJ **328**(7449), 1166 (2004)
14. Hopfgartner, N., Auer, M., Santos, T., Helic, D., Griffiths, M.D.: The effect of mandatory play breaks on subsequent gambling behavior among Norwegian online sports betting, slots and bingo players: a large-scale real world study. J. Gambl. Stud. **38**, 737–752 (2021)
15. Hutto, C., Gilbert, E.: VADER: a parsimonious rule-based model for sentiment analysis of social media text. In: Proceedings of the International AAAI Conference on Web and Social Media, vol. 8, pp. 216–225 (2014)
16. Jonsson, J., Hodgins, D.C., Munck, I., Carlbring, P.: Reaching out to big losers leads to sustained reductions in gambling over 1 year: a randomized controlled trial of brief motivational contact. Addiction **115**(8), 1522–1531 (2020)
17. Kaakinen, M., Oksanen, A., Sirola, A., Savolainen, I., Garcia, D.: Emotions in online gambling communities: a multilevel sentiment analysis. In: Meiselwitz, G. (ed.) HCII 2020. LNCS, vol. 12194, pp. 542–550. Springer, Cham (2020). https://doi.org/10.1007/978-3-030-49570-1_38
18. Latané, B.: The psychology of social impact. Am. Psychol. **36**(4), 343 (1981)
19. Low, D.M., Rumker, L., Talkar, T., Torous, J., Cecchi, G., Ghosh, S.S.: Natural language processing reveals vulnerable mental health support groups and heightened health anxiety on reddit during Covid-19: observational study. J. Med. Internet Res. **22**(10), e22635 (2020)
20. Lu, J., Sridhar, S., Pandey, R., Hasan, M.A., Mohler, G.: Investigate transitions into drug addiction through text mining of Reddit data. In: Proceedings of the 25th ACM SIGKDD International Conference on Knowledge Discovery & Data Mining, pp. 2367–2375 (2019)
21. Luquiens, A., Dugravot, A., Panjo, H., Benyamina, A., Gaïffas, S., Bacry, E.: Self-exclusion among online poker gamblers: effects on expenditure in time and money as compared to matched controls. Int. J. Environ. Res. Public Health **16**(22), 4399 (2019)
22. McNeilly, D.P., Burke, W.J.: Gambling as a social activity of older adults. Int. J. Aging Human Dev. **52**(1), 19–28 (2001)
23. Mohammad, S.M.: Obtaining reliable human ratings of valence, arousal, and dominance for 20,000 English words. In: ACL 2018–56th Annual Meeting of the Association for Computational Linguistics, Proceedings of the Conference (Long Papers), vol. 1, pp. 174–184 (2018). https://doi.org/10.18653/v1/p18-1017
24. Nagelkerke, N.J., et al.: A note on a general definition of the coefficient of determination. Biometrika **78**(3), 691–692 (1991)
25. Pellert, M., Schweighofer, S., Garcia, D.: The individual dynamics of affective expression on social media. EPJ Data Sci. **9**(1), 1–14 (2020). http://dx.doi.org/10.1140/epjds/s13688-019-0219-3
26. Raban, D.R., Moldovan, M., Jones, Q.: An empirical study of critical mass and online community survival. In: Proceedings of the 2010 ACM Conference on Computer Supported Cooperative Work, pp. 71–80 (2010)
27. Schuler, A., et al.: Gamblers anonymous as a recovery pathway: a scoping review. J. Gambl. Stud. **32**(4), 1261–1278 (2016)

28. Sharma, A., Choudhury, M., Althoff, T., Sharma, A.: Engagement patterns of peer-to-peer interactions on mental health platforms. In: Proceedings of the International AAAI Conference on Web and Social Media, vol. 14, pp. 614–625 (2020)
29. Singer, P., Flöck, F., Meinhart, C., Zeitfogel, E., Strohmaier, M.: Evolution of reddit: from the front page of the internet to a self-referential community? In: Proceedings of the 23rd International Conference on World Wide Web, pp. 517–522 (2014)
30. Syvertsen, A., Erevik, E.K., Mentzoni, R.A., Pallesen, S.: Gambling addiction Norway-experiences among members of a Norwegian self-help group for problem gambling. Int. Gambl. Stud. **20**(2), 246–261 (2020)
31. Tan, C.: Tracing community genealogy: how new communities emerge from the old. In: Twelfth International AAAI Conference on Web and Social Media (2018)
32. Warriner, A.B., Kuperman, V., Brysbaert, M.: Norms of valence, arousal, and dominance for 13,915 English lemmas. Behav. Res. Methods **45**(4), 1191–1207 (2013)

Uncovering Discussion Groups on Claims of Election Fraud from Twitter

Jose Martins da Rosa Jr[1]($\boxtimes$), Renan Saldanha Linhares[1],
Carlos Henrique Gomes Ferreira[1,2], Gabriel P. Nobre[2],
Fabricio Murai[2,3], and Jussara M. Almeida[2]

[1] Department of Computing and Systems, Universidade Federal de Ouro Preto, João Monlevade, Brazil
{jose.rosa,renan.linhares}@aluno.ufop.edu.br, chgferreira@ufop.edu.br
[2] Department of Computer Science, Universidade Federal de Minas Gerais, Belo Horizonte, Brazil
{chgferreira,gabrielnobre,jussara,murai}@dcc.ufmg.br
[3] Worcester Polytechnic Institute, Worcester, USA
fmurai@wpi.edu

Abstract. Twitter was widely used during the 2020 U.S. election to disseminate claims of election fraud. As a result, a number of works have examined this phenomenon from a variety of perspectives. However, none of them focus on analyzing topics behind the general fraud claims and associating them with user communities. To fill this gap, we propose to uncover and characterize groups of Twitter users engaging in discussions about election fraud claims during the 2020 U.S. election using a large dataset that spans seven weeks during this period. To accomplish this, we model a sequence of co-retweet networks and employ a backbone extraction method that controls for inherent traits of social media applications, particularly, user activity levels and the popularity of tweets (which together generate many spurious edges in the network), thus allowing us to reveal topics of tweets that lead users to retweet them. After extracting the backbones, we identify user groups representative of the communities present in the network backbones and finally analyze the topics behind the retweeted tweets to understand how they contributed to the spread of fraud claims at that time. Our main results show that (i) our approach uncovers better-structured communities than the original network in terms of users spreading discussions about fraud; and (ii) these users discuss 25 topics with specific psycholinguistic and temporal characteristics.

Keywords: Topic analysis · Twitter · Network backbone extraction · Community detection

1 Introduction

Social media platforms have become efficient channels for information dissemination, especially during election periods [18,26,32]. One of the most recent and

F. Hopfgartner et al. (Eds.): SocInfo 2022, LNCS 13618, pp. 320–336, 2022.
https://doi.org/10.1007/978-3-031-19097-1_20

notable examples of political exploitation of such platforms took place during the 2020 U.S. presidential election, when Twitter was reportedly abused to spread (dis)information about alleged election frauds [1,14,23,38], culminating on the violent invasion to the U.S. Capitol. At the time, a large number of accounts were suspended on the grounds of spreading content that could incite further violence.[1] Driven by these happenings, a number of studies have examined content shared on Twitter during the period from various perspectives, including the spread of hate speech [7,23] and (dis)information [6,14,38,43], as well as sentiment [5,41], and polarization [9] analyses.

In contrast, we are here interested in analyzing groups of users who contributed to the discussion spread of fraud allegations at the time by retweeting tweets on the topic, thus contributing to maintaining the discussions on the subject online. To identify such groups, we employ a network-driven approach where such groups of users are expressed in the form of communities of tightly connected nodes. Though some prior studies have also employed network models to study information spread during the period [1,9,14,38,40], they neglected a key aspect, namely the presence of edges that emerge by chance, as a side effect of the dynamics of the platform and, as such, do not contribute, and may indeed hurt, the understanding of the phenomenon under study (i.e., the online discussions) [16,21,32,33].

As an example, consider the task of modeling a *network of co-retweets* as an undirected and weighted graph where pairs of users (nodes) are connected by the number of tweets in common both retweeted (weighted edges). Such network allows us to study information spread through the discussions associated with the tweets of specific user accounts that fuel the debate. When retweeted, these tweets can be used to gauge support for public discussions through the topics they contain [17,29]. Yet, not all pairs of common retweets (i.e., co-retweets) do indeed reflect actual user discussions around a common theme (i.e., tweet). For example, two users may retweet a particular tweet simply because it has a very popular content (or content creator). Similarly, very active users naturally tend to co-retweet with many other users due to their frequent retweeting. All these co-retweets lead to (a possibly large number of) edges in the network that emerge as side effect of properties of the platform (content popularity and user activity level). As such, they do not reflect true user interactions to foster specific discussions as they can generate edges due to the aforementioned side effects. Such sporadic and spurious edges can then be considered *noise*, as they tend to overshadow the phenomenon under investigation [8,16].

To overcome such challenge, we propose to employ a backbone extraction technique to identify and remove noisy edges, thus revealing the underlying network structure of interest [16,21]. Once the backbone has been revealed, we can then proceed to extract user communities belonging to it. Prior efforts to extract the backbone of a Twitter network have applied a simple strategy that removes edges with weights below a given threshold [4,15,22,33,35]. Yet, such approach does not account for the heterogeneity of content popularity and

---

[1] https://www.nytimes.com/2021/01/11/technology/twitter-removes-70000-qanon-accounts.html.

user activity typical of social media, thus leading to information loss as entire network components may be removed [8]. In contrast, the TriBE method, which was designed to study online discussions in social media [16,21], does consider both aspects, but has never been applied to domains other than Instagram.

In this context, our goal is to *uncover and characterize groups of Twitter users driving discussions on alleged frauds during the 2020 U.S. election.* To that end, we leverage a large collection of tweets on election fraud claims, the VoterFraud dataset [1], which spans seven weeks around the election period. Our approach consists of first modeling a co-retweet network, then employing TriBE to extract the network backbone and using the Louvain's algorithm [3] to uncover representative communities of users co-retweeting tweets on fraud claims. Finally, we examine how the discussion topics driven by such communities emerge and evolve over time. Our research questions (RQ) and their respective findings are:

RQ1: What Topological Structures Emerge in the Backbone Extracted from a Co-retweet Network? By analyzing millions of retweets, we show that, by first extracting the backbone, we are able to reveal much better structured communities of users than in the original network. Such communities include thousands of users who contributed to keep the discussions on fraud claims alive by spreading the same tweets on the topic.

RQ2: What are the Properties of the Main Topics of Discussions of the Identified Communities? Despite constrained by a specific context (fraud claims), the tweets shared by users in the identified communities could be grouped into 25 discussion topics, with quite different temporal patterns. Some of these topics are widely discussed throughout the period under study, others come and go, and still, others are topical and appear only in a particular week. Notably, the psycholinguistic elements present in their content, as captured by the LIWC lexicon [34,39], are specific to each week and change as they move away from the election period, reflecting the facts and topics identified in connection with the fraud allegations.

The remainder of this paper is organized as follows. Related work is discussed in Sect. 2 while the methodology adopted is presented in Sect. 3. Section 4 describes our main findings. Finally, Sect. 5 concludes our work.

2   Related Work

Previous work has analyzed the debates on Twitter during the U.S. election, notably those related to fraud allegations, from a variety of perspectives. For example, Grimminger *et al.* analyzed the presence of hate speech among different groups of candidates' supporters [23]. Childs *et al.*, in turn, analyzed the extent to which discussions on Twitter spread to other platforms [6].

Others have followed up on Twitter's post-election suspension of many user accounts[2] to analyze the textual properties of the content shared by those

---
[2] https://www.bbc.com/news/technology-55638558.

accounts. In that direction, Chowdhury *et al.* compared the tweets of suspended users with a control group, finding that the former were more likely to violate various Twitter rules, such as sharing insults and hate speech [7]. Similarly, Zannettou studied the sharing patterns associated with tweets that were given a political warning by Twitter, focusing on the engagement of suspended users [43]. Others have performed sentiment analysis of election-related tweets, comparing sentiment estimates to election results by region and across candidates [5, 41].

Another group of studies have employed various network models to examine the characteristics of the Twitter debate on the 2020 U.S. election. For example, Sharma *et al.* used network cascade analysis to uncover narratives related to misinformation [38]. Ferrara *et al.*, in turn, analyzed the network of retweets to characterize the debate along two dimensions: (i) automation (e.g., the prevalence of bots) and (ii) distortion (e.g., manipulation of narratives, injection of conspiracies or rumors) [14]. The network of retweets was also explored by others to analyze the formation of communities, aiming at characterizing them in terms of ideology [9] and presence of suspended user accounts [1]. Tran *et al.*, in turn, examined discussions based on the common use of hashtags, by exploring a co-hashtag network [40].

In contrast to prior work, we here propose to model a network of co-retweets in which users are connected by the number of tweets they retweet in common, aiming at uncovering communities driven by the discussion topics behind those tweets. Thus, our study provides an orthogonal view compared to previous efforts. Also, we argue that such a network, like the other networks used to study the same phenomenon [1,14,38,40], may contain a number of noisy edges that are not of interest and, even more, may obfuscate fundamental aspects of the phenomenon under study. Thus, we propose to extract the network backbone prior to community identification to provide a clearer view of how discussions ob election fraud have played out on Twitter. Our decision is supported by recent results on the utmost importance of this step to the study of various phenomena in social media applications, including coordinated behavior on WhatsApp [31,32] and Twitter [19,20,33], as well as online discussions on Instagram [14,16].

3   Methodology

This section describes the methodology adopted to carry on our study.

3.1   Dataset

Our study is based on the VoterFraud[3] dataset kindly provided by the authors [1]. This is a collection of tweets collected via the Twitter API between October 23th and December 16th 2020[4]. The crawl process searched for a set of predefined keywords and hashtags related to allegations of fraud in the 2020 U.S. elections. Examples include *voterfraud*, *discardedballots*, *stopthesteal*, and *stopcheating*

---

[3] https://voterfraud2020.io/.
[4] The election week began on November 3rd 2020.

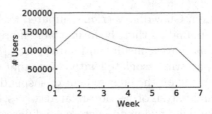

Fig. 1. Time series of the number of users per week.

When we divided the dataset into nine weekly intervals[5], we found that the first two weeks contained significantly fewer data. Therefore, we decided to discard the first two weeks and thus analyze an additional seven weeks. We also focused our analysis on the distribution of content posted by the most popular accounts. To this end, we only considered tweets from accounts that received a total of at least 5,000 retweets per week. In total, we selected 186 accounts that posted a total of 4,328 tweets and received 4,545,021 retweets from 323,912 unique user accounts over the seven weeks.

Figure 1 represents the final quantitative number of users over the analyzed weeks who tweeted or retweeted at least one tweet related to election fraud during the analyzed period. We can see that the greatest engagement occurs during the election, particularly between the first and second weeks analyzed, which includes Election Day (November 3rd, 2020). Even though the number of users is higher during this week, we can see that it is relatively high in the following weeks. In particular, six of the seven analyzed weeks contain more than 100,000 users spreading tweets about the fraud allegations.

3.2 Network Modeling

We start by dividing the analysis period into a sequence of discrete and non-overlapping time windows with a duration of one week $\Delta_T = \{1, 2, ..., 7\}$. Thus, for each time window Δ_t, we model an undirected and weighted graph $G_{\Delta_t} = (V_{\Delta_t}, A_{\Delta_t})$. The set of nodes $V_{\Delta_t} = \{v_{\Delta_t}^1, v_{\Delta_t}^2, ..., v_{\Delta_t}^i\}$ corresponds to the i users who retweeted at least once during the time window Δ_t. The set of edges $A_{\Delta_t} = \{a_{\Delta_t}^1, a_{\Delta_t}^2, ..., a_{\Delta_t}^j\}$ contains edges between two given vertices if they have retweeted at least one common tweet in Δ_t with weight w equal to the number of common retweets. Thus, our interest lies in analyzing the network that favors the spread of topics of discussion through tweets that attract these users, who consequently retweet them and contribute to the spread of such claims.

3.3 Backbone Extraction

Remember that our ultimate goal is to discover groups of users who are attracted to topics on the co-retweet network, notably, communities. However, some factors

---

[5] We consider a week from Sunday to Saturday.

inherent to social networks may obscure users' interests, such as heterogeneity in activity levels and popularity of the author and/or content. For example, assume that a particular user a retweets all tweets from a particular profile. Also assume that subsets of that profile's tweets are representative of the topics being disseminated. When groups of users retweet the tweets that are potentially interesting for those topics, edges are created between a and the other users, overshadowing their interests due to the parallel effect of a's activity level. Note that this can originate from multiple users like a in different profiles, which increases the noise in the network. Similarly, an extremely popular tweet, e.g., on a hot topic, attracts thousands of users who retweet it. However, if these users only interact with this tweet, we probably cannot say that they are actually interested in the same topics and were only attracted by the popularity factor. Conversely, we would like to focus on the interactions between users and tweets that are potential topics of discussion and were not influenced by any of these factors.

To address these challenges, we propose to identify edges using *Tripartite Backbone Extraction* (TriBE). This is a backbone extraction method proposed in the literature that takes into account these two factors, specifically the level of user activity and the popularity of tweets and their authors [16,21]. For each graph G_{Δ_t}, TriBE extracts the backbone B_{Δ_t} as follows. First, TriBE builds a null model $\widehat{G_{\Delta_t}}$ taking into account the two factors mentioned above. In this way, TriBE computes the expected weight of each edge in G_{Δ_t} analytically, as if users were randomly assigned to retweets, subject to the following constraints: (i) the set of tweet creators; (ii) the popularity of each tweet, which consists of the number of retweets it has received; and (iii) the relative proportion of a user's retweets to the tweets of a given *influencer*. Given these variables, TriBE builds a reference model $\widehat{G_{\Delta_t}}$ so that it is possible to test each edge in the original graph G_{Δ_t} and see if it has weights large enough to reject the assumption of independent user behavior according to a given *alpha* confidence level. The edges whose premise of independent behavior is rejected remain in the backbone B_{Δ_t}. In other words, given the assumptions used to build the reference model, these edges provide strong evidence that users are attracted by hidden factors, i.e., potential discussion topics contained in the tweets they retweet.

3.4 Community Detection

After extracting the backbone, we identify communities that are interested in specific discussion topics. To detect such communities, we apply Louvain's widely used community detection algorithm, which considers communities as non overlapping groups of nodes in a graph [3]. In a nutshell, it is a greedy algorithm that aims to optimize a metric called *modularity*. Modularity quantifies the relative density of edges within communities compared to a network with the same degree sequence but randomly connected nodes. Its value ranges from -1/2 to +1, with values of 0.3 or higher considered a reliable indicator of well-structured communities [30].

3.5   Topic Extraction and Characterization

To extract discussion topics shared by users on *backbone*, we use BERTopic, a state-of-the-art *framework* that combines embedding models and clustering algorithms to extract topics [24]. By generating vector representations (embeddings), BERTopic preserves the semantics of a given set of sentences and allows them to be grouped by similarity. BERTopic relies on Sentence BERT (SBERT) for the sentence embedding step [36], which has shown good performance on semantic text similarity tasks using a pre-trained model[6] [10]. Such framework has been used in several previous works, including discussion analysis on Twitter [2,11–13]. In this way, we can use vector representations from the pre-trained model for all tweets from users who remained on at least one of the backbones.

In a nutshell, BERTopic works as follows. First, the set of tweets is represented as vectors using SBERT. Then, the algorithm *Uniform Manifold Approximation and Projection for Dimension Reduction* (UMAP) is used to reduce the dimensionality of the vector space [28]. BERTopic uses UMAP to reduce the vector space (before grouping the tweets) and increase the performance of the clustering algorithms. Unlike the commonly used alternatives PCA and t-SNE, UMAP preserves the global and local features of the sentences with greater accuracy [28]. Once the representation of tweets in low-dimensional vectors (embeddings) is obtained, the HDBSCAN algorithm is used to group them into k groups (automatically defined) whose semantic representations captured by the reduced vector space are similar. By finding these groups of tweets (the so-called documents, for BERTopic), representing potentially interesting topics expressed as disjoint sets of tweets, the technique *Term Frequency-Inverse Document Frequency* (TF-IDF) is applied to extract the most discriminative words for each group and thus describe the topics to which each group of tweets (or documents) belongs [25].

Having uncovered such topics of discussion, it is possible to characterize them from different perspectives. Therefore, we summarize here how we intend to do this. Since a document (a group of sentences) may consist of tweets from users in different communities, an important analysis is to observe how these topics emerge and evolve. In particular, whether they are transient, persistent, or recurrent over time. It is also possible to analyze how interested the communities are in these topics and which ones they tend to spread more.

An important alternative for the analysis of texts from social media platforms is the study of the psycholinguistic properties that characterize them. This makes it possible to find peculiarities in the way a particular group of users communicates and explore specific themes in search of mobilization for particular contexts [27,37]. Here, we used LIWC - *Linguistic Inquiry and Word Count*, which seeks to quantify psycholinguistic properties of texts. LIWC provides insights into the emotional state, thought processes, and other measures that describe the behavior and context of the author of the texts [34,39]. To this end, this tool uses a lexical dictionary consisting of attributes (also called dimensions), each containing representative words. For example, an attribute describing texts related

---

[6] https://huggingface.co/sentence-transformers/all-mpnet-base-v2.

to "death" consists of words such as "bury", "coffin", "kill", while an attribute describing the text's relation to health consists of words such as "clinic", "flu", "pill". It should be noted that a word can belong to more than one attribute. For example, the word "death" can be part of an attribute describing texts about death and at the same time part of the attribute describing the feeling of anger presented in the text. In this work, we use the LIWC2015 English dictionary, which consists of about 6400 words associated with 125 attributes [34].

Once the dictionary is defined and applied to the sentences, LIWC calculates the percentage of attributes in each sentence. Since LIWC consists of several attributes, it is necessary to apply a strategy to select the most distinctive attributes for the analyses to be performed. Here we follow previous works and adopt the Gini index [16,27,42], which can be used to evaluate the distinctiveness of a given attribute as a function of a variable, such as topics or week. In this case, the idea is to select the most discriminative k attributes among the weeks in order to identify them as the different psycholinguistic features evolve over time.

4   Results

In this section we present our results. First, in Sect. 4.1, we describe the communities that are representative of the potential discussion groups on our backbones. We then move to topic analysis by examining the topics we uncovered and some of their characteristics in Sect. 4.2.

4.1   Discussion Groups

Recall that the discussion groups captured by the communities are extracted by TriBE from the backbone of each time window Δ_t. Using TriBE, we assume a significance level $\alpha = 0.05$ to decide whether or not an edge is preserved in the backbone from the reference model $\hat{G}$. Thus, we start our analysis by comparing the structure of the community before and after applying TriBE.

Table 1 shows the topological and community metrics for the original network and the backbone when $\Delta_t = 1$. For this time window, we can observe a decrease in the number of nodes in backbone by about 32% and edges by more than 98%. Indeed, many users and especially edges are removed from the network, indicating the presence of many noisy edges and users that had only edges of this type. As a result, the backbone is sparser and thus has a lower density and average degree. However, analyzing the structure of the communities identified by the Louvain's algorithm in both networks, we can see that the backbone extracted for TriBE has a larger number of communities[7], but it is much better structured in terms of modularity than the original network, increasing from 0.24 to 0.50.

Table 2 presents the description of such communities for the entire period analyzed. In general, we can observe that the communities found according to

---

[7] We have disregarded communities with less than 100 users.

Table 1. Comparison of original network and extracted backbone for $\Delta_t = 1$.

Network	# Nodes	# Edges	Avg. Degree	Density	# Com.	Mod.
Original	121992	651835172	10686.52	0.0876	12	0.24
Backbone	82121	8490834	206.79	0.0025	16	0.50

Table 2. Breakdown of the backbones structure for the period analyzed.

Week	# Nodes	# Edges	Avg. Degree	Avg. Clustering	Density	# Com.	Mod.
1	82121	8490834	206.79	0.35	0.0025	16	0.50
2	126723	23389461	369.14	0.31	0.0029	11	0.44
3	88779	23207352	522.81	0.40	0.0059	8	0.36
4	77183	39097031	1013.10	0.39	0.0131	8	0.39
5	96499	52956309	1097.55	0.38	0.0114	8	0.35
6	68551	32599329	951.10	0.47	0.0139	7	0.31
7	21642	3920047	362.26	0.46	0.0167	13	0.37

the reported modularity, which varies from 0.31 to 0.50, are well structured for all the analyzed weeks. In general, the backbones are much sparser, as shown by the density, the average degree of vertices and the average clustering coefficient.

4.2 Topic Analysis

To analyze the discussion topics of users belonging to these communities, we used the BERTopic framework explained in Sect. 3. For the parameterization, we followed the recommendations in the documentation to find the best compromise between the number of topics and the size of the dataset[8]. As a result, we obtain the following parameterization: the number of neighbors and the component parameters required by UMAP were set to 15 and 5, respectively. The minimum topic size was set to 15, which controls the minimum number of unique tweets on a topic. We found a total of 25 discussion topics. Table 5 in Appendix I provides the most representative words of each topic, a brief discussion of the context based on reading the most representative tweets of each topic and links related news[9]. In general, it is possible to observe the presence of multiple topics, which confirms the presence of specific discussions about fraud claims.

To illustrate how topics describe discussions in a particular context, we focus on Topics 7 and 14, whose respective keywords and a brief description of the context are shown in Table 3. Topic 7 refers to the organization of demonstrations calling for a suspension of the vote count for allegedly rigging the election

---

[8] https://maartengr.github.io/BERTopic/getting_started/parameter%20tuning/parametertuning.html.

[9] We have noted the presence of some fake news according to the Fact Check Agencies. However, we did not analyze this aspect because it is beyond the scope of this paper.

Table 3. Top discriminative words for Topic 7 and 14.

Topic	Words	Context
7	'stopthesteal', 'DD', 'Washington', 'join', 'tomorrow' 'freedom', 'plaza' 'capitol', 'noon', '14th', 'congressman', 'millionmagamarch', 'excited' 'sat', 'womenfortrump' 'marchfortrump', 'nov', 'building', 'late'	Demonstrations demanding a halt to the vote count due to allegations of fraud and the organization of a pro-Trump march leaving Freedom Plaza
14	'victim', 'voted', 'Elizabeth', 'ballot', 'Christiansen' 'waltower', 'skwiot' '2019', 'year', 'died', 'voter'	Alleged election fraud from dead votes.

Table 4. The most retweeted tweets and hashtags on Topics 7 and 14.

Topic	Tweet	Hashtags
7	So excited to have Congressman join us tomorrow for the #MarchForTrump in Washington, DC.It's not too late to join ususat, NOV 14thus12PMusFreedom Plaza - Washington, DC #stopthesteal #MillionMAGAMarch #WomenForTrump #TXgop https://t.co/y7RT3cWs9U	#stopthesteal, #millionmagamarch, #marchfortrump, #womenfortrump,
	'This is so awesome! Where are you, Governor ? #StopTheSteal https://t.co/P3lbkbBJ3y	#txgop, #protectthevote
	#StopTheSteal Rally at the Georgia State Capitol in Atlanta https://t.co/gGjyIKBGQl	
	'Proud to be your lawyer, Mr. President!!! We are fighting for this great country with you!!! us https://t.co/k6nrLYj1iV'	
	See you all this Saturday at the Freedom Plaza at noon. #StopTheSteal https://t.co/EMEyKPKrXD	
14	Elizabeth Bartman of Drexel Hill, Pennsylvania registered to vote in September 2020 and cast a ballot in last week's election. Here's the problem: Elizabeth passed away 12 years ago, in 2008. Sadly, Elizabeth has become a victim of voter fraud. https://t.co/2qgJ9ssB8Z https://t.co/'FhNAAFTqS4	#OANN, #Wisconsin, #AbsenteeBallot, #VoterFraud,
	Mrs. Deborah Jean Christiansen of Roswell, Georgia was registered to vote on October 5. Then she voted in the election. The only problem? She passed away a year and a half ago, in May 2019. Sadly, Mrs. Christiansen is a victim of voter fraud. https://t.co/6UcJ7hqEui	
	Roderick Waltower of Detroit, Michigan voted in the November election. His absentee ballot application was received on June 23, and his ballot was returned on October 19.The only problem? He passed away 13 years ago, in 2007. Sadly, Mr. Waltower is a victim of voter fraud. https://t.co/6uHtPOEF86	
	President Trump's campaign accused four Georgia voters of fraud. Said they voted 'dead' in the presidential election. We tracked two of them down, alive well. We simply knocked on a door and 96-year-old Mrs. James Blalock answered. https://t.co/n9dLA70jJB https://t.co/10cbPJTXB0'	
	John H. Granahan of Allentown, Pennsylvania voted in the November election. The problem? He passed away in 2019. Mr. Granahan is a victim of voter fraud. https://t.co/2qgJ9ssB8Z https://t.co/5Ixji1Y5eG	

fraud and supporting the then-candidate and President Donald Trump[10]. Topic 14, on the other hand, consists of tweets alleging election fraud based on the calculation of dead voters in favor of Democratic candidate Joe Biden. At the time, Donald Trump made serious allegations that dead people votes were counted to manipulate the election results[11].

To analyze the representativeness of the topics in the tweets, we then examined the most shared tweets and hashtags for both topics as shown in Table 4. For Topic 7, it can be seen that the most retweeted tweets relate to calls for protests. In addition, hashtags such as #MillionMAGAMarch, which joins the group MAGA *Make America Great Again,* show that these user groups collaborate with groups that advocate extremist policies. As with Topic 14, the tweets

---

[10] https://www.cbc.ca/news/world/trump-supporters-washington-march-1.5802409.
[11] https://www.theguardian.com/us-news/2021/dec/28/donald-trump-georgia-2020-election-dead-people.

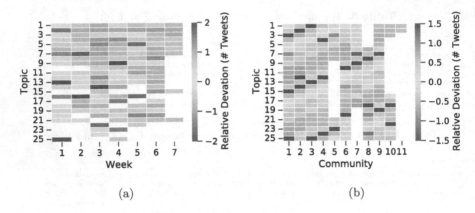

Fig. 2. (a) Distribution of topics across weeks; and (b) Distribution of tweets from communities into topics in $\Delta_t = 2$.

are representative. Moreover, a particular pattern can be observed. The tweets cite people's names, the days they voted, and the date of their deaths, suggesting fraud by the votes of the dead. However, many of the people cited were still alive at the time of the vote, according to news reports[12]. There is also some consistency in the hashtags used, where Topic 7 involving protest and Topic 14 involving fraud and a well-known pro-Trump channel such as the One America News Network[13] (OANN).

Having examined how topics emerge, we analyze how the discussion topics are distributed over the time period studied. The heatmap in Fig. 2a shows the distribution of discussion topics over the weeks. The x-axis represents the weeks and the y-axis represents the topics found. The rows are normalized by z-$score$[14] to analyze in which week a particular topic is more concentrated. The results show different patterns in the presence of topics during the analyzed period: (i) some topics (e.g., 5, 7, 9, 13, 14, 22, 23, and 25) are mainly discussed in specific weeks; (ii) others (e.g., 2 and 4) are concentrated in several weeks, not necessarily in sequence, coming and going over the weeks. (iii) some of them (e.g., 10, 15, 23, 24, and 25) are completely short-lived and are not discussed at all in some weeks; and (iv) finally, topics such as 1, 6, 11, 15, 18, and 19 are discussed with the same intensity in all weeks.

We then examine how the communities differ with respect to the topics they discuss. For this purpose, we choose the most representative week in terms of data volume, in this case $\Delta_t = 2$. Figure 2b shows a heatmap with communities on the x-axis and topics on the y-axis. Each cell shows the number of tweets posted by a given community on a given topic. Again, we normalize these values per row with the normalization z-score. In this way, we can examine the relative variation, i.e., the propensity of each community to post on a particular topic.

---

[12] https://www.bbc.com/news/election-us-2020-54874120.
[13] https://www.oann.com/.
[14] The z-score normalization is defined by $z = (x - \mu)/\sigma$.

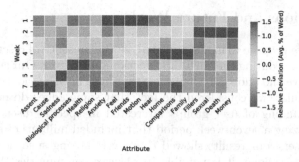

Fig. 3. Psycholinguistic characteristics of tweets related to discussion topics.

Note that the white cells indicate the absence of comments from a particular community on a topic. In general, we can see that some user communities show more interest in certain topics and share more content on certain topics. These results suggest that the discussion about election fraud was interesting to users because of certain content. Indeed, we observe similar patterns across all weeks, as explained before.

To analyze how the dynamics of the topics discussed affected the psycholinguistic properties of the discussions in general, we used LIWC to identify the most discriminative attributes in the analyzed period. Note that the definition of such attributes is based on the Gini index to identify those that vary most over time. Figure 3 shows a *heatmap* of the 18 most discriminatory attributes. Attributes are shown on the x-axis and weeks on the y-axis. Again, *z-score* normalization was performed to facilitate visualization and interpretation.

It is possible to observe the presence of groups of representative attributes over the weeks. For instance, in the first week analyzed, the attribute "Anxiety" was predominant, representing words related to worry and fear. We note that the election week belongs to such a week. Examining tweets with those attributes, we found that they reflected concern about political interference, contained exclamation points, and used the words "to keep alert" several times. Week 2, filled with tweets that included textual "Fillers" (*dunno, blah, I don't know, I mean, oh well, you know*), "Sexual" (*fuck, fucker, fucking*), and "Death" (e.g. *die, died, dies, ghost,* and *grief*) reflect allegations of fraud due to dead votes after voting began and votes were later counted. We also examined Week 6, which had as the most discriminatory attribute "Sadness" (*cry, grief, sad*), which referred to tweets whose sentiment was outrage at the Republican candidate's defeat, often claiming that Donald Trump did not lose and that voter fraud was responsible for that outcome. In summary, we note that the way accusations of fraud were discussed varied during the observed period. Earlier, for example, votes from dead people were not discussed. Later, when votes were counted, these and other dimensions were explored.

5 Conclusions and Future Work

In this paper, we propose to model and analyze the presence of discussion groups about fraud claims during the 2020 U.S. election on Twitter. Our study provides a new perspective and addresses challenges that have been overlooked in previous work. In particular, we considered the fact that some edges do not contribute to the understanding of user groups interested in specific discussions on the topic. By analyzing a seven-week period that included millions of retweets from thousands of users, our results showed that by removing such noise edges and extracting the backbone, it is possible to observe communities that are much better structured than in the original network. We also found that the tweets shared by users in these communities have up to twenty-five discussion topics that attract them in groups. Regarding the content of the topics, we unveiled that the psycholinguistic elements related to the fraud allegations changed during the analyzed period, possibly due to the dissemination strategies.

As future work, we plan to analyze the temporal relationship between the communities and topics, as both evolve together. We also intend to look for evidence of coordinated behavior in the dissemination of fake news about election fraud. Another avenue that deserves attention is to study the effects of using combined null models, i.e., backbone and modularity.

Acknowledgments. We thank the Voter Fraud Project and Abilov et al. [1] for providing the data to support our work.

Appendix I

Table 5. Keywords, description and external links related to the extracted topics.

Topic	Key Words	Contextualization	External Links
1	'fraud', 'election', 'media', 'voter', 'evidence', 'Trump'	General allegations and alleged evidence of fraud in the 2020 United States presidential election.	[1], [2], [3]
2	'fraud', 'election', 'Georgia', 'Michigan', 'county' 'ballots', 'voter', 'Nevada', 'live', 'hearing' 'Arizona', 'watch'	Allegations of fraud in various locations in the U.S. and dissemination of Arizona State Senate Hearing on Election Fraud.	[1], [2] [3],
3	'blow', 'gamechanger', 'minds', 'bam', 'see', 'watch', 'disgusted', 'outrageous', 'massive', 'awesome', 'thank'	A set of links about election fraud shared with attention-grabbing words	-
4	'DOJ', 'FBI', 'reported', 'fraud', 'department', 'bill', 'election' 'investigation', 'voter', 'account', 'spokesperson' 'affirmative', 'incorrectly','Lois' 'Lerner'	The U.S. Department of Justice (DOJ) concludes that there is no evidence of election fraud and claims that Christopher Wray would become director of FBI if Biden won the election, so FBI and the DOJ would treat the alleged election fraud with carelessness and hound conservatives.	[1], [2], [3]
5	'Biden', 'states', 'Joe', 'Trump', 'votes', 'democrats', 'fraud', 'country', 'night', 'election', 'elect', 'middle', 'bank'	Allegations that thousands of votes were stolen/suspended in Georgia in the middle of the night. Other allegations of alleged election fraud, requests for recounts, and attacks on the integrity of the election as a whole.	[1]

(*continued*)

Table 1. (*continued*)

Topic	Key Words	Contextualization	External Links
6	'Twitter', 'election', 'censoring', 'warning', 'suspended', 'Joe', 'interference' 'Col' 'content', 'Youtube', 'tweet', 'loading', 'fraud', 'legal', 'Biden', 'big', 'tech'	Accusation of election interference by 'big' 'techs' due to suspension of 'COLonel' Douglas McGregor on Twitter.	[1]
7	'stopthesteal', 'DD', 'Washington', 'join', 'tomorrow' 'freedom', 'plaza' 'capitol', 'noon', '14th', 'congressman' , 'millionmagamarch', 'excited' 'sat', 'womenfortrump' 'marchfortrump', 'nov', 'building', 'late'	Demonstrations demanding a halt to the vote count due to allegations of fraud and the organisation of a pro-Trump march leaving Freedom Plaza.	[1], [2], [3]
8	'dominion', 'voting', 'machines', 'hacked', 'companies', 'used', 'election', 'pervasive', 'americafirst', 'maga', 'dobbs', 'smartmatic', 'systems', 'intentionally'	Accusations against the "Dominion Voting" system and "Smartmatic" (systems for calculating ballots) that they were programmed for election fraud.	[1], [2]
9	'Giuliani', 'Rudy', 'breaks', 'revealed', 'pervasive', 'fraud', 'Spain', 'dept', 'sworn', 'dod', 'company', 'defense', 'evidence', 'stopped', 'election', 'case'	Statements by Rudy Giuliani, former mayor of New York, alleging the existence of voter fraud.	[1]
10	'Sidney', 'Powell', 'released', 'massive', 'attorney', 'breaking', 'election', 'kraken', 'complaint', 'fraud', 'bombshell', 'Georgia'	Alleged evidence by attorney and former prosecutor Sidney Powell about alleged fraud in the election and her attempt to invalidate the election.	[1]
11	'Graham', 'Lindsey', 'stolen', 'chairmanship', 'Georgia' 'illegally', 'complain', 'cared', 'broke', 'gop', 'pressuring', 'election', 'officials', 'care', 'silence'	Alleged abuse of power by Lindsey Graham, senator from North Caroline and allegations of manipulation of the election in Georgia.	[1]
12	'stopthesteal', 'unprecedented', 'wrong', 'everything', 'millionmagamarch' 'activity', 'Joaquin', 'flagrant' 'marchfortrump', 'phoenix', 'coming'	Topic dominated by the associated words the accusation of fraud.	[1], [2]
13	'hotline', 'calls', 'bog', 'spamming', 'voter', 'receiving', 'complaints', 'prank', 'thousands', 'night', 'hide', 'heroic'	Discussions about prank phone hotline set up by Trump campaign to report election fraud	[1], [2]
14	'victim', 'voted', 'Elizabeth', 'ballot', 'Christiansen' 'waltower', 'skwiot' '2019', 'year', 'died', 'voter'	Alleged election fraud from dead votes.	[1]
15	'instance', 'single', 'raise', 'court', 'tampering', 'Lindsey', 'Graham', 'election', 'fraud'	Demand that Senator Lindsey Graham be investigated for possible election interference.	[1]
16	'charged', 'fraudulent', 'applications', 'registration' 'submitted', 'behalf' 'California', 'laremind', 'voter', 'alleges', 'complaint', 'allegedly', 'criminal', 'social'	Accusations of electoral fraud from the addition of fraudulent votes.	[1]
17	'Patrick', 'reward', 'Dan', 'Texas', 'gov', 'million', 'offers', 'bigfoot', 'voter', 'governor', 'fraud' 'handsome', 'collect',	Lieutenant Governor Dan Patrick offers $1 million for evidence of election fraud.	[1]
18	'Fox', 'news', 'Jeanine', 'Pirro', 'newsmax', 'stirewalt', 'cancelled', 'fire', 'msnbc', 'Chris', 'sue', 'tonight', 'cnn', 'video', 'Trump'	Accusations of election interference by the Fox TV channel, for canceling the broadcast of anchorwoman Jeanine Pirro, who was supposed to present evidence of election fraud.	[1]
19	'signature', 'match', 'real', 'absentee', 'matching', 'margin', 'cycle', 'ballots', 'ignored', 'verification' 'victory', 'illegal'	Allegations of fraud by envelopes with ballots without valid signatures.	[1]
20	'americafirst', 'maga', 'algorithms', 'news', 'lawsuit' 'widespread', 'Georgia', 'detected', 'designed', 'firsthand'	Topic on legal action on new evidence of election fraud through the use of Smartmatic software.	[1]
21	'foreign', 'interference', 'intelligence', 'date', 'tuned', 'report', 'order', 'national', 'plan', 'disgusting', 'fall', 'director' 'sound' 'gov'	Accusation of foreign interference in the election.	[1]
22	'physical', 'impossibility', 'results', 'Michigan', 'ramsland', 'russ', 'election', 'fraud'	Accusations of "physical impossibility" to count the votes of the election in Michigan.	[1]
23	'Khait', 'Anna', 'Couch', 'scytl', 'Matt', 'software' 'America', 'amp', 'voter'	Disclosure of allegations of fraud in a live broadcast led by Matt Couch and Anna Khait in the software used to count the votes.	[1], [2], [3]
24	'Monica', 'Palmer', 'Abraham', 'Aiyash', 'extortion', 'threatened', 'waynecounty', 'democrat', 'breaking', 'intimidating', 'arrested'	It is alleged that politician Abraham Aiyash threatened the family of Monica Palmer, who worked in the elections, to get her to agree to the alleged fraud.	[1]
25	'priority', 'locks', 'navy', 'blatant', 'account' 'American', 'Twitter', 'video', 'breaking', 'president', 'Georgia', 'ballots', 'voter', 'fraud' 'block', 'fake'	Suspension of accounts of supporters of former U.S. President Donald Trump for spreading fake news of flagrant voter fraud of Navy ballots in Georgia.	[1]

References

1. Abilov, A., Hua, Y., Matatov, H., Amir, O., Naaman, M.: Voterfraud 2020: a multi-modal dataset of election fraud claims on twitter. In: Proceedings of the International AAAI Conference on Web and Social Media, vol. 15, pp. 901–912 (2021)

2. Altamirano, M., et al.: Unsupervised characterization of lessons according to temporal patterns of teacher talk via topic modeling. Neurocomputing **484**, 211–222 (2022)
3. Blondel, V.D., Guillaume, J.L., Lambiotte, R., Lefebvre, E.: Fast unfolding of communities in large networks. J. Stat. Mech: Theory Exp. **2008**(10), P10008 (2008)
4. Cann, T.J., Weaver, I.S., Williams, H.T.: Ideological biases in social sharing of online information about climate change. PLoS ONE **16**(4), e0250656 (2021)
5. Chaudhry, H.N., Javed, Y., Kulsoom, F., Mehmood, Z., Khan, Z.I., Shoaib, U., Janjua, S.H.: Sentiment analysis of before and after elections: Twitter data of us election 2020. Electronics **10**(17), 2082 (2021)
6. Childs, M.C., Buntain, C., Trujillo, M.Z., Horne, B.D.: Characterizing Youtube and Bitchute content and mobilizers during us election fraud discussions on twitter. In: ACM Conference on Web Science (2022)
7. Chowdhury, F.A., Saha, D., Hasan, M.R., Saha, K., Mueen, A.: Examining factors associated with twitter account suspension following the 2020 us presidential election. arXiv preprint arXiv:2101.09575 (2021)
8. Coscia, M., Neffke, F.M.: Network backboning with noisy data. In: 2017 IEEE 33rd International Conference on Data Engineering (ICDE), pp. 425–436. IEEE (2017)
9. Dai, Y.: Using 2020 U.S. Presidential election to study patterns of user influence, community formation and behaviors on twitter. Ph.D. thesis, The Pennsylvania State University (2021)
10. Devlin, J., Chang, M.W., Lee, K., Toutanova, K.: BERT: pre-training of deep bidirectional transformers for language understanding. In: Proceedings of the 2019 Conference of the North American Chapter of the Association for Computational Linguistics: Human Language Technologies, Volume 1 (Long and Short Papers). Association for Computational Linguistics, Minneapolis, Minnesota, June 2019
11. Ebeling, R., Sáenz, C.A.C., Nobre, J., Becker, K.: The effect of political polarization on social distance stances in the brazilian covid-19 scenario. J. Inf. Data Manage. **12**(1) (2021)
12. Ebeling, R., Sáenz, C.A.C., Nobre, J.C., Becker, K.: Analysis of the influence of political polarization in the vaccination stance: the Brazilian Covid-19 scenario. In: Proceedings of the International AAAI Conference on Web and Social Media, vol. 16, pp. 159–170 (2022)
13. Egger, R., Yu, J.: A topic modeling comparison between LDA, NMF, Top2Vec, and BERTopic to demystify twitter posts. Front. Soc. **7** (2022)
14. Ferrara, E., Chang, H., Chen, E., Muric, G., Patel, J.: Characterizing social media manipulation in the 2020 us presidential election. First Monday (2020)
15. Ferreira, C.H.G., Ferreira, F.M., de Sousa Matos, B., de Almeida, J.M.: Modeling dynamic ideological behavior in political networks. J. Web Sci. **7** (2019)
16. Ferreira, C.H., et al.: On the dynamics of political discussions on Instagram: a network perspective. Online So. Netw. Media **25**, 100155 (2021)
17. Finn, S., Mustafaraj, E., Metaxas, P.T.: The co-retweeted network and its applications for measuring the perceived political polarization (2014)
18. Freelon, D., Lokot, T.: Russian twitter disinformation campaigns reach across the American political spectrum. Misinformation Rev. (2020)
19. Fudolig, M.I., Alshaabi, T., Arnold, M.V., Danforth, C.M., Dodds, P.S.: Sentiment and structure in word co-occurrence networks on twitter. Appl. Netw. Sci. **7**(1), 1–27 (2022)

20. Gallagher, R.J., Reagan, A.J., Danforth, C.M., Dodds, P.S.: Divergent discourse between protests and counter-protests:# blacklivesmatter and# alllivesmatter. PLoS ONE **13**(4), e0195644 (2018)
21. Gomes Ferreira, C.H., et al.: Unveiling community dynamics on Instagram political network. In: 12th ACM Conference on Web Science, pp. 231–240 (2020)
22. Gomes Ferreira, C.H., de Sousa Matos, B., Almeira, J.M.: Analyzing dynamic ideological communities in congressional voting networks. In: Staab, S., Koltsova, O., Ignatov, D.I. (eds.) SocInfo 2018. LNCS, vol. 11185, pp. 257–273. Springer, Cham (2018). https://doi.org/10.1007/978-3-030-01129-1_16
23. Grimminger, L., Klinger, R.: Hate towards the political opponent: a twitter corpus study of the 2020 US elections on the basis of offensive speech and stance detection. In: Workshop on Computational Approaches to Subjectivity, Sentiment and Social Media Analysis (2021)
24. Grootendorst, M.: Bertopic: Leveraging Bert and C-TF-IDF to create easily interpretable topics. (2020). https://doi.org/10.5281/zenodo.4381785
25. Grootendorst, M.: Bertopic: Neural topic modeling with a class-based TF-IDF procedure. arXiv preprint arXiv:2203.05794 (2022)
26. Guerrero-Solé, F.: Community detection in political discussions on twitter: an application of the retweet overlap network method to the Catalan process toward independence. Soc. Sci. Comput. Rev. **35**(2), 244–261 (2017)
27. Malagoli, L.G., Stancioli, J., Ferreira, C.H., Vasconcelos, M., Couto da Silva, A.P., Almeida, J.M.: A look into Covid-19 vaccination debate on twitter. In: 13th ACM Web Science Conference 2021, pp. 225–233 (2021)
28. McInnes, L., Healy, J., Saul, N., Großberger, L.: Umap: uniform manifold approximation and projection. J. Open Source Softw. **3**(29), 861 (2018)
29. Metaxas, P., Mustafaraj, E., Wong, K., Zeng, L., O'Keefe, M., Finn, S.: What do retweets indicate? results from user survey and meta-review of research. In: Proceedings of the International AAAI Conference on Web and Social Media (2015)
30. Newman, M.E., Girvan, M.: Finding and evaluating community structure in networks. Phys. Rev. E **69**, 026113 (2004)
31. Nobre, G.P., Ferreira, C.H.G., Almeida, J.M.: Beyond groups: uncovering dynamic communities on the WhatsApp network of information dissemination. In: Aref, S., et al. (eds.) SocInfo 2020. LNCS, vol. 12467, pp. 252–266. Springer, Cham (2020). https://doi.org/10.1007/978-3-030-60975-7_19
32. Nobre, G.P., Ferreira, C.H., Almeida, J.M.: A hierarchical network-oriented analysis of user participation in misinformation spread on Whatsapp. Inf. Process. Manage. **59**(1), 102757 (2022)
33. Pacheco, D., Hui, P.M., Torres-Lugo, C., Truong, B.T., Flammini, A., Menczer, F.: Uncovering coordinated networks on social media: methods and case studies. Int. AAAI Conf. Web Soc. Media **21**, 455–466 (2021)
34. Pennebaker, J.W., Boyd, R.L., Jordan, K., Blackburn, K.: The development and psychometric properties of liwc2015. Technical Report (2015)
35. Rahimi, A., Cohn, T., Baldwin, T.: Twitter user geolocation using a unified text and network prediction model. In: Proceedings of the 53rd Annual Meeting of the Association for Computational Linguistics (2015)
36. Reimers, N., Gurevych, I.: Sentence-bert: Sentence embeddings using siamese bert-networks. In: Proceedings of the 2019 Conference on Empirical Methods in Natural Language Processing and the 9th International Joint Conference on Natural Language Processing (EMNLP-IJCNLP), pp. 3982–3992 (2019)

37. Resende, G., Melo, P., CS Reis, J., Vasconcelos, M., Almeida, J.M., Benevenuto, F.: Analyzing textual (mis) information shared in Whatsapp groups. In: Proceedings of the 10th ACM Conference on Web Science, pp. 225–234 (2019)
38. Sharma, K., Ferrara, E., Liu, Y.: Characterizing online engagement with disinformation and conspiracies in the 2020 U.S. presidential election. In: International Conference on Web and Social Media (2022)
39. Tausczik, Y.R., Pennebaker, J.W.: The psychological meaning of words: LIWC and computerized text analysis methods. J. Lang. Soc. Psychol. **29**(1), 24–54 (2010)
40. Tran, H.D.: Studying the community of trump supporters on twitter during the 2020 us presidential election via hashtags# maga and# trump2020. Journalism Media **2**(4), 709–731 (2021)
41. Xia, E., Yue, H., Liu, H.: Tweet sentiment analysis of the 2020 us presidential election. In: Proceedings of the Web Conference 2021, pp. 367–371 (2021)
42. Yitzhaki, S.: Relative deprivation and the Gini coefficient. Q. J. Econ. 321–324 (1979)
43. Zannettou, S.: I won the election!: An empirical analysis of soft moderation interventions on twitter. In: International AAAI Conference on Web and Social Media, pp. 865–876 (2021)

Online Social Integration and Depressive Symptoms in Adolescents

Elizaveta Sivak[✉][iD], Ivan Smirnov[iD], and Yulia Dementeva[iD]

Institute of Education, National Research University Higher School of Economics,
Moscow, Russia
elizaveta.sivak@gmail.com, ibsmirnov@hse.ru

Abstract. Social integration is known to be beneficial for mental health. However, it is not clear whether this applies to online as well as offline relationships. In this paper, we explore the association between online friendship and symptoms of depression among adolescents. We combine data from the popular social networking site with survey data on high school students ($N = 144$) and find that integration into the online network is a protective factor against depression. We also find that not all online connections are equally important: friendship ties with students from the same schools are stronger associated with depression than outside ties. In addition to friendship ties, we explore the effect of online interaction ("likes"). Overall, our results suggest that online relationships are associated with depression as well as offline friendship. However, the effect of more distant online connections is limited, while immediate social environment and peer relationships at school are more important.

Keywords: Adolescents · Depression · Digital traces · Online social integration · Psychological well-being · Social media · Social networks

1 Introduction

Social integration is vital to an individual's well-being. People who have stronger social networks are healthier [1–3] and live longer [4]. They are also less likely to be depressed [5–8]. Association between social ties and psychological well-being is well established and dates back to Durkheim's work on suicides [9].

Social environment is especially important in adolescence, as during this period of life adolescents start to spend more time in peer groups and the developmental significance of peers increases [10,11]. Based on various measures of social integration, previous research has shown that integration promotes adolescents' mental health. Protective factors associated with lower risks of depressive mood or depression include feeling connected to parents, peers, or school [12], a larger number of friends [13], and high social network centrality [14]. Adolescents who are less socially integrated have more internalizing problems, which are common among depressed children [15]. During the COVID-19 crisis, isolation in social networks and lack of interaction and emotional support were associated with negative mental health trajectories [16].

F. Hopfgartner et al. (Eds.): SocInfo 2022, LNCS 13618, pp. 337–346, 2022.
https://doi.org/10.1007/978-3-031-19097-1_21

As people increasingly use social networking sites (SNSs) for communication and maintaining friendship, researchers focus on online social integration – size and properties of online friendship networks and intensity of online contacts. It is yet not clear whether online interactions are beneficial for well-being as well as offline social ties. Previous research has shown that online social integration is linked to reduced mortality risk from the causes that are strongly related to social factors such as drug overdose and suicide but not from other causes such as cancer [17]. Online integration may enhance access to various forms of support and produce positive psychological states like a sense of belonging and self-worth, which in turn protect against distress [18]. Even though a friendship on SNS does not necessarily involve a close connection [19], a large number of online friends could remind users of their social ties and boost their self-esteem [20]. Users who have more online friends should be more likely to receive likes or comments, which are considered a symbolic token of social approval, inclusion, and support [21–23], and elicit feelings of validation, conferring positive status and regard, and thus leads to positive emotions [24,25]. Therefore, embeddedness in a large online social network may lower the risk of developing depressive symptoms.

There is evidence that social connectedness on SNSs is related to lower levels of depression and anxiety [26] and higher subjective well-being [27]. Larger networks and larger estimated audiences predicted higher levels of life satisfaction and perceived social support on Facebook [19], which in turn is associated with reduced stress and greater well-being [28]. Receiving more likes and comments was linked to greater self-esteem and happiness [23].

On the other hand, on SNSs, the probability of unflattering social comparisons increases, because comparison information, e.g. number of friends or "likes" which may serve as status and popularity cues [29], is more salient than offline [30–32] and the presented information is positively skewed [33–36].

In turn, negative social comparison on SNS is related to higher levels of emotional distress and depression [30,37–39]. This supports the hypothesis, which is based on the relative social evaluation theories of depression, that the SNSs' users may be the more susceptible to causal triggers for depression if they have a large number of online friends [29]. Larger online networks might mean more opportunities for negative social comparisons.

In this paper, we explore how online social integration is associated with depression symptoms of high school students. We measure social integration using the properties of the ego network (its overall size and the size of the densest part of the network) and the intensity of online communication. The study was conducted among students of one high school in Moscow, Russia. We used self-reported depression symptoms, information about friendship obtained using name generator, and data from the popular social networking site VK on online friendship and interactions. We studied the associations between symptoms of depression and 1) the number of online friends and structural properties of a person's network, 2) online interactions - the number of received and sent "likes". We also measure the changes in the strength of the association between "likes" (intensity of communication) and depression.

2   Methods

2.1   Participants and Procedures

The study was conducted among students of one high school in Moscow, Russia. The study was approved by the Institutional Review Board. Participation was voluntary. Students from 10th and 11th grades (16–17 years old) were informed about the study and the opportunity to participate. The researchers held group meetings with all students who self-selected to participate, in which they explained the aims of the study and what data would be collected. All participants who decided to participate, as well as one of their parents, signed an informed consent form. Students were informed that their participation was voluntary and that they could stop participation at any time and request to delete the collected data (there were no such requests to date).

The study took place over a 4-month period (November 2017–February 2018). Participants were asked to fill out an online survey at the beginning and at the end of this period. Students could participate in the survey at their own time. Both waves included items that measure depression. In the baseline survey, participants were also asked about friendship. The baseline survey was filled out by 144 students (81% girls), the endline by 78 students. Public data were gathered from profiles on VK with the participants' consent.

2.2   Measures

Depression. We used the Patient Health Questionnaire scale (PHQ-9), which is used to assess the severity of depressive symptoms [40][1]. The scale has been shown to be a valid tool in detecting depression among adolescents across various cultures [41–45].

We measured depressive symptoms twice. The test-retest reliability coefficient is 0.73 ($P < 10^{-11}$). In the analysis, we used results of the first measurement, as it has fewer missing values. According to the PHQ-9 scale, 10% of the sample had no symptoms of depression (scored 0–4), 41% exhibited mild symptoms (5–9), 26% moderate (10–14), 11.5% moderately severe (15–19), and 11.5% severe (20–27). These rates seem unusually high: previous studies that used PHQ-9 to measure depression among middle and high school students reported the prevalence of moderately severe/severe depression to be 5–9% [41,42,46,47]. In Russia, there is not enough data on the prevalence of depressive symptoms in adolescents to compare our results to. We attribute this high rate to the fact that lower rates are reported for middle and high school students (11–17 years old) while we focus only on high school students. They are 16–17 years old which is the age when the onset for depressive illnesses peaks [48]. They are also preparing for their final exams and are under high academic pressure. Moreover, the school where the study was conducted is highly selective and partners with a university: once a week students attend classes of their choice at the university. Given all this, the more appropriate reference group might be university

---

[1] https://www.phqscreeners.com/

students. For that group, the reported depression prevalence is 10–85% with a weighted mean prevalence of 30.6% [49].

Because of the high rate of students with moderately severe and severe depressive symptoms according to conventional thresholds, we use PHQ-9 severity score as a continuous variable. This severity score is known to be strongly associated with other indicators of depression and mental health, and also with the different aspects of health-related quality of life and can be used in addition to the categorical diagnostic groups [50].

Online Social Integration. We used several measures of online integration. For each participant, we measured the degree to which an individual is connected to other individuals in a network, i.e. the number of "friends" they had on VK a) among those who studied at the same school and b) overall. The majority of the participants have no more than 250 online friends overall (see Fig. 1), while several participants have more than a thousand online friends (not shown in the figure).

We also measure the intensity of communication as the number of "likes" participants received per post a) overall, b) from students from the same school. Unlike an almost static friendship network (once added, friends are rarely deleted), likes have a temporal dimension, i.e. it is possible to infer when the like was received. This allows us to look at the relationship between the number of likes and symptoms of depression at the time of the measurement of depression and before that (six months before the data collection).

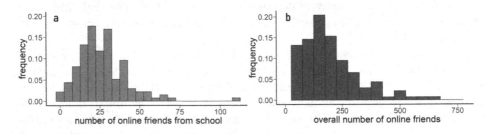

Fig. 1. The distribution of the number of online friends a) from the same school, b) overall. The median number of online friends is 22 and 157, respectively.

Finally, to understand the potential role of closely interconnected communities, we measure the size of k-core (k-core number), where k-core is the maximal subgraph in which each node has at least k connections to other nodes in the subgraph [51], or the size of the largest close-knit part of a student's network.

To compute a k-core number, the information on the whole school online network is needed. For that, we automatically select all users who indicated on VK that they are studying at the school. This includes both participants and non-participants of the study. We then collect the list of all friends of these users. We anonymized information on any non-participant and analyzed the resulting network. The size of this whole school online network is 670 students (46% of the total number of students in the school). We then computed a k-core number for each person's ego network including only their VK friends from the same school.

Offline Social Integration. We used a number of friends from the same school as a measure of offline social integration. Data on offline friendships were collected using a single name generator. In the survey, participants were asked to indicate up to 10 other students from the same school whom they considered friends. Since the sample included only 10% of all students at the school from different classes, we used unilateral friendship nominations as indicators of friendship, i.e. if at least one person named another as a friend, we considered them friends.

3   Results

We find that a higher number of offline friends is associated with severity of depressive symptoms (Pearson's $r = -0.295$; $P = 0.002$; 95% CI $[-0.461, -0.110]$). By contrast, a total number of friends on VK is not correlated with depression severity ($r = -0.096$; $P = 0.315$; 95% CI $[-0.277, 0.091]$). One potential reason is that friendship on a social networking site does not necessarily indicate a strong social connection. It is even possible to be "friends" on a social networking site without actually knowing each other.

If we consider separately the number of friends on VK from the same school and not from the same school, we find that the number of online friends from the same school is correlated with depressive symptoms ($r = -0.209$; $P = 0.028$; 95% CI $[-0.381, -0.023]$) while the number of online friends outside the school is not correlated ($r = -0.084$; $P = 0.379$; 95% CI $[-0.266, 0.103]$). Note that given the small sample size it is impossible to definitively conclude that there is no correlation between the number of online friends outside the school and depression (or between the total number of online friends and depression). However, our results suggest that even if this correlation exists it is significantly weaker than the correlation between depression and the number of friends from the school.

This result might be explained by the important role of the school's local peer community in the structure of adolescent social relations. It is the immediate social environment that a person interacts with on a daily basis. A small number of friends on VK from the same school may be a signal of unpopularity or peer rejection in this major social arena, which can threaten psychological well-being.

Research shows that it is not only the size of adolescents' social network that matters but also belonging to cohesive peer groups [52], relationships with which increase markedly in intensity and significance during adolescence [10]. We analyzed how the size of the largest close-knit group to which the person belongs (k-core number) is associated with depression symptoms.

We find that depressive symptoms are correlated with k-core number ($r = -0.204$; $P = 0.032$; 95% CI $[-0, 377, -0, 018]$) for a person's ego network of their

VK friends from the same school. So, the smaller is the dense part of a person's ego network the higher the severity of depressive symptoms. This suggests that it is not the total number of dyadic online relationships that matters but also belonging to a tightly-knit online community.

In addition to online friendship, we consider the intensity of communication in which students engage on the platform, namely exchange of likes. Instead of the total amount of received likes we consider the number of likes per post as a measure of the intensity of communication. This was necessary as people with more pronounced symptoms of depression on average write more posts ($r = 0.270$; $P = 0.006$; 95% CI $[0.076, 0.445]$)[2]. The same has been previously observed in other social networking sites such as Facebook [53,54].

We find that at the time of data collection there is a significant correlation: participants with a higher depression score receive on average less likes per post than participants with lower score ($r = -0.31$; $P = 0.005$; 95% CI $[-0.49; -0.10]$). Consistent with the previous results, the association between the number of likes received from online friends outside the school is weaker and does not reach statistical threshold ($r = -0.191$; $P = 0.067$; 95% CI $[-0.38; 0.01]$). However, six month before the data collection the correlation is non-significant ($r = -0.017$, $P = 0.899$, 95% CI $[-0.28; 0.25]$).

Thus, consistent with the expectations, the association between likes and depression symptoms is not constant and becomes weaker at time point more distant from the moment of depression measurement.

4   Conclusions

The Internet creates unique opportunities for people to connect to each other. Therefore, it might be vastly beneficial for users' psychological well-being as social ties are known to buffer against depression and other mental health issues. However, it is not yet clear whether online interactions are as beneficial for well-being as offline social ties.

In this paper, we have studied associations between online social integration and depressive symptoms in adolescents. We find that the total number of online social ties and the number of online friends outside the school is not associated with depression score. By contrast, online integration into a tightly-knit online community is a protective factor against depression. For school students, this community is online friends from the same school.

SNSs facilitate expansive social networks that grow disproportionately via distant kinds of relationships [19]. Our results suggest that this expansion of connections may be less beneficial and important in terms of mental well-being than online interactions with people from closer social groups. However, given the small sample size, it is impossible to conclude that these distant relationships are not important at all. Further studies are needed to clarify this question.

---

[2] Because of the skewed distribution, the number of post was log-transformed.

The relationship between depression and social integration is temporal in nature because both depression symptoms and social interactions are not constant over time. We have demonstrated that digital traces could facilitate studying this relationship when longitudinal survey data is not available. Specifically, we have employed information on the exchange of likes and have found that the association between the number of likes and depressive symptoms weakens further from the moment of measuring depression. This result could inform future research on the influence of online social integration on psychological well-being.

Acknowledgements. This work was supported by a grant from the Russian Science Foundation (project №19-18-00271).

References

1. Ford, E.S., Ahluwalia, I.B., Galuska, D.A.: Social relationships and cardiovascular disease risk factors: findings from the third national health and nutrition examination survey. Prev. Med. **30**(2), 83–92 (2000)
2. House, J.S., Landis, K.R., Umberson, D.: Social relationships and health. Science **241**(4865), 540–545 (1988)
3. Umberson, D., Crosnoe, R., Reczek, C.: Social relationships and health behavior across the life course. Ann. Rev. Sociol. **36**, 139–157 (2010)
4. Holt-Lunstad, J., Smith, T.B., Layton, J.B.: Social relationships and mortality risk: a meta-analytic review. PLoS Med. **7**(7), e1000316 (2010)
5. Berkman, L.F.: The role of social relations in health promotion. Psychosom. Med. **57**(3), 245–254 (1995)
6. Seeman, T.E.: Social ties and health: the benefits of social integration. Ann. Epidemiol. **6**(5), 442–451 (1996)
7. Thoits, P.A.: Mechanisms linking social ties and support to physical and mental health. J. Health Soc. Behav. **52**(2), 145–161 (2011)
8. Rosenquist, J.N., Fowler, J.H., Christakis, N.A.: Social network determinants of depression. Mol. Psychiatry **16**(3), 273–281 (2011)
9. Durkheim, E.: (1951) Suicide. Free Press, New York (1897)
10. Brown, B.B., Larson, J., Lerner, R.M., Steinberg, L.: Handbook of Adolescent Psychology. Adolescents' Relationships with Peers, 2nd edn., pp. 363–394. Wiley, Hoboken (2004)
11. Rubin, K.H., Bukowski, W.M., Parker, J.G.: Peer Interactions, Relationships, and Groups. Handbook of Child Psychology, vol. 3 (2007)
12. Costello, D.M., Swendsen, J., Rose, J.S., Dierker, L.C.: Risk and protective factors associated with trajectories of depressed mood from adolescence to early adulthood. J. Consult. Clin. Psychol. **76**(2), 173 (2008)
13. Ueno, K.: The effects of friendship networks on adolescent depressive symptoms. Soc. Sci. Res. **34**(3), 484–510 (2005)
14. Okamoto, J., et al.: Social network status and depression among adolescents: an examination of social network influences and depressive symptoms in a Chinese sample. Res. Hum. Dev. **8**(1), 67–88 (2011)
15. Liu, J., Chen, X., Lewis, G.: Childhood internalizing behaviour: analysis and implications. J. Psychiatr. Ment. Health Nurs. **18**(10), 884–894 (2011)

16. Elmer, T., Mepham, K., Stadtfeld, C.: Students under lockdown: comparisons of students' social networks and mental health before and during the Covid-19 crisis in Switzerland. PLoS ONE 15(7), e0236337 (2020)
17. Hobbs, W.R., Burke, M., Christakis, N.A., Fowler, J.H.: Online social integration is associated with reduced mortality risk. Proc. Natl. Acad. Sci. 113(46), 12980–12984 (2016)
18. Berkman, L., Kawachi, I.: Social ties and mental health. J. Urban Health 78(3), 458–467 (2001)
19. Manago, A.M., Taylor, T., Greenfield, P.M.: Me and my 400 friends: the anatomy of college students' Facebook networks, their communication patterns, and well-being. Dev. Psychol. 48(2), 369 (2012)
20. Gonzales, A.L., Hancock, J.T.: Mirror, mirror on my Facebook wall: effects of exposure to Facebook on self-esteem. Cyberpsychol. Behav. Soc. Netw. 14(1–2), 79–83 (2011)
21. Martinez-Pecino, R., Garcia-Gavilán, M.: Likes and problematic Instagram use: the moderating role of self-esteem. Cyberpsychol. Behav. Soc. Netw. 22(6), 412–416 (2019)
22. Mascheroni, G., Vincent, J., Jimenez, E.: "Girls are Addicted to Likes So they Post Semi-naked Selfies": peer mediation, normativity and the construction of identity online. Cyberpsychol. J. Psychosoc. Res. Cyberspace 9(1), 5 (2015)
23. Zell, A.L., Moeller, L.: Are you happy for me... on Facebook? The potential importance of "likes" and comments. Comput. Hum. Behav. 78, 26–33 (2018)
24. Davey, C.G., Allen, N.B., Harrison, B.J., Dwyer, D.B., Yücel, M.: Being liked activates primary reward and midline self-related brain regions. Hum. Brain Mapp. 31(4), 660–668 (2010)
25. Gunther Moor, B., van Leijenhorst, L., Rombouts, S.A., Crone, E.A., Van der Molen, M.W.: Do you like me? Neural correlates of social evaluation and developmental trajectories. Soc. Neurosci. 5(5–6), 461–482 (2010)
26. Seabrook, E.M., Kern, M.L., Rickard, N.S.: Social networking sites, depression, and anxiety: a systematic review. JMIR Mental Health 3(4), e5842 (2016)
27. Kim, J., Lee, J.E.R.: The Facebook paths to happiness: effects of the number of Facebook friends and self-presentation on subjective well-being. Cyberpsychol. Behav. Soc. Netw. 14(6), 359–364 (2011)
28. Nabi, R.L., Prestin, A., So, J.: Facebook friends with (health) benefits? Exploring social network site use and perceptions of social support, stress, and well-being. Cyberpsychol. Behav. Soc. Netw. 16(10), 721–727 (2013)
29. Blease, C.: Too many 'friends', too few 'likes'? Evolutionary psychology and 'facebook depression'. Rev. Gen. Psychol. 19(1), 1–13 (2015)
30. Appel, H., Gerlach, A.L., Crusius, J.: The interplay between Facebook use, social comparison, envy, and depression. Curr. Opin. Psychol. 9, 44–49 (2016)
31. Haferkamp, N., Eimler, S.C., Papadakis, A.M., Kruck, J.V.: Men are from Mars, women are from Venus? Examining gender differences in self-presentation on social networking sites. Cyberpsychol. Behav. Soc. Netw. 15(2), 91–98 (2012)
32. Vogel, E.A., Rose, J.P., Roberts, L.R., Eckles, K.: Social comparison, social media, and self-esteem. Psychol. Pop. Media Cult. 3(4), 206 (2014)
33. Jordan, A.H., Monin, B., Dweck, C.S., Lovett, B.J., John, O.P., Gross, J.J.: Misery has more company than people think: underestimating the prevalence of others' negative emotions. Pers. Soc. Psychol. Bull. 37(1), 120–135 (2011)
34. Chou, H.T.G., Edge, N.: "They are happier and having better lives than i am": the impact of using Facebook on perceptions of others' lives. Cyberpsychol. Behav. Soc. Networking 15(2), 117–121 (2012)

35. Qui, L., Lin, H., Leung, A.K.Y., Tov, W.: Putting their best foot forward: emotional disclosure on Facebook. Cyberpsychol. Behav. Soc. Netw. **15**(10), 569–572 (2012)
36. Lee-Won, R.J., Shim, M., Joo, Y.K., Park, S.G.: Who puts the best "face" forward on Facebook?: positive self-presentation in online social networking and the role of self-consciousness, actual-to-total friends ratio, and culture. Comput. Hum. Behav. **39**, 413–423 (2014)
37. Feinstein, B.A., Hershenberg, R., Bhatia, V., Latack, J.A., Meuwly, N., Davila, J.: Negative social comparison on Facebook and depressive symptoms: rumination as a mechanism. Psychol. Pop. Media Cult. **2**(3), 161 (2013)
38. Steers, M.L.N., Wickham, R.E., Acitelli, L.K.: Seeing everyone else's highlight reels: how Facebook usage is linked to depressive symptoms. J. Soc. Clin. Psychol. **33**(8), 701–731 (2014)
39. Lup, K., Trub, L., Rosenthal, L.: Instagram# instasad?: Exploring associations among Instagram use, depressive symptoms, negative social comparison, and strangers followed. Cyberpsychol. Behav. Soc. Netw. **18**(5), 247–252 (2015)
40. Kroenke, K., Spitzer, R.L., Williams, J.B., Löwe, B.: The patient health questionnaire somatic, anxiety, and depressive symptom scales: a systematic review. Gen. Hosp. Psychiatry **32**(4), 345–359 (2010)
41. Burdzovic Andreas, J., Brunborg, G.S.: Depressive symptomatology among Norwegian adolescent boys and girls: the patient health questionnaire-9 (PHQ-9) psychometric properties and correlates. Front. Psychol. **8**, 887 (2017)
42. Tsai, F.J., Huang, Y.H., Liu, H.C., Huang, K.Y., Huang, Y.H., Liu, S.I.: Patient health questionnaire for school-based depression screening among Chinese adolescents. Pediatrics **133**(2), e402–e409 (2014)
43. Richardson, L.P., et al.: Evaluation of the patient health questionnaire-9 item for detecting major depression among adolescents. Pediatrics **126**(6), 1117–1123 (2010)
44. Fatiregun, A., Kumapayi, T.: Prevalence and correlates of depressive symptoms among in-school adolescents in a rural district in Southwest Nigeria. J. Adolesc. **37**(2), 197–203 (2014)
45. Ganguly, S., Samanta, M., Roy, P., Chatterjee, S., Kaplan, D.W., Basu, B.: Patient health questionnaire-9 as an effective tool for screening of depression among Indian adolescents. J. Adolesc. Health **52**(5), 546–551 (2013)
46. Tsehay, M., Necho, M., Mekonnen, W.: The role of adverse childhood experience on depression symptom, prevalence, and severity among school going adolescents. Depression Res. Treat. **2020**, 5951792 (2020)
47. Leung, D.Y., Mak, Y.W., Leung, S.F., Chiang, V.C., Loke, A.Y.: Measurement invariances of the PHQ-9 across gender and age groups in Chinese adolescents. Asia Pac. Psychiatry **12**(3), e12381 (2020)
48. Young, C.B., Fang, D.Z., Zisook, S.: Depression in Asian-American and Caucasian undergraduate students. J. Affect. Disord. **125**(1–3), 379–382 (2010)
49. Ibrahim, A.K., Kelly, S.J., Adams, C.E., Glazebrook, C.: A systematic review of studies of depression prevalence in university students. J. Psychiatr. Res. **47**(3), 391–400 (2013)
50. Kroenke, K., Spitzer, R.L., Williams, J.B.: The PHQ-9: validity of a brief depression severity measure. J. Gen. Intern. Med. **16**(9), 606–613 (2001)
51. Kong, Y.X., Shi, G.Y., Wu, R.J., Zhang, Y.C.: K-core: theories and applications. Phys. Rep. **832**, 1–32 (2019)
52. Newman, B.M., Lohman, D.J., Newman, P.R.: Peer group membership and a sense of belonging: their relationship to adolescent behavior problems. Adolescence **42**(166), 241–263 (2007)

53. Frison, E., Eggermont, S.: Toward an integrated and differential approach to the relationships between loneliness, different types of Facebook use, and adolescents' depressed mood. Commun. Res. **47**(5), 701–728 (2020)
54. Scherr, S., Brunet, A.: Differential influences of depression and personality traits on the use of Facebook. Social Media+ Soc. **3**(1), 2056305117698495 (2017)

(Im)balance in the Representation of News? An Extensive Study on a Decade Long Dataset from India

Souvic Chakraborty[✉], Pawan Goyal, and Animesh Mukherjee

Indian Institute of Technology, Kharagpur, West Bengal, India
chakra.souvic@gmail.com

Abstract. (Im)balance in the representation of news has always been a topic of debate in political circles.

The concept of balance has often been discussed and studied in the context of the social responsibility theory and the *prestige press* in the USA. *Comprehensive analysis* of all these measures across a *large dataset* of the *post-truth era* comprising *different popular news media houses over a sufficiently long temporal scale* in a non-US democratic setting is lacking. For this study, we amass a huge dataset of over *four million* political articles from India for 9+ years and analyze the extent and quality of coverage given to issues and political parties in the context of contemporary influential events for three leading newspapers. We use several state-of-the-art NLP tools to effectively understand political polarization (if any) manifesting in these articles over time. We also observe that only a few locations are extensively covered across all the news outlets. Cloze tests show that the changing landscape of events get reflected in all the news outlets with border and terrorism issues dominating in around 2010 while economic aspects like unemployment, GST, demonetization, etc. became more dominant in the period 2014–2018.

Keywords: Imbalance in digital media · India · Politics · Computation journalism · Fairness · Political influence on news

1 Introduction

Indian media has been the target of blatant criticism internationally for propagation of one-sided views on specific issues and deliberate introduction of imbalance and sensationalism in reporting news[1]. Specific media houses have been consistent targets by the supporters of specific parties for propagating unbalanced views on issues benefiting some specific party. Many of these unverified news and systematic imbalances have been criticized to introduce communal disharmony and even loss of lives.

---

[1] https://www.aljazeera.com/opinions/2020/2/24/indias-media-is-failing-in-its-democratic-duty.

F. Hopfgartner et al. (Eds.): SocInfo 2022, LNCS 13618, pp. 347–369, 2022.
https://doi.org/10.1007/978-3-031-19097-1_22

So, we intend to study how (im)balanced Indian news media is and how it has changed its course over time with different ruling parties in the centre and on face of large scale events including the national election in 2014 with almost a billion voters and significant change in share of seats for parties, large scale changes in monetary policy like demonetisation and introduction of GST in 2016 & 2017 and nation-wide non-political anti-corruption movement in 2011 with huge influence and mass following having significant impact on later political discourse.

While popularity of sharebaits is a problem, a bigger problem is perhaps the reliance of the common mass on social media to get their daily news feeds Earl et al. (2001), Mitchell et al. (2015), Thurman et al. (2019). There is an increasing lack of diversity in the algorithmically driven news feeds that the social media typically presents to its readers. In many cases this leads to reinforcing the 'imbalance' among readers in the form of increased polarity of the political opinion of these readers over time Bakshy et al. (2015). This idea has been presented in the past literature in various forms like echo chambers Flaxman et al. (2016), Garrett (2009) and filter bubbles Resnick et al. (2013). Had the nature or inclination of imbalance used by newspapers been dynamic temporally or topically, it would have been less likely to influence people at large. However, recent research Vosoughi et al. (2018) in imbalance propagation suggests that typically "static" forms of imbalanced news are more likely to spread. So, once a specific imbalance is introduced by the major media houses systematically, it will act as a positive feedback loop catering to the "confirmation" of their readers and making it more difficult for the media houses to introduce a different stance contradicting the view of their readers which they themselves shaped and are identified with.

Motivation: Computational studies (apart from the manual studies done by independent journalists) in news media Budak et al. (2016), Lazer et al. (2018), Spillane et al. (2017) done till now are at most times lacking in either the number of articles examined or the time span of examination or both. One of the prime limitations of these studies is that most of them have taken a piecemeal approach. Especially, the number of large scale studies done probing Indian media is small which creates a huge gap for accountancy.

Objectives of This Work: The primary objective of this paper *is to examine a large body of news articles through various lenses of imbalances.* While most of the news media datasets available are specific to US Kiesel et al. (2018), ProQuest (2019), Thompson (2018) or Europe Corney et al. (2016), Eberl (2018) or Austraila Kulkarni (2018), they are limited to the specific regional scope in time/events, diversity of media groups etc. So, for this specific study, we mine Indian newspapers with highest readership numbers and online availability that spans over almost a decade. We make efforts to understand the temporal behavior of different forms of imbalance featuring across three news media outlets by analyzing this massive news dataset, in the Indian context. We summarize our contributions in the following section.

Key Contributions: In the following we summarize our specific contributions.

- We collect news articles for three leading Indian newspapers for a huge span of 9+ years. In addition, for every article we also separately collect various metadata like the source of the article, the headline and the URL.
- We use seven different metrics of (im)balance that are easy to compute as well as interpret, motivated by *two completely orthogonal viewpoints* generally upheld by researchers or termed important by media imbalance gatekeeping organizations.
- We compute these metrics for (im)balance month-wise for the three leading newspapers and observe the temporal trends for each kind of metrics, cluster these time series and discuss the most interesting observations.
- We use different NLP tools like word embedding association test and masked language modelling to answer several research questions in an India specific setting and discuss the implications of the results obtained. These investigations unfold various interesting trends in Indian political discussions over the years.

2 Background

In this section we first present a brief review of fairness and balance in the journalism literature. This is followed by a narration of how we build up our work on these ideas.

(Im)balance in Journalism: Fairness and balance in the press has been studied for a long time in the journalism literature. One of the early works pertains to how the prestige press is distinctly different from the media outlets with wide circulation Lacy et al. (1991). The authors perform a small scale data-driven study to show that the prestige press presents a more balanced coverage of local stories compared to wide circulation media outlets. Fico et al. (1994) studied the newspaper coverage of US in Gulf war and find that wide circulation newspapers were more likely to favor anti-war advocates than smaller ones. Fico and Soffin (1995) develop a content based technique to study the newspaper coverage of controversial issues. They find that only 7% of the stories were evenly balanced and the coverage on the Gulf war issue was most imbalanced. Fico and Cote (1999) study structural characteristics of newspaper stories on the 1996 US presidential election. One of the very important findings in this work is that event coverage was the biggest predictor of imbalanced story. Fico and Freedman (2008) study balance in election news coverage about 2006 US senate elections. They observe that women reporters provided more evenly balanced treatment of the candidate assertions. Carter et al. (2002) the authors report the structural balance in local television election coverage. Fico et al. (2008) the authors study the broadcast and cable network news coverage of the 2004 presidential election and find that broadcast networks were more balanced in their aggregate attention to the presidential candidates compared to the cable networks. In Robertson et al. (2018), the researchers studied Google searches to find partisan imbalance in widely used digital platforms. Morgan et al. (2013) studied imbalance in social media shares and of news items. On the other hand, Kulshrestha et al. (2017) studied social media imbalance for political searches. Finally, in Resnick et al. (2013) the authors study remedy techniques to limit exposure to imbalance: *strategies for promoting diverse exposure.*

The Present Work: In most of the above works, (im)balance has largely been quantified in terms of coverage. However, we posit that (im)balance can manifest in many different ways. In the following we outline these assimilating concepts from various past literature.

Coverage imbalance is the extent to which some specific entities/topics are covered in the articles by a specific media house. Coverage imbalance may originate from the inequality in the number of articles published with stories related to each major party or the amount of inkspace given to each party (even if the number of articles are equal, articles covering one party can be longer) or the amount of inkspace used to cover speeches of leaders of each political party.

For the first two metric of coverage imbalance, we take inspiration from the work of D'Alessio and Allen (2000) and Lacy et al. (1991). The equivalent of number of stories featuring a party is the number of headlines featuring that party, the ideal contender of measuring Gatekeeping imbalance D'Alessio and Allen (2000). On the other hand, we take the sentences in the content as proxy for a combined measure of fairness and balance in work of Lacy et al. (1991) to measure the amount of inkspace given to a particular party. For all the analysis we use words as the analog of inkspace here as words are the basic units of semantic information in online media.

Following the work of Lin et al. (2006), we introduce another measure of coverage imbalance, the *point of view* imbalance. The point of view from which a news story is reported matters as the editors have to choose selective viewpoints due to the constraint in space/number of words that can be used in a readably long article. While one newspaper may choose to quote the government sources, the same news story may be reported quoting the opponent leader. Thus, imbalance gets introduced if diverse viewpoints are not equally represented as discussed in the guidelines for fair reporting by FAIR[2]. We try to capture the sentences where speech of any person affiliated to a party is reported and calculate the number of words (semantic equivalent of inkspace) just like the previous cases of coverage imbalance.

Political funding can influence the news organization to create news stories favoring the party. So, it is important to check for tonal imbalance in the news-stories also. We use the same concepts of coverage imbalance for tonality as we will describe in the Methodology Section.

---

[2] https://www.fair.org.

In addition to the introduction of different perspectives on imbalance as above, we also upscale our study in two other major directions. First, we perform the analysis on a huge dataset comprising three Indian news outlets leading to a total of 3.86 million articles. Second, rather than aggregate statistics, we present temporal characteristics of the imbalance which allows us to make various important and nuanced observations.

3 Dataset

From the list of top news media by readership, published by the Indian Readership Survey (IRS) 2017 Council (2017) compiled by the Media Research Users Council (MRUC), we collect the news articles data for three popular English language newspapers in India, namely, Times of India (TOI)[3], The Hindu[4] and India Today[5], where an online archive is available. We create a date-wise repository of more than four million news articles spanning 9+ years (2010–2018) of news data crawling through the archives.

The total number of articles retrieved for TOI, The Hindu and India Today are 1,899,745, 1,032,377 & 926,922, respectively. A brief description of the year wise statistics of the political articles across the three newspapers is noted in Table 1.

Table 1. Year-wise statistics of the collected data for the chosen time range for all three newspapers. Note that for India Today the pattern is unique in that from 2011 to 2012 the circulation became 5x while from 2015 to 2016 the circulation became 0.5x. None of the other outlets indicate such stark shifts.

	TOI	The Hindu	India Today
2010	101903	74927	45297
2011	169183	75160	27135
2012	236548	86107	146634
2013	237372	88795	197139
2014	210859	106013	152260
2015	243473	204421	135898
2016	208861	192120	71155
2017	242334	117584	76800
2018	249212	87250	74604

Pre-processing of the Raw Dataset: Our data consists of the headlines of the news stories, date of publication and the content.

---

[3] https://timesofindia.indiatimes.com/archive.cms.
[4] https://www.thehindu.com/archive/.
[5] https://www.indiatoday.in/archives/.

Keyword Based Shortlisting of Articles: Our entire study is done to depict the political imbalance of different media houses in representation of news related to two major political parties of India – 'Bharatiya Janata Party'[6] and 'Indian National Congress'[7], more famous as 'BJP' & 'Congress'. We present a keyword based analysis throughout all the metrics. The set of keywords chosen for BJP (is referred to as $BJP_{keywords}$ from now on) consists of – 'Bharatiya Janata Party', 'BJP', 'Akhil Bharatiya Vidyarthi Parishad', 'ABVP', 'National Democratic Alliance', 'NDA'. The set of keywords chosen for Congress (is referred to as $Congress_{keywords}$ from now on) consists of – 'Congress' (the most popular version of the full name of the party), 'INC', 'National Students' Union of India', 'NSUI', 'United Progressive Alliance' and 'UPA'.

Motivation for the Choice of Keywords: A natural question would be why we chose only the above keywords for our experiments. The choice is motivated by the additional set of experiments that we did to fix the above set of keywords. We first chose these keywords on the basis of two criteria. We manually checked the news articles to find the important indicators and through this qualitative analysis, we found that the discussion around the parties can typically be identified with the most popular version of their names including acronyms & full names and popular acronyms of coalition governments & student organizations. Next we included the names of the personalities related to the party thereafter and observed the results are completely swayed away by the coverage of influential figures like the names of the Prime Minister or all the other names holding important offices. We argue that the political parties are distinct from the personalities affiliated to those parties or the government formed by those parties. This justifies the exclusion of these entities from our seed set since they might correspond to issues related to (i) the functioning of the government and not the party in particular or (ii) the functioning of the personalities who might hold different portfolios within the government and might have their own charismatic presence on many issues and may have a different face than being a party member only while commenting on different issues. Thus we argue that we should limit the keywords to the most popular seed set chosen alone that includes party names, acronyms, names of student wings and name of the democratic alliances where any of the two parties are the most influential ones.

4   Methodology

This section is laid out in three parts. In the first part we discuss the different metrics of imbalance. In the second part, we demonstrate how the different temporally varying metrics of imbalance can be summarised to reflect certain universal patterns. Finally, we outline a method to identify word associations that could reflect polarisation.

---

[6] https://en.wikipedia.org/wiki/Bharatiya_Janata_Party.
[7] https://en.wikipedia.org/wiki/Indian_National_Congress.

4.1 Uniform Metric of Imbalance

We adopt the method of determining imbalance from the acclaimed work of Lacy et al. (1991). For each of the metric i, that we use in the subsequent analysis, (henceforth, $metric_i$), we compute an imbalance score at the granularity of each month. Thus, for a particular month of a year, the imbalance score (henceforth, $imbalance^i_{\text{yy-mm}}$) is calculated as follows, adapting the work of Lacy et al. (1991).

$$Imbalance^i_{\text{yy-mm}} = \frac{Score_i(B^i_{\text{yy-mm}}) - Score_i(C^i_{\text{yy-mm}})}{Score_i(B^i_{\text{yy-mm}}) + Score_i(C^i_{\text{yy-mm}})} \tag{1}$$

where $B^i_{\text{yy-mm}}$ and $C^i_{\text{yy-mm}}$ correspond to the *aggregated documents* for the two political parties considered (BJP and Congress, respectively, in our case).

Next, we obtain the imbalance scores for each metric across the timeline of 2010–2018. Note that this *imbalance score has a direction*. All *positive scores correspond to a leaning toward BJP* and *all the negative scores correspond to a leaning toward Congress*. The *absolute value of the score* denotes the *imbalance without direction*. Apart from the timeline plots illustrating the imbalance with direction, we also compute the aggregate values of the absolute imbalance score for each metric averaged over the timeline of computation.

4.2 Coverage Imbalance

We have done two studies to find balance in coverage of political parties in newspapers, one on the basis of (i) the *headlines* and the other on the basis of (ii) the *content* of the article.

Headlines

Sentence Inclusion Criterion: If one or more of the BJP_{keywords} introduced in the previous section are present in the headline of a news article, we include the headline in $B^h_{\text{yy-mm}}$. Similarly, if one or more of the $Congress_{\text{keywords}}$ introduced in the previous section are present in the headline of a news article then we include that headline in $C^h_{\text{yy-mm}}$. If the headline contains keywords from both the sets of keywords, it is included in both the documents.

Score of Each Document: Each of the headlines forms one entity of attention to the general populace. So, we simply count the number of headlines included for each of the document as score of that document.

Content

Sentence Inclusion Criterion: If one or more of the BJP_{keywords} are present in a sentence of the content of a news article, we include that sentence in $B^c_{\text{yy-mm}}$. Similarly, if one or more of the $Congress_{\text{keywords}}$ are present in a sentence of the content of a news article, we include that sentence in $C^c_{\text{yy-mm}}$. If the sentence contains keywords from both the sets of keywords, it is included in both the documents.

Score of Each Document: In contrast to the headlines, content is consumed by volume of words written. As words form the atomic unit of semantic expression, we use the number of words in the whole document as the score of that particular document in case of content metric.

Point of View Imbalance

To understand which party's point of view is presented, we turn to the narrative verbs like "say" and "tell". Whereas, much research Muzny et al. (2017) has gone into quote attribution, we find that the majority of point of views presented in the newspaper is indirect speech in reported form. So, to account for both, we count the number of times a noun phrase, containing at least one keyword/keyphrase of BJP or Congress, is the subject of a sentence. Thus, we will be able to get the sentences where something said by BJP or Congress or some member of the party has been highlighted.

Sentence Inclusion Criterion: The sentence inclusion criterion is exactly similar to the one used for determination of content imbalance.

Score of Each Document: We wish to get a rough statistical estimate of the number of words used to represent the point of view of each party by this score. So, as discussed above, we pick those sentences which contain any of the forms of the narrative verbs like "say" and "tell" as the main verb and also have a subject noun phrase containing the keywords/phrases related to the specific party of the document. We thus calculate the total number of words contained in the sentences picked from each document as the score of that document.

4.3   Tonality Imbalance

Here we discuss two different forms of imbalance metrics - (i) *sentiment* imbalance and (ii) *subjectivity* imbalance.

Sentiment Imbalance

We have done sentiment analysis for the articles using the widely used VADER sentiment analyzer of NLTK[8].

Sentence Inclusion Criterion: The sentence inclusion criterion is exactly similar to the one used for coverage imbalance in content.

Score of Each Document: For each of the sentences in the BJP or Congress document, we determine the positive/negative sentiments expressed in that sentence using the VADER sentiment analyzer. Now, we get the average of the sentiments of these sentences weighted by the number of words of these sentences as the final score of the document. We use such weighting scheme to account for the semantic space as the sentiment is being expressed over the words for each sentence. So the density of the sentiments per word is a useful measure here.

---

[8] https://www.nltk.org/.

Subjectivity Imbalance

We compute various quantities here most of which pertain to some notion of subjectivity as per the standard literature. In particular, we compute *subjectivity* and uses of *superlatives* & *comparatives* in the text of the content using the TextBlob[9] & NLTK[10] library.

Sentence Inclusion Criterion: For all the measures of subjectivity, we use the same sentence inclusion criterion as the one used for coverage imbalance in content.

Score of Each Document: Sentiment and subjectivity are very related concepts. So, we use the same rationale of scoring here as used in the section of sentiment imbalance. For all these subjectivity metrics, for each of the sentences in the document we determine the score of the sentences using the aforementioned tools. Now, we obtain the average of these scores across all the sentences weighted by the number of words of these sentences as the final score of the document for each metric using the same rationale as described in the previous section.

For superlatives and comparatives, we count the average percentage of superlatives and comparatives used in the sentences where any of the party is mentioned (based on the same *keyword* based filtering), as an alternative measure of subjectivity.

Table 2. Aggregate absolute imbalance scores: an upward arrow at the left of any number denotes an imbalance toward BJP and vice versa. The highest absolute imbalance score for each metric has been highlighted in boldface.

	TOI	The Hindu	India Today
CovHead	↑**16.18**	↑9.87	↑14.72
CovCon	↓4.49	↓**11.72**	↓2.50
PoV	↑**78.31**	↑70.14	↑62.45
PosSent	↑0.44	↑**2.42**	↑0.20
NegSent	↓**2.02**	↑1.05	↓0.54
Subj	↓0.28	↓0.57	↑**1.04**
SupComp	↓1.15	↓1.96	↓**5.22**

4.4 Summary Metrics

We aggregate the documents of each of the two parties over the whole timeline to obtain two aggregate documents. Next we compute each of the above metrics using the Eq. 1, to obtain the aggregate imbalance score corresponding to each metric and each political party.

---

[9] https://github.com/sloria/textblob.
[10] https://www.nltk.org/.

5   Experiments and Results

In this section we discuss the key experiments and then detail the corresponding results.

5.1   Summary Based on Aggregation of Scores

Table 2 shows the aggregate imbalance scores for each of the newspapers across all metric for a fair quantitative comparison. We can see that there is no clear winner or loser in terms of imbalances. TOI reports the highest degree of imbalance in case of three metrics and The Hindu & India Today show highest imbalance in case of two metrics each. One peculiar point to note here is that for The Hindu, the average positive and negative sentiments are both BJP leaning. One can argue that this is counterintuitive since the density of positive sentiments in favor of one party being high for a media house in one month should imply that the density of negative sentiments has to be low in favor of that party for that month. Although intuitive, this is not obvious as both positive and negative sentiments can be expressed highly about a party if more about that party is discussed in the inkspace. For instance, at multiple time points, both the positive and negative sentiment scores for The Hindu are much above the zero line unlike the other two media houses (data not shown for paucity of space).

5.2   Imbalance in Portrayal of Different States/cities

Non-Hindi speaking states and especially states from north-east IndiaGiri (2015), Jammu & Kashmir have often alleged other parts of India of cultural exclusion[11]. We attempt to understand how much of those allegations are true and if the situation is changing over time.

City Level Analysis. We prepare a list of 25 most populous cities in India according to the census report of 2011[12] and measure how these cities are covered by the news articles. We take one entry of a city if the city is mentioned at least once in a news article. We thus calculate the share of each city for a specific media house. We illustrate this imbalance in the coverage of cities in Fig. 1.

---

[11] https://towardfreedom.org/story/indian-medias-missing-margins/.
[12] http://censusindia.gov.in/2011-Common/CensusData2011.html.

Distribution of Cities for Each Newspaper

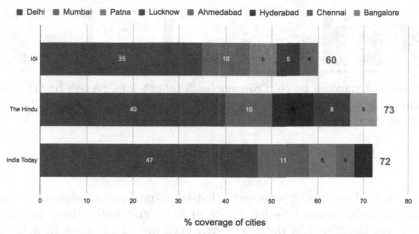

Fig. 1. Coverage of different cities by the three news outlets (only top five cities covered are shown to facilitate increased visibility).

Observation: We can see from Fig. 1 that the distribution of cities covered by each of the newspapers is heavily skewed with the most frequently covered five cities corresponding to 60–70% of the articles. Delhi and Mumbai are the two most dominant cities on this list for all the three newspapers.

We add a detailed state level analysis in the appendix section which holds the proof of state level inequality of coverage.

Is the Situation Getting Better/Worse? To better understand the trend, we attempt to quantify homogeneity using three metrics. First we convert the counts of states to probabilities by dividing them with the total number of mentions of all cities. Next we define the first metric of homogeneity as the inverse of the standard deviation of the probability distribution (since standard deviation is an established measure of homogeneity). The next two measures take a more boxed approach trying to understand if the low priority states for that particular newspaper is getting higher attention over time. Here low priority states for the second metric is the bottom 20% states and for the third metric is the bottom 50% states.

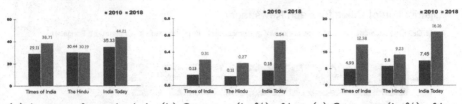

(a) Inverse of standard de- (b) Coverage (in %) of bot- (c) Coverage (in %) of bot-
viation (imbalance in cover- tom 20% states   tom 50% states
age of all states together)

Fig. 2. Trends in imbalance in coverage of states over time.

Observations: From Fig. 2, we observe that the intuitive conclusions drawn from the last analysis stands true for *Times of India* and *India Today* for all the metrics. For the Hindu in the first metric (i.e., inverse of standard deviation) we see no clear trend. However, in both the other metrics we note that the newspaper is clearly diversifying its coverage over the states.

6   Discussion and Conclusion

In this section we identify some of the possible mitigation strategies that could be adopted in view of the observations made in this paper and, thereby, point to the road ahead.

Making Imbalance Transparent: This approach would envisage to make the user aware that he/she is consuming a imbalanced news through various visualization techniques implemented on the online newspaper platforms making a topic-wise comparison between various media outlets. This might also include simple indicators like how much factual a news is or what part of the same news-story is a news item covering with what sentiment. Such a nudging practice is widely prevalent in the literature with objectives to deliver multiple aspects of news in social media Park et al. (2009) or for encouraging users to read about diverse political opinions Munson and Resnick (2010), Munson et al. (2013).

Platform Governance: With the exponential penetration of the social media, the way users consume news has seen a sea of change. Most users active on different social media platforms now consume their daily news from the news stories that are recommended by these platforms Shearer and Matsa (2018). With the explosion in the Indian smartphone market the number of such users is increasing in leaps and bounds. Such platforms can easily game the users to consume only imbalanced political news Oremus (2016). In February 2019 the United Kingdom's Digital, Media, Culture, and Sport (DCMS) committee issued a verdict in view of this rising problem. The verdict said that social media platforms can no longer hide themselves behind the claim that they are merely a 'platform' and therefore have no responsibility of regulating the content they recommend to their users Gorwa (2019). EU, recently, has also deployed mechanisms to combat imbalanced and fake news in the online world by constituting working groups that include voices from different avenues including academia, industry and civil society. For instance, in January 2018, 39 experts met to frame the 'Code of Practice on Online Disinformation' which was signed by tech giants like Facebook, Google etc. We believe that more such initiatives need to be taken worldwide to combat this problem.

The Road Ahead. Our main objective in this paper was to introduce and quantify the different forms of imbalance metrics that one is able to observe across the Indian news media outlets. This will subsequently help in better platform governance through informing readers about the extent of different kinds of imbalances present in an article they are consuming and by showing similar articles on same topic highlighting the opposite viewpoints in the recommended list helping to create a better inclusive worldview for the readers bursting the filter bubble of imbalanced news consumption. In view of the recent resurgence of debates and legal actions around platform governance Gorwa (2019), Shearer and Matsa (2018), this, we believe, is a very significant step forward. One immediate task we would like to consider is to study a wider range of media houses across different Indian languages and religious communities and observe if we get similar results. Finally, we would also like to contribute to mitigation of such imbalances through platform governance.

A Appendix

A.1 Summary Based on Time Series Clustering

For each individual imbalance metric and each newspaper, one can obtain a time series of the directed scores spanning over 9+ years. While one can always look into each such time series data to make an inference, our idea was to look for universal characteristics of imbalance across the three news outlets. To this end, we cluster the time series of imbalance scores using the standard dynamic time warping (DTW) approach. We use hierarchical agglomerative clustering to understand the similarity among the newspapers based on their temporal imbalance characteristics. In addition, this clustering technique also summarizes which of the metrics have remained closer to each other over time.

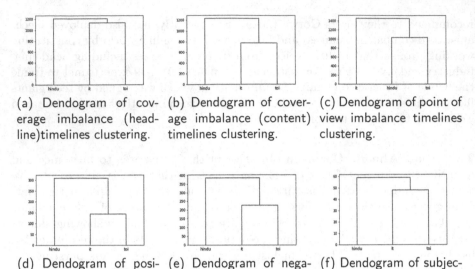

(a) Dendogram of coverage imbalance (headline)timelines clustering.

(b) Dendogram of coverage imbalance (content) timelines clustering.

(c) Dendogram of point of view imbalance timelines clustering.

(d) Dendogram of positive sentiment imbalance timelines clustering.

(e) Dendogram of negative sentiment imbalance timelines clustering.

(f) Dendogram of subjectivity imbalance timelines clustering.

Fig. 3. Dendogram of different measures of imbalances across different newspapers

Observations. We have seven different imbalance metrics namely – headlines coverage, content coverage, point of view, positive sentiment, negative sentiment, subjectivity and superlatives/comparatives. For a given news outlet therefore we shall have seven corresponding time series each spanning over 9+ years. Since there are three major news outlets in our dataset we have 21 time series in all. We cluster these 21 time series using DTW as discussed in the previous section. As evident from the results presented in the form of dendograms in Fig. 3, *Times of India and India Today exhibit stronger clustering across almost*

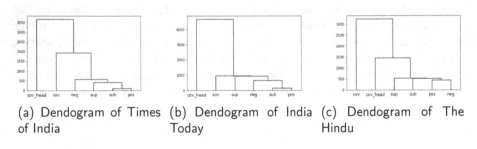

(a) Dendogram of Times of India

(b) Dendogram of India Today

(c) Dendogram of The Hindu

Fig. 4. Dendogram of different newspapers across different measures of imbalances.(Acronyms used and their full forms: cov_h: coverage imbalance in headings; cov: coverage imbalance in content; sup: superlative and comparative imbalance; pos: positive sentiment imbalance; neg: negative sentiment imbalance; subj: subjectivity imbalance)

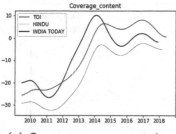

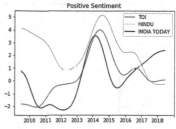

(a) Content coverage trends.   (b) Positive sentiment trends.

Fig. 5. Temporal variation of imbalance in coverage of content and positive sentiments in the news articles for the different media houses.

all the imbalance measures pointing to an interesting universal characteristic. In order to delve deeper into the dynamics, we present in Figs. 5(a) and 5(b) respectively, two representative time series plots of imbalance scores – content coverage imbalance and positive sentiment imbalance.

Content Coverage Imbalance: In Fig. 5(a), we plot the directed imbalance scores of content for each of the media houses over time. The first noticeable trend is that the media houses have distinct relative imbalance very consistent over the timeline. The Hindu has been especially consistent in maintaining a 5–10% shift in coverage toward the Congress party than the other two news organizations. Consequent to relatively higher leaning of The Hindu in coverage of the Congress party, The Hindu always remained Congress leaning (below zero in the curve) unlike its two peers. The shift between TOI and India Today is not that apparent thus providing the empirical justification of the results obtained from the DTW clustering.

Positive Sentiment Imbalance: In Fig. 5(b), we observe that The Hindu has an imbalance score higher than the zero mark throughout till 2017 showing higher density of positive sentiments toward BJP. This behavior is in drastic contrast with the other two news outlets thus providing the justification in support of the DTW results. Of course, the election year (2014, which also marked significant change in vote share and public sentiment) observes high positive sentiments in favor of BJP in general.

As a next step, we cluster the seven different time series corresponding to the respective imbalance metrics for each of the news outlets separately (see Fig. 4). For all the news outlets we again observe *a universal pattern whereby the tonality based imbalances are clustered more strongly exhibiting their distinctions with the coverage and point of view imbalances.*

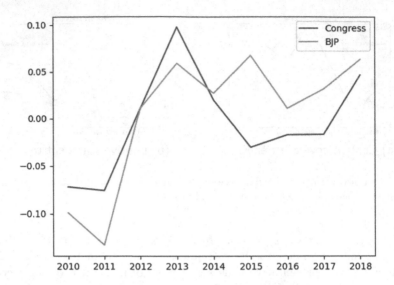

Fig. 6. Temporal variation of *popularity* of each party for the India Today corpus. The trends are very similar for the other two news outlets.

A.2   WEAT Scores to Determine Party Popularity

We calculate the differential association over time and plot that over the years. We use this distance as a proxy for popularity as portrayed by that particular news media. We illustrate the algorithm next.

Word Embedding Association Test (WEAT). In order to understand how the popularity of the political parties among the people of India has changed over time we calculate the year specific word embeddings on our corpus using methods used to measure semantic shift in words over time.

Previous research Azarbonyad et al. (2017) suggests that frequently used words have the least shift of their meaning over time. Hence we use top 1000 words in our corpus (excluding the words *BJP* and *Congress* consciously) to align the word embeddings trained for different time periods. We train word2vec Mikolov et al. (2013) with SGNS (skip-gram with negative sampling), to create embeddings for each of the year in our dataset. Let $W(t) \in \mathbb{R}^{d \times V}$ be the matrix of word embeddings learnt for year t and for vocabulary V. Following Hamilton et al. (2016), we jointly align the word embeddings while generation, using the top 10000 common words present across time periods t_1 and t_2 by optimizing:

$$R^t = \underset{Q_{t_1 t_2}^T Q_{t_1 t_2} = I}{\arg \min} \; ||QW^{t_1} - W^{t_2}||$$

For simplicity we assume $Q_{t_1 t_2} = I \forall t_1, t_2$. After alignment, we measure the WEAT score of the words *BJP* and *Congress* with the opposite set of words $A_1 = \{\text{good, honest, efficient, superior}\}$ and $A_2 = \{\text{bad, dishonest, inefficient, inferior}\}$ using the algorithm presented in Brunet et al. (2019).

The differential association of a word c with word sets A_1 and A_2 is given by

$$g(c, A_1, A_2, w) = \underset{a \in A_1}{\overset{mean}{}} \cos(w_c, w_a) - \underset{b \in A_2}{\overset{mean}{}} \cos(w_c, w_a)$$

where w is the set of word embeddings, w_x is the word embedding for the word x.

Now, the WEAT score is calculated as

$$B_{weat}(w) = \frac{g'(s_1) - g'(s_2)}{\underset{s_3 \in S_1, S_2}{SD} g(s_3, A_1, A_2, w)}$$

where

$$g'(s_i) = \underset{s_i \in S_i}{\overset{mean}{}} g(s_1, A_1, A_2, w)$$

Here the word sets S_1 and S_2 are the keywords related to the political parties, as already discussed previously.

From Fig. 6, it is evident that *BJP* gained popularity in news very fast post 2011, surpassing popularity of *Congress* in 2014, the year of legislative assembly election when incumbent *BJP* overthrew the ruling Congress government. We also see the popularity of *Congress* increasing again since 2016, the year of demonetization, that possibly had a strong impact on the economy of India and specially on the poorest ones of the country.[13]

A.3 State Level Analysis of Inequality in Coverage

Now we attempt to understand if the situation is similar in state level and if *yes*, then which states are covered poorly. We collect all the state names from the census report of 2011 (see footnote 12) and search for their occurrence across the corpus. We note the number of articles a specific state is mentioned in and plot the same. We do this experiment for all the three newspapers and for each newspapers, we once plot for only 2010, once only for 2018 to understand the evolving trend.

Observations: Figure 7 holds the evidence that the states of Jammu & Kashmir, states in the north-east and some non-Hindi speaking states like Orissa or Jharkhand are squarely ignored by all the three newspapers. Hindu seems to stand out in coverage of states from the other two newspapers covering mostly south Indian states. Looking at the maps comparatively from 2010 to 2018, it seems that the situation is improving and more states are getting covered by the national newspapers over time though equality among the states may be a long way.

---

[13] https://www.bbc.com/news/world-asia-india-46400677.

B   Further Insights

In order to obtain further insights, we perform a *cloze* task Taylor (1953), i.e., a task that requires completion of a sentence by correctly predicting the masked/hidden word. For instance, in the following cloze task – "Sun is a huge ball of $\langle mask \rangle$, "fire" is a likely completion for the missing word. Given a cloze test, well-known language models like RoBERTa Liu et al. (2019), produce a sequence of tokens with their corresponding probabilities to fill the given blank in the input sentence. We train RoBERTa (initialized with RoBERTa-base Liu et al. (2019)) for each of our newspapers for each year present in the corpus separately for 20000 iterations following the language model training procedure described in Khalidkar et al. (2021). This results in a total $3 * 9 = 27$ different models. We use these models (representative/mouthpiece of each newspaper at different times of the 9 years in our corpus) to answer the following three questions – (a) can one track the changing priorities for India as depicted by each news media house? (b) how are these newspapers reporting popularity of one party over the other, for these 9 years? and (c) how are newspapers presenting perception about the Indian economy?

Table 3. Top tokens increasingly and decreasingly accepted as answer in 2018 for the cloze task (a) & (c).

Probe	RoBERTa$_{(TOI)}$		RoBERTa$_{(Hindu)}$		RoBERTa$_{(IT)}$	
	2010 ⟶ 2018		2010 ⟶ 2018		2010 ⟶ 2018	
	↑ 2018	↓ in 2018	↑ 2018	↓ 2018	↑ 2018	↓ 2018
The main issue in India is $\langle mask \rangle$	unemployment, water, terrorism, jobs, farmers, corruption, employment, women, agriculture, reservation, fuel, caste, GST, development, food	Kashmir, migration, terror, Afghanistan, security, India, democracy, Pakistan, elections, insecurity, peace, violence, inflation	unemployment, corruption, employment, water, GST, development, jobs, reservation, agriculture, poverty, immigration, housing, governance, money, food	Kashmir, terrorism, terror, prices, India, Pakistan, trade, Afghanistan, inflation, peace	unemployment, corruption, poverty, education, GST, water, Aadhaar, malnutrition, pollution, agriculture, farmers, immigration, inequality, healthcare, democracy	terrorism, Kashmir, terror, Afghanistan, security, Pakistan, trade, inflation, development
The economy of India is $\langle mask \rangle$	growing, strong, slowing, weak, stagnant, thriving, developing, intact, poor, healthy, deteriorating, flourishing, bleeding, backward, expanding	crumbling, shrinking, dying, suffering, divided, rotting, exploding, changing, broken, paralyzed, declining, collapsing, reeling, weakening, fragile	shrinking, crumbling, dead, collapsing, destroyed, slowing, falling, broken, bleeding, different, intact, deteriorating, poor	growing, vibrant, stagnant, flourishing, struggling, strong, booming, recovering, healthy, thriving, weak, improving, stable, fragile, sound	changing, suffering, shrinking, developing, huge, dying, broken, transforming, declining, great, poor, weak, stagnant, flourishing	growing, robust, booming, slowing, improving, fragile, contracting, thriving, strong, evolving, stable, good, expanding, recovering, vibrant

Can One Track Changing Priorities? To understand the changing priorities of India as a nation over the last decade, we propose the following cloze task query – "The main issue in India is $\langle mask \rangle$". We attempt to understand how RoBERTa's answer changes for this specific query from 2010 to 2018. To this purpose, we take a union of top 50 tokens given as output for RoBERTa$_{2010}$ and RoBERTa$_{2018}$. We then rank the top tokens which underwent maximum positive change from 2010 to 2018 as an answer to the cloze test (i.e. the tokens which are more accepted as answer in 2018 than in 2010 for the cloze test). We also rank the top tokens which underwent maximum negative change from 2010 to 2018 as an answer to the cloze test (i.e. the tokens which are less accepted as answer in 2018 than in 2010 for the cloze test). We show maximum of 15 such tokens in order of probability (higher to lower).

Analysis and Observations: From Table 3, we see a similar pattern reverberating across the news media houses. The focus of India in 2018 is more on economic issues like *unemployment, jobs, corruption, poverty, GST, food* and *reservation* and less on border issues like *Kashmir, Pakistan, Afganistan* and *security*. More basic demands like *food, housing, water* and *agriculture* are popping up in 2018. We showed these results to 9 Indians in verse with the events in Indian government. All of them unanimously agreed that these are due to the changing landscape of events affecting India from 2010 to 2018. The period 2008–2010 saw a lot of coordinated bombing and shooting attacks by terrorists on Mumbai, the economic capital of India resulting in mass killings and injuries. These issues mainly related to the India-Pakistan border conflicts emerge in the words popping up in the 2010 newspapers. Between 2014–2018, on the other hand, India saw various economic reforms in the form of introduction of GST, demonetization, stress on online transactions and implementation and linking of AADHAR (an unified database of citizens like social security number in US) with banking for continuation of banking services. All these together led to the increase of priority of economy related words in these news outlets.

How are These Newspapers Reporting Popularity? We attempt to understand how popularity of one party over the other is reported in these newspapers and how they are similar or different from each other. We define voting preference toward a specific political party $\langle p \rangle$, $\forall \langle p \rangle \in \{$ *"BJP", "Congress"* $\}$ as:

$$V_{pop}(\langle p \rangle) = P_{RoBERTa}(\langle mask \rangle = \langle p \rangle | input = prompt) \qquad (2)$$

where

$$prompt = \text{"This election people will vote for } \langle mask \rangle \text{."} \qquad (3)$$

Further, we normalize these values to probabilities toward any of the two parties, arbitrarily selected to be *BJP* (plotting both is redundant as $p_{congress} = 1 - p_{bjp}$) as

$$Pr_{pop}(\text{"BJP"}) = \frac{V_{pop}(\text{"BJP"})}{V_{pop}(\text{"BJP"}) + V_{pop}(\text{"Congress"})} \qquad (4)$$

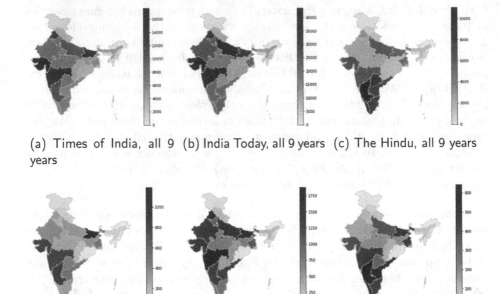

(a) Times of India, all 9 years   (b) India Today, all 9 years   (c) The Hindu, all 9 years

(d) Times of India, 2010   (e) India Today, 2010   (f) The Hindu, 2010

(g) Times of India, 2018   (h) India Today, 2018   (i) The Hindu, 2018

Fig. 7. Number of articles mentioning each state for different newspapers across different time periods

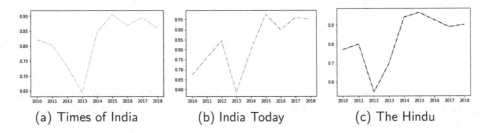

(a) Times of India   (b) India Today   (c) The Hindu

Fig. 8. Popularity of BJP over Congress quantified from the results of Cloze test 4, plotted over the years

How are These Newspapers Reporting Economic Prosperity? We attempt to understand how media houses are reporting economic prosperity of India over time. Using the probe "The economy of India is ⟨mask⟩", we report the most probable outputs in Table 3.

Observations: We plot the probabilities in favor of "BJP" over time for each news media house in Fig. 8. We observe that once again all the news media groups show a very similar pattern with the period 2012–2013, a year before the national election, to be the inflection point. The opposition 'BJP' could defeat the incumbent 'Congress' government with a large margin following gain in popularity in 2010–2011 largely due to corruption charges against the 'Congress' which resulted in nationwide protest and a very influential anti-corruption movement in the capital. We see the popularity of 'BJP' with respect to 'Congress' only rose in the years following the election which seems intuitive as 'BJP' won the 2019 election also with huge majority and increased vote share than 2014[14]. Also, an interesting observation is that a huge policy failure like demonetization which arguably influenced the fall of GDP due to extreme shrinkage of money in circulation[15] and nationwide increase in economic inequality did not decrease the popularity of 'BJP' very significantly though a dip in popularity is observed in 2016 for all the news media houses. For cloze test (c), we see Hindu and India Today both reporting similarly about the economy with higher negative words for economy in 2018 which resonates with the ground truth of GDP growth rate for India but ToI interestingly reports the opposite trend.

References

Azarbonyad, H., Dehghani, M., Beelen, K., Arkut, A., Marx, M., Kamps, J.: Words are malleable: computing semantic shifts in political and media discourse. In: CIKM (2017)

Bakshy, E., Messing, S., Adamic, L.A.: Exposure to ideologically diverse news and opinion on Facebook. Science **348**, 1130–1132 (2015)

Brunet, M.-E., Alkalay-Houlihan, C., Anderson, A., Zemel, R.: Understanding the origins of bias in word embeddings. In: ICML, pp. 803–811 (2019)

Budak, C., Goel, S., Rao, J.M.: Fair and balanced? Quantifying media bias through crowdsourced content analysis. Public Opin. Q. **80**(S1), 250–271 (2016). https://doi.org/10.1093/poq/nfw007

Carter, S., Fico, F., McCabe, J.A.: Partisan and structural balance in local television election coverage. JMCQ **79**, 41–53 (2002)

Corney, D., Albakour, D., Martinez, M., Moussa, S.: What do a million news articles look like? In: Proceedings of the First International Workshop on Recent Trends in News Information Retrieval Co-located with 38th European Conference on Information Retrieval (ECIR 2016), Padua, Italy, 20 March 2016, pp. 42–47 (2016). http://ceur-ws.org/Vol-1568/paper8.pdf

---

[14] https://en.wikipedia.org/wiki/Results_of_the_2019_Indian_general_election.

[15] https://www.theguardian.com/world/2018/aug/30/india-demonetisation-drive-fails-uncover-black-money.

Media Research Users Council. Indian Readership Survey: 2017 (2017)

D'Alessio, D., Allen, M.: Media bias in presidential elections: a meta-analysis. J. Commun. **50**(4), 133–156 (2000)

Bennett, S.E., Rhine, S.L., Flickinger, R.S.: Assessing Americans' opinions about the news media's fairness in 1996 and 1998. Polit. Commun. **18**(2), 163–182 (2001)

Eberl, J.-M.: Lying press: Three levels of perceived media bias and their relationship with political preferences. Communications (2018). https://doi.org/10.1515/commun-2018-0002

Fico, F., Cote, W.: Fairness and balance in the structural characteristics of newspaper stories on the 1996 presidential election. JMCQ **76**, 124–137 (1999)

Fico, F., Freedman, E.: Biasing influences on balance in election news coverage: an assessment of newspaper coverage of the 2006 U.S. senate elections. JMCQ **23**, 23–39 (2008)

Fico, F., Soffin, S.: Fairness and balance of selected newspaper coverage of controversial national, state, and local issues. JMCQ **72**, 621–633 (1995)

Fico, F., Ku, L., Soffin, S.: Fairness, balance of newspaper coverage of U.S. in Gulf war. NRJ **15**, 30 (1994)

Fico, F., Zeldes, G.A., Carpenter, S.M., Diddi, A.: Broadcast and cable network news coverage of the 2004 presidential election: an assessment of Partisan and structural imbalance. Mass Commun. Soc. **11**(3), 319–339 (2008)

Flaxman, S., Goel, S., Rao, J.M.: Echo chambers online?: Politically motivated selective exposure among internet news users. Public Opinion Q. **80**, 298–320 (2016)

Garrett, R.K.: Echo chambers online?: Politically motivated selective exposure among internet news users. J. Comput.-Mediated Commun. **14**, 265–285 2009

Giri, N.A.: Content analysis of media coverage of North East India. Mass Communicator Int. J. Commun. Stud. **9**(1), 4–8 (2015)

Gorwa, R.: The platform governance triangle: conceptualising the informal regulation of online content (2019). https://tinyurl.com/yb6hsys5

Hamilton, W.L., Leskovec, J., Jurafsky, D.: Diachronic word embeddings reveal statistical laws of semantic change. In: ACL (2016)

Khadilkar, K., KhudaBukhsh, A.R., Mitchell, T.M.: Gender bias, social bias and representation: 70 years of B^Hollywood. arXiv preprint arXiv:2102.09103 (2021)

Kiesel, J., et al.: Data for PAN at SemEval 2019 task 4: hyperpartisan news detection, November 2018. https://doi.org/10.5281/zenodo.1489920

Kulkarni, R.: A million news headlines (2018). https://doi.org/10.7910/DVN/SYBGZL

Kulshrestha, J., et al.: Quantifying search bias: investigating sources of bias for political searches in social media. In: Proceedings of CSCW, pp. 417–432 (2017)

Lacy, S., Fico, F., Simon, T.F.: Fairness and balance in the prestige press. JMCQ **68**, 363–370 (1991)

David, M.J., et al.: The science of fake news. Science **359**(6380), 1094–1096 (2018)

Lin, W.-H., Wilson, T., Wiebe, J., Hauptmann, A.: Which side are you on? Identifying perspectives at the document and sentence levels. In: Proceedings of (CoNLL-X) (2006)

Liu, Y., et al.: A robustly optimized BERT pretraining approach. arXiv preprint arXiv:1907.11692 (2019)

Mikolov, T., Chen, K., Corrado, G., Dean, J.: Efficient estimation of word representations in vector space. In: ICLR (2013)

Mitchell, A., Gottfried, J., Matsa, K.E.: Millennials and political news: social media - the local TV for the next generation? Pew Research Center Survey (2015). https://www.journalism.org/2015/06/01/millennials-political-news/

Morgan, J.S., Lampe, C., Shafiq, M.S.: Is news sharing on twitter ideologically biased? In: Proceedings of CSCW, pp. 887–896 (2013)

Munson, S.A., Resnick, P.: Presenting diverse political opinions: how and how much. In: Proceedings of the SIGCHI Conference on Human Factors in Computing Systems, CHI 2010, pp. 1457–1466 (2010)

Munson, S.A., Lee, S.Y., Resnick, P.: Encouraging reading of diverse political viewpoints with a browser widget. In: Proceedings of ICWSM (2013)

Muzny, G., Fang, M., Chang, A., Jurafsky, D.: A two-stage sieve approach for quote attribution. In: EACL (2017)

Oremus, W.: Of Course Facebook is Biased (2016). https://tinyurl.com/y8zq9nqz

Park, S., Kang, S., Chung, S., Song, J.: NewsCube: delivering multiple aspects of news to mitigate media bias. In: Proceedings of the SIGCHI Conference on Human Factors in Computing Systems, CHI 2009, pp. 443–452 (2009)

ProQuest. ProQuest Historical Newspapers (2019). https://www.proquest.com/libraries/academic/news-newspapers/pq-hist-news.html

Resnick, P., Garrett, R.K., Kriplean, T., Munson, S.A., Stroud, N.J.: Bursting your (filter) bubble: strategies for promoting diverse exposure. In: Proceedings of CSCW Companion, pp. 95–100 (2013)

Robertson, R.E., Jiang, S., Joseph, K., Friedland, L., Lazer, D., Wilson, C.: Auditing partisan audience bias within google search. Proc. ACM Hum.-Comput. Interact. 2(CSCW), 148:1–148:22 (2018)

Shearer, E., Matsa, K.E.: News Use Across Social Media Platforms (2018). https://tinyurl.com/y4awgo2p

Spillane, B., Lawless, S., Wade, V.: Perception of bias: the impact of user characteristics, website design and technical features. In: WI (2017)

Taylor, W.L.: "Cloze procedure": a new tool for measuring readability. Journalism Q. 30(4), 415–433 (1953). https://doi.org/10.1177/107769905303000401

Thompson, A.: All the News (2018). https://components.one/datasets/all-the-news-articles-dataset/

Thurman, N., Moeller, J., Helberger, N., Trilling, D.: My friends, editors, algorithms, and i: examining audience attitudes to news selection. Digital C 7(4), 447–469 (2019)

Vosoughi, S., Roy, D., Aral, S.: The spread of true and false news online. Science 359(6380), 1146–1151 (2018)

Short Papers

Deception Detection with Feature-Augmentation by Soft Domain Transfer

Sadat Shahriar[✉], Arjun Mukherjee, and Omprakash Gnawali

University of Houston, Houston, TX 77004, USA
sshahria@cougarnet.uh.edu, arjun@cs.uh.edu, odgnawal@central.uh.edu

Abstract. In this era of information explosion, deceivers use different domains or mediums of information to exploit the users, such as News, Emails, and Tweets. Although numerous research has been done to detect deception in all these domains, information shortage in a new event necessitates these domains to associate with each other to battle deception. To form this association, we propose a feature augmentation method by harnessing the intermediate layer representation of neural models. Our approaches provide an improvement over the self-domain baseline models by up to 6.60%. We find Tweets to be the most helpful information provider for Fake News and Phishing Email detection, whereas News helps most in Tweet Rumour detection. Our analysis provides a useful insight for domain knowledge transfer which can help build a stronger deception detection system than the existing literature.

Keywords: Deception · BERT · LSTM · Phishing · Fake news · Rumour

1 Introduction

Deception in the text implies a deliberate attempt of a sender to misconstrue an affair or create a false impression [2]. Deception in the text can occur in multiple domains like News, Tweets, Emails, and research has been done to detect deception in domain-specific settings [13,16,19]. Although deceivers use their con in each domain with a unique style, all kinds of deception have the same agenda of deceiving people. Hence, detecting deception in one domain can be leveraged with detection in the other domain. In this paper, we perform a soft domain transfer by investigating how to harness the power of deception detection in domain A to detect deception in domain B. We also investigate the effectiveness of domain transfer when the source domain is non-deceptive.

Researchers looked at deception from a holistic point of view in the hope of capturing the nuances in the style of deception [12]. However, it is not clear if such a clear pattern exists since deceptions in different domains are very different. Additionally, further investigation is needed to quantify the "help" received from one domain to the other. To this end, there is a significant research gap in

© The Author(s), under exclusive license to Springer Nature Switzerland AG 2022
F. Hopfgartner et al. (Eds.): SocInfo 2022, LNCS 13618, pp. 373–380, 2022.
https://doi.org/10.1007/978-3-031-19097-1_23

achieving the domain knowledge transfer. We define *Deceptive Domain* as different sources of the information through which deception occurs, and we use fake news, phishing emails, and rumours as deception in different domains. As non-deceptive domains, we use Newsgroup topics, sentiment detection, and Wikipedia ontology detection. Therefore, we formulate our first research question as (**RQ1**): Can knowledge transfer from different domains help improve deception detection? Additionally, our second research question is posed as (**RQ2**) Between the deceptive and non-deceptive domains, which set of domains are most helpful in detecting deception? To answer these questions, we train six different BERT and LSTM models [3, 6] for three deceptive and three non-deceptive domains. We collect the intermediate-layer information of the target domain and harness the power of the external domain by combining the intermediate-layer and train a Fully-Connected Deep Neural Network (FC-DNN) to detect deception. In this way of feature augmentation, we leverage the knowledge of other domains in the FC-DNN model by injecting that knowledge into the input information.

The significance of this study is manifold. First, in many domains, deceptive data is significantly scarce. For example, individuals and corporations are reluctant to share the phishing emails they receive to evade embarrassment [1]. Second, with the influx of social media, the information is flown through different domains when a new event emerges. For example, the emergence of COVID-19 created a significant misinformation upsurge in news, tweets, and Facebook posts; thus, learning deception by relying on one domain only results in missing other domain information. Finally, this study can guide researchers to lay out a selective knowledge transfer scheme from different domains and find the generalized pattern of deception. The novelty of our work is, to the best of our knowledge, this is the first work that explores the effectiveness of domain transfer in deception detection, and opens up new avenues of further promising research.

2   Related Works

Hernández-Castañeda et al. proposed a cross-domain deception detection using SVM, where the datasets were of opinions on different topics [5]. They aimed to find a general set of features in different experimental train-test settings. Similar research was done by [14] and [9]. In the Fake News detection task, Pèrez-Rosas et al. performed cross-domain experiment on two different datasets and showed the challenges of generalizability [11]. Gautam and Jerripothula used Spinbot, Grammarly and GloVe-based method to for cross-domain fake news detection [4]. However, these research were done to make the deception detection system topic-agnostic rather than mediums-of-deception agnostic. Hence, harnessing the deception-detection capability in the cross-domain setting remains an unexplored area.

3   Dataset

For the Email domain, we use a phishing email dataset from the Anti-Phishing Pilot at ACM IWSPA 2018 [17]. The training set has 5092 legitimate and 629 phishing emails, and the test data size is 4300, with 3825 legitimate and 475 phishing emails. We label phishing emails as deceptive and non-phishing as non-deceptive. For the News domain, we use LIAR dataset [18], which comes with six labels of the news, namely, True, Mostly-True, Half-True, Mostly-False, False, Pants-on-Fire False. We consider the first two as non-deceptive text, and the last four as deceptive following the work in [15]. In the training set, the Fake and non-Fake news distribution are 792 and 5092, respectively, and in the test set, we have 475 and 3825, respectively. For the Tweet domain, the PHEME dataset is used, which had 2402 rumour texts, and 4023 non-rumour texts [20]. We label rumour tweets as deceptive and non-rumour tweets as non-deceptive.

For non-deceptive tasks, three datasets are used. The IMDB movie review dataset comes with 50,000 reviews, labeled as positive or negative [10]. The 20 newsgroups dataset consists of around 18000 samples with labels on newsgroups posts about 20 topics [7]. The Wikipedia topic classification dataset consists of 342,782 articles with 9 topic classes [8]. We randomly sample 10,000 texts for each non-deceptive domain and use 80–20 ratio for the train-test.

4 Methodology

We use two neural models– the Bidirectional Encoder Representations from Transformers (BERT) model and Long Short-Term Memory (LSTM) model as baseline methods [3,6]. The BERT model is built with transformer layers consisting of encoders and decoders with self-attention capability. We fine-tune our baseline self-domain BERT model, extract the model's last [CLS] layer, and use an FC layer and a softmax for the downstream classification task. LSTMs are an efficient variation of Recurrent Neural Network (RNN) with added long-term dependency solution. We use the sequence of words as the input of a two-layer LSTM model and use an FC layer on top to classify the text.

For the feature augmentation process, we perform the Intermediate Layer Concatenation (**ILC**), which is explained in Fig. 1. For the BERT model, we extract the self-domain trained [CLS] layers of different domains and concatenate them, representing our target domain's augmented feature set. Similarly, for the LSTM model, we extract the output from the final LSTM layer representation of different domains and concatenate them. The augmented feature set is then fed to a 2-layer Fully-Connected (FC) model to detect deception. Finally, all the network hyperparameters are set using validation sets generated by sampling 20% data from the training set.

5 Results and Discussion

The Table 1 shows the performance of feature augmentation with different deception domains using the BERT-based ILC models. For the Email domain, we observe that the News domain improves the F1 score of phishing detection by 2.31% and the Tweet domain improves the performance by 4.89%. While both Tweet and News domains are combined, we observe a performance boost in

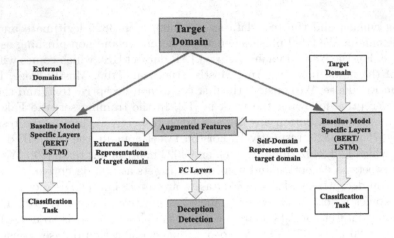

Fig. 1. Feature augmentation by soft domain transfer to improve deception detection. We augment the deceptive features by concatenating the intermediate layer representation of baseline models of both target and external domains and the augmented features are fed to a FC network to detect deception.

F1-score by 6.60%. For News and Tweet domain, we also observe an improved performance with deceptive feature augmentation. Emails help detect fake news by 0.75%, and Tweets help by 1.69%. Tweet rumour detection gets performance improvement of 1.36% from News and 1.14% from Email domain. However, compared to the News and Tweet, performance improvement is higher in the Email domain. Being a pretrained model, BERT is more likely to perform well with public texts like News and Tweet, and thus the baseline model achieves a better understanding of deception in these two domains. Hence, the augmentation from other deceptive domains improves phishing email detection more than deception detection in other domains.

Table 1. Cross-domain deception detection based on BERT models. **E**, **T**, and **N** stands for Email, Tweet and News respectively. For example, "ILC-TN" stands for ILC model where Tweet and News domains are combined.

Domains	Baseline – BERT		ILC – EN		ILC – TN		ILC – ET		ILC – ETN	
	F1	ACC	F1	ACC	F1	ACC	F1	ACC	F1	ACC
Email	80.99	95.41	83.31	96.03	–	–	85.88	96.79	**87.59**	**97.39**
News	76.88	63.55	77.63	63.93	78.57	**67.80**	–	–	**78.80**	67.56
Tweet	80.34	84.79	–	–	81.70	86.23	81.48	85.99	**82.07**	**86.77**

We further investigate the effectiveness of cross-domain feature augmentation by projecting the data to a 2-D subspace using Singular Value Decomposition (SVD) method. Figure 2 clearly shows an improved feature separation while

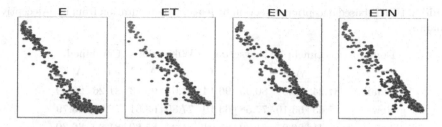

Fig. 2. SVD-reduced representation (BERT model) of Email domain with their self-domain features vs intermediate layer concatenated features with different deception domains. Blue points represent non-deception and red points represent deception (Color figure online)

Tweet and News domains are added with Email, increasing the distance between the deceptive and non-deceptive samples' center of cloud by 50.23%, when all three domains are concatenated.

Using the LSTM-based feature augmentation technique, we compromise overall performance, but unlike BERT, we do not use a pretrained model. Therefore, we observe a consistent performance improvement in all three deception domains (Table 2). In the Email domain, like the BERT-based ILC model, the Tweet domain helps the most, and overall improvement is up to 3.97%, with a combined augmentation. Tweets are the most helpful domain both for Email and News. However, the best performance is obtained while all three domains are combined, giving a performance raise of 4.82% in the News domain and 3.39% in the Tweet domain. As standalone domains, News helps the Tweet domain most, providing a boost of 1.76% in the F1-score.

Table 2. Cross-domain deception detection based on LSTM models.

Domains	Baseline – LSTM		ILC – EN		ILC – TN		ILC – ET		ILC – ETN	
	F1	ACC	F1	ACC	F1	ACC	F1	ACC	F1	ACC
Email	71.23	92.23	72.04	92.45	–	–	74.96	94.68	**75.20**	**94.87**
News	72.71	62.03	74.69	62.43	75.45	63.18	–	–	**77.53**	**63.59**
Tweet	73.11	77.16	–	–	74.87	79.29	74.18	79.00	**76.50**	**82.13**

Next, we investigate deception detection performance while augmented with non-deceptive domains using BERT models. From Table 3, we observe that Sentiment and Wikipedia slightly improve the performance of phishing email detection, and with combined domains, it improves by 0.27% in F1-score. For the News domain, Wikipedia helps the most, and overall we get a 1.16% improvement in F1 score with all the domains combined. The Sentiment is the most helpful domain for detecting rumour in Tweets, improving the performance by 1.07% in the F1-score, and with the combined domains, the improvement is 1.55%. We

Table 3. BERT-based deception detection by feature augmentation from non-deceptive domains.

Domains	Sentiment		Newsgroup		Wikipedia		Combined	
	F1	ACC	F1	ACC	F1	ACC	F1	ACC
Email	81.24	96.09	80.95	96.14	81.04	96.13	81.26	96.09
News	77.43	63.10	77.58	63.19	77.89	63.51	78.05	63.79
Tweet	81.41	86.07	81.32	85.91	81.24	85.80	81.89	86.30

also find a similar performance with LSTM-based ILC models, with the best performance in combined domains, improving the Email, News, and Tweet domain deception detection by 2.60%, 5.04%, and 3.10% respectively (Table 4).

From the above discussion, we find that the feature augmentation from different domains helps improve the deception detection task. However, the performance boost is greater when the external domain is deceptive than a non-deceptive one, and thus, a soft domain transfer takes place.

Table 4. LSTM-based deception detection by feature augmentation from non-deceptive domains.

Domains	Sentiment		Newsgroup		Wikipedia		Combined	
	F1	ACC	F1	ACC	F1	ACC	F1	ACC
Email	73.18	93.41	71.49	92.18	72.17	92.77	73.83	94.11
News	72.80	61.97	72.96	62.11	75.50	63.37	76.48	63.41
Tweet	73.93	78.32	73.00	77.91	75.17	81.56	76.21	82.02

6   Conclusion and Future Work

Despite the research on deception detection in many existing domains, there is a research gap on how to harness cross-domain deception detection by transferring the knowledge gained from one domain to the other. In this paper, we bridge the gap using an intermediate-layer concatenation approach from the neural model. There are several future research directions for this work. First, our analysis is limited to three domains only. Several other domains, e.g., reviews, Facebook posts, and Whatsapp message forwards, can also be explored for cross-domain deception detection. Furthermore, we use only one dataset in each domain. Additional research with more datasets in these domains will help solidify our hypothesis.

Acknowledgements. The research was supported in part by grants NSF 1838147, ARO W911NF-20-1-0254. The views and conclusions contained in this document are those of the authors and not of the sponsors. The U.S. Government is authorized to reproduce and distribute reprints for Government purposes notwithstanding any copyright notation herein.

References

1. Aassal, A.E., Moraes, L., Baki, S., Das, A., Verma, R.: Anti-phishing pilot at ACM IWSPA 2018 evaluating performance with new metrics for unbalanced datasets, pp. 2–10. http://ceur-ws.org/Vol-2124/#anti-phishing-pilot
2. Burgoon, J.K., Buller, D.B.: Interpersonal deception: III. Effects of deceit on perceived communication and nonverbal behavior dynamics. J. Nonverbal Behav. **18**(2), 155–184 (1994). https://doi.org/10.1007/BF02170076
3. Devlin, J., Chang, M.W., Lee, K., Toutanova, K.: BERT: pre-training of deep bidirectional transformers for language understanding. ArXiv abs/1810.04805 (2019)
4. Gautam, A., Jerripothula, K.R.: SGG: Spinbot, grammarly and glove based fake news detection. In: 2020 IEEE Sixth International Conference on Multimedia Big Data (BigMM), pp. 174–182 (2020)
5. Hernández-Castañeda, Á., Calvo, H., Gelbukh, A., Flores, J.J.G.: Cross-domain deception detection using support vector networks. Soft. Comput. **21**(3), 585–595 (2016). https://doi.org/10.1007/s00500-016-2409-2
6. Hochreiter, S., Schmidhuber, J.: Long short-term memory. Neural Comput. **9**(8), 1735–1780 (1997)
7. Lang, K.: NewsWeeder: learning to filter netnews. In: Proceedings of the Twelfth International Conference on Machine Learning, pp. 331–339 (1995)
8. Lehmann, J., et al.: DBpedia - a large-scale, multilingual knowledge base extracted from Wikipedia. Semant. Web **6**, 167–195 (2015)
9. Li, J., Ott, M., Cardie, C., Hovy, E.: Towards a general rule for identifying deceptive opinion spam. In: Proceedings of the 52nd Annual Meeting of the Association for Computational Linguistics (Volume 1: Long Papers), Baltimore, Maryland, pp. 1566–1576. Association for Computational Linguistics, June 2014. https://doi.org/10.3115/v1/P14-1147. https://aclanthology.org/P14-1147
10. Maas, A.L., Daly, R.E., Pham, P.T., Huang, D., Ng, A.Y., Potts, C.: Learning word vectors for sentiment analysis. In: Proceedings of the 49th Annual Meeting of the Association for Computational Linguistics: Human Language Technologies, Portland, Oregon, USA, pp. 142–150. Association for Computational Linguistics, June 2011. http://www.aclweb.org/anthology/P11-1015
11. Pérez-Rosas, V., Kleinberg, B., Lefevre, A., Mihalcea, R.: Automatic detection of fake news. In: COLING (2018)
12. Shahriar, S., Mukherjee, A., Gnawali, O.: A domain-independent holistic approach to deception detection. In: Proceedings of the International Conference on Recent Advances in Natural Language Processing (RANLP 2021), pp. 1308–1317 (2021)
13. Shu, K., Sliva, A., Wang, S., Tang, J., Liu, H.: Fake news detection on social media: a data mining perspective. ACM SIGKDD Explor. Newsl. **19**(1), 22–36 (2017)
14. Sánchez-Junquera, J., Villaseñor-Pineda, L., Montes-y-Gómez, M., Rosso, P., Stamatatos, E.: Masking domain-specific information for cross-domain deception detection. Pattern Recogn. Lett. **135**, 122–130 (2020). https://doi.org/10.1016/j.patrec.2020.04.020. https://www.sciencedirect.com/science/article/pii/S0167865520301422
15. Upadhayay, B., Behzadan, V.: Sentimental LIAR: extended corpus and deep learning models for fake claim classification (2020)
16. Varshney, G., Misra, M., Atrey, P.K.: A survey and classification of web phishing detection schemes. Secur. Commun. Netw. **9**(18), 6266–6284 (2016)

17. Verma, R.M., Zeng, V., Faridi, H.: Data quality for security challenges: case studies of phishing, malware and intrusion detection datasets. In: Proceedings of the 2019 ACM SIGSAC Conference on Computer and Communications Security, CCS 2019, pp. 2605–2607. Association for Computing Machinery, New York (2019). https://doi.org/10.1145/3319535.3363267
18. Wang, W.Y.: "Liar, liar pants on fire": a new benchmark dataset for fake news detection. In: Proceedings of the 55th Annual Meeting of the Association for Computational Linguistics (Volume 2: Short Papers), Vancouver, Canada, pp. 422–426. Association for Computational Linguistics, July 2017. https://doi.org/10.18653/v1/P17-2067. https://www.aclweb.org/anthology/P17-2067
19. Zubiaga, A., Aker, A., Bontcheva, K., Liakata, M., Procter, R.: Detection and resolution of rumours in social media: a survey. ACM Comput. Surv. (CSUR) **51**(2), 1–36 (2018)
20. Zubiaga, A., Hoi, G.W.S., Liakata, M., Procter, R.: PHEME dataset of rumours and non-rumours, October 2016. https://doi.org/10.6084/m9.figshare.4010619.v1

User-Based Stance Analysis for Mitigating the Impact of Social Bots on Measuring Public Opinion with Stance Detection in Twitter

Ali Almadan[(✉)] and Mary Lou Maher

The Department of Software and Information Systems, The University of North
Carolina at Charlotte, Charlotte, NC 28223, USA
{aalmadan,mmaher9}@uncc.edu

Abstract. Stance detection is the task of detecting the standpoint of a
user towards a target of interest, such as a controversial topic. Stance detection has various applications such as surveying and polling the public as
an alternative to traditional instruments to measure public opinion. One of
the implications of using stance detection on Twitter data to measure public opinion is the prevalence of social bots that can impact the measured
public opinion. In this paper, we propose a user-based stance analysis to
mitigate the impact of social bots on measuring public opinion from stance
detection in Twitter. In contrast to a tweet-based stance analysis, the user-
based stance analysis shows a minimal impact of social bots on measured
public opinion for all stance classes: favor, against, and neutral.

Keywords: Public opinion · Stance detection · Stance analysis ·
Social bots

1 Introduction

Social media platforms provide a medium for users to freely express their opinions towards various issues [3,17]. While sentiment analysis, or opinion mining,
has long been used to analyze public opinion, recent studies have shown a mis-
alignment between text polarity and the user's standpoint towards the target
[1,8,24]. On the other hand, stance detection is argued to better align with
public opinion. Therefore, it can be seen as an alternative or a complement to
traditional instruments to measure public opinion [16]. However, one implication
of using Twitter as a measure of public opinion is the presence of social bots [14].

To understand the impact of social bots on the measured public opinion
and how such impact can be mitigated, we analyze the stance by using two
analysis approaches: tweet-based and user-based stance analyses. In a tweet-
based approach, the stances of favor, against, and neutral *tweets* are aggregated
and visualized separately on daily basis. In contrast, a user-based stance analysis
approach makes the *user* the center of the analysis by inferring the stance of
the user from their tweets as users are the unit of analysis for public opinion.

F. Hopfgartner et al. (Eds.): SocInfo 2022, LNCS 13618, pp. 381–388, 2022.
https://doi.org/10.1007/978-3-031-19097-1_24

Therefore, the stances of favor, against, and neutral users are aggregated and visualized. In this paper, we aim to answer the following research question:

- **RQ)** How does a user-based stance analysis mitigate the impact of social bots on measured public opinion in Twitter?

To answer the research question, we collect and analyze English tweets and bot scores associated with the accounts contributing to the vaccination discussion on Twitter by following these two analysis approaches. This study provides insights for researchers to minimize the impact of bots on their measurement of public opinion and improve the robustness of their measurement of public opinion using stance detection.

2 Background and Related Work

2.1 Social Bots

In social media research, social bots are automated programs that exhibit human-like behavior and generate and spread content on social media [14]. Social bots can be benign or malicious. While benign bots (also called good, helpful, and useful) automatically generate helpful information such as news and weather reports, malicious bots are widely used to spread false information and influence public opinion. Social bots can influence public opinion by tweeting and retweeting content on Twitter.

Recent research studies suggest that bots contribute to the discussion of sensitive topics such as politics and the vaccination debate [10,22]. In 2016, bots played a role in manipulating public opinion in the US presidential elections [7,9]. In one study [11], researchers found that bot accounts tweet with higher frequency than non-bot accounts. To the best of our knowledge, the literature lacks studies that investigate the impact of bots on tweet-based and user-based stance analysis as measures of public opinion.

2.2 Stance Detection

Stance detection, also known as stance prediction and classification, on Twitter is the task of automatically determining the standpoint expressed in a tweet towards a target of interest, such as a person, topic, organization, issue, or claim [3,17]. Stance detection is different from sentiment analysis, another well-known NLP task, where the latter focuses on determining the polarity of the text in a tweet [18]. A fundamental difference between the two tasks is that sentiment analysis is intended to determine the polarity of the tweet (positive, negative, or neutral). On the other hand, stance analysis intends to determine the users' attitude towards the target based on their tweets (favor, against, neutral).

Most stance detection studies are concerned with improving the performance of stance detection algorithms [2,5,20,23,25]. However, some studies have gone beyond the algorithm and used stance detection for the application of measuring public opinion. One study followed a tweet-based stance analysis to analyze public opinion towards masks during the COVID-19 pandemic [12]. In another study [6], the researchers followed a user-based stance analysis as a measure of public opinion towards vaccination in Italy. In the work of [15], the authors followed a user-based stance analysis approach to gauge public opinion towards Brexit. However, previous studies have not considered the impact of social bots on tweet-based and user-based stance analyses.

3 Data Collection and Classification

To answer our research question, we collected tweets related to vaccination using Twitter's streaming API between August 7, 2021 and November 28th, 2021. During this period, some COVID-19 vaccines, such as the Pfizer and Moderna vaccines, were widely available to the population and individuals used Twitter to express their opinion about vaccination. We elected to use the streaming API as opposed to the historical API to be able to collect account information before any account is deleted or suspended. To ensure reliable data collection, we set up the data stream on Amazon Web Services (AWS). To filter the stream, we used general vaccine-related keywords and hashtags from the literature to examine pro- and anti-vaccination (ProVax and AntiVax) users on Twitter. For example, we used the hashtag #vaccineswork to filter tweets in favor of vaccination and the hashtag #vaccinefraud to filter tweets against vaccination. We include the full list of keywords and hashtags in Appendix A. The final dataset has 15,813,362 original tweets and 3,286,474 unique users. We excluded retweets and quotes because they do not necessarily indicate endorsement [19].

To identify bot accounts in our data, we used Botometer V4 to assess whether an account exhibits an automated behavior [13]. Botometer assigns bot scores between 0 and 1, where a score of 0 indicates the account is unlikely to be a bot and a score of 1 indicates the account is likely to be a bot. Botometer has English and Universal scores, where the former incorporates language-specific features. Since our data consists of English tweets only, we used the English scores.

In this research, we do not use the numerical bot scores. Instead, our interest is to assign the accounts binary labels (bot or non-bot) based on the numerical value. Therefore, a threshold had to be selected. For the purpose of assigning binary labels to accounts (bot vs. non-bot) in this paper, we reviewed the Botometers's instructions and threshold for assigning labels based on the scores as follows:

- 0.00 <= score <= 0.39: Likely not bot
- 0.40 <= score <= 0.60: Unclear
- 0.61 <= score <= 1.00: Likely bot

To minimize the impact of bot misclassification on the analysis, we considered accounts with bot scores below 0.40 to be non-bot accounts and accounts with bot scores above 0.61 to be bot accounts. Therefore, we discarded the unclear accounts with bot scores between 0.40 and 0.60.

In our exploratory analysis, we found that bot accounts do not survive suspension for a long period of time, especially if they violates Twitter's terms of service. This aligns with the findings of [11]. To ensure that we collect the bot scores before they become unavailable due to the deletion or suspension of the accounts, we retrieved the bot scores while the tweets were being streamed. As soon as we streamed the data, we used our AWS architecture to fully automate the bot score collection and processing. Once a Twitter data file is complete and has 100,000 tweets, a program reads the file and maintains a list of the unique users in the file. Then, the program feeds the list of unique users to Botometer to check the likelihood of the account being a bot. Following this method, we report that the number of accounts that were deleted or suspended when retrieving the bot scores was only 1% of the total accounts. Our final bot dataset has 3,245,504 unique users with their associated bot scores.

For stance detection, we used stance labels that are specific to vaccination: ProVax, AntiVax, and Neutral. We automatically classified the stance of each tweet towards vaccination using a state-of-the-art stance classifier [21] which is publicly available[1]. The CT-BERT++ classifier was trained on tweets before COVID-19 and during COVID-19 after the outbreak between 2019 and 2021, and the authors report an average macro F1 score of 0.775. The classifier was also validated using a different manually labeled Twitter dataset [4], resulting in a macro average F1 score of 0.83 for the ProVax and AntiVax stance classes. Using the classifier, we classified all tweets in the dataset into three stance classes: ProVax (43%), AntiVax (39%), and Neutral (18%).

4   Analysis and Discussion

Stance detection provides a classification for each tweet. Since public opinion is associated with individual users rather than individual tweets, we include in our analysis of the results of stance detection both a tweet-based and a user-based aggregation. We explore the effect of a user-based analysis on the impact of social bots on measured public opinion and compare it to a tweet-based analysis. We examined the presence of bots in our data and found that on average 15% of the accounts that tweeted on a particular day were bot accounts. We also note that bot accounts were present in all the ProVax, AntiVax, and Neutral stance classes. Table 1 shows examples of tweets posted by bot and non-bot accounts.

We aggregate the tweet-based stance for one day by calculating the ratio of tweets in each class (ProVax, AntiVax, and Neutral) as classified by the classifier to the total number of tweets that day. The tweet-based stance ST for a stance class c on a specific day i is measured as shown in Eq. 1.

$$ST_{c,i} = \frac{t_{c,i}}{t_i} \tag{1}$$

where $c = \{ProVax, AntiVax, Neutral\}$, $t_{c,i}$ is the number of tweets that belong to class c for day i, and t_i is the total number of tweets for day i.

---

[1] https://github.com/sohampoddar26/covid-vax-stance.

Table 1. Examples of tweets posted by bot and non-bot accounts

Tweet	Account type	Stance
Wouldn't it be easier, cheaper, and healthier for everyone to get the vaccine so we don't need these ambulances? We could wear masks until that happens	Non-bot	ProVax
No. The vaccine is a magnetic device to track us	Non-bot	AntiVax
I thought she was comparing vaccines	Non-bot	Neutral
The evidence that the vaccine is SAFE all the studies that make up the FULL CLINICAL TRIALS - which any vaccine or drug has before it goes to market	Bot	ProVax
They're not "vaccine passports," they're movement licenses. It's not a vaccine, it's experimental gene therapy. "Lockdown" is at best completely pointless universal medical isolation and at worst ubiquitous public incarceration. Call things what they are, not their euphemisms	Bot	AntiVax
BREAKING: San Francisco to require proof of COVID vaccine to enter restaurants, bars, gyms, etc., becoming first major U.S. city to do so	Bot	Neutral

We followed two steps to identify the user-based stance. First, we determine the daily stance for each unique users from the stance of their tweets, where a user's stance is defined by the stance of the majority of their tweets for a specific day. Second, we calculate the user-based stance SU for a stance class c on specific day i as shown in Eq. 2.

$$SU_{c,i} = \frac{u_{c,i}}{u_i} \tag{2}$$

where $c = \{ProVax, AntiVax, Neutral\}$, $u_{c,i}$ is the number of users that belong to class c for day i, and u_i is the total number of users for day i. We assume that a user's stance will typically remain constant for a short period of time, such as 24 h, and when there are specific days in which their stance changes, we can use the majority stance for that day.

A comparison of tweet-based and user-based stance analyses with and without bots is shown in Fig. 1. The blue dotted lines represent the stance with bots and the orange solid lines represent the stance without bots. We observe a visible difference between tweet-based stance with and without bots for ProVax, AntiVax, and Neutral stances. This is evidence that tweet-based stance analysis is sensitive to the presence of bots. We observe that the user-based stance with bots and the user-based stance without bots are visually identical at the same scale as tweet-based stance. Bots are designed to automate the spread of content and to do so, bots tend to tweet with high frequency. In our data, the top 10 tweeting accounts were bots guiding users to locations where vaccination was available. Therefore, these bots did not have a polarized stance. However, bots could play a different role for other stance targets. Because tweet-based stance analysis considers *individual tweets* regardless of whether they were posted by the same account, the increased frequency of bot tweets has an impact on

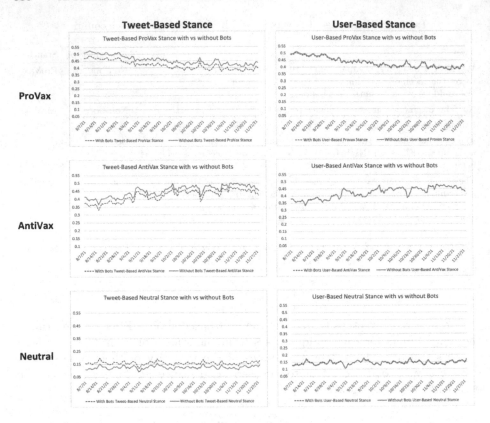

Fig. 1. Tweet-based and user-based stance analysis with and without bots (Color figure online)

measuring public opinion. Our analysis shows that the user-based stance analysis is more robust to the presence of bots because each bot is considered an *individual user* and the increased frequency of bot tweets does not impact the measure of public opinion.

5   Conclusion

This paper describes and compares two approaches for measuring public opinion with stance detection from Twitter data: tweet-based and user-based analyses. We found that tweet-based stance is sensitive to bots, and there was a minimal impact of bots on measuring public opinion with user-based stance analysis. The results of this study provide insights for researchers who intend to use stance detection for measuring public opinion from Twitter data. Although we show that there is a difference between tweet-based and user-based stance analyses in mitigating bots' impact on measuring public opinion about vaccines, we note that this may be context sensitive. The paper provides a method to investigate whether a user-based stance analysis mitigates the impact of bots for other stance targets.

A   Appendix: Data Collection

To collect tweets related to the vaccination discussion, we used the following keywords and hashtags:

Keywords: 'vaccine', 'vaccines', 'vaccination', 'vaccinations'
Hashtags: '#antivaxxers', '#antivax', '#antivaxxer', '#vaccineagenda', '#vaccineswork', '#novaccineforme', '#antivaccination', '#novaccinemandate', '#vaccinesprotect', '#vaccines4results', '#vaccinesaregenocide', '#novaccineforme', '#vacccinessavelives', '#vaxwithme', '#vaccineinjury', '#vaccinedeath', '#vaccinedamage', '#novaccine', '#vaccinefraud', '#vaccineskill', '#vaccinesarepoison'

References

1. Aldayel, A., Magdy, W.: Assessing sentiment of the expressed stance on social media. In: Weber, I., et al. (eds.) SocInfo 2019. LNCS, vol. 11864, pp. 277–286. Springer, Cham (2019). https://doi.org/10.1007/978-3-030-34971-4_19
2. Aldayel, A., Magdy, W.: Your stance is exposed! Analysing possible factors for stance detection on social media. Proc. ACM Hum.-Comput. Interact. **3**(CSCW), 1–20 (2019)
3. AlDayel, A., Magdy, W.: Stance detection on social media: state of the art and trends. Inf. Process. Manag. **58**(4), 102597 (2021)
4. Almadan, A., Maher, M.L., Pereira, F.B., Guo, Y.: Will you be vaccinated? A methodology for annotating and analyzing Twitter data to measure the stance towards COVID-19 vaccination. In: Arai, K. (ed.) FICC 2022. LNNS, vol. 438, pp. 311–329. Springer, Cham (2022). https://doi.org/10.1007/978-3-030-98012-2_24
5. Augenstein, I., Rocktäschel, T., Vlachos, A., Bontcheva, K.: Stance detection with bidirectional conditional encoding. arXiv preprint arXiv:1606.05464 (2016)
6. Bechini, A., Ducange, P., Marcelloni, F., Renda, A.: Stance analysis of Twitter users: the case of the vaccination topic in Italy. IEEE Intell. Syst. **36**(5), 131–139 (2020)
7. Bessi, A., Ferrara, E.: Social bots distort the 2016 US presidential election online discussion. First Monday **21**(11), 14 (2016)
8. Bestvater, S., Monroe, B.: Sentiment is not stance: target-aware opinion classification for political text analysis. Polit. Anal., 1–22 (2022). https://doi.org/10.1017/pan.2022.10
9. Boichak, O., Jackson, S., Hemsley, J., Tanupabrungsun, S.: Automated diffusion? Bots and their influence during the 2016 U.S. presidential election. In: Chowdhury, G., McLeod, J., Gillet, V., Willett, P. (eds.) iConference 2018. LNCS, vol. 10766, pp. 17–26. Springer, Cham (2018). https://doi.org/10.1007/978-3-319-78105-1_3
10. Broniatowski, D.A., et al.: Weaponized health communication: Twitter bots and Russian trolls amplify the vaccine debate. Am. J. Public Health **108**(10), 1378–1384 (2018)
11. Chu, Z., Gianvecchio, S., Wang, H., Jajodia, S.: Who is tweeting on Twitter: human, bot, or cyborg? In: Proceedings of the 26th Annual Computer Security Applications Conference, pp. 21–30 (2010)

12. Cotfas, L.A., Delcea, C., Gherai, R., Roxin, I.: Unmasking people's opinions behind mask-wearing during COVID-19 pandemic-a Twitter stance analysis. Symmetry **13**(11), 1995 (2021)
13. Davis, C.A., Varol, O., Ferrara, E., Flammini, A., Menczer, F.: BotOrNot: a system to evaluate social bots. In: Proceedings of the 25th International Conference Companion on World Wide Web, pp. 273–274 (2016)
14. Ferrara, E., Varol, O., Davis, C., Menczer, F., Flammini, A.: The rise of social bots. Commun. ACM **59**(7), 96–104 (2016)
15. Grčar, M., Cherepnalkoski, D., Mozetič, I., Kralj Novak, P.: Stance and influence of Twitter users regarding the Brexit referendum. Comput. Soc. Netw. **4**(1), 1–25 (2017). https://doi.org/10.1186/s40649-017-0042-6
16. Joseph, K., et al.: (Mis)alignment between stance expressed in social media data and public opinion surveys. arXiv preprint arXiv:2109.01762 (2021)
17. Küçük, D., Can, F.: Stance detection: a survey. ACM Comput. Surv. (CSUR) **53**(1), 1–37 (2020)
18. Liu, B., et al.: Sentiment analysis and subjectivity. In: Handbook of Natural Language Processing, vol. 2, pp. 627–666 (2010)
19. Metaxas, P., Mustafaraj, E., Wong, K., Zeng, L., O'Keefe, M., Finn, S.: What do retweets indicate? Results from user survey and meta-review of research. In: Proceedings of the International AAAI Conference on Web and Social Media, vol. 9, pp. 658–661 (2015)
20. Mohtarami, M., Baly, R., Glass, J., Nakov, P., Màrquez, L., Moschitti, A.: Automatic stance detection using end-to-end memory networks. arXiv preprint arXiv:1804.07581 (2018)
21. Poddar, S., Mondal, M., Misra, J., Ganguly, N., Ghosh, S.: Winds of change: impact of COVID-19 on vaccine-related opinions of twitter users. In: Proceedings of the International AAAI Conference on Web and Social Media, vol. 16, pp. 782–793 (2022)
22. Stukal, D., Sanovich, S., Bonneau, R., Tucker, J.A.: Detecting bots on Russian political Twitter. Big Data **5**(4), 310–324 (2017)
23. Sun, Q., Wang, Z., Li, S., Zhu, Q., Zhou, G.: Stance detection via sentiment information and neural network model. Front. Comput. Sci. **13**(1), 127–138 (2019)
24. Tachaiya, J., Irani, A., Esterling, K.M., Faloutsos, M.: SentiStance: quantifying the intertwined changes of sentiment and stance in response to an event in online forums. In: Proceedings of the 2021 IEEE/ACM International Conference on Advances in Social Networks Analysis and Mining, pp. 361–368 (2021)
25. Zhang, Q., Yilmaz, E., Liang, S.: Ranking-based method for news stance detection. In: Companion Proceedings of the Web Conference 2018, pp. 41–42 (2018)

'You Are Big, S/he Is Small' Detecting Body Shaming in Online User Content

Varsha Reddy[1]([✉])(ID), Harika Abburi[1](ID), Niyati Chhaya[1,2](ID),
Tamara Mitrovska[3](ID), and Vasudeva Varma[1](ID)

[1] IIIT-Hyderabad, Information Retrieval and Extraction Lab,
Gachibowli, Hyderabad, Telangana, India
varshareddy842@gmail.com, vv@iiit.ac.in
[2] Adobe Research, Bengaluru, Karnataka, India
nchhaya@adobe.com
[3] MIT, Computer Science and Artificial Intelligence Lab, Cambridge, USA

Abstract. Body shaming, a criticism based on the body's shape, size, or appearance, has become a dangerous act on social media. With a rise in the reporting of body shaming experiences on the web, automated monitoring of body shaming posts will help rescue individuals, especially adolescents, from the emotional anguish they experience. To the best of our knowledge, this is the first work on body shaming detection, and we contribute the dataset in which the posts are tagged as body shaming or non-body shaming. We use transformer-based language models to detect body shaming posts. Further, we leverage unlabeled data in a semi-supervised manner using the GAN-BERT model, as it was developed for tasks where labeled data is scarce and unlabeled data is abundant. The findings of the experiments reveal that the algorithm learns valuable knowledge from the unlabeled dataset and outperforms many deep learning and conventional machine learning baselines.

Keywords: Body shaming · Semi-supervised learning · Transformers · Classification

1 Introduction

Body shaming refers to treating individuals unjustifiably based on their physical appearance. Historically, manifested in verbal communications, physical discrimination is now rampant in social media conversations. Studies establish the severe impact of body shaming on targeted individuals' mental and physical health, often leading to social anxiety and depression, especially body dysmorphic disorders(BDD). The negative impact of this discrimination is most observed in pre-teen, and school students [9], making it even more critical to curtail. Given a large number of body shaming content on public platforms, both in textual and visual forms, automatic identification of body shaming may help policy-makers and social scientists fight these phenomena. We believe automated detection

© The Author(s), under exclusive license to Springer Nature Switzerland AG 2022
F. Hopfgartner et al. (Eds.): SocInfo 2022, LNCS 13618, pp. 389–397, 2022.
https://doi.org/10.1007/978-3-031-19097-1_25

methods can lead to mitigation of the propagation and promotion of this type of abusive content resulting in controlling the negative impact on society.

Sexism-related discrimination [16] and abusive language detection [15] from social media have recently gained popularity in academia. However, studies focusing on physical discrimination in online user content are limited. Online shaming can manifest in various ways. Here, we focus on physical appearance-based discrimination, i.e., body shaming. [16] introduces body shaming as a significant category of discrimination found in self-reported discrimination instances available online via the Everyday Sexism Project[1]. Their dataset contains 542 posts that include discrimination based on physical appearance. Their work does not present a study or methods specific to physical discrimination. In [14], authors look at shaming in media and news, and [12] presents a study mapping body shaming to BDD in teenage girls. [1] presents a detailed analysis of the occurrence of body shaming on social media without providing computational models using machine learning approaches. There is a significant visual element in this type of discrimination as well. [10] looks at discrimination detection from vlogs and [8] studies these phenomena from visual and text content in memes. None of these aim at automated detection of physical discrimination from the textual content.

In this work, we focus on detecting body shaming from the text available in Instagram posts[2]. We introduce a dataset of 2159 posts with binary labels that define the existence or absence of body shaming. We also leverage a large unlabeled dataset to test and benchmark several deep-learning and statistical machine learning models for detecting body shaming, modeled as a semi-supervision problem. Through experiments, we establish the superiority of transformer-based models, i.e., BERT [6] with adversarial learning, GAN-BERT [5] over all other baselines for body-shaming detection in social media posts using textual information only, reducing the overhead of visual cues and large labeled datasets. The key contributions of this work include,

- This is the first work on classifying the body shaming posts explicitly. We created the dataset consisting of 2159 posts that are tagged as either body shaming or non-body shaming.
- We investigate the state-of-the-art transformers for the task of body shaming detection.
- We explore the semi-supervised BERT with adversarial learning (GAN-BERT) to leverage the information present in the unlabeled data for this task. It yields superior results to many traditional machine learning and deep learning baselines.

2   Dataset

The dataset was created in two stages: textual data collection and labeling. We first consider 542 posts from Parikh et al. [16], labeled as body shaming, as the

---

[1] https://everydaysexism.com/.
[2] www.instagram.com.

first path of our dataset. The remaining posts are scraped from Instagram with specific hashtags to create a collection of potential interest. The hashtags are-**body shaming, fat shaming, skinny shaming, mom shaming, victim shaming, and body image**. We scraped 52000 posts, non-English posts were ignored, resulting in 44617 posts. We reserve a random subset for labeling and formed an unlabeled dataset with 44617 posts. Each post was annotated by two annotators, referring to the guidelines that a social scientist frames before doing the annotations[3]. Any post with "Objectionable comments or behaviour concerning appearance including the promotion of certain body types or standards." is tagged body-shaming. We combined the posts the annotators agreed upon with the initial 542 posts and finally formed a dataset of 2159 posts, of which 736 are positive, and 1423 are negative. Example posts are shown in Table 1. Our dataset is available here[4].

Part-of-Speech Tags: Table 2 shows the top 10 words across different parts of speech tags for the positive class.

Language Analysis: We provide a linguistic analysis of this labeled data using EMPATH [7], a tool for analyzing text across lexical categories (similar to Linguistic Inquiry and Word Count (LIWC) [17]). We focus on the EMPATH scores for *Body, Shame, Shape and Size, Hate,* and *Sexual* categories. Details concerning how the EMPATH scores are computed can be found in EMPATH 2016 [7]. Table 3 shows the scores for these EMPATH categories for both the classes of body shaming. For each category, we compute the EMPATH scores for all posts tagged with that class label and then calculate the average across all posts for that class to obtain the category-level scores. Significantly higher scores indicate the role of language here.

2.1 Ethical Concerns

We abide by the ethical principles concerned with the privacy and anonymity of users. Our dataset contains only publicly available posts. The author's usernames are not saved or used, which could contain sensitive information about the user's identity.

3 Benchmark Models

We model body shaming detection as a binary classification task. A GAN-BERT based semi-supervised approach is evaluated along with several transformer-based and baseline methods.

---

[3] (Guidelines for annotation.)

[4] https://github.com/Harikavuppalala/Bodyshaming_classification/tree/master/data.

Table 1. Samples from the labeled dataset

Post	Label
Walking home from college and random male stranger thinks its acceptable to pass judgement on my appearance, you're ugly	1
The first message I ever got on FaceBook was "You have fat ti**ies baby."	1
The instructor in my yoga class called the women darling and the men boss	0
You never know what someone is going .Be kind, fat shaming is real be kind	0

Table 2. Top 10 words across PoS tags and High frequency Bi-grams for the Body Shaming (positive) class

Features	Words
Nouns	body, people, weight, time, way, thing, someone, day, year, woman
Adjectives	fat, much, many, good, healthy, first, skinny, big, happy, last
Pronouns	my, you, it, me, they, we, your, their, myself, our
Bi-grams	(lose, weight) (look, like) (feel, like) (make, feel) (body, image) (body, shaming) (weight, loss) (people, think) (gain, weight) (first, time)

Table 3. Linguistic analysis of the labeled dataset

Empath feature	Body shaming	Non-Body shaming
Body	472	383
Shame	276	207
Shape and size	295	178
Hate	231	165
Sexual	100	96

3.1   GAN-BERT

GAN-BERT [5] is built on top of BERT [6] based on the SS-GAN [19]. It is primarily applicable in a semi-supervised setting with abundant unlabeled and scarce labeled data. It comprises two components during BERT's fine-tuning stage - Discriminator(D) and Generator(G). G's responsibility is to generate fake samples mimicking the original dataset from a fixed sized random vector. D's goal is to determine whether the input is fake and, in turn, classify the real inputs into the right class label in case of a labeled real sample. The model has loss components from both D & G. We take an 85–15 split of the labeled data for training and validation and experiment with different random subsets of the complete unlabeled data. We tune the batch size in the range of 8–64, max sequence length from 16–100, and learning rate between 1e-4 and 1e-5. We find that a batch size of 64, a max sequence length of 64, and a learning rate of 2e-5 give the best results.

3.2 Transformer Based, Traditional ML, DL Models

We consider the performance of **transformer based models**, namely BERT [6], RoBERTa [13] and XLNet [20]. We train all the layers of the pre-trained model, including the final classification layer, as part of the fine-tuning procedure in all cases. We take the bert-base-cased, roberta-base, and xlnet-base-cased pre-trained models and experiment with different max sequence lengths ranging from 32 to 300. We experimented with the batch size with values ranging from 8 to 64. The best model setting on the validation data for all the models was with a batch size of 8, a max sequence length of 128, a learning rate of 4e-5, cross-entropy loss, and Adam optimizer.

Under the **Traditional Machine Learning (ML) models category**, we experiment with SVM [3], Logistic regression [4], and XGBoost [2]. We use three sentence embedding schemes BERT, ELMo [18], and Tf-Idf embeddings. We do not fine-tune the model parameters in BERT and ELMo here. We experimented with other prominent embedding methods, but we reported only BERT and ELMo as they performed best. For Tf-idf char, we consider 1–5 n-grams. We perform hyper-parameter tuning using Grid search to obtain the best model parameters in each case. We tune the C value for a range of 1e-2 to 1e3 for both SVM and Logistic models. For SVM, we experiment with RBF, sigmoid and linear kernels. We tune the max_depth parameter of XGboost. For all the classifiers, we perform class balanced loss computation to tackle the imbalance in the dataset.

For all the methods considered in the **Traditional Deep Learning (DL) models category**, we feed the model with BERT and ELMo word embeddings and finally pass the sentence vector obtained to an Multi layer perceptron classification layer. We have experimented with different dimensions of the RNN and attention output, different filter sizes, and the number of filters wherever applicable. We have experimented with the following:

BiLSTM and BiLSTM-Attention: The word embeddings correspond to each post are fed through a bidirectional LSTM and with the attention scheme from [21].

CNN: Word vectors of a post are passed through convolutional and max-over-time pooling layers.

C_BiLSTM: This method is based on the multi-label sexual harassment classification [11], in which convolution is applied to the word embeddings, and feature maps are stacked along the filter dimension to generate a sequence of window vectors. They are finally fed into a BiLSTM to obtain the final sentence vector.

4 Results

We report prediction accuracy across the various approaches described so far. Our code & hyper parameters are available here[5]. For all experiments, we reserve 15% of the entire data as unseen test data. We use the same test data across all experiments for uniformity. We further split the remaining 85% data in the ratio of 85:15 for training and validation, respectively. We report the results on an average of 3 runs on the test data for all the experiments.

Table 4. Comparing Trad. ML & DL Baselines

	Approach	Embedding	Accuracy	F1
Trad. ML	SVM	BERT	0.901	0.893
	Logistic	BERT	0.910	0.901
	Xgboost	BERT	0.890	0.876
	SVM	Elmo	0.920	0.910
	Logistic	Elmo	0.930	**0.900**
	Xgboost	Elmo	0.901	0.890
	SVM	Tf-idf char	0.912	0.890
	Logistic	Tf-idf char	0.903	0.893
	Xgboost	Tf-idf char	0.930	0.899
	SVM	Tf-idf word	0.850	0.840
	Logistic	Tf-idf word	0.840	0.823
	Xgboost	Tf-idf word	0.840	0.793
Deep learning	C-BiLSTM	BERT	0.907	0.764
	BiLSTM + Attn	BERT	0.917	0.791
	BiLSTM	BERT	0.907	0.784
	CNN	BERT	0.922	0.794
	C_BiLSTM	Elmo	0.932	0.807
	BiLSTM + Attn	Elmo	0.929	0.801
	BiLSTM	Elmo	0.944	0.830
	CNN	Elmo	**0.947**	0.839

Table 4 provides the results for various traditional ML & DL baselines as described in Sect. 3. It is observed that among all the combinations of features and classifiers experimented within this trad. ML setup, **Logisitic Regression with ELMo embeddings** performs best. For the DL baselines, it is observed that **CNN with ELMo embeddings** performed well. Table 5 shows the results for various transformer-based models along with the GAN-BERT approach. The

---

[5] https://github.com/Harikavuppalala/Bodyshaming_classification.

Table 5. Transformers and semi-supervised approach. L refers to labeled, and UL refers to unlabeled posts. Semi-supervised method outperforms supervised transformer-based baselines.

	Approach	Accuracy	F1
Transformers	BERT	0.946	0.919
	RoBERTa	0.959	0.937
	XLNet	0.962	0.944
GAN-BERT approach	2K (L)+5K (UL)	0.970	0.969
	2K (L)+15K (UL)	0.975	0.975
	2K (L)+25K (UL)	0.977	0.975
	2K (L)+35K (UL)	**0.977**	**0.976**
	2K (L)+43K (UL)	0.972	0.972

results show that the transformer models performed well compared to deep learning and traditional ML baselines. The best results are observed with **XLNet**. For the **GAN-BERT model**, we show the results with different amounts of unlabeled data (UL) along with 1835 (2k) labeled data (L). The results show that with any ratio of unlabeled data, the performance is superior compared to any supervised methods. When we have large unlabeled data and want to leverage the useful information in it, the GAN-BERT model is suitable. It also gives superior accuracy and F1 score compared to any other baseline model. However, the traditional ML and DL models are computationally less expensive. We can choose these models when we prefer model simplicity over accuracy.

5   Conclusion

We create a dataset for body-shaming classification consisting of 2159 posts and discuss the properties of this data through various analyses. We are committed to following ethical practices, including safeguarding users' privacy and anonymity. We also explore several transformer models and semi-supervised GAN-BERT to leverage the unlabeled data for the task of body shaming detection. Experimental results show that the semi-supervised approach performs well compared to the several baselines. Directions for future work include expanding the labeled data and exploring more ways of utilizing the unlabeled data to create a robust, novel framework to categorize physical discrimination in social media posts.

References

1. Cassidy, L.: Body Shaming in the Era of Social Media. Interdisciplinary Perspectives on Shame: Methods, Theories, Norms, Cultures, and Politics (2019). 157 pages

2. Chen, T., Guestrin, C.: XGBoost: a scalable tree boosting system. In: Proceedings of the 22nd ACM SIGKDD International Conference on Knowledge Discovery and Data Mining, pp. 785–794. KDD 2016, ACM, New York, USA (2016). https://doi.org/10.1145/2939672.2939785

3. Cortes, C., Vapnik, V.: Support-vector networks. Mach. Learn. **20**(3), 273–297 (1995). https://doi.org/10.1007/BF00994018

4. Cox, D.R.: The regression analysis of binary sequences. J. Roy. Stat. Soc. Ser. B (Methodol.) **20**(2), 215–232 (1958)

5. Croce, D., Castellucci, G., Basili, R.: GAN-BERT: generative adversarial learning for robust text classification with a bunch of labeled examples. In: Proceedings of the 58th Annual Meeting of the Association for Computational Linguistics, pp. 2114–2119 (2020)

6. Devlin, J., Chang, M.W., Lee, K., Toutanova, K.: BERT: pre-training of deep bidirectional transformers for language understanding. arXiv preprint arXiv:1810.04805 (2018)

7. Fast, E., Chen, B., Bernstein, M.S.: Empath: understanding topic signals in large-scale text. In: Proceedings of the 2016 CHI Conference on Human Factors in Computing Systems, pp. 4647–4657 (2016)

8. Fersini, E., Gasparini, F., Corchs, S.: Detecting sexist meme on the web: a study on textual and visual cues. In: 2019 8th International Conference on Affective Computing and Intelligent Interaction Workshops and Demos (ACIIW), pp. 226–231 (2019). https://doi.org/10.1109/ACIIW.2019.8925199

9. Gam, R.T., Singh, S.K., Manar, M., Kar, S.K., Gupta, A.: Body shaming among school-going adolescents: prevalence and predictors. Int. J. Commun. Med. Public Health (Gujarat) **7**(4), 1324–1328 (2020)

10. Jaman, J.H., Hannie, M.S.S.: Sentiment analysis of the body-shaming beauty vlog comments (2020)

11. Karlekar, S., Bansal, M.: SafeCity: understanding diverse forms of sexual harassment personal stories. In: Proceedings of the 2017 Conference on Empirical Methods in Natural Language Processing (EMNLP), pp. 2805–2811 (2018)

12. Lestari, S.: Bullying or fat shaming? the risk factors of body dysmorphic disorder (BDD) in teenage girls. JARSSH **4**(1) (2019)

13. Liu, Y., et al.: RoBERTa: a robustly optimized BERT pretraining approach. arXiv preprint arXiv:1907.11692 (2019)

14. Muir, S.R., Roberts, L.D., Sheridan, L.P.: The portrayal of online shaming in contemporary online news media: a media framing analysis. Comput. Hum. Behav. Rep. **3**, 100051 (2021)

15. Nobata, C., Tetreault, J., Thomas, A., Mehdad, Y., Chang, Y.: Abusive language detection in online user content. In: Proceedings of the 25th International Conference on World Wide Web, pp. 145–153 (2016)

16. Parikh, P., et al.: Multi-label categorization of accounts of sexism using a neural framework. In: Proceedings of the 2019 Conference on Empirical Methods in Natural Language Processing and the 9th International Joint Conference on Natural Language Processing (EMNLP-IJCNLP), pp. 1642–1652 (2019)

17. Pennebaker, J.W., Boyd, R.L., Jordan, K., Blackburn, K.: The development and psychometric properties of liwc2015. Tech. rep. (2015)

18. Peters, M.E., et al.: Deep contextualized word representations. In: Proceedings of the 2018 Conference of the North American Chapter of the Association for Computational Linguistics: Human Language Technologies, Volume 1 (Long Papers), pp. 2227–2237. Association for Computational Linguistics, New Orleans, Louisiana (2018). https://doi.org/10.18653/v1/N18-1202, https://aclanthology.org/N18-1202

19. Salimans, T., Goodfellow, I., Zaremba, W., Cheung, V., Radford, A., Chen, X.: Improved techniques for training GANs. arXiv preprint arXiv:1606.03498 (2016)

20. Yang, Z., Dai, Z., Yang, Y., Carbonell, J., Salakhutdinov, R., Le, Q.V.: XLNet: generalized autoregressive pretraining for language understanding. arXiv preprint arXiv:1906.08237 (2019)

21. Yang, Z., Yang, D., Dyer, C., He, X., Smola, A., Hovy, E.: Hierarchical attention networks for document classification. In: Proceedings of the 2016 Conference of the North American Chapter of the Association for Computational Linguistics: Human Language Technologies, pp. 1480–1489 (2016)

Unpacking Gender Stereotypes in Film Dialogue

Yulin Yu[(✉)], Yucong Hao, and Paramveer Dhillon

University of Michigan, Ann Arbor, MI 48109, USA
{yulinyu,yucongh,dhillonp}@umich.edu

Abstract. The representation of gender stereotypes in films profoundly impacts societal values and beliefs since they reflect and can potentially reinforce prevailing social norms. Hence, it is crucial to unravel how such stereotypes arise from gender portrayal in films. In this paper, we decompose the gender differences portrayed in movies along several socio- and psycho-linguistic dimensions. In particular, we consider gender disparities in four dialogue dimensions: 1) the degree of assertion, 2) the degree of confirmation, 3) the valence of emotions, and 4) the topic. Empirical analyses show that the valence of emotions expressed in the dialogue explains the most variation in gender disparity. Moreover, for certain kinds of dialogue, such as those occurring between different gender actors, the topic of discussion is also a strong predictor of gender differences.

Keywords: Computational social science · Gender inequality · Movie

1 Introduction

The construct of gender and its portrayal in popular media has attracted researchers in various disciplines. Of particular interest are gender depictions in film dialogue since movies profoundly impact individual beliefs and help shape the social mores [2]. Films specifically and media more generally are known to reflect as well as reinforce prevailing social norms [10]. All these factors, coupled with the easy availability of dialogue data, make movies a perfect testbed for studying gender differences by computational social scientists [5,11,18–20].

Several social, cultural, and psychological factors are known to determine gender differences. Past research has shown that the correlates of gender identity including occupations, gender roles, and interpersonal relationships are some such factors [3,12–14,17]. One can summarize these factors along four key conversational dimensions, 1) *the degree of assertion*, 2) *the degree of confirmation*, 3) *valence of emotions*, and, 4) *the topic of dialogue*. [9,21] discuss how these four dimensions can capture gender differences. For *degree of assertion*, they find that women have a higher tendency to use tentative words, whereas men are more assertive in expressing their opinions [3,13,15]. Women also tend to give positive responses to their interlocutors, unlike men, who are more likely to interrupt their interlocutors, which leads to women having a *higher degree*

F. Hopfgartner et al. (Eds.): SocInfo 2022, LNCS 13618, pp. 398–405, 2022.
https://doi.org/10.1007/978-3-031-19097-1_26

of confirmation in their interactions [12]. As far as *valence of emotions* is concerned, women express more positive emotions, while men show more negativity in their emotions, e.g., anger [17]. Finally, in terms of *dialogue topics*, women tend to discuss their families, friends, and acquaintances, whereas men are more preoccupied with showing off their work and achievements [13].

We conjecture that these socio-cultural dimensions of gender stereotype also apply to movie dialogues since they represent innate gender propensities in conversations. So, in this paper, we test the hypothesis of how these four socio-cultural and psychological dimensions of gender differences explain femininity (as measured by gender ladenness) in movies. In particular, we ask two research questions in this paper: **RQ1:** Which of the four dimensions of gender stereotype are associated with femininity in film dialogues? **RQ2:** How is femininity perceived in same and mixed-gender conversations in movies? How do the various stereotypes differentially associate with femininity in mixed- and same-gender interactions in movies?

2   Empirical Setup

We seek to unpack the impact of the four socio-cultural dimensions of gender stereotype just discussed on the representation of femininity in movie dialogues. Next, we decompose these estimates to compute the differential impact of the stereotypes on femininity depiction in mixed- and same-gender conversations. However, before we dive deep into our analyses, we describe our data and feature extraction pipeline.

Table 1. Description of various socio-cultural dimensions. Men and women stereotypes listed are the LIWC categories, e.g., tentative, certain, etc. The words in the brackets are examples of words in that specific stereotype LIWC category.

Socio-cultural dimension	Women Stereotype (LIWC Category)	Men Stereotype (LIWC Category)
Degrees of assertion	Tentative (e.g., wonder, unknown, confusing)	Certain (e.g., absolute, definitely, fact, must)
Degrees of confirmation	Assent (e.g., agree, indeed, okay)	Negate(e.g., can't, cannot, doesn't)
Valence of emotion	Positive (e.g., excellent, amazing)	Negative (e.g., emptiness, irrational, unfair)
Dialogue topics	Home (e.g., bed, garden, house)	Work (e.g., project, achieve, agent)

2.1   Data

Our dataset comes from the Cornell Movie-Dialogues Corpus [5], which is a collection of dialogues from 617 film scripts. The dataset was automatically generated from publicly available movie scripts, and to the best of our knowledge, it is the largest available dataset of its kind. The dataset contains 304,713 lines of dialogue from English-language movies from 1930 to 2010. Most scripts are tagged with cast lists, IMDB information, genre, release year, and conversation label. Every line of dialogue is also tagged with the speaker (character name) and speaker gender. Since we are interested in studying the differential expression of stereotypes in movies, we only considered movies with both male and female characters. It left us with a total of 503 movies.

2.2   Feature Extraction

Below we describe how we featurize the femininity and gender stereotype variables.

Femininity: We define *femininity* as the difference in feminine-associated words used by females in their movie dialogue compared to males. We use the *gender ladenness* lexicon, which captures a specific word's underlying feminine or masculine association. The lexicon scores the gendered tendency of each word on a scale from -1 to +1. More negative values are generally associated with masculine words, and positive values are associated with femininity. For example, the gender ladenness score of the word "actor" is -0.182 and for the word "actress" is +0.675. The gender-ladenness lexicon was generated via crowdsourced annotations on 925 words [4]. Later, the dictionary was expanded from 925 words to 274,596 words by scoring the unlabeled words based on semantic similarity [16]. We use the gender ladenness lexicon to compute femininity, as shown in Eq. 1. μ_{GL}^{F} represents the average gender ladenness of a movie calculated using just the female dialogue, and μ_{GL}^{M} is the average gender ladenness of a movie computed using just the male dialogue.[1]

$$\text{Femininity} = \mu_{GL}^{F} - \mu_{GL}^{M} \tag{1}$$

We chose to represent the femininity score as the difference between the averaged gender ladenness score of female and male dialogues since we want to capture the directional change in femininity. Female dialogue typically has a higher femininity score than male dialogue; however, through exploratory analysis, we found that many male conversations had higher gender-ladenness scores (or were more feminine) than female conversations. Pinpointing this directional change can help us better understand language usage in the movies.

Dimensions of Gender Stereotype: As described earlier, we calculate gender stereotypes in movie dialog along four key socio-cultural dimensions. These dimensions are 1) degrees of assertion, 2) degrees of confirmation, 3) valence of emotion, and 4) dialogue topics. These four dimensions are motivated by the fact that they are highly representative since: First, they cover various words that

---

[1] We compute the gender ladenness scores using only the 274,596 words in the lexicon and dropped out-of-vocabulary words. We also removed stopwords as well as words that occurred less than 50 times in the movie scripts.

are used to indicate essential aspects of gender identities, including occupations, gender roles, interpersonal relationships, and psychology and emotions. Second, the four dimensions contain words that mean both semantics and moods. Thus we can measure both the literal meanings of words and the unspoken implications of language. Third, these socio-cultural dimensions have been shown to effectively reflect gender differences in the feminist linguistics literature [9,21].

We use the Linguistic Inquiry and Word Count (LIWC) dictionary to compute stereotypes corresponding to the socio-cultural dimensions [23]. Essentially, we define the female and male stereotypes in each of the four dimensions using a LIWC category. For example, for the dimension *degree of assertion*, we define the women stereotype using the LIWC category "tentative" and the male stereotype using the category "certain". Recall that [3,13,14] showed women tend to be tentative in their speech, whereas men are more likely to be certain. Similarly, we identify LIWC categories for other stereotypes. The full list (along with sample words from each LIWC category) is shown in Table 1. Next, based on the LIWC categories, we compute the variable *stereotype* similarly as we computed *femininity*. The calculation is shown in Eq. 2.

$$\text{Stereotype} = \mu^F_{LIWC} - \mu^M_{LIWC} \tag{2}$$

μ^F_{LIWC} represents the averaged LIWC output for each of the eight stereotypes shown in Table 1 using just the female dialogue and μ^M_{LIWC} represents the corresponding output for the male dialogue.

2.3   Model Specifications

We use a simple linear model—ordinary least squares (OLS) regression —to quantify the relationship between the various gender stereotypes and femininity in the movie dialogues. We chose OLS regression owing to its simplicity and its statistical properties [1]. Of course, we do not rule out non-linearity in the relationship, but we are less interested in higher-order effects, typically captured by non-linear models. Our model specification is shown in Eq. 3.

$$\text{Femininity}_i = \alpha + \sum_{k=1}^{8} \text{Stereotype}_{ik} + \epsilon_i \tag{3}$$

Femininity and Stereotype describe the femininity and stereotype variables, which are calculated as described earlier. The subscript i indexes the movies and k indexes the stereotypes described in Table 1. α is the movie-specific intercept, and ϵ represents the Gaussian error term.

Next, we are interested in assessing the differential impact of the stereotypes on femininity based on whether the dialogue was between mixed-gender or same-gender actors. Our model specification for the second research question is shown in Eq. 4.

$$\text{Femininity}_j = \alpha + \text{MixedGender}_j + \sum_{k=1}^{8} \text{Stereotype}_{jk}$$
$$+ \sum_{k=1}^{8} \text{Stereotype}_{jk} \times \text{MixedGender}_j + \epsilon_i \tag{4}$$

The binary variable MixedGender_j denotes whether the dialogue is between actors of different genders ($\text{MixedGender}_j=1$) or between same-gender actors ($\text{MixedGender}_j=0$). j indexes the various dialogues in a movie; they can either be mixed-gender or same-gender. The various *interaction terms* estimate the differential impact of a particular stereotype on femininity for mixed-gender conversations in the movie.

Table 2. Regression estimates obtained from Eqs. 3,4. *Note:* 1) Heteroskedasticity Robust standard errors are shown in parenthesis next to the coefficient, 2) ***$p \leq .01$, **$p \leq .05$, *$p \leq .1$

	Femininity (Eq. 3)	Femininity (Eq. 4)
Intercept	0.47***(.042)	1.17***(0.11)
PosEmotion	0.32***(0.05)	0.36**(0.14)
NegEmotion	-0.27***(0.04)	-0.11***(0.02)
Assent	-0.07(0.05)	-0.052(0.182)
Negate	-0.13***(0.05)	0.08(0.09)
Tentative	0.04(0.04)	-0.05(0.10)
Certain	0.06(0.04)	-0.07(0.11)
Home	0.05(0.05)	-0.16(0.12)
Work	-0.14***(0.04)	-0.08(0.12)
MixedGender		-1.07***(0.12)
PosEmotion× MixedGender	-	-0.18(0.15)
NegEmotion× MixedGender	-	-0.09(0.12)
Assent× MixedGender	-	-0.04(0.19)
Negate × MixedGender	-	-0.03(0.10)
Tentative × MixedGender	-	0.05(0.11)
Certain × MixedGender	-	0.12(0.12)
Home × MixedGender	-	0.26**(0.13)
Work × MixedGender	-	-0.08(0.13)
Number of Observations	503	597
R-squared	0.226	0.293
F-statistic	14.51	12.01

3   Results and Discussion

RQ1-Gender Stereotype Decomposition: Looking at the first column of results in Table 2 we can make a few observations. First, we can see that gender stereotypes corresponding to three of the four socio-cultural dimensions (valence of emotion, dialogue topic, and degree of confirmation) have a significant association with the representation of femininity in movie dialogues. These associations are not only statistically significant, but they are also practically significant, which is evident based on the substantial point estimates of these variables. The positive point estimate of the "PosEmotion" suggests a unit increase in its value results in an increase (0.32) in the value of "Femininity." Along similar lines, we see unit increases in "NegEmotion," "Negate," and "Work" being associated with corresponding decreases in "Feminity." These results confirm our hypothesis that an increase in female-related socio-cultural stereotypes leads to increased femininity in the movie dialogue. Conversely, an increase in male-related stereotypes results in a decrease in femininity.

Among the three stereotypes that are significantly associated with femininity, *valence of emotion* has the most substantial impact on the degree of femininity depiction in movie dialogue. This finding corroborates similar findings by media scholars who have called the film "an emotional machine" that uses intense emotion to construct the plot, create characters, and elicit viewers' affective responses [7, 22].

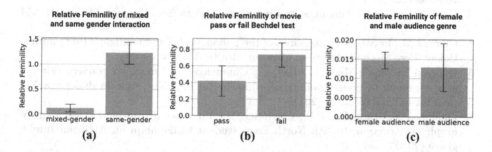

Fig. 1. Plots showing standardized mean of femininity with 95% confidential interval in (a) mixed and same-gender interaction (b) movies pass or fail Bechdel test) (c) movies in genres favored by female audiences (f-aud) and male audiences (m-aud)

RQ2-Differential Impact of Stereotype in Same and Mixed-gender Interactions: We can make two key observations by examining the results from the second column in Table 2. First, the negative coefficient on the "MixedGender" variable suggests that same-gender conversations are associated with larger femininity depiction in movie dialogues. This observation is consistent with the "chameleon effect" in language, which indicates that a speaker will adapt more to their interlocutor in a mixed-gender conversation than in a same-gender conversation [5]. Moreover, women are believed to possess more interpersonal sensitivity and are more willing to show respect or support their interlocutors [15].

Based on these findings, we can conclude that in mixed-gender conversations, women tend to get assimilated to how their male interlocutors speak either out of the unconscious "chameleon effect" or out of their interpersonal sensitivity, hence resulting in the decrease in femininity in mixed-gender conversations. Second, we observe that the feature *Home* has a positive coefficient. This deviates from our prediction: while it is significantly associated with an increase in femininity in mixed-gender conversations (the coefficient of interaction term "Home × MixedGender"), it associates with a decrease in femininity in same-gender conversations (the coefficient of "Home"). A potential explanation for this phenomenon is the "actor effect," which posits that in mixed-gender conversations, speakers tend to use masculine- or feminine-preferential language per their biological sex due to traditionalism and prevalent social norms [8]. Although the "chameleon effect" and the "actor effect" seem to produce opposite results, they account for different components of mixed-gender conversations, including the speaker's sensitivity to interpersonal relationships and the influence of prevalent gender norms on language use.

References

1. Angrist, J.D., Pischke, J.S.: Mostly Harmless Econometrics: An Empiricist's Companion. Princeton University Press (2008)
2. Cape, G.S.: Addiction, stigma and movies. Acta Psychiatrica Scandinavica **107**(3), 163–169 (2003)
3. Carli, L.L.: Gender, language, and influence. J. Pers. Soc. Psychol. **59**(5), 941–951 (1990)
4. Clark, J.M., Paivio, A.: Extensions of the paivio, yuille, and madigan (1968) norms. Behav. Res. Methods Instrum. Comput. **36**(3), 371–383 (2004)
5. Danescu-Niculescu-Mizil, C., Lee, L.: Chameleons in imagined conversations: a new approach to understanding coordination of linguistic style in dialogs. arXiv preprint arXiv:1106.3077 (2011)
6. Dhillon, P.S., Talukdar, P.P., Crammer, K.: Inference-driven metric learning for graph construction. In: 4th North East Student Colloquium on Artificial Intelligence (2010)
7. Feng, D., O'Halloran, K.L.: The multimodal representation of emotion in film: integrating cognitive and semiotic approaches. Semiotica **2013**(197), 79–100 (2013)
8. Fitzpatrick, M.A., Mulac, A., Dindia, K.: Gender-preferential language use in spouse and stranger interaction. J. Lang. Soc. Psychol. **14**(1–2), 18–39 (1995)
9. Holmes, J.: Women, language and identity. Journal of Sociolinguistics **1**(2), 195–223 (1997). https://onlinelibrary.wiley.com/doi/abs/10.1111/1467-9481.00012, eprint: https://onlinelibrary.wiley.com/doi/pdf/10.1111/1467-9481.00012
10. Holtzman, L.: Media Messages: What Film, Television, and Popular Music Teach Us About Race, Class, Gender, and Sexual Orientation. Routledge, 2 edn. (2014). https://doi.org/10.4324/9781315702469, https://www.taylorfrancis.com/books/9781315702469
11. Kagan, D., Chesney, T., Fire, M.: Using data science to understand the film industry's gender gap. Palgrave Commun. **6**(1), 1–16 (2020)
12. Kollock, P., Schwartz, P., Blumstein, P., Blumstein, P.: Sex and power in interaction: conversational privileges and duties. Am. Soc. Rev. **50**, 34–46 (1985)

13. Lakoff, R.T.: Language and Woman's Place: Text and Commentaries. Oxford University Press (2004)
14. Leaper, C., Ayres, M.M.: A meta-analytic review of gender variations in adults' language use: talkativeness, affiliative speech, and assertive speech. Pers. Soc. Psychol. Rev. **11**(4), 328–363 (2007). https://doi.org/10.1177/1088868307302221
15. Leaper, C., Robnett, R.D.: Women are more likely than men to use tentative language, aren't they? a meta-analysis testing for gender differences and moderators. Psychol. Women Quart. **35**(1), 129–142 (2011)
16. Malandrakis, N., Narayanan, S.S.: Therapy language analysis using automatically generated psycholinguistic norms. In: Sixteenth Annual Conference of the International Speech Communication Association (2015)
17. Newman, M.L., Groom, C.J., Handelman, L.D., Pennebaker, J.W.: Gender differences in language use: an analysis of 14,000 text samples. Discourse Process. **45**(3), 211–236 (2008)
18. Ramakrishna, A., Martínez, V.R., Malandrakis, N., Singla, K., Narayanan, S.: Linguistic analysis of differences in portrayal of movie characters. In: Proceedings of the 55th Annual Meeting of the Association for Computational Linguistics (Volume 1: Long Papers), pp. 1669–1678 (2017)
19. Sap, M., Prasettio, M.C., Holtzman, A., Rashkin, H., Choi, Y.: Connotation frames of power and agency in modern films. In: Proceedings of the 2017 Conference on Empirical Methods in Natural Language Processing, pp. 2329–2334 (2017)
20. Schofield, A., Mehr, L.: Gender-distinguishing features in film dialogue. In: Proceedings of the Fifth Workshop on Computational Linguistics for Literature, pp. 32–39 (2016)
21. Talbot, M.: Gender stereotypes: reproduction and challenge. In: Holmes, J., Meyerhoff, M. (eds.) The Handbook of Language and Gender, pp. 468–486. Blackwell Publishing Ltd, Oxford, UK (2003). https://doi.org/10.1002/9780470756942.ch20
22. Tan, E.S.: Emotion and the Structure of Narrative Film: Film As An Emotion Machine. Routledge (2013). Google-Books-ID: 5khUAQAAQBAJ
23. Tausczik, Y.R., Pennebaker, J.W.: The psychological meaning of words: LIWC and computerized text analysis methods. J. Lang. Soc. Psychol. **29**(1), 24–54 (2010)

Nostalgic Analysis of Location Based Tweets

Larissa Gao[1], Lingzi Hong[2], and Afra Mashhadi[1]

[1] Computing and Software Systems, University of Washington, Bothell, USA
{gao14,mashhadi}@uw.edu
[2] Information Science, University of North Texas, Denton, USA
Lingzi.Hong@unt.edu

Abstract. Social media posts have been increasingly used as mediums for gaining insight into a wide spectrum of people's experiences including those in relation to physical spaces. We examine features of social media posts that characterized users' memories of different visited Points-of-Interest (POI). Our results revealed that these recall of memories often mention other users, making them a collective experience. Furthermore, our analysis shows that nostalgic tweets are more than just tweets that mention the past but include an intertwine the past experiences with a positive outlook on the future and present. We also note that while these tweets do not mention specific locations in their content, their originating geo-location reflects places with a greater sense of belonging present.

Keywords: Nostalgia · Location-based social network · NLP

1 Introduction

Recent years has seen a great number of analysis investigating social media platforms as a window of understanding people's experiences when visiting various points of interest (POIs). For instance, geolocated Tweets have helped assess park usage in United States cities as shown by [6,8] and in Birmingham, United Kingdom [18]. Other studies of location-based social networks have focused on the quality of users' experiences through a range of methods such as sentiment analysis [1,13].

However, little attention has been given to nostalgic longing and shared recall experiences in different locations. The nostalgic conversations online have been studied from the perspectives of public health [7,19] and marketing [3,9,10]. Researchers found nostalgic activities usually evoke psychological benefits such as increased optimism [4] and a sense of belongings [26], which could help with campaigns and marketing of brands or products. Nostalgia on social media also enables users to build online communities to share common interests, values, and experiences [14]. Although nostalgic activities on social media are commonly seen, few studies have paid attention to the understanding of nostalgic activities on social media to improve the experience of users in sharing memories. Naini et al. have

F. Hopfgartner et al. (Eds.): SocInfo 2022, LNCS 13618, pp. 406–413, 2022.
https://doi.org/10.1007/978-3-031-19097-1_27

proposed a ranking for social media posts for reminiscence as a way to facilitate recall of events through memorable posts [16]. There is a lack of study on the comprehensive analysis of nostalgic conversations on social networks.

In this paper, we are interested in understanding the attributes of reminiscence and nostalgic longing in relation to recalling experiences that connect the online (social media platform) and offline world. We are to uncover: *what are the features that may characterize social media posts on a collective memory of a visited point of interest (POI)?* To answer this question, we study the shared recall experience of people by collecting 500,000 geo-tagged tweets corresponding to hashtags related to nostalgic longing. We analyze these tweets from the perspective of *what* these posts mention, *what time entities* (i.e., when) they recall and what location entity (i.e., *where*) the memory takes place. Our analysis of this dataset shows that these nostalgic conversations are more than just mentions of the past but are combined by *positive* outlook on the future and present. Furthermore, our analysis reports that while these memories do not specifically mention locations in the content of the tweet, the geo-location property of these tweets presents a positive sentiment with places of association where users may feel a greater sense of belonging (e.g., churches, schools). We also show that the mention of the past is independent of the type of locations where the tweet originated from. Finally, a great number of our tweets include mentions of other users reflecting that conversations are of a *collective* memory of the past.

2   Related Work

Nostalgia in Social Psychology. Nostalgic posts refer to the ones to collect memories or develop activities associated with past events. Many researchers from the field of Psychology have paid attention to the phenomenon of people engaging in nostalgic activities. Wildschut et al. discovered that nostalgic narratives usually evoked more positive than negative psychological effects [24]. Researchers also identified nostalgia as a resource for self-identification and positive self-esteem [23] and the past-oriented emotion in nostalgia usually extends to psychological benefits that lead to increased optimism for the future [4]. During the COVID-19 pandemic, collective nostalgia on social media such as Twitter has been seen as a method to comfort individuals in the status of isolation, fear, and a loss of freedom [15].

Nostalgia in Social Networks. Understanding the collective memories and how users engage in nostalgic activities online is important. The design of social interactions and networked socially together shape the social media memory practices. Social interactions are incentives for people to uncover interesting and evocative moments while becoming constraints for users to determine what to share [12]. Sumikawa et al. found that collective memories are selective with a focus on a certain time in history through a quantitative analysis of tweets on reminiscence. A better understanding of the nostalgic content can help the designs for time-aware recommendation systems or search applications [22].

Additionally, marketing researchers found nostalgic practices on social media could result in greater intention to pass along the message, a more positive attitude towards the nostalgic product and brand, and a better brand-consumer relationship [14,26]. Several studies have used machine learning or natural language processing (NLP) techniques to study nostalgic posts on social media. Davalos et al. conducted content analysis on nostalgic posts on Facebook. They identified themes that are most popular and found the nostalgic posts are usually more emotional with both positive and negative emotions and have concurrent use of past- and present-tense words, which shows a bittersweet character [5]. Sumikawa et al. conducted a temporal analysis to analyze which years are strongly remembered, an entity analysis to understand what types of entities are the most popular in collective memory, which past and present entities are mentioned together, and the semantic categories of hashtags [22]. Ferrario et al. designed machine learning algorithms using NLP features to differentiate reminiscence posts from general conversations to understand the characteristics of nostalgic expressions [7].

3   Dataset and Methods

Dataset: To collect tweets, we used Twitter's official search API2 with an academic license allowing us to access the entire historical pipeline of Twitter. To make sure that we collected tweets that refer to the reminiscence of the past or are related to the collective memory of past events/entities, we performed a bootstrapping procedure including hashtag-based crawling of data. We first defined seed hashtags including **#throwbackthursday** and **#tbt** as identified by a previous study [21]. We then formed a query using these hashtags and collected **geo-tagged** tweets. This allowed us to collect 500,000 tweets that correspond to a real-world experience but also include a recall component.

Methods: To answer the proposed research question, we analyzed the content of the tweets to identify what type of past references they contain, what type of locations they mention, and where they originate from.

Location-Entity Categorization. To identify the location entities mentioned in tweets, we used spaCy [11], a natural language processing library. We then defined categories of location entities, created a set of common keywords for each category, annotated each location entity using the dictionary. This enables us to analyze the category of location entities instead of specific locations. The error rate of location entity annotation was 5.73%.

Time-Entity Categorization. We used HeidelTime [20], which is an effective temporal tagger with a specialized option for tweet processing to extract temporal references. HeidelTime outputs normalized temporal expressions according to the TIMEX3 annotation standard. This tool is known to have a high recall and precision of over 90%. Using a dictionary of keywords, we then grouped the time entities mentioned in tweets into references to the past, present, and future.

We further separated the time entities into various granularity of times (shorter than a day), days, weeks, months, seasons, and years.

Geo-location Categorization. To understand what type of places tweets originated from, we reverse-geocoded the geo tagged locations of tweets using the Nominatim API [17]. We extracted latitude and longitude coordinates from the bounding box and used these to query the API. The resulting location information included an "amenity" tag indicating the location name, e.g. "Starbucks" or "X High School". We used the amenity of each location (e.g., coffee shop, school) for further analysis. Additionally, we categorized each location into three distinct classes as a public, semi-public, or private space. Finally, we performed sentiment analysis using the RoBERTa transformers model [25], which was trained on an English Twitter corpus.

4   Results

In this section, we present the results of our analysis from three perspectives: *what* do the nostalgic tweets mention, *what time entities* (i.e., when) they recall, and what location entity (i.e., *where*) the collective memory recalls and what type of location does the nostalgic tweet takes place (i.e., geo-location).

4.1   What Do the Nostalgic Tweets Mention

We first quantified the percentage of nostalgic tweets that included user entities, i.e., mentioned other users. We found that almost half of our dataset (45% of nostalgic tweets) mentioned other users. We conducted a T-test to compare the positive sentiment of tweets with user mentions and without. Results showed that tweets *with* user mentions (M = 0.600, Sd = 0.363) are significantly more positive than tweets *without* user mentions (M = 0.488, Sd = 0.370); t = −16.65, p = <0.001. The result indicated that collective memories with social connections display more positive sentiment.

To identify the word content of the nostalgic tweet, we used spaCy's part-of-speech tagging function to identify the nouns mentioned in each tweet. These tokens were normalized using Natural Language Toolkit [2]. We manually removed noisy entities, including time entities and non-English words. Finally, we aggregated the count of each unique token and found the top 10 mentioned objects were "love", "couple", "music", "freshman", "beach", "friend", "family", "age", "thanksgiving", and "lifestyle", which showed the type of social relations and activities in Twitter users' collective memories.

4.2   Time Entity Analysis

Out of our entire dataset 35% of tweets had a time entity mentioned in their content. Past *years* and past *weeks* were the most frequently mentioned time entities (Fig. 1A). For both present and future type of entities, *weeks* and *years* were the most frequently mentioned. As expected, mentions of the past were more frequent than mentions of the present. Mentions of the present were more frequent than mentions of the future. We analyzed the sentiment of tweets with entities of the past, present, and future combined with the granularity of times, days, weeks, months, seasons, and years. The findings, Fig. 1B, show that for all categories except times, mentions of the past had the lowest positive sentiment, and mentions of the future were the most positive, showing that users were more positive about the future compared to the past and present, echoing previous psychological work [4].

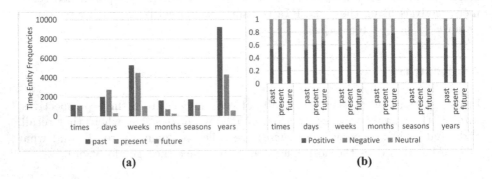

Fig. 1. A) Frequency of time entities B) Sentiment analysis of time entities

4.3   Location Entity Analysis

Our analysis of the nostalgic tweets shows that only 4% of the tweets recalled a location entity. Out of those, the most frequently mentioned location entity category was "street", followed by "park", "region", "continent", and "state" (Fig. 2A). Based on the results, users notably tend to refer to geographic locations and outdoor locations such as "street" and "parks" in nostalgic tweets, suggesting that nostalgic recollections are linked to public places. Our sentiment analysis of location entities shows that among the top 20 most frequently mentioned location entities, the entities with the highest positive sentiment rate were "coast", "planet", "continent", "restaurant", and "mountain". Out of the entire set of data, "paradise" was the location entity that had the overall highest positive sentiment rate, reflecting the language that users employ to recall their positive memorable locations (Fig. 2B).

We compared the positive sentiment of nostalgic tweets *with location entities* versus those *without*. The T-test shows tweets *without* mentioning of locations (M = 0.513, Sd = 0.374) showed more positive sentiment than tweets *with* location entities (M = 0.485, Sd = 0.375); t = 5.226, p = 1.737e−07. It is hypothesized that users memorizing other locations might be missing other places or less satisfied with their current situation.

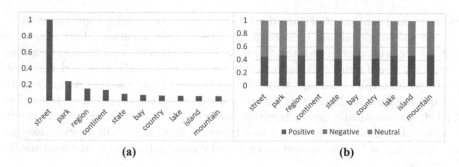

Fig. 2. A) Normalized frequency of location entities B) their sentiment analysis

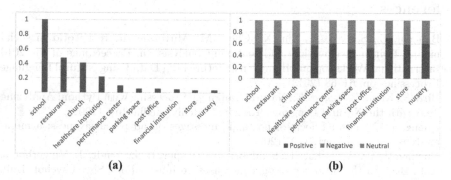

Fig. 3. A) Normalized frequency of geolocations B) Sentiment analysis of geolocations

4.4   Geo-location Analysis

Our analysis of geo-tagged location categories showed that "schools" were the most popular location that people tweeted from, followed by "restaurants", "churches", "healthcare institutions", and "performance centers" (Fig. 3). Nostalgic tweets originating from financial institutions are the most positive and from parking spaces are the most negative.

To understand what type of locations are associated with what type of recall experiences, we cross-referenced public and semi-public locations with specific years referenced in tweets. We found that there was little difference in terms of the past recalls between the distributions of public spaces and semi-public spaces. The Jensen-Shannon distance between the public and semi-public distribution was 0.103, indicating little difference across the two distributions.

5   Discussion

Our work creates direction for future researchers to design models for the identification of nostalgic tweets based on the revealed characteristics. We observed the frequency and sentiment of named entities of nostalgic tweets, focusing particularly on the temporal and location references and geo-locations. Our next step analysis includes identifying the themes, time references, and location entities mentioned in different geolocations. The preliminary study analyzed nostalgic tweets with certain hashtags, while we recognized that many nostalgic tweets may not use such hashtags. Our future work includes the design of systems that can help automatically detect nostalgic tweets for a more comprehensive study of collected memories in location-based tweets. The findings will provide insights for the design of location-based recommendations and services on social media platforms.

References

1. Baucom, E., Sanjari, A., Liu, X., Chen, M.: Mirroring the real world in social media: Twitter, geolocation, and sentiment analysis. In: Proceedings of the 2013 International Workshop on Mining Unstructured Big Data Using Natural Language Processing, pp. 61–68 (2013)
2. Bird, S., Klein, E., Loper, E.: Natural Language Processing with Python: Analyzing Text with the Natural Language Toolkit. O'Reilly Media, Inc. (2009)
3. Cheng, Y., Yan, X.: Effects of nostalgic messages on ad persuasiveness: a meta-analysis. Int. J. Advert. 1–25 (2022)
4. Cheung, W.Y., Wildschut, T., Sedikides, C., Hepper, E.G., Arndt, J., Vingerhoets, A.J.: Back to the future: nostalgia increases optimism. Pers. Soc. Psychol. Bull. **39**(11), 1484–1496 (2013)
5. Davalos, S., Merchant, A., Rose, G.M., Lessley, B.J., Teredesai, A.M.: 'The good old days': an examination of nostalgia in Facebook posts. Int. J. Hum Comput Stud. **83**, 83–93 (2015)
6. Donahue, M.L., Keeler, B.L., Wood, S.A., Fisher, D.M., Hamstead, Z.A., McPhearson, T.: Using social media to understand drivers of urban park visitation in the Twin Cities, MN. Landsc. Urban Plan. **175**, 1–10 (2018)
7. Ferrario, A., Demiray, B., Yordanova, K., Luo, M., Martin, M., et al.: Social reminiscence in older adults' everyday conversations: automated detection using natural language processing and machine learning. J. Med. Internet Res. **22**(9), e19133 (2020)
8. Hamstead, Z.A., Fisher, D., Ilieva, R.T., Wood, S.A., McPhearson, T., Kremer, P.: Geolocated social media as a rapid indicator of park visitation and equitable park access. Comput. Environ. Urban Syst. **72**, 38–50 (2018)
9. Havlena, W.J., Holak, S.L.: & quot; the good old days& quot observations on nostalgia and its role in consumer behavior. ACR North American Advances (1991)
10. Holak, S.L., Havlena, W.J.: Feelings, fantasies, and memories: an examination of the emotional components of nostalgia. J. Bus. Res. **42**(3), 217–226 (1998)
11. Honnibal, M., Montani, I.: spaCy 2: natural language understanding with Bloom embeddings, convolutional neural networks and incremental parsing (2017)
12. Jacobsen, B.N., Beer, D.: Quantified nostalgia: social media, metrics, and memory. Soc. Media+ Soc. **7**(2) (2021). https://doi.org/10.1177/20563051211008822
13. Jurgens, D., Finethy, T., McCorriston, J., Xu, Y., Ruths, D.: Geolocation prediction in Twitter using social networks: a critical analysis and review of current practice. In: Proceedings of the International AAAI Conference on Web and Social Media, vol. 9, pp. 188–197 (2015)

14. Koetz, C., Tankersley, J.D.: Nostalgia in online brand communities. J. Bus. Strat. **37**(3), 22–29 (2016)
15. Lee, W., Kao, G.: "You know you're missing out on something": collective nostalgia and community in Tim's Twitter listening party during COVID-19. Rock Music Stud. **8**(1), 36–52 (2021)
16. Naini, K.D., Kawase, R., Kanhabua, N., Niederée, C., Altingovde, I.S.: Those were the days: learning to rank social media posts for reminiscence. Inf. Retrieval J. **22**(1), 159–187 (2018). https://doi.org/10.1007/s10791-018-9339-9
17. OpenStreetMap contributors: planet dump (2017). https://planet.osm.org. https://www.openstreetmap.org
18. Roberts, H., Sadler, J., Chapman, L.: Using Twitter to investigate seasonal variation in physical activity in urban green space. Geo Geogr. Environ. **4**(2), e00041 (2017)
19. Stevens, R.C., et al.: Exploring substance use tweets of youth in the united states: mixed methods study. JMIR Public Health Surveill. **6**(1), e16191 (2020)
20. Strötgen, J., Gertz, M.: Multilingual and cross-domain temporal tagging. Lang. Resour. Eval. **47**(2), 269–298 (2013). https://doi.org/10.1007/s10579-012-9179-y
21. Sumikawa, Y., Jatowt, A.: Annotated dataset of history-related tweets. Data Brief **38**, 107344 (2021)
22. Sumikawa, Y., Jatowt, A., Düring, M.: Digital history meets microblogging: analyzing collective memories in Twitter. In: Proceedings of the 18th ACM/IEEE on Joint Conference on Digital Libraries, pp. 213–222 (2018)
23. Vess, M., Arndt, J., Routledge, C., Sedikides, C., Wildschut, T.: Nostalgia as a resource for the self. Self Identity **11**(3), 273–284 (2012)
24. Wildschut, T., Sedikides, C., Arndt, J., Routledge, C.: Nostalgia: content, triggers, functions. J. Pers. Soc. Psychol. **91**(5), 975 (2006)
25. Wolf, T., et al.: Transformers: state-of-the-art natural language processing. In: Proceedings of the 2020 Conference on Empirical Methods in Natural Language Processing: System Demonstrations, pp. 38–45. Association for Computational Linguistics, October 2020. https://www.aclweb.org/anthology/2020.emnlp-demos.6
26. Youn, S., Jin, S.V.: Reconnecting with the past in social media: the moderating role of social influence in nostalgia marketing on Pinterest. J. Consum. Behav. **16**(6), 565–576 (2017)

OMGMO: Original Multi-modal Dataset of Genetically Modified Organisms in African Agriculture

Daniel Grzenda[1]([✉]) [iD], Trevor Spreadbury[1], Joeva Rock[2] [iD], Brian Dowd-Uribe[3,4], and David Uminsky[1]

[1] University of Chicago, Chicago, IL 60637, USA
grzenda@uchicago.edu
[2] University of Cambridge, Cambridge CB2 1TN, UK
[3] University of San Francisco, San Francisco, CA 94117, USA
[4] Montpellier Advanced Knowledge Institute on Transitions, 34090 Montpellier, France

Abstract. Genetically modified (GM) crops can be a tool to address food security, climate change, and environmental sustainability in Africa. However, despite nearly three decades of developing GM crops for explicit use on the African continent, very little is known about this research, and very few crop varieties have moved from development to use by farmers. This paper introduces a collection of three multi-modal datasets to provide insight into the social, political, and economic actors shaping the future of GM crop development in Africa. Our interdisciplinary team compiled a dataset of GM crops in the research development pipeline, a collection of financial disclosures of funders supporting GM crop research, and a collection of over 2 million articles on agriculture and GM crop reporting from African media. We demonstrate the effectiveness of combining these pertinent datasets to aid in social science analysis of the social, political, and economic landscape of agricultural biotechnology in Africa.

Keywords: Multi-modal data · Genetically modified organisms · Data science · International development · Africa · Agriculture · Genetically modified crops

1 Introduction

Proponents claim that genetically modified (GM) crops – often simply referred to as "GMOs" – can be a tool to combat persistent food insecurity, the effects of climate change, and environmental sustainability challenges in Africa [1]. GM crops have been under development on the continent for over 25 years to address these issues. However, much of this research, including the institutional arrangements and financial sources stewarding it, are not well known by the public [2].

The current gold standard for information on the development of GM crops is the International Service for the Acquisition of Agri-biotech Applications (ISAAA). The ISAAA is a not-for-profit international organization that provides information related to agricultural biotechnology and builds support for it worldwide. One of the main services provided by the ISAAA is the GM Approval Crop Database, which shares information on the commercial development of GM crops.

Notably, the ISAAA dataset has several shortcomings. The ISAAA receives funding from the biotechnology industry, leading some to question whether it is a fair and objective source of information [3]. The ISAAA only provides data on crops that have been approved for commercialization, leaving out a large number of GM crops in other development stages. By using the approval process as a reporting mechanism, the ISAAA leaves out key information on the development of these GM crops. Finally, the ISAAA contains an incomplete list of the organizations involved in the development of each of these crops.

Another area where little information is available is who funds GM research on the continent, and which types of institutional arrangements lead to successful GM crop commercialization. The ISAAA dataset does not include this financial data. What is known about financial support is scattered across different newspaper accounts and journal articles, and is not comprehensive. There is no publically available data on the for-profit, public-private or public institutional arrangements stewarding GM crop research.

Despite these shortcomings, ISAAA's database remains widely cited in the literature on GM crops in Africa [1]. An additional database by CropLife [4], which has not been updated since 2017, is also cited in the literature [5]. These cases, all from the last two years, demonstrate both an interest in better understanding GM crop research in Africa, and an opportunity to serve more complete data on this topic.

Thus, to address these shortcomings, we combined multiple datasets on GM crops in Africa. We argue that this data, and its delivery via a user-friendly website, is an important advancement in public awareness of GM crop development in Africa. Still more, this data can be used to understand whether and how GM crops can address multiple challenges on the African continent.

2 Multi-modal Datasets

The research presented in this paper is a product of mBio (Mapping Biotechnologies in Africa), an interdisciplinary project with the goal of building robust datasets that give a more detailed view of the development of biotechnologies in Africa. The mBio project achieves this goal by collecting and cleaning data from a variety of sources, and serving these datasets through a public portal. The project is composed of an interdisciplinary team of data and social scientists: Grzenda, Spreadbury, and Uminsky are all data scientists and lead the automated data collection, data cleaning and merging, and analysis aspects of the project. Rock and Dowd-Uribe are both social scientists who have extensive research experience on GM crops in Africa [6, 7] and lead mBio's qualitative data gathering and analysis.

Our broad methodological and thematic expertise permitted a wide methodological net to be cast. Each dataset had a distinct data collection process. The first dataset we will discuss is focused on developing research methods for the collection of data on GM crop development outside of the ISAAA database.

2.1 Crop Data

GM crops must go through a series of research stages before they reach farmers' fields. These stages, which we conceptualize as development, research trials, approval, and commercialization, are all essential components of developing a GM crop. While the ISAAA provides data on crops that have been approved for commercial release, their dataset does not contain information on crops in any of the other stages, including, crucially, whether a crop approved for commercialization is actually commercialized. Here we develop a dataset that includes GM crops at all stages, including those that are currently or once were under development. We also include, where appropriate and available, information about the parent crop varieties onto which GM traits have been conferred. We categorize crops by these development stages and their activity status to provide additional granularity to the dataset. By doing this, we develop a more holistic and current view of biotechnology crop development in Africa.

We gathered and collated this data in four key ways. First, we combined two lists of GM crops under development in Africa that Dowd-Uribe and Rock had previously compiled using keyword searches in multiple languages and analyzing project reports and websites. Second, we employed graduate student research assistants to update these lists by analyzing project reports, donor websites, news sources, and other gray literature. Third, we scraped the ISAAA database. With these individual datasets in place, we next reviewed and revised each entry for consistency and uniformity. Given that data was gathered across a wide variety of sources with different naming conventions and level of detail in reporting, this task proved difficult. Here, we leveraged the expertise of our interdisciplinary team: Rock and Dowd-Uribe assessed and edited each entry. The final step was to clean the dataset further for precision, ensuring uniformity across all labels (e.g. crop name). In total, the crop data we collected includes: country of approval; names of the developers involved; information regarding the public or private distinction of the developers; information on geographic location of the developers' headquarters; the non-profit status of each of the partners; the name of the crop and any alternative, trade, or scientific names; the crop variety; any commercial traits conferred to the crop; the genes that were modified; its food, feed, and cultivation authorization; stage of development; status; and any information found about its legal and biosafety statuses.

The dataset generated from this process includes 231 instances of genetically modified crop varieties being developed across 19 countries in Africa. Overall, we identified 83 different developers, including but not limited to national research institutes, non-governmental organizations (NGOs), universities, and private companies. An overview of all crop varieties under research grouped by crop can be seen in Fig. 1 (below). In total, we found evidence of 23 distinct crop types that have been genetically modified, including maize, cotton, and banana (see Fig. 1). Figure 2 and Fig. 3 illustrate development stage and status by country.

Our dataset provides the most comprehensive public data on GM crops in Africa to date. This is evidenced when comparing our dataset to the current gold standard, the ISAAA dataset. To illustrate, as of 2021, the ISAAA dataset contains data on 166 GM crops in Africa, while our dataset contains 231 instances and more detailed metadata on each of these events. Additionally, the ISAAA's sole focus on countries that have approved GM crops for commercialization results in only listing 8 African countries in their database; our dataset contains information on 19 countries. Together, these examples illustrate how including a wide set of data sources and examining GM crops across development stages provides a more comprehensive view of GM crop development in Africa.

2.2 Financial Data

To gather a better sense of the organizations and financial resources being invested in GM crop research, we paired our more complete GM crop dataset with financial data. We did so in two key ways. First, we scraped, standardized, and linked data from the Securities and Exchange Commission of the United States (SEC) 990 forms, which nonprofit organizations are required to file annually, of institutions known to be major supporters and/or developers of GM crops in Africa, including: the Rockefeller Foundation, the Donald Danforth Plant Science Center, the Howard G. Buffett Foundation, and the Bill & Melinda Gates Foundation (BMGF). These documents disclose information about the flow of funding to projects and other organizations. Second, we scrapped the funding database of the US Agency for International Development (USAID). USAID is not only a major source of funding for GM crop research in Africa, they also – along with other funders such as the BMGF – fund media projects aimed at building public and political support for agricultural biotechnology across Africa [3].

In total, these sources provided information about 48,476 distinct transactions from non-profits, 2,423 of which were sent to organizations and projects in Africa, of which 616 were associated with agriculture. One surprising finding came from the 990 forms of the African Agricultural Technology Foundation (AATF). AATF liaises with private companies and public research institutions to broker public-private partnerships that develop GM crops throughout Africa [8]. Two such projects are the WEMA and TELA maize projects, respectively. Both projects partner with Monsanto (and subsequently Bayer, who acquired Monsanto in 2018), who licensed "its commercial drought-tolerance and insect-protection traits royalty free" to the project [9]. Media coverage of this agreement has largely applauded Monsanto/Bayer for working towards "humanitarian purposes" [10]. However, we found that between 2008–2020, AATF compensated Monsanto $45,940,909 in independent contractor services for the WEMA and TELA projects. While the details of these services are unclear, these transactions have to date been unexplored, and raise additional questions about the potential complexities of public-private partnerships developing GM crops.

As a whole, our financial data report funding for GM crops that emanates from US-based non-profits. This presents valuable but partial insight into the myriad actors and interests involved in GM crop development in Africa (and elsewhere) [8]. This view into the funding landscape does not include data from other public (sometimes reported) and private (unreported) stakeholders. This limitation is a finding itself: further research is needed to gain a fuller picture of the overall funding landscape.

2.3 Media Data

Finally, to collect data on how GM crops are portrayed in African media, we leveraged Factiva, a news aggregation service, as a research tool to obtain a large set of articles.

We filtered to only obtain articles that originated in Africa and mentioned "crop", "agri-culture", "genetically modified", "genetically modified organism", and/or "GMO". We searched over all articles written in English, French, or Portuguese. Together they total over 1.96 million articles published between January 1, 1997 and June 15, 2022. After restricting the articles to those with more than 50 words from known media sources in Africa, there were 1.06 million articles. Many of these articles were published in more than one country, but the top 10 countries by article count can be found in Table 1.

3   Discussion

Reviewed together, these datasets begin to shed light on important questions driving our research. The first larger question we can answer is where, geographically, is most GM crop research and GM crop commercialization? GM crop research is ongoing in 14 countries, whereas 40 countries do not have any current research. Within those countries with research, over half is concentrated in just two countries, South Africa and Nigeria (see Fig. 3). Many of the crop varieties approved in each of these countries, however, do not have clear evidence of commercialization (see Fig. 4). For instance, while Nigeria has approved 28 crop varieties, only one has actually been commercialized. Moreover, many countries have complex legal regimes when it comes to GM crops. For instance, while Egypt technically "prohibits importing and planting GMO seeds" [11], research into GM crops is active and ongoing within the country [12, 13].

Our dataset also helps to answer which crops are targeted for genetic modification, and which traits are most utilized. Figure 1 shows the dominant crop researched in Africa is maize, which comprises over 37% of the entries in our dataset. The three most dominant crops, maize, cotton, and soybean, comprise 62.3% of the dataset. These three crops are also the most dominant GM crops globally [14]. Similarly we found that both herbicide tolerance and insect resistance were the two most often conferred traits for GM crops. These traits were found in 41% and 48% of crop varieties respectively in our updated dataset. The high prevalence of these traits is mirrored in GM crop usage around the world [14].

Moreover, our dataset shows that 32 GM crop varieties have ever reached the com-mercialization stage: cotton (15), maize (15), cowpea (1), and soybean (1). All either contain herbicide resistance, insect tolerance, or both. Three of the commercialized cot-ton varieties reflect different parent hosts of the same GM trait. Only 29 of these com-mercialized varieties are still active. The 29 active varieties are present in 7 countries, but geographically concentrated: South Africa hosts 21 of the active varieties, while the others are split across Eswatini (2 varieties), Ethiopia (2 varieties), with Kenya, Malawi, Nigeria and Sudan each with one commercialized variety.

Additionally, by mapping the different developers involved in GM crop development, our research sheds light on who is driving GM crop research, and which institutional combinations have been successful at bringing GM crop varieties to commercialization. Only 13% of GM crop varieties under research are driven entirely by African-based institutions (see Fig. 5). None of these 31 crop varieties have made it to the commer-cialization stage. Moreover, 94% of commercialized GM crop varieties were achieved by entirely for-profit institutions. Those GM crop varieties which were driven by either public-private partnerships or all public institutions only produced two commercialized GM crop varieties (see Fig. 6). Within the dataset there are only 12 crops which are supported solely by African not-for-profit organizations. Four are located in Egypt and the remainder are in South Africa. All but two of these crops have had development suspended. These data complicate an oft-repeated narrative that GM crop development is primarily driven by public African organizations. Moreover, they shed light on what types of partnerships have been able to move crops from the lab to farmers' fields [15].

Our initial analysis of the funding sources for GM crop research aligns with our findings from the updated crop dataset. Figure 7 breaks down the flow of money from the non-profit organizations highlighted above to each African country. As expected, South Africa and Nigeria are both in the top 3 countries receiving funding. Kenya is also at the top of this list, which is also expected given that it is home to AATF. Interestingly, these three countries also top the list of those publishing articles regarding GMOs in Africa, as shown in Table 1.

4   Conclusion and Future Work

Above we demonstrate the effectiveness of collecting and combining datasets from a variety of sources. The initial crop dataset provides expansive and novel insights into the research pipeline of biotechnologies in Africa. We extend the value of this dataset and provide a more holistic view of biotechnology development in Africa by combining this dataset with an analysis of institutions supporting African biotechnology development, and social context through the media analysis of local African media coverage of biotechnologies.

Today, October 19, 2022, we release our updated crop dataset to be widely available. We hope this dataset will serve as a resource for researchers, community members, and policymakers interested in the development of GM crops in Africa. We will continue to make regular updates to the dataset, including providing the community with ways to submit revisions or entries omitted from our database, to ensure its accuracy and timeliness.

Having a more accurate representation of the development pipeline of GM crops has led to additional questions in the financial and media datasets. In addition to releasing the crop dataset today, we plan to publish a derivative dataset generated from the processing and analysis of both the financial data in 990 forms and the media articles collected for this project. Other future work will include analyzing the articles using NLP methods and extracting more complete information about the main actors.

Appendix

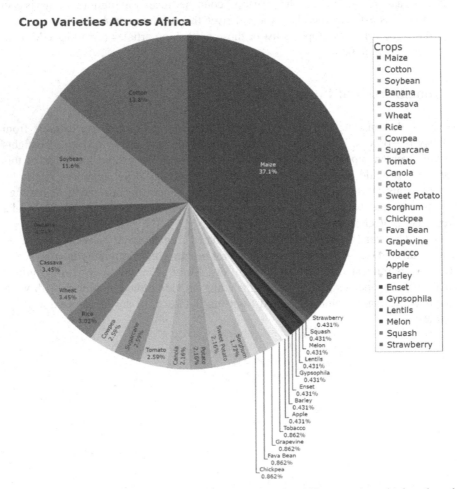

Fig. 1. An overview of GM crop variety development on the African continent broken down by crop type.

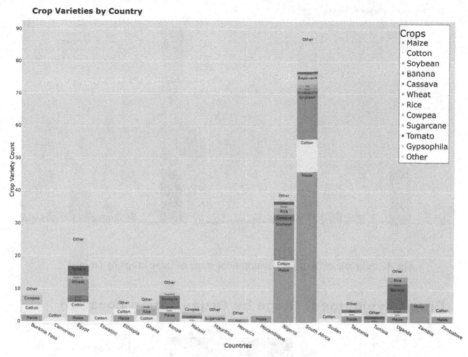

Fig. 2. A breakdown of GM crop varieties in Africa, by country.

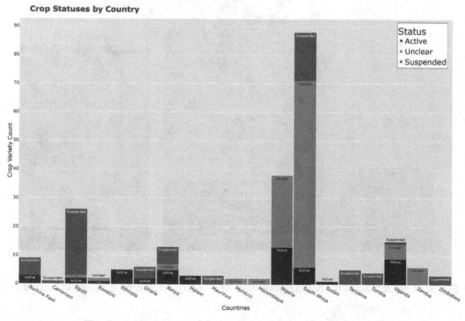

Fig. 3. A breakdown of the statuses of these crops by country.

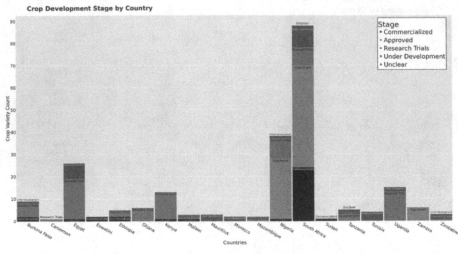

Fig. 4. A breakdown of the development stage of these crops by country

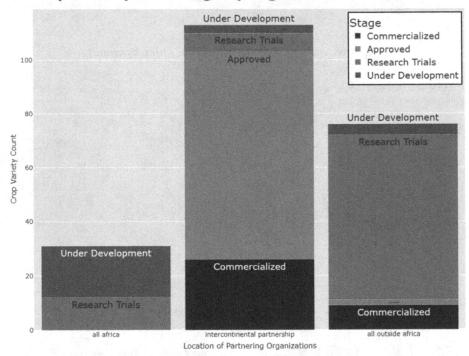

Fig. 5. A breakdown of the development stage of crops by developers' geographic locations

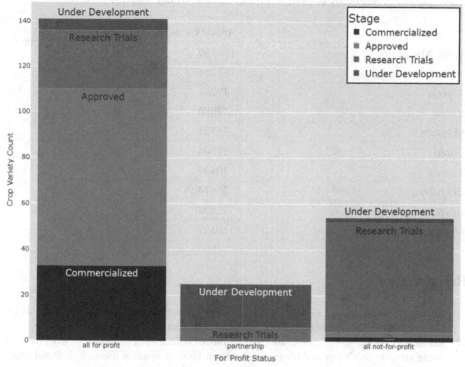

Fig. 6. A breakdown of the development stage of crops by developers' for/non-profit status.

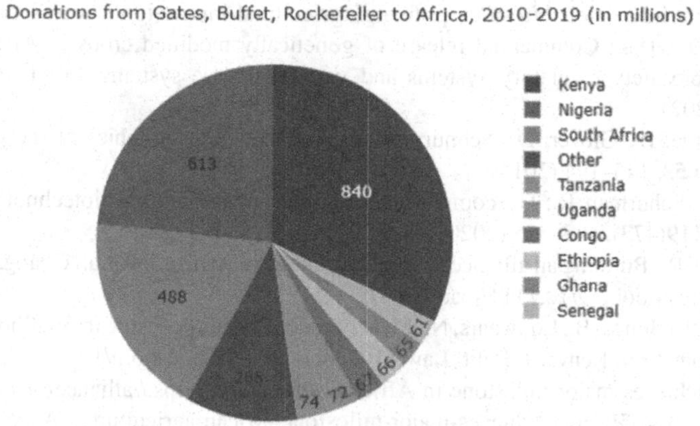

Donations from Gates, Buffet, Rockefeller to Africa, 2010-2019 (in millions)

Fig. 7. A breakdown of the funding from select non-profit organizations to the African continent.

Table 1. Articles published in African media containing keywords "crop", "agriculture", "genetically modified", "genetically modified organism", and/or "GMO" (top 10).

Country	Article count
South Africa	186150
Nigeria	182244
Algeria	47791
Kenya	37080
Morocco	31721
Ghana	31504
Tunisia	30437
Zimbabwe	23614
Egypt	22537
Uganda	19527

References

1. Gbadegesin, L.A., et al.: GMOs in Africa: status, adoption and public acceptance. Food Control 109193 (2022). https://doi.org/10.1016/j.foodcont.2022.109193
2. Schnurr, M.A., Dowd-Uribe, B.: Anticipating farmer outcomes of three genetically modified staple crops in sub-Saharan Africa: insights from farming systems research. J. Rural Stud. **88**, 377–387 (2021). https://doi.org/10.1016/j.jrurstud.2021.08.001
3. Rock, J.S.: We Are Not Starving: The Struggle for Food Sovereignty in Ghana. Michigan State University Press, East Lansing (2022)
4. Agricultural Innovation. https://croplife.org/agricultural-innovation/. Accessed 20 Aug 2022
5. Akinbo, O., et al.: Commercial release of genetically modified crops in Africa: interface between biosafety regulatory systems and varietal release systems. Front. Plant Sci. **12**, 605937 (2021)
6. Dowd-Uribe, B., Glover, D., Schnurr, M.A.: Transgenic geographies of the global South. Geoforum **53**, 145–194 (2014)
7. Rock, J.S., Schurman, R.: The complex choreography of agricultural biotechnology in Africa. Afr. Aff. **119**(477), 499–525 (2020)
8. Schurman, R.: Building an alliance for biotechnology in Africa. J. Agrar. Chang. **17**, 441–458 (2017). https://doi.org/10.1111/joac.12167
9. Munyi, P., De Jonge, B., Louwaars, N.: Plant breeders' rights licensing in smallholder farming: observations from Kenya. J. Polit. Law **11**(2), 45–60. https://doi.org/10.5539/jpl.v11n2p45
10. WEMA achieves major milestone in African agriculture. https://allianceforscience.cornell.edu/blog/2018/05/wema-achieves-major-milestone-african-agriculture/. Accessed 20 Aug 2022
11. Egypt considers planting genetically-modified seeds due to high prices of grain: Lawmaker. https://www.egypttoday.com/Article/1/114491/Egypt-considers-planting-genetically-modified-seeds-due-to-high-prices. Accessed 20 June 2022
12. Egypt' agriculture scientists at Atomic Energy Authority produces new strain of wheat resistant to salinity, water scarcity. https://www.egypttoday.com/Article/1/115421/Egypt'-agriculture-scientists-at-Atomic-Energy-Authority-produces-new-strain. Accessed 20 June 2022

13. Dessoky, E.S., Ismail, R.M., Elarabi, N.I., Abdelhadi, A.A., Abdallah, N.A.: Improvement of sugarcane for borer resistance using Agrobacterium mediated transformation of cry1Ac gene. GM Crops Food **12**, 47–56 (2021). https://doi.org/10.1080/21645698.2020.1809318

14. Stone, G.D.: Genetically Modified Crops. https://oxfordre-com.ezp.lib.cam.ac.uk/anthropology/view/10.1093/acrefore/9780190854584.001.0001/acrefore-9780190854584-e-296. https://doi.org/10.1093/acrefore/9780190854584.013.296. Accessed 20 June 2022

15. 10 things everyone should know about GMOs in Africa. https://allianceforscience.cornell.edu/10-things-everyone-should-know-about-gmos-in-africa/. Accessed 21 June 2022

Changes in Policy Preferences in German Tweets During the COVID Pandemic

Felix Biessmann[1,2(✉)]

[1] Berlin University of Applied Sciences, Berlin, Germany
[2] Einstein Center Digital Future, Berlin, Germany
felix.biessmann@bht-berlin.de

Abstract. Online social media have become an important forum for exchanging political opinions. In response to COVID measures citizens expressed their policy preferences directly on these platforms. Quantifying political preferences in online social media remains challenging: The vast amount of content requires scalable automated extraction of political preferences – however fine grained political preference extraction is difficult with current machine learning (ML) technology, due to the lack of data sets. Here we present a novel data set of tweets with fine grained political preference annotations. A text classification model trained on this data is used to extract policy preferences in a German Twitter corpus ranging from 2019 to 2022. Our results indicate that in response to the COVID pandemic, expression of political opinions increased. Using a well established taxonomy of policy preferences we analyse fine grained political views and highlight changes in distinct political categories. These analyses suggest that the increase in policy preference expression is dominated by the categories pro-welfare, pro-education and pro-governmental administration efficiency. All training data and code used in this study are made publicly available to encourage other researchers to further improve automated policy preference extraction methods. We hope that our findings contribute to a better understanding of political statements in online social media and to a better assessment of how COVID measures impact political preferences.

Keywords: Policy preference extraction · Text classification · Social media

1 Introduction

The past decades have shown two trends that are becoming increasingly interdependent: Political campaigns take place online in social media. And at the same time online content for individual users is recommended using automated machine learning (ML) systems that are often optimized for user engagement or other proxy metrics for economic profit. These mechanisms can increase visibility of polarizing content and simultaneously enforce a bias towards existing user preferences.

© The Author(s), under exclusive license to Springer Nature Switzerland AG 2022
F. Hopfgartner et al. (Eds.): SocInfo 2022, LNCS 13618, pp. 426–435, 2022.
https://doi.org/10.1007/978-3-031-19097-1_29

During the COVID pandemic, global platforms such as online social media allowed users to directly express their preferences for or against the measures taken by governments, such as lockdowns or vaccination programs. Analysing these policy preferences can yield valuable insights that could help to improve governmental policies. The large amount of content requires methods for automated extraction of policy preferences. Recent trends in machine learning (ML) towards bigger and more powerful language models could help to improve policy preference extraction. However there are few training data sets that contain annotations for fine grained policy preferences [9]. The lack of high quality annotated data sets with political information impedes the development of better models for automated detection of policy preferences.

Here we present a data set of online social media content, Twitter posts, with fine grained political annotations as defined in [24]. The data set is used to train a text classification model that predicts policy preferences from social network posts. On a larger corpus of tweets collected from 2019 to 2022 the model is used to predict policy preferences before and during the COVID pandemic. Analyses of automatically extracted policy preferences suggest that the amount of policy preferences expressed on Twitter increased after the first lockdown. Leveraging a fine grained political viewpoint taxonoomy we can investigate which policy preferences were expressed in those political tweets. To summarize, the main contributions of this study are:

- A data set of German tweets with fine grained political preference annotation
- A novel text classification model
- An analysis of policy preferences before and during the COVID pandemic

2   Related Work

The general topic of automated information extraction from online socia media has been widely studied and different approaches have been proposed, including supervised ML methods, such as text classification [11], and unsupervised methods, such as topic models, or extensions thereof [1,7,8]. Many of these methods are dedicated to trending topic extraction. Since not all trending topics are related to the political discourse a large fraction of these methods do not lend themselves easily to the invesigation of policy preferences.

A number of studies have explored automated extraction of policy preferences, for a comprehensive overview we refer the interested reader to [9]. There have been many studies exploring traditional ML techniques for ideology detection and policy preference extraction [21] as well as approaches based on more recent natural language processing models, such as Recurrent Neural Networks [12] or more recently also Transformers [17].

The authors of [9] highlight that training ML models for automated extraction of fine grained policy preferences expressed in online social media content remains challenging. Primarily this is due to the fact that annotating this data requires expertise that can not as easily be crowdsourced, as the annotation of hate speech for instance. Annotation of policy preferences requires domain expertise and in particular experience with policy preferences as expressed in online media.

There are some publicly available data sets that can be used for training ML models that detect policy preferences in text data. One of the largest and best curated data sets is the corpus of the Manifesto Project [23] which contains over 1,500,000 quasi-sentences, extracted from over 1,500 party manifestos, and annotated according to a well established category scheme of 56 policy categories [24]. This data has been used by researchers to investigate policy preferences [15] and there have been efforts to train ML models on this data to make predictions on online social media texts [6,16,18]. However the texts of party manifestos are written in a different style than posts in online social media. Hence models trained on the manifesto data usually do not work well on online social media texts. Other data sets focus more on texts in online social media but these often focus on a small set of political policy preferences [2,4,10,13].

Table 1. F1 scores for tweets in the test set for the top 10 (according to F1) political categories. The complete list can be found in the Appendix, Table 3.

	Precision	Recall	F1-score	Support
Controlled economy +	1.00	0.67	0.80	3.0
Europe -	0.80	0.75	0.77	16.0
Environmentalism +	0.76	0.70	0.73	90.0
Democracy +	0.63	0.74	0.68	77.0
Anti-imperialism +	1.00	0.50	0.67	2.0
Economic orthodoxy +	0.57	0.67	0.62	6.0
Europe +	0.56	0.64	0.60	14.0
Undefined	0.58	0.55	0.57	271.0
Infrastructure +	0.43	0.80	0.56	20.0
Foreign special +	0.50	0.55	0.52	11.0
...				
Accuracy			0.46	1214
Macro avg	0.30	0.31	0.30	1214
Weighted avg	0.46	0.46	0.46	1214

3   Training Data Set

For annotating training data with fine grained policy preferences we sampled tweets from a corpus of German tweets [14]. The tweets were sampled between August 2019 and March 2022 and filtered using the following criteria:

User Interaction. We selected tweets that were interacted with in some form (likes, retweets, quotes) at least once.

Relevance. We used a ML model (see below) trained on the Manifesto Project corpus [23] to estimate the political relevance of each tweet. To increase the usefulness of the annotated data set we tried to cover all labels of the Manifesto Project's category scheme by selecting for each week only the top 5 tweets that were predicted as the most likely for each political category by an ML model trained on German party manifestos [23].

The filtered set of tweets were then annotated by two experts trained by researchers of the Manifesto Project. The annotation was performed in a custom written web app and later using labelstudio [22]. Annotators were instructed to label a tweet with one of the 56 political categories of the Manifesto Project codebook [24].

Additionally annotators provided the label undefined for tweets that could not be associated with any of the relevant political categories. If the tweet contained an image, annotators also considered the image content for the annotation. Context beyond the actual tweet content was not taken into account. Exceptions were tweets that replied to or commented on another tweet. In that case the original tweet was also considered. These replied-to tweets are, to keep the data set simpler, not part of the data set but can be retrieved via the url of the annotated tweet.

In the current version of the data set there are 6097 unique tweets and the most frequent political categories annotated are shown in Table 2 (Appendix). Note that the majority of tweets is labeled as undefined, despite the filtering with the ML model. This is an indication that the data set contains useful negative examples for training better models. The data set is released and available for research purposes [5].

4   Evaluation of Policy Preference Predictors

To establish a simple baseline for policy preference extraction on the PoliTweet data set we used the TextPredictor module of the autoML package AutoGluon [3,19]. The model was trained on a V100 NVIDIA GPU with a pretrained BERT model checkpoint (bert-base-german-cased) on the entire German part of the manifesto corpus [23] and 4883 annotated tweets from the training data set in Sect. 3; 1214 annotated tweets were held out for testing the model. In Sect. 2 we list the results for the top 10 political categories that could be predicted with highest F1 score by the model; the full list of results for all categories is listed in the Appendix, Table 3. Note that while the overall prediction performance is below 0.50 F1 score (macro or class-frequency weighted), these results are still encouraging. Fine grained political viewpoint extraction is a challenging task and even when trained on the manifesto corpus, the classification performance for all categories with extensive tuning and leveraging state-of-the-art ML models often stays below an F1 score of 0.5 [20].

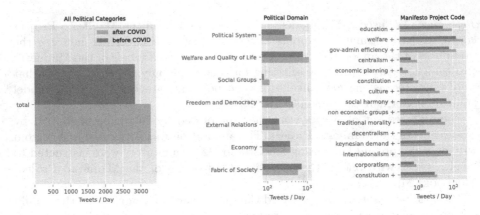

Fig. 1. Increases in political tweets after the first COVID lockdown in Germany. Policy preferences were extracted with a text classifier. *Left:* After the first lockdown the total number of political tweets per day increases. *Middle:* Strong increases were observed in the broad political category of `political system` and `welfare`; note the log scale on the x-axis. *Right:* Fine grained policy preferences show a strong increase in *pro education, pro welfare* and *pro government administration efficiency*

5   Policy Preferences After COVID Lockdown

The model as trained in Sect. 4 was then applied to the entire twitter corpus [14] between 2019 and 2022 and filtered using the relevance and activity criteria as mentioned in Sect. 3. We applied additional relevance filters to extract only tweets expressing political views. All tweets for which the category `undefined` was amongst the top 3 predictions of the text classification model were considered irrelevant and filtered out. The histograms of policy preferences in the remaining tweets were then compared before and after the COVID lockdown onset in Germany. In Fig. 1 we show histograms of political views expressed in tweets before and after onset of the first lockdown.

Overall our results suggest that the number of political tweets increased after the first lockdown. Investigating the fine grained political categories we find that this increase is driven by an increased number of tweets categorized as *pro education, pro welfare* and *pro government administration efficiency*. These changes in policy preferences of tweets could reflect the negative impact that COVID measures such as lockdowns had: many employes lost their jobs, many needed to teach their children at home and all administrational processes were substantially slowed down due to the poor digitalization in German administration.

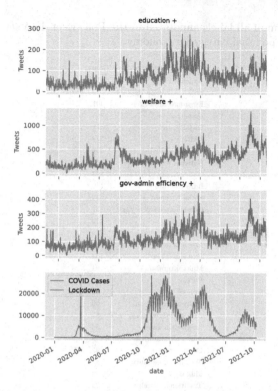

Fig. 2. Number of tweets over time in those political categories that exhibit a strong increase after the first lockdown in Germany. Bottom panel shows an overview of COVID cases reported from Robert-Koch-Institutel, lockdown starts are indicated in blue. While the first lockdown did not result in strong increases of Tweets with political preferences, during the second COVID wave political preferences in the categories *pro education, pro welfare* and *pro government administration efficiency* were expressed more often than before.

In Fig. 2 timelines are shown for the political categories *pro education, pro welfare* and *pro government administration efficiency*, which exhibit the largest change after onset of the COVID lockdown as shown in Fig. 1. The bottom panel in Fig. 2 shows the onsets of lockdowns and COVID case numbers. The strongest impact of lockdown measures with respect to political policy preferences on Twitter appears to develop during the second wave of the pandemic.

Table 2. Histogram of all labels annotated in the PoliTweet data set according to the Manifesto Project political category taxonomy.

Political category	Count
Undefined	1318
Freedom/human rights +	502
Environmentalism +	401
Democracy +	395
Social justice +	379
Welfare +	343
Political authority +	337
National way of life +	241
National way of life -	198
Infrastructure +	136
Social harmony +	133
Gov-admin efficiency +	131
Labour +	130
Education +	119
Law and order +	112
Free enterprise +	104
Multiculturalism -	94
Europe +	90
Europe -	63
Political corruption -	60
Anti-growth economy +	57
Internationalism +	54
Multiculturalism +	49
Constitution +	47
Traditional morality +	43
Military -	43
Traditional morality -	42
Market regulation +	41
Productivity +	41
Military +	37
Foreign special +	33
Agriculture +	33
Welfare -	31
Economic orthodoxy +	31
Culture +	28
Marxist analysis +	25
Economic goals	25
Non economic groups +	19
Peace +	15
Incentives +	15
Controlled economy +	13
Nationalization +	12
Protectionism +	10
Keynesian demand +	10
Internationalism -	10
Anti-imperialism +	10
Decentralism +	9
Centralism +	5
Middle class +	5
Foreign special -	5
Protectionism -	4
Labour -	3
Minority groups +	2
Education -	2
Economic planning +	1
Constitution -	1
Total	6097

Table 3. F1 scores for tweets of all political categories in the test set.

	Precision	Recall	F1-score	Support
Controlled economy +	1.00	0.67	0.80	3.0
Europe -	0.80	0.75	0.77	16.0
Environmentalism +	0.76	0.70	0.73	90.0
Democracy +	0.63	0.74	0.68	77.0
Anti-imperialism +	1.00	0.50	0.67	2.0
Economic orthodoxy +	0.57	0.67	0.62	6.0
Europe +	0.56	0.64	0.60	14.0
Undefined	0.58	0.55	0.57	271.0
Infrastructure +	0.43	0.80	0.56	20.0
Foreign special +	0.50	0.55	0.52	11.0
Education +	0.38	0.76	0.51	17.0
Marxist analysis +	0.50	0.50	0.50	6.0
Social justice +	0.46	0.52	0.49	69.0
Internationalism +	0.39	0.50	0.44	14.0
Freedom/human rights +	0.45	0.43	0.44	97.0
Political authority +	0.41	0.43	0.42	60.0
Decentralism +	0.33	0.50	0.40	2.0
Traditional morality -	0.43	0.38	0.40	8.0
Protectionism +	0.33	0.50	0.40	2.0
Law and order +	0.37	0.42	0.39	24.0
Social harmony +	0.42	0.35	0.38	23.0
Political corruption -	0.36	0.38	0.37	13.0
Agriculture +	0.50	0.29	0.36	7.0
Constitution +	0.33	0.40	0.36	10.0
National way of life -	0.33	0.36	0.35	36.0
Multiculturalism -	0.38	0.33	0.35	18.0
Culture +	0.29	0.40	0.33	5.0
Military -	0.33	0.31	0.32	13.0
Macro avg	0.30	0.31	0.30	1214.0
Welfare +	0.37	0.24	0.29	82.0
Market regulation +	0.33	0.25	0.29	12.0
National way of life +	0.30	0.29	0.29	48.0
Military +	0.22	0.33	0.27	6.0
Peace +	0.17	0.33	0.22	3.0
Labour +	0.25	0.19	0.22	21.0
Gov-admin efficiency +	0.21	0.19	0.20	32.0
Free enterprise +	0.19	0.15	0.17	20.0
Protectionism -	0.00	0.00	0.00	2.0
Centralism +	0.00	0.00	0.00	1.0
Welfare -	0.00	0.00	0.00	8.0
Traditional morality +	0.00	0.00	0.00	9.0
Corporatism +	0.00	0.00	0.00	0.0
Incentives +	0.00	0.00	0.00	2.0
Economic goals	0.00	0.00	0.00	8.0
Productivity +	0.00	0.00	0.00	6.0
Education -	0.00	0.00	0.00	1.0
Nationalization +	0.00	0.00	0.00	0.0
Multiculturalism +	0.00	0.00	0.00	4.0
Minority groups +	0.00	0.00	0.00	0.0
Foreign special -	0.00	0.00	0.00	1.0
Anti-growth economy +	0.00	0.00	0.00	9.0
Keynesian demand +	0.00	0.00	0.00	1.0
Internationalism -	0.00	0.00	0.00	3.0
Non economic groups +	0.00	0.00	0.00	1.0
Accuracy			0.46	1214
Macro avg	0.30	0.31	0.30	1214
Weighted avg	0.46	0.46	0.46	1214

6 Conclusion

This study presents three main contributions, a) a data set of German tweets with fine grained political preference annotation, b) a novel text classification model trained on that data and c) an analysis of policy preferences before and during the COVID pandemic. Our preliminary analyses of tweets during the COVID pandemic showed a pronounced increase in political tweets overall and in particular also in certain fine grained political categories. These findings are not from a representative sample and have several other limitations, such as the predictive performance of the text classification model for some classes, especially in rare categories. Nonetheless we believe the data set, the model and the experimental results are an important step towards more scalable and more fine grained policy preference extraction in German online social media. We hope that our contributions will encourage other researchers to improve current state-of-the-art models for policy preference extraction in research and applications.

Acknowledgements. We thank Jonas Bauer for conceptualizing, implementing and maintaining the first data annotation setup, Teo Chiaburu for setting up labelstudio, Marvin Müller and Maren Krumbein for annotating tweets, Pola Lehmann for training the annotators and valuable feedback on the analyses, Johannes Hoster for analyses and Philipp Staab for valuable discussions on sociological aspects.

References

1. Aiello, L.M., et al.: Sensing Trending Topics in Twitter. IEEE Trans. Multimedia **15**(6), 1268–1282 (2013)
2. Aksenov, D., Bourgonje, P., Zaczynska, K., Ostendorff, M., Schneider, J.M., Rehm, G.: Fine-grained classification of political bias in german news: A data set and initial experiments. In: Proceedings of the 5th Workshop on Online Abuse and Harms (WOAH 2021), pp. 121–131 (2021)
3. AutoGluon: https://github.com/awslabs/autogluon
4. Barbera, P., Jost, J., Nagler, J., Tucker, J., Bonneau, R.: Replication Data for: Tweeting from Left to Right: Is Online Political Communication More Than an Echo Chamber? (2015). https://doi.org/10.7910/DVN/F9ICHH
5. Biessmann, F.: Politweets https://zenodo.org/record/6570856#.YqH6khMzaAk
6. Biessmann, F., Lehmann, P., Kirsch, D., Schelter, S.: Predicting political party affiliation from text. PolText 2016 14, 14 (2016)
7. Biessmann, F., Papaioannou, J.M., Harth, A., Jugel, M.L., Muller, K.R., Braun, M.: Quantifying spatiotemporal dynamics of twitter replies to news feeds. In: IEEE Int. Work. Mach. Learn. Signal Process. MLSP (2012). https://doi.org/10.1109/MLSP.2012.6349806, iSSN: 21610363
8. Bießmann, F., Papaioannou, J.M., Braun, M., Harth, A.: Canonical trends: Detecting trend setters in web data. In: Proc. 29th Int. Conf. Mach. Learn. ICML 2012. vol. 2, pp. 1247–1254 (2012)
9. Doan, T.M., Gulla, J.A.: A survey on political viewpoints identification. Online Soc. Netw. Media **30**, 100208 (2022)

10. Gilardi, F., Gessler, T., Kubli, M., Müller, S.: Replication Data for: Social Media and Policy Responses to the COVID-19 Pandemic in Switzerland (2021). https://doi.org/10.7910/DVN/BKGZUL
11. Gryc, W., Moilanen, K.: Leveraging Textual Sentiment Analysis with Social Network Modelling: Sentiment Analysis of Political Blogs in the 2008 U.S. Presidential Election. In: Bertie Kaal, I.M., van Elfrinkhof, A. (eds.) From Text to Polit. Positions Text Anal. across Discip, pp. 47–70 (2014). https://doi.org/10.1075/dapsac.55.03gry
12. Iyyer, M., Enns, P., Boyd-Graber, J., Resnik, P.: Political Ideology Detection Using Recursive Neural Networks. In: Proceedings of the 52nd Annual Meeting of the Association for Computational Linguistics (Volume 1: Long Papers). pp. 1113–1122. Association for Computational Linguistics, Baltimore, Maryland (2014). https://doi.org/10.3115/v1/P14-1105, https://aclanthology.org/P14-1105
13. Kiesel, J., et al.: Semeval-2019 task 4: Hyperpartisan news detection. In: Proceedings of the 13th International Workshop on Semantic Evaluation, pp. 829–839 (2019)
14. Kratzke, N.: Monthly samples of german tweets (2020). https://doi.org/10.5281/zenodo.3633935
15. Krause, W.: Appearing moderate or radical? radical left party success and the two-dimensional political space. West Eur. Polit. 43(7), 1365–1387 (2020)
16. Phillips, J.B., Woodman, V.: Party system fragmentation, social cleavages, and social media: New zealand's 2017 election campaign on facebook. Aust. J. Polit. Sci. 55(3), 293–310 (2020)
17. Schick, T., Schütze, H.: Exploiting Cloze Questions for Few Shot Text Classification and Natural Language Inference. Tech. Rep. arXiv:2001.07676, arXiv (Jan 2021). https://doi.org/10.48550/arXiv.2001.07676
18. Schwarz, J.: Detecting political ideology in youtube comments using machine learning. In: Seminar Social Media and Business Analytics (2019)
19. Shi, X., Mueller, J., Erickson, N., Li, M., Smola, A.: Multimodal automl on structured tables with text fields. In: 8th ICML Workshop on Automated Machine Learning (AutoML) (2021)
20. Subramanian, S., Cohn, T., Baldwin, T.: Hierarchical Structured Model for Fine-to-coarse Manifesto Text Analysis. Tech. Rep. arXiv:1805.02823, arXiv (May 2018)
21. Thomas, M., Pang, B., Lee, L.: Get out the vote: Determining support or opposition from Congressional floor-debate transcripts. Tech. Rep. arXiv:cs/0607062, arXiv (Jun 2012)
22. Tkachenko, M., Malyuk, M., Holmanyuk, A., Liubimov, N.: Label Studio: Data labeling software (2020–2022), https://github.com/heartexlabs/label-studio, open source software available from https://github.com/heartexlabs/label-studio
23. Volkens, A., et al.: The manifesto data collection. manifesto project (mrg/cmp/marpor). version 2021a (2021). https://doi.org/10.25522/manifesto.mpds.2021a
24. Werner, A., van Rinsum, L.: Manifesto coding instructions. In: 5th re-revised edition. Tech. rep., Berlin: WZB Wissenschaftszentrum Berlin für Sozialforschung (2021)

Bullying in Online Brand Communities-Exploring Consumers' Intentions to Intervene

Jan Breitsohl[1] (ID), Nadia Jiménez[2](✉) (ID), Phil Megicks[3] (ID), Ioannis Krasonikolakis[4] (ID), Stratos Ramoglou[3] (ID), Ulf Aagerup[5] (ID), and Catherine Happer[1] (ID)

[1] University of Glasgow, Glasgow G12 8QQ, UK
{jan.breitsohl,catherine.happer}@glasgow.ac.uk
[2] University of Burgos, C/Hospital del Rey s/n, 09001 Burgos, Spain
nhjimenez@ubu.es
[3] University of Southampton, University Road, Southampton SO17 1BJ, UK
{P.R.Megicks,S.Ramoglou}@soton.ac.uk
[4] University of Kent, Canterbury CT2 7FS, UK
I.Krasonikolakis@kent.ac.uk
[5] Halmstad University, SE-301 18 Halmstad, Sweden
ulf.aagerup@ju.se

Abstract. Research on the psychological and marketing-related predictors of bystanders' intentions to intervene when consumers are bullied in online brand communities is scarce. Using Structural Equation Modelling and Process Analysis, we investigate bystanders' concern for social appropriateness as key psychological influence that drives intervention intentions, and further consider two novel moderators. Specifically, when brand followers perceive the victim to be a rival, the effect of social appropriateness on intention to intervene is weaker than when the victim is a supporter. Moreover, when brand followers perceive the community to have a stronger consciousness of kind, the effect of social appropriateness on intention to intervene is more emphasised compared to when the consciousness of kind is perceived to be lower. The same is true for the moderation effect of shared rituals and sense of moral responsibility.

Keywords: Bystanders · Intentions to intervene · Social appropriateness

1 Introduction

Research on consumers who bully other consumers in online brand communities (OBC) is scarce, and mostly relies on qualitative observations of consumer comments (e.g. [3]). Recently, authors have started to explore what brands can do to intervene in consumer bullying [4]; yet, the possibility of bystanding consumers intervening on behalf of the brand has largely been neglected. Bystanders are consumers who are not directly involved in the consumer-to-consumer bullying interaction, i.e. they are neither the victim nor the bully. This paper aims to explore why, and under which conditions, bystanders are likely

F. Hopfgartner et al. (Eds.): SocInfo 2022, LNCS 13618, pp. 436–443, 2022.
https://doi.org/10.1007/978-3-031-19097-1_30

to intervene in bullying interactions between consumers in online brand communities. In psychology, one of the key determinants for a bystander to intervene in cyberbullying is related to the perceived social appropriateness of doing so. Lennox & Wolfe for instance suggests that those with a high sense of social appropriateness are more likely to feel obliged to intervene when faced with inappropriate behaviors [13]. Similar findings have been reported in a social media context [17]. Recent qualitative work in Marketing suggests two marketing-related factors that further whether someone remains a passive bystander who does not get involved, or whether someone decides to intervene (i.e. becoming an 'upstander' [18]). Most notably, it is proposed that bystanders will consider whether the victim of bullying is someone who supports the same brand as they do (brand supporter), or someone who supports a different brand (brand rival) (e.g. [8]); and that bystanders will reflect upon whether the online brand community within which the bullying took place is characterised by a sense of belonging between its members (consciousness of a kind), a perceived sense of moral obligation between members to help one another (moral responsibility), and a visible set of norms and values that dictate intra-community behaviors (shared rituals) [16]. Therefore, we test whether consumers concern for social appropriateness has a significant influence on bystanders' intention to intervene, and whether this is moderated by the identity of the victim (brand rival vs supporter) and the online brand community character.

In doing so, we contribute to the marketing literature by offering quantitative insights gathered via direct enquiry with consumers (i.e. survey data) on the predictors, and underlying mechanisms, that lead to consumers' intention to intervene when a consumer is bullied in an online brand community. Theoretically, we enrich the literature by introducing bullying bystander theory to a marketing paradigm, by testing novel, marketing-focused moderators, and by highlighting that concepts which have previously been explored in positive consumer-to-consumer interactions can also advance a negative (i.e. bullying) research paradigm. As such, we address calls for research on bullying interactions between consumers in OBCs [6, 7], and the lack of research on the dark side of company hosted social media pages in general [1]. For practitioners, our findings indicate circumstances under which brands may rely on consumers to deal with bullying, without having to get involved. Moreover, we show that nurturing factors related to the community character can enhance the likelihood for consumers to become upstanders, hence offering concrete means to foster consumer engagement in form of bystander interventions.

We propose the conceptual model as depicted in Fig. 1, and follow an exploratory (rather than hypotheses-based approach), given the lack of current knowledge related to c2c (consumer-to-consumer) bullying. Our model is based on the following tentative propositions:

1) A strong concern for social appropriateness increases the likelihood to intervene when exposed to cyberbullying in online brand communities
2) However, this will depend upon two brand-related moderators:

First, the victim's identity. It is conceivable that a consumer is more likely to consider social appropriateness in the decision to intervene when the victim is a supporter of the same brand, and less likely to do so when the victim is a brand rival.

Second, the character of the brand community. Arguably, a consumer is more likely to consider social appropriateness in the decision to intervene the more he/she perceives three community characteristics to be present, and less likely to do so when they are less evident.

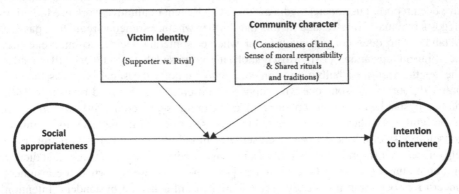

Fig. 1. – Conceptual model

2 Method

We recruited 1263 participants through the Qualtrics online panel who were users of OCB on Facebook. Participants were 82% female, mostly aged between 25–44 (61.4%) with an income between $1,000–$6,000 per month (71%). Most participants visited Facebook daily (85.4%) and indicated reading users' comments at least 'often' (79.4%).

Embedded within an online questionnaire, participants were shown the screenshot of a simulated bullying interaction in an OBC on Facebook, designed in close relation to observational evidence presented in prior work [3, 8]. To increase the personal relevance of our experiment, we asked participants to enter the name of a brand they follow on Facebook into a textbox, which was then carried forward into the scenarios and measurement items. Following participants entered the brand's name; they were then randomly channelled to a scenario showing a post of their brand and a negative statement from a "fictitious victim" (Michael); containing the manipulation of victim identity (e.g., I support D&G and like the brand a lot, but recently D&G has become really awful) or a brand rival (e.g., I do not support D&G and always preferred its competitors, especially since D&G has recently become really awful). Afterwards, another consumer, Pete, bullies Michael by using various swearwords and harassing comments (e.g. Shut up Michal you are an idiot).

Participants then reported their concern for social appropriateness via the adapted scale from [13]. The intention to intervene was measured via [14] scale. Concerning moderator variables, the three dimensions of perceived Brand Community Character (i.e., consciousness of kind, shared rituals and traditions and sense of moral responsibility) were measured with the [16] scale. We measured all items on a scale from 1 (strongly disagree) to 7 (strongly agree).

To analyze the measurement properties of our constructs, we used partial least squares (PLS) and bootstrap analysis with 5000 subsamples [9]. Standard psychometric guidelines suggest cut-off values of 0.7 for Cronbach alpha (α), 0.5 for average variance extracted (AVE) and .6 for composite reliability (CR) [2], all of which the employed constructs exceed. Details about measurement are illustrated in Table 1.

Table 1. Measurement model estimation and descriptive statistics

Construct	Items	Loadings	Mean	SD
Concern for social appropriateness (α: 0.806; CR: 0.874; AVE: 0.700)	When I am uncertain how to act in a social situation, I look to the behavior of others for cues	0.844	3.72	1.81
	I try to pay attention to the reactions of others to my behavior in order to avoid being out of place	0.733	4.36	1.72
	It is my feeling that if everyone else in a group is behaving in a certain manner, this must be the proper way to behave	0.923	3.10	1.71
Consumer intention to intervene (α:0.945; CR:0.964; AVE:0.900)	If I had seen these comments* on Facebook, I would feel obliged to personally intervene	0.967	3.08	1.70
	If I had seen these comments* on Facebook, I would feel personally responsible to intervene	0.932	2.86	1.67
	If I had seen these comments* on Facebook, I would consider it as my duty to personally intervene	0.948	2.73	1.65
Consciousness of kind (α:0.920; CR: 0.933; AVE: 0.737)	I perceive that the members of this fanpage feel a sense of belonging to this group	0.790	5.37	1.32
	I perceive that this fanpage gives its members the feeling that they belong together	0.835	5.18	1.40
	I perceive that there is a sense of we-ness among this fanpage's members	0.864	5.21	1.41
	I perceive that the members of this fanpage feel that they are part of the group	0.951	5.44	1.26

(*continued*)

Table 1. (*continued*)

Construct	Items	Loadings	Mean	SD
	I perceive that the members of this fanpage feel interconnected	0.844	5.16	1.29
Shared rituals and traditions (α:0.854; CR: 0.896; AVE: 0.633)	I perceive that this fanpage defines its behavior-relevant norms and values visibly to the public	0.736	4.78	1.38
	I perceive that the members of this fanpage live their common values	0.796	4.57	1.36
	I perceive that there is a common culture in this fanpage	0.817	4.86	1.33
	I perceive that shared rituals and traditions are practiced and lived in this fanpage	0.795	4.34	1.40
	I perceive that the members of this fanpage use a common system of values and symbols	0.830	4.47	1.44
Sense of moral responsibility (α:0.917; CR: 0.941; AVE: 0.800)	I perceive that the members of this fanpage help each other	0.899	4.70	1.57
	I perceive that the members of this fanpage support each other	0.929	4.86	1.54
	I perceive that the members of this fanpage act cooperatively among each other	0.890	4.68	1.60
	I perceive that the members of this fanpage show solidarity	0.860	4.82	1.50
Victim identity	0 = Supporter; 1 = Rival	N.A	N.A	N.A

Note: N.A.: Not applicable; * Referring to simulated bullying interaction in an OBC.

Supporting discriminant validity [12], the square root of the AVE exceeded the inter-correlations of each construct with the other constructs, and the Heterotrait-Monotrait (HTMT) ratio of correlations showed that all latent variables were lower than 0.85 (see Table 2). We also assessed the common method variance (CMV) using Harman's single-factor test [15], and found that the percentage variance explained by a single factor is 39.6%, indicating a lack of concern for CMV.

Table 2. Correlation matrix and Heterotrait-Monotrait (HTMT) ratio

	(1)	(2)	(3)	(4)	(5)
(1) Concern for social appropriateness	**0.837**	0.120	0.103	0.176	0.068
(2) Consumer intention to intervene	0.121	**0.949**	0.022	0.098	0.038
(3) Consciousness of kind	0.074	-0.028	**0.858**	0.705	0.753
(4) Shared rituals and traditions	0.157	0.089	0.608	**0.795**	0.763
(5) Sense of moral responsibility	0.065	-0.035	0.687	0.672	**0.895**

Note: the main diagonal (in bold) shows the square root of the average variance extracted (AVE). The correlations between latent variables are presented below the diagonal and above the diagonal the ratio HTMT.

3   Results

After validating the measurement model, the next step was to analyze the proposed structured model and related hypotheses. The root mean square residual (SRMR) was found to be 0.057, that suggests a good fit model [11]. The estimation of the hypothesized direct relationship was then tested (Fig. 1). Consistent with our expectations, the positive influence of concern for social appropriateness in intention to intervene in simulated bullying interaction in an OBC is corroborated (β:0.121; t-value: 4.135).

Using Process Macro, we performed a moderation analysis (model 1, [10]). We use concern for social appropriateness as the independent variable and intention to intervene in simulated bullying interaction in an OBC as the dependent variable (hypothesis 1), and the respective 3 continuous variables (i.e., consciousness of kind, shared rituals and traditions and sense of moral responsibility) and 1 categorical variable (i.e., victim identity), as moderator variables. Table 3 depicts the moderation analysis results. The subgroups for the variables are shown and subsequently examined at $\pm$ 1 SD above and below the variable's mean, as suggested by [5]. Results indicated a significant moderation for all moderators at p. > 0.05, except shared rituals and traditions which was significant at p. > 0.1.

Table 3. Results for moderation analysis

Variable		Subgroups	Conditional effects		95% CI	
			Coef.	SE	ULCI	LLCI
Victim identity		a: supporter	0.19	0.046	0.28	0.10
(Interaction coefficient: −0.13; ULCI: −0.253 and LLCI: −0.015)		b: rival	0.05	0.039	0.13	−0.02
Perceived Brand Community Character dimensions as moderators						
Consciousness of kind (Interaction coefficient: 0.06;ULCI: 0.104 and LLCI: 0.012)		a: weaker (−1 SD) b: stronger (+1 SD)	0.04 0.17	0.043 0.037	0.12 0.25	−0.04 0.10
Shared rituals and traditions (Interaction coefficient: 0.04;ULCI: 0.086 and LLCI: −0.006)		a: weaker (−1 SD) b: stronger (+1 SD)	0.04 0.14	0.042 0.037	0.13 0.21	−0.03 0.06
Sense of moral responsibility (Interaction coefficient: 0.07;ULCI: 0.112 and LLCI: 0.034)		a: weaker (−1 SD) b: stronger (+1 SD)	−0.00 0.20	0.044 0.038	0.08 0.27	−0.09 0.13

Note: Coef.: Coefficient; CI: Confidence Interval; ULCI: Upper limit and LLCI: Lower limit.

References

1. Appel, G., Grewal, L., Hadi, R., Stephen, A.T.: The future of social media in marketing. J. Acad. Mark. Sci. **48**(1), 79–95 (2020)
2. Bagozzi, R.P., Yi, Y.: On the evaluation of structural equation models. J. Acad. Mark. Sci. **16**(1), 74–94 (1988)
3. Breitsohl, J., Roschk, H., Feyertag, C.: Consumer brand bullying behaviour in online communities of service firms. Presented at the (2018). https://doi.org/10.1007/978-3-658-22424-0_13
4. Breitsohl, J., Jimenez, N., Roschk, H.: Investigating consumers' motives for consumer brand-cyberbullying on social media. Inf. Soc. **38**(1), 1–12 (2022)

5. Cohen, J., Cohen, P., West, S. G., & Aiken, L. S.: Applied Multiple Regression/Correlation Analysis for the Behavioral Sciences. Routledge (2013)
6. Dineva, D., Breitsohl, J., Garrod, B.: Corporate conflict management on social media brand fan pages, J. Mark. Manage. 1–20 (2017)
7. Dineva, D., Breitsohl, J., Garrod, B., Megicks, P.: Consumer responses to Conflict-management strategies on Non-profit social media fan pages. J. Interact. Mark. **52**, 118–136 (2020)
8. Ewing, M.T., Wagstaff, P.E., Powell, I.H.: Brand rivalry and community conflict. J. Bus. Res. **66**(1), 4–12 (2013)
9. Hair, J., Hult, G., Ringle, C., Sarstedt, M., Thiele, K.: Mirror, mirror on the wall: a comparative evaluation of composite-based structural equation modeling methods. J. Acad. Mark. Sci. **45**(5), 616–632 (2017)
10. Hayes, A.F., Montoya, A.K., Rockwood, N.J.: The analysis of mechanisms and their contingencies: PROCESS versus structural equation modeling. Australas. Mark. J. (AMJ) **25**(1), 76–81 (2017)
11. Henseler, J.: Composite-based structural equation modeling: Analyzing latent and emergent variables. Guilford Publications, New York, UK (2020)
12. Henseler, J., Ringle, C.M., Sarstedt, M.: A new criterion for assessing discriminant validity in variance-based structural equation modeling. J. Acad. Mark. Sci. **43**(1), 115–135 (2014). https://doi.org/10.1007/s11747-014-0403-8
13. Lennox, R.D., Wolfe, R.N.: Revision of the self-monitoring scale. J. Pers. Soc. Psychol. **46**(6), 1349–1364 (1984)
14. Obermaier, M., Fawzi, N., Koch, T.: Bystanding or standing by? How the number of bystanders affects the intention to intervene in cyberbullying. New Media Soc. **18**(8), 1491–1507 (2016)
15. Podsakoff, P.M., Organ, D.W.: Self-reports in organizational research: problems and prospects. J. Manag. **12**(4), 531–544 (1986)
16. Relling, M., Schnittka, O., Sattler, H., Johnen, M.: Each can help or hurt: Negative and positive word of mouth in social network brand communities. Int. J. Res. Mark. **33**(1), 42–58 (2016)
17. Su, L.Y.F., Scheufele, D.A., Brossard, D., Xenos, M.A.: Political and personality predispositions and topical contexts matter: effects of uncivil comments on science news engagement intentions. New Media Soc. **23**(5), 894–919 (2021)
18. Wong-Lo, M., Bullock, L.: Digital metamorphosis: examination of the bystander culture in cyberbullying. Aggress. Violent. Beh. **19**(4), 418–422 (2014)

Late-Breaking Papers

Towards an Expectation-Oriented Model of Public Service Quality: A Preliminary Study of NYC 311

Julia Hsin-Ping Hsu[1], Jieshu Wang[2], and Myeong Lee[1]

[1] George Mason University,Fairfax, VA 22030, USA
{hhsu2,mlee89}@gmu.edu
[2] Arizona State University,Tempe, AZ 85281, USA
jwang490@asu.edu

Abstract. The 311 system has been deployed in many U.S. cities to manage non-emergency civic issues such as noise and illegal parking. To assess the performance of 311-mediated public service provision, researchers developed models based on execution time and the status of execution. However, research on user satisfaction suggests that the level of individuals' perception is asymmetric with respect to the quality of services, because negative experiences have a stronger impact on people's dissatisfaction than positive experiences do for satisfaction. Informed by the uneven nature of human satisfaction regarding positive and negative service quality, we propose an expectation-based model that measures the quality of public services by adapting the asymmetric function that reflects different perceptions of positive and negative experiences. Our preliminary analysis using the NYC 311 and Census data provides an initial assessment of the model's validity.

Keywords: 311 System · Expectation-oriented model · Expectancy disconfirmation · The quality of public service

1 Introduction

311 systems were initially deployed in the 1990s in many cities in North America as a dedicated telephone number that provides residents with access to non-emergency municipal services such as fixing potholes and picking fallen trees. Over the years, many U.S. cities have adopted the 311 systems to improve communication between residents and public agencies about non-emergency civic issues [29]. These systems have evolved into complex platforms that can be now accessed through multiple channels including mobile apps and websites. Residents can report a variety of civic issues with geographic locations through local 311 systems and keep track of whether, how, and when the issues are resolved. At the same time, 311 systems regularly collect and share large amounts of geo-tagged requests through open data portals. The richness of those data allows to conduct in-depth studies on urban dynamics.

F. Hopfgartner et al. (Eds.): SocInfo 2022, LNCS 13618, pp. 447–458, 2022.
https://doi.org/10.1007/978-3-031-19097-1_31

In major U.S. cities, the 311 systems have improved local governments' ability to monitor residents' needs, deliver public services efficiently, and in some cases manage disasters, enhancing accountability and improving resident-government relationship [29]. Many municipal governments rely on the reports filed in the 311 systems to identify and locate civic issues and deliver public services. In doing so, efforts of pinpointing urban issues are "crowdsourced" to local residents, facilitating public participation and service co-production [4,15,21].

Because the 311 data provides a comprehensive understanding of public service provision for different types of issues, many researchers have analyzed the data to study citizen engagement [36], citizen satisfaction [20], propensity to contact governments [19], equity and biases of using the 311 system [8,13–15], and disaster management [2,26]. Despite the studies, assessing the effectiveness of 311 systems in managing public services has been a challenging task for both governments and researchers as technological systems are part of a larger socio-technical system where social and technological systems dynamically co-shape each other's behavior and outcomes [3].

Researchers have applied different approaches to measure the effectiveness of public service provision. Some researchers focused on human perception by measuring the level of people's satisfaction with local governments and public services through surveys [9,27,28,37]. Others leveraged objective measures such as execution time (i.e., the time it takes to address the request) and the case status (i.e., whether the issue is resolved or not) (e.g., [7]). Although both approaches provide meaningful means to assess the effectiveness of public service provision, there are methodological gaps. The human-focused approach that measures residents' satisfaction with public services (e.g., survey) is costly and has a risk of sampling and perception biases. Meanwhile, measuring the effectiveness of services based on execution time and case status can achieve objectivity but cannot take residents' perceptions of service quality into account. Filling this methodological gap requires the consideration of both measurement objectivity and people's perception of service quality. Specifically, there is a need to develop a computational model that considers both the objective measurement from 311 data and the asymmetric nature of human perception on service quality [6].

To this end, we propose an expectation-oriented model of public service quality by adapting (1) the Expectancy-Disconfirmation Model (EDM), which has been used to understand citizen satisfaction with public services [38] and (2) Cheung and Lee's model of asymmetric user satisfaction [6]. The proposed computational model quantifies the quality of public services by taking into account the asymmetric nature of human perception on service quality within the objective measurement of execution time. This study offers a framework to quantify urban service quality through public online data. The proposed model can provide governments and policymakers with a tool to evaluate public service performance, with an enhanced accuracy of the measurement. Using this tool, governments can identify places with low service quality, locate under-served communities, and improve service quality accordingly in a more targeted fashion. Researchers can benefit from the computational model in assessing the quality of public services as well as urban inequality moderated by technical systems, which is a key topic in computational social science. Combining with other urban data such as socio-economic status and civic engagement data, the proposed model has potential to examine and improve the systematic inequality of urban environments.

2 Related Work

2.1 Civic Technology and Inequality

Previous research has found that civic technologies often surface or exacerbate inequality, such as the systematic under-representation of minority groups [13]. For example, López and Farzan reported a low level of participation from women and people of color on civic discourse forums [16]. At the community level, researchers have reported correlations between 311 reports and socio-economic characteristics, such as community wealth, education, employment status, and housing prices [34]. The use of civic technology is also shaped by individual-level characteristics such as the access to internet and mobile devices, trust in government, existing civic engagement, and territoriality [23,24]. Social interactions (e.g., words from friends and families [35]), previous interaction with the government [19], and successful experience of using the systems [30]) are found to affect the adoption of civic technologies.

Given these factors that range from individual to community levels that may shape technology-mediated inequality in local communities, the precision in measuring system performance is the key to understanding the dynamics of urban inequality. Because inequality and biases are often formed based on certain qualities of life (e.g., income level, access to opportunities, service quality), measuring the performance of 311 systems is the basis for studying technology-driven inequality and biases.

2.2 User Satisfaction Measurements

The performance of 311 systems manifests as public service quality, which is closely related to user satisfaction. User satisfaction has been modeled in different ways. Research in Network Communication assessed user satisfaction with the quality of service (QoS) through a logistic function, where user's sensitivity to the QoS degradation and acceptable region of operation are considered [17,25]. In the area of Public Administration, citizen satisfaction is measured in different ways. Some researchers focused on human perspectives by measuring the level of people's satisfaction with public services through surveys [9,27,28,37]. Others leveraged objective measures such as execution time and the case status. For example, a recent study introduced a Spatial-Temporal FTiS model to examine the level of public service quality that used execution time and the completeness of the issue as proxies of satisfaction [20]. Although both approaches provide meaningful means to assess the effectiveness of public service provision, methodological gaps exist due to the asymmetric nature of human perception of service quality.

2.3   Expectancy-Disconfirmation Model (EDM) of User Satisfaction

Among the approaches to understanding user satisfaction, the EDM model, a conceptual framework originally used for studying customer satisfaction in Marketing research [22], has been adapted and used in public service-related research [5,12,32,33]. The EDM model explains that residents tend to compare the perceived performance of public service against their prior expectations. Specifically, if the performance is better than expected (i.e., positive disconfirmation), they are satisfied, whereas if the performance is worse than expected (i.e., negative disconfirmation), the opposite [5,38].

While studies that use the EDM model assume a symmetrical relationship between user satisfaction and perceived service quality (e.g., [18]), Cheung and Lee suggest that this relationship is more complex and asymmetrical [6]. They conducted an online survey to collect data of user satisfaction with an e-portal and identified that the relationship between these two factors are asymmetrical by fitting the level of user satisfaction with a natural logarithm function. The results suggested that, in many cases, negative perceived performance had a stronger impact on user satisfaction than positive perceived performance did, which is consistent with some previous work [10,11,31].

While the studies focusing on perceived service quality using the EDM model help understand residents' satisfaction with public services, most of these studies relied on survey data and did not consider the asymmetrical nature of expectancy disconfirmation. Another stream of research indicated the asymmetrical nature of user satisfaction, but is still limited to survey-based measurements in online contexts. Filling this gap, we develop an expectation-oriented model that measures the quality of public service through an asymmetric function that reflects different human perceptions of positive and negative experiences.

3   Proposed Model and Analysis Method

We collect New York City's 311 (NYC311) data for 2019 to provide an initial assessment of the proposed model. Because residents' satisfaction would be affected by their initial expectations of public services imposed by local governments, *Service Level Agreement (SLA)* is used as the baseline expectations for each type of service in NYC311 [1]. SLA is an expected service execution time included in the confirmation message when a resident submits a 311 request. The quality of public service is modeled as:

$$service\_quality(x) = \begin{cases} (1 + e^{\alpha}) \frac{1}{1 + e^{-\alpha x}} & \text{if } x \geq 0 \\ (1 + e^{\alpha}) \frac{1}{1 + e^{-\beta x}} & \text{if } x < 0 \end{cases} \tag{1}$$

$$x = \frac{T_{SLA} - t_e}{T_{SLA}} \tag{2}$$

where t_e is the execution time; x is the disconfirmation, calculated by normalizing the execution time using the pre-defined number of hours specified in the SLA; α

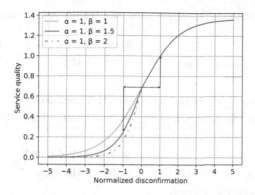

Fig. 1. Models of service quality with different settings of Parameters

and β reflect people's different perception of positive and negative service quality. Specifically, α is the growing steepness of positive effect and β is the decreasing steepness of negative effect ($\alpha \leq \beta$). α and β are parameters that could be adjusted in different contexts. Finally, the score is normalized by $(1 + e^{\alpha})$ so that the service quality score ranges from 0 to 1. Figure 1 shows different models depending on varying parameters. Our analysis uses $\alpha = 1$ and $\beta = 1.5$, so that negative disconfirmation has a stronger impact on the service quality.

After calculating the service quality score for each individual report in NYC 311, we compute the median service quality score for each census tract (i.e., the third-smallest administrative unit in U.S. cities) to quantify the tract-level service quality. To provide an initial assessment of our model's validity, we examine the relationship between the tract-level service quality (DV) and socioeconomic variables (i.e., median household income and educational attainment) as IVs. A Poisson regression model is used as the analytical model. This model and the arrangement of IVs and control variables (e.g., types of report) are consistent with that of Clark et al.'s study [8], so as to ensure the robust testing of validity.

4 Preliminary Results

4.1 Service Quality and Socioeconomic Status

We examine our model with the five most common report types (i.e., noise - residential, heat and hot water, illegal parking, blocked driveway and large item collection) in NYC 311. Table 1 shows the summary statistics of variables and the regression results, where educational attainment is positively related to the service quality, and the median household income is negatively related to it. This result is consistent with some of the previous findings in [7].

Table 1. Descriptive statics of variables and results of the poisson regression

Variables	Mean	SD	Coeff	S.E	2.5%	97.5%
DV: Median service quality score	0.766	0.185				
IVs						
% Population with a BA degree or higher	34.341	19.892	0.001***	0.000	0.001	0.002
Median household income (in USD 1,000s)	71.128	34.699	-0.001***	0.000	-0.001	-0.000
CVs						
% Pop. non-white	55.879	29.295	0.000**	0.000	0.000	0.000
Number of requests in tract in 1000s	0.082	0.107	0.035***	0.010	0.016	0.053
Types of report (categorical variables)			***			

***$p < 0.001$ **$p < 0.01$ *$p < 0.05$

4.2   Revealing Inequality in Public Service Delivery

Our model can help reveal inequality of public service delivery for a specific category. Figure 2 in Appendix A shows two examples of comparing the median execution time (traditional approach) and median service quality score (our model) in each census tract of NYC regarding two 311 request types—blocked driveway (Fig. 2a and 2b) and large item collection (Fig. 2c and 2d). The expected execution time specified in the SLA for blocked driveway is 8 h while that for large item collection being 48 h. The middle points of the color coding (yellow) in each of the four panels in Fig. 2 represent the cases when the median execution time in a tract is equal to the expected execution time. As shown in Fig. 2, the geographic disparity of service quality scores (right panels) is largely consistent with that of execution time (left panels). Nevertheless, the service quality score maps (right) make the tracts with low service quality more salient. For instance, the color of census tracts on Staten Island at the southwest corner of NYC in Fig. 2d is darker in red than that in Fig. 2c. This salient map helps identify areas with low service quality that could be otherwise considered as being less serious if execution time itself were used solely as a proxy for service quality.

4.3   Assessing General Public Service Quality Across Departments

In NYC, different types of 311 reports are assigned to corresponding departments within the government to resolve. Because of the different natures of report types, expected execution times are different across the departments. For instance, the expected execution time in SLA for "large item collection" is 2 d, while "noise complaints" are expected to be addressed within 8 h. Therefore, it is challenging to compare overall service quality across the geographical regions. Our model offers the possibility of computing robust aggregate scores across reporting types, which is more accurate than using execution times themselves.

Figure 3 in Appendix B compares the execution time-based approach (Panel a) and the service quality score-based approach (Panel b) in assessing general service quality. The aggregated execution time of set A of reporting types in census tract i $(T_{A,i})$ is computed as the weighted sum of median execution times across the available types (five types in our analysis):

$$T_{A,i} = \sum_{a \in A} \left(\frac{n_{a,i}}{\sum_{b \in A} n_{b,i}} \cdot \frac{t_{u,i} - \min_{\forall c \in C} t_{a,c}}{\max_{\forall c \in C} t_{a,c} - \min_{\forall c \in C} t_{a,c}} \right) \tag{3}$$

where $n_{a,i}$ denotes the number of 311 reports in tract i regarding issue a $(a \in A)$, $t_{a,i}$ denoting the median execution time of type a issues in tract i, and C denoting the set of all census tracts $(i \in C)$. Similarly, the aggregated public service quality score of reporting type set A in census tract i $(S_{A,i})$ is computed as:

$$S_{A,i} = \sum_{a \in A} \left(\frac{n_{a,i}}{\sum_{b \in A} n_{b,i}} \cdot s_{a,i} \right) \tag{4}$$

where $s_{a,i}$ is the median quality score of issue type a in tract i.

Then, the two panels in Fig. 3 show similar patterns—most neighborhoods in Brooklyn have a better-than-average service quality; communities in eastern Queens have their public service delivered relatively slowly; Manhattan enjoys fairly good public services; and Staten Island is quite average but situation varies across areas like Port Ivory and South Shore.

However, the two panels are quite different in details. A large proportion of Bronx has longer execution times than average according to Fig. 3a. Conversely, the same areas in Fig. 3b are presented with quite good quality scores. Qualitative inspection into this inconsistency suggests that our proposed model can be considered a more accurate proxy in describing service quality. For instance, the Parkchester community in Bronx shows low execution time (0.226) yet a fair level in aggregated quality score (0.748). Nevertheless, each type of issues in Parkchester has a median execution time shorter than expectation—60 h for heat and hot water issues $(T_{SLA} = 72)$, 6.5 h and 4.5 h for illegal parking and noise, respectively $(T_{SLA} = 8)$. This example suggests that the general public service in Parkchester is better than expectation, implying that service quality score is more accurate than execution time in assessing aggregated public service quality.

Another example is Yorkville, a neighborhood in the Upper East Manhattan, where three of the four 311 types were resolved faster than expectation. However, one request for large item collection took 20 d to solve. This single outlier led to an aggregated execution time higher than 98.2% of all census tracts. Meanwhile, aggregated service quality scores (0.76) computed using our proposed model suggests accurately that issues are generally resolved on time. Similar discrepancy can be observed in the areas highlighted with purple ellipse in the two panels.

This suggests that using aggregated execution times after normalization to understand general service quality can be misleading, because the distribution of execution time varies significantly across the types. Our model can eliminates the impact of outliers and ensure the objective neutral scores based on SLA.

5   Discussion and Future Work

It is worth noting that in our proposed model, the sensitivity of the quality score to execution time changes depending on two factors related to human perception. First, quality score is more sensitive when the specified time in SLA is smaller. In other words, when SLA time is shorter, quality score varies more in a unit execution time than the case with a longer SLA. We note that this characteristic of the model is consistent with human perception. For example, a noise complaint is expected to be resolved within 8 h while a large item collection is expected to be addressed within 3 d. Because of the different levels of urgency perceived by the residents regarding the two issues, the meaning of "one hour" would be very different. Being late by one hour for a noise complaints would affect resident's satisfaction level to a greater extent than being late by one hour for a large item collection. Secondly, quality score is more sensitive when execution time does not deviate much from SLA and is substantially less sensitive in extreme cases. This also makes sense from a human perception perspective. For example, a resident should perceive similar service quality if an issue is solved in 5 min or 10 min (with the service quality score ≈ 1), because both cases would be equally very fast. Likewise, if an issue takes an extremely long time to be resolved, residents' dissatisfaction level would be similar regardless of whether it took 5 or 6 months (≈ 0).

In addition, our preliminary results show that socioeconomic status is associated with public service quality. While some of these patterns are consistent with previous work [7], further investigation and sensitivity tests are necessary to understand the general dynamics of how socioeconomic factors are related to the level of public service quality. Moreover, as Van Ryzin pointed out, measuring disconfirmation by subtracting the execution time from expectation could overestimate the effect of expectation [33], which is not completely addressed in our model. More investigations are needed to adapt the model in different contexts. Despite the limitations in the empirical implications of the results, this study (1) offers a novel layer of information regarding urban conditions and resident perception of public service provision in the city and (2) provides an initial assessment of the proposed model's external validity. Through further sensitivity tests and the validation of the model based on surveys and other triangulation methods, we believe that this approach will further benefit local governments, information scientists, and public administration researchers who study user satisfaction and service quality.

Acknowledgment. This work is supported by the National Science Foundation under Grant No. (1816763 and 2217706). We thank NSF, reviewers, and the committee.

A   Example Comparisons Between Execution Time and Quality score

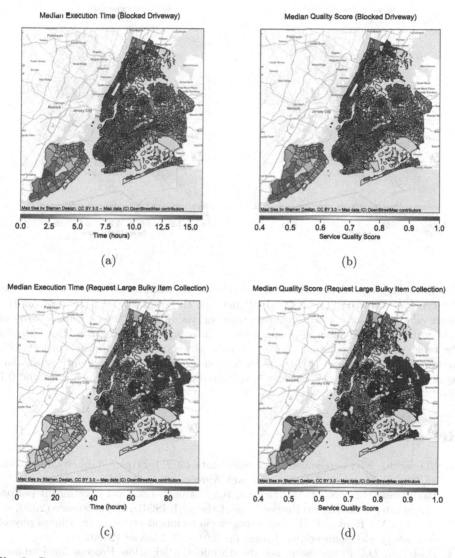

Fig. 2. Comparison between execution time and service quality score of two types of 311 reports in NYC on census tract level. Panel (a) and (b) are about report type "blocked driveway," while Panel (c) and (d) are about "large item collection" type. The middle points of the color coding (yellow) represent the neutral values in each case. Solving an issue exactly on time results in a quality score around 0.7 given the preset parameters $\alpha = 1$ and $\beta = 1.5$. Therefore, the neutral values in Panel (b) and (d) are set to 0.7. Tracts with longer median execution time or lower quality score are colored in red, while tracts with shorter execution time or higher quality score are colored in green. (Color figure online)

B   Comparison Between Aggregated Execution Time and Aggregated Quality Score

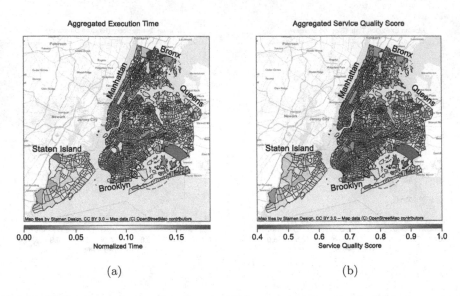

(a)   (b)

Fig. 3. (a) Aggregated execution time and (b) aggregated service quality scores across five types of 311 reports in NYC. In Panel (a), the color legend is centered at the mean value of the aggregated execution times across all census tracts, which is around 0.09 in this case, and about 98% census tracts have aggregated execution times within the range of the color legend. Any tract with longer execution time is colored with the darkest red. In Panel (b), the color legend is centered at the quality score that represents the scenario where service is delivered exactly on time, which is around 0.7 given the preset parameters $\alpha = 1$ and $\beta = 1.5$. (Color figure online)

References

1. 311 service level agreements: Nyc open data (2021). https://data.cityofnewyork.us/City-Government/311-Service-Level-Agreements/cs9t-e3x8
2. Baghersad, M., Zobel, C.W., Behara, R.: Evaluation of local government performance after disasters. In: Proceedings of the 17th ISCRAM Conference (2020)
3. Bauer, J.M., Herder, P.M.: Designing socio-technical systems. In: Philosophy of technology and engineering sciences, pp. 601–630. Elsevier (2009)
4. Brabham, D.C.: Crowdsourcing the Public Participation Process for Planning Projects. Planning Theory **8**(3), 242–262 (Aug 2009). https://doi.org/10.1177/1473095209104824, number: 3 Publisher: SAGE Publications
5. Chatterjee, R., Suy, R.: An overview of citizen satisfaction with public service: based on the model of expectancy disconfirmation. Open J. Soc. Sci. **7**(4), 243–258 (2019)
6. Cheung, C.M., Lee, M.K.: User satisfaction with an internet-based portal: an asymmetric and nonlinear approach. J. Am. Soc. Inform. Sci. Technol. **60**(1), 111–122 (2009)

7. Clark, B.Y., Brudney, J.L.: Citizen representation in city government-driven crowdsourcing. Comput. Supported Coop. Work (CSCW) **28**(5), 883–910 (2019). https://doi.org/10.1007/s10606-018-9308-2

8. Clark, B.Y., Brudney, J.L., Jang, S.G., Davy, B.: Do advanced information technologies produce equitable government responses in coproduction: an examination of 311 systems in 15 us cities. Am. Rev. Pub. Adm. **50**(3), 315–327 (2020)

9. Collins, B.K., Kim, H.J., Tao, J.: Managing for citizen satisfaction: is good not enough? J. Public Nonprofit Aff. **5**(1), 21–38 (2019)

10. Fullerton, G., Taylor, S.: Mediating, interactive, and non-linear effects in service quality and satisfaction with services research. Canadian J. Adm. Sci./Revue Canadienne des Sci. de l'administration **19**(2), 124–136 (2002)

11. Hamilton, D.L., Zanna, M.P.: Differential weighting of favorable and unfavorable attributes in impressions of personality (1972)

12. James, O.: Evaluating the expectations disconfirmation and expectations anchoring approaches to citizen satisfaction with local public services. J. Pub. Adm. Res. Theo. **19**(1), 107–123 (2009)

13. Kontokosta, C., Hong, B., Korsberg, K.: Equity in 311 reporting: Understanding socio-spatial differentials in the propensity to complain. arXiv preprint arXiv:1710.02452 (2017)

14. Kontokosta, C.E., Hong, B.: Bias in smart city governance: How socio-spatial disparities in 311 complaint behavior impact the fairness of data-driven decisions. Sustain. Cities Soc. **64**, 102503 (2021)

15. Lee, M., Wang, J., Janzen, S., Winter, S., Harlow, J.: Crowdsourcing Behavior in Reporting Civic Issues: The Case of Boston's 311 Systems. In: Academy of Management Annual Meeting Proceedings (AOM) (2021)

16. López, C., Farzan, R.: Designing for digital inclusion: a post-hoc evaluation of a civic technology. In: Ciampaglia, G.L., Mashhadi, A., Yasseri, T. (eds.) SocInfo 2017. LNCS, vol. 10539, pp. 572–588. Springer, Cham (2017). https://doi.org/10.1007/978-3-319-67217-5_34

17. Mazza, D., Tarchi, D., Corazza, G.E.: A user-satisfaction based offloading technique for smart city applications. In: 2014 IEEE Global Communications Conference. pp. 2783–2788. IEEE (2014)

18. McKinney, V., Yoon, K., Zahedi, F.: The measurement of web-customer satisfaction: an expectation and disconfirmation approach. Inform. Syst. Res. **13**(3), 296–315 (2002)

19. Minkoff, S.L.: Nyc 311: A tract-level analysis of citizen-government contacting in New York city. Urban Affairs Rev. **52**(2), 211–246 (2016)

20. Mohammadi, R., Taleai, M., Alizadeh, S., Abbasi, O.R.: STFTiS: Introducing a spatio-temporal FTiS model to investigate the level of citizens' satisfaction of 311 non-emergency services. Trans. GIS **26**(2), 980–1016 (2022)

21. Nam, T., Sayogo, D.S.: Government 2.0 collects the wisdom of crowds. In: Datta, A., Shulman, S., Zheng, B., Lin, S.-D., Sun, A., Lim, E.-P. (eds.) SocInfo 2011. LNCS, vol. 6984, pp. 51–58. Springer, Heidelberg (2011). https://doi.org/10.1007/978-3-642-24704-0_10

22. Oliver, R.L.: A cognitive model of the antecedents and consequences of satisfaction decisions. J. Market. Res. **17**(4), 460–469 (1980)

23. O'Brien, D.T., Offenhuber, D., Baldwin-Philippi, J., Sands, M., Gordon, E.: Uncharted Territoriality in Coproduction. The Motivations for 311 Reporting. J. Pub. Adm. Res. Theor. **27**(2), 320–335 (2017). https://doi.org/10.1093/jopart/muw046

24. Pak, B., Chua, A., Moere, A.V.: FixMyStreet Brussels: socio-demographic inequality in crowdsourced civic participation. J. Urban Technol. **24**(2), 65–87 (2017). https://doi.org/10.1080/10630732.2016.1270047

25. Pal, S., Das, S.K., Chatterjee, M.: User-satisfaction based differentiated services for wireless data networks. In: IEEE International Conference on Communications, 2005. ICC 2005. 2005. vol. 2, pp. 1174–1178. IEEE (2005)

26. Pamukcu, D., Zobel, C.: Characterizing 311 system reactions to a global health emergency. In: Proceedings of the 54th Hawaii International Conference on System Sciences, p. 2216 (2021)

27. Reddick, C.G.: The adoption of centralized customer service systems: a survey of local governments. Govern. Inform. Quart. **26**(1), 219–226 (2009)

28. Ryzin, G.G.V.: The measurement of overall citizen satisfaction. Pub. Perform. Manage. Rev. **27**(3), 9–28 (2004)

29. Schellong, A., Langenberg, T.: Managing citizen relationships in disasters: Hurricane wilma, 311 and miami-dade county. In: 2007 40th Annual Hawaii International Conference on System Sciences (HICSS'07), pp. 96–96. IEEE (2007)

30. Sjoberg, F.M., Mellon, A.J., Peixoto, T.C.: The effect of government responsiveness on future political participation. Tech. Rep. 99519, The World Bank (2015). https://documents.worldbank.org/curated/en/637241467995637358/The-effect-of-government-responsiveness-on-future-political-participation

31. Taylor, S.E.: Asymmetrical effects of positive and negative events: the mobilization-minimization hypothesis. Psychol. Bull. **110**(1), 67 (1991)

32. Van Ryzin, G.G.: Expectations, performance, and citizen satisfaction with urban services. J. Policy Anal. Manage. **23**(3), 433–448 (2004)

33. Van Ryzin, G.G.: Testing the expectancy disconfirmation model of citizen satisfaction with local government. J. Pub. Adm. Res. Theor. **16**(4), 599–611 (2006)

34. Wang, L., Qian, C., Kats, P., Kontokosta, C., Sobolevsky, S.: Structure of 311 service requests as a signature of urban location. PLoS ONE **12**(10) (2017). https://doi.org/10.1371/journal.pone.0186314

35. Wu, W.N.: Citizen relationship management system users' contact channel choices: digital approach or call approach? Information (Switzerland). Information **8**(1), 8 (2017). https://doi.org/10.3390/info8010008

36. Wu, W.N.: Features of smart city services in the local government context: a case study of San Francisco 311 system. In: International Conference on Human-Computer Interaction, pp. 216–227. Springer (2020)

37. Wu, W.N., Jung, K.: A missing link between citizen participation, satisfaction, and public performance: evidences from the city and county of San Francisco. Int. J. Pub. Sector Perform. Manage. **2**(4), 392–410 (2016)

38. Zhang, J., Chen, W., Petrovsky, N., Walker, R.M.: The expectancy-disconfirmation model and citizen satisfaction with public services: a meta-analysis and an agenda for best practice. Pub. Adm. Rev. **82**(1), 147–159 (2022)

A Heterophily-Based Polarization Measure for Multi-community Networks

Sreeja Nair[1]([⊠])(ID) and Adriana Iamnitchi[2](ID)

[1] University of South Florida, Tampa, USA
sreejas@usf.edu
[2] Maastricht University, Maastricht, Netherlands
a.iamnitchi@maastrichtuniversity.nl

Abstract. This work proposes a heterophily-based metric for quantifying polarization in social networks where multiple ideological, antagonistic communities coexist. This metric captures node-level polarization and is built on user's affinity towards other communities rather than their own. Node-level values can then be aggregated at the community, network, or sub-network level, providing a more detailed map of polarization. We tested our metric on the Polblogs network, White Helmets Twitter interaction network with two communities and the VoterFraud2020 domain network with five communities. We also tested our metric on dK-random graphs to verify that it results in low polarization scores, as expected. Finally, we compared our metric with two widely used polarization measures: Guerra's polarization index and RWC.

Keywords: Polarization · Communities · Heterophily

1 Introduction

Different polarization metrics have been proposed in the literature from several vantage points, including network topology [13,14,17], content semantics and sentiment [5,7]. Current network-based polarization measures [13,14,17] are tailored based on the assumption that a polarized network consists of two opposing communities. According to Esteban et al. [11], individuals can be grouped into multiple, antagonistic communities in a polarized society. Most efforts on measuring polarization assume that the polarized networks consist of exactly two antagonistic groups, and thus need to ignore the neutral nodes, or add them to one of the extreme groups. Our metrics address this limitation by acknowledging the existence of multiple communities.

This paper proposes a heterophily-based polarization metric called "cross-community affinity" that can be applied to networks with two or more communities with conflicting positions, goals, and viewpoints. We consider these communities are placed equi-distantly in a one-dimensional space. This assumption is supported by two facts: First, it allows us to compare with other metrics in the literature. Second, it reflects the datasets we use for our empirical evaluation.

© The Author(s), under exclusive license to Springer Nature Switzerland AG 2022
F. Hopfgartner et al. (Eds.): SocInfo 2022, LNCS 13618, pp. 459–471, 2022.
https://doi.org/10.1007/978-3-031-19097-1_32

The cross-community affinity of a node represents the node's affinity to communities with a different ideology than its own. Our proposed metric measures the node-level value that can be aggregated to any higher level, such as the community level, the network level, or any sub-network level. With this approach, we can understand which nodes or communities contribute most to polarization, enabling a more detailed picture and the possibility of directing interventions to particular nodes.

The rest of the paper is structured as follows. Section 2 presents the relevant works in this area. Section 3 explains the metric we propose. Section 4 describes the datasets used in this study and reports the results of experiments performed. Section 5 summarizes the results and discusses the future work.

2   Polarization Metrics in the Literature

Measuring polarization using structural characteristics inferred from network representations of social or political systems is a common topic in the literature, along with two other approaches: survey-based approaches [9], which measure distributional properties of public opinion through surveys; and content-based approaches [4,8,21], which use NLP tools to identify opposing groups on the network.

Conover et al. [6] suggest that polarization has a significant impact on the structures of social networks because it results in the formation of two groups that are well connected within themselves but have few ties to one another. Guerra et al. [14] present a polarization metric that centers on investigating nodes that belong to the community boundary, which captures the concepts of antagonism and polarization. Another polarization metric, the Polarization index [17], measures how far apart two groups are in terms of ideology, assuming their populations are equal. Garimella et al. [13] established the Random Walk Controversy (RWC) metric, which uses the random walk to see how likely information is to stay inside or reach out to other groups. Salloum et al. [20] examine the polarization measures mentioned above via simulations and demonstrate that all of them produce high polarization scores even for random networks with density and degree distributions close to typical real-world networks.

However, these metrics are developed based on the assumption that the polarized network consists of exactly two communities. In this paper, we propose a heterophily-based polarization metric called cross-community affinity, which measures the affinity of a node to other clusters rather than its own.

3   Cross-community Affinity: A Heterophily-Based Polarization Metric

We propose a new polarization metric called cross-community affinity to serve two specific objectives. First, it should adapt to a variable number of ideological groups connected by different antagonizing forces. Second, we want this metric to be applicable to different granularity, from node to full network and other network-based groupings in between.

As in previous work [13,14], the basis of this polarization metric is a node's connectivity with groups other than its own. In order to capture that, we introduce a heterophily-based metric consistent with its definition [15] that captures how a node is connected to different groups via both direct and indirect links. We assume the polarization of a network is the inverse of the average cross-community affinity, that is:

$$Polarization = -\ Avg.\ cross\text{-}community\ affinity$$

In order to define the metric, we use the following intuition. First, a network can have multiple communities. We assume a constant between 0 and 1 represents an ideological distance between different groups. Intuitively, a connection with an ideologically opposite node should weigh differently than a connection with an ideologically similar node. In a political system, one could consider the difference between a far right—far left connection vs. a leaning right and center political positioning connection. To account for the ideological difference between communities, we define communities as being in a one-dimensional space and equally spaced apart. The datasets(described in Sect. 4.1) we looked at implicitly position themselves on the one-dimensional space. Specifically, our use of the VoterFraud2020 dataset labeled using Media Bias Fact Check considers political orientation in a uni-dimensional space. We are providing a weight factor to represent the ideological distance. For simplicity, we consider that the distance between consecutive communities is constant and equal to $\frac{1}{|C|-1}$, where C is the number of communities (as shown in Appendix A.4). This assumption can, of course, be relaxed in a scenario in which, for example, the ideological distance between extreme left and leaning left in smaller than between leaning left and center.

Second, we assume that both direct and indirect connections can have an impact on a node's cross-community affinity. However, as well accepted in the literature [12], indirect connections have a much smaller impact on one's beliefs than direct connections. It has been empirically observed by Friedkin [12] that people's awareness of others' actions is restricted to people who were either in direct contact or had at least one contact in common. Moreover, the impact of such connections is typically a function of the overall number of connections a node has: the more neighbors, the less the impact of any one neighbor may be. To implement this, we assume that the ideological difference between nodes from the same community is -1. This value was chosen such that a node's affinity for its community reduces its cross-community affinity.

We thus define cross-community affinity(CCA) of a node i as the sum between the effects of its direct neighbors and indirect neighbors on its ideological openness:

$$CCA(i) = DNE(i) + \alpha \times INE(i) \tag{1}$$

where DNE(i) is the direct neighbor effect on node i and INE(i) the indirect neighbor effect on node i. α is the impact factor of the indirect neighbor effect. For simplicity we consider $\alpha = 1/h$, where h is the number of social hops between node i and the given set of nodes (in this case h = 2).

We consider the direct neighbor effect on node i as the sum of the relative impact of i's direct neighbors as follows:

$$DNE(i) = \sum_{c \in C} w_{(s(i),c)} \times \frac{k_c(i)}{k(i)} \qquad (2)$$

where C is the set of communities in the network, $s(i)$ is the community to which node i belongs, $w_{(s(i),c)}$ is the ideology based distance between i's community and community c. $k_c(i)$ denotes the number of neighbors of i in the community c and $k(i)$ denotes the total number of neighbors of i. Similarly, we consider the indirect neighbor effect on i as the average of the relative effects of its 2-hop neighbors over all different communities.

$$INE(i) = \frac{1}{|C_{N(i)}|} \sum_{c \in C_N(i)} ANE_c(i) \qquad (3)$$

where $C_{N(i)}$ is the set of communities in the i's neighborhood and $|C_{N(i)}|$ is the number of communities in the i's neighborhood. ANE_c represents the average neighbor effect of i's immediate neighbors by examining neighbors' neighborhood. We calculate the individual neighbor effect of each neighbor of node i to determine how their neighbors are distributed throughout the communities. To determine the impact of neighbor j on node i we calculate neighbor effect(NE) j on i as follows:

$$NE(j,i) = \sum_{g \in C} w_{(s(i),g)} \times \frac{k_g(j)}{k(j) - 1} \qquad (4)$$

where g is the community to which node j's neighbors belong, $w_{(s(i),g)}$ is the ideology distance between i's community and community g, $k_g(j)$ represents the number of j's neighbors in community g and $k(j)$ is the total number of j's neighbors, from which we exclude i.

$CCA(i)$ has a value ranging from -1.5 to 1.5. The $CCA(i)$ is minimum ($CCA(i) = -1.5$) if all nodes in the immediate and two-hop neighborhood belong to the same community as node i. If all neighbors up to two hops away are in the node's extreme opposite community, the cross-community affinity is maximum ($CCA(i) = 1.5$). Cross-community affinity can thus be aggregated at different granularities, from node-specific to any grouping of nodes in the networks, whether connected or not by, for example, averaging the node-specific affinity. A node-specific cross-community affinity can tell whether the node contributes to the network polarization. The network-level polarization P can thus be obtained as the negative average cross-community affinity:

$$P = -\frac{1}{|N|} \sum_{i \in N} CCA(i) \qquad (5)$$

where N is the set of nodes in the network. Appendix A.3 shows the different scenarios of a network and their respective CCA.

4 Empirical Evaluation

We evaluate our proposed metric on networks with different numbers of ideological groups. We use three datasets: Polblogs [3] and White Helmet Twitter interaction network [19] which each have two antagonistic communities, and the VoterFraud2020 domain network [18], with five communities.

4.1 Datasets

The Polblogs network [3] is a publicly available network of hyperlinks between political blogs about politics leading up to the 2004 United States presidential election. Each node in this network is labelled as either conservative (right) or liberal (left). Edges are the interaction between blogs such as citation, blogroll links etc. We consider the network as an undirected labelled network.

White Helmets Twitter dataset is the interaction network [19] based the tweets on White Helmets for a period from April 2018 to April 2019. Each node in this network is labelled as either pro-White Helmets or anti-White Helmets.

The VoterFraud2020 domain network [18] is derived from the publicly available VoterFraud2020 dataset [2], a Twitter dataset related to voter fraud claims about the US 2020 Presidential election. In this network, nodes are the web domains of URLs posted in tweets, and links connect domains that were tweeted by the same user. This network of websites is structurally divided into communities. Each node is labeled based on its media bias and credibility using publicly available source Media Bias Fact Check (MBFC) [1]. The labels are: right, right-center, center, left-center, and left. However, after this labeling strategy, 75.6% of the nodes remained unknown because they are not included in the MBFC database. To assign labels to the 'unknown' nodes, we relabelled them as the dominant label in the node's direct neighborhood. That is, we started with unlabeled nodes with the largest proportion of labeled nodes in their one-hop neighborhood and labeled them as the majority. We recursively applied this methodology until all nodes were labeled. Edge distribution of this network is depicted in Appendix A.1 Table 1 shows the network properties of Polblogs, White Helmets twitter network and VoterFraud2020 domain network. Appendix A.2 depicts the visual representation of these datasets.

Table 1. Network properties of Polblogs, White Helmets twitter network and the VoterFraud2020 domain network.

	Nodes	Edges	Average degree	Assortativity	Clustering Coefficient
Polblogs	1224	16715	27.3	−0.22	0.32
White Helmets	9024	11641	2.6	−0.47	0.14
VoterFraud2020	2461	48189	39.2	−0.33	0.68

4.2   Cross-community Affinity in the Polblogs Network

Polblogs networks has two communities: conservative (right) and liberal (left). The edges connecting two communities are only 9%. 50.9% nodes (623 nodes) have connections to the opposite community. First, the ideology-based distances between these two communities are defined. As discussed in the preceding section, the ideology-based distance between the same communities is -1. In contrast, the connection to the most polar community gets the maximum weight of 1. In the Polblogs network, the weights between conservative-conservative and liberal-liberal are -1 and the weight between conservative and liberal is 1.

We compute the average cross-community affinity value across each community and the entire network to determine cross-community affinity at the community and network levels. Using Eq. 5, the polarization score of conservative is 1.13, liberal is 1.0, and the network is 1.07. These values indicate that the communities and the whole network are polarized. One of the key benefits of having a metric that captures polarization at the node level is that, (Appendix A.2 Fig. 3a) we can determine which nodes contribute to the polarization.

Next, we evaluate how the metric works on a random graph. Our intuition is that randomizing the network should reduce polarization [20]. We generates a set of random networks using dK series [16]. dK-series generate random graphs that preserve desired prescribed properties of the original. $0K$ $(d = 0)$ creates the Erdös-Rényi network with the same average node degree as the original graph. $1K$ $(d = 1)$ creates the configuration model, fixing the degree sequence of the original graph. As compared to the polarization score of 1.07, the average polarization value for generated $0K$ is 0.58 and $1K$ is 0.02. These networks have lower polarization score than the original Polblogs network, which means that they are less polarized. This observation gives us confidence that measuring polarization using the methodology we proposed captures random behavior.

4.3   Cross-community Affinity in the White Helmets Twitter Interaction Network

We conducted a similar experiment on the White Helmets Twitter network. Around 73% of users are anti-White Helmets, and 27% are pro-White Helmets. The size of the communities is significantly different from the Polblogs, where it has an almost similar size for communities (52% and 48%). The connection between anti-White Helmets and pro-White Helmets users is 0.3%. Only 0.2% of users have interaction with the opposite community. As in the Polblogs experiment, we used -1 for the ideology-based distance between the same communities and 1 for the opposing communities. The polarization score for the network and each community is 1.49. The score indicates that the network is highly polarized.

Next, we created a set of 0K and 1K graphs for the White Helmets Twitter dataset. The average polarization score for 0K graphs is 0.94 and for 1K graphs is 0.35. Consistent with the Polblogs results, the random graphs generated for White Helmets also yield lower polarization score indicating they are less polarized.

4.4   Cross-community Affinity in the VoterFraud2020 Domain Network

Next the experiment is conducted on the VoterFraud2020 domain network with five communities. Given that there are five communities in the network, the distance between two adjacent communities is defined as $1/(|C| - 1)$, or $1/4$ (Appendix A.4). The polarization scores computed using Eq. 5 for each community are: right: 0.88; right-center: -0.34; center: -0.19; left-center: 0.62; left: 0.05; and for the entire network: 0.61. The right-center and center communities are less polarized compared to other communities. That is because the right-center has a comparatively higher number of edges to the right community. Similarly, the center community contains more links to left-center and right. Even if the network-level polarization score shows that the network is polarized, the community-level polarization score reveals that two communities do not contribute to the polarization state of the network. Using only a network-level polarization score, it is impossible to determine how different communities contribute to polarization, thus obscuring information that might be useful in limiting damage or directing intervention.

We also created random networks via dK-distributions. A set of random graphs with same number of nodes and same average degree (0K) are generated. The average polarization score for $0K$ graphs is -0.06 and $1K$ graphs is 0.02 compared to the original network's score is 0.61. The polarization value dropped for the random networks even when the network's degree sequence was preserved. More experiments on VoterFraud2020 domain network are shown in Appendix A.5

4.5   Comparision with Exisiting Polarization Metrics

In this section, we compare our cross-community affinity metric with two widely used polarization metrics: Guerra's polarization index (PI) [14] and random walk controversy score (RWC) [13]. The RWC score has been described as state-of-the-art [10,22]. The range of polarization values for PI is -0.5 to 0.5, and RWC is -1 to 1. Our metric P ranges from -1.5 to 1.5. The higher the value, the higher the polarization. Table 2 shows the polarization value calculated using P, PI, and RWC. We can see that polarization values reduce consistently for Polblogs random networks. The PI value for White Helmets-0K increased compared to

Table 2. Comparison of polarization value calculated by P, PI, and RWC

	Polblogs			WhiteHelmets			VoterFraud2020		
	Original	0K	1K	Original	0K	1K	Original	0K	1K
P	1.07	0.58	−0.00	1.49	0.94	0.34	0.61	−0.06	0.02
PI	0.18	−0.02	−0.32	0.22	0.34	0.02	N/A	N/A	N/A
RWC	0.42	0.22	−0.05	0.92	0.45	−0.04	N/A	N/A	N/A

the original White Helmets dataset. This shows that the PI failed to capture the randomness of the network. P and RWC show a consistent drop in value, indicating that random networks show low or no polarization. The results also show that our metric works consistently as the current state-of-the-art metric, RWC. PI and RWC for VoterFraud2020 are N/A because of multiple communities.

According to Salloum et al. [20], RWC displays a severe problem related to hubs. RWC captures how likely a random user on either side is to be exposed to an authoritative user (higher degree node) from the opposing side. Even in a non-polarized network, a random network with one or more hubs can keep the random walker confined to its community, producing a high polarization value. CCA calculates a polarity score for each node separately. So, having one or more hubs will not affect our metric. Another issue with RWC is that we need to specify the parameter 'k,' which represents the number of authoritative users in each group. While doing experiments, we noticed that the same graph produces different polarization scores with a value 'k' change. So we need to be extra mindful while using RWC. Another limitation of RWC acknowledged by the author [13] is that it reports low controversy score for the Karate Club network with 34 nodes and 78 edges. The author mentions that the graph may be too small for random-walk-based measures to function correctly. According to the literature the RWC score for the Karate Club network is 0.11 whereas our polarization metric shows 1.02. Our polarization metric performs appropriately for networks with small size.

5   Summary

This paper proposes the cross-community affinity polarization metric as a new way to measure polarization. The cross-community affinity is a heterophily-based measure that captures the connectedness of nodes to groups other than their own. It has two specific goals. First, it adapts to a different number of ideological groups. Second, it applies to various levels of granularity, ranging from individual nodes to entire networks, as well as other network-based groups in between. The network-level polarization score can be obtained as the negative of average cross-community affinity. We evaluate our proposed metric on networks with multiple ideological groups. In addition, we compared them to randomized versions of our network datasets generated using dK distributions. The results show lower polarization values for the randomized networks. We also compared our metric with two widely used existing polarization metrics.

Our work has limits that merit mentioning. First, for simplicity we consider ideological difference to be a one-dimensional space. Second, our metric is now tailored to undirected unweighted networks. These are essential agenda items for future research. With a metric that captures polarization at the node level, it is possible to determine which nodes or communities contribute to the polarization. Assessing how distinct communities contribute to polarization is feasible, providing knowledge that may be valuable for limiting damage or directing intervention.

Appendix A   Additional Materials

A.1   Edge Distribution of VoterFraud2020 Domain Network

Figure 1 depicts the distribution of edges to communities after relabelling unknown based on the dominant label in the node's direct neighborhood. The majority of the edges in the right community are to themselves. Left-center also has most of its edges to left-center and right.

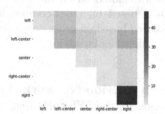

Fig. 1. Heatmap of the edge distribution between communities in the VoterFraud2020 domain network with five communities: left, left-center, center, right-center, right.

A.2   Visual Representation of Datasets

Polblogs. Figure 2a shows the visualization of Polblogs community structure. Light green represents liberal and red represents conservative. Figure 3a displays the Polblogs network colored based on the cross-community affinity of each node. The greater the value, the lighter the shade. Different nodes have distinct hues, which demonstrates that their values vary. The figure is dominated by a darker hue, indicating that the majority of nodes have low cross-community affinity values, resulting in a polarized network.

(a) Polblogs communities   (b) WH communities   (c) VoterFraud2020 communities

Fig. 2. (a) The Polblogs interaction network: light green represents liberal nodes, and red represents conservative; (b) The White Helmets Twitter network. The colors red represents anti-White Helmets and green represents pro-White Helmets; (c) The Voter-Fraud2020 domain network, with colors reflects the node's political orientation: red for right, orange for right-center, yellow for center, green for left-center and blue for left.

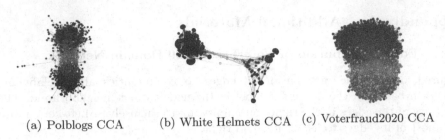

(a) Polblogs CCA   (b) White Helmets CCA   (c) Voterfraud2020 CCA

Fig. 3. (a) The Polblogs network colored based on cross-community affinity (b) The White Helmets Twitter colored based on cross-community affinity. (c) The Voter-Fraud2020 domain network colored based on cross-community affinity. The darker the color, the lower the value, thus higher polarization.

White Helmets Twitter Interaction Network. Figure 2b depicts the visual representation of communities in the WhiteHelmet interaction network. The colors red represents anti-White Helmets and green represents pro-White Helmets. Figure 3b displays the White Helmets network colored based on the cross-community affinity of each node. The greater the value, the lighter the shade. The figure is dominated by a darker hue, indicating a polarized network.

VoterFraud2020 Domain Network. The visual representation of communities in the network is shown in Fig. 2c. The color reflects the political orientation of the nodes, with red for right, orange for right-center, yellow for center, green for left-center, and blue for left. The right (47.4%) and the left-center (35.5%) constitute the majority of the network. The center has 7.4% nodes, the left has 6.1%, and the right-center has 3.6% nodes. Figure 3c shows the VoterFraud2020 domain network colored based on nodes' cross-community affinity value. Darker hue means low cross-community affinity. Overall, the graph shows darker shade indicating that the network is polarization.

A.3   Scenarios of Network for CCA Calculation

Figure 4 depicts various scenarios of a network with seven nodes and two communities: red and green. For each scenario, the cross-community affinity for node v is provided. In scenario Fig. 4a all the immediate neighbors and two-hop neighbors of node v are members of the same community, indicating the absence of cross-community affinity. In this instance, $CCA(v)$ has a value of -1.5. Similarly, in scenario Fig. 4f, all neighbors inside a two-hop neighborhood belong to the opposing community, resulting in a node with maximum cross-community affinity, where, $CCA(v)$ equals 1.5. $CCA(v) = 0$ in the Fig. 4d, because the neighborhood of node v is equally distributed among both communities.

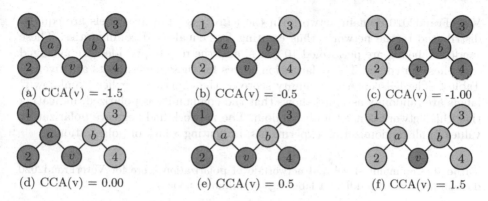

Fig. 4. Different scenario of a network with 7 nodes and two communities: red and green. The cross-community affinity of node v, $CCA(v)$ is shown. (Color figure online)

A.4   Ideological Distance for Five Communities

Table 3 shows the distance between communities in a scenario in which we consider $C = 5$. Right and left communities are on the ends of the spectrum. As a result, the distance between them is 1.

Table 3. The ideological distance between 5 communities for VoterFraud2020 domain network

	Right	Right-center	Center	Left-center	Left
Right	−1	1/4	2/4	3/4	1
Right-center	1/4	−1	1/4	2/4	3/4
Center	2/4	1/4	−1	1/4	2/4
Left-center	3/4	2/4	1/4	−1	1/4
Left	1	3/4	2/4	1/4	−1

A.5   Relabelling VoterFraud2020 Domain Network

We randomized the labeling of the nodes of VoterFraud2020 domain network to see the effect on the polarization metric. We relabelled the network in three ways. In the first case, we randomly relabelled "unknown" without altering the community size of labeled nodes. We determined the number of "unknown" required by each community to maintain the community sizes. Then, "unknown" was arbitrarily assigned to each community. Even though we relabel "unknown" only, 75.6% of nodes in the network are "unknown", making the network at least 75% random.

In the second case, we relabelled all the nodes in the network randomly but kept the number of nodes in each community the same as in the original

VoterFraud2020 domain network. In the third case, the five labels are equally distributed to the network, thus creating five equal-sized communities. These random labeling are performed 10 times, and the results provided are averaged over these outcomes. The polarization scores for these experiments are given in Table 4. The left-center community score in the experiment where "unknown" labels are randomly assigned shows that the community is polarized, indicating that this network is not totally random. The network had negative polarization values in all randomization experiments, indicating a lack of polarization.

Table 4. Community-level and network-level polarization score for VoterFraud2020 domain network with different labellings of unknown nodes.

	Original network	Random labelling of "unknown"	Random labelling keeping the original community sizes	Random labelling with equally divided community sizes
Right	0.88	−0.52	−0.44	−0.40
Right-center	−0.34	−0.37	−0.20	−0.18
Center	−0.19	−0.04	−0.09	−0.21
Left-center	0.62	0.11	−0.22	−0.26
Left	0.05	−0.38	−0.48	−0.48
Network	0.61	−0.20	−0.28	−0.31

References

1. Media Bias/Fact Check News. https://mediabiasfactcheck.com/. Accessed 25 July 2022
2. Abilov, A., Hua, Y., Matatov, H., Amir, O., Naaman, M.: Voterfraud 2020: a multi-modal dataset of election fraud claims on Twitter. In: ICWSM (2021)
3. Adamic, L.A., Glance, N.: The political blogosphere and the 2004 U.S. election: Divided they blog. In: Proceedings of the 3rd International Workshop on Link Discovery, LinkKDD 2005, pp. 36–43. Association for Computing Machinery, New York (2005)
4. Belcastro, L., Cantini, R., Marozzo, F., Talia, D., Trunfio, P.: Learning political polarization on social media using neural networks. IEEE Access **8**, 47177–47187 (2020)
5. Borge-Holthoefer, J., Magdy, W., Darwish, K., Weber, I.: Content and network dynamics behind egyptian political polarization on Twitter. In: Proceedings of the 18th ACM Conference on Computer Supported Cooperative Work & Social Computing, pp. 700–711 (2015)
6. Conover, M., Ratkiewicz, J., Francisco, M., Gonçalves, B., Menczer, F., Flammini, A.: Political polarization on Twitter. In: Fifth International AAAI Conference on Weblogs and Social Media, January 2011
7. Darwish, K.: Quantifying polarization on twitter: the kavanaugh nomination. In: Weber, I., Darwish, K.M., Wagner, C., Zagheni, E., Nelson, L., Aref, S., Flöck, F. (eds.) SocInfo 2019. LNCS, vol. 11864, pp. 188–201. Springer, Cham (2019). https://doi.org/10.1007/978-3-030-34971-4_13

8. Demszky, D., Garg, N., Voigt, R., Zou, J.Y., Gentzkow, M., Shapiro, J.M., Jurafsky, D.: Analyzing polarization in social media: Method and application to tweets on 21 mass shootings. In: NAACL (2019)
9. DiMaggio, P., Evans, J., Bryson, B.: Have American's social attitudes become more polarized? Am. J. Sociol. **102**(3), 690–755 (1996)
10. Emamgholizadeh, H., Nourizade, M., Tajbakhsh, M.S., Hashminezhad, M., Esfahani, F.N.: A framework for quantifying controversy of social network debates using attributed networks: biased random walk (brw). Soc. Netw. Anal. Min. **10**, 1–20 (2020)
11. Esteban, J., Ray, D.: On the Measurement of Polarization. Econometrica **62**(4), 819–851 (1994)
12. Friedkin, N.E.: Horizons of observability and limits of informal control in organizations. Soc. Forces **62**(1), 54–77 (1983)
13. Garimella, K., Morales, G., Gionis, A., Mathioudakis, M.: Quantifying controversy in social media. ACM Trans. Soc. Comput. **1**, May 2015
14. Guerra, P.H.C., Meira, W., Cardie, C., Kleinberg, R.D.: A measure of polarization on social media networks based on community boundaries. In: ICWSM (2013)
15. Lozares, C., Verd, J.M., Cruz, I., Barranco, O.: Homophily and heterophily in personal networks. from mutual acquaintance to relationship intensity. Quality & Quantity 48, September 2014
16. Mahadevan, P., Krioukov, D., Fall, K., Vahdat, A.: Systematic topology analysis and generation using degree correlations. ACM SIGCOMM Computer Communication Review 36, June 2006
17. Morales, A.J., Borondo, J., Losada, J.C., Benito, R.M.: Measuring political polarization: Twitter shows the two sides of Venezuela. Chaos: Interdisciplinary J. Nonlinear Sci. **25**(3), 033114 (2015)
18. Nair, S., Iamnitchi, A.: The polarized web of the voter fraud claims in the 2020 US presidential election. In: Workshop Proceedings of the 15th International AAAI Conference on Web and Social Media. International Workshop on Social Sensing (2021)
19. Nair, S., Ng, K., Iamnitchi, A., Skvoretz, J.: Diffusion of social conventions across polarized communities: an empirical study. Social Network Analysis and Mining 11, December 2021
20. Salloum, A., Chen, T.H.Y., Kivelä, M.: Separating polarization from noise: comparison and normalization of structural polarization measures. In: Proceedings of the ACM on Human-Computer Interaction 6(CSCW1), April 2022
21. Yang, M., Wen, X., Lin, Y.R., Deng, L.: Quantifying content polarization on Twitter. In: 2017 IEEE 3rd International Conference on Collaboration and Internet Computing (CIC), pp. 299–308 (2017)
22. Ortiz de Zarate, J., Di Giovanni, M., Feuerstein, E., Brambilla, M.: Measuring Controversy in Social Networks Through NLP, pp. 194–209. Springer International Publishing (09 2020)

Decoding Demographic *un*-fairness
from Indian Names

Vahini Medidoddi, Jalend Bantupalli, Souvic Chakraborty(✉),
and Animesh Mukherjee

Indian Institute of Technology, Kharagpur, West Bengal, India
chakra.souvic@gmail.com

Abstract. Demographic classification is essential in fairness assessment in recommender systems or in measuring unintended bias in online networks and voting systems. Important fields like education and politics, which often lay a foundation for the future of equality in society, need scrutiny to design policies that can better foster equality in resource distribution constrained by the unbalanced demographic distribution of people in the country.

We collect three publicly available datasets to train state-of-the-art classifiers in the domain of gender and caste classification. We train the models in the Indian context, where the same name can have different styling conventions (Jolly Abraham/Kumar Abhishikta in one state may be written as Abraham Jolly/Abishikta Kumar in the other). Finally, we also perform cross-testing (training and testing on different datasets) to understand the efficacy of the above models.

We also perform an error analysis of the prediction models. Finally, we attempt to assess the bias in the existing Indian system as case studies and find some intriguing patterns manifesting in the complex demographic layout of the sub-continent across the dimensions of gender and caste.

Keywords: Caste · Gender · Fairness · Demographic bias · India

1 Introduction

The *name* of a person can convey various demographic features of the individual. This demographic information plays a crucial role in multiple studies related to racial inequality, recommendation systems, biomedical studies, hate-speech target identification, group sentiment analysis etc. [1,4,5,14,15]. Consequently, much work has been done on demographic classification and a variety of online web APIs and tools capable of predicting demographics from user name [2,3, 11]) exist. Most of this research work, however, is focused on US demographics [12,14], and many of the works [2,3,11,14] build classifiers that require a proper division of the first name, middle name, and last name to work. So, we introduce caste and gender-specific datasets on Indian demographics, which hosts one-seventh of the world population. Indian names vary significantly over states

© The Author(s), under exclusive license to Springer Nature Switzerland AG 2022
F. Hopfgartner et al. (Eds.): SocInfo 2022, LNCS 13618, pp. 472–489, 2022.
https://doi.org/10.1007/978-3-031-19097-1_33

when compared to other countries due to high religious, ethno-demographic and linguistic variance[1]. Also, Indian names do not always fall under the division of first/middle/last name, primarily because the name of a person may contain the name of their ancestors (e.g., Avul Pakir Jainulabdeen Abdul Kalam, former President of India - here the first name of the person is Abdul). Indian names may also contain the name of father in the name of a woman. This can make gender or race detection difficult in faulty name segmentation.

So, to achieve a realistic outcome for name to demography detection, we train our classifiers as an end-to-end sequence classification task, overcoming the need for a segmentation model. The Indian society is divided by gender and caste, unlike the US demographics, divided by races. Thus we focus on caste and gender prediction in this study. To summarize, the objective of this study is to predict the gender and the caste from any complete Indian name overcoming the need to build a segmentation model. We list down our contributions in this paper below.

1. Toward fulfilling the classification objective, we build large datasets acquiring already public data of India-wide examination records and parsing electoral rolls containing over 7.63 million unique names.
2. We demonstrate the efficacy of our model through several case studies and make interesting observations about caste and gender based discrimination in India both online and on the ground.
3. We show that there has been an upward trend of participation in competitive exams among women and backward classes over the years. We perform a multi-dimensional study to understand the nuance of caste and gender-based discrimination present in Indian society to help policymakers make data-driven choices.
4. We perform state-wise chronological analysis to understand the efficacy of discrimination-limiting practices/laws implemented in the Indian states.
5. We also analyze the Indian social media 'Koo' to understand the degree of representation a weaker section of the Indian society has on the web and its improvement over time.

We have opensourced our codebase encouraging further research[2].

2   Related Work

Gender Classification: Hu et al. (2021) [8] inferred gender from user first names (US data) using character based models. They further conclude that using complete names results in better prediction results compared to only first names. [16] (2011) inferred gender from Facebook data with an accuracy of 95.2% for users in the NYC area using their first names. Muller et al. (2016) [10] inferred gender from Twitter usernames with 80.4% accuracy. Tripathi and Faruqui (2011) [18] presented a SVM based approach for gender classification

---

[1] https://www.britannica.com/place/India/Indo-European-languages.
[2] https://github.com/vahini01/IndianDemographics.

of Indian names using n-gram suffixes and features based upon morphological analysis, obtaining a F1-score of 94.9%. We refer the reader to Kruger et al. (2019) [9] for a comprehensive survey on gender detection models based on textual data. There are also a few commercial APIs available for gender detection: Gender API [2], Onograph API [11], Genderize API [7]. We have used these APIs as baselines.

Ethnicity Classification and Demographic Bias: Classifying the ethnic category, one of the most telling demographic property of a user, provides an essential data add-on for social science research. Other important applications include biomedical research, population demographic studies, and marketing toward a specific group of individuals [1], [17]. Despite numerous applications, ethnic information of users are often not directly available.

To bridge this gap, Sood et al.(2018) [14] made use of registered voters in Florida to infer race and ethnicity from names obtaining a F1-score of 0.83 using LSTMs. Ambedkar et al. [1] presented a model that classifies names into 13 cultural/ethnic groups with data extracted from Wikipedia. Giles et al. [17] proposed a name-ethnicity classifier that identified ethnicity from personal names in Wikipedia with 85% accuracy.

The Present Work: Studies on computational bias in Indian datasets are rare due to unavailability of good published datasets [6]. In this work, we specifically focus on India and attempt to quantify bias in diverse Indian datasets across the two major dimensions Indian Society is divided along- caste and gender. To this purpose we collected *multi-year* data from (i) electoral records of different Indian states, (ii) data corresponding to the India wide 10th and 12th standard examination, (iii) data corresponding to the top Indian engineering and medical entrance examinations and (iv) data from one of the fastest growing Indian social network. We use pre-trained transformer models to obtain better gender and caste classification performance and perform various case studies using the prediction from the best models to gain insights into the underlying demographic biases based on gender and caste in India.

3   Datasets

We use datasets for two purposes: training models and conducting case studies. We collected three massive datasets[3] to gather training data on diverse Indian names from the Central Board of Secondary Education (CBSE), the All India Engineering Entrance Examination (AIEEE), and the Electoral Rolls (ER).

To conduct case studies on the social media data, we resorted to the Koo social network[4]. For educational data in addition to the multi-year CBSE (standard X and XII) and the AIEEE data mentioned earlier we also included the All India Pre Medical Test (AIPMT) data.

---

[3] Detailed stats are available in Appendix A.

[4] https://www.kooapp.com/.

CBSE Dataset

Data for Training Models – The Central Board of Secondary Education (CBSE) keeps a record of all students' grades[5]. We scraped a sample of about 100K records from their website for the 2014 and 2015 academic years. CBSE data includes information such as the student's name, father's name, mother's name, and grades. It comprises information from students in the 12th grade during the previous years. In this dataset, the gender labels for students are not available. However the name of the father and the mother of every student are present. This gives us an easy way to get the names and the corresponding gender labels.

Data for Case Study – We collected CBSE grade 10 student data from 2004 to 2010 and CBSE grade 12 data from 2004 to 2012 to conduct the case studies. The number of unique names in the CBSE grade 10 and grade 12 datasets are 70.09% and 73.12% respectively.

AIEEE Dataset

Data for Training Models – The All India Engineering Entrance Examination (AIEEE) is a national examination for admission to engineering colleges. The AIEEE data records[6] used for training corresponded to the years 2009, 2010, and 2011. It includes the students' names, state and caste categories - general/reserved (i.e., OBC/SC/ST)[7], the fathers' and the mothers' names.

Data for the Case Study – The marksheets of students for AIEEE exams spanning the years 2004 to 2011 are randomly sampled and gathered for the case studies.

ER Dataset: Electoral roll data is gathered from the electoral roll websites of each state government. We collected only English language data from these rolls. We show the states considered for the gender classification in Table 4(Appendix).

AIPMT Dataset: The All India Pre-Medical Test (AIPMT) is a test for admission to medical schools in India. The AIPMT data obtained spans over the years 2004 to 2011. This dataset is solely used to conduct case studies and provides information on 435,288 students with 327,665 (75.27%) unique names.

Social Media Dataset: Apart from educational data for our case studies, we also gathered data from Koo[8] which is a rapidly growing social network in India. For our study we have used the data of all Koo users that has been recently released by [13]. We applied our models to this dataset and analyzed the degree of representation based on caste and gender, as shown in Sect. 7.

---

[5] https://resultsarchives.nic.in.
[6] maintained in the same website as CBSE.
[7] https://en.wikipedia.org/wiki/Scheduled_Castes_and_Scheduled_Tribes.
[8] https://www.kooapp.com/feed.

4   Methodology

We can determine the gender/caste from a user's name using either the first or full name. In India, extracting the first name from the full name is dependent on the state, religion and local culture; for example, the first name appears as the final word in the name in certain states for certain religions. Hence we used a person's full name as input for both gender and caste classification tasks.

4.1   Classification Models

Baselines and Models: We used the top APIs available as baselines: Gender API [2], Genderize API [11], and Forebears API [7]. For non-DL models, we use logistic regression and SVM. We use CharCNN and CharLSTM as neural models trained from scratch. We used BERT, mBERT, IndicBERT, and MuRIL as pretrained neural models. Details are added in Appendix A.2.

Table 1. Performance of the models(Accuracy) for gender and caste classification.

Model	Gender classification			Caste classification - AIEEE Data	
	CBSE	ER	AIEEE	Complete Name	Name & State
LR	91.03	73.55	87.38	68.71	69.62
SVM	93.82	46.85	85.31	61.73	64.82
Char-CNN	96.18	89.74	94.13	71.57	73.21
Char-LSTM	95.81	90.41	94.72	71.61	73.38
BERT	96.97	**92.56**	**96.06**	72.62	**74.70**
MuRIL	**97.07**	92.49	95.97	71.91	73.79
IndicBERT	96.32	91.52	94.59	70.66	72.86
mBERT	96.80	92.50	95.84	**73.05**	74.61

5   Experimental Setup

Gender and Caste Labels: Only binary categories – male and female – are used for gender classification task. As for the caste, the categories that one finds are *General* (upper caste people who did not face historical discrimination and benefited from the caste system), *Scheduled Caste* (SC: who were discriminated historically), *Scheduled Tribe* (ST: who were out castes and faced the maximum discrimination), and Other Backward Castes (OBC). For the purpose of this study, we divide castes into broad groups: General and Reserved (SC/ST/OBC for whom the government guarantees reservation to ensure a level-playing field).

Repetition of Names: Many names in our datasets repeat. Thus it is possible that test points (chosen randomly) can overlap with the training points. In order to avoid this, we run our experiments on unique names only. The label for this instance is the majority label of all the individual instances of the name. For our experiments we use a train-test split of 70:30. More details related to dataset division is included in Appendix A.

6 Results

Main Results: The main results are noted in Table 1. We observe that simple ML models like LR and SVM do not perform well. Character based models show greater improvement over LR, SVM for gender detection showing the benefits of the choice of character sequences for this task. Transformer based models perform best for both gender and caste classification with no clear winner among them. Overall, MuRIL does well in gender classification and mBERT in caste classification.

Baseline APIs: We have used only 500 unseen instances due to API request limit per day for each of these baselines. For a set of randomly chosen 500 data points, we observe that the transformer based models (MuRIL and mBERT) by far outperform all the three baselines (see Table 2). Among the baselines, Onograph performs the best.

Cross Dataset Evaluation. From Table 3 we see that models trained on CBSE and AIEEE datasets (having similar pan-India demographics) perform well on each other's test sets. Further, the models trained on the ER dataset perform

Table 2. Comparison with baseline APIs. All results are on a held out set of 500 data points.

	Model	ER	AIEEE	CBSE
APIS	Gender [2]	53.2	64.0	81.0
	Onograph [11]	71.46	82.00	92.8
	Genderize [7]	49.79	63.86	82.38
Models	MuRIL-CBSE	74.85	89.00	97.00
	MuRIL-ER	93.81	94.20	97.40
	MuRIL-AIEEE	77.45	95.40	97.60
	BERT-CBSE	77.05	86.20	97.20
	BERT-ER	93.81	94.20	97.00
	BERT-AIEEE	76.25	97.00	97.60

Table 3. Performance in a cross-dataset setting

Model	Train	Test	Accuracy	F1-Score
MuRIL	ER	CBSE	97.31	97.28
	ER	AIEEE	95.40	95.31
	CBSE	ER	78.03	77.93
	CBSE	AIEEE	90.82	90.72
	AIEEE	ER	79.47	79.35
	AIEEE	CBSE	97.03	97.00
BERT	ER	CBSE	97.31	97.28
	ER	AIEEE	94.94	94.84
	CBSE	ER	78.27	78.15
	CBSE	AIEEE	89.64	89.50
	AIEEE	ER	79.66	70.53
	AIEEE	CBSE	96.99	96.96

reasonably well when tested on CBSE and AIEEE datasets but the reverse setups perform poorly due to lesser representation of north-eastern states in CBSE/AIEEE data.

7   Decoding Unfairness Across Gender and Caste Lines

We use social media datasets, longitudinal educational records, and electoral roll datasets to identify and quantify the inter-sectional bias caused by caste and gender prejudice. We also display the results over an 8-year period to better understand how government-sponsored social programs and globalization are influencing Indian society and reducing unfairness in resource distribution.

For all these studies, we have used the MuRIL-based model, which is also shown to be one of the top-performing models.

To understand the state and evolution of discrimination in the current Indian system, we draft the following set of research questions (**RQ**):

- **RQ1**: Is the representation of females (no reservation) and backward castes (reserved) in *public education* increasing over time?
- **RQ2**: Is the representation of females (no reservation) and backward castes (reserved) in *competitive engineering/medical entrance exams* increasing over time?
- **RQ3**: Are females and backward caste people less represented in the Indian social networks?
- **RQ4**: How vocal are the females and backward caste voices (#followers*#posts) in Indian social media?

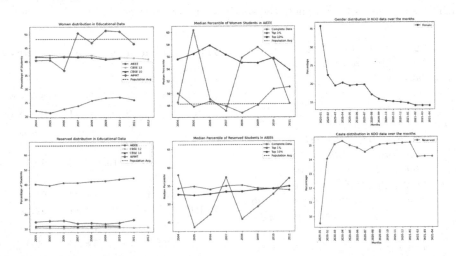

Fig. 1. Distribution of women and backward castes are shown in the left most figure. Middle figure displays the median percentile in the same. The right most diagram shows the temporal evolution of women and backward caste people in Koo

7.1   Impact of Social Bias on Education

RQ1 & RQ2: *Is the representation of females (no reservation) and backward castes (reserved) in public education and competitive exams increasing over time?*

Indian Government has the promise of equality embedded in its emblem, and the reservation system was introduced as a mechanism to ensure the continuous integration of backward caste people into the mainstream social structure. This reservation system ensures equality of representation in government institutes of higher education and workplaces by reserving some seats for backward class people who have faced historic injustice.

However, a similar system does not exist for women. Hence, we try to understand the system's effect on education for both gender and caste divisions.

In Fig. 1, we plot the ratio of women and backward castes in the sampled dataset for each year and each exam. We observe that for AIEEE, women's representation has steadily increased from 2005 to 2010. Also, the engineering exam AIEEE saw much lower participation from women when compared to the medical entrance exam AIPMT or the board exams CBSE 10th and CBSE 12th grade. In the medical examination AIPMT, women's representation has increased and has achieved the population average from 2007. In the CBSE 10th and CBSE 12th grade, we see a stable representation of women over time.

However, the representation of backward castes in the medical entrance exam and both the board exams has remained extremely low all over time. AIEEE, the engineering entrance exam, stands out here with much higher representation from backward castes, and the participation is also slightly increasing with time.

In Fig. 1 we plot the median percentile attained by women and backward castes for each year and each exam. While the average percentile for the whole dataset will be the 50th percentile, this metric, when applied to a specific community, will tell us the meritocratic position of that community, i.e., whether that community is doing better relative to other communities or lesser and how that position is changing over time concerning specific exams. We have the ranks available only for AIEEE data, so we try to analyze only this data. We see that women have achieved equality in percentile and are doing better than men in later years. However, the same is not valid for backward caste students. The above percentile changes show need for exam-specific policy modifications. For women, the inequality is mostly in participation, and women need more encouragement to participate in competitive exams, whereas backward class students need better support to score higher in the competitive exams.

7.2   Impact of Social Bias on Online Media and Web Representation

RQ3: *Are women and backward caste people less represented in the Indian social networks?*

We analyze the Indian social network 'Koo'[9] to investigate the extent of representation of women and lower caste people in this network. We use the

---

[9] https://www.kooapp.com/.

massive dataset with 4 million usernames and metadata from Koo provided by [13]. Using our classifier, we predicted the caste and the gender of these names. In Figure 1, we plot the ratio of women and backward castes in the network for each month across Koo's existence. We observe that upper caste people of India mostly occupied Koo during its inception stage; however the situation quickly changed over time with a slightly higher representation from the lower caste people. On the other hand, women's distribution continuously decreased in this Indian social network.

RQ4: *How vocal are the women and backward caste voices (#followers*#tweets) on Indian social media?*

We quantify the overall 'voice' of a group by the sum of the #followers*#tweets for each person in that group. As we do not have the number of followers data for each month, we only compute the aggregate statistics at the end of the last month in the dataset. The ratio of male voice to the female voice in the network is 3.59. Similarly the ratio of the general to the backward class voice is 10.47. These results demonstrate a striking inequality. Further we observe that a random message posted on the platform is 37.58 times more likely to be from a forward caste male than a backward-caste female.

8   Conclusion and Future Work

The paper introduced various large-scale datasets of Indian names and extensively explored the possibility of gender and caste detection from these names. We showed that the state-of-the-art APIs do not perform well on the task of gender detection from Indian names; in contrast, the recent transformer based models performed extremely well in this task. Further, to the best of our knowledge, this is the first large-scale caste classification task undertaken to understand the existing demographic disparities in across India. Through a series of rigorous case studies we have shown the gender and caste based biases that exist in basic and higher education as well as in the representation in social media. We have also opensourced our codebase for further research and contribution. In future, we will like to consider more caste varieties and data from all states for a nuanced evaluation.

A   Appendix

A.1   Dataset Statistics

Table 4 displays the dataset stats.

Table 4. The table below contains information on datasets that are used to train models and conduct case studies.

Gender classification		
Data (full)	Female	Male
CBSE	194423	194413
ER	10405236	11632598
AIEEE	358522	358522
CBSE-breakup	Female	Male
2014	25779	31573
2015	51744	63434
ER-breakup	Female	Male
Daman	53391	53605
Manipur	580415	589948
Meghalaya	748820	737951
Nagaland	253274	295039
Arunachal	292158	292544
Delhi	966324	1430743
Sikkim	76145	88209
Goa	372029	361380
Mizoram	134305	158144
AIEEE-breakup	Female	Male
2009	66286	84615
2010	70826	91687
2011	68965	89490
Caste classification		
AIEEE	Reserved	General
2009	47681	64892
2010	54703	68163
2011	57262	65810
Case study - education data		
Dataset	Total	Unique names
AIEEE	665227	525631
CBSE 10	487080	341430
CBSE 12	378123	276476
AIPMT	435288	327665
Case study - social media data		
Dataset	Total	Valid names
Koo	4061670	1761958

A.2   Baseline APIs and Models

We used a bunch of APIs available for gender classification as baselines and compared them with the results obtained from our transformer based methods. *Gender API* [2]: Gender-API.com is a simple-to-implement solution that adds gender information to existing records. It receives input via an API and returns the split-up name (first name, last name) and gender to the app or the website. According to the website, it will search for the name in a database belonging to the specific country, and if it is not found, it will perform a global lookup. If it cannot find a name in a global lookup, it performs several normalizations on the name to correct typos and cover all spelling variants.

Onograph API [11]: OnoGraph is a set of services that predicts a person's characteristics based on their name. It can predict nationality, gender, and location (where they live). The services are based on the world's largest private database of living people, which contains over 4.25 billion people (as of July 2020). According to the documentation, "OnoGraph's results are the most accurate of any comparable service; and it recognizes around 40 million more names than the nearest comparable service."

Genderize API [7]: It is a simple API that predicts a person's gender based on their name. The request will generate a response with the following keys: name, gender, likelihood, and count. The probability denotes the certainty of the gender assigned. The count indicates the number of data rows reviewed to calculate the response.

A.3   Model Description

Logistic Regression: We concatenate the different parts of the name and compute character n-grams. Next we obtain TF-IDF scores from the character n-grams and pass them as features to the logistic regression model.

SVM: The objective of the support vector machine algorithm is to identify a hyperplane in N-dimensional space (N = the number of features) that categorizes the data points clearly. Then, we accomplish classification by locating the hyperplane that best distinguishes the two classes. There are several hyperplanes that might be used to split the two groups of data points. Our goal is to discover a plane with the greatest margin or the greatest distance between data points from both classes.

Char CNN: Character-level CNN (char-CNN) is a well-known text classification algorithm. Each character is encoded with a fixed-length trainable embedding. A 1-D CNN is applied to the matrix created by concatenating the above vectors. In our model, we utilize 256 convolution filters in a single hidden layer of 1D convolution with a kernel size of 7.

Char LSTM: A name is a sequence of characters. Like char-CNN, each character of the input name is transformed into trainable embedding vectors and provided as input. Our model employs a single LSTM layer with 64 features and a 20% dropout layer.

Transformer Models

- We choose BERT for demographic categorization, using full names as inputs because it has proven to be highly efficient in English data sequence modeling.
- mBERT is trained using a masked language modeling (MLM) objective on the top 104 languages with the largest Wikipedia.
- IndicBERT is a multilingual ALBERT model that has only been trained on 12 major Indian languages[10]. IndicBERT has much fewer parameters than other multilingual models.
- MuRIL is pre-trained on 17 Indian languages and their transliterated counterparts. It employs a different tokenizer from the BERT model. This model is an appropriate candidate for categorization based on Indian names because it is pre-trained on Indian languages.

Hyperparameters

LR: learning rate = 0.003, n-gram range = (1–6)
SVM: kernel=rbf, n-gram range = (1–6), degree = 3, gamma = scale
Char CNN: learning rate = 0.001, hidden layers = 1, filters = 256, kernel size = 7, optimizer = adam
Char LSTM: learning rate = 0.001, dropout = 0.2, hidden layers = 1, features = 64, optimizer = adam
Transformer models: models = [bert-base-uncased, google/muril-base-cased, ai4bharat/indic-bert, bert-base-multilingual-uncased], epochs = 3, learning rate = 0.00005

A.4   Results

More detailed results are given in Tables 5 and 6.

Handling of Corner Cases: As a name can be common across both genders or caste, we use majority voting inorder to label a name with binary label for both gender and caste classification tasks. In case of equality we considered arbitrarily decided labels.

---

[10] IndicBERT supports the following 12 languages: Assamese, Bengali, English, Gujarati, Hindi, Kannada, Malayalam, Marathi, Oriya, Punjabi, Tamil, and Telugu.

A.5   Error Analysis - Baseline APIs vs Our Models

Table 7 lists some of the best and worst test cases for the best performing baselines and the best performing transformer based models. Both these types of models perform the best when the first name (first word) is a good representative of the gender (e.g., Karishma Chettri). Baselines usually fail in three cases: the presence of parental name or surname (e.g., Avunuri Aruna), longer names where gender is represented by multiple words (e.g., Kollipara Kodahda Rama Murthy), and core Indian names (e.g., Laishram Priyabati, Gongkulung Kamei). The main reason for the better performance of transformer models might be that they are trained on complete names and larger datasets. As a result, they handle the complexity of Indian names. However, both these types of models tend to fail in presence of unusual and highly complicated names (e.g., Raj Blal Rawat, Pullammagari Chinna Maddileti).

Table 5. Performance of the models for gender classification on each dataset.

Gender classification						
Model	CBSE		ER		AIEEE	
	F1-Score	Accuracy	F1-Score	Accuracy	F1-Score	Accuracy
LR	90.93	91.03	73.23	73.55	87.24	87.38
SVM	93.69	93.82	37.91	46.85	85.12	85.31
Char-CNN	96.12	96.18	89.72	89.74	94.54	94.13
Char-LSTM	95.75	95.81	90.23	90.41	94.62	94.72
BERT	96.94	96.97	**92.52**	**92.56**	**95.99**	**96.06**
MuRIL	**97.04**	**97.07**	92.45	92.49	95.90	95.97
IndicBERT	96.28	96.32	91.48	91.52	94.48	94.59
mBERT	96.76	96.80	92.46	92.50	95.76	95.84

Table 6. Performance of the models for caste classification on AIEEE dataset.

Caste classification - AIEEE Data				
Model	Complete name		Name & State	
	F1-Score	Accuracy	F1-Score	Accuracy
LR	68.64	68.71	69.58	69.62
SVM	53.82	61.73	59.58	64.82
Char-CNN	71.18	71.57	72.74	73.21
BERT	**71.80**	72.62	**73.99**	**74.70**
MuRIL	71.57	71.91	73.04	73.79
IndicBERT	69.72	70.66	72.03	72.86
mBERT	71.34	**73.05**	73.60	74.61

Table 7. Table listing some common errors by the best performing baselines and the best performing transformer models. Here **W** stands for wrong and **C** stands for correct. And **XX** denotes the model, API results respectively; for e.g., **WC** lists names where transformer predicted wrong while API predicted correct. The letter in bracket denotes the gender (M for male and F for female). The listed names have multiple instances in the datasets. So none of the names uniquely identify any person

Dataset	CC		CW
CBSE	Himanshu Bharatia (M)		Vijay Laxmi Soni (F)
	Sudha Chaturvedi (F)		Gang Shyam Herau (M)
ER	Karishma Chettri (F)		Chingakham Romita (F)
	Shekhar Sethi (M)		Ramesh Kasarlekar (M)
AIEEE	Suguna (F)		Indra Kumar Singh Bundela (M)
	Sudeep Agrawal (M)		Avunuri Aruna (F)
Dataset	WC		WW
CBSE	Sharmil arora (M)		Raj Blal Rawat (F)
	Ramkanwar gund (F)		Vimal Soni (M)
ER	Jmod Kyrsian (F)		Embha Lyngdoh (M)
	Esphorlin Thongnibah (M)		Basanta Thapa (F)
AIEEE	Tazeen Husain (F)		Dogin Yapyang (F)
	Zakki Khan (M)		Pullammagari Chinna Maddileti (M)

A.6 Case Studies - Values of Median Percentile

Table 8 displays values that are plotted in the left plot of Fig. 1.

A.7 Case Studies - State Wise Results

To understand state wise distribution of Caste and Gender, we answer following additional research questions(ARQ).

- **ARQ1**: Which states in India have the highest representation of females and backward castes in higher education compared to its population?
- **ARQ2**: Which states in India have been successful in achieving a significant decrease in bias toward females and backward castes over time? Which states are lacking in this aspect?

ARQ1: *Which states in India have the highest representation of females and backward castes in higher education compared to its population?*

The AIEEE dataset has the state information for each data point. We also collect the state wise population record from Census 2011[11]. We compute the population normalized fraction of women and backward caste people writing the AIEEE 2011 exam. From the plotted results in Fig. 2, we observe that the top

---

[11] https://en.wikipedia.org/wiki/2011_Census_of_India.

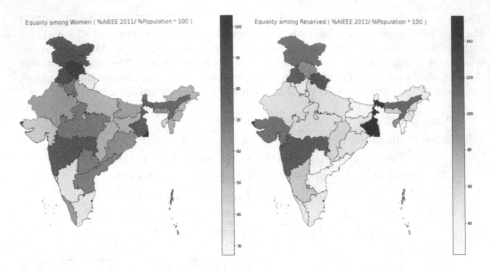

Fig. 2. Population normalized distribution of women and backward caste students in AIEEE 2011 data across Indian states.

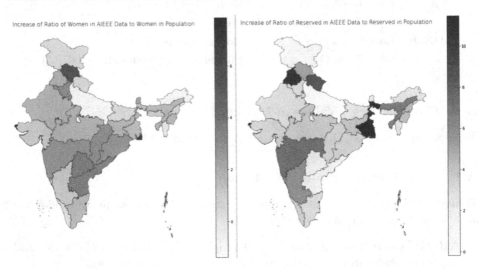

Fig. 3. Rate of change of population normalized percentage of women and backward caste students across Indian states appearing in AIEEE exams.

states with population normalized higher representation of women writing the AIEEE exam are Jammu & Kashmir, Himachal Pradesh, Punjab, West Bengal, and Maharashtra. Similarly, the states with population normalized higher representation of backward castes writing the AIEEE exam are West Bengal, Maharashtra, Punjab, Uttarakhand, and Jammu & Kashmir. We believe that the education policies of these states could act as a suitable guidance to improve the condition of the other Indian states.

Table 8. Median perctile of Women and Reserved students in AIEEE data

Dataset	Women			Reserved		
	All Data	Top 1%	Top 10%	All Data	Top 1%	Top 10%
AIEEE 2004	50.00	48.53	55.60	54.31	57.81	52.67
AIEEE 2005	47.82	60.38	56.48	54.87	43.68	52.43
AIEEE 2006	48.67	49.08	57.88	54.06	47.23	52.78
AIEEE 2007	47.90	47.14	56.35	54.99	57.38	53.40
AIEEE 2008	46.78	55.85	55.03	55.20	45.97	53.46
AIEEE 2009	48.10	57.56	54.98	54.35	49.39	53.98
AIEEE 2010	50.71	55.55	55.82	54.22	52.8	54.28
AIEEE 2011	51.04	48.35	53.83	53.88	57.14	54.94

ARQ2: *Which states in India have been successful in achieving a significant decrease in bias toward females and backward castes over time? Which states are lacking in this aspect?*

One way to measure the reduction (increase) in bias would be to check for the increase (decrease) in the population normalized percentage of women and backward caste over time. To this purpose, we obtained the rate of change of population normalized women and backward class candidates taking the AIEEE exam. For each state, the rate of change is measured as the slope of the best fit line (linear regression) of the year versus population normalized percentage scatter plot. The year range considered was 2004 to 2011.

From Fig. 3, we observe that the most successful states in reducing the gender inequality are Himachal Pradesh, Andhra Pradesh (Seemandhra and Telangana), Haryana and Maharashtra. With respect to reducing caste inequality we find West Bengal, Punjab, Uttarakhand, Maharashtra, Karnataka are the most successful.

Table 9. Gender and caste breakup (%) in the Koo data.

	General	Reserved
Male	73.26	12.66
Female	12.52	1.56

Table 10. % users at in the oldest 1% data sorted by creation date.

	General	Reserved
Male	67.1	12.66
Female	17.65	2.58

Table 11. % users at in the most recent 1% data sorted by creation date.

	General	Reserved
Male	73.44	13.84
Female	11.22	1.50

Table 12. % users in the top 1% data sorted by number of followers.

	General	Reserved
Male	63.87	9.00
Female	24.65	2.47

Table 13. % users in the bottom 1% data sorted by number of followers.

	General	Reserved
Male	74.91	12.08
Female	11.74	1.27

A.8   Distribution of Caste and Gender in Koo

In Table 9 we show the % breakup of the cross-sectional categories in the Koo dataset. We observe that the largest representation is from the general category males while the smallest is from the reserved category females. In the latest time point (see Table 11) we observe higher female representation than in the oldest time point (see Table 10). The % of females (both general and reserved) in top 1% users sorted by followers is relatively larger than in the bottom 1% followers (see Tables 12 and 13). This is exactly the opposite (see Tables 12 and 13) for males (both general and reserved). We believe that a possible reason could be that women have closed coteries of followership.

A.9   Ethical Implications

Like any other classification task, it can also be potentially misused when in the hands of malicious actors. Instead of reduction of bias, the same technology can be used to enforce discrimination. Hence, we request the researchers to exercise caution while using this technology as some demography classification APIs are already publicly available. Further, to keep personally identifiable data private, we opensource the codebase to collect the datapoints instead of sharing the datasets, a policy ubiquitous for social science researchers.

References

1. Ambekar, A., Ward, C.B., Mohammed, J., Male, S., Skiena, S.: Name-ethnicity classification from open sources. In: KDD, pp. 49–58. Association for Computing Machinery, New York, NY, USA (2009)

2. Gender API. https://gender-api.com (2021)
3. Name API. https://www.nameapi.org/en/home/ (2021)
4. Chakraborty, S., Dutta, P., Roychowdhury, S., Mukherjee, A.: CRUSH: contextually regularized and user anchored self-supervised hate speech detection. In: Findings of the Association for Computational Linguistics: NAACL 2022, pp. 1874–1886. Association for Computational Linguistics, Seattle, United States (2022). https://doi.org/10.18653/v1/2022.findings-naacl.144. https://aclanthology.org/2022.findings-naacl.144
5. Chakraborty, S., Goyal, P., Mukherjee, A.: Aspect-based sentiment analysis of scientific reviews. In: Proceedings of the ACM/IEEE Joint Conference on Digital Libraries in 2020, pp. 207–216. JCDL 2020, Association for Computing Machinery, New York, NY, USA (2020). https://doi.org/10.1145/3383583.3398541
6. Chakraborty, S., Goyal, P., Mukherjee, A.: (IM) balance in the representation of news? an extensive study on a decade long dataset from India. International Conference on Social Informatics, SocInfo (2022). arXiv preprint arXiv:2110.14183
7. Genderize. https://genderize.io/ (2021)
8. Hu, Y., Hu, C., Tran, T., Kasturi, T., Joseph, E., Gillingham, M.: What's in a name? - gender classification of names with character based machine learning models (2021)
9. Krüger, S., Hermann, B.: Can an online service predict gender? on the state-of-the-art in gender identification from texts. In: Proceedings of the 2nd International Workshop on Gender Equality in Software Engineering, pp. 13–16. GE 2019. IEEE Press, Canada (2019). https://doi.org/10.1109/GE.2019.00012
10. Mueller, J., Stumme, G.: Gender inference using statistical name characteristics in twitter. In: Proceedings of the The 3rd Multidisciplinary International Social Networks Conference on Social Informatics 2016, Data Science 2016. MISNC, SI, DS 2016, Association for Computing Machinery, New York, NY, USA (2016). https://doi.org/10.1145/2955129.2955182
11. Onograph. https://forebears.io/onograph/ (2021)
12. Parasurama, P.: raceBERT - a transformer-based model for predicting race and ethnicity from names (2021). arXiv preprint arXiv:2112.03807
13. Singh, A.K., et al.: What's kooking? characterizing india's emerging social network, koo. In: Proceedings of the 2021 IEEE/ACM International Conference on Advances in Social Networks Analysis and Mining, pp. 193–200. Association for Computing Machinery, New York, NY, USA (2021)
14. Sood, G., Laohaprapanon, S.: Predicting race and ethnicity from the sequence of characters in a name (2018)
15. Swami, S., Khandelwal, A., Shrivastava, M., Akhtar, S.: LRTC IIITH at IBEREVAL 2017: stance and gender detection in tweets on catalan independence. In: CEUR Workshop Proceedings 1881, 199–203 (2017), 2nd Workshop on Evaluation of Human Language Technologies for Iberian Languages, IBEREVAL (2017)
16. Tang, C., Ross, K., Saxena, N., Chen, R.: What's in a name: a study of names, gender inference, and gender behavior in facebook. In: Xu, J., Yu, G., Zhou, S., Unland, R. (eds.) Database Systems for Advanced Applications - 16th International Conference, DASFAA 2011, International Workshops, pp. 344–356 (2011)
17. Treeratpituk, P., Giles, C.L.: Name-ethnicity classification and ethnicity-sensitive name matching. In: Proceedings of the Twenty-Sixth AAAI Conference on Artificial Intelligence, pp. 1141–1147. AAAI2012, AAAI Press, Canada (2012)
18. Tripathi, A., Faruqui, M.: Gender prediction of Indian names. In IEEE Technology Students' Symposium, pp. 137–141. IEEE, Kharagpur (2011). https://doi.org/10.1109/TECHSYM.2011.5783842

Mitigating Harmful Content on Social Media Using an Interactive User Interface

Gautam Kishore Shahi[✉] and William Kana Tsoplefack

University of Duisburg-Essen, Duisburg, Germany
gautam.shahi@uni-due.de

Abstract. With the rapid growth in the number of users on social networking sites (SNS), harmful content has also been fueled enormously over time. The purpose of harmful content is usually to mislead or harm or deceive an individual or a group of users. This study focuses on two types of harmful content: hate speech and misinformation. Alongside existing methods to detect misinformation and hate speech, users are still not well informed about the content description. This study proposes an interactive user interface, 'TweetInfo', for analysing information consumption towards harmful content by providing metainformation about social media posts. The study aims to explore the consumption of harmful content by users by providing an interactive user interface which flags harmful content and provides metadata about the post by doing content analysis and standard platform without the above features. The effectiveness of the proposed TweetInfo is measured using a user study conducted with 30 participants. TweetInfo reduces the spread of harmful content compared to the standard platform. While there are still interactions with bots on both platforms, verified accounts are also involved in propagating harmful content.

Keywords: Misinformation · Hate speech · Information behaviour · TweetInfo · Interactive user interface

1 Introduction

Social media has evolved over the last decade and become a source of information for most people, especially Twitter and Facebook [1]. The world is spending more time on social media and interacting with different content. Over time, exposure to harmful social media content has increased, affecting mental health and multiplying social isolation. Harmful content tends to spread faster than non-harmful content, and these posts have a wider reach among users [2]. For users, it is difficult to identify the truthfulness of the content [3]. Harmful content may be shared as a post or hidden under external sources such as links or as advertisements by links.

Despite having guidelines on social networking sites (SNS), the real-time implementation is inferior, allowing social media users to create user-generated content (UGC) without verifying the content [4]. Users browse the content and

F. Hopfgartner et al. (Eds.): SocInfo 2022, LNCS 13618, pp. 490–505, 2022.
https://doi.org/10.1007/978-3-031-19097-1_34

share it without checking the authenticity of the content [5]. SNS provide access to multimodal user-generated content from all over the world [6]. Social media platforms are well known for spreading harmful content like misinformation or hate speech [7,8]. For users, it is hard to verify the authenticity of the information. Hence, users interact with harmful content and spread it through shares, likes, and comments, sometimes resulting in social crimes such as mob lynching and cyberbullying [9]. SNS such as Twitter, Facebook, and YouTube are working on strategies to minimise harmful content on their platforms and respect free speech for all [10]; however, users have no option to receive notifications or filter options to get more information about a particular category of social media post, and especially no information regarding the content and authenticity of the post.

Much research has been done in hate speech detection and fake news classification; however, those systems are limited to a sample dataset, platform, and language and cannot provide an option to flag the real-time content on SNS. Thus users are not aware of the truthfulness of the UGC. To solve this problem, we propose an interactive user interface, 'TweetInfo'. The proposed interface allows users to flag harmful content as per their choice and interact with social media posts on their timelines. We first analyse the elements required to flag the harmful content and implement it in the user interface. The metainformation for each tweet is generated via the procedure of content analysis. The proposed method will create awareness about the content and reduce the consumption of harmful content by users. In other words, TweetInfo provides an option to filter social media posts along with providing metainformation about social media posts based on content analysis, enabling users to customise their content timeline. In this study, we pose and confront the following research question:-

RQ How can we reduce the consumption of harmful content by providing an interactive user interface?

To answer the research question, we have developed two user interfaces, one without any customisation option called standard platform and another is 'TweetInfo' with a customisation option. We propose seven different tags for customising the user interface based on the literature. From the customisation, we generate metainformation for each tweet. Using the customised option, users can choose to filter hate speech or misinformation. Then to measure the effectiveness of the proposed system, we conduct a user study among selected participants. We consider social impact theory to examine the differences in consuming harmful content on standard and TweetIno platforms. According to Latané, influence relies on the dimensions of strength, which describe features of a source, immediacy, meaning the closeness of the source, and the number of sources [11]. We gathered demographic information and their experience with harmful content and asked some questions to measure the effectiveness of TweetInfo in reducing the consumption of harmful content from participants.

Our contribution is to provide an approach to design the interactive user interface and analyse user behaviours in consuming harmful content. The proposed approach can create public awareness while browsing the UGC in the long run.

The following sections are arranged as follows: the Related Work section describes the past research and highlights the theoretical background to support our analysis, and the Methodology section describes the approach used in the study. The Result section discusses the study's findings, the Discussion section discusses our observation and conclusion, and the Future Work provides concluding points and aspects of the future work.

2   Related Work

This section describes the background of online harm, interactive systems and social impact theory as theoretical background.

2.1   Online Harm

Online harm is behaviour online which may hurt a person physically or emotionally. It could be harmful information that is posted online or information sent to a person [12]. Online harm is not new; it is available in several forms, like cyberbullying, hate speech, and misinformation. With the growth in the number of users on SNS, it evolved across different formats like images, text, and videos. An individual could initiate online harm to a target group. The psychological effects of online abuse on individuals can be extreme and lasting [13]. Online harm in the form of hate speech, cyberbullying, and personal attacks are common issues [13]. Previous research has been done in English and other widely spoken languages to detect online harm like hate speech. In this study, we cover the two types of online harm, hate speech and misinformation; they are discussed below-

Hate speech is speech or expression that shares harmful content that targets an individual or group based on race, gender, age, or religion [14]. Research shows that the amount of hate speech on social media sites is increasing, and several users are regularly targeted. Hate speech can be further classified as offensive and profane [15]. Research has been published on hate speech in multiple languages, and topics [16]. Still, a real-time hate speech detection system is not implemented on SNS, and users are unaware of the content while browsing.

Misinformation is defined as incorrect or misleading information. Misinformation can be categorised into several different categories like false, partially false [7,17,18]. Research on rumours is closely related, and the terms are often used interchangeably" [7]. The amount of misinformation is higher on platforms like Twitter, Facebook, and YouTube [6,19], WhatsApp [20]. Also, several methods are being tested to detect the misinformation on social media sites [21–23]. Still, the user is not able to check the correctness of the social media post while browsing.

2.2   Interactive User Interface

Social media has been part of our lives for the last two decades; several social media platforms exist with different targeted users. However, social media interfaces have lagged behind user expectations. McMinn et al. proposed a new tool for the visualisation of events. The tool detects, tracks, and summarises the event in real-time [24]. Hana et al. conducted a user study to measure satisfaction with the Facebook interface among users in Saudi Arabia and found that due to differences in culture and way of writing styles, users are not satisfied with the Facebook interface [25]. The reason is that Facebook is designed based on western culture. In another study, the author proposed an interactive approach to identify the age and gender of the post with the involvement of the user to get the feedback [26]. Previously, the author used the linguistic feature to hate speech detection, and data visualisation [27]. In another approach, an interactive user approach has been developed to search the existing database, scrape social media using keywords, annotate data through a dedicated platform, and contribute new content to the database [28]. Shu et al. developed FakeNewsTracker for tracking, detecting, and analysing fake news from social media [29]. Despite several interactive systems, none of them allows users to customise the content on the timeline and explain the content of the social media post.

To solve the problem of online harm and the research gap in user interaction with social media posts, we proposed an interactive user interface(TweetInfo). TweetInfo provides an interactive platform for content filtering, more options on the timeline like dislike, share, and detailed content analysis of the given social media post. It also provides background information if it is misinformation or hate speech.

2.3   Theoretical Background

The speed of harmful content on social media depends on social influence. Some post gets viral and propagates across different social media platform. To analyse social influence, we used the social impact theory. The Social impact theory proposes that influence depends on strength, immediacy, and number. The impact directly depends on strength, immediacy, and number [11,30]. We can consider the numerical features like a friend and follower count as strengths on social media platforms like Twitter. The immediacy expresses time and space proximity to the target of influence. The number could be considered as account age and verified status. So, in this study, we analyse the impact of harmful posts on the propagation of misinformation and hate speech. Also, to make aware that if there is any direct impact of account type (verified), account age. We compare the impact by measuring how users interacted with different tweets based on the above values.

3   Methodology

In this section, we describe the steps involved in analysing the consumption of online harm using an interactive user platform. The approach is further divided into two parts, i.e., collecting data, data analysis for the design of an interactive social media platform and a user study to measure its effectiveness. For the development of TweetInfo, we have considered the layout of Twitter as the reference because the collected dataset was based on Twitter, and our research is based on textual data only. An overview of the steps involved in the methodology is shown in Fig. 1. The steps are defined as follows-

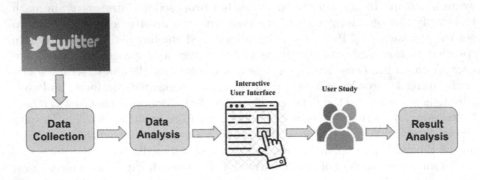

Fig. 1. A pipeline for the creation of TweetInfo

3.1   Data Collection

For our study, we have collected data from two different sources. The first data set consists of misinformation tweets. The second is a collection of hate speech tweets into two categories racism and sexism. The details are explained below-.

Dataset I: For hate speech, we have used data from the abusive dataset [31], which provides the manually annotated data for hate speech on racism and sexism. The data is collected using search terms like "MKR", "Asian drive", "feminazi", "immigrant", "nigger", "sjw", "WomenAgainstFeminismWe". We randomly sampled 500 tweets from 16,914 tweets mentioned for this work.

Dataset II: For misinformation, we have used data from COVID-19 misinformation tweets [7]. The dataset focuses on the propagation of misinformation about COVID-19. The dataset contains tweets in false and partially false categories and links the news articles to support the misinformation mentioned. The dataset was an extension of the FakeCovid corpus and automatically fetched the labels for each tweet [32]. We randomly sampled 489 tweets from 1,500 tweets.

Both data sets were made available as tweet IDs and labels on Github. We wrote a Python program to fetch tweets. We excluded the tweet ID if it was already deleted. From both datasets, we filtered 989 tweets for analysis and stored them in a database. The sampled data used in the study is available at GitHub[1].

---

[1] https://github.com/Gautamshahi/tweetinfo.

3.2   Data Analysis

In this step, we discuss the data analysis and prepossessing, and we prepare the list of tags, which can be presented as metainformation. For the data preprocessing, we have used the NLTK toolkit [33] to preprocess tweets to calculate the sentiment analysis. We calculated the account age for each Twitter handle, defined as the time difference between the account creation date and 30th April 2021. Based on the prior research, we have used language(categorical), country(categorical), hate speech(binary), sentiment(numeric), gender(binary) tweet Category(categorical), misinformation(binary), bot(binary), verified account(binary) as metainformation. A short description of the list of tags is discussed in Table 1. Detailed information about each tag and the extraction process is explained as follows.

Hate Speech: Hate speech is one of the most commonly occurring phenomena on social media. So, we decided to flag the tweet as hate speech or not. The dataset also contains the subcategory of Sexism and Racism. We have given two options to filter the post, one based on hate speech and another based on the category of hate speech, i.e., "sexist" and "racism" values. Adding a new column in the dataset will categorise whether or not a tweet is hate speech. Both options are binary values, so selecting the value will include it on the timeline.

Misinformation: Misinformation is spread over all social media platforms, and it is hard to mitigate the spread of misinformation. Even though some misinformation is debunked, they are still available on social media platforms. Dataset II contains the tweets and a link to the fact-checked articles, which debunk the misinformation. The fact-checked link is used as background truth to provide an explanation for the misinformation. In the metainformation, we provide a link to the fact-checked article only if it is misinformation; otherwise, it is empty. Both hate speech and misinformation are mutually exclusive in this study because these datasets gather from two different sources.

Sentiment: Sentiment is the way of measuring the emotions of the tweets; usually, hateful tweets have a negative sentiment. We have calculated the sentiment for both datasets. For sentiment calculation, we have used Vadersentiment analysis tool [34]. The score is computed by summing each word's valence scores in the lexicon, adjusted according to the rules, and then normalised to be between -1 (most extreme negative) and +1 (most extreme positive).

Language: Nowadays, social media platforms are multilingual. User browses the content in their native language. We provided the option to browse the content as per their language choice. The tweets are available in two languages, i.e., English and Spanish. Users can filter the contents using the language filter.

Bot: Social Bot is an agent that communicates more or less likely an original account. Bots are programmed for both good and harmful activity. We have considered bot as an element for metainformation. We have checked each Twitter user using to BotoMeter API [35]. The API gives a score in the range of 0 to 5. According to the interpretation score rule related, the scale is from 0 to 5, with zero for a human being in most cases and five for the opposite of a bot.

Table 1. A short description of the metainformation applied to TweetInfo

Element	Description	Example
Hate Speech	Language expresses prejudice against a person from a group or a particular group, primarily based on race, religion, or sexual orientation.	Let's kill **** and kill them for fun[a]
Misinformation	Misinformation is information which is shared accidentally without an intention to harm	A Dean Koontz novel written in 1981 predicted the outbreak of the coronavirus![b]
Tweet Category	Tweet category is a subcategory of Hate speech to identify the particular kind of hate speech	Sexism
Sentiment	Sentiment is an estimate of the emotion contained in the text	Negative
Language	Language used in the text	English
Bot	A Twitter bot is a type of bot software that controls a Twitter account via the Twitter API	Yes
Verified Account	Twitter gives a blue badge on Twitter to inform people know that an account of public interest is authentic	Yes
Gender	Gender of the author who publishes the tweets	Male
Country	The location from where the tweets are posted by the user	India

[a] https://twitter.com/nikmahnasty/status/1393115982705532931
[b] https://twitter.com/mattmfm/status/1258750892448387074

Verified Account: Twitter has an account verification feature. Usually, Twitter checks the popular account and verifies it based on the given information. If the profile is verified, it shows a blue tick mark. Usually, people tend to trust more on these accounts because they are verified and might be famous people. The attribute's value is a binary form (yes or no). The issue is trivial whether an identity is verified or not.

Gender: We identified the gender of the Twitter handle using the gender detection tool and provided an option to filter the content based on gender. This option is not available in the filter, but we generate it from the tweet.

Country: Using the geo-location information of tweets, we have identified the tweets' location and got the user's country. We also added them as metainformation for filtering the timeline based on the country. This option is not available in the filter, but we generate it from the tweet to highlight the origin location of the tweet.

3.3   Design of Interactive User Interface

In a later stage, we implemented the proposed social media platform based on Twitter data. We have designed an interactive user interface to enable users with the option to customise their timeline after filtering the social media posts. The user can also use the filter to determine the type of content on their timeline based on the metainformation. We have built two different user interfaces, one with an option to customise called Standard platform and another without an option to customise called TweetInfo, which can be accessed online[2]. Presently, for the user interface, we have used pre-classified tweets stored in a database as mentioned in Sect. 3.1. It contains labels for hate speech, misinformation, bot, hate keyword, tweet category, language, and country. The following steps have been followed in the development of TweetInfo. We have tested the developed interactive user system using a user study; the details of interactive platforms are given below.

Standard Platform. The standard platform is developed without the option of metainformation. The user can interact with an interface similar to Twitter. Users can browse the tweet and react to like, retweet, reply, and dislike. The visual of the standard platform is shown in Fig. 2.

TweetInfo Platform. In the TweetInfo, we have presented a modified interface with a customisation option. We have provided the customised user interface using the filter button on the right-hand side. Participants can choose the filter option to customise the content on their timeline. Users must check the box parameter and click on search to filter the tweets. By default, all radio buttons are set as no. Until now, hate speech and misinformation are mutually exclusive (users can not use both options simultaneously). In Table 1, we have provided the list of options available for customisation and their description. On the timeline, each tweet contains an icon to provide the metainformation in the pop-up window. The metainformation provides the details of tweets from the content analysis. The visual of the TweetInfo platform and metainformation is shown in Fig. 3. For example, Fig. 4 shows an example of a misleading tweet and its metainformation in Fig. 5.

Fig. 2. Standard Platform without an option of filtering content, similar to Twitter

Fig. 3. TweetInfo: an interactive system for visualisation of tweets

---

[2] https://gautamshahi.github.io/tweetinfo/.

3.4   User Study

To measure the effectiveness of interactive user interfaces using customisation options, we have conducted a user study with both user interfaces and have conducted post-survey feedback. This study aims to measure the differences between hate speech consumption and misinformation on social media. We have provided two platforms - one gives an option to customise the content as per the user's interest, and another is without a customisation option. We observe the differences in browsing and consumption of the contents in two different settings.

Fig. 4. An example of a misinformation tweet

Fig. 5. Metainformation of a misinformation tweet with a link to the fact-checked article

Table 2. Instructions to use the customisation button on Tweetinfo

Element	Usability
Hate speech	This button allows the user to remove the hateful tweet from your timeline. It has the binary value yes and no; with the checkbox yes, you will allow hate speech on the timeline, while no will remove all hate speech tweets. By default, it includes all tweets from the database
Misinformation	This button allows the user to remove the misinformation tweet from your timeline. Yes, with the radio button, you will allow misinformation on the timeline, while no will remove all misleading tweets. By default, it includes all tweets from the database
Verified	If you want to include only verified accounts, then you can choose yes. With option no, it will remove all non-verified accounts
Sentiment	Provides an option to filter the tweets based on positive, negative, and neutral tweets. You can select the positive, negative, and neutral tweets with the radio button
BOT	It allows you to include or remove the bot account from your timeline. It has the binary value yes and no. Choosing yes will enable the bot on the timeline with the radio button, while no will remove all bot accounts. By default, it includes both a bot and a non-bot account
Tweet Category	It relates to hate speech if you want to remove the sexist or racist tweet
Language	In general, tweets are in multiple languages, but you can choose the tweets based on the language. Currently, the majority of tweets are in English and Spanish language only

We have provided an overview of the platform and have explained the instructions; each user was asked to respond to at least ten tweets in terms of like, retweet and dislike, and they can use the icon to get the metainformation of the tweets. Detailed instruction for using the filter option is shown in table 2.

Questionnaire. To find out the opinion of participants by utilising the features suggested and supporting future work on mitigating the misinformation and hate speech on social media, a survey is an excellent option to maximise efficiency by making data immediately accessible for more statistical analysis. After interacting with the online interface, we asked the participants to participate in a survey to gather feedback. In the survey, we have asked 28 questions: demographic details, user background, knowledge about hate speech and misinformation, and previous encounters with it. We have asked for the willingness to opt for the customisation features and the importance of different customisation options. We have also asked about the significance of selection elements used for metainformation. In the end, we have asked about the benefits of using the interactive interface for managing online harm, all kinds of questions having a rating of one to five with a text for open suggestions. The list of questionnaires used for the survey is shown in Table 4.

Participant Selection. For selecting the participants, we have used a mailing list, social media posts on Facebook, and word of mouth in our research group. Due to the COVID-19 situation, we have conducted the entire study remotely. The participants used their laptops for the study. We have provided detailed instructions for user study and questionnaires for getting feedback. We have hosted both interfaces online using Heroku[3] and require a credential to use the application. Overall, 42 participants(25 Males & 17 Females) participants with a median age of 37 years from eight countries agree with the survey. All the participants were graduates, 16 were students in the university, and 26 were working professionals. We asked them to evaluate both the standard and TweetInfo platform for the study. Thirty-five participants completed the online study, but 30 completed both the online and post-survey. For the analysis, we used results from 30 participants.

4   Results

To measure the effectiveness of the given interactive user interface in consuming hate speech and misinformation. In this section, we have explained the results obtained from the user study. We have recorded each click activity of the user while using the standard and TweetInfo user interface. A detailed description of the number of participants who interacted with the TweetInfo and the standard system is shown in Table 3. For TweetInfo, each user interacted with different customisation options, bot, hate speech, misinformation and sentiment were highly used filter options.

---

[3] https://dashboard.heroku.com/.

Table 3. Description of user's interaction with Tweetinfo and Standard user interface as click counts

Timeline	Standard	TweetInfo
User's profile	12	4
Like	102	33
Retweet	79	30
Comment	22	11
Dislike	25	33
Share	8	10
Misinformation	142	61
Hate speech	45	34
Bot account	8	8

In terms of source, verified Twitter handle spread more misinformation than hate speech. Also, misinformation tweets have more retweets and favourites (like) than hate speech, indicating that if the verified Twitter handle shares some misleading content, it diffuses faster. Few verified accounts spread misinformation and hate speech.

To measure the reduced interaction with harmful content, we combined the click result for the hate speech and misinformation tweets from TweetInfo and the standard platform, respectively. Overall, we got eight misinformation and 15 hate speech tweets common. We used this data to test the significance. The propagation of tweets can be measured as the value of likes and retweets [36]. We have considered likes and retweets to measure the differences between both interfaces. Chi-square tests have been used to compare percentages of retweets and likes within each setup and the percentages of bot account and sentiment score. Results indicate that users interact with misinformation or hate speech while using the standard platform. Study indicate that: The interaction with misinformation tweets differs significantly between TweetInfo and the standard user interface, $X2$ $(2, N = 8) = 0.32$, $p < 0.1$. Also, the interaction with hate speech tweets differs significantly between TweetInfo and the standard user interface, $X2$ $(2, N = 15) = 0.55$ $p < 0.1$. We have also tested the test for bot account and sentiment score, and users interact more with bot accounts and negative sentiment with misinformation which is not true in the case of hate speech. In terms of click count of tweets on both user interfaces. The user interacts less with the misinformation and hate speech on TweetInfo, while both platforms share equal numbers for bot interaction. Overall with the interactive system, there is a reduction in the consumption of harmful content.

Apart from the quantitative comparison, in the survey, we have asked for feedback about the current tags for customisation of content and have also asked the suggestion for the changes. The user voted the idea, implementation, and visualisation of metainformation on a scale of 0–5. The results show that the proposed elements for metainformation help customise content on the timeline. 73% of participants are satisfied with the proposed idea and user interface. At the same time, 23% participants suggested several new elements like highlighting fake accounts, which often spread harmful content. Political influence to flag the tweet as politically polarised, timestamp to filter the tweets with date, dislike counts to show the user reactions, and more tweet categories to filter the tweets on the timeline.

5 Discussion

With the user study, each participant confirmed that they had experienced misinformation while 96.67% users experience hate speech in their daily lives. 46.67 % of people experience misinformation every day, 33.3 % confirm that they experience it once a week, 13.33 % once a month, and the remaining 0.67% once a year. In contrast to misinformation, 53.3% of people experience hate speech every day, 20 % confirm that they experience it once a week, 23.33 % once a month, and the remaining 0.33% never experienced hate speech. Overall it indicates that around 60–70% of users are regularly experiencing either hate speech or misinformation. It suggests the dominance of harmful content on social media.

The study explains the importance of interactive user interface in reducing the consumption of online harm. With the interactive user interface, only 35% participants interacted with misinformation and hate speech. Around 76% find it useful for mitigating online harm. It shows the participant's willingness to use the system. Also, from the survey, 83.3% of users accepted they wanted some customisation.

For both platforms, people interact with a verified account that shares misinformation and hate speech which relates to the proposed theory to the number of social impact theories and aligns with the findings of previous work [7]. But the quantity of hate speech from the verified account is more compared to misinformation. Following the trend, old accounts are more involved in spreading misinformation than hate speech. Overall verified accounts, old accounts having more followers are less engaged in spreading hate speech but regularly involved in spreading misinformation. The harmful content from verified account gets more retweets and likes, which propagates for a longer time and is related to immediacy. Usually, misinformation gets more retweets and likes compared to hate speech, but the retweet and likes increase if a verified account publishes it. Hence, harmful content posted by a verified account propagates faster [36]. We also found that the participants often interact with older accounts with more followers.

Table 4. List of questionnaires asked participants and obtained value

No.	Question	Scale	Median	Mean
1	What is your gender?	Categorical	–	–
2	How old are you?	Numeric	25	28
3	Which country are you currently living in?	Categorical	–	–
4	What is the highest level of education you have completed?	Categorical	–	–
5	What do you do professionally?	Categorical	–	–
6	How often do you use these social media services? [Twitter]	Categorical	–	–
7	What is your goal when you use social media platforms like Twitter?	Categorical	–	–
8	Have you encountered any fake news (misinformation) on social media?	Categorical	–	–
9	Have you encountered any hate speech on social media?	Categorical	–	–
10	Would you like an option to access content on social media with filter options based on content and authenticity?	Binary	–	–
11	Would you like to get the content analysis of the tweet?	Binary	–	–
12	Would you like to customise your social media platform?	Binary	–	–
13	Are attributes displayed in the metainformation helpful?	Numeric	4	3.7
14	How satisfied are you with the metainformation displayed?	Numeric	4	3.8
15	Is getting metainformation improving the understanding of user tweets?	Numeric	4	3.7
16	How will you rate the difficulties faced using the metainformation option?	Numeric	3	2.7
17	What other information would you like to see in the metainformation field?	Text	–	–
18	Are you satisfied with the presentation of the customisation options?	Numeric	4	3.9
19	How will you rate the difficulties faced using the filter option?	Numeric	3	2.8
20	How satisfied are you with the proposed option for customisation?	Numeric	4	3.8
21	Which option is most suitable for the filter button for customisation?	Text	–	–
22	Would you like to have more filter options? If yes, what other information would you like to see on this filter field?	Text	–	–
23	How would you rate the idea of Tweetinfo?	Numeric	4	3.9
24	How do you like the idea of the filter option?	Numeric	4	4
25	How do you like the idea of metainformation?	Numeric	4	3.9
26	Do you believe it will help to reduce the spread of fake news?	Numeric	4	3.7
27	Do you believe it will help to reduce the spread of hate speech?	Numeric	3.7	4
28	What would you like to change in the TweetInfo?	Numeric	3.6	4

6   Conclusion and Future Work

In this work, we presented an interactive system that is capable of providing an option for customisation. TweetInfo provides additional information based on content analysis like sentiment, language, and the author's gender. We have implemented the system with two datasets on hate speech and COVID-19 misinformation previously collected from Twitter. The results show that the interactive user interface, which provides an option to filter and metainformation, helps reduce the propagation of harmful content.

Presently, we have explored the user responses on the interactive user interface using pre-classified data. An extension of this work is possible by using the browser plugin's real-time metainformation on Twitter. Another extension could be to choose the robust model for the classification and provide explainability to the tweets if classified as misinformation or hate speech. Overall we find that with the interactive system, participants interact less with hate speech and misinformation. Also, popular and credible accounts are more involved in the spread of misinformation. We also expect that the social media platforms could adopt the proposed concepts to provide a customisation option.

In future work, we could increase the dataset size and add more features for the customisation. We can also extend a user study to larger participants in a different experimental setup to get diverse feedback from users. The work could be implemented as a practical implication to mitigate the consumption of harmful content on social media platforms.

References

1. Lappas, D., Karampelas, P., Fessakis, G.: The role of social media surveillance in search and rescue missions. In: Proceedings of the 2019 IEEE/ACM International Conference on Advances in Social Networks Analysis and Mining, ASONAM 2019, pp. 1105–1111, New York, NY, USA, 2019. Association for Computing Machinery
2. Mathew, B., Dutt, R., Goyal, P., Mukherjee, A.: Spread of hate speech in online social media. In: Proceedings of the 10th ACM Conference on Web Science, WebSci 2019, pp. 173–182, New York, NY, USA, 2019. Association for Computing Machinery
3. Atodiresei, C.-S., Tănăselea, A., Iftene, A.: Identifying fake news and fake users on twitter. Procedia Comput. Sci. **126**, 451–461 (2018)
4. Kaplan, A.M., Haenlein, M.: Users of the world, unite! the challenges and opportunities of social media. Bus. Horiz. **53**(1), 59–68 (2010)
5. Luca, M.: User-generated content and social media. In: Handbook of media Economics, vol. 1, pp. 563–592. Elsevier (2015)
6. Shahi, G.K., Majchrzak, T.A.: Amused: an annotation framework of multimodal social media data. In: Sanfilippo, F., Granmo, OC., Yayilgan, S.Y., Bajwa, I.S. (eds.) ITA. INTAP 2021. CCIS, vol. 1616, pp. 287–299. Springer, Cham (2022). https://doi.org/10.1007/978-3-031-10525-8_23
7. Shahi, G.K., Dirkson, A., Majchrzak, T.A.: An exploratory study of COVID-19 misinformation on twitter. Online Soc. Netw. Media **22**, 100104 (2021)

8. Nandini, D., Schmid, U.: Explaining hate speech classification with model-agnostic methods (2022)
9. Keipi, T., Näsi, M., Oksanen, A., Räsänen, P.: Online hate and harmful content: cross-national perspectives. Taylor & Francis (2016)
10. Ruwandika, N.D.T., Weerasinghe, A.R.: Identification of hate speech in social media. In: 2018 18th International Conference on Advances in ICT for Emerging Regions (ICTer), pp. 273–278 (2018)
11. Latané, B., Wolf, S.: The social impact of majorities and minorities. Psychol. Rev. **88**(5), 438 (1981)
12. Wright, J., Javid, S.: Online harms white paper, April 2019 (2019)
13. Mishra, P., Yannakoudakis, H., Shutova, E.: Tackling online abuse: a survey of automated abuse detection methods. arXiv preprint arXiv:1908.06024 (2019)
14. Fortuna, P., Nunes, S.: A survey on automatic detection of hate speech in text. ACM Comput. Surv. (CSUR) **51**(4), 1–30 (2018)
15. Modha, S., et al.: Overview of the HASOC subtrack at fire 2021: hate speech and offensive content identification in English and Indo-Aryan languages and conversational hate speech. In: Forum for Information Retrieval Evaluation, pp. 1–3 (2021)
16. Vidgen, B., Derczynski, L.: Directions in abusive language training data: garbage in, garbage out. arXiv preprint arXiv:2004.01670 (2020)
17. Shahi, G.K., Struß, J.M., Mandl, T.: Overview of the CLEF-2021 CheckThat! lab task 3 on fake news detection. In: Working Notes of CLEF 2021-Conference and Labs of the Evaluation Forum, CLEF2021, Bucharest, Romania (online) (2021)
18. Köhler, J., et al.: Overview of the clef-2022 checkthat! lab task 3 on fake news detection. Working Notes of CLEF (2022)
19. Röchert, D., Shahi, G.K., Neubaum, G., Ross, B., Stieglitz, S.: The networked context of COVID-19 misinformation: informational homogeneity on youtube at the beginning of the pandemic. Online Soc. Netw. Media **26**, 100164 (2021)
20. Kazemi, A., Garimella, K., Shahi, G.K., Gaffney, D., Hale, S.A.: Research note: tiplines to uncover misinformation on encrypted platforms: a case study of the 2019 Indian general election on whatsApp. Harvard Kennedy School Misinformation Review (2022)
21. Nakov, P., et al.: The CLEF-2021 CheckThat! Lab on Detecting Check-Worthy Claims, Previously Fact-Checked Claims, and Fake News. In: Hiemstra, D., Moens, M.-F., Mothe, J., Perego, R., Potthast, M., Sebastiani, F. (eds.) ECIR 2021. LNCS, vol. 12657, pp. 639–649. Springer, Cham (2021). https://doi.org/10.1007/978-3-030-72240-1_75
22. Nakov, P., et al.: Overview of the CLEF–2021 CheckThat! Lab on Detecting Check-Worthy Claims, Previously Fact-Checked Claims, and Fake News. In: Candan, K.S., et al. (eds.) CLEF 2021. LNCS, vol. 12880, pp. 264–291. Springer, Cham (2021). https://doi.org/10.1007/978-3-030-85251-1_19
23. Nakov, P., et al.: The CLEF-2022 CheckThat! Lab on Fighting the COVID-19 Infodemic and Fake News Detection. In: Hagen, M., et al. (eds.) ECIR 2022. LNCS, vol. 13186, pp. 416–428. Springer, Cham (2022). https://doi.org/10.1007/978-3-030-99739-7_52
24. McMinn, A.J., et al.: An interactive interface for visualizing events on twitter. In: Proceedings of the 37th International ACM SIGIR Conference on Research & Development in Information Retrieval, pp. 1271–1272 (2014)
25. Almakky, H., Sahandi, R., Taylor, J.: The effect of culture on user interface design of social media-a case study on preferences of Saudi Arabians on the Arabic user interface of facebook. World Acad. Sci. Eng. Technol. Int. J. Soc. Behav. Educ. Econ. Bus. Ind. Eng. 9(1), 107–111 (2015)

26. Beretta, V., Maccagnola, D., Cribbin, T., Messina, E.: An interactive method for inferring demographic attributes in twitter. In: Proceedings of the 26th ACM Conference on Hypertext & Social Media, pp. 113–122 (2015)
27. Capozzi, A.T., et al. Computational linguistics against hate: Hate speech detection and visualization on social media in the" contro l'odio" project. In: 6th Italian Conference on Computational Linguistics, CLiC-it 2019, vol. 2481, pp. 1–6. CEUR-WS (2019)
28. Vrysis, L., et al.: A web interface for analyzing hate speech. Future Internet **13**, 80 (2021)
29. Shu, K., Mahudeswaran, D., Liu, H.: FakeNewsTracker: a tool for fake news collection, detection, and visualization. Computational and Mathematical Organization Theory **25**(1), 60–71 (2018). https://doi.org/10.1007/s10588-018-09280-3
30. Harkins, S.G., Latané, B.: Population and political participation: a social impact analysis of voter responsibility. Group Dyn. Theory Res. Pract. **2**(3), 192 (1998)
31. Waseem, Z., Hovy, D.: Hateful symbols or hateful people? predictive features for hate speech detection on twitter. In: Proceedings of the NAACL Student Research Workshop, pp. 88–93, San Diego, California, June 2016. Association for Computational Linguistics
32. Shahi, G.K., Nandini, D.: FakeCovid - a multilingual cross-domain fact check news dataset for COVID-19. In: Workshop Proceedings of the 14th International AAAI Conference on Web and Social Media (2020)
33. Loper, E., Bird, S.: NLTK: the natural language toolkit. arXiv preprint arXiv:cs/0205028 (2002)
34. Hutto, C.J., Gilbert, E.: Vader: a parsimonious rule-based model for sentiment analysis of social media text. In: Eighth International AAAI conference on weblogs and social media (2014)
35. Davis, C.A., Varol, O., Ferrara, E., Flammini, A., Menczer, F.: BotOrNot: a system to evaluate social bots. In: Proceedings of the 25th International Conference Companion on World Wide Web, WWW 2016 Companion, pp. 273–274, Republic and Canton of Geneva, CHE (2016). International World Wide Web Conferences Steering Committee
36. Stieglitz, S., Linh, D.X.: Emotions and information diffusion in social media-sentiment of microblogs and sharing behavior. J. Manage. Inf. Syst. **29**(4), 217–248 (2013)

Author Index

Printed in the United States
by Baker & Taylor Publisher Services